The Economic Structure of Intellectual Property Law

The Economic Structure of Intellectual Property Law

William M. Landes

Richard A. Posner

The Belknap Press of
Harvard University Press

Cambridge, Massachusetts, and London, England | 2003

Library of Congress Cataloging-in-Publication Data

Landes, William M.
  The economic structure of intellectual property law /
William M. Landes, Richard A. Posner.
    p.   cm.
  Includes bibliographical references and index.
  ISBN 0-674-01204-6
  1. Intellectual property—United States.
  2. Intellectual property—Economic aspects.
  I. Posner, Richard A.   II. Title.

  KF2979.L36   2003
  346.7304′8—dc21   2003050882

Contents

Introduction   *1*

1   The Economic Theory of Property   *11*

2   How to Think about Copyright   *37*

3   A Formal Model of Copyright   *71*

4   Basic Copyright Doctrines   *85*

5   Copyright in Unpublished Works   *124*

6   Fair Use, Parody, and Burlesque   *147*

7   The Economics of Trademark Law   *166*

8   The Optimal Duration of Copyrights
    and Trademarks   *210*

9   The Legal Protection of
    Postmodern Art   *254*

10   Moral Rights and the Visual Artists
     Rights Act   *270*

11   The Economics of Patent Law   *294*

12   The Patent Court:
     A Statistical Evaluation   *334*

13   The Economics of Trade Secrecy Law   *354*

14   Antitrust and Intellectual Property   *372*

15   The Political Economy of Intellectual
     Property Law   *403*

Conclusion   *420*

Acknowledgments   *425*

Case Index   *427*

Author Index   *430*

Subject Index   *435*

Introduction

Awareness that intellectual property raises distinctive economic issues long predates the modern law and economics movement. By "intellectual property" we mean ideas, inventions, discoveries, symbols, images, expressive works (verbal, visual, musical, theatrical), or in short any potentially valuable human product (broadly, "information") that has an existence separable from a unique physical embodiment, whether or not the product has actually been "propertized," that is, brought under a legal regime of property rights. Intellectual property as we are defining it is ancient in origin; trademarks in their approximate modern sense, as indicators of the source of traded goods, were in common use in ancient Rome.[1] Even the "modern" idea that propertizing intellectual property may be necessary if there are to be adequate incentives to create it dates back to the Middle Ages. The landmarks in its history include the Venetian Patent Act of 1474, the English Statute of Monopolies of 1624, the petition of the English Stationers' Company to Parliament in 1643,[2] the Statute of Anne (the English Copyright Act of 1710),[3] the patent and copyright clause of the U.S. Constitution of 1787,[4] the U.S. patent and copyright statutes of 1790, and the French Patent Act of 1791. Economic analysis of intellectual property can be dated to brief discussions by Smith, Bentham, Mill, and other classical economists and by early twentieth-century economists such as Pigou, Taussig—and perhaps most notably

---

1. See Abraham S. Greenberg, "The Ancient Lineage of Trade-Marks," 33 *Journal of the Patent Office Society* 876, 879–880 (1951).

2. See Arnold Plant, "The Economic Aspects of Copyright in Books," in Plant, *Selected Economic Essays and Addresses* 57, 65–67 (1974 [1934]).

3. 1709 according to the calendar then in use; 1710 according to the modern calendar. See Lyman Ray Patterson, *Copyright in Historical Perspective* 3 (1968).

4. Authorizing Congress to "promote the Progress of Science and Useful Arts, by securing for limited Times to Authors and Inventors the exclusive Right to their respective Writings and Discoveries." U.S. Const., art. I, § 8, cl. 8.

Arnold Plant, who published pathbreaking articles on patents and copyrights in the 1930s.[5]

But it was not until the 1970s that sustained publication of economic analyses of the various forms of intellectual property began. Since then the literature has ballooned.[6] This is a reflection of the growth of economic analysis of law generally, the growing importance of intellectual property in the national and world economy, and a powerful movement, again both national and international, for expanded rights over such property; this movement has resulted in a number of legislative, executive, and judicial initiatives discussed in this book. Throughout the 1970s and well into the 1980s (and in some quarters into the 1990s),[7] there was a widespread belief in the United States that the nation was in decline, that it was being outcompeted by other nations, particularly Japan, and that the decline could be halted only by a renewed emphasis on technological innovation as a stimulus to economic growth. An era of rapid legal change began in 1976 with a major overhaul of the copyright law by Congress. Of particular significance for judicial policy was the creation in 1982 of the U.S. Court of Appeals for the Federal Circuit, which was given a monopoly of appeals in patent cases.

Here are some of the fruits of the new emphasis on technological innovation and the growing enthusiasm for intellectual property rights generally. Between 1985 and 2001 the annual number of patents issued by the U.S. Patent and Trademark Office increased from 111,000 to 269,000.[8] Over the same period the percentage of federal civil cases involving disputes over intellectual property doubled.[9] Between 1980 and 2001 membership in the Intellectual Property Section of the American Bar Association grew from 5,526 to 21,670—and the growth in just the last five years of that period was 39 percent, exceeding all categories other than the closely related "Science and

5. See Plant, note 2 above, and Plant, "The Economic Theory concerning Patents for Inventions," in id. at 35. See generally Gillian K. Hadfield, "The Economics of Copyright: An Historical Perspective," 38 *Copyright Law Symposium* 1 (1992).

6. For a useful survey, see Peter S. Menell, "Intellectual Property: General Theories," in *Encyclopedia of Law and Economics*, vol. 2: *Civil Law and Economics* 129, 130–156 (Boudewijn Bouckaert and Gerrit De Geest eds. 2000).

7. See, for example, Lester Thurow, *Head to Head: The Coming Economic Battle among Japan, Europe, and America* (1992).

8. See U.S. Patent and Trademark Office, "U.S. Patent Activity 1790–Present," *http://www. uspto.gov/web/offices/ac/ido/oeip/taf/reports.htm* (utility patents only, granted to U.S. residents only). The rate of growth in the number of trademarks and copyrights is similar. For more detailed patent statistics (also limited, however, to utility patents issued to U.S. residents), see Table 12.2 in Chapter 12, and for copyright statistics, see Figure 8.2 in Chapter 8.

9. "United States District Courts—National Judicial Caseload Profile," in Administrative Office of the U.S. Courts, *Federal Court Management Statistics* (1974–2000).

Technology." The number of law journals specializing in intellectual property, technology, and art has risen from two in 1980 to twenty-six today, and while in 1981 the University of Chicago Law School offered seven courses or seminars in tax and one in intellectual property, the ratio is now five to five.[10] Economic journals published five articles in 1982 whose titles contained terms indicating intellectual property and 235 in 2000.[11] Between 1980 and 2000 the average annual growth rate of scientific and engineering employment in the United States was 4.9 percent, more than four times the overall annual growth rate in employment,[12] while between 1983 and 2000 the number of persons employed as authors rose at an annual rate of 8.7 percent and as designers at an annual rate of 9.2 percent.[13] And between 1987 and 1999, a period of only twelve years, annual U.S. receipts from foreign trade in intellectual property rose from $10 billion to $36.5 billion, versus U.S. payments to foreign owners of intellectual property in 1999 of only $13 billion.[14]

The figure of $36.5 billion may seem meager in light of frequent claims that intellectual property is America's biggest export. U.S. exports of high-technology products such as computers and electronic equipment amounted in 1998 to $190 billion out of total exports of $690 billion[15] (28 percent) and exports of copyright-based industries including films and computer software were $89 billion in 2001.[16] But of course these figures include a great deal of hardware (such as computers and CDs) as well as the intellectual property that is embodied in or sold with the hardware. Nevertheless it is apparent that intellectual property is a large and growing part of the U.S. economy in general and of U.S. foreign trade in particular.

Our own collaborative work on intellectual property began in the mid-1980s, with articles on the economics of trademark law and copyright law, at

10. University of Chicago Law School, *Announcements* (1981–2001).

11. Computed from OCLC FirstSearch: Advanced Search for "Intellectual Property," "Copyright," "Patent," and "Trademark," in *EconLit.*, *http://newfirstsearch.oclc.org* (visited Aug. 12, 2002).

12. See National Science Foundation, "Science and Engineering Workforce: Profile of the U.S. S&E Workforce," *http://www.nsf.gov/sbe/srs/seind02/c3/c3s1.htm.*

13. U.S. Bureau of the Census, *Statistical Abstract of the United States: 2000*, at 416, tab. 669.

14. National Science Foundation, "Science and Engineering Indicators: 2002," tab. 6.1, *http://www.nsf.gov/sbe/srs/seind02/append/c6/at06-01.xls;* National Science Foundation, "Industry, Technology and the Global Marketplace: U.S. Technology in the Marketplace," tab. 6.6, *http://www.nsf.gov/sbe/srs/seind02/c6/c6s1.htm.* All these export figures are in 1997 dollars.

15. See id.

16. See Stephen E. Siwek, *Copyright Industries in the U.S. Economy: The 2002 Report* 6 (2002).

a time when it was still necessary to justify the economic perspective on law to the legal profession—and to many economists and policymakers as well. That is no longer the case with regard to bodies of law that regulate primarily commercial relations, which is a generally apt description of the laws pertaining to intellectual property. Today it is acknowledged that analysis and evaluation of intellectual property law are appropriately conducted within an economic framework that seeks to align that law with the dictates of economic efficiency.[17] Throughout the book we shall be examining cases, doctrines, and principles from the standpoint of whether they are efficient in an economic sense and, if not, how they might be changed to make them efficient.

Other perspectives from which to view intellectual property law besides the economic can be found in the scholarly literature.[18] For example, copyright and patent law have long been defended by reference to Locke's theory that labor creates an entitlement to its fruits. But since (to sound a frequent theme in this book) intellectual creation is a cumulative process—each creator of "new" intellectual property building on his predecessors—and since copyright and particularly patent law give a long-term property right to someone who may have won the race to come up with the new expressive work or new invention by just a day, it is unclear to what extent an intellectual property right can realistically be considered the exclusive fruit of its owner's labor.[19]

A different philosophical approach to intellectual property law builds on Hegel's emphasis on the possession of property as a mark of the free man. From this it has been argued that perhaps intellectual property should be inalienable,[20] in the same way that freedom itself is inalienable (that is, one is not allowed to sell oneself into slavery). Steps toward that conclusion include the doctrines of *droit de suite* (which gives the creator of an expressive work an indefeasible right to royalties even if he assigns his copyright), examined briefly in Chapter 2, and moral rights, which we take up in Chapter 10. We point out in these chapters that a person's freedom is diminished rather than enlarged by limiting his right to sell his property in exchange for money that he can use to buy things he needs or wants more.

17. See, for example, Symposium, "Taking Stock: The Law and Economics of Intellectual Property Rights," 53 *Vanderbilt Law Review* 1727 (2000). For a useful collection of articles, see *The Economics of Intellectual Property*, 4 vols. (Ruth Towse and Rudi Holzhauer eds. 2002).

18. For a nice summary and critique, see Robert P. Merges, Peter S. Menell, and Mark A. Lemley, *Intellectual Property in the New Technological Age* 2–12 (2d ed. 2000).

19. See Wendy J. Gordon, "A Property Right in Self-Expression: Equality and Individualism in the Natural Law of Intellectual Property," 102 *Yale Law Journal* 1533 (1993); Alfred C. Yen, "Restoring the Natural Law: Copyright as Labor and Possession," 51 *Ohio State Law Journal* 517 (1990).

20. See references in Merges, Menell, and Lemley, note 18 above, at 11.

We are skeptical that the noneconomic theories of intellectual property have much explanatory power or normative significance, but we do not pursue the issue further in this book. The complexity and heterogeneity of modern intellectual property and of the legal doctrines, both statutory and common law, that define and regulate that property are too great to enable even a comprehensive *economic* analysis within the confines of a single volume. The book places particular emphasis on copyright, followed by trademarks, patents, and trade secrets, while glancing occasionally at the tort right of publicity, the social norm against plagiarism, and the common law doctrine of misappropriation stemming from the *INS* case (see Chapter 4), all being forms of intellectual property protection in a practical economic sense. Our emphasis on copyright is inevitable, given that most of the legal, especially statutory, ferment in intellectual property law in recent decades has concerned copyright law, probably because of the extraordinary advances in the technology of copying. However, because we frequently refer to trademarks, patents, and trade secrets for purposes of comparison in the chapters mainly devoted to copyright, any seeming "imbalance" in favor of copyright is not so great as might appear from the chapter headings. If anything, by our emphasis on copyright we are redressing an imbalance in the economic literature: there is much more economic scholarship on patents than on copyrights[21] and little on trademarks and trade secrecy. And *that* imbalance is unfortunate, given that so many recent legal developments have been about copyright.

A quick tour of the chapters will give a further indication of our emphases. Chapter 1 analyzes the economics of property in general, thus situating intellectual property in a larger theory of optimal property rights. Chapter 2 sets forth a general economic theory of copyright protection, which is then formalized in Chapter 3.[22] We emphasize the difficulty of determining the optimal scope of that protection in light of advances in technology and changes in the concept of creativity, and especially in light of the underemphasized role of the public domain as a source of vital inputs into the creation of new expressive works. Chapter 4 continues the analysis with an examination of the fundamental doctrines of copyright law, namely the requirement of independent creation, the nonprotection of ideas and facts, the copyright owner's ex-

21. For a glimpse of the disparity, see Nancy Gallini and Suzanne Scotchmer, "Intellectual Property: When Is It the Best Incentive System?" 2 *Innovation Policy and the Economy* 51 (2002).

22. Several other chapters contain either mathematical models or econometric empirical analyses, but the mathless reader should have no difficulty reading around these technical portions of the book. Indeed, the book presupposes none but the most elementary acquaintance with either economic theory or intellectual property law. We hope that it will appeal to a general audience of educated persons interested in intellectual property and not merely to specialists.

clusive control of derivative works, and the defense of fair use. Chapter 5 turns to copyright in unpublished works, and to the controversial issue of when copying from such works should be deemed a fair use. Continuing the discussion of fair use, Chapter 6 explores its application to parodies and cognate genres (burlesque and satire) but also brings trademarks into the discussion because more parody cases have involved trademarks than copyrights.

Chapter 7 focuses exclusively on trademarks. We argue that the principal doctrines of trademark law can be explained as efforts to optimize the value of trademarks in reducing consumer search costs—even in cases in which trademark infringement is charged on the basis of dilution of the plaintiff's mark rather than consumer confusion, though we register some concern about possible extensions of antidilution doctrine. Chapter 8 turns to the durational limitation on copyright, but with a concluding section on the duration of trademarks. We raise in that chapter the neglected issue of copyright's role in preventing "congestion" of expressive works and resulting loss in value. We advocate a return to a system of renewable terms in place of the system created by the Copyright Act of 1976, which other than in cases of work for hire creates a single nonrenewable term now of seventy years after the author's death; the copyright term for works of hire is also very long.[23]

Chapters 9 and 10 take up additional issues of copyright law. These are the applicability of copyright protection to styles of modern art that emphasize the conceptual over the expressive, such as "Appropriation Art," and the introduction of moral rights into American law in the Visual Artists Rights Act. Chapter 9 emphasizes the tension between the protection of conceptual art by copyright law and copyright law's fundamental distinction between ideas, which are not protectable, and expression, which is. We also raise the general question whether copyright is important for unique works of art, such as paintings and sculptures. In Chapter 10, besides describing and evaluating the Visual Artists Rights Act, we discuss the work for hire doctrine and also make our lone empirical attempt to explain why intellectual property law has been expanding.

Chapter 11 discusses patents. We link them closely to trade secrets (the subject of Chapter 13), arguing that the strongest case for patent protection—though not necessarily for so expansive a concept of patentability and patent duration as the law has adopted—is that, given trade secret law, which we argue should not be abolished and which in any event is not going to be abolished, some degree of patent protection is necessary to minimize social costs that trade secret law would create if inventors had no patent option. At

---

23. Chapter 8 is one of several chapters that contain empirical analyses, which we believe may have an interest independent of the particular analytical uses that we make of them.

the same time, as we show in Chapter 13, trade secret law fills certain gaps in patent law; in effect trade secret law necessitates patent law, and patent law necessitates trade secret law.

Amid this discussion Chapter 12 considers the effect on patent law and practice of perhaps the single most significant institutional innovation in the field of intellectual property in the last quarter-century, namely the creation in 1982 of the U.S. Court of Appeals for the Federal Circuit with exclusive jurisdiction over patent appeals.

Chapter 14 examines the major antitrust problems presented by intellectual property, particularly patents and copyrights. Such common terms as "patent monopoly" and "copyright monopoly" are not merely figures of speech. Although most patents and copyrights do not confer substantial monopoly power on their owners, some do, and more are feared to.

In Chapter 15 we take up the political economy of intellectual property law; that is, we explore the political forces that have determined its evolution and present scope, emphasizing the role both of interest groups (as in conventional public-choice analysis), and of a free-market ideology that may sometimes go overboard in its generally salutary enthusiasm for property rights, in the expansion of intellectual property rights in recent decades. The Conclusion recapitulates a few of our main points and lists some of the unanswered questions that our analysis leaves us with.

Although the book covers a lot of ground, some important topics are omitted, notably compulsory licensing of intellectual property, foreign intellectual property laws, and intellectual property treaties.[24] Others are scanted. For example, while we discuss a number of issues relating to intellectual property rights in computer software and to the impact of the Internet on intellectual property law, readers who believe that these are *the* central issues of that law today will be disappointed with our coverage. Unfortunately, it would extend an already long book unduly to try to cover these issues in the depth that they deserve.

We discuss remedies in intellectual property cases from time to time but, except with regard to trade secrecy, not systematically.[25] A point to bear in mind is that when intellectual property is "propertized," that is, made subject to a regime of legally enforceable property rights, the rights holders should have the full range of remedies that owners of physical property have. For ex-

---

24. See, for example, Alan S. Gutterman and Bentley J. Anderson, *Intellectual Property in Global Markets: A Guide for Foreign Lawyers and Managers* (1997); John F. Duffy, "Harmony and Diversity in Global Patent Law," 17 *Berkeley Technology Law Journal* 685 (2002).

25. For a workmanlike discussion of intellectual property remedies from an economic perspective, see Roger D. Blair and Thomas F. Cotter, "An Economic Analysis of Damages Rules in Intellectual Property Law," 39 *William and Mary Law Review* 1585 (1998).

ample, if a patent is deliberately infringed by a more efficient producer than the patentee, so that his profits from the infringement exceed the patentee's loss, the patentee should be permitted to claim the infringer's profits. By thus making the infringement worthless to the infringer, the law forces would-be users of the patent to negotiate with the owner, thus substituting a market transaction for a legal one.

When market transaction costs are low, as is generally the case when one person thinks he can use another's property more efficiently than the owner can, efficiency requires remedies that coerce the would-be user into negotiating with the owner rather than just taking the owner's property subject to a court's determining what price (damages) he shall be forced to pay for it—a less efficient method of resource allocation. This fundamental insight of the economic analysis of the common law[26] is applicable to intellectual property and illustrates one of the themes of the book—that the economic principles that inform and explain property law can guide thinking about intellectual property law as well. The principal difference between the law of intellectual property and the law of physical property is that transaction costs tend to be much higher in the former case. This difference argues for less extensive propertization of intellectual than of physical property. But once a judgment is made that a particular "parcel" of intellectual property should be owned, the standard analysis of remedial options is applicable.

We impart unity to our analysis by making heavy use of the economics of property, and to those economics we devote, as mentioned, the first chapter. But because of the significant economic differences between conventional physical property, such as land, and intellectual property, an analysis of the economics of property in general can only be a starting point. As the invaluable Plant pointed out, in the case of physical property "the institution of private property makes for the preservation of scarce goods, tending (as we might somewhat loosely say) to lead us to 'make the most of them,'" and it is "generally true that there is not a sufficient concentration of ownership of the supplies of a particular good, and of all the easily substitutable alternatives for it, to enable the owners to control the prices of the property they own. Neither the withholding, nor the disposal of the property of any one owner will in general affect appreciably the price of the commodity in question."[27] In contrast, "property rights in patents and copyright make possible the *creation* of a scarcity of the products appropriated which could not otherwise be maintained . . . The beneficiary is made the owner of the entire supply of a product for which there may be no easily obtainable substitute."[28]

---

26. See, for example, Richard A. Posner, *Economic Analysis of Law*, pt. 2 (6th ed. 2003).
27. Plant, "The Economic Theory Concerning Patents for Inventions," note 5 above, at 36.
28. Id. (emphasis in original).

Plant is not the only responsible economic student of the subject to have raised important questions about the social value of intellectual property rights.[29] Others have proposed systems of government prizes or rewards for creators of valuable intellectual property.[30] A better alternative—given the danger that a rewards system would be hopelessly politicized, with grossly debilitating effects on economic efficiency, as well as likely to have misallocative effects similar to those created by enforcing intellectual property rights—might be simply leaving the market for intellectual property to find its own way, as it did before there were enforceable rights to such property.

We cannot ignore such fundamental questions, because they bear on many of the issues of intellectual property law that we discuss. But neither can we answer them to our complete satisfaction. The economic case for abolishing intellectual property rights has not been made. But neither economic theory nor empirical evidence enables a ringing endorsement of any complete body of intellectual property law other than trademark law, which protects "property" in only an attenuated sense. We do, however, find pretty solid economic support for a degree of trade secrecy protection close to what we have and for a degree of copyright and patent protection as well, but possibly a lesser degree than we have.

Given the emphases of the existing scholarly and popular literature concerned with intellectual property, it may come as a surprise to many readers that the economic arguments that we make for intellectual property protection are not based primarily on a belief that without legal protection the incentives to create such property would be inadequate. That belief cannot be

29. See the interesting discussion in Fritz Machlup and Edith Penrose, "The Patent Controversy in the Nineteenth Century," 10 *Journal of Economic History* 1 (1950). Among other skeptical analyses of intellectual property law, see Robert M. Hurt and Robert M. Schuchman, "The Economic Rationale of Copyright," 56 *American Economic Review* 421 (1966), an article that stimulated the modern interest in the economics of copyright law. Important skeptical articles by Stephen Breyer and Adam Jaffe are cited in Chapter 1. The skeptical position is powerfully argued in Lawrence Lessig, *The Future of Ideas: The Fate of the Commons in a Connected World* (2001).

30. As advocated, for example, in Steven Shavell and Tanguy Van Ypersele, "Rewards versus Intellectual Property Rights," 44 *Journal of Law and Economics* 525 (2001). For a comparison more favorable to intellectual property law, see Gallini and Scotchmer, note 21 above. Closely related to reward systems are compulsory licensing schemes, in force in several copyright domains but subject to the same objections based on politicization. See Robert P. Merges, "Contracting into Liability Rules: Intellectual Property Rights and Collective Rights Organizations," 84 *California Law Review* 1293 (1996). As Merges points out in another article, these schemes actually retard the emergence of voluntary arrangements for overcoming transaction-cost problems in the enforcement of intellectual property rights, arrangements such as the blanket licenses issued by performing-rights organizations (ASCAP and BMI and their foreign counterparts). See Robert P. Merges, "Of Property Rules, Coase, and Intellectual Property," 94 *Columbia Law Review* 2655 (1994).

defended confidently on the basis of current knowledge. The concerns we highlight have rather to do with such things as optimal management of existing stocks of intellectual property, congestion externalities, search costs, rent seeking, and transaction costs.[31]

The complexity of the subject and the degree to which economic analysis of intellectual property remains inconclusive, if not indeterminate,[32] should warn the reader not to expect this book to be much like our other, similarly entitled book, *The Economic Structure of Tort Law* (1987), though they are alike in being the first book-length economic analyses of their respective fields of law. A nonstatutory field, tort law comprises a relatively small body of general doctrines that have an impressive intellectual unity. A reasonably straightforward and intuitive economic analysis can make that unity perspicuous and show it to be (or so we argued, and continue to believe) generally efficient. In contrast, intellectual property law is a complex amalgam of frequently amended federal statutes, together with common law principles, both state and federal, and some state statutes; and the economic issues are considerably more intricate. Still, economics has much to contribute to an understanding of intellectual property law—much of which does seem, as in the case of tort law, to be shaped by efficiency considerations—and to its incremental reform, though definitive recommendations for *fundamental* change cannot be supported on the basis of existing knowledge.

One of the major contributions of economic analysis to law has been simplification, enabling enhanced understanding. Economics is complex and difficult but it is less *complicated* than legal doctrine and it can serve to unify different areas of the law. We shall demonstrate how economics can bring out the deep commonality, as well as significant differences, among the various fields of intellectual property law and between intellectual property law and the law governing physical property. Economics can reduce a mind-boggling complex of statutes, amendments, and judicial decisions to coherency. By cutting away the dense underbrush of legal technicalities, economic analysis can also bring into sharp definition issues of policy that technicalities may conceal. That too is an aim of the book.

---

31. Edmund W. Kitch deserves recognition for his early effort to shift thinking about intellectual property from the creation of incentives to other economic ends. See Kitch, "The Nature and Function of the Patent System," 20 *Journal of Law and Economics* 265 (1977). We question the particulars of his analysis in Chapter 11 but not its significance in the history of economic thought about intellectual property.

32. The literature on the economic effects of patents is especially inconclusive. See, for example, Vincenzo Denicolò, "Patent Races and Optimal Patent Breadth and Length," 44 *Journal of Industrial Economics* 249 (1996), and Chapter 11 of this book.

1

The Economic Theory of Property

The economics of property rights in physical property are now well understood, and its basic elements can be summarized fairly briefly.[1] These elements provide, though only with adjustments, the tools for understanding the essential economic characteristics of intellectual property and for evaluating the pros and cons, the scope and limits, of property rights in intellectual goods. With intellectual property scholarship becoming more and more specialized, there is a danger of losing sight of the continuity between rights in physical and in intellectual property and thus the utility of using what economics has learned about the former to assist analysis of the latter.

The danger is exacerbated by a tendency among economic analysts of intellectual property to reduce the entire problem of intellectual property rights to a tradeoff between "incentive" and "access." Because intellectual property is often copiable by competitors who have not borne any of the cost of creating the property, there is fear that without legal protection against copying the incentive to create intellectual property will be undermined. At the same time, legal protection against copying, by enabling the creator of the intellectual property to charge a price for copies (of which his property right makes him a monopolist) in excess of his marginal cost, prevents access to (use of) the intellectual property by persons who value that access at more than the marginal cost but less than the price. We shall argue that to reduce the problem of intellectual property to this tradeoff is to oversimplify greatly; to ignore entire bodies of intellectual property law, notably trademark law; and, of particular pertinence to this chapter, to obscure the legal and economic continuity between physical and intellectual property. Not that the incentive-access tradeoff is nonexistent or even unimportant; but there is much else to consider in an economic analysis of intellectual property law.

---

1. See, for example, Richard A. Posner, *Economic Analysis of Law,* ch. 3 (6th ed. 2003); for a fuller treatment, see *Property Rights: Contract, Conflict, and Law* (Terry L. Anderson and Fred S. McChesney eds. 2003).

A property right is a legally enforceable power to exclude others from using a resource—all others (with exceptions unnecessary to get into here, such as the government when exercising its eminent domain power), and so with no need to make contracts with would-be users of the resource forbidding their use. If *A* owns a pasture, he can, with the backing of the courts and the police, forbid others to graze their cattle on it. He does not have to negotiate with them an agreement entitling him to exclusive use; that would be an infeasible alternative because the whole world could threaten to graze their cattle on his property in order to be paid by him not to do so. Conversely, if *B* wants to have the exclusive use of the pasture, he must acquire it on terms acceptable to *A*. Thus a property right includes both the right to exclude others and the right to transfer the property to another.

Benefits

Property rights confer two types of economic benefit, static and dynamic. The former is illustrated by a natural (that is, uncultivated) pasture. If the owner cannot exclude others from using his pasture, there will be overgrazing. Unless law or contract (or maybe custom) intervenes, users of the pasture will ignore the costs they impose on each other in reducing their animals' weight by making the animals expend more energy in grazing in order to find enough to eat.[2] This is not, by the way, a hypothetical example. The enclosure movement in England transformed common pastures into private property. Although much criticized on grounds of distributive (in)justice, the movement increased agricultural productivity enormously,[3] though less by eliminating crowding of pastures than by reducing transaction costs. Enclosure made it unnecessary to get the agreement of all users of the pasture before it could be put to other uses,[4] thus facilitating movement from lower-valued to higher-valued uses of land. Reducing transaction costs is the very

2. This argument for property rights comes from Frank Knight, "Some Fallacies in the Interpretation of Social Cost," 38 *Quarterly Journal of Economics* 582 (1924), though the example he used was traffic congestion. Although we are using the pasture example as an example of a static benefit of property rights, it has a dynamic dimension as well, since overgrazing will deplete the pasture prematurely. We return to this point in discussing intellectual property congestion externalities in Chapter 8.

3. See, for example, J. R. Wordie, "The Chronology of English Enclosure, 1500–1914," 36 *Economic History Review* (n.s.) 483, 504–505 (1983).

4. See Donald N. McCloskey, "The Persistence of English Common Fields," in *European Peasants and Their Markets* 73, 85–87 (William N. Parker and Eric L. Jones eds. 1975); Carl J. Dahlman, *The Open Field System and Beyond: A Property Rights Analysis of an Economic Institution* 175 (1980).

raison d'être of property rights, as we just saw in contrasting them with contract rights.

The counterpart to the common pasture in intellectual property is the public domain (the *intellectual* public domain, that is, for there is also a public domain in physical things, mainly roads, parks, and waterways).[5] The term refers to the vast body of ideas and expression that are not copyrighted, patented, or otherwise propertized. Because the enclosure movement has been criticized, some critics of intellectual property law who would like to see the public domain enlarged emphasize the analogy between the common pasture and the public domain and between the enclosure movement and the movement, which has been gathering steam since the mid-1970s and which we will encounter again and again in this book, to enlarge the scope and duration of rights in intellectual property.[6] It is important therefore to emphasize the contribution that the enclosure movement made to agricultural productivity. But it does not follow that rampant propertization of information and other intellectual goods would have similarly beneficent effects. Indeed, we doubt that it would. It is easy to imagine agriculture without common pastures but difficult to imagine a system under which, for example, every possible combination of words, symbols, colors, and other marks of identification were owned, so that to launch a new brand one would have to buy a trademark.

The dynamic benefit of a property right is the incentive that possession of such a right imparts to invest in the creation or improvement of a resource in period 1 (for example, planting a crop), given that no one else can appropriate the resource in period 2 (harvest time). It enables people to reap where they have sown. Without that prospect the incentive to sow is diminished. To take an example from intellectual property, a firm is less likely to expend resources on developing a new product if competing firms that have not borne the expense of development can duplicate the product and produce it at the same marginal cost as the innovator; competition will drive price down to marginal cost and the sunk costs of invention will not be recouped. This prospect provides the traditional economic rationale for intellectual property rights, though it involves as we shall see a significant degree of oversimplification. The possibility that such rights might also confer static benefits, eliminating congestion externalities comparable to those of the common pasture with which we began, has been neglected because of the widely held belief that intellectual property, not being physical, cannot be worn out, crowded,

5. See Carol M. Rose, "The Comedy of the Commons: Custom, Commerce, and Inherently Public Property," 53 *University of Chicago Law Review* 711 (1986).

6. See, for example, James Boyle, "Fencing Off Ideas: Enclosure and the Disappearance of the Public Domain," *Daedalus*, Spring 2002, p. 13, and references cited there.

or otherwise impaired by additional uses. It is a "public good" in the economist's sense that consumption of it by one person does not reduce its consumption by another. More accurately, it has public-good characteristics, for we shall show that in some circumstances propertizing intellectual property can prevent overuse or congestion in economically meaningful senses of these terms.

The very term "public good" is misleading, moreover. It sounds like a good produced by the government as opposed to the private sector. That is true of public goods that people cannot be excluded from having the benefit of even if they don't contribute to the cost of supplying the goods. The clearest example is national defense. Many public goods, however, including intellectual property, are excludable in the sense that it is possible to condition access to them on payment. Such goods need not be provided by government.

Both the static and the dynamic benefits of property rights presuppose, as we noted at the outset, that there are too many potential users of the property for transactions with all of them to be economical. When transaction costs—which in general, though not in every case, rise with the number of contracting parties—are low, Ronald Coase's well-known analysis of transaction costs implies that enforceable contract rights are all that society needs, beyond some underlying set of entitlements so that the parties have something to contract about, to attain optimal use and investment.[7] That is not the only situation in which property rights may be dispensable, even undesirable, from a social standpoint. If, though tradable at low cost, a good, however valuable it may be in the sense of utility conferred on the possessor, is not scarce (that is, if it has no *exchange* value),[8] if the costs of enforcing property rights are disproportionate to the value of the rights, or if the costs of appropriating someone's valuable good are prohibitive quite apart from any legal sanctions, the social value of property rights will be slight or even negative.[9] These qualifications will loom large in this book; we shall see that "depropertizing" intellectual property rights may sometimes be the soundest policy economically. Even the strongest defenders of property rights acknowledge the economic value of preserving public domains—that is, of ar-

7. See R. H. Coase, "The Problem of Social Cost," 3 *Journal of Law and Economics* 1 (1960). The entitlements required to get the contract process going need be no more elaborate than simple possessory "rights." So long as *A* "has" something that *B* wants, and vice versa, there is the possibility of a transaction.

8. Goods may be very valuable, but if they are in infinite supply their price will be zero and so they will have no exchange (market) value. That was Adam Smith's distinction between water and diamonds.

9. See Harold Demsetz, "Toward a Theory of Property Rights," 57 *American Economic Review Papers and Proceedings* 347, 350–353 (May 1967), where these tradeoffs were first clearly identified.

eas in which property is available for common use rather than owned—even in regard to physical property and *a fortiori* in regard to intellectual property.[10]

Consider the following, we trust uncontroversial, example. Judicial decisions are not copyrighted; they are all in the public domain and thus a "commons" available for all to use without a license. Because they are produced as a byproduct of the operation of a court system, it is unlikely that more would be produced if they were copyrighted. Nor is it likely that more would be better. It is true that if judges were paid according to the use others make of their opinions, for example by citing them, the quality of judicial opinions could well increase; but the quantity would probably rise as well and this would increase lawyers' research costs and might make the law less knowable and coherent than if there were fewer opinions, because an increase in the number of opinions increases the likelihood of inconsistent rulings. Most important, the transaction costs of obtaining licenses by the myriad of lawyers, litigants, judges, and law professors who make copies of judicial decisions would be immense.

It does not follow that government should never assert copyright in its documents, though that is the law at present. The conventional argument that if the government copyrighted the documents it produces or patented its inventions the public would pay twice, first in the taxes used to finance the creation of the document or invention and second in the part of the purchase price that reflected the copyright or patent monopoly,[11] is incorrect. If correct, it would mean that government should never charge a fee for any service. It would be correct only if the government permitted private persons or firms to copyright government documents. Something like this is the government's policy with respect to patents, as we shall see in Chapter 11. But if instead government asserted copyright in order to be able to sell its documents for higher prices by forbidding their being copied, it could reduce taxes. In other words, copyrighting of government documents would merely be a switch from taxes to user fees as the method of financing the government's expressive works. Such a switch is often a way of economizing on the costs of government and might be so with regard to many kinds of government doc-

10. See, for example, Richard A. Epstein, "Steady the Course: Property Rights in Genetic Material" (University of Chicago Law School, John M. Olin Law and Economics Working Paper No. 152 [2d ser.], May 22, 2002).

11. A caveat is necessary here: in using the conventional terms "copyright monopoly" or "patent monopoly" we do not mean to suggest that every copyright and every patent should raise warning flags for antitrust enforcers. Most copyrights and patents do not confer enough market power to raise any kind of antitrust issue, as we shall emphasize in Chapter 14, where we discuss the application of antitrust law in intellectual property markets.

ument. True, the higher prices charged for such documents would cause a deadweight loss by deflecting consumers to substitutes for the copyrighted document that might cost society more to produce. But it would not necessarily be a greater deadweight loss than that brought about by the higher taxes required to finance the creation of the documents when lower prices are charged for them.

Costs

The costs of property rights are severalfold. First is the cost of transferring such rights (transaction cost). If it is too high, a property right may prevent optimal adjustments to changing values. Suppose that a factory is assigned a property right to the use of a river that runs beside it because the river is more valuable as a sewer than for recreation, but that as the years go by the relative values of these uses reverse. If the recreational users are numerous, the transaction costs of their buying the right to use the river from the factory may exceed the value of the right to them. In such a case a liability rule would be better, whereby the factory could be induced to discontinue its use of the river by being made to pay damages equal to the costs of the pollution to recreational users. The rule would reallocate the use of the river in accordance with changed values without requiring a transaction.

Transaction costs tend to be high in the case of intellectual property even when there are only a few transactors, actual or potential, in the picture. The reason is the frequent difficulty of identifying such property because by definition it has no unique physical site. This is true even of unique works such as paintings, since a painting may be photographed or otherwise copied, and the copies sold as prints or affixed to other salable objects such as mugs and calendars. What the original and the copies have in common—"the picture," we might call it, or even "the work of art"[12]—is a nonmaterial object separate from the painting itself. The transaction costs involved in selling the original are not likely to be especially high; the problem comes with the transfer of interests in the picture itself, that is, the transfer of the right to make copies (the copyright) and subsets of that right. Such rights are difficult to define because while the original itself is a definite, visible, physical object, what we are calling "the picture" is not, so there might be a question whether something that looked very much like the original was a copy that infringed the copyright or an independent creation that merely resembled the original.

The second major cost of a property rights system, and again one of partic-

---

12. See Oswald Hanfling, "The Ontology of Art," in *Philosophical Aesthetics: An Introduction* 76 (Oswald Hanfling ed. 1992).

ular importance to intellectual property, arises from a common motive for obtaining a property right, the motive that economists refer to as "rent seeking." Economic rent is a return over and above the cost of generating the return; it is pure profit, and so worth incurring costs to obtain, even if the costs exceed the social benefit from the undertaking, as they will often do. Suppose a sunken ship has a salvage value of $1 million that could be realized at a cost of only $100,000. The potential gain to the salvager—the economic rent or pure profit from salvaging the sunken ship—is thus $900,000 if a property right in the sunken ship can be acquired. The competition to realize that gain by acquiring the property right may gobble up all or most of the potential rent, transforming it into a deadweight social loss unless the pell-mell competition speeds up the salvage process enough to produce an increase in present value that offsets the added cost.

The example assumes that the original owner of the ship abandoned it, so that it is unowned. If it has not been abandoned, the owner can auction off the right to salvage the ship to the lowest bidder, that is, the salvage company that demands the least for salvaging the ship. There will be no rent-seeking problem because competition among bidders will drive the price of the salvage down to its cost, including a reasonable profit measured by the opportunity cost of the resources used in the salvage—and that profit is not a rent but merely the reimbursement of a cost.

In the case of abandonment, property law ameliorates rent-seeking problems by sometimes giving the first committed searcher the exclusive right to conduct the search operation. Thus in *Treasure Salvors, Inc. v. Unidentified Wrecked & Abandoned Sailing Vessel*,[13] we read that "persons who actually reduce lost or abandoned objects to possession and persons who are actively and ably engaged in efforts to do so are legally protected against interference from others, whereas persons who simply discover or locate such property, but do not undertake to reduce it to possession, are not . . . The law acts to afford protection to persons who actually endeavor to return lost or abandoned goods to society as an incentive to undertake such expensive and risky ventures; the law does not clothe mere discovery with an exclusive right to the discovered property because such a rule would provide little encouragement to the discoverer to pursue the often strenuous task of actually retrieving the property and returning it to a socially useful purpose and yet would bar others from attempting to do so." By shifting rent-seeking activity to an earlier stage and eliminating duplicative expenditures on search at later

13. 640 F.2d 560, 572–573 (5th Cir. 1981). We thank James Krier for this reference. Similar cases, involving capture of whales, are discussed in Robert C. Ellickson, *Order without Law: How Neighbors Settle Disputes* 196–296 (1991), and Richard A. Posner, *Frontiers of Legal Theory* 210 (2001). See also the *Haslem* case, discussed later in this chapter.

stages, a committed-searcher doctrine may limit overall expenditures on rent seeking. This is not certain, however, as we shall point out in considering the patent law version of the doctrine in Chapter 11.

The legal protection of intellectual property gives rise to serious problems of rent seeking because intellectual goods are waiting, as it were, to be discovered or invented, just like the sunken ship whose owner has abandoned it. The term "patent race" has been coined to describe an intellectual property counterpart to the salvage example. Well before the term "rent seeking" had entered the economics lexicon, George Stigler observed that "the prospects of monopoly pricing [of patents] will lead to such a scale of investment in producing knowledge that it will return only the competitive rate of return on average."[14] The excess over the optimal investment, minus any social benefit produced by the additional investment, is the waste produced by rent seeking.

The third cost of property rights is the cost of protection. It includes not only the expenses incurred by police, property owners, and courts in enforcing laws against trespass and theft but also the cost of a fence used to mark boundary lines, the cost of a toll booth used to enforce a property right in a road or a bridge, and the cost of a registry used to record land titles. In some instances the total costs will exceed the benefits of propertization. The owner of a shopping center who does not charge separately for the use of the shopping center's parking lot, instead treating it as a commons, has decided that the cost of charging for the use of the lot would exceed the benefit in enabling him to build a smaller lot by encouraging more economical use of it by his customers.

Intellectual property tends to be particularly costly to protect. An idea or other intellectual product cannot be seen in the way a piece of land can be or described with the precision possible in a map. The land may have been transferred by inheritance for many generations, but, unless it is located on a shifting shoreline, it is the same piece of land, recorded in the same land registry on a map with unchanged specifications. To trace the descent of an idea (or image, verbal formula, and so on), which has no spatial limits, is much more difficult. Moreover, the public-good character of intellectual property, of which more below and in the next two chapters, can make it difficult to prevent misappropriation and to exclude free riders in the absence of special legal protections. A related point is the greater difficulty of detecting unauthorized uses. If A steals B's car, B will discover the theft quickly because the theft prevents his using his car. He will report the theft promptly and take ac-

---

14. George J. Stigler, "A Note on Patents," in Stigler, *The Organization of Industry* 123, 124 (1968). Stigler's paper was published for the first time in his 1968 book; we do not know when it was written.

tion to get his car back. Not so for intellectual property. If *A* reproduces *B*'s copyrighted work, *B* may not discover this for a long time (or ever) because the reproduction does not deprive him of the use of his work but only of the exclusive use of it. Moreover, this reproduction may take place in another state or country.[15]

A fence or other measure taken to enforce a property right may reduce output by restricting the use of the property, and if so this is as much a cost of the property right as the cost of the fence is. Suppose the owner of a shopping center does charge for the use of his parking lot; then, given that the demand for the use of the lot will not be perfectly inelastic other than perhaps in the very short run (if it had zero elasticity in the long run, the profit-maximizing price would be infinite), there will be less use of the lot than if access to it were "free." Some waste will result, for example, on days in which, the lot being empty, an additional user would impose no cost yet might be deflected by the price charged by the owner to a more costly activity, such as shopping at a less convenient shopping center that offers free parking. Granted, that waste may be more than offset on days when there is substantial traffic at the shopping center. If there is a charge for parking, then on those days instead of shoppers queuing up for scarce parking spaces, fewer drivers (not necessarily fewer shoppers) will choose to park at the mall and this will make it easier for those willing to pay to find a space. Substituting a price for queuing saves real resources, because price is a transfer from drivers to the owner of the shopping center whereas queuing imposes a social cost because it involves an expenditure of time. Such a saving is less likely in the case of intellectual property because of its public-good character. If price deflects users of a zero-marginal-cost good (such as space in an empty parking lot) to costly substitutes, there is no offsetting benefit from reducing crowding. And so to the extent that the use of intellectual property by one person does not interfere with its use by others, there is no crowding effect that one might want to alleviate by imposing a price for such use.

The public-good character of intellectual property is pronounced. In the case of farmland, whether cultivated or uncultivated, adding a user will, as we pointed out in discussing the example of the overgrazed pasture, impose costs on the existing user(s). So the fact that a fence keeps additional users out need not impose a net cost on users as a group, and if not, the only cost of the property right will be the fence. In our shopping-center example—which distantly echoes the discussion by Harold Hotelling and other economists in the first half of the twentieth century of the optimal pricing of goods, such as bridges, that have a very high ratio of fixed to marginal

15. These points were noted by Justice Holmes in *White-Smith Music Publishing Co. v. Apollo Co.*, 209 U.S. 1, 18–20 (1908) (concurring opinion).

costs[16]—charging for the use of the parking lot may have some misallocative effect. For once the lot is built, if it is large enough to accommodate customers at peak shopping hours it will often have excess capacity, at which times the marginal cost of providing parking for additional shoppers may, as we saw, be zero. At those times the lot is a public good and the marginal cost of another user will be zero (ignoring trivial wear and tear). When the lot is crowded, marginal cost will turn positive because the use of the lot by some customers will be depriving others of that use.

Often and not merely exceptionally, adding users will impose no costs on previous users of intellectual property. One farmer's using the idea of crop rotation does not prevent any other farmer from using the same idea. It is true that when more farmers use crop rotation, output will rise and price will fall, hurting farmers already using crop rotation. But the price effects of the diffusion of the idea are purely pecuniary externalities because the losses to the farmers are completely offset by the gains to consumers; there is no reduction in the aggregate value of the society's economic resources.[17] However, when the marginal cost of using a resource is zero, excluding someone (the marginal purchaser) from using it by charging a positive price for its use creates a deadweight loss, in addition to the out-of-pocket cost of enforcing exclusion by fences, security guards, police, lawyers, and registries of title deeds, because the price deflects some users to substitute goods that have a positive marginal cost. This loss is rarely significant in the case of physical property because, as we said, it brings with it a benefit: it avoids crowding in the pasture and shopping-center cases, and worse when joint consumption is not possible. More broadly, it allocates scarce resources to their highest-valued uses. Two people can't eat the same radish or wear the same pair of shoes at the same time. There must be a mechanism for allocation, and normally the most efficient is the price system. Hence Plant's point that intellectual property rights create scarcity whereas property rights in physical goods manage scarcity.

But the point is incomplete. Unless there is power to exclude, the incentive to create intellectual property in the first place may be impaired. Socially desirable investments (investments that yield social benefits in excess of their social costs) may be deterred if the creators of intellectual property cannot recoup their sunk costs. That is the *dynamic* benefit of property rights, and the result is the "access versus incentives" tradeoff: charging a price for a public good reduces access to it (a social cost), making it artificially scarce (Plant's

16. We abstract from any costs of congestion. Just as in the overgrazing case, the effect of traffic congestion on a bridge is that each driver imposes a cost (a time cost, in this case) on the other drivers. This is a marginal cost because it varies with the amount of use of the bridge.

17. When an externality results in a net reduction in the value of output, as in the case of pollution, rather than merely in a transfer of wealth, it is referred to as a "technological" externality.

point), but increases the incentive to create it in the first place, which is a possibly offsetting social benefit.

The Cost-Benefit Tradeoff

The fact that intellectual property rights tend to be more costly, in all the ways we have indicated, than rights in physical property has several implications that form the core of our inquiry in this book. First, we can expect intellectual property law, to the extent it is guided by a concern with economic efficiency, to endeavor to reduce the costs of these rights. Second, we can expect that one way the law will do this is by imposing limitations on intellectual property rights that go beyond what is found in the domain of physical property. An example is the requirement that an invention, to be patentable, must not be an obvious application or extension of existing technology. This requirement prevents the obtaining of a property right in circumstances in which deadweight loss and excessive rent seeking would be serious problems. "Obviousness" implies a low cost of discovery and development and so a large potential gap between value and cost and therefore a rich opportunity to obtain economic rents. As a precondition to obtaining a property right, the requirement of nonobviousness has no counterpart in the law of physical property.

Another example is the limited duration of patents, which has only a distant cousin in that law (the doctrine of adverse possession, which, as we'll see shortly, enables title to physical property to be extinguished by the passage of time under special conditions). The durational limitation further limits rent seeking by putting a ceiling, though a high one, on a patent's expected value. It also responds to the high cost of tracing an idea over a long period of time in which it may have become embodied in a great variety of products and processes. That is a transaction cost because it increases the cost of licensing the idea.

Third, an extension of the second point, the high social costs of intellectual property rights create uncertainty as to whether on balance such rights are, from an overall social standpoint, cost-justified at all.[18] Intellectual property rights are an add-on to the physical property rights that the creators of intel-

---

18. The leading skeptic remains, as noted in the Introduction, Arnold Plant. See the two articles by him cited there in notes 2 and 5. See also, for example, Stephen G. Breyer, "The Uneasy Case for Copyright: A Study of Copyright in Books, Photocopies, and Computer Programs," 84 *Harvard Law Review* 281 (1970), and Adam B. Jaffe, "The U.S. Patent System in Transition: Policy Innovation and the Innovation Process," 29 *Research Policy* 531, 539–540 (2000). These two articles take a moderately skeptical position on copyright and patent, respectively—not calling for abolition but opposing extension. Many similar articles could be cited and some will be in later chapters.

lectual property uncontroversially possess. A writer has a property right in his time, his word processor, and his original manuscript. An artist has a property right in his painting. An inventor has a property right in his time, his laboratory, his equipment, his drawings. These property rights, together with certain personal rights such as the right to bodily integrity and the right not to be defrauded, enable the writer, the artist, and the inventor to create intellectual property, which none of them could do if, for example, it were lawful to break into a writer's laptop and steal and publish under one's own name the compositions found there. Because the producers of intellectual property have these rights, a great deal of intellectual property would be created even if there were no property rights in intellectual goods as such. We know this because an enormous quantity (and quality) of intellectual property was produced before there were such rights and because even today a great deal of the intellectual property that is produced would be produced even if they did not exist—some because produced with no hope of significant financial gain, some because financed by means other than sale, and some because the costs can be recouped before competitors can duplicate it, since, as we just pointed out, the preparatory stages in the creation of intellectual property are protected by the normal rights that people have to privacy and physical property. It is true that when these rights are used to protect intellectual property, they are discussed under the rubric of "trade secrecy," normally regarded as a branch of the law of intellectual property. But we shall see in Chapter 13 that trade secrecy law doesn't, for the most part anyway, create intellectual *property* rights.

A further reason for skepticism about the social value of expansive intellectual property rights is the access versus incentives tradeoff: these rights reduce the demand for intellectual property by inserting a wedge between price and marginal cost, creating deadweight loss that must be balanced against the disincentive effects of denying the creator of such property a remedy against copiers. Another point, emphasized by Arnold Plant who in this respect was anticipating a much later economic literature on the rent seeking of cartelists and other monopolists, is that intellectual property protection might result in too much intellectual property being produced rather than too little (or perhaps both, for different types of intellectual property). Such protection creates a monopoly, in the literal sense in which a person has a monopoly of the house he owns but occasionally in a meaningful economic sense as well because there may be no good substitutes for a particular intellectual work. Monopoly profits are not available in most endeavors, so the prospect of obtaining such profits, just as in our sunken-ship example, attracts into the creation of intellectual property resources that might be socially more productive in more competitive sectors of the economy where they would earn only a normal return on investment. If someone has the bright idea that a particular intersection is a good location for a gas station, and builds one at one corner of the intersection, he cannot prevent someone else from appropriating his idea by building a gas station at the opposite corner. A fundamental principle of American law is that competition is not a tort, that is, an invasion of a legally protected right. Freedom to imitate, to copy, is a cornerstone of competition and operates to minimize monopoly profits.

Plant remarked that publishers defend intellectual property by pointing to the many books that fail in the market, their costs being defrayed by the profits generated by the occasional success. The implicit assumption underlying this defense is that either those failed books are a "success" in a meaningful though not commercial sense because they confer an external benefit by increasing the stock of knowledge, or that there is such profound uncertainty about which books will "make it" in the marketplace that publishers could not afford to publish books unless the successful ones generated revenue far in excess of the fixed costs of producing them, in just the same way that the revenue from a gusher must cover the costs of the dry holes that any sound plan of exploring for oil must anticipate. An alternative possibility, however, is that the costs of the failed books are, at least to a considerable extent, just like the costs of the unsuccessful treasure hunters—they are waste induced by competition for economic rents.[19]

On the other side of the question whether to recognize rights in intellectual property is the potentially debilitating effect of free riding on the production of goods that involve a high ratio of fixed to marginal costs, a characteristic of intellectual property related to its public-good character.[20] Coase and others pointed out in criticism of Hotelling that if the owner of a bridge were forbidden to charge users because the marginal cost of their use was zero, the question how to finance the construction of the bridge in the first place would be acute.[21] The government would have to pay for it and how would the government discover whether the demand for the bridge was sufficient to warrant the cost of building it? If users are willing to pay in the aggregate an amount sufficient to cover its cost, at least we'll know that the

19. One possible but not terribly attractive response to Plant's point would be to provide similar legal protection to substitute activities. That is an argument for "business method" patents (see Chapter 11): if ideas for new business methods cannot be patented while new technological methods can be, there may be an inefficient diversion of intellectual talent and other resources from the first type of innovation to the second.

20. Some public goods, such as air, do not involve any costs of production. But of course the fact that a good has a zero marginal cost does not mean that it cost nothing to produce. Its costs of production will, however, be by definition fixed costs.

21. See, for example, R. H. Coase, "The Marginal Cost Controversy," 13 *Economica* (n.s.) 169 (1946); Posner, note 1 above, at 370–371.

market values the bridge more than alternatives. That is one of the social advantages of a public good's being excludable.

Likewise, if the fixed costs of intellectual property—the costs incurred before a single sale is made—are very high and the marginal costs very low, and if, as implied by marginal costs being low, the costs of duplication are slight, then in the absence of intellectual property rights either the intellectual property will not be created or the government may have to finance it through a system of grants or rewards to writers and inventors. (We say "may," not "will," because there may be alternative sources of funding, such as private patronage.) Apart from the objection that such a system would be bound to be politicized, as it would involve substituting a governmental determination of the value of particular types of intellectual property for a market determination, it would not solve the access problem (that is, the misallocative effect of charging a price in excess of marginal cost). Or rather it would solve it only at the cost of creating another access problem. The money for the grants and rewards would have to be raised by taxation, and all feasible forms of taxation drive a wedge between price and marginal cost, just like the pricing of intellectual property when rights in such property are recognized. This is the same issue as whether to finance the production of government documents by taxation or by the government's copyrighting the documents, thus enabling them to be sold at a price that covers the costs of creating them.

Ideally, in deciding how broad or narrow an intellectual property right to recognize, one would want to classify different forms of intellectual property according to the output likely to be produced with and without the recognition of such a right and grant such recognition only to those forms in which output would be seriously suboptimal without it. So in areas of intellectual property where fixed costs were low or other incentives besides the prospect of royalty income were present in force, intellectual property protection would be slight or would even be withheld altogether. Unfortunately, the empirical studies required to make such a classification have never been undertaken; and there is a danger that such a classification could become a political football, with politically favored producers of intellectual property being granted broader rights than others (to some extent this may already be happening). Note finally that when costs of duplication are high, free riding may be eliminated, and intellectual property protection may therefore become relatively unimportant. ("Relatively" because intellectual like physical goods may create congestion externalities.) This was true for works of visual art until such derivative works as prints, decorative plates, statuettes, postcards, mugs, and T-shirts, sold in museum shops, became a source of significant income for owners of copyrighted art.

Paper versus Possessory Titles

A crucial issue in the economics of property, including intellectual property, is the choice between possession and paper titles as grounds of ownership. Both methods are used, and for both physical and intellectual property. Either would be inefficient if universalized. A universal system of paper titles assumes that everything is already owned[22] and permits transfers only by formal conveyance (for example, the delivery of a deed); it is therefore useless for establishing rights over property newly created, never owned, or once owned but abandoned. Such a system would also leave undefined the status of nonowners who nevertheless have the exclusive use of property, such as tenants or licensees. And it would be helpless to deal with the inevitable mistakes to which a system of paper rights gives rise. The other polar regime, in which rights to the exclusive use of property are made to depend on physical control of the property or, in the case of trademarks, on sale in commercially meaningful quantities of the product or service that the trademark designates, entails heavy investments in the maintenance of such control. It also makes no provision for rights to future as distinct from present use. For example, the appropriation system of water rights that is in force in the western states of the United States, under which one acquires a right to water by possessing, that is, using, water (in irrigation, for example), encourages wasteful present use as a method of staking a claim to the future use of the water. The future use may be sufficiently valuable to the possessor to make the present wasteful expenditure worthwhile from his standpoint even though a system of paper rights would be more efficient from an overall social standpoint. That is a danger in conditioning the right to enforce a trademark, as U.S. law does, on the trademark holder's having actually begun to sell the trademarked product, though the problem is alleviated somewhat by permitting "intent to use" trademark registrations (see Chapter 7).

An efficient legal regime of property rights thus is likely to be a mixed system, combining paper rights with possessory rights. Consider, for example, whether unowned property should be obtainable only by possession or also by grant or some other nonpossessory method. The general answer is, only by possession. Suppose a new, and to simplify analysis an uninhabited, continent were discovered. It would not be efficient to give the discoverer title to the entire continent before he had taken possession of it in the sense of occupying all or at least most of it. Such an enormous reward would induce excessive investment in exploration, assuming competition in the exploration mar-

---

22. An exception—the acquisition of title by a grant—is discussed below.

ket. The explorer who discovered the continent just one day before his rivals would obtain the continent's entire value. The prospect of obtaining a value so greatly in excess of his cost of discovery would induce him, and likewise his rivals, to incur additional costs (above the minimum cost of discovery) that would exceed the marginal benefit of those additional exertions.

Recall the earlier example of maritime salvage and assume that the exclusive right to exploit the newly discovered continent is worth $X and that if there were only one potential discoverer he would spend $.1X to discover it and discovery would take him two years. If there are ten potential discoverers, each with an equal chance of winning the race, each will (assuming they are not risk-averse) spend up to $.1X to come in first. But now suppose that the race would cause the continent to be discovered a year earlier; given the time value of money, early discovery would increase the discovery's present value, say to $1.1X. But the increase in value ($.1X) would fall far short of the added cost ($.9X). The race would thus be wasteful from a social standpoint, though if one of the contestants has much lower costs than the others, so that it is apparent from the start that if there is a contest (and the contestants have equal access to the capital markets to finance the expense of the contest) he will win, the others will forbear to compete, and so there will be no race.[23]

An alternative, which resembles the committed-searcher doctrine noted earlier and which we consider in Chapter 11, is to grant the first searcher the exclusive right to the discovery—but then rents may be incurred to become the first searcher.

Probably the most efficient alternative to basing ownership of previously unowned property on either discovery or a grant is to base it on physical occupation. This reduces the net reward to being first and so alleviates to some extent the problem of excessive investment by forcing the would-be owner to incur the costs of occupation. It also tends to allocate resources to those persons best able to use them productively, for they are the people most likely to be willing to incur the costs involved in possession. A discoverer who could obtain title to the entire continent just by declaration or filing would promptly turn around and sell off most or all of the land because he would not be the most efficient developer of all of it. Transaction costs are minimized if the people who are actually going to possess the land are given the ownership right in the first place. That was the procedure followed in the Homestead Act. Parcels of 160 acres were granted to people who wanted to

23. See Dean Lueck, "First Possession," in *New Palgrave Dictionary of Economics and the Law*, vol. 2, p. 132 (Peter Newman ed. 1998).

farm. An alternative would have been to give a real estate company the whole public domain and let the company subdivide it; transaction costs would probably have been higher.

An analogy from intellectual property is the American rule against obtaining a trademark simply by registration, with no present or imminent use. Or consider patent rights: the patent grant is a piece of paper, but you cannot get it until you have actually invented something. We shall see in Chapter 11 that there is debate over how far along in the inventive process one should be required to be in order to be entitled to the critical piece of paper.

Oliver Wendell Holmes discussed a case in which the plaintiff entrusted a safe to the defendant to sell for him and the defendant found some banknotes, evidently the plaintiff's, in a crevice in the safe before he sold it. The plaintiff was held entitled to get the banknotes back; the defendant was not their "possessor" in the eyes of the law.[24] Finding lost property is a valuable service and should be encouraged.[25] But just as with the discovery of new continents, giving a finder the entire value of his find could lead to overinvestment in trying to find things of value. (A discoverer is a kind of finder.) If the agent in Holmes's case had been a specialist in finding forgotten items in safes, then he could have negotiated to purchase the safe and any contents found in it. That is the way in which connoisseurs profit from their skills—they buy from owners who do not realize the full value of their art.

An additional problem with a legal rule of "finders keepers," which has no counterpart in the case of discovery of a new continent, is that giving the finder of lost property its entire value may lead owners to overinvest in safeguarding their property. That problem has been discussed with reference to proposals to give title to finders of long-lost works of art.[26] Better than giving the finder ownership is entitling him, under the law of restitution, to com-

24. Oliver Wendell Holmes, Jr., *The Common Law* 225–226 (1881). For a modern case, involving a painting, see Mucha v. King, 792 F.2d 602 (7th Cir. 1986).

25. Oddly, though, this is less true of currency than of other valuable goods. A successful hunt for sunken artifacts enriches the world's stock of valuable goods, whereas a successful hunt for sunken currency (assuming it has no historical value) merely shifts wealth to the finder by increasing the stock of money and giving him the amount by which it has increased, so that the entire resources consumed in the hunt are a deadweight loss. Hence the rule that "treasure trove" (currency and bullion) escheats to the government rather than becoming the property of the finder. See Posner, note 1 above, at 36–37. This is an example of a legal doctrine that, like the committed-searcher doctrine, can be interpreted as being designed to minimize rent seeking.

26. See William M. Landes and Richard A. Posner, "The Economics of Legal Disputes over the Ownership of Works of Art and Other Collectibles," in *Economics of the Arts* 177 (Victor A. Ginsburgh and Pierre-Michel Menger eds. 1996).

pensation from the owner for the costs of finding and returning the property.[27] That is also better than dividing the found property between the original owner and the finder. Unless the property is readily divisible, a division will reduce its total value (not a problem with a sheaf of banknotes, however), and so the parties would have to expend resources on negotiating a transfer of one party's share to the other, or both parties' shares to a third party, in order to preserve the property's integrity and economic value. The extreme case of inefficient division would be giving the head of a recovered statue to the finder and the rest of the statue to the original owner.

In the case discussed by Holmes, the owner of the safe owned the banknotes. Suppose he didn't. Or suppose someone leaves his wallet, containing money, at a supermarket checkout counter; a customer picks up the wallet; and the owner never claims it. Should the customer be entitled to retain possession of the wallet and money, or should the supermarket be entitled to it? The argument for the customer is that since it was he who found it, he deserves a reward; the supermarket did nothing. But if, knowing that he will be able to keep the wallet if the owner doesn't claim it, the customer walks off with it, it is less likely to be returned to the owner than if it were left to be found by a supermarket employee. For when the owner of the wallet discovers its loss he will check in the places he has visited that day, and the search will quickly lead him back to the supermarket.

The supermarket case illustrates the legal distinction between lost and mislaid items, "lost" meaning that the owner doesn't realize the property is missing. Not realizing that, he is unlikely to search for it, and so the law awards lawful possession of lost property to the finder rather than, as in the case of mislaid property, to the owner of the place where it is found. Still, lost property is not abandoned property, so as between the finder and the owner, the latter has the superior right. But abandoned property is an important category, especially of intellectual property, given the durational limitations of patents and copyrights and the frequent forfeiture of trademarks. When property is abandoned, the law's choice is between "depropertizing" it, so that anyone can use it but no one can establish an exclusive right to its use,

27. See Nadalin v. Automobile Recovery Bureau, Inc., 169 F.3d 1084 (7th Cir. 1999), and cases cited there; William M. Landes and Richard A. Posner, "Salvors, Finders, Good Samaritans, and Other Rescuers: An Economic Study of Law and Altruism," 7 *Journal of Legal Studies* 83 (1978); Saul Levmore, "Explaining Restitution," 71 *Virginia Law Review* 65 (1985). A case similar to that of the safe, also discussed by Holmes, is where "a stick of timber comes ashore on a man's land" (presumably without his knowing it). "He thereby acquires a 'right of possession' as against an actual finder who enters for the purpose of removing it." Holmes, note 24 above, at 223 (footnote omitted). The optimal solution may be to give the finder a reward while giving the property right to the landowner—assuming the stick of timber was unowned when it washed ashore.

and allowing it to be reappropriated, which may make for more efficient use but also may incite rent seeking by competing would-be reappropriators.

Rent seeking incited by excessive rewards provides another argument against allowing the customer-finder in our supermarket example to keep unclaimed mislaid property: his reward may greatly exceed his cost. True, it is only ex post that the customer-finder obtains this reward; that is, it is only if the owner did not claim his property. And this means that the finder's *expected* reward may have been small, since most people who lose valuable property make an effort to recover it. But since an employee of the supermarket would probably have found the wallet shortly after the customer did, the value of the customer's finding it may have been slight—in fact negative, for the owner will have more difficulty reclaiming it from a customer than from the supermarket even if the customer is required to leave his name and address with the supermarket.

The case of the safe with the hidden banknotes sheds light on whether physical control should be required for the maintenance as well as acquisition of ownership. The general answer is "no" because such a requirement would lead to wasteful expenditures and also discourage specialization. To grasp the second point, imagine that a tenant were deemed the owner of the leased premises because the landlord, by virtue of the lease, loses physical control over them (that is, the landlord cannot barge into the premises during the term of the lease). It is more sensible to recognize the joint possession of landlord and tenant and to parcel out the right to take legal action to protect their possessory interests between them in accordance with comparative advantage in particular circumstances. So in cases in which dispossession by an intruder takes place so late in the term that the tenant has little incentive to sue, or cases in which the infringement is more harmful to the landlord than to the tenant (for example, if the tenant is dispossessed by a dealer in illegal drugs, who proceeds to frighten away the other tenants), or cases in which the tenant simply lacks the resources to litigate against the infringer, the landlord though not in possession should be permitted to sue.

Not that joint possession is unproblematic. Transaction costs are higher if the law, rather than placing the right to the use of property in one person, requires two or more people to agree with each other on how the property is to be used. The law deals with this problem by allowing each joint owner to insist on the partition of the property so that it becomes reconfigured as separate parcels each controlled by only one person. Of course this won't be permitted if the partition would greatly reduce the value of the property, as in our earlier example of the statue. In such cases—which are common in the case of intellectual property—efficiency requires a presumption that the entire object is the thing possessed. The blanket licenses issued by performing-rights organizations such as ASCAP are a dramatic example of minimizing transaction costs by aggregating control, in that case by treating a multitude of bits of property (individual songs) as a single lump under one management. Another example is that while copyrights and patents are indivisible, when they are jointly owned the law allows each joint owner the full use of the property right, thus minimizing transaction costs. The difference between this example and that of the statue is the public-good character of intellectual as distinct from physical property. Each joint owner of a copyright can incorporate elements of the copyrighted work into his own future intellectual property, and each joint owner of a patent can work to improve the invention, without interfering (at least physically) in the activity of the other joint owner or owners.

Suppose that a tract of land was previously unowned, unclaimed, and unoccupied, and there is no paper title to it. The first possessor is therefore the owner. But what if he isn't continuously present on the land? If someone now occupies the land, is *he* the possessor? Surely not, as otherwise owners would make wasteful expenditures on fencing and patrolling land. It is one thing to condition acquisition of title to newly found property on possession. But once title is acquired by this route, it should be enough for the maintenance of that title to record it in a public registry of deeds in order to warn away accidental trespassers. That is a cheaper method of notice than elaborate signage and fencing, let alone the kind of present, pervasive use that might reasonably be required to obtain title to *terra incognita*. It is another example of why a system of purely possessory property rights would be uneconomical. It is also an example of the perils of generalizing about the law and specifically about moving too quickly by the route of analogy from physical to intellectual property. For in the case of trade secrets, the possessor in order to be allowed to complain about the theft of his secret information *is* required to have taken active measures to keep it secret. The social purpose of trade secrecy would be thwarted if trade secrets had to be recorded in public registries, and so an alternative method of warning off infringers is necessary and it involves the possessor's taking measures that make clear to the world that the information in question is indeed a secret and may not be used without his permission. This in turn implies, in contrast to the law of physical property, that finders of trade secrets *are* keepers. If you leave your trade secret, as distinct from your wallet, "lying around," rather than as it were under lock and key, someone who "finds" your secret invention becomes a rightful possessor of it—but of course not its exclusive rightful possessor, since it is no longer secret.

Title records are not infallible. Nor do they ordinarily record abandonment. If a new occupier of land formally owned by another makes clear that he is claiming the land and the owner does nothing to contest the claim for years, the law shifts the ownership of the land to the new occupier, who is said to have acquired ownership by "adverse possession." The requirement of adverseness (implicit in our stipulating that the new occupier "is claiming" the land) is essential. Otherwise a tenant whose lease extended for the period of years required to obtain ownership by prescription (that is, by passage of time) would, at the end of that period, have become the owner of the leased property.

The tenant's possession is not "owner-like"; the adverse possessor's is. The root difference lies in the possessor's intent, which can often be inferred from such objective indicia as the existence of a lease, the behavior of the owner (whether itself "owner-like"), and the behavior of the possessor (for example, whether he makes permanent improvements to the property, implying that he thinks himself the owner). We shall see something akin to adverse possession at work in the trademark field; sellers are often dispossessed of their trademarks because a trademark has become in the public mind the name of something other than the particular seller's brand.

Adverse possession, understood as a method of shifting ownership without benefit of negotiation or a paper transfer, is one answer to the question when should property be deemed abandoned, that is, returned to the common pool of unowned resources. Economics teaches that this should happen when it is likely to promote the efficient use of valuable resources. The clearest case of abandonment is when a possessor deliberately "throws away" the property, in effect voluntarily returning it to the common pool. His act signifies that the property has no value in his hands. And so by deeming the property abandoned and therefore available for reappropriation by someone else, the law encourages the reallocation of the property to a higher-valued use without burdening the system with negotiation costs. Similarly, the owner who does not react to the adverse possession of his property for years is indicating that he does not value the property more than the cost of taking the minimum steps necessary to maintain his property right; that is the economic meaning of abandonment.

In allowing property rights to be obtained in abandoned property, the law tracks the economist's presumptive preference for propertized property over commons. It allows property to be withdrawn from the public domain and privatized. But as we have already noted, this is a source of potential worry when the public domain in question consists of intellectual property. The more costly property rights are to transact over—and we have seen that intellectual property rights are likely to be highly costly to transact over—the greater the danger that allowing goods that are in the public domain to be privatized will have inefficient results. In the extreme case, if transaction costs were prohibitive, allowing the public domain to be privatized would eliminate it as a source of inputs into future intellectual property created by anyone other than the owner of the particular bit of formerly public, now privatized intellectual property.

When an owner actually throws away his property—something done all the time, even with land, as when an owner defaults on his mortgage or allows his land to be seized by the government for nonpayment of real estate taxes—this indicates that after deducting the costs of owning the property, he values it at zero dollars or less, and so any finder who bothers to take the property is certain to be someone who values it more. Negotiation is not required in such a case in order to certify that the appropriation of the property by the finder is indeed a value-maximizing transaction; the costs of negotiation would be a deadweight loss. In other cases market transactions are a more efficient method of moving property to its highest-valued use than coerced transactions are, provided transaction costs are low. But often they are high even when the property in question is as conventional as a parcel of land. The owner may be unknown. More commonly, the exact boundaries of his property are unknown, which is why the adverse possessor doesn't know that he's encroaching or the owner that his property is being encroached upon. Such problems are particularly acute in the case of intellectual property. It is not bounded in space or, except for its beginning, in time, and not being physical it is indestructible as well as having no spatial limits.

The law treats the abandonment of intellectual property differently. Once it is abandoned, it becomes part of the public domain and property rights cannot be obtained in it. The difference in legal treatment is explicable by reference not only to the higher transaction costs of intellectual compared to physical property, but also to the traditional emphasis on the role of intellectual property rights in providing incentives to create such property. Once it has been created and abandoned, there is no felt need, from the standpoint of incentivizing, to allow its reappropriation. This may be too limited a standpoint, however, as we shall explore in subsequent chapters, particularly Chapter 8.

We noted that the right of adverse possession is confined to cases in which the adverse possessor is acting in good faith—that is, he really believes the property is his. Otherwise the doctrine would encourage coercive property transfers in settings of low transaction costs. Confined to cases in which the true owner cannot easily be identified or found or seems clearly to have abandoned the property, the doctrine fulfills a basic function of law conceived economically, that of mimicking the market in cases in which high transaction costs either prevent it from bringing about an efficient allocation of resources or, as in the case of abandonment, would be a pure waste. Yet we shall point out repeatedly in this book instances in which the law allows intellectual property to be taken deliberately, without claim of ownership, and without compensation to the current owner, because of high transaction costs—which may indeed be the most important factor that explains the differences between the law of intellectual property and the law of physical property.

Adverse possession can also be thought of as a method of correcting paper titles in settings in which market-transaction costs are high;[28] it improves rather than challenges the system of property rights. By the time an undiscovered owner, or the owner of property of unknown scope, wakes up and asserts his rights, evidence may have faded and the adverse possessor may have relied on a reasonable belief that he is the true owner of the property in question. Thinking the property his he may have made an investment in it that will be worthless if he loses the property to the original owner—to whom, however, the property may be worthless, as indicated by his having slept on his rights. When there is a gross disparity in the value that the only competitors for a good attach to it, transaction costs are likely to be high as each competitor vies for the largest possible share of that value. Suppose the land is worth $1 million to the adverse possessor (perhaps because he believes there are mineral deposits on it) and only $10,000 to the original owner (who disbelieves this). Then at any sale price between $10,000 and $1 million both parties will think themselves made better off by a sale. But each will be eager to engross as much of the difference as possible, and that may make it difficult for them to agree on a price without protracted bargaining; ultimately they may not agree, especially if they want to obtain or maintain a reputation for being hard bargainers.

The doctrine of adverse possession is rarely if ever invoked in intellectual property cases. Yet something quite like it operates in the trademark area; we shall see an example in the "March Madness" case discussed in Chapter 7, where a senior user lost a trademark right to a junior one. Trade secrecy law contains an echo of adverse possession because by failing to take precautions to keep his invention (or customer list, business plans, or other information) secret, the possessor of the trade secret shows that he doesn't value it highly. And the fixed duration of patents and copyrights, a very rough counterpart to adverse possession, has among other purposes simplifying the system of paper titles to intellectual property so that the creation of new and the use of old intellectual property are not encumbered by excessive costs of transacting with existing owners. The fixed duration corresponds to the period of prescription (or statute of limitations) at the end of which physical property is

28. Thomas W. Merrill, "Property Rules, Liability Rules, and Adverse Possession," 79 *Northwestern University Law Review* 1122 (1985).

lost to an adverse possessor. In both cases the effect is to clear the decks of stale paper titles. A major difference, however, is that adverse possession shifts ownership from one person to another, whereas the expiration of a fixed-duration intellectual property rights eliminates ownership and makes the work a part of the public domain.

Sometimes an intention to abandon property can be inferred from negligence in the use of it. The neglectful possessor both implies by his conduct that the property is not worth much to him and creates the impression among potential finders that the property has indeed been abandoned and is therefore fair game. Deeming the property abandoned in these circumstances becomes a method of reducing transaction costs and increasing the likelihood that the property will be shifted to a more valuable use. Our trade secrecy example illustrated this point.

The close relation between, as well as the interdependence of, possession and paper titles as methods of establishing property rights should be clear by now and also the historical priority of the former. Just like a deed of title recorded in a public registry, possession, provided it is "open and notorious," as the cases on adverse possession say, is a way of notifying the world of the existence of a claim.[29] It was the only feasible way in the earliest stages of society. The fence is prior to the paper title as a method of announcing a property right and something like it continues to figure in trademark and trade secrecy law, and in copyright law as well. Before a 1988 amendment to the Copyright Act of 1976, notice had to be affixed to the published work for it to be copyrighted. The amendment dispensed with the requirement of formal notice. But because by virtue of the 1976 Act copyright now attaches automatically to any expressive work once it is fixed in a tangible medium, the work itself is notice of the property right. The decision whether to require a physical act in order to obtain or maintain a possessory right involves trading off the costs of the particular act that communicates a claim against the benefits of clear communication. The more elaborate the required acts, the more unmistakable the communication, which is efficient because the clear public definition of property rights lowers transaction costs and tends to optimize investment; but also the more costly this form of notice becomes.

The costs of the most elaborate acts of notice by possession—acts of complete, continuous, and conspicuous occupation—will often outweigh the benefits. That is why, to recur to an earlier point, a lesser degree of active possession will suffice to maintain a property right than would be neces-

---

29. This function of possession is emphasized in Carol M. Rose, "Possession as the Origin of Property," 52 *University of Chicago Law Review* 73 (1985).

sary to acquire it, a point illustrated by the colorful old case of *Haslem v. Lockwood*.[30] The plaintiff had raked horse manure dropped on the public streets into heaps that he intended to cart away the next day, which was the earliest he could obtain the necessary transportation. The defendant beat him to the punch. The plaintiff sued for the return of the manure and won. The original owners of the manure, who were the owners of the horses that had dropped it, had abandoned the manure; the plaintiff had found it. He took possession by raking it into heaps, and the heaps were adequate notice to third parties, such as the defendant, that the manure was no longer abandoned property available to be reappropriated. To have required the plaintiff, in order to protect his property right, to go beyond the heaping of the manure—to fence it, or watch continuously over it, or arrange in advance to have a cart in place to remove the manure as soon as it was heaped—would have increased the cost of the transaction by which manure worthless to the original owner became a valuable commodity, without generating offsetting benefits.

When property is stolen, it is not deemed abandoned. The purchaser from the thief, even if wholly and reasonably ignorant of the tainted source of his possession, has no right against the original owner. This rule can be defended as reducing the gain from and hence the likely incidence of theft; but there is more to a sound economic analysis, as is brought out by the issue of property rights in stolen art.[31] Many works of art were stolen during World War II, which ended more than half a century ago. It can be argued that if the original owner has done nothing to try to recover the work in all that time, his title should be cut off lest the current owner be reluctant to exhibit the work for fear of alerting his dormific predecessor; the work should be deemed "abandoned." Were this the rule, original owners would have an incentive to take additional precautions to prevent the theft of their art.

But creating such an incentive is not the unalloyed benefit that it may seem. The cost of these precautions, precautions that might include refusing to allow the art to be exhibited widely, have to be balanced against the cost of additional efforts by the purchaser to prevent the discovery of the theft. They also have to be balanced against the additional search costs that an original owner will incur to discover his stolen art if he is entitled to get it back even from a bona fide purchaser from the thief. If the costs in concealment by the purchaser and search by the owner, under a system in which the original owner prevails, do not greatly exceed the costs in owners' precautions under

30. 37 Conn. 500 (1871).
31. See Landes and Posner, note 27 above.

a system in which the bona fide purchaser prevails, the undesirability of making stolen goods more readily marketable is likely to tip the balance against allowing the purchaser to acquire title.

Yet we have noted several times now that trade secrecy law strikes the opposite balance. This is a reminder that the traditional law of property, economically understood, though invaluable as a source of insights for understanding intellectual property law in economic terms, cannot be mechanically extrapolated to that law. The differences are as important as the similarities. Neglect of this point may be responsible for the possibly uncritical expansion in intellectual property rights that we try to explain in the last chapter.

A final difference of great importance between physical and intellectual property is that, despite our example of continental discovery and our reference to the Homestead Act, almost all physical property available for private ownership is already owned. The government is no longer in the business of giving away property rights to land, and as a result all transactions involving land (and personal property as well, that is, physical property that is not land) are private. But in the case of intellectual property, the government remains very much in the business of making ad hoc grants. Every year, government creates hundreds of thousands, maybe millions, of new property rights in intellectual property by issuing copyrights, patents, and trademarks. Government's much deeper involvement in intellectual than in physical property makes it perilous to extrapolate uncritically to the domain of intellectual property from the deservedly high repute in which the system of property rights in land and other physical property is held.

2

How to Think about Copyright

In this chapter we present an informal economic model of optimal copyright protection that will be formalized in the next chapter, and in succeeding chapters we consider how well the principal doctrines (such as fair use) and other features (such as limited duration) of copyright law line up with our economic analysis. We discuss in this chapter the technological, cultural, legal, and economic factors that determine the number and character of expressive works created and then examine the modes of exploitation of the created works. These are the building blocks of the formal model developed in the next chapter.

By "expressive work" we mean any work that might be a candidate for copyright protection under modern law. The term is not ideal, though we haven't been able to think of a better one. Copyright protection is not limited to works of the imagination, such as novels and operas and paintings, but extends to nonfiction, certain data compilations, and even machine-readable computer software. The protection, however, is of the form or configuration in which an idea is expressed, as distinct from the idea itself, the protection of which is the domain of patent and trade secret law rather than of copyright law.

The Creation and Distribution of Expressive Works

The cost of producing a book or other expressive work (we start by talking just about books and later branch out to other forms of expression) has two components. The first is the cost of creating the work. We assume that it does not vary with the number of copies produced or sold, since it consists primarily of the author's time and effort plus the cost to the publisher of soliciting and editing the manuscript and setting it in type. Consistent with copyright usage, we call the sum of these costs the "cost of expression." It is, to repeat, a fixed cost. The second component, the cost of producing the actual copies, increases with the number of copies produced, for it is the cost of printing, binding, and distributing individual copies. It is thus a variable cost.

37

We shall generally ignore differences in costs or incentives between authors and publishers, instead using "author" or "creator" to mean both. In doing this we elide a number of interesting economic questions involving the relation between author and publisher. These include whether the author's right to reclaim copyright from assignees after a specified period of years (currently thirty-five), and the closely related (because also the conferral of an inalienable right) *droit de suite,* now gaining a foothold in American law, which entitles artists to claim royalties on resales of their art by initial (or subsequent) purchasers of it, increase or reduce the incentive to create new works.[1] Economic analysis suggests, contrary to intuition, that these laws reduce the incentive to create intellectual property by preventing the author or artist from shifting risk to the publisher or dealer. He is prevented because he cannot contract away his right of reclamation. A publisher who must share any future speculative gains with the author will pay him less for the work, so the risky component of the author's expected remuneration will increase relative to the certain component. If risk-averse, the author will be worse off as a result. And if he dies before the event that vests his right (the passage of thirty-five years, in the case of the recapture right, or the resale of his work, in the case of *droit de suite*), he will have received no part of the value of the copyright that survived that event, since he was not permitted to sell that value. Notice also that if the law creating *droit de suite* applies to works created before it was passed, it favors established artists at the expense of new ones, because it gives them an unbargained-for return on those works, while reducing the price that collectors are willing to pay for new works.[2]

But if authors are indeed risk-averse, and publishers risk-neutral because they have a portfolio of books and are corporations whose shareholders can eliminate firm-specific risk by holding a diversified portfolio of stocks, why are authors usually compensated by royalties rather than paid a lump sum to assign the copyrighted work to the publisher, who would then bear the entire risk of the book's failing or succeeding in the market? The answer probably is that by tying the author's compensation to the realized rather than anticipated success of the book, the royalty contract increases the author's incentive to produce a commercial success. And the variability of the author's income stream ("risk" in the sense in which economists use the word in discussing risk aversion, risk preference, and risk neutrality) is minimized because authors who actually live on their royalties usually receive nonrefundable advances against royalties, thus shifting risk back to the publisher. Other authors—academics, for example—have a steady source of income, namely

1. See Jeffrey M. Perloff, "Droit de Suite," in *The New Palgrave Dictionary of Economics and the Law,* vol. 1, p. 645 (Peter Newman ed. 1998).

2. See Richard E. Caves, *Creative Industries: Contracts between Art and Commerce* 282 (2000).

a salary, which reduces the riskiness of their overall income (salary plus royalties).

The demand curve for copies of a given book will be negatively sloped because there are good but not perfect substitutes. The publisher will produce copies up to the point where marginal cost equals marginal revenue. The resulting difference between price and marginal cost, summed over the number of copies sold, will generate revenues to offset the cost of expression. The offset may not be perfect; it may fall short or exceed the cost of expression because it is based not on that cost, a sunk cost that does not affect a rational seller's price, but rather on the elasticity of demand and on marginal cost.

Since the decision whether to create the work must be made before the demand for copies is known, it will be a "go" only if the difference between expected revenue and the cost of making copies equals or exceeds the cost of expression. And because the cost of creating equivalent works differs among authors, the number of works created, as distinct from the number of copies of a given work, will increase until the return from the last work created just covers the (increasing) cost of expression.

Two qualifications should be noted. First, the demand for copies of a given work depends not only on the number of copies but also on the number of competing works. The more there are, the lower will be the demand for any given work. Thus the number of works and the number of copies per work will be determined simultaneously, and the net effect of this interaction will be to reduce the number of works created.

Second, price discrimination is often feasible in the case of intellectual property because individual works are not perfect substitutes for each other and arbitrage can often be prevented or at least limited. Thus a publisher will commonly charge higher prices for hardcover editions of a work and later reduce the price for the part of the market that is willing to wait for the paperback edition to appear. Similarly, the prices charged by exhibitors for first-run movies will generally be higher than the prices in the aftermarket (consisting of second-run theaters, home video cassettes, pay television, cable television, network television). Price discrimination increases revenue and thus the number of works produced, though it may not increase the number of copies of each work. A price discriminator substitutes for a single price for all units a schedule of prices, some of which will be higher than that single price and will thus reduce sales to the segment of his market charged those higher prices; and that reduction may be equal to, greater than, or less than the increase in sales to customers charged a lower price.[3]

3. See F. M. Scherer and David Ross, *Industrial Market Structure and Economic Performance* 494–496 (3d ed. 1990); Paul A. Samuelson, *Foundations of Economic Analysis* 42–45 (1947); Joan Robinson, *The Economics of Imperfect Competition* 188–195 (1933).

Many economists believe that discrimination is more likely to expand than to reduce output or leave it unchanged,[4] but there is no firm theoretical or empirical basis for this belief.[5] Even perfect price discrimination—where the seller charges a different price at each point on his demand curve—would produce the competitive output (because the perfectly discriminating seller would proceed down the demand curve to its intersection with his marginal cost curve, charging a different price at every point on the demand curve in this interval) only if the cost of administering the discriminatory scheme were ignored. In any event the information about consumer demands that would be required in order to be able to practice perfect price discrimination is not obtainable at any cost that would make it worthwhile.[6]

In the absence of copyright protection the market price of a book or other expressive work will eventually be bid down to the marginal cost of copying, with the result that the work may not be produced in the first place because the author and publisher may not be able to recover their costs of creating it. We say "may not" rather than "will not" because these costs may be modest, and the head start over competitors, who cannot duplicate a work instantaneously (unless, perhaps, it is a digital work that can be disseminated over the Internet), may enable the charging of a price sufficiently above marginal cost to enable the creator's fixed costs to be recouped. The problem of recoupment is magnified, however, by the fact that the author's cost of creating the work, and many publishing costs (for example, editing costs), are incurred before it is even known what the demand for the work will be. Because demand is uncertain, the difference between the price and marginal cost of the successful work must not only cover the cost of expression but also compensate for the unavoidable risk of failure. If a copier can defer making copies un-

4. See, for example, Robinson, note 3 above, at 201; Scherer and Ross, note 3 above, at 494–496; Peter O. Steiner, Book Review, 44 *University of Chicago Law Review* 873, 882 (1977); and, with particular reference to intellectual property, Jerry A. Hausman and Jeffrey K. MacKie-Mason, "Price Discrimination and Patent Policy," 19 *RAND Journal of Economics* 253 (1988). We give an example in Chapter 14 of where price discrimination seems likely to increase output.

5. See Dennis W. Carlton and Jeffrey M. Perloff, *Modern Industrial Organization* 290–291 (3d ed. 2000); Jean Tirole, *The Theory of Industrial Organization* 152–158 (1988); Hal R. Varian, "Price Discrimination," in *Handbook of Industrial Organization,* vol. 1, pp. 597, 629–633 (Richard Schmalensee and Robert D. Willig eds. 1989).

6. Hausman and MacKie-Mason, note 4 above, emphasize a different social advantage of price discrimination, that it may enable the opening of new markets. A promotional price cut, however, is not really price discrimination; it is a form of advertising. Price discrimination should also be distinguished from Ramsey pricing, which means pricing inversely to the elasticity of demand for a firm's products but with a zero-profit constraint. See Richard A. Posner, *Economic Analysis of Law* 371–372 (6th ed. 2003). If customers can be separated, Ramsey pricing maximizes output. But it requires public-utility-type regulation, to prevent the firm from seeking to maximize profits instead of output.

til he knows whether the work is a success, the potential gains from free riding on expression are enhanced because the difference between the price and marginal cost of the original work will rise to compensate for the uncertainty of demand, thus creating a bigger profit potential for copiers.

Uncertainty has, it is true, an upside as well as a downside, and there is no reason to think that on average the predicted demand for a book exceeds the realized demand. So if a publisher has a diversified list, expected and realized outcomes will tend to converge. The greater the uncertainty, therefore, the larger and more diversified in their publications we can expect publishers to be. Nevertheless even a diversified publisher will be at risk of losing his upside if his competitors are free to copy his successful works.

Factors That Would Limit Copying Even in the Absence of Copyright Law

A number of factors, besides the head start noted in the preceding section, would limit the effect of copying in preventing the creator of an original work from recouping the cost of creating it, even in the absence of copyright law. Some of these points are elaborated further either later in this chapter or in subsequent chapters.

1. *The copy may be of inferior quality and hence not a perfect substitute for the original.* In the case of books and other printed matter, the copier may not be able to match the quality of paper or binding of the original or the crispness of the printing, and there may be errors in transcription. None of these is a very important impediment to good copies any longer. But in the case of unique works of art—such as a painting by a well-known artist—a copy, however accurate, may be such a poor substitute in the market that it will have no negative effect on the price of the artist's work. (Compare the price of an original Rembrandt to the price of a copy so exact that only an expert could tell the difference.) Indeed, the copy may have a positive effect on that price by serving as advertising for the artist's works, though it may also deprive him of income from selling derivative works, such as prints and postcards of his painting.[7] Perfect copies of computer software may be economically inferior, too, because they come without instruction materials or warranties that users may want.

Similarly, museum shops would have a significant locational advantage in the market for posters, replicas, and other derivative artworks even in a world without copyright. This is an example, writ small, of the general point, much

---

7. Museum-shop derivative works, not limited to prints, are a growing phenomenon. See Chapter 9. Derivative works are discussed in Chapter 4.

emphasized in the literature on patents, that a firm that already has a monopoly of intellectual property (entry being for some reason impeded) does not need intellectual property rights.

2. *Copying may itself involve some original expression—as when the copy is not a literal copy but involves paraphrasing, deletions, marginal notes, and so on—and so may have a positive cost of expression.* In other words, the copier may incur his own fixed costs, and not only those just mentioned but also set-up costs, such as the cost of rekeying or photographing the words of the original work. Still, the copier's average cost will usually be lower than the original creator's because it will not include the author's time or the cost of soliciting and editing the original manuscript. Moreover, modern technology has greatly increased the speed and accuracy of copying and lowered its costs. "Rekeying" or "photographing" the words in a book are anachronisms. The book can be scanned into a computer that will generate typeface as clear and elegant as the plates (another anachronistic term in this context) from which the original was printed. In the case of e-books, the book is sold in machine-readable form, as are music CDs, which can be inserted into a computer and their contents uploaded into the computer's hard drive. It remains the case that when the copier cannot take a completely free ride on the creator's investment in expression and his other fixed costs, the need for copyright protection is reduced; but this is an observation of diminishing significance.

3. *Copying takes time, so there will be an interval during which the original publisher will not face competition.* Because the cost of production normally is inverse to time,[8] generally a copier will be unable to produce copies at a reasonable cost until sometime after the work that he is copying is put on the market. But modern technology has reduced the time it takes to make copies, as well as enabled perfect or near-perfect copies to be made at low cost, and as a result the importance of copyright protection has increased for many types of expressive work. Not for all, though. For works that are faddish or otherwise ephemeral (the typical newspaper article, for example)—where demand is initially strong but falls sharply after a brief period—copyright protection may not be needed to assure the creator of the work a fully compensatory return. The cost of such works must be recouped over a short period of time, which will often exceed the time required for duplicating the work and marketing the duplicate.

This continues to be a factor in the case of drama. If most plays have only a short run (as was true in Shakespeare's day, just as in ours, though plays were often revived some time after their initial run), by the time a pirate acquires the script and produces the play the public may have lost interest in it. What

---

8. See Armen A. Alchian, "Costs and Outputs," in *Readings in Microeconomics* 159, 165 (William Breit and Harold M. Hochman eds., 2d ed. 1971).

is more, an exact copy of a play is impossible because the copier will have to find his own actors, director, etc., in order to be able to perform the play. Granted, if the play had prospects of being developed into a movie, copiers would have a shot at beating the owner of the play to the punch. This possibility might induce the owner to skip the play version and move directly to making the movie—an example (one of many) of potentially costly self-protective measures to which creators of expressive works might resort in the absence of copyright protection. The copier's movie would not be an exact duplicate of the play owner's movie version because there would be different actors, etc., but it might be close enough to kill the market for the owner's version if the copier's came out first.

4. *There are contractual alternatives to copyright protection for limiting copying.* One is licensing the original work on condition that the licensee not make copies of it or disclose it to others in a way that would enable them to make copies. Like trade secrecy, contractual prohibitions on copying may be costly to enforce and feasible only if there are few licensees. But the feasibility condition is satisfied in an important class of copyrightable expression, namely computer software programs sold directly by the manufacturer to the consumer by means of a license that forbids the consumer to make and sell copies. Where, however, widespread distribution of a copyrighted work through middlemen is necessary to generate an adequate return to the author, contractual prohibitions will not prevent widespread copying, because the author (or publisher) will not have a contract with each of the potential buyers of unauthorized copies. Anyway, the costs of enforcing contracts with a multitude of individuals would be prohibitive. This is also a problem with enforcing copyright, except that the concept of contributory infringement often enables the copyright owner to concentrate his enforcement activities against one or a handful of large firms, the enablers of the copyright violations by individual consumers. (There is, however, a corresponding doctrine in contract law: tortious inducement of a breach of contract.)

5. *Technological fixes can limit copying.* Computer files (and digital files more broadly) can generally be quickly, inexpensively, and accurately copied and the copies disseminated both cheaply—sometimes indeed at zero cost—and virtually instantaneously. But encryption software can make the cost of unauthorized copying of computer files prohibitive by physically preventing the purchaser of the software product from duplicating the copy that he buys. The law can make encryption more effective. The Digital Millennium Copyright Act[9] forbids reverse engineering of encryption devices for the purpose of facilitating unauthorized electronic copying of copyrighted recordings.

---

9. 17 U.S.C. §§ 1201 et seq. See Universal City Studios, Inc. v. Corley, 273 F.3d 429 (2d Cir. 2001).

Encryption can actually provide greater protection for expressive work than copyright law does. This is not only because copyrights are often infringed, owing to costs of detection and litigation that make it impossible to achieve 100 percent compliance with copyright law, but also because encryption circumvents the defenses to copyright infringement, notably fair use—not to mention the durational limitation of copyright. (Contractual restrictions in a license can do the same thing.) It is also the case, however, that by increasing the cost of sharing copyrighted works encryption can reduce their value. Thus encryption increases the copyright owner's revenues on one margin but reduces it on another. The net effect is uncertain but, unless encryption itself is very costly, it probably is positive.

Although encryption makes copyright protection less vital to the creators of intellectual property, it does so at a social cost that may be quite high. This point is actually obscured by the analogy of physical property. It would be odd to complain about a law that forbade would-be trespassers to tear down the fences that property owners put around their property to prevent trespass; and there is a sense in which that is all that a law against de-encryption ("circumvention" is the more common term) through reverse engineering does. But the difference is that property rights of perpetual duration and with no fair use exception are efficient in the case of physical property, but not in the case of intellectual property because of the social value of the intellectual public domain. If encryption is to replace copyright for digital works because the cost of copying such works in the absence of encryption is zero or close to it and enforcement of copyright law against infringers of copyright in such works is for one reason or another ineffectual, it would seem that the same limitations, such as limited term and a fair use exception, should be placed on encryption protection (or, for that matter, on license terms having the same effect) as are placed on copyright protection. This would depend, however, on the feasibility and cost of engineering the necessary modifications in encryption programs, as well as on the cost of government regulation of technology.

The optimum configuration and use of encryption and circumvention technology in the recording industry could not be achieved simply by repealing the Digital Millennium Copyright Act. Producers of digital works would have an incentive to improve their techniques of encryption in order to frustrate efforts at reverse engineering (though this would depend on the cost and likely efficacy of such efforts given the likely response of the reverse engineers). To the extent that these efforts succeeded, encryption would provide greater protection of intellectual property rights than copyright law. Moreover, these efforts would set off an "arms race" between producers of intellectual property who wanted to prevent copying and the would-be copiers, and the costs incurred in the arms race would be classic rent-seeking costs.

They would be likely to exceed the costs of rent seeking engendered by copyright law if encryption potentially provided greater protection for intellectual property than copyright law does.

Because of discounting to present value, and because many digital (like other) works are ephemeral, technological extensions of the duration of intellectual property protection are unlikely to impose major social costs beyond the costs of the technology itself and of the arms race that it might touch off. This, however, assumes that the technology is adopted when the copyrighted work is first created. It is more likely to be adopted shortly before the copyright expires. Until then the copyright owner may be quite content with enforcing his legal remedies. In fact, because of discounting to present value, it would rarely be cost-justified for him to incur the upfront cost of technology designed to lengthen the copyright term when the copyrighted work was first created. With his legal remedies about to disappear, however, as the copyright term neared its end, the copyright holder would have an incentive to encrypt his copyrighted work if the work still had commercial value and if copies in the possession of buyers were not usable for making good copies at low cost after the copyright expired (such copying would of course be lawful). If he did encrypt the work shortly before the copyright expired, the deadweight loss from preventing copying would begin to accrue almost immediately.

Durational extensions to one side, the extinction of fair use copying by technological or contractual means could impose heavy social costs. We emphasize the economic value of fair use copying throughout this book, and indeed advocate the expansion of the fair use privilege.

A possible partial solution to the concerns just expressed would be to punish the use of circumvention technology only when it was used to infringe copyright.[10] Circumvention technology used to enable copying after the expiration of the copyright term, or to enable fair use copying, would be lawful. But if it were used to enable copying that infringed the copyright on the copied work, the user (the infringer or contributory infringer) would be given a heavier punishment for the infringement, like the enhanced sentence for drug offenses when the offender uses a gun in his drug dealings.

6. *"Copiability" may enhance the value of the original, so that the copyright owner indirectly appropriates some of the value of the copies.* A book is more valuable to the customer if he can make copies of chapters that may be of particular value to him. A CD is more valuable to the purchaser if he can upload

---

10. This was suggested to us by Lawrence Lessig in conversation. Lessig has been in the forefront of those concerned that encryption and other technological fixes may give copyright owners greater protection from copying than copyright law envisages. See Lessig, *Code, and Other Laws of Cyberspace,* ch. 10 (1999).

it into his computer and transmit it over the Web to a friend, perhaps in exchange for a CD owned by the friend. Libraries will pay more for a scholarly journal if they can make copies free of charge for faculty, and the higher price may compensate the journal's publisher for the reduction in revenues from faculty subscriptions.[11] A museum will pay more for a work of art that it can make posters of for sale in its museum shop. Even pirating of software, about which the software industry complains so loudly, is not all loss to software producers. It may create a demand on the part of the pirates for complementary products made by the manufacturer of the pirated software.[12] It may also discourage the formation of a market in lawful or unlawful copies, since piracy is an alternative to purchasing copies as well as originals and so reduces copiers' markets. By accelerating the spread of the work, moreover, piracy may help the creator of the work to obtain a network monopoly (see Chapters 4 and 14). The fair use doctrine recognizes the frequent complementarity between an original and its copies, as does the growing practice of publishers of offering the buyers of their books and journals "free" on-line versions that enable the downloading and printing of selected portions of a work, as well as global searches.

The ability of the original creator to appropriate the benefits of copying by his customers depends basically on the cost of selling directly to the copy recipients and on the cost of copying. If the customer can provide a copy to another person at a lower cost than the original creator could, the latter is likely to benefit even though he does not make a sale.[13] The copy bought by the customer is more valuable to him if he can make a copy for someone else, a friend or relative for example. The clearest case in which unauthorized copying can actually benefit the owner of the copyright is where the recipient of the copy could not afford to pay anything for it. Much sharing of copyrighted work within the family is of this character, and forbidding it would hurt, not help, the original creator by reducing the value of the work to the buyer without generating any offsetting income. The cheaper it is for a customer to

11. See S. J. Liebowitz, "Copying and Indirect Appropriability: Photocopying of Journals," 93 *Journal of Political Economy* 945 (1985). There is, however, a crucial difference between the CD and the journal cases: only in the latter case can the publisher price discriminate and thus appropriate much of the value of his customers' copying by charging a higher price to the big copiers (the journals). See Benjamin Klein, Andres V. Lerner, and Kevin M. Murphy, "The Economics of Copyright 'Fair Use' in a Networked World," 92 *American Economic Review Papers and Proceedings* 205, 206 (May 2002).

12. The terms "complement" and "complementarity" recur throughout the book, and it is important that they be clearly understood. Two goods are complements of each other if a fall in the price of one increases the demand for the other. They are substitutes if a fall in the price of one reduces the demand for the other.

13. See Stanley M. Besen and Sheila N. Kirby, "Private Copying, Appropriability, and Optimal Copying Royalties," 32 *Journal of Law and Economics* 255 (1989).

make copies, however, the likelier it is that copying will be so widespread as to deprive the original creator of income that he would have obtained from selling copies directly to the recipients of his customers' copies. In the limit, if the first customer could make an indefinite number of copies at a lower cost than the price the original creator would have to charge to recoup his fixed costs, unauthorized copying would prevent that recoupment.

This discussion casts additional light on the issue of copyright piracy. When the pirate is unable or unwilling to pay the price charged by the copyright owner, that owner is not deprived of any revenue; the pirate was not a potential purchaser. This is an important respect in which copyright theft, and theft of intellectual property generally, differs from theft of physical property. If a thief steals a Rolls-Royce from the dealer's lot, it is no consolation to the dealer that the thief was not a potential customer because he could not afford to pay the dealer's price; the theft deprived the dealer of the opportunity to sell the Rolls to someone else. But when the purchaser of a software program makes a copy for someone else, he does not reduce the number of copies in the software producer's inventory. If the someone else was not a potential purchaser from the producer, the producer loses nothing from the unauthorized copying. Weak demand for drugs (for example, to treat AIDS in Africa) is an example of how piracy need not reduce the sales revenue of an intellectual property owner.[14]

We are not suggesting that piracy is harmless, let alone beneficial, to creators of expressive works and should therefore be permitted. The fact that some recipients of pirated copies would not have paid for them does not imply that all or most would not have paid. Creators of expressive works do obtain and enforce copyright, as they would not do if piracy benefited them on balance. No copying "privilege" for those unwilling to pay the copyright owner's price would be feasible because the law could not distinguish between those who really were unwilling to pay and those who faked their unwillingness in order to avoid having to pay. And while small-scale, private, noncommercial copying among family and friends will often enable the original creator to charge a sufficiently higher price to offset completely the loss of revenue from selling fewer copies, this will not always be true. Sharing of digital files with friends over the Internet is the germ of Napster-like copyright erosion (see Chapter 4). Some degree of sharing of copyrighted work, however, even if the sharing involves copying, as when one family member makes a photocopy of an article and sends it to another, can be considered either to be fair use or to be implicitly licensed by the copyright holder; these come to the same thing.

14. See Jagdish Bhagwati, "Patents and the Poor," *Financial Times* (U.S. ed.), Sept. 17, 2002, p. 13.

7. *Many authors derive substantial benefits from publication that are over and beyond any royalties.* This is true not only in terms of prestige, celebrity, and other forms of nonpecuniary income, but also in terms of pecuniary income in such forms as a higher salary for a professor who publishes than for one who does not,[15] or greater consulting income, or, for popular authors, performers, and other creators of intellectual property, income from lectures and even product endorsements. Publishing is an effective method of self-advertisement and self-promotion. The social norm against plagiarism reinforces the conferral of prestige by publishing; to the extent that the norm is enforced, whether by ostracism, ridicule, or other means, it ensures that the author will obtain recognition, if not always royalties, from the works he publishes. The label of "plagiarist" can ruin a writer, destroy a scholarly career, blast a politician's chances for election, and cause the expulsion of a student from a college or university; and so the norm against plagiarism helps to secure for original authors a return, though not necessarily a pecuniary one, for their originality.

Although we said we weren't going to discuss relations between authors and publishers, the discussion in the preceding paragraph suggests a possible (though quite possibly illusory) conflict of interest between them that is worth noting. Authors, especially academic ones, may prefer minimal copyright protection because it expands access to their works, which enables them to gain more income, both pecuniary and nonpecuniary, from lecture fees, academic promotion, and enhanced academic prestige than they lose in royalties from book sales. These benefits do not accrue to the publisher and so do not offset the loss of revenues that a reduction in copyright protection implies. However, the author can compensate the publisher by accepting lower royalties and advances and, in some instances, by paying the publisher to publish his work.[16] Academic publishing is roughly consistent with this model. Authors of journal articles, for example, are rarely paid for their contributions; in some cases they actually pay the journal, normally from grant funds, to publish their articles.

8. *Reductions in the cost of copying help copyright owners by reducing their own production costs.* The word "copies" has two distinct referents. It refers to

---

15. See, for example, Steve Swidler and Elizabeth Goldreyer, "The Value of a Finance Journal Publication," 53 *Journal of Finance* 351 (1998) (finding that "the present value of the first top finance journal article is between $19,493 and $33,754, with the additional result of large returns to subsequent publications"); Daniel C. Hamermesh, George E. Johnson, and Burton A. Weisbrod, "Scholarship, Citations and Salaries: Economic Rewards in Economics," 49 *Southern Economic Journal* 472 (1982); Howard P. Tuckman and Jack Leahey, "What Is an Article Worth?" 83 *Journal of Political Economy* 951 (1975).

16. This point was overlooked in American Geophysical Union v. Texaco, 60 F.3d 913, 927 (2d Cir. 1994).

the output of a copier; but it also refers to the physical output of the producer of the copied work, and it is the second usage on which we want to focus now. The publisher obtains revenues by selling copies of the books he publishes. The lower the cost of making copies, the lower his production costs will be and the greater, other things being equal, will be the demand for his books. Modern technology has brought about dramatic reductions in the cost of manufacturing the copies on which publishers earn their revenues, especially when cost is adjusted for higher quality. Think of the CD in comparison to the methods of distributing music in the nineteenth century, or television and video recorders as alternative methods of movie distribution to movie theaters. Think of how a publisher can economize on inventory costs by retaining only a digital copy of his backlist and printing out hard copies only when he receives an order. Think of how quickly and cheaply a digitized book can be revised and updated—thereby obsoleting pirated copies of the original edition.

In short, technological developments, growth of markets, falling transportation costs, and new methods of distribution have combined to increase enormously the ability of the producer of an expressive work to obtain revenues from the sale of copies. We are mindful of the old joke about the businessman who lost money on every sale but hoped to make it up in volume. But even if without copyright protection a publisher could not recover as high a percentage of his fixed cost of expression in the price of the book, so long as that price covers his marginal cost and makes *some* contribution to the recovery of his fixed cost, the more copies he sells the more of that fixed cost he will recover.

The greatly improved dissemination of intellectual property largely explains the "superstar" phenomenon.[17] Consider two concert pianists, one (A) slightly better than the other (B) on balance (that is, trading off technical virtuosity against sensitivity, platform presence, and other desired qualities). Suppose that most of the income of a concert pianist nowadays derives not from performing or teaching but from recording. Since recordings of the same piece of music are close substitutes, a consumer has no reason to buy recordings made by B rather than those made by A unless there is a significant difference in price, and there need not be. Even if A receives a higher royalty from his contract with the record company than B could command, the added cost to the record company may be offset by the economies of a larger output. A may thus end up with a very substantial income from recording and B with a zero income from it, though A may be only a 2 percent better pianist and the difference in quality may be discernible by only a small per-

17. See Sherwin Rosen, "The Economics of Superstars," 71 *American Economic Review* 845 (1981).

centage of the music-loving public. Of course, if recordings made by A can be copied at very low cost, A's royalties will decline—the record company will not be able to afford to pay high royalties when its copying competitor pays none. Yet the royalties that the superstar phenomenon generates are mostly economic rent, with few incentive effects (we'll give examples shortly). The only really serious concern about such copying, therefore, is that it may prevent the record company from recovering costs that it incurs in producing and marketing that are unrelated to the expense of the artist. But many of these will have to be borne by the copier as well. The copier can, it is true, avoid "dry hole" costs by holding off on copying until a work proves to be a hit. But by holding off he gives the producer of the original work a head start that may be decisive in a market such as the market for popular music, since even hit songs have a very short commercial half-life.

9. *The cost of expression has fallen in many areas of intellectual property.* What we are calling the cost of expression includes all the fixed costs of an expressive work, which is to say, roughly speaking, the costs incurred before the first copy is sold. These costs can be divided into the creative and the developmental. In the case of a novel, the creative costs are the time and effort of the novelist in producing an acceptable manuscript and the developmental costs are those incurred by the publisher in putting the manuscript into publishable form, printing the first run, arranging for distribution and advertising, and so forth. Computerized printing and the World Wide Web will soon enable authors to become self-publishers at greatly reduced developmental as well as variable costs, and by selling directly to consumers over the Internet they can contractually bind the purchasers not to make or sell copies. This may enable them to obtain more protection against copying than copyright law provides. There are similar possibilities for other forms of expressive work, including both music and artworks. The same technological advances that have greatly reduced the quality-adjusted cost of copying are reducing the cost of expression, raising the cost of copying by enabling it to be restricted contractually or technologically and on both counts reducing the importance of copyright protection as a means for enabling the recovery of the cost of expression.

The foregoing nine points constitute the case against an incentive-motivated need for copyright (an equivocal case, though, in the case of such copyright substitutes as contract and encryption)—and especially against an incentive-motivated need for very long copyright terms. For even with regard to expressive works especially vulnerable to being promptly and perfectly and widely copied, such as a CD and many types of computer software, it is unclear that manufacturers would require copyright protection lasting more than a few years in order to be able to recover the reasonable cost of creating the work. (The qualification in "reasonable" is necessary because the greater copyright protection is, the likelier it is that many of the costs of expression are costs engendered by rent seeking.) Copyright skeptics like to add that intellectual property was produced in considerable quantity and quality long before there were any copyright laws,[18] but this point is misleading. For centuries after the invention of the printing press, books continued to be very expensive to produce. More precisely, the *variable* costs of printing—the costs that varied with the number of copies printed, such as the cost of paper and ink—were high both absolutely and relative to the fixed costs of expression,[19] which tended to be modest because most books were translations or reissues of familiar works, such as the Bible (which was both), all of which were in the public domain. There was still the set-up cost, but the copier had a set-up cost too before the modern era of computerized printing from a scanned copy. The higher the cost of a copy relative to that of the original, the smaller is the advantage to the copier from not having borne any part of the cost of creating the original. For example, if that cost (what we are calling the cost of expression) is only 1 percent of the total cost, the copier will derive only a 1 percent cost advantage over the original publisher from not bearing it.

Moreover, before there was formal copyright law there were limited functional equivalents of a sort that would not be available today if copyright were abolished.[20] In England publishers of particularly expensive or politically sensitive books, such as the Bible and law books, were sometimes given printing patents, the equivalent of copyright, by the Crown. And because the Stationers' Company had a monopoly of the books registered by it, a member of the company could obtain the equivalent of copyright protection by producing a book—or even just by buying a copy of it—and registering it. The Company was composed of printers and booksellers rather than authors, but this is a detail of no economic significance. The author owned the manu-

---

18. On the history and prehistory of copyright law—which appears to have emerged first in fifteenth-century Venice, along with patent law—see Joseph Loewenstein, *The Author's Due: Printing and the Prehistory of Copyright* (2002); Arnold Plant, "The Economic Aspects of Copyright in Books," in Plant, *Selected Economic Essays and Addresses* 57, 58–79 (1974 [1934]); Bruce W. Bugbee, *The Genesis of American Patent and Copyright Law,* ch. 2 (1967); Brander Matthews, *Books and Play-Books,* ch. 1 (1895); Salathiel C. Masterson, Comment, "Copyright: History and Development," 28 *California Law Review* 620 (1940).

19. See Henri-Jean Martin, *The History and Power of Writing* 237–239 (1994).

20. See Lyman Ray Patterson, *Copyright in Historical Perspective* 20–142 (1968); see also John Feather, "From Rights in Copies to Copyright: The Recognition of Authors' Rights in English Law and Practice in the Sixteenth and Seventeenth Centuries," in *The Construction of Authorship: Textual Appropriation in Law and Literature* 191 (Martha Woodmansee and Peter Jaszi eds. 1994); Mark Rose, *Authors and Owners: The Invention of Copyright* 9–12, 17 (1993); David Saunders, *Authorship and Copyright* 47–51 (1992). Parallel developments in sixteenth-century France are traced in Cynthia J. Brown, *Poets, Patrons, and Printers: Crisis of Authority in Late Medieval France* (1995), and in sixteenth-century Germany in Fedor Seifert, *Von Homer bis Richard Strauss: Urheberrecht in Geschichten und Gestalten,* ch. 9 (1989).

script, without access to which the Company could not publish, and so the Coase Theorem implies that the terms the author got were the same or at least similar to what they would have been had the author rather than the Company owned the copyright equivalent. (Erosion of the monopoly of the Stationers' Company provides part of the backdrop to the first English Copyright Act, enacted in 1710.)[21] Milton's contract for the sale of the uncopyrighted *Paradise Lost* to a publisher in 1667 shows that a member of the Stationers' Company would pay authors a significant sum for the author's promise not to sell copies of his work to anyone else—in effect, for the right to publish his work.[22] This is as the Coase Theorem would lead us to expect.

Before freedom of expression became generally applauded, publishing was often believed to impose negative externalities—so there was less, sometimes no, desire to encourage it. The absence of copyright law in Imperial China, despite the fact that printing had begun there centuries before it began in the West, has been attributed in part to the emphasis that Chinese culture placed on continuity with the past, and to its suspicion of novelty, both of which attitudes encouraged what we would consider (depending on the precise meaning of the word, on which more later) plagiarism.[23] Renaissance Europe was more hospitable to novelty. But the prevalence of censorship then and indeed for a long time afterward shows that intellectual creativity was feared as well as valued and that the encouragement of literary output by the generous bestowal of authors' rights would not have been considered a prudent policy.

A related point that will play a major role in our formal analysis in the next chapter is that the absence of copyright protection is, paradoxical as this may seem, a benefit to authors as well as a cost to them. It reduces the cost of writing by enabling an author to copy freely from his predecessors. Shakespeare would have had to work harder, and so might have written fewer plays, had he not been able to copy gratis from works of history and literature, sometimes, as we shall see, verbatim. The less that originality is valued, the less

21. See Benjamin Kaplan, *An Unhurried View of Copyright,* ch. 1 (1967); Philip Wittenberg, *The Protection of Literary Property,* ch. 1 (1968). The history is more complicated than the summary in the text, however. See Patterson, note 20 above, chs. 6–7.

22. See Peter Lindenbaum, "Milton's Contract," in *The Construction of Authorship,* note 20 above, at 177; Patterson, note 20 above, at 73–74. The author could not grant outright the right to publish because the existence of censorship meant that no one had a legal right to publish. Id. at 73.

23. See William P. Alford, "Don't Stop Thinking about . . . Yesterday: Why There Was No Indigenous Counterpart to Intellectual Property Law in Imperial China," 7 *Journal of Chinese Law* 3, 29–32 (1993). Alford also mentions limited literacy and absence of corporate bodies capable of large-scale commercial innovation as factors discouraging the creation of intellectual property law. Id. at 20. These factors would have reduced the demand for copying and increased the cost, making copyright law less needful.

valuable to authors and readers is copyright protection, which encourages originality.

That was then and this is now; and one of the changes has been an upward valuation of originality. Yet even today the importance of copyright for internalizing the cost of expression is easily exaggerated. The cost of writing is very low for many excellent writers—it is mainly the time cost to the author—so authors can afford to do some writing even if they have little or no hope of obtaining royalties or other income from their writing because they lack copyright protection. This would not be true if writing were a full-time occupation, but most writers write only part time even if they are well paid for writing. And as we noted earlier, many writers receive nonmonetary rewards from writing that in addition they often can commute into money. A famous author will be invited to give lectures or teach, awarded prizes, asked for endorsements. Indeed, the more emphasis a culture places on originality, the greater the rewards to originality even if copying is cheap, quick, and accurate; the rewards don't necessarily have to come in the form of legal remedies against copiers.

A related point is that copyright protection is important only if an author is seeking payment for his writing from book buyers. He may instead have a patron who pays him to write, or may receive a public subsidy for writing, or—this is increasingly common—may be paid to teach writing or literature, with the understanding that he will use his free time to write, so that his teaching income is implicitly a writing income as well. And most scholars receive few copyright royalties, yet, as noted earlier, scholarly publication has a significant effect on academic incomes. Patronage lives.

We must not ignore the publishers, however. Given substantial fixed costs of publication and easy copiability, publishers may need copyright protection in order to be able to recover their fixed costs even if they don't have to pay a cent for the expressive content of what they publish. And often they don't—often they publish books that are in the public domain, such as the Starr Report. In the case of academic books, as we have noted, the publisher may require a subvention from the author, in effect exacting a negative royalty. But these very arguments show that the case for copyright based on publishers' fixed costs is far from airtight. Publishers can't copyright works in the public domain, yet they publish them anyway. When, as is normally the case with intellectual property, the fixed costs of production are a high fraction of total costs, so that average total costs are declining over the full range of feasible output, we have natural monopoly; and natural monopolists are hard to compete against. The copier, though not bearing all the fixed costs borne by the original publisher, will have some fixed costs and he will find it hard to recoup them if in response to his entry the original publisher reduces his cost to or near marginal cost, which he is quite likely to do.

We shall note a counterexample in Chapter 11—that patentees of branded drugs tend (or tended—the practice is changing) not to reduce price when the patent expires and competition from generics erupt, but rather to cede the low-price segment of their market to the generics. This is possible because many customers do not consider the generic a perfect substitute for the branded product despite its chemical identity. This makes it easier for the producer to recover his fixed costs. Brand loyalty is nowhere near as important a factor in the market for books as in the market for drugs, but it is not wholly absent. The key is trademarks. The trademark on the drug identifies it as a branded product distinct from its generic substitute. Were there no copyright law, the publisher of the original work would be careful to identify it as the version authorized by the writer. The copier of a book, to avoid trademark infringement, would have to disclaim that it was the authorized version. Some readers would pay a premium for the authorized work.

What is more, publishers publish copies of original works published by other publishers, whether under license or because those works have fallen into the public domain, as well as their own original works. Anything that makes copying cheaper, such as withdrawal of copyright protection, creates new publishing opportunities. The larger the public domain, the larger the number of works that a publisher can publish without having to negotiate a license or pay royalties.

Consider now the enormous incomes of top producers of intellectual property, whether they are software writers, rock stars, actors and actresses, celebrity authors such as former President Clinton (who received an $8 million advance for a book about his presidency), or top Hollywood producers and directors.[24] A very large fraction of these incomes appear to be rents, that

---

24. "Power 100," *Forbes Magazine*, July 8, 2002, p. 123, estimates the *annual* income for 2002 of Britney Spears at $39.2 million, Madonna at $43 million, Oprah Winfrey at $150 million, Tom Clancy at $47.8 million, George Lucas at $200 million, Stephen King at $52.4 million, Bill Clinton at $25 million, and Meg Ryan at $25 million. In the entire *Forbes* list of 100 celebrities, only four have annual incomes below $10 million, and although Lucas and Winfrey are the highest earners, a number of the others on the list have incomes higher than some whom we have given as examples—Britney Spears, for example, ranks only 25 on the basis of income. Most of the earnings of the 100 celebrities are from copyrighted works or from endorsements and other "publicity rights," a form of intellectual property discussed in subsequent chapters. One effect on celebrity performers of reduced copyright protection owing to increased piracy, especially of music CDs, is noted in a recent newspaper article: "Internet piracy, greater media choices and declining CD sales have forced music companies to work harder to persuade consumers to buy music. Artists must go on exhaustive promotion campaigns, showing up on morning news shows and prime-time specials. They must be more open to fans than they were a decade ago. As a result, artists are more willing to risk overexposure." Lynette Holloway, "Keeping J. Lo in Spotlight Has Risks for Her Career as Well as Rich Rewards," *New York Times* (natl. ed.), Dec. 9, 2002, pp. C1, C12. The article is about Jennifer Lopez, the actress and singer, whose 2002 income according to the *Forbes* list was $37 million.

is, income in excess of the recipient's opportunity costs. (This is related to the superstar phenomenon.) And since these rents are costs to publishers, reducing or eliminating them, provided it didn't kill the geese that lay the golden eggs, might benefit publishers more than it harmed them.

Appearances may deceive; it may be that the expected as distinct from the realized return to the creation of intellectual property is low, and that if it fell farther because the realized income was lower it would no longer be high enough to attract good people into the field. But the argument can be turned on its head. Because huge rents accrue to the most successful creators of intellectual property by virtue of the monopoly power conferred by copyright, people whose social product might be greater in other fields in which monopoly returns are not obtainable are attracted into the creation of intellectual property, hoping to hit the jackpot.

Think of all the books, movies, television shows, and songs that bomb in the marketplace. If publishing (broadly defined) is a competitive industry, industry profits in an economic sense will be zero in equilibrium even though some published works will be hugely profitable. The profits will be competed away by the publishing of speculative works most of which lose money. The costs incurred in these losing ventures are social as distinct from merely private losses if the ventures are themselves an artifact of the rents that the occasional success generates.

By way of comparison, imagine that a cartel or government regulation increased the price of wheat above its cost: more wheat might be produced than the market would buy at the fixed price, and the excess supply would be stored and left to rot in warehouses. The cost of producing and storing this extra wheat would be a deadweight loss. Copyright works differently but with a similar result. It does not place a floor under the price of a book, but by penalizing copying it enables the owner of the copyright to charge a higher price per copy not offset by a higher cost, just as if nonmembers of a wheat cartel were fined for producing wheat.

In the formal model in the next chapter we treat the expected penalty from copyright infringement as an addition to the marginal costs of unauthorized copiers (infringers) of copyrighted works. If the penalty is zero, then the price for copies charged by the copyright holder would be driven down to his marginal cost, assuming that the marginal costs apart from the penalty are the same for the copyright holder and for the copiers. If the expected penalty is positive (that is, the copyright is valid and infringed, and enforcement costs are not prohibitive), copiers will face a higher marginal cost curve than the copyright holder does. The copiers' penalty-related marginal cost curve will be upward sloping, since a limited amount of copying will not involve much risk of liability but as the copying becomes more extensive the expected penalty will rise. This will limit the copiers' ability to compete, just as in a dominant-firm model in which the higher marginal costs of the fringe firms enable the dominant firm to charge a price in excess of marginal cost even though it does not have 100 percent of the market. In the limiting case in which copyright enforcement drives unauthorized copying to zero, the price charged by the copyright holder will be based on the elasticity of demand for the copyrighted work (which now will equal the elasticity of demand facing the copyright holder because there is no unauthorized copying) and on his marginal cost.

The increase in net revenue enabled by copyright protection draws resources into the creation and production of new books. Indeed, this is the incentive-based argument for copyright protection. The question is not whether copyright creates incentives to make expressive works, but whether it creates such powerful incentives that it leads to socially wasteful expenditures on creating and producing such works. It is true that the additional expenditures may make for a higher-quality product, but that is also true in our wheat example; cartel members frequently transform rents into costs by engaging in nonprice competition that produces more quality, at a higher price, than consumers want. If they wanted it, it would be provided under competition.

Consider the humble example of academic publishing. Academic publishers often derive much of their income from their "backlist," that is, from continuing sales of books published in previous, sometimes long-previous, publishing seasons. This income is used to finance current publication of academic books, most of which fail to generate income sufficient to cover their cost. Without copyright, a backlist wouldn't be worth much, and the number of books published by universities would decline. What would be the social loss? On the one hand, it can be argued that even those academic books (the majority) that are marginal in a commercial sense generate unusually large external benefits, by adding much more to the stock of knowledge than books intended primarily for entertainment or books dealing in scandal and other ephemera. On the other hand, these academic books, which often sell only a few hundred copies each and rarely yield significant income to their authors, could easily be disseminated to their tiny readership in electronic or samizdat form. Their publication as books may be an artifact of copyright rather than a response to a social need.

Although for the reasons that we have been exploring it is difficult, indeed probably impossible, to say whether copyright is necessarily a good thing or a bad thing from the standpoint of optimizing the production of expressive works,[25] it is easy to spot particular distortions that a copyright law corrects.

25. For a good discussion, see Björn Frank, "On an Art without Copyright," 49 *Kyklos* 3 (1996).

Without copyright protection, authors, publishers, and copiers would have inefficient incentives with regard to the timing of various decisions. Publishers, in order to lengthen their head start, would be reluctant to engage in prepublication advertising and even to announce publication dates in advance, and copiers would have an incentive to install excessively speedy production lines. There would be increased incentives to create ephemeral works because the gains from being first in the market for such works would be likely to exceed the siphoning of revenues to copiers. There would also be incentives for vertical integration, since publishers, by taking over the retail outlets at which their books were sold, could use contract to prevent the buyers of its books from making copies. Dramatists would be reluctant to publish their plays, since it is difficult to copy a play by attending a performance and memorizing the actors' speeches (though audience members would also have to be prevented from taping the performance). There would be a shift toward the production of works that are difficult to copy; authors would be more likely to circulate their works privately rather than widely to lessen the risk of copying; and contractual and technological restrictions on copying would multiply.

Particularly to be emphasized are the costs of defensive measures akin to those taken by possessors of physical property who lack legal protection. (They are not "owners" because ownership is a legal status.) In the case of inventions, defensive costs are likely to take such forms as maintaining extreme secrecy in laboratories and plants and binding employees by strict covenants not to compete. In the case of expressive works such as novels, fear that a copier would be the first to publish the work might stimulate the author or publisher to purchase a safe in which to keep his manuscript, hire guards, restrict the number and circulation of drafts, and even publish the work in a premature, incomplete state. These measures not only would be costly but might incite potential copiers to undertake equally or more costly countermeasures. In the software industry, where piracy is rife, producers resort to such measures of protection against copying as "supplying large manuals, use of which is closely associated with the running of the program, tight contractual arrangements, providing manuals on paper difficult to copy, and regular updates which—some cynics might suggest—contain few facilities which advance the use of the software concerned."[26] Society can reduce the total costs incurred in defensive measures against piracy by providing effective enforcement of property rights in intellectual property, just as it can reduce the total costs of defensive measures against crime by deterring crime by means of threat of punishment.

26. John Gurnsey, *Copyright Theft* 120 (1995).

Copyright, however, causes its own distortions in the market for expressive works. By discouraging copying, it discourages the historically very important form of artistic creativity that consists of taking existing work and improving it. For example, Shakespeare's characteristic mode of dramatic composition was to borrow the plot and most of the characters—and sometimes some of the actual language—from an existing work of history, biography, or drama and to embroider the plot, add some minor characters, alter the major ones, and write most, or more commonly all, of the dialogue. Shakespeare made up Antony's great funeral oration in *Julius Caesar;* no part of it is in his source, North's translation of Plutarch. However, for the description of Cleopatra in *Antony and Cleopatra* Shakespeare merely edited the North-Plutarch description, though he did so brilliantly and vastly improved it. Here is North:

> She disdained to set forward otherwise, but to take her barge in the river of Cydnus, the poope whereof was of gold, the sailes of purple, and the owers [oars] of silver, which kept stroke in rowing after the sounde of the musicke of flutes, howboyes, citherns, violls, and such other instruments as they played upon in the barge. And now for the person of her selfe: she was layed under a pavillion of cloth of gold of tissue, apparelled and attired like the goddesse Venus, commonly drawen in picture: and hard by her, on either hand of her, pretie faire boyes apparelled as painters doe set forth god Cupide, with litle fannes in their hands, with the which they fanned wind upon her.[27]

And here is the corresponding passage in Shakespeare:

> The barge she sat in, like a burnished throne,
> Burnt on the water. The poop was beaten gold;
> Purple the sails, and so perfumèd that
> The winds were lovesick with them. The oars were silver,
> Which to the tune of flutes kept stroke, and made
> The water which they beat to follow faster,
> As amorous of their strokes. For her own person,
> It beggared all description: she did lie
> In her pavilion—cloth-of-gold of tissue—
> O'erpicturing that Venus where we see
> The fancy outwork nature. On each side her

27. Plutarch, "The Life of Marcus Antonius" (translated by Sir Thomas North, 1579), in *Narrative and Dramatic Sources of Shakespeare,* vol. 5, pp. 254, 274 (Geoffrey Bullough ed. 1964).

Stood pretty dimpled boys, like smiling Cupids,
With divers-colored fans, whose wind did seem
To glow the delicate cheeks which they did cool,
And what they undid did.[28]

And here for good measure, to show that the older notion of creativity is not dead, though it is constrained by copyright, is T. S. Eliot's version of the barge scene in Part II of *The Waste Land:*

The Chair she sat in, like a burnished throne,
Glowed on the marble, where the glass
Held up by standards wrought with fruited vines
From which a golden Cupidon peeped out
(Another hid his eyes behind his wing)
Doubled the flames of sevenbranched candelabra
Reflecting light upon the table as
The glitter of her jewels rose to meet it.

Mention of Eliot is apropos because the echoing of the literature of the past has been a common device of modernist literature; one is not just talking about a vanished era of literary conventions. Joyce's *Ulysses* is a famous example of modernist borrowing. Kafka borrowed heavily from Kleist and Dickens. The first stanza of Yeat's great poem "The Second Coming" contains borrowings from two of Shelley's poems.[29] Modern writers, living in the age of copyright, are perforce limited to taking from the public domain unless they are willing to try to negotiate a license from a copyright holder, or (an exception we discuss in Chapter 6) they wish to parody a copyrighted work, or they are content with a sufficiently loose paraphrase to avoid infringement under the "substantial similarity" standard (see Chapter 4), or they take so little as to bring them within the fair use defense to infringement. Even the Romantic poets' notorious equation of creativity with originality was a considerable exaggeration of their actual practice. Coleridge, seemingly the most "original" of the Romantics, borrowed heavily, to the point of committing plagiarism, from other writers.[30]

The pervasiveness of borrowing in literature is captured in Northrop

28. *Antony and Cleopatra,* act II, sc. 2, ll. 201–215 (David Bevington ed 1988).

29. Harold Bloom, *Shelley's Mythmaking* 93–94 (1959).

30. See Norman Fruman, *Coleridge, the Damaged Archangel* (1971); Françoise Meltzer, *Hot Property: The Stakes and Claims of Literary Originality* 2–3 (1994). Thomas Mallon, *Stolen Words,* ch. 1 (1989), discusses plagiarism by Coleridge and Thomas De Quincey, as well as the earlier, flagrant plagiarisms of Laurence Sterne in *Tristram Shandy.* For many examples of allusion in Romantic poetry, see Christopher Ricks, *Allusion to the Poets,* pt. 1 (2002).

Frye's dictum that "poetry can only be made out of other poems; novels out of other novels."[31] Frye has some tart words about copyright. He notes the challenge to the assumptions underlying the copyright law posed by "a literature which includes Chaucer, much of whose poetry is translated or paraphrased from others; Shakespeare, whose plays sometimes follow their sources almost verbatim; and Milton, who asked for nothing better than to steal as much as possible out of the Bible."[32] What Chaucer, Shakespeare, and Milton *did* with inherited or borrowed themes and sources—which if the originals were under copyright today would constitute copyright infringement—exemplified a higher order of creativity than is commonly attained by works of literature that are fully original in the copyright sense. Under a regime of copyright law, Shakespeare might have had to get a license from North in order to be allowed to compose one of his most beautiful passages.[33] To repeat, though inhibited by copyright law this older form of creativity retains a foothold in modern culture; to the examples given earlier we can add appropriation art (see Chapter 9), which as the name implies borrows heavily from previous work, and jazz improvisation, which often works off existing melodies, with the creativity lying in the variations added by the improviser.

Infringement, Plagiarism, and the Role of Personality and Originality in Copyright Law

A plagiarist and a copyright infringer are both copycats; the difference is that the plagiarist is trying to pass off the copied work as his own while the infringer qua infringer is merely trying to appropriate value generated by property that belongs to someone else, namely the holder of the copyright on the writing or other work that the infringer has copied. (The infringer will be a plagiarist as well if he states or implies that his copy is an original work.)

31. Northrop Frye, *Anatomy of Criticism: Four Essays* 97 (1957).

32. Id. at 96. See also id. at 95–104.

33. "Might," not "would," because Plutarch's and therefore North's account purports to be factual, and factual assertions, as we'll see in Chapter 4, are not copyrightable, though their arrangement and wording are. Notice also that if Plutarch's account but not North's was in the public domain, then Shakespeare (or anyone else) could translate and edit Plutarch's account without violating North's (hypothetical) copyright. But a translator can copyright his translation; and Shakespeare obviously was copying North's translation rather than copying the original, and so infringing North's (hypothetical) copyright. If Plutarch's works were copyrighted and Shakespeare were deemed to be copying expression and not just facts, Shakespeare would be infringing that copyright as well. Eliot, however, would be able to get away with his pastiche by a combination of the substantial-similarity test and the fair use doctrine, since his is a loose paraphrase except for the first line, where he just changed "barge" to "Chair."

There is no copyright infringement if the "stolen" intellectual property is not property at all because it is not under copyright but instead is in the public domain, or if what is copied consists of facts or ideas rather than the form in which they are expressed, or if the copying is insulated from liability by the doctrine of fair use, which permits brief passages (and sometimes more) of a book to be quoted in a review or critical essay. And we'll point out in Chapter 6 that the parodist of a copyrighted work is permitted by the doctrine to copy as much of that work as is necessary to enable readers to recognize the copying work as a parody. Fair use would also allow a writer to quote a passage from another writer just to liven up his narrative. But in that case the omission of quotation marks—passing off another writer's writing as one's own— would be more like fraud than like a "fair" use of another writer's work.

Plagiarism[34] may tentatively be defined as *unacknowledged* copying whether or not in violation of copyright law, whereas copyright infringement is unlawful copying whether or not the original author is acknowledged. Although plagiarism sounds like a worse offense from a moral standpoint than mere copyright infringement, we know that literary, artistic, theatrical, and music history is full of noble plagiarisms. But what these examples show is that, contrary to our initial stab at definition, not all unacknowledged copying, even if it is of vast swatches rather than mere bits of previously published work, is "plagiarism" in the pejorative sense. Although there was no explicit acknowledgment of copying in the examples we gave (except *The Waste Land,* to which Eliot appended endnotes identifying most of his borrowings) or could give from the literary tradition, such as what Shakespeare did to North and Plutarch (neither of whom most members of Shakespeare's audiences would even have heard of), neither was there any likelihood of deception. Either the reader was intended to recognize that copying was going on, as in the case of Milton's borrowings from the Bible,[35] or the reader had no particular expectations concerning the ratio of original to copied material in a given work.

Deception is thus the essence of "plagiarism" in the pejorative sense. One of the reasons plagiarism in that sense is so reprobated is that it seems so gratuitous; the copier can take all he wants without being a plagiarist so long as he merely acknowledges that he is copying. Plagiarism is so often made subject to sanctions that seem disproportionate to the harm the plagiarist causes

34. On which see generally *Perspectives on Plagiarism and Intellectual Property in a Postmodern World* (Lise Buranen and Alice M. Roy eds. 1999).

35. That is, Milton was *alluding* to the Bible, not plagiarizing it in the sense of pretending that *Paradise Lost* was completely original—that he had invented Adam and Eve, Satan, the Garden of Eden, the eating of the forbidden fruit, the expulsion from Eden, and so forth. The distinction between allusion and plagiarism is stressed in Ricks, note 30 above, at 219–240.

for a related reason: precisely because the plagiarist attempts to conceal his act, it is often very difficult to detect. This is true of the student's plagiarized term paper and to a lesser extent of the professor's plagiarized scholarly article. These are genuine frauds because they may lead the reader to take steps, such as giving the student a good grade or voting to promote the professor, that he would not take if he knew the truth.[36] By inducing such actions, plagiarism of the deceptive kind causes harm—to the honest student (assuming that grading is on a curve) and to the academic or other writer whose reputation for originality is impaired by a successful plagiarism. The latter harm is reduced, however, often to zero, if the person plagiarized from is dead. Plagiarism can be a form of fraud, but, like copyright infringement, it is not a real theft. If a thief steals your car, you are out the market value of the car; but if a writer copies material from a book you wrote, you don't have to replace the book. At worst, the plagiarist obtains a reputation that he does not deserve (that is the element of fraud in plagiarism), but the principal victim is not the person whose work he copies, but those of his own competitors who scruple to enhance their own reputations by such means. In contrast to plagiarism, *acknowledged* copying can provide advertising for the author of the original work, yet without derogating from any rights under copyright law that that author may have.

Interestingly, plagiarism is not a legal category; plagiarizing is not a crime or a common law tort or a violation of any intellectual property statute. This illustrates the absence from the law of any *general* principle that appropriating intellectual property created by another person is wrongful, although particular forms of misappropriation are sometimes forbidden, as

---

36. An intermediate case is that of popular historians who, as in the celebrated instances of the late Stephen Ambrose and of Doris Kearns Goodwin, quoted passages from previous historians' work without quotation marks but with a footnote reference. They may have felt that the readability of their work would be impaired if they had to interrupt their smooth, fast-paced narratives by confessing that "a predecessor of mine, ___, has said what I want to say next better than I can, so rather than paraphrase him here, indented and in quotation marks, I give you the following passage from his book ___." Since a footnote does not signal verbatim incorporation of material from the source footnoted, the fact that Ambrose and Goodwin footnoted their "thefts" does not exonerate them from the charge of plagiarism but did reduce the cost of discovering it; this is relevant to how severely they should be criticized, since as mentioned in the text the difficulty of detecting plagiarism is one of the reasons it is criticized as severely as it is. Moreover, the element of fraud was attenuated because readers of popular histories are not professional historians and don't care how original the historian they are reading is. The public wants a good read, a good show, and the fact that the book or the play is the work of many hands, as in truth most art and entertainment are, is of no consequence to it. But there is some harm both to competing historians and to the authors of the works stolen from. The prevalence and hence social costs of plagiarism may be declining because computer search programs have made it easier to detect plagiarism.

we'll point out from time to time in subsequent chapters. Some plagiarisms, however, may be actionable as trademark infringements. Titles, like other short phrases, are not copyrightable; but if a writer were to appropriate the title of a famous book in circumstances in which readers were fooled into thinking that in buying his book of that title they were buying the famous book, this could constitute trademark infringement. Usually, however, the plagiarist is not trying to pass off his work as that of another writer.

No element of fraud, deception, or passing off is involved in the noble plagiarisms of the cultural tradition, where the copier adds value (making his use of the original "transformative" in the copyright sense discussed in subsequent chapters) and where the copying itself, to the extent intended to be recognized as such (as in our Milton example), enriches the new work. Plagiarism is also innocent—indeed, efficient—when no *value* is attached to originality; so judges, who try to conceal originality and pretend that their decisions are foreordained, "steal" freely from each other without attribution. Judges cite cases a lot but rarely mention the author of the opinion they are citing; nor will the reader ordinarily recognize the author from the name of the case or bother to look him up.

Historically the "no value" qualification has been of great importance. The high value that modern people place on originality is a relatively recent phenomenon. It is related to the movement from anonymous to identified authorship—to what might be called the rise of "personality." *Webster's Third New International Dictionary* give several definitions of the word, including "the fact of being an individual person," "the complex of characteristics that distinguishes a particular individual or individualizes or characterizes him in his relationships with others," and "the social characteristics of commanding notice, admiration, respect, or influence through personal characteristics." Personality thus signifies human individuality and, as in the last definition, a striving for recognition as a separate, distinctive, and admirable individual. When personality is not recognized, we have anonymity. The "author," conceived of as a writer who infuses his personality into his writing, is thus to be contrasted with the ghostwriter, who tries (or tried—for the practice is changing) to conceal his personality.

The concept of personality, in the sense of individuality and the concomitant notion of expressive works as the emanation of individual creativity, is central to the copyright laws, although it is most conspicuous in the variant of copyright protection, just now gaining a foothold in American law, that goes by the name of "moral right" and that, crudely stated, prevents tampering with an artist's work even if he has assigned the copyright to someone else (see Chapter 10). The rise of copyright in tandem with the growing disapproval of plagiarism may reflect the increased value that people attach to personality in the sense in which we are using the term. Creativity in Shakespeare's day was defined as creative imitation, implying subordination of the creator's originality to that of an earlier creator or creators. A new work was essentially a collaboration with an old one. This understanding downplayed the individuality, the personality, of the creator of the new work. With the rise of the Romantic movement in philosophy, literature, art, and music, creativity became reconceived as the expression of personality. Copyright was thereby given a boost because copying can be a way of impairing or appropriating personality. Plagiarism and forgery are other concepts used to protect personality by limiting copying, and they too underwent expanded definition with the rise of Romantic theories of creativity.

Personality figures in trademark law as well, once we understand that a firm or other institution can have personality in the sense of individuality, just like a natural person. A name-brand product has personality; the generic version of the product does not. Not only do brand names reduce consumer search costs, as we shall argue in Chapter 7, but famous brands are "celebrities" in their own right, whose logos fashion-conscious people wear proudly on their clothing. Personality is also central to the tort right of privacy, especially but not only the branch of the right that goes by the name of the "right of publicity"—the right of a person (a right valuable mainly to celebrities) to control the use of his or her name or picture for advertising and other commercial purposes.[37] The advent and expansion of this right, too, may be related to the decline of anonymity in the authorship not only of books but also of newspaper and magazine articles. It has become commonplace for the name of the ghostwriter of a ghostwritten book to appear on the title page under the name of the (nominal) author. And student notes and comments in law reviews now usually carry the name of the student author (a practice formerly unheard of), however heavily the work may have been edited. The *auteur* movement has sought with some success to obtain recognition of a movie's director as the author of the movie, while at the same time, and only superficially inconsistently, the acknowledgment of contributions to a book or other creative project by readers of drafts, by editors, by family members, and by secretaries and other clerical personnel is increasingly the norm and indeed is becoming mandatory in some forms of writing. Works ostensibly of scholarship increasingly include tidbits of autobiography. Name-brand products are a relatively recent development too.

The increasing social and legal recognition of personality is related to changes in the costs and benefits of personalized versus anonymous production of goods, both tangible and intangible. Three changes are central. The

---

37. See Huw Beverley-Smith, *The Commercial Appropriation of Personality* 174–187 (2002).

first is in the size of the market. The smaller the market for some product, the easier it is for consumers to identify the producer without an identifying mark, whether that mark is the name or signature of the producer, in the case of a book or a work of art, or a logo in the case of a less "creative" product or service. Modern, typically large, markets are, tellingly, said to be "impersonal." Their impersonality creates a demand for information, and the demand is compactly supplied by means of brand names, logos, and other personalizing devices. Think of the increased importance that academics attach to issues of priority, originality, volume of published work, citations and other acknowledgment in published work, and plagiarism. Modern academic markets are large, indeed international, so academics cannot create a reputation by word of mouth as easily as they once could; they need a visible stamp of personality.

A market may be so small that production for it cannot be financed by consumers; the producers may require private patronage or public subsidy. If consumers are not paying, they will be less interested in identifying the producer. The smaller the market, moreover, the less important it is to motivate producers by enabling them to appropriate a large part of the social benefits of their work. Despite Samuel Johnson's quip that only fools don't write for money, there have always been talented people who wrote or composed or painted because of the personal satisfaction it gave them rather than because of the pecuniary income that they obtained. If the demand for a class of work is small, the efforts of the self-motivated producers may be sufficient to satisfy it.

The second economic change that bears on the rise of the personality factor in law, norms, and commerce is closely related to the first, the size of the market. The cost of information about the quality of goods and services has risen as a result of an increased number of products and producers, increased product variety and complexity, and increased specialization, which reduces the amount of information that consumers have about the design and production of the products they use. (Consumers do not make their own tools or grow their own food any more.) The higher the cost of information, the more difficult it is to evaluate a product and hence the greater is the value of knowing who produced it. More products, in other words, are today what economists call "credence goods"—goods that one buys on the basis of faith in the producer rather than on the basis of one's ability to evaluate the product directly by examining it. This is true of cultural products as well as of ordinary consumer products.

Although there are thus considerable benefits to giving legal recognition to the producer's personality, the costs of that recognition must not be ignored. They have largely to do with the collaborative nature of most production, a characteristic that the Romantic emphasis on genius has obscured and that is the third variable in the cultivation and recognition of personality that we emphasize. Most creative work depends heavily, though to a degree that the creator himself may take pains to conceal, on previous work. The more the appropriation of previous work is burdened by costs of transacting with its creator, whether those costs are rooted in copyright law or, less likely, in the antiplagiarism norm (less likely because the norm does not forbid copying as such but only unacknowledged copying), the higher will be the cost of creative work in the present and future. This is an example of collaboration between generations but there is also of course much simultaneous collaboration, as in joint authorship and the creation of multimedia works such as opera and film. Here too the effort to give legal protection to the personality of each contributor may create formidable transaction costs.

The rise of personality and the resulting emphasis on individual distinction have implications for the supply of intellectual property as well as for its demand. The more originality is prized, the less interested the ablest writers will be in doing creative imitation, especially when it takes the form of revising recently published work. Shakespeare remains greatly admired, but his method is rarely emulated by distinguished writers and artists of today. And so a possible source of pressure for curbing the rise of copyright protection is eliminated.

Although analysis of the rise of personality as a valued asset is helpful in explaining the demand for copyright and related forms of legal protection of intellectual property, it does not establish the socially efficient level of copyright protection. That depends on many things, including the elasticity of demand for copies of an expressive work. If that elasticity is very high, as in the case of popular music, copyright protection can result in a drastic reduction in output as the copyright holder raises price to maximize profits,[38] yet supply might dry up without copyright protection. The efficient level of protection is found at the point at which the social benefits from further protection just equal the social costs. Above that point, additional protection increases costs more than benefits; below it, the benefits of strengthening copyright protection are greater than the resulting costs.

Copyright Protection and the Cost of Expression

Copyright's effect on subsequent producers of intellectual property requires particular emphasis. Creating a new expressive work typically involves bor-

---

38. See Paul Romer, "When Should We Use Intellectual Property Rights?" 92 *American Economic Review Papers and Proceedings* 213 (May 2002).

rowing or building on material from a prior body of works, as well as adding
original expression to it. A new work of fiction, for example, will contain the
author's expressive contribution but also characters, situations, plot details,
and so forth that were invented by previous authors. We gave some examples
earlier; here are some more. An influential copyright treatise, applying the
test of "substantial similarity" that many courts use, concludes that *West Side
Story* would infringe *Romeo and Juliet* if the latter were copyrighted.[39] If so,
then *Measure for Measure* would infringe the (hypothetical) copyright on an
earlier Elizabethan play, *Promos and Cassandra;* Doctorow's novel *Ragtime*
would infringe Heinrich von Kleist's novella *Michael Kohlhaas;* and *Romeo
and Juliet* itself would have infringed Arthur Brooke's *The Tragicall Historye
of Romeo and Juliet,* published in 1562, which in turn would have infringed
several earlier *Romeo and Juliets,*[40] all of which probably would have infringed
Ovid's story of Pyramus and Thisbe—which in *A Midsummer Night's Dream*
Shakespeare staged as a play within the play: another infringement of Ovid's
"copyright." Had the Old Testament been under copyright, *Paradise Lost*
would have infringed it, as would Thomas Mann's novel *Joseph and His
Brothers.* There is worse: in the case of ancient authors, like Homer and the
authors of the Old Testament, we do not know their sources and therefore
do not know to what extent these authors were originals and to what extent
they were copiers.

These examples could be multiplied indefinitely. And they are not limited
to literature. A new work of music may borrow tempo changes and chord
progressions from earlier works. And just as sophisticated literature is often a
reworking of an ancient folk tale, so classical music frequently builds on folk
melodies (think only of Dvorak, Bartok, and Copland) and often "quotes"
(as musicians say) from earlier classical works.[41] To the amateur listener, at
least, the last movement of Brahms's *First Symphony* sounds virtually identical
to the last movement of Beethoven's *Ninth Symphony*. And think of the innu-
merable "variations on" a theme by an earlier composer—Beethoven on a
theme composed by Mozart, Brahms on a theme by Handel, Rachmaninoff
on a theme by Paganini, and so forth.

The same thing is found in painting. Manet's most famous painting,
Déjeuner sur l'herbe, contains extensive and unmistakable copyings from ear-

39. See Melville B. Nimmer and David Nimmer, *Nimmer on Copyright,* vol. 4, §
13.03[A][1][b], pp. 13–33 to 13–34 (2002).

40. See *Narrative and Dramatic Sources of Shakespeare,* note 27 above, vol. 1, pp. 269–283.

41. For numerous examples, see S. S. Dale, "Musical Quotations," 96 *Musical Opinion* 623
(1973). See also Eric Cross, "Vivaldi's Operatic Borrowings," 59 *Music and Letters* 429 (1978);
William Klenz, "Brahms, op. 38: Piracy, Pillage, Plagiarism or Parody?" *Music Review,* Feb.
1973, p. 39.

lier works by Raphael, Titian, and Courbet, among others.[42] There are numerous examples from opera and musical theater, such as *My Fair Lady*, based on Shaw's play *Pygmalion;* Britten's opera *Billy Budd,* based on Melville's novel; and Verdi's Shakespearean operas. And from movies,[43] such as *High Society,* based on *The Philadelphia Story, High Anxiety,* based on *Vertigo,* and *Silk Stockings,* based on *Ninotchka,* as well as remakes, such as the 1978 remake of the 1956 classic, *Invasion of the Body Snatchers,* and the several remakes of Hitchcock's *The Thirty-Nine Steps.*[44] Woody Allen's movie *Play It Again, Sam* "quotes" a famous scene from *Casablanca*. The popular Meg Ryan-Tom Hanks comedy *You've Got Mail* is a remake of the great 1940 Jimmy Stewart-Margaret Sullavan comedy *The Shop around the Corner*. Popular genres, such as the farce, the detective story, and the spy thriller, tend to become formulaic, with the result that if copyright protection were expansively construed, the scope for creative imitation would be truncated. Think of the heavy debt that *From Russia with Love* owes to Hitchcock's thrillers *To Catch a Thief* and *North by Northwest* (themselves derivative from earlier Hitchcock thrillers), or that Michael Caine's late thriller *Blue Ice* owes to his first thriller, *The Ipcress File*. Such examples could be multiplied ad infinitum. (Consumers of popular culture crave variety but variety within a narrow compass—in effect, endless variations on a handful of tried and tested themes.) Countless movies, moreover, are based on books, such as *The Thirty-Nine Steps* on John Buchan's novel of that name or *For Whom the Bell Tolls* on Hemingway's novel. All these are examples of derivative works, which under modern copyright law require authorization from the owner of the copyright on the original.

The less extensive copyright protection is, the more an author, composer, painter, or other creator can borrow from previous works without a license yet without thereby infringing copyright, and the lower, therefore, the costs of creating a new work. In some of the examples that we have given, however, the original was copyrighted and the copy was authorized by the copyright owner. What is at stake in determining the scope of copyright protec-

42. See Michael Fried, *Manet's Modernism—Or, The Face of Painting in the 1860s* 150–151 (1996). Manet, as Fried explains, was a particularly relentless borrower from earlier painters, though he is widely regarded as the first, and one of the very greatest, modern artists. On the derivation of Manet's other most famous painting, *Olympia,* from Titian's *Venus of Urbino,* see id. at 152–154; T. J. Clark, *The Painting of Modern Life: Paris in the Art of Manet and His Followers* 93–94 (1984). See also Peter Schjeldahl, "The Spanish Lesson: Manet's Gift from Velázquez," *New Yorker,* Nov. 18, 2002, p. 102: Manet's "emulation of Velázquez and other Spanish artists was not merely a matter of influence. It was pretty much a straight steal."

43. See Don Harries, *Film Parody* (2000).

44. See *Play It Again, Sam: Retakes on Remakes* (Andrew Horton and Stuart Y. McDougal eds. 1998).

tion is not whether copyrighted works may lawfully be copied, but whether the right to copy is controlled by the owner of the copyright on the original work.

Even if copyright law forbade all unauthorized copying from a copyrighted work, authors would still copy. But they would copy works whose copyright protection had run out, or they would disguise their copying, engage in costly searches to find public domain substitutes for the copyrighted works that they would prefer to use as inputs, or, as we have just noted, incur licensing and other transaction costs to obtain permission to copy such works. The effect would be to raise the quality-adjusted cost of creating new works—the cost of expression, broadly defined—and thus, paradoxically, perhaps lower the number of works created.

This analysis implies that copyright holders might well find it in their self-interest, ex ante, to limit the scope and duration of copyright protection. To the extent that a later author is free to borrow material from an earlier one, the later author's cost of expression is reduced; and from an ex ante viewpoint every author is both an earlier author from whom a later author might want to borrow material and the later author himself. In the former role he desires maximum copyright protection for works he creates, but in the latter he prefers minimum protection for works created earlier by others. True, the first generation of authors, having no one to borrow from, will have less incentive to strike the optimal balance than later ones. Later generations of authors may also differ among themselves on where to set the level of copyright protection; authors expecting to borrow less than they are borrowed from will prefer more copyright protection than those expecting to be net borrowers. Ex ante, however—which is to say before anyone knows whether he is likely to be a net "debtor" or "creditor"—authors should be able to agree on the level of copyright protection. A fundamental task of copyright law viewed economically is to determine the terms of this hypothetical contract, or in other words to strike the optimal balance between the effect of copyright protection in encouraging the creation of new works by reducing copying and its effect in discouraging the creation of new works by raising the cost of creating them.

A further complication should be noted. Although in the short run broadening copyright protection shrinks the public domain, in the long run it may expand it. To the extent that broader protection elicits more expressive works by increasing their profitability, then, given the limited duration of the copyright term, the additional works, though copyrighted, will become a part of the public domain when their copyright term expires. The future public domain is nourished by copyright. However, this consideration has only limited significance when the copyright term is very long, as it is by virtue of the

Copyright Act of 1976 and the further lengthening of the term by the Sonny Bono Copyright Term Extension Act (see Chapter 8). Because of discounting to present value, extensions of the copyright term beyond twenty or twenty-five years have little incentive effect (and thus do not bring forth a significant number of additional expressive works to enrich the public domain when the copyright on those works expires), but greatly diminish the size of the public domain, especially since all extensions of the copyright term have been applied to existing as well as new works. We address the issue of optimal duration in Chapter 8; Chapter 4 focuses on issues of scope.

A final caveat: throughout this chapter our emphasis has been on the effect of copyright on the production of expressive works. In the terms introduced in Chapter 1, the emphasis is on the dynamic as distinct from the static benefits and costs of copyright. But we shall see in Chapter 8 that there may be static benefits of copyright as well. Copyright may correct certain congestion externalities in the market for expressive works. These benefits, which previous scholarship on copyright has largely overlooked or denied, must be kept in mind in any overall assessment of the social value of copyright.

3

A Formal Model of Copyright

As explained in the last chapter, while standard economic models of copyright emphasize the incentive-access tradeoff, we emphasize in addition the tradeoff between the incentive and cost-of-expression effects of varying the level of copyright protection. In order to incorporate this insight in a tractable formal model, we make several simplifying assumptions: that creators and copiers produce quality-adjusted copies that are perfect substitutes,[1] that demand is not subject to uncertainty, that the cost of expression is the only fixed cost of an expressive work, and that the marginal costs of creators, though not of copiers, are constant. We shall let p denote the price of a copy, $q(p)$ the market demand for copies of a given work, x and y the number of copies the creator and the copiers produce, respectively (so $q = x + y$), c the creator's marginal cost of a copy, and e the cost of expression. We denote the level of copyright protection by $z \geq 0$, so that $z = 0$ signifies no copyright protection and $z = 1$ signifies complete protection—no copying is permissible without the copyright holder's consent. The amount of copyright protection depends on such things as how alike two works must be before infringement will be found, the elements in a work that are protected, the duration of protection, and the efficacy and cost of enforcement. We subsume all these factors in our single index of copyright protection, z.

We assume that copiers, like fringe firms in a market with a dominant firm, supply copies up to the point where price equals marginal cost and that their marginal cost increases (not necessarily steeply) as both the number of copies and the level of copyright protection increase.[2] Given our earlier assumption that the author's[3] marginal cost (c) is constant, increasing marginal cost for

---

1. A copier might, of course, produce a copy only half as good as one produced by the author. In that event, on a quality-adjusted basis two copies made by the copier would be weighted as one.

2. We explained the significance of this assumption in Chapter 2.

3. Remember that we are using "author" and "creator" interchangeably and ignoring the difference between author and publisher.

copiers is a necessary assumption; otherwise copiers would produce all copies, in which event the work would not be created, or no copies, in which event the degree of copyright protection would not present an interesting question.

More important, it is *realistic* to assume that copiers will have increasing marginal costs. Recall that the copying that takes place at a given level of z is lawful. Some of it will be by consumers (for example, home taping of television programs) and some by producers who incorporate the author's work into their product (for example, fair use copying). The higher z is, the less the amount of such lawful copying. At a given level of $z < 1$, however, there will be some types of copying that require consumers and producers to use only a small amount of their own resources. They will be able to free ride on the author's work, and so the cost of copying will tend to be low. Other types of copying will be more costly, and here free riding will be less important. Such differences should generate differences in the cost of copying among copiers and so lead to rising marginal costs for the copiers as a group (rising because if demand falls, more of it will be supplied by the copiers having the lowest marginal costs).

The copiers' supply curve can thus be written as

$$y = y(p, z) \tag{1}$$

with $y_p > 0$ and $y_z < 0$.[4] The author's profits are

$$\Pi = (p - c)x - e(z), \tag{2}$$

and substituting for x we have

$$\Pi = (p - c)[q(p) - y(p, z)] - e(z), \tag{3}$$

4. That is, an increase in market price, or decrease in copyright protection, will evoke additional supply. We can derive the copiers' supply curve from their cost as follows. Denote the total cost of copying for copiers $M = M(y, z)$ where $M_y > 0$ (= marginal cost), $M_{yy} > 0$, $M_z > 0$, $M_{zz} \geq 0$, and $M_{yz} > 0$. That is, marginal cost is positive and increases with the number of copies. We assume that z increases both the total and marginal cost of copies (M_y) because, as z increases, the amount of protected material in a given work will rise, so that copiers must add more of their own material or make greater alterations in the copy to avoid infringement. This factor will tend to make copying more costly. To simplify, we assume that $\partial M_{yy}/\partial z = 0$—that is, that the rate of change in marginal cost is independent of z. Since copiers operate where $p = M_y(y, z)$, we have $y_p = \partial y/\partial p = 1/M_{yy} > 0$ and $y_z = \partial y/\partial z = -M_{yz}/M_{yy} < 0$. Note that y_z denotes the shift to the left in the copier's supply curve as z increases, so that at each price copiers make fewer copies.

where $e(z)$ denotes the author's cost of expression, which is higher the greater copyright protection is.[5]

Let the author's gross profits, R in our notation, equal his revenue from selling copies minus the cost of making those copies, or $(p - c)x$. We show later that R increases as z increases. The author will create a work only if

$$R \geq e(z), \tag{4}$$

since otherwise his profits (equation (2)) would be negative.

Let N equal the total number of (equivalent) works that are created. Our assumption that the cost of expression, $e(z)$, will differ among authors—some authors will be more efficient at creating equivalent works and so their costs will be lower than those of other authors—implies that with free entry of authors into the business of creating new works, N will rise until the cost of expression of the marginal author equals R. The supply of works will equal

$$N = N(R, z), \tag{5}$$

where $N_R > 0$ and $N_z < 0$.

The net effect on N of an increase in copyright protection (z) depends on the balance between two effects because the increase leads to both a movement up the supply curve of works (as R increases) and an upward shift of the supply curve as z drives up the cost of expression. Thus $dN/dz = N_R(dR/dz) + N_z$. At low levels of z, the revenue-enhancing effect of limiting copying by free riders should dominate, so that $dN/dz > 0$. When z is very low, few or no works may be created, since free riding by copiers may prevent any author from covering his cost of expression.[6] So N will increase as z increases, at least up to some level, say $\bar{z}$. Beyond $\bar{z}$ we assume that increases in the cost of expression to marginal authors will dominate, so that the number of works will begin to fall. That is, $dN/dz > 0$ for all $z < \bar{z}$, $dN/dz = 0$ at $\bar{z}$, and $dN/dz < 0$ for all $z > \bar{z}$.

5. Our model is similar to one used by Salop and Scheffman to analyze how a dominant firm selects strategies that raise both its and its rivals' costs. See Steven C. Salop and David T. Scheffman, "Cost Raising Strategies," 36 *Journal of Industrial Economics* 19 (1987). In our model copyright protection is like a strategy that raises both the rivals' (copiers') marginal cost and the dominant firm's fixed cost (the creator's cost of expression).

6. If, however, the copier's marginal cost is much higher than the original author's marginal cost, copyright protection may not be necessary for the author to be able to cover his full cost of expression, as we know from our earlier discussion. In such a case the principal effect of increasing z, even at low levels, will be to raise the cost of expression and thus lower N. In our formal model we assume away conditions that would make the optimal amount of copyright protection equal zero.

The intuition behind these results is straightforward. Some copyright protection is necessary to generate incentives to incur the costs of creating easily copied works. But too much protection can raise the costs of creation to a point at which current authors cannot cover their costs even though they have complete copyright protection for their own originality. The key issue is how the level of protection, z, here modeled as a single index, is set along several dimensions that include withholding protection from ideas as opposed to expression, giving copyright holders rights over derivative uses, and permitting unauthorized copying that satisfies fair use criteria.

Optimal copyright protection depends not only on the number and cost of original works but also on the number and cost of copies of each original work. Once created, an expressive work can be exploited in many ways, and they need not be mutually exclusive. The author (or publisher, remember) of a novel may sell copies, sell to a magazine prepublication rights to publish selections, and license derivative works such as a play, musical, movie, translation, or condensation. Similarly, he may license the characters in his novel for a comic book or television series or for a line of clothes. In the next chapter we distinguish between copiers who make identical copies of a work and those who create derivative works, since the former have a greater impact on the incentive to create the original work. For now, we treat all different ways to exploit a work identically and call them the making and selling of copies.

Figures 3.1 and 3.2 may help to convey an intuitive understanding of how copyright protection (z) simultaneously determines the price of a copy (p), the number of copies produced by the creator of the expressive work (x), the number of unauthorized copies (y), the economic returns to creating a work (R), and the total number of works created (N).

Figure 3.1 illustrates the market for copies. The demand curve for copies produced by the creator of the expressive work is derived by subtracting the copiers' supply curve ($y = y(p, z^0)$) from the market demand for copies. The creator of the expressive work then sets marginal cost (c) equal to the marginal revenue from the derived demand curve. This yields a price of p^0, quantities of copies produced by the creator and copier of x^0 and y^0 respectively, and total number of copies of q^0 ($= x^0 + y^0$). In equilibrium, the creator of the expressive work earns gross profits shown by the shaded area labeled R^0. Notice that the copiers' marginal cost or supply curve depends on the level of copyright protection—as z increases, $y(z)$ rotates to the left—which in turn affects prices, output, and the gross profits earned by the copyright holder: an increase in z increases p, x, and R and lowers y and q.

In the market for the creation of new expressive works, depicted in Figure 3.2, the number of works (N) increases with an increase in copyright protection to the point at which the cost of the marginal author's expression, which

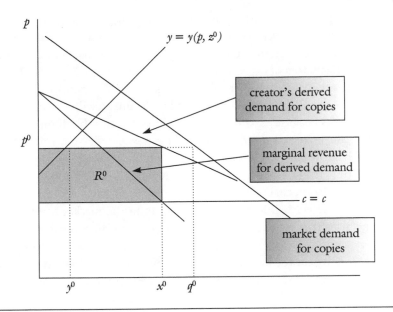

Figure 3.1. The market for copies

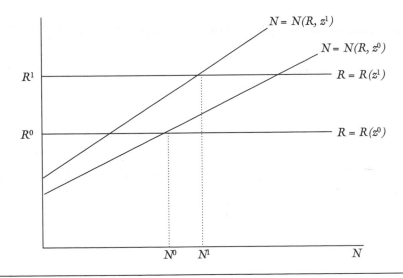

Figure 3.2. The market for new works

we assume differs among authors and is therefore increasing in N, equals his return. Assume that copyright protection is initially set at z^0, which in turn determines the equilibrium values in Figure 3.1 and in particular the gross profits (R^0) of creators of expressive works. From Figure 3.2 we can then determine the equilibrium number of new works; it is N^0. If copyright protection increases, the R curve will shift upward to R^1 but so will the supply curve N of new works because expanding copyright protection by diminishing the public domain increases the cost of creating new intellectual property. Although N is shown as increasing from N^0 to N^1 as copyright protection expands, the net effect of an increase in z on N actually is ambiguous—and for the additional reason that an increase in N brought about by an increase in z has a feedback effect by increasing competition in the market for expressive works and thus dampening the effect of the increase in z on the copyright holder's revenue.

Below we solve for the level of z that maximizes social welfare, but the considerations determining this maximum can be seen in Figures 3.1 and 3.2. In the market for copies (Figure 3.1), an increase in z produces a greater deadweight loss because the price of a copy increases and the number of copies sold decreases. The increase in z also increases the creator's gross profits, R, which in turn leads to both a movement up and a shift to the left in the supply curve of new works in Figure 3.2. The first effect creates social welfare in the form of producer surplus, while the second reduces producer surplus. Overall social welfare is maximized when the marginal benefit of increasing z in higher producer surplus exactly balances the reduction in welfare in the market for copies plus the reduction in producer surplus in Figure 3.2 as the supply curve of new works shifts upward.

The Price of a Copy

The author will choose the price that maximizes his profits in equation (2). This requires that p satisfy

$$[q(p) - y(p, z)] + (p - c)(q_p - y_p) = 0, \tag{6}$$

which can be rewritten as

$$p\{1 - F/[\varepsilon^d + \varepsilon^s(1 - F)]\} = c, \tag{7}$$

where F is the fraction of copies made by the author, $1 - F$ the fraction made by copiers, ε^d the elasticity of demand for copies, and ε^s the elasticity of supply of the copiers ($\varepsilon^s = y_p(p/y)$). The price per copy will be greater the less elastic the demand for copies, the less elastic the copiers' supply curve, and the larger the author's share of copies relative to that of copiers, which in turn will be larger the lower the author's cost of making copies relative to that of copiers.[7]

We can determine the effect on price of changes in the level of copyright protection (z), and in the author's marginal cost of copying, by totally differentiating p in equation (6) with respect to z and c. This yields

$$dp/dz = y_z/S > 0, \tag{8}$$

$$dp/dc = (q_p - y_p)/S > 0, \tag{9}$$

where S equals $\partial^2\Pi/\partial p^2$, which is negative from the second-order condition for profit maximization. Increases in z and c increase the price of a copy and reduce the total number of copies sold—provided, of course, that copiers' output is still positive. If not, increases in z will have no effect on the price and output or the number of copies; the author will be a monopolist and will not need any copyright protection.

We are also interested in the effect of changes in z on the author's gross profits (that is, before deducting the cost of expression) and on the number of copies made by author and copiers (again assuming that copiers have a positive output). The change in gross profits (R) from a small change in z is given by

$$dR/dz = -(p - c)y_z > 0. \tag{10}$$

Since y_z in equation (8) is the reduction in the quantity supplied by copiers as z increases (holding p constant), the change in the author's gross profits for a small increase in z will equal the difference between price and the author's marginal cost multiplied by the increased number of copies he supplies, an increase that in equilibrium will just match the reduction in copies supplied by copiers.

Although the author's gross profits will increase with greater copyright protection until copiers cease making copies—after which additional copy-

7. We assume that the second-order condition for a maximum is satisfied—that is, that

$$\partial^2\Pi/\partial p^2 = 2(q_p - y_p) + (p - c)(q_{pp} - y_{pp}) < 0.$$

8. dR/dz equals

$$d(p - c)x/dz = dp/dz + (p - c)\{q_p(dp/dz) - [y_p(dp/dz) + y_z]\}.$$

Collecting terms yields

$$d(p - c)x/dz = dp/dz[x + (p - c)(q_p - y_p)] - (p - c)y_z.$$

Since $x + (p - c)(q_p - y_p) = 0$ from the first-order profit-maximizing condition, the first term in the above expression vanishes, leaving the expression in the text.

right protection can yield no benefit since there are no more competitors to exclude—net profits need not rise. The cost of expression to authors of copyrighted works increases as copyright protection increases, because of transaction costs, acquisition costs (the license fee charged by the owner of a copyrighted work that the new producer wants to incorporate in his work), and substitution costs (finding some equivalent in the public domain to the copyrighted input that the new producer would most like to use). And so the less material an author (not a copier) can borrow from other copyright holders without infringing their copyrights unless he has licenses from them, the greater will be his cost of expression. The change in net profits from increases in z will be positive or negative depending on whether

$$-(p - c)y_z - e_z < \text{or} > 0. \tag{11}$$

The sign of inequality (11) bears on the earlier question of whether an increase in copyright protection will increase or decrease the number of new works created. A positive sign for the marginal work (or author) means that an increase in z increases gross profits by more than the cost of expression, so net profits will rise and the number of works will increase. A negative sign means that greater copyright protection will reduce the number of works.

We speculated earlier that at low levels of z the revenue-enhancing effect would dominate while at higher levels the cost-enhancing effect would dominate. Inequality (12) enables us to be more explicit about the factors that affect the relation between z and the number of works. Since gross profits equal the cost of expression for the marginal author, inequality (11)—the condition for whether z increases or decreases the number of works—can be rewritten in percentage terms:

$$-\tilde{y}_z(y/x) - \tilde{e}_z < \text{or} > 0, \tag{12}$$

where $\sim$ denotes percentage change brought about by a change in z. This expression is more likely to be negative the smaller the copiers' share relative to the author's share (that is, the smaller is y/x). Since the copiers' share will fall and the author's rise as z increases, inequality (12) is more likely to be negative at higher than at lower levels of copyright protection. So, consistent with our earlier conjecture, the revenue-enhancing effect of increasing copyright protection diminishes as the level of protection increases.

The percentage change in the copiers' supply brought about by a change in the level of copyright protection, $\tilde{y}_x$, will be greater the larger the increase in the copiers' marginal cost as z increases and the lower the rate of increase in marginal cost with respect to a change in the number of copies—that is, the lower their supply elasticity.[9] This has two implications. The first is that the more difficult it is for copiers to avoid infringing the author's copyright by substituting other inputs for the protected part of the author's work because the protected part is bigger, the greater will be the increase in the copiers' marginal cost. The greater, therefore, will be the increase in the author's gross profit, and so the more likely is the number of works to increase as copyright protection expands. If copiers produce only exact copies or, equivalently, slavish imitations, there will be, by definition, no other inputs to substitute for the author's work, and therefore an increase in z will tend to have a large positive effect on the copiers' marginal cost curve and so on the number of works created.

Second, the smaller the difference in efficiency or cost of copying among copiers (which depends in turn on the similarity of the uses that copiers make of the author's work), the more elastic the copiers' supply or marginal cost will be and the larger therefore will be the increase in the author's gross profit as z increases. This, too, makes it more likely that expanding copyright protection will increase the number of works created. Alternatively, if copiers use the author's work in diverse ways, the marginal cost of copying is likely to be less elastic and so an increase in copyright protection will have a smaller effect on the author's gross profits.

What happens to the number of copies produced by copiers and by the author as the level of copyright protection rises? Since price will rise, the total number of copies will fall. The change in the copiers' output (y), however, will depend on the net effect of two offsetting effects. As z rises, the copiers' supply curve will shift to the left ($y_z < 0$), reducing y. But the increase in p will lead to a movement up the supply curve, increasing y.

Regarding the number of copies sold by the author (x), and recalling that $x = q - y$ and that an increase in copyright protection raises price and lowers the total number of copies sold, the author will sell more copies only if y declines by more than the reduction in q. That is indeed the most likely outcome, however. Since an increase in z raises the residual demand faced by the author, he would normally be expected to sell more. But if the elasticity of the residual demand curve declines sufficiently as it shifts outward, the author may produce less at the new equilibrium price. This is simply an illustration of the well-known proposition that an increase in demand may reduce the optimal output of a monopolist if the elasticity of demand declines sufficiently with the increase.

9. Recall that $-y_z = M_{yz}/M_{yy}$, where M_y denotes the copiers' marginal cost. Hence $-y_z$ will tend to be greater the greater the increase in the copiers' marginal cost as z increases and the smaller the increase in their marginal cost as y increases (that is, the flatter or more elastic the copiers' marginal cost curve).

Welfare Effects of Copyright Protection

To model the effects of copyright protection on economic welfare, let w equal the standard measure of economic welfare (the sum of consumer and producer surplus) in the market for copies of a single work before the cost of creating the work is deducted:

$$w = \int_{p^*}^{\infty} q(p)dp + (p^* - c)[q(p^*) - y(p^*, z)] + \int_{p_0}^{p^*} y(p, z)dp \quad (13)$$

The first term is consumer surplus at p^* (the profit-maximizing price set by the author), the middle term is the author's gross profits, and the last term is the copiers' profits.[10]

Net welfare equals $w - e(z)$, where $e(z)$ is the cost of creating the particular work and is a function of the scope of copyright protection. The change in net welfare with respect to a change in z equals

$$\partial[w - e(z)]/\partial_z = (p^* - c)\{q_p(dp^*/dz) - [y_p(dp^*/dz) + y_z]\}$$
$$+ \int_{p_0}^{p^*} y_z dp - e_z \neq 0. \quad (14)[11]$$

This complicated expression has a simple interpretation. The first term is the change in the author's surplus from a change in the scope of copyright protection. It depends on the difference between price and the author's marginal cost and on the change in the number of copies he sells; for the term in brackets is merely the difference between the change in total copies and the number of copies sold by copiers. Normally the author will sell more copies when z increases because the copiers' marginal costs will rise.

Notice that at the margin copiers generate no consumer or producer surplus, because they equate marginal cost to price. As for the last two terms in equation (14), $\int_{p_0}^{p^*} y_z dp$ is negative because an increase in z increases the

---

10. Notice that p_0 is the minimum price at which copiers are willing to produce a copy. Since we assume that copiers incur no fixed costs, the number of copies at p_0 is zero—that is, $y(p_0, z) = 0$.

11. From equation (13) we have

$$\partial w/\partial z = -q(p^*)(dp^*/dz) \quad (i)$$
$$+[q(p^*) - y(p^*, z)](dp^*/dz) + (p^* - c)[q_p(dp^*/dz) - (y_p(dp^*/dz) - y_z] \quad (ii)$$
$$+ y(p^*, z)(dp^*/dz) - y(p^0, z)(dp^0/dz) + y_z dp \quad (iii)$$

where (i) denotes the reduction in consumer surplus ($dp^*/dz > 0$); (ii) the change in the author's profits, which depend on both the change in price and the change in the number of copies he produces (which may be positive or negative); and (iii) the change in the copier's surplus, which depends on the increase in price, the increase in his costs, and the change in the number of copies he produces. Combining the terms in $\partial w/\partial z$ yields equation (14).

total cost to copiers of the copies they produce; $-e_z$ is also negative because the cost of expression increases with the amount of copyright protection.

An increase in copyright protection is likely to reduce the welfare benefits (consumer plus producer surplus) generated by a given work, assuming it will be created. Both the increase in the cost of creating the work and the increase in the cost to copiers reduce welfare, and only rarely will these increases be offset by cost savings resulting from the shift in producing copies from copiers to the author, a shift that will be larger the lower the author's marginal cost relative to that of the copiers. For the cost savings are obtained only on the additional units produced by the author, while the cost increase affects all copies produced by copiers plus the cost of expression.

Total welfare, however, depends on the number of works created as well as on the consumer and producer surplus generated by a given work assuming it is created; and the number of works may rise as copyright protection expands even though welfare per work falls. The traditional analysis emphasized the tradeoff between the benefits of copyright protection in encouraging the production of works and the losses from reducing access to the works by consumers. If one defines "access" as the sum of consumer and producer surplus generated by a single work, access is indeed likely to fall as copyright protection increases. But it falls because of factors—the increase in copiers' costs *and* in the cost of expression—that are ignored in the traditional view. That view stresses losses to consumers from higher prices—a factor that drops out of our analysis.

Let total welfare equal

$$W = W[N, w, E(N, z)].\tag{15}$$

W will be an increasing function of both N, the number of (equivalent) works created, and w, the consumer and producer surplus per work before deducting the cost of creating the work, and will be a decreasing function of E, the total costs of creating works (including the cost of administering and enforcing the copyright system). In turn, E will be an increasing function of both N and z (that is, $E_N > 0$ and $E_Z > 0$).[12] We assume for convenience that equation (15) can be rewritten as

$$W = f(N)w - E(N, z),\tag{16}$$

12. Note that $E_{NN} > 0$ because authors will differ in the costs of creating works, and as the economic return from creating works increases, higher-cost authors will find it economical to create works. $E_{Nz} > 0$ because increasing copyright protection will raise the cost to all authors of creating works. Administrative and enforcement costs are likely to rise both with the number of works created, holding constant z, and with the level of copyright protection, holding constant N, since more works will be registered and more infringement suits brought. One possible offset, however, is that an increase in copyright protection will deter some infringers. In that event, the number of suits may fall despite the greater incentive to pursue infringement claims as z increases.

where $f_N > 0$ and $f_{NN} < 0$—that is, there is diminishing marginal utility as the number of works created increases.

Maximizing W with respect to z yields

$$\partial W/\partial z = f_N N_z w + f(N) w_z - (E_N N_z + E_z) = 0, \tag{17}$$

or, equivalently,

$$N_z(f_N w - E_N) = -f(N) w_z + E_z, \tag{18}$$

where $N_z = (\partial N/\partial R)R_z + (\partial N/\partial z)$ and $w_z = (p^* - c)(dx/dp)(dp/dz) + \int_{p^0}^{p^*} y_{zdp}$ (see equation (14)).[13] We denote by z^* the level of z that maximizes W. The right-hand side of equation (18) will be positive at z^* in the typical case because an increase in z will lower producer and consumer surplus per work (that is, w_z is negative) and raise the cost of expression for all works and increase administrative and enforcement costs ($E_z > 0$).[14]

N_z measures the response of the number of works created to an increase in copyright protection. As we saw earlier, it can be either positive or negative. However, when z is set optimally, N_z will be positive. For suppose that N_z were negative at z^*. Since the same level of N could be attained at a lower z (because N increases initially and then falls as z rises), a lower z would yield a higher level of W. Not only would $E(N, z)$ be lower (since it is a positive function just of z when N is unchanged, and z would now be lower), but w (consumer and producer surplus per work before deducting the cost of expression) would be higher at a lower z for reasons explained in the previous section.

We can therefore eliminate from our analysis levels of z at which $N_z < 0$. The only exception would be where w fell as z fell—that is, where the loss in producer surplus from substituting copies made by copiers for those made by authors exceeded the reduction in copiers' costs as z fell, provided that, in addition, this effect was large enough to offset the reduction in E as z fell. We showed earlier, however, that w is likely to rise as z falls. Moreover, if total welfare were maximized when N_z was negative, this would turn the traditional rationale for copyright protection upside down. Instead of encouraging the production of works, copyright would discourage them in equilibrium, and instead of reducing access it would increase access (defined, as before, in terms of welfare per work).

Another consideration, not captured in our formal model but working in

13. We assume that the second-order condition for a maximum is satisfied, that is, that $\partial^2 W/\partial z^2 < 0$.

14. The right-hand side of equation (18) could be negative in the unlikely event that w increased and enforcement costs decreased as z increased, and these changes more than offset the increased cost of expression. In that event, z^* would be at a level sufficient to eliminate all copying.

the same direction, is that as N rises a point may be reached at which any further increase will raise each author's cost of expression and hence E_N, the marginal cost of expression. With more and more copyrighted works, the amount of public domain material—unappropriated materials suitable for inclusion in a new work—will fall. It will then cost more to create a new work. This problem would be particularly serious if "ideas" (in the sense used in copyright law) as well as expression were copyrightable. They are not, as we shall see in the next chapter, and our explanation will be based on the relation between z and N developed in our formal model.

Several implications of our formal model should be noted, some of which will figure in subsequent chapters:

1. At z^*, the amount of producer and consumer surplus per work (w) weighted by f_N must exceed the cost of creating the marginal work;[15] otherwise the left-hand side of equation (18) would be negative. This implies that the optimal amount of copyright protection is greater for classes of work that are more valuable socially (that is, the higher w is relative to the cost of creating the work). The left-hand side of equation (18) would rise initially, relative to the right-hand side, requiring an increase in z to restore equilibrium. Contrary to our model, the law has resisted efforts to vary the term or otherwise alter the amount of copyright protection depending on the perceived social value of different classes of expressive work. This may be the correct second-best solution, however, because of the invitation to politicization of the copyright process and resulting rent seeking that would be tendered if copyright protection varied among classes of work. The more heterogeneous the class of persons affected by a law, the more difficult it is for them to organize a politically effective interest group to make the law more favorable to them.

2. Optimal copyright protection requires that z^* be set *below* the level that maximizes the number of works created. The latter would require that $N_z = 0$ (assuming that N increases initially and later decreases as z increases), which would make the left-hand side of equation (18) zero. To put this differently, strengthening copyright protection beyond z^* would increase the incentive to create more works ($N_z > 0$) but would not be worth the costs in reduced welfare per work, the higher costs of expression (for works that would have been created anyway at a lower value for z), and the greater administrative and enforcement costs. This conclusion formalizes the tradeoff between the cost of expression, which copyright protection increases, and the incentive effect of copyright in encouraging the creation of expressive works.

3. It follows from equation (18) that the greater the responsiveness of N to

---

15. E_N also includes the incremental cost of administering and enforcing the copyright system that results from an increase in N. Note that since $E_{NN} > 0$, w will also exceed the full cost of creating each work at z^*.

an increase in z (that is, the greater N_z at each level of z), the greater the optimal value of copyright protection must be to reach equilibrium. In turn, N_z will be greater (as z increases) the greater the increase in gross profits (R) (which is greater the greater the difference between p and c and the bigger the reduction in copies made by copiers as z increases), the smaller the increase in the cost of expression for the marginal author, and the smaller the rate of increase in the marginal cost of expression as N_z increases and hence the smaller the difference among authors in the cost of creating works. In other words, optimal copyright protection will tend to be greater the more responsive the supply of new works is to increases in such protection, and this responsiveness will depend on both the costs of creating new works and the costs of producing unauthorized copies. The higher the costs of new works and the lower the costs of producing unauthorized copies, the greater the optimal scope of copyright protection.

4. We know that the optimal extent of copyright protection tends to rise with the value of a work (w) and that w will be greater the greater the demand for the work and the lower the marginal cost of making copies. Hence if rising incomes and technological advances enlarge the market for a representative work and the cost of copying declines, copyright protection should expand. This suggests a possible efficiency explanation for why copyright protection has, indeed, expanded over time. But it is highly conjectural because the model does not specify the optimal extent of that expansion, which may have gone too far, as subsequent chapters will suggest.

5. Suppose that w falls only slightly as copyright protection expands. Then the right-hand side of equation (18) will be smaller and the optimal level of copyright protection will rise. Put differently, the less that welfare per work is reduced by copyright protection, the higher will be the optimal level of that protection because an expansion in copyright protection increases the number of expressive works.

6. The more the cost of expression rises as z increases (that is, the greater is E_z), the smaller will be the optimal amount of copyright protection. This suggests that if it is feasible to differentiate in infringement proceedings between individuals who make literal copies and those who use copyrighted material to create derivative works by adding new expression to the copyrighted original, there should be broader copyright protection against the former group than against the latter—and there is.

7. Finally, and obviously (but sensibly), the formal analysis implies that the lower the cost of administering and enforcing a copyright system and the more responsive authors are to pecuniary incentives, the greater will optimal copyright protection be.

4

Basic Copyright Doctrines

The model developed in the preceding two chapters can help explain a number of features of copyright law. We examine several of them here and others (primarily fair use, discussed briefly in this chapter, and the length of the copyright term) in subsequent chapters.

Copying versus Re-Creation

We begin with the nature of the protection that a copyright gives its owner. In contrast to a patent or trademark, a copyright protects only against copying; unintended re-creation of the copyrighted work ("independent," that is, inadvertent, duplication) is not actionable.[1] Liability for intentional copying is, however, strict in the sense that it is no defense that the copier reasonably believed that the work was in the public domain.

Economic analysis suggests two reasons why inadvertent duplication is not actionable. The first is the added cost to an author of checking countless copyrighted works to avoid inadvertent duplication. In terms of our formal model, this cost (if actually incurred—a qualification the significance of which will appear shortly) would increase $e(z)$ (the cost of expression as a function of copyright protection) and lower social welfare, because both net welfare per work ($w - e(z)$) and the number of works created would fall. True, the author's gross revenues might rise if the reduction in the amount of

---

1. Although we can think of an exception: an art critic meticulously analyzes and inspects a famous painting of, say, Niagara Falls. By microscopic study of the brushwork, pigments, and other design elements, he is able to determine the exact place and time of day and of the year at which the painting was made and to compile a set of instructions that if followed exactly would enable an amateur to make an identical painting of Niagara Falls without ever having seen the famous painting. Even though the amateur had not knowingly copied the painting, this would not be independent duplication; he would be an infringer and the art critic a contributory infringer.

inadvertent duplication raised the demand for his work or made that demand less elastic.[2] But since inadvertent duplication of copyrighted works is rare except in the area of popular music, discussed below, the net effect of making it unlawful would probably be to lower social welfare unless it was *so* rare that no author or publisher would bother to search for copyrighted precursors.

In contrast to copyright, inadvertent infringements of patents are actionable. The difference makes economic sense. A patent is issued only after a search by the applicant and by the U.S. Patent and Trademark Office of prior patented inventions. This procedure is feasible because it is possible in most cases to describe an invention compactly and to establish relatively small classes of related inventions beyond which the searchers need not look. (Software patents may be an exception.) The procedure enables an inventor to avoid at reasonable cost inadvertently duplicating an existing patent. In the case of trademarks, inadvertent infringements are also actionable. Two features of trademarks make this feasible. One is that a trademark is protected only if it is used in commerce; the other is that many trademarks are registered. Both the use-in-commerce requirement and registration provide readily available information to firms that are considering adopting a new trademark as to whether another firm has already asserted ownership in the mark.

In contrast, the Copyright Office does not search copyrighted works before issuing or registering a copyright—in fact, copyright is not issued; it is simply asserted by the author or publisher. Registration is possible, and confers significant remedial advantages,[3] but is not required for copyright protection to attach and, more important, is not conditioned on persuading the Copyright Office that the work is original rather than a duplication of previous work.[4] There are many millions of pages of copyrighted material, any one

---

2. If we include in y, the copiers' supply of copies, the copies made by inadvertent duplication, an expansion in the scope of copyright protection to make inadvertent duplication unlawful would shift both the copiers' supply curve and the author's residual demand curve upward.

3. A suit for infringement cannot be brought until the copyright is registered, but the copyright can be registered at any time before the suit is brought; the holder of the copyright can wait till the last minute to register. However, to be entitled to obtain in such a suit statutory damages (fixed damages, up to $150,000, not requiring proof of actual injury) and reimbursement of one's attorney's fees from the defendant if one wins one's infringement suit, the copyright must have been registered either within three months of first publication or before the infringement occurred. See 17 U.S.C. §§ 408, 411–412, 504–505.

4. However, part 202 of the regulations of the Copyright Office denies registration for certain classes of work that do not meet the statutory criteria for copyright, such as words and short phrases and works consisting entirely of noncopyrightable information, such as a standard calendar that contains no original authorship.

page of which might contain a sentence or paragraph that a later writer might by pure coincidence duplicate so closely that he would be considered an infringer if he had actually copied the words in question or if copying were not a prerequisite of liability.

Inadvertent word for word duplication is of course extremely unlikely if more than a phrase or a sentence is involved, but word for word duplication is not required for infringement, only substantial similarity, and this can happen by accident in descriptions of the same phenomenon, for example, two accounts of the same boxing match. If all copyrighted works were in digital form and posted on an accessible Web site, a search for duplication would be feasible; it is the same point that we made in Chapter 2 concerning the increased feasibility, in our digital age, of detecting plagiarism. But they are not.

What is infeasible (at present) for the Copyright Office is also infeasible for the author. He cannot read all the copyrighted literature in existence in order to make sure that he has not inadvertently duplicated some copyrighted material. A further impediment is that unpublished expressive works are copyrighted too, provided only that they are fixed in some tangible medium; how is an author to search them? The problem does not arise in patent law because, as we'll see in Chapter 11, a prior invention does not bar the issuance of a patent unless it was known and used.

The cost of preventing inadvertent duplication of copyrighted work would be so great, and the benefits in terms of higher revenues (and therefore the amount of damages if such duplication were actionable) so slight because of the rarity of such duplication, that, as we have suggested, even if inadvertent duplication were actionable no writer or publisher would make an effort to avoid it and therefore the increase in the cost of expression would probably be slight. But social welfare would still be reduced. At best we would have a system of strict liability that had no significant allocative effects; it would not deter duplication. As explained in the literature on negligence and strict liability in tort law, the costs of such a regime are wasted from the standpoint of overall economic welfare because their only product is an occasional transfer payment.[5] The transfer here would be from the accidental infringer to the owner of the copyright on the material inadvertently duplicated.

The second reason for not deeming inadvertent duplication infringement is that it does not involve free riding. Since the second work is independently created, its author incurs the full cost of expression. If the works are com-

---

5. See William M. Landes and Richard A. Posner, *The Economic Structure of Tort Law* 70, 115–116 (1987).

pletely identical—a remote possibility, to say the least[6]—competition between the two works could drive the price of copies down to marginal cost and prevent either author from recovering his cost of creating the work. But it is quite likely that enough differences between the two works will remain to enable both authors to obtain sufficient revenue to enable them to recover their respective costs of expression. This is particularly likely if neither author is the marginal author, whose gross revenues would just cover the cost of expression if there were no accidental duplication to siphon off revenues from him.

A significant legal difference between literary and musical copyright is that inadvertent duplication may infringe a songwriter's copyright if his song has been widely performed.[7] Since most popular songs have simple melodies and the number of melodic variations is limited, the possibility of inadvertent duplication of several bars is significant. Widespread playing of these songs on the radio makes it likely that the second composer will have had access to the original work, which both increases the likelihood of inadvertent duplication and reduces the cost of avoiding it. If proof of intentional duplication were required for infringement in these circumstances, composers of popular songs would have little copyright protection. Yet even here it is not inadvertent duplication per se that is being punished but unconscious copying, although some cases of genuine re-creation will be caught in the liability net by the tests that the courts use.

To distinguish in the music area between copying and genuine re-creation, the courts trade off access by the alleged infringer to the work allegedly infringed against the similarity of the two works. If there is a strong showing of similarity, it is more likely that the original work was indeed copied, and in such a case the copyright owner can prevail even if he presents only weak evidence that the defendant had access to the original work. But if the differences between the original work and its alleged copy are substantial, the

6. Recall Judge Learned Hand's remark in Sheldon v. Metro-Goldwyn Pictures, 81 F.2d 49, 54 (2d Cir. 1936), that "if by some magic a man who had never known it were to compose anew Keats's Ode on a Grecian Urn, he would be an 'author,' and, if he copyrighted it, others might not copy that poem, though they might of course copy Keats's." Hand thought such inadvertent duplication a remote possibility ("magic"). He was right. In fact the probability of inadvertent duplication of Keats's poem word for word is vanishingly small—much too small to justify courts in treating it as a litigable question, that is, one fairly open to doubt.

7. For example, in ABKO Music, Inc. v. Harrisongs Music, Ltd., 722 F.2d 988, 997–999 (2d Cir. 1983), the court found that George Harrison's "My Sweet Lord" had infringed "He's So Fine," recorded by the Chiffons. "He's So Fine" had been one of the most popular songs in the United States and England during the same year that Harrison (a former member of the Beatles) composed "My Sweet Lord." The court found infringement even though it also found that Harrison had copied the Chiffons' song unconsciously rather than deliberately.

copyright owner will be required to present strong evidence of access to rebut the defense of independent re-creation.

Similar reasoning provides one explanation for the rule that short phrases (such as "Return Unused Portion for a Refund" or "Self-Addressed Envelope Enclosed") are not copyrightable. The shorter the phrase, the likelier is independent duplication; and it is difficult by the methods of litigation to distinguish between it and deliberate copying.[8] But there is more to the rule than that. Since the cost of thinking up a short phrase is normally small, copyright protection should not be necessary to create adequate incentives for its creation. Still other economic reasons for the rule are discussed below.

But what exactly *is* copying? We know that it need not be word for word to constitute infringement, for, if it were, copyright protection would be largely illusory. Instead the standard is substantial similarity. No precise rule can be laid down as to how much variation ("originality," in unhelpful copyright jargon) is required to avoid a finding of substantial similarity, but economic analysis suggests the following test: an alleged copy of a copyrighted work is infringing if it is a close substitute, in the market, for the expressive aspect of the work and so would cut significantly into the demand for the work. One economics textbook might be a close substitute for another even though no sentences in the second book were paraphrases of sentences in the first and the choice and sequence of topics were different. But the second would be a close substitute only by virtue of the similarity of the ideas, and ideas, as we are about to see, are not copyrightable. In contrast, if the second book were such a close paraphrase of the first that a careless reader might not even notice that it *was* a different book, it would be a close substitute along its expressive dimension as well as along the dimension of ideas, and so it would be infringing. It would be infringing even if it stole just one chapter from the previous book; the theft would make the later book a closer substitute because it was using the original author's words as well as his ideas.

The reason we called the requirement of "originality" unhelpful is its confusing echo of the statutory requirement of "novelty" for obtaining a patent (see Chapter 11). Novelty, along with utility and nonobviousness, and the requirement of prescreening by the Patent and Trademark Office to determine

---

8. See Douglas Lichtman, "Copyright as a Rule of Evidence" 17 (University of Chicago Law School, John M. Olin Law and Economics Working Paper No. 151 [2d ser.], May 2002). Outside of popular music, inadvertent duplication (as opposed to inadvertent infringement, where there is no intention to copy copyrighted material) is rare. Here are two examples. In an episode of the television series *Murphy Brown*, a writer of children's books allegedly infringed a work that had been read to him as a child, though he had no recollection of that event. More commonly, a painter may "copy" from his own earlier works without being aware that he is copying. If he no longer owns the copyright in the earlier work, his current work may be an infringement.

whether the applicant has met these conditions, is a condition of patentability because patents, partly because they do forbid independent duplication, confer potentially great monopoly power; if they were too easily obtainable, there would be significant rent seeking and deadweight losses. Copyrights confer less protection against competition; and the less original the copyrighted works are, the less protection the copyrights confer because originality is highly prized by consumers of expressive works. The main function of conditioning copyright protection on a showing of some originality is not to reduce monopoly power but to lighten the evidentiary burden on the courts of having to decide whether two virtually indistinguishable works (indistinguishable because they contain trivial amounts of original expression—maybe both are copies, with negligible alterations in format, of the same railroad timetable) were independently created or one was copied from the other; and for this purpose a minimal requirement of originality is sufficient. We shall explore this point in discussing derivative works later in this chapter, and shall also point out that many such works are indeed close substitutes for the original work. Not all, however; the translation of a book into a foreign language may not take any of the market from the original if the people in the foreign land do not read books written in the language of the original work. As a final complication, sometimes even verbatim copying does not make the copy a market substitute for the original and so does not infringe (more on this later).

Let us come back for a moment to the example of the two economics textbooks that are close substitutes even though none of the sentences is the same or even a close paraphrase of a sentence in the other book and there are enough other differences as well, for example in the arrangement of chapters, to preclude a finding of copyright infringement. Nevertheless they are both expressive works, and they are close substitutes. This complicates the analysis in the preceding chapters of the effect of expanding copyright protection on the output of expressive works. In the formal model presented in Chapter 3, N (the number of different expressive works, as distinct from the number of copies of a given work) increases as z (the level of copyright protection) increases, but only up to the level, $\bar{z}$, beyond which increases in the cost of expression to marginal authors due to higher input costs caused by copyright protection dominate the effect of a higher z on copiers' marginal costs. In addition, however, an increase in N brought about by an increase in copyright protection increases competition among creators of expressive works because, as in our example of the economics textbooks, many copyrighted works are substitutes for other copyrighted works. So there will be more substitutes if N is higher. They will not be as close substitutes, given the increase in z that caused N to rise, as was possible before. But the additional substitutes will increase the demand elasticity in the market for copies of a given work and thus lower the equilibrium price of a copy. This in turn will diminish the positive impact of expanding copyright protection on the expected return to creators of expressive works and so blunt the effect of a higher z on N.[9] As a result of this feedback effect, expanding copyright protection has, beyond some point, a somewhat self-defeating character, though by the same token the feedback effect reduces access costs by limiting the increase in the price of copies brought about by the expanded protection.

Idea versus Expression

Copyright law protects expression but not ideas.[10] To illustrate, if an author of spy novels copies a portion of an Ian Fleming novel about James Bond, he is an infringer. If, inspired by Fleming, he decides to write a novel about a British secret agent who is a bon vivant, he is not an infringer. If an economist reprints Ronald Coase's article on social cost without permission, he is an infringer; but if he expounds the Coase Theorem in his own words, he is not. As these examples suggest, the "ideas" that copyright does not protect tend to be different in fictional and nonfictional works, and so we will discuss them separately. In nonfiction they are ideas in the conventional sense in which scientists, philosophers, and other theoreticians deal in ideas. In fiction, as well as in other works of imagination, such as paintings and musical compositions, they tend to fall into one of two categories. The first consists of standard, often hackneyed, themes or plots (the murder of a woman by her irrationally jealous husband, but not the specific plot of *Othello*), stock characters (the idea of a talking animal, but not Mickey Mouse), literary techniques (such as the obtuse narrator, but not the obtuse narration in Ford Madox Ford's *The Good Soldier*), familiar subject matter and locales, perspective and other conventions in painting for depicting depth, and musical conventions suggestive

9. This point is suggested by a recent paper on patents. See Tomas J. Philipson and Frank R. Lichtenberg, "The Dual Effects of Intellectual Property Regulations: Within- and Between-Patent Competition in the US Pharmaceuticals Industry" (University of Chicago, George J. Stigler Center for the Study of the Economy and the State, Working Paper No. 178, Oct. 12, 2002). We return to the point in Chapter 11.

10. "In no case does copyright protection for an original work of authorship extend to any idea, procedure, process, system, method of operation, concept, principle, or discovery, regardless of the form in which it is described, explained, illustrated, or embodied in such work." 17 U.S.C. § 102(b). Ideas may sometimes be protected in other ways, by contract law, for example. Or, if A discloses an idea to B on the implicit understanding that if B uses the idea he will pay A, A will be protected under the doctrine of quasi-contract or unjust enrichment. See Minniear v. Tors, 266 Cal. App. 2d 495 (1968). See also the discussion of trade secrecy in Chapter 13 and of the misappropriation doctrine later in this chapter.

of suspense, dread, or joy. Such "ideas" are commonplace, and so their presence both in the original copyrighted work and the alleged infringing work does not support a finding of copying—the "infringer" could easily have picked up the ideas from works in the public domain. Second, there are profound or original ideas, techniques, and so forth—"ideas" (broadly understood) that are not just, as it were, lying around, but instead are the invention of the creator of the original copyrighted work. Twentieth-century examples include Cubism, stream of consciousness narration, the hard-boiled-detective story, and twelve-tone music. These are not protected by copyright either, not because they are commonplace (they are not) but because conferring a monopoly on the inventor is probably not necessary either to elicit an optimal supply of such innovations or to prevent congestion externalities as a consequence of their being unowned.

IDEAS IN IMAGINATIVE WORKS Suppose the N works in the formal model in Chapter 3 express the same idea differently; for example, each work might be a different novel about a romance between young people who belong to different social classes or religious faiths and whose parents are feuding. If copyright protected the first author's idea, the cost of expression to each of the remaining $N - 1$ authors would increase because each would have to invest time and effort in coming up with an original idea for his work, or to substitute additional expression for the part of his idea that overlapped the first author's, or to incur licensing and other transaction costs to obtain the right to use the first author's idea.

We can write the full cost of creating a work as $e(z) + i$, where i is the cost of obtaining the ideas used in the work. If copyright law protected ideas, i would become $i(z)$ and would rise, and probably $e(z)$ would rise also because the author would substitute more of his own expressive material for i, since e and i are used in variable proportions to create a work. The net effect of protecting ideas would therefore be to reduce the number of works created (in the limit, to one, although mention of Professor Coase reminds us that the Coase Theorem makes this outcome unlikely), so that social welfare (see equation (16) in the preceding chapter) would fall. It is true that the copiers' costs would also rise if copyright protected ideas, because copiers generally use the author's ideas as well as his way of expressing them. But the offset would probably be small. Copiers copy expression either unlawfully, in which case the marginal deterrence from protecting ideas is likely to be small, or lawfully, for example because their copying is deemed a fair use. In either case copyright protection for ideas would have a negligible effect on the copier's cost of copying. Even if protection did increase the gross profits of the $N - 1$ authors and thus offset partially the reduction in N, social welfare would fall because both N and welfare per work would fall.

The traditional explanation for why only expression is protected emphasizes the welfare losses from a monopoly of an idea. We emphasize instead the increase in the cost of creating works and the resulting reduction in the number of works, rather than the higher price (per copy) that is normally associated with monopoly. Suppose our N authors did not know which one would be the first to come up with an idea that the other $N - 1$ authors would use. Since the investment required to come up with the kind of new idea likely to be embodied in an expressive work usually is low relative to the costs in time and effort of expressing the idea (we'll give examples shortly), and since the originator of the idea will probably obtain a normal return in one form or another from being first in the market even without receiving copyright protection, the N authors, behind a veil of ignorance, would probably agree to a rule that gave legal protection to expression but denied it to ideas.[11]

The copyrighting of ideas would also encourage rent seeking, as in the hypothetical case of the undiscovered continent discussed in Chapter 1. Could the inventor of the detective story copyright that entire genre? The inventor of tragedy, of comedy, of the tale of star-crossed lovers, of the sonnet, the rhymed couplet, opera, and so forth? If we are right that the costs of developing a new idea are likely to be low in most cases relative to the potential reward from licensing the idea to others, there would be a mad rush to develop and copyright ideas. Resources would be sucked into developing ideas with minimal expression,[12] and the ideas thus developed would be banked in the hope that a later author would pay for their use. There would be copyright equivalents of patent races—the reason for such races being precisely that a patent grants exclusive control over an idea that may have broad application and as a result immense commercial value. This is another reason for not allowing the copyrighting of individual words, titles, and short phrases.

A final concern is with the administrative costs involved in enforcing rights in ideas. Courts would have to define each idea, set its boundaries, determine its overlap with other ideas, and, most difficult of all, identify the original idea in the work of the alleged infringer. True, the total administrative and enforcement costs of operating a copyright system might actually shrink if ideas were protected because fewer works would be created. But since the optimal level of copyright protection for expression takes account of the costs of enforcement, our first point—the decline in social welfare that is brought about by a reduction in the number of works created—incorporates the savings in

11. In a more complicated model the demand for copies would depend not only on the number of copies, as in our model, but also on the number of competing works. In that case legal protection of ideas would, in addition to its other effects, raise the price of copies.

12. In other words, *abstract* ideas, because they would cover the broadest range of subsequent works. See Michael Steven Green, "Copyrights in Facts" (forthcoming in *Indiana Law Journal*).

administrative and enforcement costs from a reduction in the number of protected works. Those savings reduce but do not eliminate the welfare loss from fewer works. There would be a further loss because authors would encounter sharply increased transaction costs in attempting to license materials under copyright since those materials would include ideas as well as expression.

Novels illustrate these points well. The novelist creates a novel by combining familiar and therefore easily recognizable characters and situations (many of which go back to the earliest writings that have survived from antiquity, and doubtless earlier)—i—with his particular choice of words, incidents, and dramatis personae—e. He does not create or buy the familiar characters and situations that he uses. Unlike the ideas for which patents can be obtained, most of the "ideas" found in fiction are not new and the novelist acquires them at zero cost, either from observation of the world around him or from works long in the public domain. This is not because novelists are lazy and uninventive. It is because most works of fiction that anyone would want to copy appeal to a mass audience—regardless of the author's intentions—and to do this, especially over an extended period of time as in the case of the classics, a work must be relatively impervious to cultural change. It therefore must deal, to a considerable extent anyway, with the recurrent problems of the human condition—with the commonplaces of life, the recurrent situations, the familiar human types (what Elizabethans called "humors"), standard narratives. That is why paraphrasing literature tends to yield merely bromides and banalities. Ideas in literature are not like the ideas of science or philosophy; they are more like painters' subjects. And as they comprise a quite limited stock of situations, narratives, and character types, to recognize property rights in them would overreward the earliest writers and deplete the stock of literary raw material available for later writers without fee. It would also create baffling evidentiary problems because of the point just made that works of literature do not endure unless they depict permanent features of the human condition. If Homer had not lived, eventually someone else would have written a poem about revenge, gods, and a war over a beautiful woman. Yet once the *Iliad* is in existence, it becomes hard to determine whether subsequent authors of works on these themes are copying the *Iliad* or copying life. We have given literary examples but similar examples from music, painting, and other expressive activities abound.

We have identified real problems with extending copyright to ideas but must not exaggerate them. The magnitude of the problems depends on the length of the copyright term. If it were forever, the problems would be staggering. The shorter it is, the less severe the problems, especially if we are correct that literature and the arts tend by their nature to draw on an ancient stock of subject matter, narrative forms, and the like. But there are exceptions—think of such twentieth-century cultural innovations as the comic book, the animated cartoon, film noir, modern dance, cubism, and abstract expressionism. The impact on these cultural forms of even a short copyright term could be profound and largely negative.

An important class of ideas found in works of the imagination consists of technique, such as the sonnet form, the five-act play, stream of consciousness writing, perspective in painting, the pointed arch, and serial composition in music. A reason for denying copyright protection in such cases, besides the excessive monopoly power that protection would confer in many of them, is that technique is harder to copy well than a work embodying the technique. It is easy to copy someone else's sonnet—but try writing one! With copies likely to be costly, slow to appear, and imperfect, the originator of a technique will be able to recoup some and perhaps all of his fixed costs even if he has no property right in the technique, as opposed to the copyright of his own works that utilize the technique.

Notice, however, that by allowing authors carte blanche to copy genre, technique, style, and even—to a significant though not unlimited extent—plot and characters from previous authors, all in the name of the idea-expression distinction, copyright law discriminates among types of literary work and by doing so may be distorting writers' choices of which genres to work in. A lyric poem receives maximum protection from copyright law because the verbal pattern is almost everything in poetry, and it is verbal pattern that copyright law protects most securely. Maximum protection is not complete protection. If the poem employs a new meter (such as dactylic hexameter) or a new form (such as the sonnet), the poet will not be able to prevent the copying of the meter or the form. But novels and plays, in which plot and character often are more important than the specific choice of words (which is why novels and plays are easier to translate well than poems), receive less protection than poetry.

IDEAS IN DISCURSIVE WORKS   In the case of Professor Coase, the reason for confining copyright protection to the form in which he expressed the Coase Theorem, and not extending it to the theorem itself, is less obvious. The theorem was not obtained at zero cost but reflected decades of study and thought. And it is novel and nonobvious in senses that lend themselves to objective determination, as in the case of patentable ideas but not of aesthetic ideas.[13] But precisely because the theorem is a powerful analytical construct,

---

13. But it probably would not have been patentable even as a "business methods" patent (see Chapter 11), had such patents been recognized when Coase invented the theorem, because it has no commercial applications and thus is not "useful" within the meaning of the patent statute.

copyright protection would yield the inventor substantial royalty income over and above the considerable nonpecuniary (as well as indirect pecuniary) income that accrues to a major theoretician. Every economist who wanted to apply or extend the Coase Theorem would have to get a license from Coase, though the fair use doctrine would privilege an economist who wanted to test or challenge the theorem. Coase's total income might well exceed the cost of invention, creating a problem of rent seeking. Indeed, this is implicit in the fact that he created (or discovered) the theorem without the prospect of copyright protection of it; the question is the effect such protection would have on academics facing similar opportunities.

The cost of enforcement of a copyright on the theorem would also be greater than if the article itself had been copied. Often it would be hard to tell whether an article in economics was really using the Coase Theorem; the author (if he did not want to pay a royalty) would make every effort to explain his results in different terms. Furthermore, mathematical and scientific (including social-scientific) ideas often are discovered simultaneously, or nearly so; this would make it difficult to determine whether an alleged infringer was a copier or an independent inventor. Some economists have even argued that Coase's theorem was nothing new; that he was just saying that there are gains from trade when trade is feasible.[14] Coase himself has argued that the real significance of his article was in drawing attention to the importance of transaction costs. So would all subsequent economic analysis of transaction costs, such as this book, require a license from Professor Coase if the ideas found in expressive works, along with the expression itself, were copyrightable?

Clearly the bare-bones concept of "originality" that suffices when copyright is limited to expression would have to be revised in the direction of patent law if copyright were extended to ideas. Yet mention of patent law is a reminder of the importance of distinguishing between ideas that are the fruits of basic research and those that are the fruits of applied research. The prime difference from an economic standpoint is that the former lack immediate commercial applications. Patent law does not permit the fruits of basic as distinct from applied research to be patented, yet the ideas found in discursive as distinct from imaginative writing are mainly of a basic-research character, such as the Coase Theorem itself. To allow them to be copyrighted would upset a balance deliberately and intelligently struck by patent law, while to grant copyrights in applied ideas would be stepping directly on the toes of the patent statute. It is true that there is overlapping patent and copyright pro-

14. See Deirdre N. McCloskey, "The Good Old Coase Theorem and the Good Old Chicago School: A Comment on Zerbe and Medema," in *Coasean Economics: Law and Economics and the New Institutional Economics* 239, 240–241 (Steven G. Medema ed. 1998).

tection of some computer software, but this is because some software can both satisfy the requirements of patentability and be an expressive work. Ideas are not expressive works.

A final point regarding the Coase Theorem, and one with application to issues of patentability as well, has to do with the reward system in science and the academy generally. Precisely because a fruit of truly basic research has by definition no immediate or foreseeable commercial applications, the incentives for basic research have to come elsewhere than from the market for commercial goods and services. They come from academic salaries and from the prestige that accrues to successful scientists and other academics, and the salaries are in turn a function to a considerable extent of that prestige. Academics compete with one another to maximize their reputation, and success in that competition depends on the widespread adoption of their creative ideas, "copies" of which—uses of which by other academics—have therefore a high degree of complementarity with the ideas themselves.[15] This implies that ordinarily academics would license their ideas at a zero fee, and if so, since licensing is not costless, this is a further argument against copyright or patent protection of such ideas.

The Merger of Ideas and Expression

Some ideas can be expressed only in one or a very few ways, so that protecting expression fully would as a practical matter prevent anyone but the author from using the idea. Copyright protection is construed narrowly in such cases to avoid excluding others from using the idea. In copyright jargon, expression indispensable to function—"functional expression"—is not copyrightable. This is the same principle that, as we shall see in Chapter 7, denies trademark protection to "functional" trademarks, for example, trademarks consisting of features, such as shape, that may be essential to the operation of the trademarked product.

The leading case on functional expression is *Baker v. Selden*.[16] Selden had published a book describing a bookkeeping system that he had invented, and he illustrated the book with blank bookkeeping forms. Baker copied the forms, rearranging columns and using different headings, and sold them to people who wanted to use Selden's system. This was held not to be infringement, since otherwise Selden would have had a monopoly over his bookkeeping system that he could have exploited by insisting that anyone wanting

15. See Green, note 12 above.
16. 101 U.S. 99 (1879). See also Morrissey v. Procter & Gamble Co., 379 F.2d 675 (1st Cir. 1967), where the rationale for denying copyright protection is explained in terms highly congruent with our analysis.

to use the system buy the forms necessary for using it from him. Formally, if r denotes the use of Selden's new bookkeeping system, s the system itself, and t the blank account forms in the book,

$$r = f(s, t) \tag{1}$$

where both s and t are required to produce r, so that if Selden controls either s or t, he has a monopoly of r as well.

It might seem that without copyright protection Selden could not even have prevented Baker from copying his entire book, but this is not correct. Had Baker published a book that copied verbatim (or by close paraphrase) the expository portions of Selden's book, he would have been guilty of infringement. If he wanted to sell the forms together with explanatory material, he had to write that material himself; the expressive part of Selden's book was thus protected. Likewise only Selden or his licensees (he had licensed the copying of the forms before Baker's unauthorized copying) could represent their forms as "officially authorized by Selden."

Is denial of copyright protection for Selden's forms the optimal result? Denying him the right to copyright his forms might have prevented him from recouping the expense in time and effort of inventing a new bookkeeping system. But this is unlikely. There are other ways in which he could have cashed in on such a notable commercial innovation. Consider pirated computer software. Consumers might prefer to pay for the original software just to get the instructions manual that comes with it, and likewise bookkeepers might have preferred to get the forms together with Selden's own explanation of how to use them. Granting him copyright protection might well have overcompensated him, raising the spectre of rent seeking, as well as have created deadweight losses in the market for account forms by raising the price of those forms above their marginal cost.

More important, copyright is designed to protect expression, not the invention of new business methods, however original, ingenious, and socially valuable. Whether a new system of bookkeeping should be treated as intellectual property—today's counterpart to Selden might have been able to obtain a business-methods patent—is a question that should be faced head on rather than being elided by giving the new system legal protection as an expressive work. It would have been a similar mistake to have allowed the zipper's inventor to copyright the zipper. Copyright would have given him a monopoly going far beyond the zipper's expressive aspect, since no one else could have designed a zipper that would look sufficiently unlike the original inventor's as not to infringe his copyright. We have a body of law for determining when inventors should be given a property right in their invention, but it is patent law, not copyright law.

Similar reasoning furnishes still another reason why short phrases (such as "Money-Back Guaranty") are not copyrightable. If a seller could copyright phrases that were essential to the sale and marketing of his product, it would be difficult for other sellers to compete effectively with him.

The rule of *Baker v. Selden* bears on whether copyright protection for computer software[17] extends to the visual "desktop" on which the computer operator views icons representing documents, files, programs, and so on, and to the organization and sequence by which the operator is led through a program. Because a given desktop display ("user interface") or program sequence can be generated by a variety of different programs, the copyright on the machine code that is the program itself does not cover these visual aspects of computer use. The question is whether they are separately copyrightable by analogy to a painting—a visual display that could be generated by a variety of different processes too. The argument against copyrightability is that the visual aspects in question may have become so well accepted as a standard in the computer market (in the same way that the QWERTY keyboard is the standard for typing) that copyright protection would enable the copyright holder to exclude from the market competing manufacturers of software. The counterargument is that the "idea" is the display of documents or other data, or sequences of steps, on a screen, and the "expression" the particular visual symbology. The argument continues that the mere fact that a particular set of symbols has become the industry standard is a tribute to the expressive skills of the particular manufacturer and should not be deemed to convert expression into idea.

The debate should be resolved not by the semantics of the words "idea" and "expression" but by the economics of the problem and, specifically, by comparing the deadweight costs of allowing a firm to appropriate what has become an industry standard with the disincentive effects on originators if such appropriation is forbidden. The deadweight costs could be large—large enough to raise serious antitrust issues (see Chapter 14)—if the inventor of the QWERTY keyboard had been able to copyright the arrangement of the letters constituting the keyboard, or if the first person to produce a clock or watch with its characteristic face consisting of numbers arranged in a circle with minute and hour hands rotating through them could have copyrighted the face. But Disney's copyrighting a watch face configured to look like Mickey Mouse left plenty of alternative configurations for competitors to adopt. The disincentive effects of denying copyrightability to a standard may be small, since there are apt to be significant returns over and above those generated by copyright protection to a firm that achieves such a position

---

17. On which see the thorough analysis in Peter S. Menell, "Envisioning Copyright Law's Digital Future" (forthcoming in *New York University Law Review*).

(though competition to be the owner of the standard is likely to reduce the expected return to the normal, competitive level); and the narrowly expressive aspects of the display are protected, which limits the amount of free riding.

A variant of the standards issue is presented by intermediate copying, illustrated by *Sega Enterprises Ltd. v. Accolade, Inc.*[18] Sega manufactured both copyrighted video games and a console or monitor on which the games could be played. Accolade wanted to manufacture games that would also run on Sega's consoles. To do this it needed access to Sega's copyrighted computer source code to discover the interfaces by which to "hook" a program to the operating code in a Sega console. It gained that access by reverse engineering Sega's video games. The information it obtained in this fashion enabled it to manufacture video games compatible with Sega's consoles. Its games did not infringe any copyright owned by Sega, and the information that Accolade obtained about the interfaces was not information that Sega could have copyrighted, because it was an idea.[19] But to obtain this information Accolade had copied the entire source code, which was copyrighted. The only use it made of the copies was to generate noninfringing works, and the only effect of liability would thus have been to impede Accolade's competing with Sega in the market for video games, an anticompetitive result not sanctioned by any policy of the copyright statute. The court sensibly held that the copying was a fair use and therefore noninfringing.

Another application of *Baker v. Selden* concerns the copying of architectural works. Architects' plans, blueprints, etc., can be copyrighted, and if they are then copied without authorization the copier is an infringer, though entitled by the "intermediate copying" exception just discussed to use the noncopyrightable ideas contained in the plans.[20] But what if someone copies not the plans or some ornamental sculptural work attached to the building's façade but the building itself (its shape, proportions, cladding, and so on), which contains expressive as well as design elements, constructed from the plans? Is he an infringer? In cases preceding the statute discussed next, the law's answer sensibly was "no."[21] A building is functional as well as formal or decorative. If the architect could prevent the copying of the design elements visible in the building, he would have greater property-right protection than

18. 977 F.2d 1510 (9th Cir. 1992).

19. A "method of operation" within the meaning of section 102(b). See note 10 above.

20. Unless they are covered by a design patent or the copier cannot get hold of them—but in the *Demetriades* case, cited in the next note, the plans had been filed with a municipal agency and were open to public inspection.

21. See, for example, Imperial Homes Corp. v. Lamont, 458 F.2d 895, 898 (5th Cir. 1972); Demetriades v. Kaufmann, 680 F. Supp. 658, 666; 698 F. Supp. 521, 527 n. 6 (S.D.N.Y. 1988).

copyright law envisages. The building built without the aid of the architect's plans corresponds to the desktop display generated without access to the originator's software.

Yet in the Architectural Works Protection Act of 1990, Congress amended the copyright statute to enable the copyrighting of "the overall form [of the building] as well as the arrangement and composition of spaces and elements," though not of "individual standard features."[22] This is a dubious extension of copyright protection. The copying of a building without access to the building plans, which, as just seen, are copyrightable under traditional principles, is likely to be extremely costly. Far from being able to free ride on the original, the copier is likely to incur higher costs in making his copy of the building. A person who wanted to duplicate a building designed by a distinguished architect would therefore ordinarily prefer to hire the architect or his firm rather than try duplicating it on the basis of the visible aspects of the building[23]—and for the further reason that he would be thought a cheapo otherwise. And it is rare for buildings to give rise to derivative works (a potential source of income for architects), though not unknown—think of statuettes of the Empire State Building and the Eiffel Tower.

It would be different if an architect or builder wanted merely to copy the external, nonfunctional, purely ornamental features of another building. That could be done easily enough without access to the building plans. But that type of copying would not be protected by the doctrine of *Baker v. Selden*, because preventing the copying would not prevent duplication of any of the functional features of the building.

It is surprising that there have been few cases under the Architectural Works Protection Act; indeed, we have found—what is rare in a new statute bristling with potential interpretive issues—only one substantial opinion.[24] The case involved the copying of a developer's copyrighted tract house (the "Louisa") rather than of a house designed by a distinguished architect; and so duplication without hiring the architect was quite feasible. Since developers offer only a limited number of design choices to their customers, allowing duplication would, by enabling an unlimited number of identical houses to be put on the market, reduce the distinctiveness and hence value of the original developer's product—a person loses face by living in a house identical to the houses everyone else lives in. Since the "Louisa" was already duplicated in

---

22. 17 U.S.C. § 101; see also id., § 102(a)(8).

23. The *Demetriades* case, notes 20 and 21 above, is an exception; the defendant copied a $2 million house built by the plaintiff and tried to build on a lot located only a few houses away from the original.

24. Richmond Homes Management, Inc. v. Raintree, Inc., 862 F. Supp. 1517 (W.D. Va. 1994), affirmed in part and reversed in part, 1995 WL 551274 (4th Cir. Sept. 18, 1995).

the development, however, the negative effect of one more copy was probably slight. In any event, the case has little if anything to do with enabling the creator of an expressive work to recoup his fixed costs. It belongs rather with the cases discussed in Chapter 7 that forbid nonconfusing duplication of a trademark in order to prevent the trademark from losing its distinctiveness.

Still another way to think about the merger of idea and expression in cases such as *Baker* and *Sega* is in terms of incremental incentives. If there is only one way conveniently to express a commercially valuable idea, the inventor will have a powerful incentive to invest the necessary resources in creating the proper form for the expression of the idea; for otherwise his idea will be worth much less. When there are legal or other means of internalizing the invention externality itself, there is no need to protect the expression as well in order to induce the creation of the idea. Returning once more to the Coase example, we point out that while in the merger cases expression is incidental to idea, this is not true of Coase's article, in which, besides presenting the Coase Theorem (though not describing it in those terms), Coase gave illustrations of it, compared it with previous approaches, defended it, and discussed its implications for law, economics, and public policy, all in a distinctive prose style. As the subsequent literature on the Coase Theorem demonstrates, there are an indefinite variety of expressive forms in which to articulate, defend, attack, qualify, and illustrate Coase's idea.

Facts versus Expression

Merger of idea and expression is rarely a problem in fiction, given the rejection of copyrightability of literary genres, techniques, and familiar human types. The different expressive forms in which to cast these public domain elements are well-nigh infinite. In between works of fiction, on the one hand, and works in which the variety of possible expression is so constrained that expression is deemed entirely merged into idea *(Baker v. Selden)*, on the other hand, are works of nonfiction. The facts that form the subject matter of such a work may or may not dictate the expression; if they do, it is a case of merger and copyright protection should be denied. Thus the first author of a history of the United States should not be allowed to copyright the sequence of events narrated, since that would impede any subsequent author in writing a narrative history of the United States covering the same period as the first author. We say "impede" rather than "preclude" because the subsequent author could always argue that he had based his narration on the facts of history as revealed by noncopyrighted primary sources rather than on any copyrighted history book. When the "originality" of a work consists mainly in the disclosure of facts, it will often be difficult to determine whether a subsequent author's similar work is a copy of the previous work or a work of independent creation because there will be other routes of access to facts besides the previous work. The more likely independent creation is, the more costly and uncertain the litigation of a claim of copyright infringement will be, and this becomes an argument for denying copyright protection.

This could be a factor in a *Baker v. Selden* type of case as well. Baker might have argued that his forms (unless word for word the same as Selden's, or—what would have been especially persuasive evidence distinguishing copying from independent creation—if they contained the same typographical or other mechanical errors as Selden's) duplicated Selden's forms simply because there was only one way in which to express Selden's noncopyrightable bookkeeping system and thus that they were actually an independent creation.

Copyright does not protect facts. The excluded categories of idea and of fact are similar. Compare a surgeon's copyrighting his article describing a new procedure for breast implants, and obtaining by virtue of the copyright a right to prevent anyone else from publishing a description of the procedure, with an astronomer's copyrighting his article describing his discovery of a planet in a distant galaxy and obtaining thereby a right to prevent anyone else from mentioning the planet. In both cases the effect of allowing copyright would be to provide legal protection for activities (in both, forms of research, but the first producing an idea and the second disclosing a fact) that are different from expression.

Yet the copyright statute explicitly authorizes the copyrighting of compilations, defined as works "formed by the collection and assembling of preexisting materials or of data that are selected, coordinated, or arranged in such a way that the resulting work as a whole constitutes an original work of authorship."[25] On one level, virtually every expressive work is a compilation of preexisting materials, namely words (in the case of books or articles—unless the author makes up the words, as in the case of Lewis Carroll's poem "Jabberwocky"), or lines and colors in the case of paintings, or 0's and 1's in the case of computer code. But the significance of compilation in copyright law is that compilations merely of facts are copyrightable, and this creates tension with the noncopyrightability of the facts themselves. In *Feist Publications, Inc. v. Rural Telephone Service Co.*, the Supreme Court resolved the tension against the copyrightability of the compilation at issue in that case.[26] Rural, the plaintiff, a small telephone company, published a phone book, as did Feist, the defendant; Feist's covered eleven service areas, Rural's being

25. 17 U.S.C. § 101; see also id., § 103.
26. 499 U.S. 340 (1991).

one. Feist was not a phone company and so didn't have access to people's telephone numbers. It sought licenses from the phone companies serving the various service areas, and when Rural refused to grant it a license Feist went ahead anyway and copied names and numbers from Rural's phone book, precipitating Rural's suit. Since Rural distributed its phone book free of charge, it is hard to see how it could have been injured by Feist's copying. It may well have been helped; Feist's directory made searching for phone numbers easier and thus may have increased phone usage.

But the deeper problem with Rural's suit (which it lost) was that facts and compilation were merged in Rural's directory in the same sense in which idea and expression had merged in Selden's forms in *Baker v. Selden*. To place the names of telephone subscribers in alphabetical order is to arrange preexisting materials. But as there is no other satisfactory way to arrange them, giving the arranger a copyright of the phone directory (the white pages, not the yellow pages, which enable greater flexibility in selection and arrangement) gives him practical control over the preexisting materials, the facts, in this case the names and numbers themselves.

The point is not that there is no free riding in such a case; there may be; and depending on the cost of obtaining the facts, free riding may discourage socially useful activities. But as they are activities distinct from expression, the question whether and by what means to establish property rights in them should be addressed on its own terms rather than answered uncritically by a mechanical extension of copyright law to nonexpressive activities.

The issue is acutely posed by recent developments in the creation and copying of digital data. Huge electronic databases are being created at great cost yet the copying of an entire such database, also electronically, is often cheap and virtually instantaneous, inviting massive free riding on large investments. Copyright is of little help because the data in these databases are not arranged by the compiler; they are merely available to be searched by the user; the user's search engine replaces the compiler's traditional creative function of arrangement. The question whether and in what form to extend property rights to the creators of such databases, rather than forcing them to rely on contract enforcement and other self-help (for example, encryption, corresponding to a fence designed to keep trespassers from entering one's land), requires careful consideration rather than automatic extension of copyright law to electronic databases.[27]

A common law doctrine creates a limited property right in facts; it goes by

27. See J. H. Reichman and Pamela Samuelson, "Intellectual Property Rights in Data?" 50 *Vanderbilt Law Review* 51 (1997); Green, note 12 above; Stephen M. Maurer and Suzanne Scotchmer, "Database Protection: Is It Broken and Should We Fix It?" 284 *Science* 1129 (1999).

the name of "misappropriation" and is most famously illustrated by the Supreme Court's decision in *International News Service v. Associated Press*.[28] That decision no longer is authoritative, having been based on the federal courts' subsequently renounced authority to formulate common law principles in suits arising under state law though brought in federal court, usually under the diversity jurisdiction. The AP and INS competed in gathering news and selling it to newspapers. During World War I, INS, which was owned by William Randolph Hearst, who had sympathized with the Germans in the early part of the war, was barred by British and French censors from sending war dispatches to the United States. So it copied AP's dispatches from the East Coast newspapers in which they were published and published them in Hearst's West Coast newspapers at the same hour, because of the difference in time zones, and then in Hearst's East Coast newspapers only a few hours later. There was no copyright infringement, because news, consisting as it does of facts, or what are believed to be facts, is not copyrightable (the precise form in which they are expressed may be, but that was not the issue). There was no theft of a trade secret, since AP's dispatches were public. And there was no trademark infringement. Nevertheless the Supreme Court held that AP was entitled to enjoin INS's copying, since otherwise AP would have a diminished incentive to incur the costs of obtaining the news. It was a straightforward case of free riding.

The doctrine of the *INS* case is recognized in some states and has given rise to some interesting cases.[29] We discuss just three. In *Board of Trade v. Dow Jones & Co.*,[30] the Chicago Board of Trade created a futures contract based on the Dow Jones index of thirty industrial stocks. The contract enabled speculation on moves in this widely followed index. In a suit by Dow Jones, the Supreme Court of Illinois held that the Board had misappropriated Dow Jones's rights in its index. The result is unsound from an economic standpoint. Dow Jones is a publisher rather than a stock exchange and had no plans for or likely prospects of creating a futures contract. Hence the Board's copying of Dow Jones's index inflicted no present or prospective injury other

28. 248 U.S. 215 (1918). See Richard A. Epstein, "*International News Service v. Associated Press:* Custom and Law as Sources of Property Rights in News," 78 *Virginia Law Review* 85 (1992), esp. pp. 112–119.

29. See Douglas G. Baird, "Common Law Intellectual Property and the Legacy of *International News Service v. Associated Press*," 50 *University of Chicago Law Review* 411 (1983). An argument for broader use of misappropriation doctrine to plug holes in the patent statute is made in Douglas Gary Lichtman, "The Economics of Innovation: Protecting Unpatentable Goods," 81 *Minnesota Law Review* 693 (1997). The doctrine's affinity to the right of publicity mentioned in Chapter 2 is discussed in Huw Beverley-Smith, *The Commercial Appropriation of Personality* 176–177 (2002).

30. 456 N.E.2d 84 (Ill. 1983).

than a loss of licensing revenues that had never been anticipated in the first place—and the futures contract would have been an advertisement for the index and hence for Dow Jones. Nor could it be argued with a straight face that without the licensing revenues that it might be able to extract from the Board if it had a right to prevent the Board from creating the futures contract, Dow Jones would be unable to recoup its fixed costs in creating and maintaining the index. The index had been created without anticipation of licensing revenues, and its maintenance requires little if anything more than occasionally replacing one of the thirty stocks in order to maintain adequate diversification.

A year later another court in a similar case reached the opposite result.[31] The USGA, the governing body of amateur golf, establishes rules and regulations for the game and conducts tournaments. It developed a formula for computing the handicaps of golfers, which enable players of different ability to compete with each other on a nominally equal basis.[32] The defendant, Data-Max, obtained the formula (presumably by lawful means) and offered a service by which a golfer could obtain an updated handicap based on the USGA's formula. In effect, the service provided access to the formula at a lower cost than if the golfer had had to obtain the information either from the USGA itself or from a golf club authorized by the USGA to administer the formula. So that was a benefit. And although Data-Max was unquestionably free riding on the USGA's creation and promotion of the formula, there was, as in the *Dow Jones* case, no possibility that this free riding might cause USGA to abandon the formula. The court refused to enjoin Data-Max, on the ground that misappropriation, to be actionable, requires an injury to the plaintiff in his primary market.

In the third case, *National Basketball Association v. Motorola, Inc.,*[33] the National Basketball Association, which owned the copyright on the broadcasts of NBA games, tried to enjoin the defendant's "SportsTrax" service. Employees of the defendant would watch an NBA game on television and at frequent intervals phone in the score, time remaining, and other crucial information to a computer that would compile, process, and format the information and transmit it to pagers sold by the defendant to fans. The defendant's service was not a copyright infringement, because all it was taking

31. U.S. Golf Association v. St. Andrews Systems, Data-Max, Inc., 749 F.2d 1028 (3d Cir. 1984).

32. Thus, if a golfer having a handicap of ten strokes is playing against a golfer with a handicap of three strokes, the latter must complete the game with at least eight fewer strokes than his opponent to win. The handicap is determined by the golfer's previous scores adjusted for the difficulty of the courses in which he obtained those scores.

33. 105 F.3d 841 (2d Cir. 1997).

from the copyrighted broadcasts were facts (the games themselves, unlike theatrical plays, may not be copyrightable, because the moves made by the players are not prescribed). It might seem this would leave a void for misappropriation doctrine to fill. But the federal copyright statute preempts not only state laws that seek to curtail the protection that the federal statute grants owners of intellectual property, but also state laws that provide protection that the copyright statute deliberately withholds. The statute has been interpreted to deny protection to ideas, facts, and other nonexpressive material embedded in expressive works, not as an oversight but as a deliberate federal policy to preserve a public domain consisting of the noncopyrightable contents (such as facts and ideas) in copyrightable works.[34] The Constitution as we know authorizes Congress to create copyright, but leaves the details to Congress, and the exclusion of facts and ideas is one way in which Congress has fine-tuned the copyright authority conferred on it. The result of that fine tuning is that a state may not grant blanket protection in the name of misappropriation to the factual matter in a copyrighted broadcast.

But the court went on to say that if there is more than copying involved in the defendant's conduct, a state's providing a remedy to a person injured by that conduct is not preempted. We do not find this a very satisfactory explanation or see how it fits a case in which all that the defendant is doing, as in the *INS* case, is copying facts found in an expressive work. What the court should have said was that Congress probably didn't mean by the limitations that it imposed on copyright to forbid states to punish the copying of facts in situations in which unlimited free copying would eliminate the incentive to create the facts in the first place. For in such a case the congressional policy of assuring that facts remain in the public domain available for use by all without fee would be defeated; there would be no facts of the type involved in the case in the public domain.

The court formulated the elements of the right to sue for misappropriation this way: "(i) the plaintiff generates or collects information at some cost or expense; (ii) the value of the information is highly time-sensitive; (iii) the defendant's use of the information constitutes free-riding on the plaintiff's costly efforts to generate or collect it; (iv) the defendant's use of the information is in direct competition with a product or service offered by the plaintiff; (v) the ability of other parties to free-ride on the efforts of the plaintiff would so reduce the incentive to produce the product or service that its existence or quality could be substantially threatened."[35] The meat is in (v), with (i) through (iv) identifying the conditions in which the criterion stated in (v) is

34. Id. at 849–850.
35. Id. at 852 (citations omitted).

likely to be satisfied. The criterion may amount to saying that states can protect fact gathering without running afoul of the preemption provision in the federal copyright statute only if the defendant's conduct is likely to deter the plaintiff or others similarly situated from creating the facts that the defendant has copied.

Applying the test to SportsTrax, the court found no misappropriation. The NBA was not going to give up sponsoring basketball games or broadcasting them merely because a few people would not watch them because of the substitute provided by the defendant's service. In fact the service was designed for people who wouldn't watch the game anyway. There may have been some substitution of the service for the broadcasts, and hence some diminution in the advertising revenues of the NBA's member teams, but if so it must have been very slight.

Thus in all three cases the cost-internalization rationale for conferring rights over intellectual property failed as a matter of fact, leaving the benefit to consumers from additional services without offsetting cost. No doubt in all three cases the defendant could at some price have obtained a license from the plaintiff, but this would have imposed transaction costs; and the license fee, depending on how computed, would have operated to limit access to the new services.

Derivative Works

A derivative work is a translation into a different language, or a transformation into or adapation for a different medium ("translation" in a broader sense).[36] Illustrations are a German translation of an English play, the movie version of a play, Tom Stoppard's play *Rosencrantz and Guildenstern Are Dead* (a derivative work from *Hamlet*), *My Fair Lady* vis-à-vis *Pygmalion*, photographs of a painting, a wind-up Mickey Mouse doll, and a porcelain plate with scenes taken from a movie. Section 106(2) of the Copyright Act gives the owner of the copyright on the original work the exclusive right to prepare a derivative work.[37] This has been interpreted to mean that the unauthorized preparer of a derivative of a copyright work cannot copyright even

36. The Copyright Act defines a derivative work as "a work based upon one or more preexisting works, such as a translation, musical arrangement, dramatization, fictionalization, motion picture version, sound recording, art reproduction, abridgment, condensation, or any other form in which a work may be recast, transformed, or adapted." 17 U.S.C. § 101. Thus a derivative work must either be in one of the specific forms named or be "recast, transformed, or adapted." Lee v. A.R.T. Co., 125 F.3d 580, 582 (7th Cir. 1997).

37. 17 U.S.C. § 106(2).

the original expression that he has added to that work.[38] In effect, then, the owner of the copyright on the original work has a monopoly of the derivative works. The term "derivative work" must not be taken literally, however. If there is no copying of copyrighted material, the fact that a work derived from, in the sense of being inspired or suggested by, a previous work does not make the second work an infringement of the first.[39]

The copyright owner can license the making of, without the right to sell, a derivative work, perhaps so a buyer of a copy can adapt it to his special needs; this is so common in the case of computer software that Congress has legislated that it is not an infringement for the software purchaser to modify it for his personal use.[40] The owner of the copyright on the original work, or his licensee, can also copyright the derivative work (more precisely, the new expression in it), provided it satisfies the modest requirement of incremental originality. If the original work is in the public domain (*Hamlet* for example), then anyone can make and copyright a derivative work, though again the copyright protection is limited to the expressive elements added to the original by the author of the derivative work.

The case for giving the owner of a copyrighted work control over derivative works is a subtle one. It is not, as one might think, to enable the creator of the original to recoup his cost of expression. By definition the derivative work is an imperfect substitute; often it is no substitute at all. A person who is in the market for an original painting priced at $20,000 will not be interested in a $50 photograph of the painting. A German who cannot read English will not buy the English original if there is no German translation. There are exceptions, of course; for example, a movie based on a book might reduce, though more likely expand, the demand for the book.

Even when there is no element of substitution or complementarity whatsoever—that is, even when the derivative work is not part of the copiers' supply

38. See, for example, Pickett v. Prince, 207 F.3d 402, 405–407 (7th Cir. 2000); Melville B. Nimmer and David Nimmer, *Nimmer on Copyright,* vol. 1, § 3.06 (2002); Mark A. Lemley, "The Economics of Improvement in Intellectual Property Law," 75 *Texas Law Review* 989, 992 (1997). There is an exception if the original expression added by the unauthorized preparer of a derivative work is clearly detachable from the original work itself, so that no confusion, or disruption of the copyright owner's plans for the exploitation of his work, would be created by allowing the unauthorized preparer to copyright his original expression. See Pickett v. Prince, above, 207 F.3d at 407; Williams v. Broadus, 2001 WL 984714 (S.D.N.Y. Aug. 24, 2001); Anderson v. Stallone, 1989 WL 206431 (C.D. Cal. Apr. 25, 1989); Paul Goldstein, *Copyright,* vol. 1, § 2.16, p. 2:209 n. 11 (2d ed. 2002). Another exception is discussed below.

39. See Paul Goldstein, "Derivative Rights and Derivative Works in Copyright," 30 *Journal of the Copyright Society* 209, 229 (1983).

40. See 17 U.S.C. §§ 117(a)(1), (b).

curve (see equation (15) in Chapter 3), so that the demand faced by the author for the original is independent of the demand for the derivative work—giving the original author the exclusive right over derivative works will increase his expected income. But since it is uncertain whether *any* copyright protection, let alone the amount conferred by current law, is necessary to enable authors and publishers to recover the fixed costs that must be incurred to generate the socially optimal output of expressive works, it would be speculative to conclude that without control over derivative works authors and publishers would be unable to cover those costs. What is true is that some works would not be created without the expectation of revenues from derivative works (an example is a novel written in the expectation that it will be made into a movie), just as some products would not be produced if producers were forbidden to price discriminate.

To understand the best economic case for giving the owner of the original work control over derivative works even if the demands for the original and the derivatives are unrelated, one must first consider why derivative works should be copyrightable at all. Imagine the situation of the translator unable to obtain copyright protection for his contribution to the derivative work, viewed as the joint product of him and the original author. To translate *The Brothers Karamazov* into English is an enormously time-consuming task of the same general character as the expressive activities that copyright protects; indeed, translation is a vital part of literary expression, and of expression generally. If the translator could not obtain a copyright of the translation, he might be unable to recover the cost of his time; anyone would be free to copy the translation without having incurred that cost, and so could undersell him at a profit.

This analysis may seem to imply that the derivative, not original, author should be allowed to copyright the derivative work (the entire work, not just his added expression) even if the original is not in the public domain. But that could distort the timing of publication of both the original work and the derivative works. The original author, eager to maximize his income from the work, would have an incentive to delay publishing it until he had created the derivative works as well (or arranged for their creation by licensees), in order to gain a head start over any would-be authors of such works. There is also a risk of congestion externalities from an uncoordinated proliferation of variants of the same original.

The most compelling reason for vesting the original author with control over derivative works is to minimize transaction costs. Suppose Dostoevsky's heir owned the copyright on the original Russian version of *The Brothers Karamazov,* but an American owned the copyright on the English translation. A publisher who wanted to bring out a new edition of that translation would have to deal with two copyright holders. Transaction costs would be reduced if one person owned both copyrights. Of course, even if they were separately owned to begin with, one of the owners could buy the other's copyright. But such a transaction, with its attendant costs, can be avoided if the law places the power to obtain both copyrights in the same person to begin with—which in effect is what it does. What is more, there is no reason to stop with two. There could be hundreds of derivative works of a popular original. A popular movie, for example, might give rise to a multitude of ancillary products ranging from lunch boxes to toy dolls to electronic games, all incorporating characters from the movie. Another derivative work would be unlikely to infringe *all* of them—many of them the author might be unaware of—but to be on the safe side he would have to obtain a license from each copyright owner of a derivative work to which he had or might be claimed to have had access. The transaction costs would often be not merely high, but prohibitive.

But if it thus is optimal for the original author to control the derivative works, why not deny copyright protection to them? A copyright is a right to exclude; if no one can copyright a derivative work, anyone who makes such a work is an infringer of the original work—except, of course, the author of the original work. It might seem, therefore, that denying copyrightability to derivative works would give the original author the same legal protection he would enjoy under a rule that allowed only him to copyright a derivative work. Not so. If the derivative work is made shortly before the expiration of his copyright on the original work and contains a significant amount of new expression that was costly to create, the author may lack an adequate incentive to create the derivative work unless it can be copyrighted. In addition, proof of infringement is simplified if the author can enforce a copyright in a derivative work, for then there is no need to decide whether the infringer's derivative work is similar enough to the original to infringe it; it is enough that it is a close copy of the derivative work. And by enabling the author's property right to be subdivided, the copyrightability of derivative works facilitates transactions; compare time-sharing and other subdividings of more conventional property rights. In the case of a movie based on a book, for example, the producer will invariably acquire the copyright on the movie, the derivative work, because he is best able to exploit derivative uses of the movie, for example video cassettes, adaptations for television, posters, advertisements, and colorization. And in cases in which the original is in the public domain, there is no copyright owner to prevent the copying of a translation or other derivative work, and so the incentive to prepare such works would be impaired if derivative works could not be copyrighted.

One can imagine a system—it would resemble patent law's treatment of improvement patents—in which a nonlicensee would be entitled to make a derivative work "on spec," hoping that the owner of the copyright on the original work would license the derivative work from him, though knowing that he could not sell his derivative work without such a license because it would infringe the original work. Creativity might be stimulated and transaction costs actually reduced if a prospective creator of a derivative work could make the work without first having to persuade the owner of the original work that it was a worthwhile venture.[41] That is essentially the regime created by patent law, which allows nonlicensees to obtain patents on significant improvements on an existing patent and thus creates a situation ("blocking patents") in which if the owner of that patent would like to use the improvement he must obtain a license from the improver, while the improver cannot use his improvement without a license from the owner of the original patent. As we explain in Chapter 11, however, the case for patentable though unauthorized improvement patents is stronger than the case for copyrightable though unauthorized derivative works, primarily because it is much more difficult and costly to obtain a patent than a copyright, and so the use of improvement patents merely to hem in the original patentee is less of a danger than would be the case if unauthorized authors of derivative works could copyright those works.

For obvious reasons, a derivative work to be copyrightable must have some expressive elements not found in the original work; otherwise it would be a straight copy rather than a derivative work in an interesting sense. Consider a wind-up Mickey Mouse doll that looks just like the copyrighted Mickey Mouse cartoon character; the commercial success of the doll depends on its being an exact replica of the Walt Disney character. Since this mechanical "translation" of the figure into a new medium involves no expression, copyright protection is not required to prevent free riding by third parties on the cost of expression incurred by the author of the derivative work, as it was in our example of an English translation of Dostoevsky. This is not to say that anyone is free to make the mechanical translation. It is a copy and therefore infringing unless made by the author of the original work or a licensee of that author. The point is only that nothing is gained, at least in terms of enhancing incentives to create expressive works, by allowing the identical copy to be copyrighted. But we must make a qualification for the case, illustrated by photography of works of art, where the creativity of the derivative work consists precisely in the fidelity with which it reproduces the visual impression created by the original; we give an example in Chapter 9.

41. See Jed Rubenfeld, "The Freedom of Imagination: Copyright's Constitutionality," 112 *Yale Law Journal* 1, 48–59 (2002). For some evidence, see Salil Kumar Mehra, "Copyright and Comics in Japan: Does Law Explain Why All the Cartoons My Kid Watches Are Japanese Imports?" (forthcoming in *Rutgers Law Review*).

With that qualification, a derivative work that is identical to the copyrighted original should not be copyrightable (not that a photograph of a work of art ever actually looks *identical* to the original, so maybe photography is not an exception after all). The reason is the limited term of a copyright. Suppose the copyright on the original Disney character expires in 2020, and in 2000 Disney makes a mechanical translation and is able to copyright it. In 2021 someone publishes an exact copy of the Disney character. Disney will argue that the copier copied not the character on which the copyright has expired but the separately copyrighted mechanical translation. It will be a difficult dispute to resolve by the imperfect methods of litigation, even though in theory the copyright on the derivative work covers only the incremental expression, so that anyone is free to copy the original component of the derivative work if the copyright on the original work has expired, provided that he does not also copy the expression added by the derivative work. This is a potential problem with allowing photographs to be copyrighted,[42] or even highly realistic paintings. Two photographs of a public domain sculpture may look identical; but is this because one is a copy of the other or because they are both photographs of the same thing? This might be a problem with a photo of a work of art as well.

In the case of derivative works that are based on works in the public domain, for example a modern edition of Adam Smith's *Wealth of Nations,* the case for copyright protection of the derivative work is stronger, so we would expect a weaker requirement of incremental expression than for derivatives of copyrighted works. The original author (or his heirs), lacking copyright in such a case, is not able to prevent free riding on the expression contained in the derivative work; therefore the incentive to create the derivative work will be impaired if it cannot be copyrighted by its creator.

To determine the presence of incremental and hence copyrightable expression requires comparison between the original and the derivative. Some courts have required that the increment (call it "incremental originality") be significant. They worry that if the threshold is set too low and the copyrights on original and derivative works happen to be in different hands (recall that one reason for allowing the copyrighting of derivative works is to allow an unbundling of the original author's rights), the costs of determining infringement could be prohibitive.[43] If the derivative work is only trivially different from the original (imagine, for example, translating John Steinbeck's novels from the 1930s into "modern" American prose), it may be impossible by the imperfect methods of litigation to make a reliable determination of whether

42. See Goldstein, note 35 above, vol. 1, § 2.11.1.1, pp. 2:124–2:125.

43. See Gracen v. Bradford Exchange, 698 F.2d 300 (7th Cir. 1983); Pickett v. Prince, 207 F.3d 402 (7th Cir. 2000); L. Batlin & Son, Inc. v. Snyder, 536 F.2d 486, 490 (2d Cir. 1976) (en banc); Durham Industries, Inc. v. Tomy Corp., 630 F.2d 905 (2d Cir. 1980).

an infringing work was copied from (and hence infringed) the derivative work, the original, or both.[44] That was our Mickey Mouse example, except there the copyrights were in the same hands.

The outer bounds of the concept of derivative work are unclear. Suppose a book contains a very detailed description of some scene; is a painting of that scene a derivative work? Or, approaching the issue from the opposite direction, is an exact description of a painting a derivative work of the painting? It may be, we suggested earlier,[45] if it is an algorithm that enables an exact copy of the painting to be generated more or less mechanically. But that is an exceptional case,[46] and if we lay it to one side the answer to both questions is "no." Not only because the amount of free riding is limited in both cases since the copying is creative rather than mechanical, and not only because the "copy" is not a close substitute for the original—for these are characteristics of many derivative works—but because in both examples the expressive element of the "copy" dominates the expressive element in the original. There is an analogy to the patent doctrines of equivalents and reverse equivalents, discussed in Chapter 11. The doctrine of equivalents enables a patentee to enjoin a copy of his patented invention that varies in only trivial respects from the invention described in his patent. These equivalents are like derivative works, that is, "copies" because they are substantially similar though not identical to the original. But if the second invention, though it overlaps the first, is so much more inventive as to make the first invention really just an immaterial variation of it, the reverse doctrine of equivalents clicks in and the second inventor does not need a license from the first.

And likewise Leonardo da Vinci's painting *The Last Supper*, though based on the description of the event in the Bible, owes very little to the expressive content of that description; the expressive content added by Leonardo wholly dominates his indebtedness to his source. The same is true, in reverse as it were, of the verbal descriptions of Bruegel paintings in Michael Frayn's novel *Headlong*. When the expressive element in the "copy" so clearly dominates the expressive content borrowed from the "copied" work, it is apparent that the "copy" has significant independent value, and in that event transaction costs—an impediment to realizing that value—can be minimized by refusing to find infringement. Since there is little competition between visual and verbal expressive works, the cost to the original creator of unlicensed borrowing is low. Another way to put the point is that, in the posited circumstances, the grant of a license by the owner of the "copied" work would be a

44. The evidentiary significance of copyright doctrines is discussed, both generally and with specific reference to the doctrine of the cases cited in the preceding note, in Lichtman, note 8 above.

45. See note 1 above.

46. For additional discussion of this issue, see Chapter 9.

near certainty, the license fee would be slight, and therefore allowing unlicensed copying approximates the free-market solution, but without transaction costs.

Fair Use

"Fair use" is a doctrine that allows some copying of the expressive elements of a copyrighted work (that is, the elements actually protected by the copyright) without deeming the copier an infringer, even though the copyright holder has not authorized the copying;[47] we just gave two examples. Most lawyers doubt that any general theory can explain the cases that invoke the doctrine. Such a view is reinforced by section 107 of the Copyright Act of 1976. Section 107 codified the fair use doctrine, which judges had created as a federal common law supplement to the previous copyright statutes.[48] Section 107 states that "the fair use of a copyrighted work . . . for purposes such as criticism, comment, news reporting, teaching . . . scholarship or research, is not an infringement of copyright," and that to decide whether a particular use is fair the "factors to be considered [by the court] shall include (1) the purpose and character of the use, including whether such use is of a commercial nature or is for nonprofit educational purposes; (2) the nature of the copyrighted work; (3) the amount and substantiality of the portion used in relation to the copyrighted work as a whole; and (4) the effect of the use upon the potential market for or value of the copyrighted work." Factors (1) and (2) are largely empty, except that (1) suggests a preference for noncommercial educational uses, picking up the reference earlier in the statute to "teaching . . . scholarship or research," and plays a role in parody cases, as we'll see in Chapter 6; it is not and ordinarily should not be given much weight, since most expressive activity is commercial and so are most fair use copies. Factor (4) fails to distinguish between a use that impairs the potential market or value of the copyrighted work by criticizing it from a use that impairs the copyrighted work's market or value by free riding on the work. Only factor (3) points in an economic direction, and it is somewhat misleading, as we shall see. Fortunately, the statutory factors are illustrative only and leave ample room for the exercise of judicial discretion.

THE HIGH TRANSACTION COST, NO HARM CASE   Suppose the costs of a voluntary exchange are so high relative to the potential benefits that no exchange is feasible between a user of a copyrighted work and its owner. User might be willing to pay Owner a sum that the latter would gladly

---

47. We discuss the fair use doctrine at further length in the next two chapters.
48. 17 U.S.C. § 107.

accept to consent to the use of the work, but the cost of negotiating such a license is likely to be prohibitive in relation to the benefit if, for example, all User wants to do is quote a brief passage. In such a case the fair use privilege confers a clear benefit on User but does not harm Owner; it imposes no out-of-pocket cost on him and it "deprives" him of a benefit (that is, imposes an opportunity cost) that transaction costs would in any event prevent him from receiving. The copier is neither a firm selling copies nor a potential purchaser of copies, so his projected use affects neither the supply of copies nor the demand for them.

Several qualifications are necessary. First, although transaction costs are prohibitive in our example, we could substitute for the existing property-rights approach—which in the absence of the fair use doctrine would prevent User from making any use of Owner's work—a liability rule under which the user would not have to negotiate with the copyright holder but would merely be required to pay damages (if any) ex post. However, transaction costs under this approach would also be high relative to the potential benefit, which would mainly be a slight extra incentive to create the work in the first place. Often users are numerous, and this would make for a high cost of arranging compensation and a large number of legal proceedings. And the potential fee or damages per user might be so small—perhaps zero—that enforcement proceedings would often be infeasible, although the class-action device would mitigate this problem somewhat. A compulsory licensing scheme is another possibility, but any such government regulation would be likely to entail substantial costs. (As mentioned in the Introduction, we do not discuss compulsory licensing schemes.)

Second, fair use, if too broadly interpreted, might sap the incentive to develop innovative market mechanisms that reduce transaction costs and make economic exchanges between copyright holders and users feasible.[49] Performing-rights organizations, such as the American Society for Composers, Authors, and Publishers (ASCAP) and Broadcast Music, Inc. (BMI) and their counterparts in other countries, are efficient market responses to copyright problems caused by high transaction costs.[50] The number of users (radio and television stations, restaurants, hotels, night clubs, movie producers, and so on) of copyrighted music is so great that individual negotiations with copyright holders to acquire performance rights are infeasible. The performing-rights organization acquires nonexclusive rights from copyright holders and offers would-be users for a flat fee a blanket license to play any songs in

49. See Edmund W. Kitch, "Can the Internet Shrink Fair Use?" 78 *Nebraska Law Review* 880 (1999).

50. Recently, other organizations have emerged to facilitate licensing of journal articles (the Copyright Clearance Center) and of reproductions of artworks (the Visual Artists and Gallery Association and the Artists Rights Society, which we discuss in Chapter 10).

the organization's vast inventory. Usage is monitored and the fees distributed among the composers in accordance with how often each composer's songs are played. Since performing-right distributions are an important source of composers' incomes, a fair use exception for performance might significantly reduce the pecuniary incentive to compose music.

Third, even if there are many users and it is too costly to negotiate individual licenses for part of the original work, a few users may be willing to purchase the whole thing. (So it is a slight exaggeration to refer to this fair use category as that of "no harm.") Suppose you want to photocopy a chapter from a book. Although individual negotiations may be infeasible, you might, if forbidden to photocopy the chapter, purchase the book. Still, the "transaction cost," though no longer prohibitive, would be very high: it would be the difference between the price of the book and the value to the copier of the chapter that he copied.

THE NEGATIVE HARM, IMPLIED CONSENT CASE A book reviewer has a fair use privilege to quote brief passages from the book. If the reviewer quoted so much of the book that the review became a substitute for the copyrighted work itself, that would be infringement. Book reviews *are* often substitutes for the entire book, not because of extensive quotation, but rather because they summarize the ideas in the book—and ideas are not protected by copyright.

Conventional legal analysis of the reviewer's privilege has the fair use doctrine striking a balance between the author's interest in royalties and the interest of the reviewer and his readers in free access to limited portions of the work. The first stage of economic analysis reconceives the doctrine as economizing on transaction costs, though they need not be prohibitive as in our previous discussion. Since book reviews are a substitute for advertising, were there no fair use doctrine a publisher would usually license reviewers to quote at no charge brief passages from the books he publishes. By giving reviewers in effect an automatic royalty-free license, the fair use doctrine avoids the costs of explicit transactions between publishers and reviewers that would yield the identical outcome.

There is a more fundamental reason for the reviewer's privilege. Because a book is an experience good rather than a search good,[51] accurate information

---

51. An experience good is one the qualities of which do not become apparent until the consumer has had the experience of actually using the product, as distinct from a search good, whose qualities are apparent at the time of purchase. See Dennis Carlton and Jeffrey M. Perloff, *Modern Industrial Organization* 454–457 (3d ed. 2000). The book is actually an intermediate case. One can inspect a book by flipping through it at a bookstore, much as one inspects a melon by squeezing it to see whether it's ripe. The difference is that the inspection of a book takes longer and that there are too many books to be able to sample them in this way.

obtained in advance about books is likely to increase the demand for them. Without a fair use privilege, however, a publisher might not authorize quotation by reviewers apt to review a particular book unfavorably, or might condition the license on the reviewer's deleting critical portions of the review. Publishers as a whole would not be better off under such a regime because under it readers would tend to discount favorable reviews, knowing there was some probability that the favor had been procured by permission to quote the book. Ex ante, publishers as a group are better off if reviewers are free to quote without permission, for this makes reviews a *credible* form of book advertising (credible because uncensored)—and free to the publisher, to boot—that on average increases the demand for the works reviewed.[52] That is why we call this fair use category the "negative harm, implied consent" case.

It is the theory on which home video recordings of copyrighted television programs for purposes of time-shifting were held in the Betamax case to be protected by the fair use doctrine.[53] By enabling a viewer to watch a program at a more convenient time—a program he might have missed altogether if he could not have changed the time at which to watch it—the video recorder expands the program's viewing audience. That is the theory, but in actuality copyright holders are probably harmed by video recording because advertisers pay only for viewers who are likely to watch commercials, and recording a program makes it easy for viewers to fast-forward through the commercials.

Sony, the defendant in the Betamax case, was not charged as an infringer—the (alleged) infringers were the television viewers who used Sony's VCR system to record programs on tape for viewing at a different time. Recognizing the impracticability of a copyright owner's suing a multitude of individual infringers ("chasing individual consumers is time consuming and is a teaspoon solution to an ocean problem"),[54] the law allows the copyright holder to sue a contributor to the infringement (a "contributory infringer" in legal lingo) instead, in effect as an aider and abettor. The economic rationale of imposing liability for contributory infringement is similar to the economic rationale of the tort of inducing a breach of contract.[55] If a breach of contract (or violation of a copyright license, which is a contract) can be prevented by either *A*

---

52. If publishers knew in advance that their books were likely to receive negative reviews and they could suppress them on copyright grounds, they might be better off, even though consumers of books would be worse off. The suppression of an unfavorable review would be comparable to an ordinary seller's concealing a defect in his goods.

53. See Sony Corp. of America v. Universal City Studios, Inc., 464 U.S. 417 (1984); Wendy J. Gordon, "Fair Use as Market Failure: A Structural and Economic Analysis of the Betamax Case and Its Predecessors," 82 *Columbia Law Review* 1600 (1982).

54. Randal C. Picker, "Copyright as Entry Policy: The Case of Digital Distribution," 47 *Antitrust Bulletin* 423, 442 (2002).

55. See Landes and Posner, note 5 above, at 222–225.

(a party to the contract or license) or *B*, and the cost of prevention is lower for *B*, it makes sense to have a legal mechanism for placing the ultimate liability on *B*. It is cheaper to enjoin Sony from selling VCRs than it is to enjoin the millions of purchasers of VCRs.

But while many of Sony's customers, perhaps most, were infringers, others were not; and the Supreme Court ruled that as long as there were substantial noninfringing uses (time-shifting, and also recording of religious and other noncommercial programs that the owners of the copyrights on these programs did not object to being recorded), Sony could not be guilty of contributory infringement. This ruling has been criticized as failing to balance the harm from the infringing uses against the benefit from the noninfringing ones.[56] The former might indeed be greater. But striking the correct balance might be impossible, since from a social standpoint the harm is not the reduction in copyright revenues but the reduction in consumer and producer surplus caused by the impact of infringement on the creation of new copyrighted works. One must not confuse the question whether liability would promote economic welfare with the question what remedy is necessary to deter violations if liability is imposed. The first question is one of social benefits and costs, but private benefits and costs dominate the second because a violator will not be deterred unless the private costs, including the expected punishment costs, of violation exceed the private benefits, and the victim will not be compensated (and if he is not compensated he may engage in inefficient self-protection) if the remedy does not reimburse him for the private costs that he incurred as a result of the violation. Thus, once it is decided that a particular act is infringing, the copyright owner is entitled to either his loss or the violator's gain even though neither amount may correspond to the social cost of the violation.

Another way to approach the Betamax case is to ask what outcome minimizes transaction costs. It is the Court's, since it would be extremely costly for Sony to have to obtain a license from all owners of copyrights on television programs in order to be able to sell VCRs.

An alternative solution to the dilemma created by the Betamax system would have been to require Sony to modify the system to eliminate the fast-forward option. Whether this would be efficient would depend not only on the manufacturing cost but also on the loss to the consumer from not being able to use the fast-forward option for noninfringing purposes.[57]

Note finally that while ordinarily the negative harm-implied consent cate-

56. See Picker, note 51 above, at 444–445.
57. See William M. Landes and Douglas Lichtman, "Indirect Liability for Copyright Infringement: Napster and Beyond," *Journal of Economic Perspectives* 113 (Spring 2003).

gory involves copying brief excerpts from the copyrighted work, the "brief passages" category, like statutory factor (3)—the one we said seemed to point in the right direction ("the amount and substantiality of the portion used in relation to the copyrighted work as a whole")—cannot be taken as absolute: in the Betamax case entire copyrighted works were copied.

An issue similar to the one presented in the Betamax case, though not necessarily one that should be resolved the same way, is presented by cases involving music-sharing services, such as Napster. Its defenders argued (unsuccessfully in the *Napster* case itself)[58] that its service, which enabled owners of CDs to transmit the music on them over the Internet to anyone who had an Internet address and software for downloading music, was lawful under the standard laid down in the Betamax case. The service might increase the demand for copyrighted music by enabling more people to listen to music and thus discover performers and performing groups whose recordings they might want to buy. It might also increase the value of a recording by enabling the recording to be used as currency in the shared-music network. And some of the music available through Napster was in the public domain, either because it had never been copyrighted or because the copyright on it had expired. Moreover, some people used Napster's service to listen to music that they owned in CD form, because they found it more convenient to dial up on their computer than to listen to the music on a CD player—a form of space-shifting similar in its effects to time-shifting.[59]

But if everyone subscribed to Napster's service, record companies might find themselves able to sell only one copy of each recording they made! That is an extreme case, of course, but illustrates the potentially great negative impact of the service on the record companies' ability to recover their fixed costs by selling their recordings.[60] Yet there were substantial noninfringing uses of Napster's service, just as there were in the Betamax case. And again as in that case, the transaction costs involved in obtaining licenses from the copyright holders of music recordings would have been high, though lower than in the Betamax case because the performance rights to most popular music are controlled by just two entities, ASCAP and BMI.

Less problematic than Napster is the kind of music-sharing service offered by MP3.com, which made copies of recordings and placed them in an Inter-

58. See A&M Records, Inc. v. Napster, Inc., 239 F.3d 1004 (9th Cir. 2001).

59. See Lawrence Lessig, *The Future of Ideas: The Fate of the Commons in a Connected World* 194 (2001).

60. Should e-books ever catch on, publishers will face the same risk to their business as the recording industry does. See Matt McKenzie, "Book Publishers Tune In to Napster Debate," *Seybold Report on Internet Publishing*, Oct. 2000, p. 4.

net-accessible database[61] but allowed access to them only if the person seek-ing access proved that he owned the CD version of the recording. The ser-vice enabled music enthusiasts in effect to listen to their recordings when they were not at home, and since it presupposed ownership of the CD, the negative impact on the recording company was minimized. Indeed, the im-pact may have been positive. The access offered enabled the subscriber to MP3.com's service to obtain greater value from his purchase of a CD, and when enough purchasers subscribed this might enable the recording compa-nies to raise their prices. Nevertheless MP3.com's service was held to be in-fringement.[62]

Our last example of the negative harm-implied consent category involves "Beanie Babies."[63] As a marketing gimmick, Ty, the manufacturer of Beanie Babies (which Ty copyrights as "soft sculptures," in copyright jargon), delib-erately creates a shortage of each Beanie Baby by charging a very low price and not producing enough copies to clear the market at that price. As a re-sult, a secondary market is created, just like the secondary market in works of art. The secondary market gives widespread publicity to Beanie Babies, and the shortage that creates the secondary market stampedes children into nag-ging their parents to buy them the latest Beanie Babies. The appeal is to the competitive conformity of children—but also to the mentality of collectors. When the defendant, PIL, published *Beanie Babies Collector's Guide* in 1998, some Beanie Babies were selling in the secondary market for thousands of dollars, though others were selling for little more than their original purchase price. The range was vast, creating a demand for collectors' guides.

Ty acknowledged that a collectors' guide to a series of copyrighted works is no more a derivative work than a book review is. Indeed, a collectors' guide is very much like a book review, which is a guide to a book. Both are critical and evaluative as well as purely informational; both are likely to expand the de-mand for the underlying copyrighted works; and ownership of a copyright does not confer a legal right to control public evaluation of the copyrighted work. But although Ty does not sell photographs of Beanie Babies, such pho-tographs are derivative works, and PIL's books included photographs of the *entire* line of Beanie Babies—and is that not just like the book reviewer who copies the entire book or, worse, the entire *oeuvre* of the author whom he's

---

61. Direct, not contributory; for MP3.com is actually a copier, which Napster was not—Napster merely facilitated sharing of music uploaded to computers by the owners of CDs. From an economic standpoint, this is a distinction without a difference. Compare the "intermediate copying" case, Sega Enterprises Ltd. v. Accolade, Inc., text at note 18 above.

62. See UMG Recordings, Inc. v. MP3.com, Inc., 92 F. Supp. 2d 349 (S.D.N.Y. 2000).

63. See Ty, Inc. v. Publications International Ltd., 292 F.3d 512 (7th Cir. 2002).

reviewing? It is not, because a collectors' guide, to compete in the marketplace, has to be comprehensive. Given that Ty can license (in fact has licensed) the publication of collectors' guides that contain photos of all the Beanie Babies, a competitor forbidden to publish photos of the complete line could not compete, and the result would be to deliver into Ty's hands a monopoly of Beanie Babies collectors' guides.

But if Beanie Babies collectors' guides are indeed a complement to Beanie Babies (and they are), and Ty has a monopoly of Beanie Babies (and it does), how could Ty get a second monopoly profit by taking over the guides market? The higher the price it charges for collectors' guides, the lower will be the demand for the guides and hence for collecting Beanie Babies and so the less effective will be Ty's strategy of marketing Beanie Babies as collectibles. This is the sort of question that has engendered skepticism among economists about the antitrust rule against tie-in agreements (see Chapter 14). But there are two possible responses here. The first is that Ty may have wanted to suppress criticism of its product in these guides. Its licenses gave it veto power over the content of the collectors' guides published by its licensees; the unlicensed PIL guides contained criticisms of Ty's product and business. The analogy to book reviews is close.

The other possible explanation is that Ty was engaged in price discrimination. Persons who bought collectors' guides were probably the most enthusiastic collectors, who would have been willing to pay higher prices for Beanie Babies. But when a new Beanie Baby first hits the stores, everyone pays an identical price. By licensing the right to publish guides, Ty can charge a high enough licensing fee to enable it to capture some of the surplus received by persons who have less elastic demands for Beanie Babies.

THE POSITIVE HARM, PRODUCTIVE USE CASE   Our third and last fair use category involves some harm to the copyright holder in lost revenues, but the harm is more than offset by the sum of the benefits to others and the savings in the transaction costs that would be incurred if licensing were required. The Beanie Babies case illustrates this category also. PIL's collectors' guide consisted of photographs of Beanie Babies plus commentary. To decide fair use in such a case is like trying to decide whether an allegedly infringing work is substantially similar to the work from which it copied, and is therefore infringing. The court has to try to sort out the contribution to the new product of the original copyright holder and the alleged infringer. The inputs into a work of fiction include characters, situations, plot details, and so on invented by previous authors and not yet so standard or hackneyed that they are considered part of the elementary repertory of stock characters and situations on which all authors should, as we explained earlier in distinguishing ideas from expression, be free to draw. The more substantial the contribution that the later author makes to the expressive domain by his use of copyrighted materials in his work, the less likely his work is to be deemed "substantially similar" to theirs, or, equivalently, the more likely his use of those materials is to be deemed a fair use.

Courts refer to this permitted use of copyrighted elements as a *productive* (or *transformative*) use, as distinct from simply a *reproductive* (or *superseding*) one. A productive use is one that lowers the cost of expression and thus tends to increase the number of original works, while a reproductive use simply increases the number of copies of a given work, reduces the gross profits of the author, and reduces the incentives to create works. Not surprisingly, a fair use defense is more likely to prevail if the use is productive than if it is merely reproductive, as we shall see in the next chapter. Yet the Betamax case found a merely reproductive use of the copyrighted work to be fair use— though, as we pointed out earlier, time-shifting has the potential to transform a reproductive use into one that actually benefits the copyright owner by enabling some viewers to see a work who could not do so at the scheduled time. The question for an economist is not production or transformation versus reproduction or supersession, as such, but the impact of the copying on the demand for the original and the potential cost savings and other benefits that are likely to arise from reducing the cost of creating a new work that builds upon the original copyrighted work. As the Betamax case illustrates, the impact on the original work can be positive even if the copier adds nothing to the work itself.

5

Copyright in Unpublished Works

The legal protection of unpublished expressive works, such as letters, diaries, journals, reports, or drafts that the copyright owner would or might publish in the future, was traditionally the domain of common law (state-enforced) rather than statutory (federal-enforced) copyright. The tradition has been changed, as we shall explain, but after as well as before the change the judicial tendency was to give unpublished works stronger copyright protection than published or widely disseminated works by defining fair use more narrowly. We must consider whether the tendency is economically sound.

We begin by asking why unpublished works should receive any legal protection at all. The question is not why it should be a crime to steal someone's manuscript, the answer to which is obvious, but why, if the writer loses the manuscript, or reads it at a lecture and someone in the audience records it, the writer should be able to enjoin the publication of the work, as undoubtedly he can.[1] Economics suggests a twofold answer: that the author of an expressive work is in the best position to determine when and in what form to publish it (whether, for example, it is finished), and that if the author did not have legal remedies he would incur excessive costs of self-protection. A major cost would be forgoing opportunities to try out one's ideas by limited dissemination of drafts of the work; there is an analogy here to the effect on willingness to lend works of art for exhibition if the rights of owners are easily extinguished (see Chapter 1) and also to the effect on efforts to keep inventions secret if they are not patentable (see Chapters 11 and 13).

---

1. See, for example, Estate of Martin Luther King, Jr., Inc. v. CBS, Inc., 194 F.3d 1211 (11th Cir. 1999).

Fair Use of Unpublished Materials

So there is an economic rationale for recognizing copyright in unpublished works, but it does not preclude application of the fair use doctrine, which after all is about copying copyrighted works. Yet claims to fair use of unpublished works have fared badly. In *Harper & Row, Publishers, Inc. v. Nation Enterprises,*[2] an unnamed source provided the *Nation* magazine with galleys of ex-President Gerald Ford's memoirs, soon to be published by Harper & Row. Paraphrasing and quoting from the memoirs, the *Nation* rushed into print what it believed to be a "hot" article on Ford's decision to pardon Richard Nixon. In ruling for Harper & Row in its copyright infringement suit against the *Nation,* the Supreme Court held that the unpublished nature of the work was a key factor negating a defense of fair use.

In *Salinger v. Random House,*[3] the Second Circuit enjoined the publication of Ian Hamilton's biography of J. D. Salinger until Hamilton deleted from the galley proofs quotations from and close paraphrases to about thirty unpublished letters that Salinger had written between 1939 and 1962. The recipients of the letters or their estates had donated the letters to various university libraries, which had given Hamilton access to them. The court said that unpublished "works normally enjoy complete protection against copying any protected expression."[4]

The same court faced a similar question in *New Era Publications v. Henry Holt & Co.*[5] A highly critical biography of L. Ron Hubbard, the founder of the Church of Scientology, quoted extensively from his unpublished letters and diaries in an effort to expose him as a charlatan, paranoiac, and bigot. Although refusing to enjoin publication of the book because the plaintiff had delayed suing until two years after learning of its planned publication, the court left open the possibility of monetary damages and suggested that it would have enjoined publication had the suit been brought earlier.

These decisions, especially the two Second Circuit cases involving biographies, are controversial. *Newsweek* magazine ran an article entitled "The End of History?" that quoted Arthur Schlesinger, Jr., as saying that if the Hubbard decision had been the law when he wrote his three-volume history *The Age of Roosevelt,* he would still be two volumes short.[6] Congress in 1992 amended the copyright statute to provide that "the fact that a work is unpub-

2. 471 U.S. 539 (1985).
3. 811 F.2d 90 (2d Cir. 1987).
4. Id. at 97.
5. 873 F.2d 576 (2d Cir. 1989).
6. David A. Kaplan, "The End of History? A Copyright Controversy Leads to Self-Censorship," *Newsweek,* Dec. 25, 1989, p. 80.

lished shall not itself bar a finding of fair use if such finding is made upon consideration of all the above factors."[7]

The cases present a number of questions that economics can help to answer: Should a work that is unlikely ever to be published get more or less copyright protection than a work that is intended to be published in the future, perhaps the near future? (Salinger's letters were not written with the intention of their being published, while Ford's memoirs were about to be published.) Should the way in which the unpublished material is used matter? (In the *Salinger* and *New Era* cases the unpublished materials were parts of larger biographical works, while in the *Nation* case the article was based entirely on material from Ford's memoirs without any significant commentary or analysis.) And why should the copyright in letters belong to the letter writer rather than to the recipient who "owns" the letter and has the right to sell it, destroy it, show it to friends, or give it to a university library, but (because he is not the copyright holder) not to make copies of it?

Ownership of the Work versus Ownership of the Copyright on the Work

A fundamental feature of copyright law that the last question flags and that we have thus far in this book taken for granted is that ownership of the copyright of a work is separate from ownership of the individual copies of the work. This division of ownership is vital to securing the benefits of copyright law because of the rule that any joint owner of a copyright can license its use without the consent of his co-owners, though he must account to them for the profits from the license. If every owner of a Batman comic book were also a joint owner of the copyright, someone wanting to make and sell copies would have no difficulty persuading one of the millions of joint owners to license him for a pittance to make an unlimited number of copies. (Actually, it would be even cheaper for him to buy a copy himself and thus become one of those owners.) The price of a copy sold by the original author could not include any premium for the right to license further copies, because competition among the owners of copies would compress the price of copies to their marginal cost.[8] If to solve this problem the law required the consent of the

---

7. 17 U.S.C. § 107. The "above" reference is to the statutory fair use factors that we discussed in Chapter 4. The courts had not (quite) held that there can never be a fair use defense for copying unpublished materials, and so the effect of the amendment is unclear, though it has generally been interpreted as expressing congressional disapproval of *Salinger* and *New Era*.

8. See Stanley M. Besen and Sheila Nataraj Kirby, "Private Copying, Appropriability, and Optimal Copying Royalties," 32 *Journal of Law and Economics* 255 (1989). However, competition may be limited by the requirement that an owner of a jointly owned work who licenses it must share the licensing revenues with his co-owners.

joint owners to be obtained, the transaction costs would be utterly prohibitive; someone wanting to copy the Batman characters for a movie, television series, or clothing collection would have to obtain licenses from millions of copyright holders. The alternative of the copyright holder's retaining title to every Batman comic book and leasing (not selling) them to readers is only a little more attractive.

The argument for divided ownership is weakened in the case of copyright on unique works of art, such as a painting or a sculpture. Copying is likely to be limited and in addition may require physical access to the artwork. If the copyright is valuable, the purchaser of the painting will be willing to pay a higher price for the work (and copyright). This is unlike our book example, where if each owner of a copy also owned the copyright, the price of the copyright could be zero or close to it, depending on the sharing requirement.

In these circumstances transaction costs can be minimized by uniting ownership of the copyright with ownership of the physical work, so that sale of the work automatically transfers to the buyer the copyright as well. In some cases the artist will be in a better position to exploit future uses of the work, and in those cases efficiency requires that the copyright remain with the artist. Automatic transfer is therefore appropriate only as a default provision in the contract for the sale of the physical work, a provision the parties to the contract can waive if they want. In the era of common law copyright, transfers of copyrights on unpublished works were governed by state law, and the approach that we have suggested was the rule in a number of states. It was called the "*Pushman* presumption," after *Pushman v. New York Graphic Society.*[9] The 1976 Act, in bringing most of what had formerly been common law copyrights under federal law, subjected them to the federal rule that requires an explicit written transfer of a copyright.[10]

The case for giving the writer of a letter the copyright, and thus for separating the copyright from the physical work—the letter itself, which is the property of its recipient—falls between the Batman comic and the unique work of art. Separation increases the incentive to write letters by increasing their potential value to the writer but reduces the incentive of recipients to preserve rather than discard them. Separation may also raise transaction costs because publication of the letter will require the publisher to negotiate with both the letter writer, who owns the copyright, and the recipient, who owns the letter itself and thus controls access to its contents unless the writer retained a copy.

Further consideration suggests that separation is the more efficient approach after all, although this conclusion leaves open the question whether in

9. 39 N.E.2d 249 (N.Y. 1942).
10. See 17 U.S.C. §§ 202, 204(a).

some circumstances the fair use privilege should be available. The preservation rationale for fusing copyright with physical ownership of letters has become unimportant because of widespread photocopying; the writer of a letter will usually retain a copy—and his incentive to do so is greater when he owns the copyright, since then if he discards the letter he is discarding potentially valuable property. More and more correspondence is in the form of e-mail, moreover, and so a copy is automatically retained by the sender—in fact it is almost impossible to delete it from either his or the recipient's computer. Copies may also be retained on various servers or archived on CDs.

If for these reasons the writer of a letter or the sender of an e-mail can be counted on to retain a copy of the letter or the e-mail, obtaining the right to publish will require negotiations with only one person. This is important because there is rarely any interest in publishing a single letter. Much more common is the publication of the collected letters of X or excerpts from them in a biography of X. Typically X will have corresponded with many individuals, so that if he has retained copies of his correspondence, fewer transactions will be necessary for obtaining publication rights than if permission has to be obtained from the numerous recipients of X's letters. Admittedly, however, this is not a complete solution because the publisher or biographer may want to publish both sides of the subject's correspondence.

Fair Use Analysis

Two of the three rationales proposed in the preceding chapter for the doctrine of fair use provide little if any support for applying the doctrine to unpublished works. The concern with avoiding high transaction costs assumes that a voluntary exchange would have taken place except for those costs, and the fact that a work is unpublished will often mean that its author doesn't want to transact over it. Anyway, there are likely to be only two parties (or possibly three if the potential user must negotiate with both the owner of the work and the copyright holder), and so the cost of transacting with the copyright owner should be small relative to the benefits of using the unpublished work. The implied-consent rationale applicable when there are strong complementarities between the original work and the copy, as in the case of book reviews, fails as well, because the unpublished nature of the work signals that the copyright owner has no present interest in publication. The third rationale—some harm to the copyright holder, but it is outweighed by the productive character of the copy—has more force. The use of unpublished materials in a published work may enhance the value of the latter, sometimes greatly, without depriving the author of those materials of substantial, or any, revenues. But this is provided that he intends never to publish them, and it neglects privacy and other costs that publication may impose on him.

There is no per se rule against the fair use of an unpublished work, as was reasonably clear even in the Second Circuit[11] before Congress amended section 107 of the copyright statute in 1992. The negative judicial attitude had up to then been influenced by narrowly "legal" considerations, historical in character.

Under the Copyright Act of 1909, unpublished works were protected primarily by state common law (although an unpublished work could be federally copyrighted by being registered with the Copyright Office, and about 30 percent of all federally copyrighted works were of this character),[12] while published works were protected by federal law—which preempted state law within the domain of the federal statute, as continues to be the case—so long as certain formalities such as notice were satisfied. (We need not concern ourselves with those formalities or with the precise meaning of "publication," a term left undefined in the 1909 Act.) So there were few occasions for applying federal fair use principles to unpublished works.

The Copyright Act of 1976 eliminated most common law copyright by changing the onset of federal statutory protection from the moment of publication to the moment that a work is fixed in a tangible form. Federal statutory protection now begins when a letter or other document is written, leaving no room for common law protection of writings. Only works not fixed in a tangible form, such as improvised speeches and live jazz performances, remain subject to common law copyright. So Salinger's and Hubbard's letters and private papers came under the protection of federal copyright law.

Publication continued to have a role in relation to fair use, however, because of the codification of the fair use doctrine by the 1976 Act. The legislative history indicates that Congress intended the codification "to restate the present judicial doctrine of fair use, not to change, narrow, or enlarge it in any way."[13] Since state common law did not recognize a fair use defense to copying unpublished works, except for works that were so widely disseminated that as a practical matter they *were* published,[14] the unpublished nature of a work weighed heavily against finding fair use, though it is not clear that by codifying the judicial doctrine of fair use Congress meant to freeze it; there was no indication of that in the statute itself. At all events, the 1992

11. Wright v. Warner Books, Inc., 953 F.2d 731 (2d Cir. 1991), authorized the copying of very brief excerpts of unpublished materials from author Richard Wright's letters and diary in a biography of Wright. The brevity was such that the biography could not have been accepted in the marketplace as a substitute for a published edition of his letters and diary.

12. Based on data for new copyright registrations in *Annual Reports of the Register of Copyright*, 1975–1977, published by the U.S. Copyright Office.

13. H.R. Rep. No. 94-1476, 94th Cong., 2d Sess. 66 (1976).

14. The common law also carved out a narrow exception, irrelevant to our discussion, for publication of unpublished material in legal proceedings and publication that was necessary in order to defend one's reputation from charges made by the letter writer or others.

amendment cleared the air, at the same time undermining the decisions with which we began insofar as they were influenced by the statutory history that we have just recounted.

Whether as a matter of sound economic policy fair use should extend to unpublished works is a surprisingly complex question. Answering it requires distinguishing between two categories of such works. The first consists of works that the author does not intend ever to be published. Both the *Salinger* and *New Era* cases involved such works. Salinger had a powerful desire for privacy, as evidenced by his reclusive life in New Hampshire. He had published nothing in more than twenty years and had evinced no interest in publishing his letters despite their estimated market value of more than half a million dollars. The Church of Scientology, the owner of the copyrights in Hubbard's works, wanted to block the publication of Hubbard's private papers in order to conceal his unpublished views, which, if publicly known, would have adverse financial and other effects on the Church. Because the copyright statute protects expression and not facts, theories, opinions, or ideas, whether contained in published or unpublished writings, it would not shield the unpublished letters and private papers of Salinger and the Church of Scientology from public view entirely; the owners of the unpublished writings would be free (except as forbidden by the law of defamation or conceivably by privacy law) to publish the ideas contained in them. Still, there would be some incremental loss to the copyright holders from publication of the writings themselves. This is evidenced by their willingness to incur the costs of suing and to suffer the unfavorable publicity generated by their suits, even though they were seeking injunctive relief rather than damages and so would not obtain any money from prevailing in the litigation.

The other category of unpublished materials consists of those the author intends to publish in their current or revised form or to incorporate into a larger work. The *Nation* case is a good illustration because the prepublication rights to publish excerpts from Ford's memoirs had been sold to *Time* magazine and the book was about to be published. The distinction between the two categories is actually one of degree, because there is always some uncertainty about future publication. Not only may a writer or his heirs have a change of mind about not publishing, but the writer might have had no intent at all with regard to eventual publication when he wrote the work in question.

A further distinction to note, picking up one of the elements of the fair use doctrine discussed in the last chapter, is between merely "reproductive" uses of unpublished materials and "productive" uses. The publication of an unannotated set of Salinger letters would be reproductive, while the use of those letters to enrich a biography of Salinger would be productive. We first consider the second case, that is, the productive use of unpublished materials not intended for publication. We limit our consideration to materials likely to be of interest to biographers, critics, reporters, and historians.

A Model of the Effects of Copyright Protection of Unpublished Materials Not Intended for Eventual Publication

The author of an unpublished work (a letter, say) initially had to decide whether to write it at all. The benefits to him from writing it would be whatever positive value he derived from communicating in this form. The costs would depend not only on the time and effort that he expended on composing and sending the letter, and on such incidental expenses as postage, but also on the expected harm, appropriately discounted to present value, should the letter eventually be published by someone (by arrangement with the recipient) without the letter writer's permission. This expected harm would depend on both the probability and the amount of harm from publication, with the probability depending on how famous the author is or may become, the likelihood the letter will be destroyed or misplaced, and the value of the letter to potential biographers. Fame is not a necessary condition, however, given current interest in social history, often history told "from the bottom up," though biographies of utterly obscure figures remain rare.

The harms from publication might include a loss of privacy, diminished reputation, and, as a result of the second harm, lost earnings. The magnitude of such harm would be influenced by the author's personal discount rate, since any publication will be in the future—and by the scope of copyright protection for unpublished materials, specifically the availability of the fair use defense to someone who copied and published the letter.

A formal model will help us sort out these considerations. Let g equal the net gain (which may be positive or negative) to the author of unpublished materials after deducting all costs, as in

$$g = b - p(z)h, \tag{1}$$

where b is the benefit of creating the unpublished work to its author (net of costs) before deduction of h, the harm to the author from publication, and $p(z)$ is the probability that the material not intended for publication will be published in the future, say by a biographer of the writer, so that $p(z)h$ is the expected harm from publication (we can ignore for now discounting to present value). The probability depends on z, which we recall from Chapter 3 is the level of copyright protection (here for unpublished materials); we can think of it simply as the fraction of the unpublished work that cannot lawfully be copied without the author's consent. When $z = 1$, p can be assumed to be close to zero[15] because it is unlawful for subsequent authors to copy any of the unpublished materials. Even without any copyright protection for unpublished works (that is, $z = 0$), they may remain unpublished simply because there may be no interest in writing a biography of the author of the unpublished materials, the materials are unimportant to a biographer, or they have been lost or destroyed. Indeed, these circumstances are so common that for most unpublished materials p is close to zero even if $z = 0$.

The decision to write a letter or keep a diary will depend on whether g is greater or less than zero; equivalently, whether b/h is greater or less than $p(z)$. Obviously if the benefit equals or exceeds the harm even before discounting for the probability (less than one) of publication, the level of copyright protection will not affect the decision, which will be to write. Unpublished works would undoubtedly be created in profusion even without any copyright protection, common law or statutory, at all, not only because b often will exceed the discounted value of h but also because p (< 1 even if there is no copyright barrier to publication) will often be small as well; consider an obscure person writing notes to members of his family. Copyright protection matters only in cases in which b is smaller than h. In those cases the greater z is and the smaller p is, the more likely $b/h > p(z)$ and therefore the more likely the unpublished work is to be created.[16]

Let Q denote the aggregate quantity of unpublished materials not intended for publication.

$$Q = Q[p(z), b/h, x], \tag{2}$$

where $p(z)$ and b/h are now the average values of these variables calculated over the population of potential authors of unpublished materials and x denotes the combined effect of all other relevant factors, such as the number of persons capable of creating unpublished materials of interest to biographers

15. But not zero, for even when $z = 1$, $p(1) > 0$ because enforcement is imperfect, and anyway copyright law does not prevent a biographer from copying ideas, theories, or facts contained in unpublished materials, so there remains a positive probability that the unpublished materials will be used and will harm the letter writer. Whether $p(1)$ equals or exceeds zero is not critical to our analysis, though a more general formulation of the model would allow for h (as well as p) to depend on z in order to register the effect, for example, of increasing z in reducing the amount of copying of expression but not of ideas.

16. We assume that as z increases, p_z decreases at a decreasing rate ($p_{zz} > 0$)—that is, as z increases, the effectiveness of copyright protection increases but at a decreasing rate.

or historians. Q will be greater the greater on average b/h is and the smaller on average p is, which in turn will be smaller the broader copyright protection, z, is.[17] Q can be rewritten as

$$Q = q_0 + q(z) \tag{3}$$

where q_0 is the quantity of unpublished materials not intended for publication that would be generated were there no copyright protection (that is, unpublished materials in which $b/h > p(0)$) and $q(z)$ is the additional quantity generated by such protection ($q_z > 0$).[18] Since q_0 is the quantity of unpublished materials created by persons for whom $b/h > p(0)$, it will be greater the greater on average b/h is and the lower on average the probability that unpublished materials will be copied even if copying is lawful.

Q is strictly quantitative; what about possible qualitative effects of publication? Fear of publication may cause the writer of a letter to be less honest and candid than he would be if he were confident that the letter would never be published. True, the fact that it *is* a letter, meaning that it's going to be read by someone else and owned by that someone, who may lawfully decide to show it to a third party or parties or even sell it, should do much of the work in inducing the writer to be discreet. But not all. People distinguish between exposing themselves to a limited range of acquaintances (or even acquaintances of acquaintances) and exposing themselves to the world at large. The difference is recognized in the tort law of privacy, which provides a remedy for invasion of the right of privacy only when the invasion consists

17. Notice that Q_z (the increase in Q per unit increase in z) is positive but decreasing in z. Suppose there are L potential writers of one letter each. The ith individual's decision to write will depend on whether $g_i >$ or < 0, or whether $b_i/h_i >$ or $< p_i$. Assume a uniform distribution for b_i/h_i between a and c (where $a < c$, $a > 0$, and $c > 1$) across the L individuals, and assume that p_i is the same for all individuals ($= p$). The latter assumption is not as unrealistic as it may appear because the unpublished materials may be created before each author has much information on the likelihood of publication, and thus individual differences in p are likely to be small. Then the fraction of persons who write letters equals $[c - p(z)]/(c - a)$ for each value of z, and $Q = L[c - p(z)]/(c - a)$. The effect on Q of an increase in z is $Q_z = -Lp_z/(c - a) > 0$, which will be greater the greater the absolute value of p_z is, the larger L is, and the narrower the range of b/h among individuals is (that is, the smaller is $c - a$). Note that $Q_{zz} < 0$, assuming $p_{zz} > 0$.

18. To simplify the notation, we have suppressed p, b/h, and x from Q in equation (3) although b/h and x will affect q_0 and q, and z will affect q indirectly through its effect on p. Using the same notation as in the previous note, we have

$$q_0 = [(c - p(0))/(c - a)] \tag{i}$$

and

$$q(z) = [(p(0) - p(z))/(c - a)]L. \tag{ii}$$

of *publicizing,* that is, disseminating widely (as by publication), some private fact.

We know from previous chapters that whenever a property right is denied there is a danger that the denial will induce the taking of defensive measures (for example, in the case of land, building a strong fence) that may be more costly than the enforcement of a property right would be. Concealing in one's letters one's true thoughts and feelings because one lacks a secure property right in the letters would be a type of fence and could involve significant social costs of two kinds. The first would be the cost to recipients of the letters and to subsequent users (for example, readers in university libraries to which the recipients might have donated the latters) in diminished information and insight concerning the writer. The second would be the same diminution in value to biographers (and others who write about the author of the letters, but we'll use biographers as representative of the entire set of such writers) who include the letters in published works. We begin with the second cost, which is part of a larger picture of the benefits and costs to biographers of copyright protection of unpublished materials.

Copyright protection for unpublished materials benefits biographers by making it more likely that such materials will be created in the first place and thus be potentially available for use in a biography and also that they will be more honest and candid and therefore of higher quality from the biographer's standpoint. At the same time, copyright protection reduces the lawful use that a biographer can make of such materials, including materials that would have been created even without copyright protection. Limiting his right to quote and closely paraphrase unpublished materials will make it harder for him to portray the subject accurately to the reader and may expose him to criticisms that he has distorted the underlying source materials.[19] Just as the most effective way to impeach the credibility of an expert witness is to show that his prior testimony or academic writings contradict his current testimony, so a critical biography may best accomplish its purpose by quoting from its subject's unpublished materials. Extensive quotations may also enliven the biography and make good reading, even when paraphrasing would communicate the content of the unpublished materials equally well. Above all, because the way in which a person expresses himself is an important clue to his personality, a biography that contained nothing in the language of the

19. In a review of Hamilton's biography of Salinger, Mordechai Richtler, who had access to Salinger's letters, claimed that Hamilton had mischaracterized them. Richtler, "Summer Reading: Rises at Dawn, Writes, Then Retires," *New York Times,* June 5, 1988, § 7, p. 7. Such a charge would have been less likely had Hamilton not been required to remove quotations from Salinger's letters and rewrite his book.

subject would be as incomplete as if the biographer had been forbidden to disclose facts about the subject that illuminated his character.[20]

Let N be the number of biographies, $\alpha = \alpha(z, Q)$ a function that transforms N into quality-adjusted biographies, and X the quality-adjusted number. Thus

$$X = \alpha N. \tag{4}$$

We can think of $\alpha(> 1)$ as the quality "boost" to a biography given by the biographer's being able to include unpublished materials. We assume that if no unpublished materials are available to a biographer, either because none are created or copyright protection is so broad that none can be used, then $\alpha = 1$. Since this is also the case of a purely reproductive use of unpublished materials, in discussing the class of cases in which $\alpha > 1$ we are discussing productive uses. Equation (4) formalizes the insight that the more unpublished materials not protected by copyright, the higher the quality of biographies. So α is greater the less copyright protection there is for unpublished materials ($\partial\alpha/\partial z = \alpha_z < 0$), holding Q (the quantity of unpublished materials) constant, and the greater the quantity of unpublished materials is ($\partial\alpha/\partial Q = \alpha_Q > 0$), holding z constant.

But what about the reticence point—that the quality of unpublished materials not intended for publication may be reduced if the writer fears that they will be published against his will? We can adjust for it by interpreting our assumption that if Q is held constant, $\alpha_z < 0$—that is, that the quality of biography is inverse to the amount of copyright protection—to mean that the effect of stronger copyright protection in depriving biographers and other writers of the right to publish unpublished materials outweighs its effect in increasing the honesty and candor of such materials. We shall give some reasons why we think this interpretation plausible a little later.

The net effect of increasing copyright protection for unpublished works on X, holding N constant, is given by

$$\partial X/\partial z = (\alpha_z + \alpha_Q Q_z)N \tag{5}$$

20. The importance to biography and other critical writings of quotation of unpublished materials is emphasized in Pierre N. Leval, "Toward a Fair Use Standard," 103 *Harvard Law Review* 1105, 1113–1119 (1990). (Judge Leval was the trial judge in both the *Salinger* and *New Era* cases. In both cases he upheld the fair use defense and was reversed—mistakenly, as our analysis will show.) The importance of extensive quotation is even greater in works of literary analysis than in biographies. See Sundeman v. Seajay Society, Inc., 142 F.3d 194 (4th Cir. 1998), which involved a literary analysis of an unpublished novel of the once well-known novelist Marjorie Kinnan Rawlings. The publisher of the literary analysis won.

and is positive or negative depending on whether the marginal benefit of increasing $Q (= \alpha_Q Q_z > 0)$ is greater or less than the marginal loss from reducing the permissible use of unpublished materials ($\alpha_z < 0$). The value of X is maximized with respect to z for each value of N when $\alpha_z + \alpha_Q Q_z = 0$, that is, when the marginal benefits and marginal costs, with regard to the quality-adjusted stock of biographies, of increasing the scope of copyright protection are equal.

Using E (for expression) to denote the cost of creating an expressive work (as in Chapter 3), we can write the cost of expression of N biographies as

$$E = E(N). \tag{6}$$

We assume that E_N is positive (the cost of writing one biography is positive) and increasing because the cost of writing biographies will differ among biographers.[21] Some writers will be more efficient than others, and N will increase until the cost of creating an additional biography just equals the expected net revenue from selling copies of the work. Expected net revenue is the producer surplus in the market in which copies of books are sold. The marginal biography will earn just enough producer surplus to cover its cost of expression. All other biographers will earn producer surplus above the cost of creating the work.

To simplify further, we assume that the N biographies are equivalent in the sense that each faces an identical demand curve for copies that is downward sloping (indicating that biographies are not perfect substitutes for each other, although the elasticity of demand for any work is likely to be high) and that the marginal cost of making copies is identical for each work. This implies that both the price and number of copies sold of each biography are the same and hence that each biography earns identical net revenues or producer surplus in the market for copies.

Let the producer surplus earned per biography equal $\alpha (= X/N)$ multiplied by $s (=$ producer surplus when $\alpha = 1)$, so that the higher the quality of the work, the greater the demand for it and so the greater the producer surplus.[22] In

21. We used a more complicated cost-of-expression function in Chapter 3, making that cost depend on both N and z, which affects N because the more one can lawfully borrow from prior works the lower is the cost of creating new ones. An alternative formulation of the model in this chapter would assume that copyright protection for unpublished materials affects $E(N)$ through its effect on Q—that is, that the quantity of unpublished materials lowers the cost of creating biographies rather than raising their quality. Both approaches yield similar implications. We chose the quality approach because it seemed more intuitive.

22. These are simplifying assumptions. We could introduce differences both in the demand for copies of biographies and the cost of making copies and interactions between the number of biographies created and the demand for copies of a particular biography. This would greatly complicate the presentation without changing the basic results.

equilibrium the number of biographies will increase until $E_N = s\alpha$, or in words until the marginal cost of expression equals the producer surplus earned in the market for copies of books, which is assumed to be equal for all biographies. The supply curve of biographies can be written as

$$N = N(\alpha, s, z), \tag{7}$$

where N is an increasing function of producer surplus, s. Whether greater copyright protection for unpublished materials raises or lowers N depends on whether z raises or lowers α.[23] The greater α is, the greater will be the (positive) response of N to an increase in s, since each additional biography will earn a greater return because of its higher quality.

The optimal amount of copyright protection is the level of z that maximizes social welfare subject to the constraint that N increase to the point at which $E_N = s\alpha$. Social welfare (W) will equal the product of the number of quality-adjusted works published—in this case biographies—and the sum of consumer and producer surplus per biography minus the cost of expression, as in

$$W = X(c + s) - E(N), \tag{8}$$

where c is consumer surplus per quality-adjusted biography and the other terms are as defined before.

Social welfare in equation (8) is created only by *published* works. This is an arbitrary limitation, relaxed later. The creator of unpublished materials and the limited number of persons who may have access to them are members of society too. They derive benefits from such materials, especially when the materials are honest and candid rather than guarded and self-serving, and the creator may derive additional benefits from keeping the materials from becoming public. While the number of such persons is likely to be small relative to the number with access to published and widely disseminated works, the benefits from unpublished materials are realized in the present while the benefits from published works that incorporate the unpublished materials are deferred. Furthermore, the number of persons who create unpublished ma-

---

23. The number of biographies created will increase until in equilibrium producer surplus equals the marginal cost of expression (that is, the cost of writing the marginal biography) or until $s\alpha = E_N$. The slope of the supply curve of N (with z constant) is $dN/ds = \alpha/E_{NN}$, which is positive from the assumption of increasing marginal cost. Also, $dN/dz = s(\alpha_z + \alpha_Q Q_z)/E_{NN}$, which is greater or less than zero depending on whether $(\alpha_z + \alpha_Q Q_z)$ is greater or less than zero, or whether the marginal benefit of increasing Q is greater than the losses from reducing the lawful use of Q as z increases. Notice that the condition for whether N increases or decreases with respect to a change in z is identical to whether X increases or decreases with respect to z. See equation (5).

terials of potential interest to future biographers and historians will greatly exceed the number of published biographies and histories, though not the readership for those works. That is, Q will exceed N, although the larger the gap the lower p will be and so the lower the expected harm per unit of Q.

Social welfare (in our limited social welfare function) is maximized when $W_z = 0$, or equivalently when

$$(\alpha_z + \alpha_Q Q_z)N(c + s) + \alpha N_z(c + s) - E_N N_z = 0, \tag{9}$$

which simplifies to[24]

$$(\alpha_z + \alpha_Q Q_z)[N(c + s) + cE_N/sE_{NN}] = 0. \tag{10}$$

Since the terms in brackets are positive, W is maximized when $(\alpha_z + \alpha_Q Q_z) = 0$, which is the expression for maximizing the average quality (α) per biography or the output of quality-adjusted biographies (x) holding N constant (see equation (5)).[25]

The intuition behind equation (10) is that the optimal level of copyright protection for unpublished works is constrained by the fact that a biography will be written only if the expected return is as great as the cost of expression. The number of biographies will thus increase until producer surplus per book ($s\alpha$) just equals marginal cost (or, identically, the cost of the marginal biography). Since s (or producer surplus per unit of quality) is given, the law will maximize the number of biographies by choosing a level of z, call it z^*, that maximizes α, or average quality, because that will yield the highest producer surplus per biography. Since z^* maximizes $s\alpha$ and therefore the equilibrium number of biographies, it also maximizes total producer surplus after deduction of the cost of expression ($\alpha sN - E(N)$).[26] And since each N yields, by assumption, a constant consumer surplus of αc, z^* maximizes $W = \alpha N(c + s) - E(N)$.

W is maximized when $(\alpha_z + \alpha_Q Q_z) = 0$, which requires that z^* be set at a level where the marginal gain from allowing biographers to quote additional unpublished material just equals the marginal harm from reducing the quantity of unpublished material as copyright protection weakens. This implies that some copying of unpublished materials must be allowed in order to maximize social welfare, contrary to the view that the fair use defense should

24. Because $E_N = s\alpha$ in equilibrium (that is, the marginal cost of expression equals producer surplus) and $N_z = s(\alpha_z + \alpha_Q Q_z)/E_{NN}$.

25. The second-order condition for a maximum ($W_{zz} < 0$) is satisfied because it requires $\alpha_{zz} < 0$, since the other terms in W_{zz} equal zero from the first-order conditions. We assume that α_{zz} is negative because it is likely that q will increase at a decreasing rate as z increases.

26. Social welfare would be greater if N increased until E_N equaled the sum of consumer and producer surplus per biography rather than equaling just producer surplus. But then the marginal biography would not cover its cost of expression.

never be available in a case of unpublished work. Also, z^* will be lower the greater is $q_0/q(z)$—the ratio of unpublished materials that would be produced were there no copyright protection of such materials to the additional quantity that is produced only because of copyright protection. If the ratio is high, the welfare losses from restricting the copying of unpublished materials will tend to dominate any increase in benefits brought about by increases in Q (the total stock of unpublished materials not intended for publication), and copyright protection for unpublished works should be set at a low level. Similarly, the less responsive the supply of unpublished materials is to such protection (that is, the lower Q_z is), the smaller will be the benefits of increasing z and so the smaller z^* will be.

The ratio $q_0/q(z)$ is likely to be high and Q_z low: copyright protection is unlikely to have a big impact on the quantity of unpublished materials because the probability that unpublished materials will eventually be copied and published by someone else usually is slight and only weakly related to z. The expected harm to the author of unpublished materials from publication is therefore likely to be slight and it must be further discounted because publication, if it occurs at all, will occur in the future. The relevant harm, moreover, is the *incremental* harm caused by publication, which will tend to be small because copyright protects expression but not ideas, facts, theories, and so forth.

Nor is weak copyright protection likely to cause writers of unpublished materials to trim their sails much. A letter is written to someone; a diary often is expected to be read by someone, if only the writer's literary executor. A writer who trusts the intended reader will be candid even if he has no copyright protection at all, while if he distrusts the intended reader he will be uncandid even if he has full copyright protection, given that it will not protect him against revelation of the ideas in the letter or diary. Either way, copyright is unlikely to influence his behavior significantly.

The formal model ignored differences among classes of unpublished works that could affect the optimal scope of copyright protection. Consider the distinction between letters and diaries. Since the writer of a letter reveals its content to the recipient, who in turn may reveal it to others or may deposit it in a library where others will be able to read although not copy it, the incremental harm from eventual publication will be smaller than in the case of a diary not intended for anyone else to read. And the smaller the incremental harm, the greater will $q_0/q(z)$ be and the lower, therefore, the optimal level of protection. Cutting the other way, however, is the fact that the materials likely to be most valuable to a biographer are precisely those very private papers whose publication may cause the greatest harm to their author, since the more private they are the more likely they are (relative to letters, which are at best semiprivate) to contain information discreditable to him.

The formal model also equated the quantity of unpublished materials to the quantity available to biographers or other subsequent would-be users, though the two quantities actually are not identical. Not only will some material be lost between creation and use, but the incentive to preserve such materials, and the related decision whether to destroy them—particularly should it become clear at some later date that the materials may fall into unfriendly hands—may depend on the level of copyright protection. When the difference between the quantity of unpublished materials created and those preserved for future use is taken into account, the ratio $q_0/q(z)$ may be smaller and Q_z larger than we have suggested is likely. But copyright protection still is unlikely to have much effect on the incentives to preserve unpublished materials. Again the relationship between sender and recipient must be considered. Often when the recipient of unpublished materials destroys them because they are compromising, he is acting as the agent of the writer, and then the analysis is the same as in the preceding paragraph: copyright will not be important.

The model ignored the cost of administering copyright protection in unpublished materials. That cost is of course positive and suggests that optimal copyright protection for such materials should be weaker than the model implies. Technological factors are also relevant: the declining incentive to communicate in written form because of the greater availability of substitutes such as the telephone and low-cost travel (substitutes for letter writing that probably increase Q_z and so imply a greater scope of copyright protection) versus the effect of photocopying, scanning devices, and computers in reducing the cost of making and storing copies, which increases the likelihood that unpublished materials will be preserved regardless of incentives created by copyright protection.

Before concluding definitively that some and maybe a good deal of copying of unpublished materials should be permitted, we must expand our social welfare function to take account of the net benefits of copyright protection of unpublished materials to their creators and persons intended to have access to the materials. These benefits, $G(z)$, are greater the broader the scope of copyright protection for unpublished materials (that is, $G_z > 0$).

Adding G to the social welfare function yields

$$W = X(c + s) - E(N) + G(z). \tag{11}$$

Maximizing W with respect to z requires

$$(\alpha_z + \alpha_Q Q_z)[N(c + s) + cE_N/sE_{NN}] + G_z = 0. \tag{12}$$

Since $G_z > 0$, the first set of terms must be negative—not zero as before. This requires an increase in the optimal z beyond z^* to the point where the marginal losses from restricting the use of unpublished materials exceed the marginal gains to biographers from increasing Q. Let z^{**} equal the value of z that satisfies the expanded social welfare function. The difference between z^{**} and z^* will probably be small because the negative value $(\alpha_z + \alpha_Q Q_z)$ is weighted by terms that include the full consumer and producer surplus from the published works that make use of the unpublished materials and because of the reasons given earlier for doubting that the expected harm of publication to the author of unpublished materials is likely to be great.

Another reason for excluding G from the social welfare function, or at least discounting it steeply, is consumer surplus. z^* is a second-best solution because W is maximized subject to the constraint that the cost of the marginal biography (E_N) equals producer surplus (αs) in the market for copies of the work. The full social value of the marginal biography, however, is the sum of producer and consumer surplus $(\alpha(s + c))$. Since the biographer doesn't capture the consumer surplus, too few biographies are created. Excluding G from the social welfare function results in a lower z^*, a higher α, and therefore a greater value for N, countering the incentive to create too few biographies.

Private and social harm must also be distinguished. An author of unpublished materials is likely to object to their being published because they reveal his disreputable or unethical behavior. Knowing in advance that copyright protection for such materials was weak might induce him to behave better, thus raising social welfare (so G might actually be negative). This is one of the reasons for doubting that privacy is always a social good.[27] It is possibly in recognition of this fact that the tort right of privacy has never prevented the intended recipient of a letter, or anyone else who has lawful access to a private document, from "spilling the beans." It would be paradoxical to use copyright law to give people greater privacy than the body of law that is *designed* to strike the correct balance between privacy and the public's right to know. A risk remains that knowledge that discreditable jottings were not protected by copyright would induce people to be more discreet in those jottings. Since the private cost of discretion is likely to be less than its social cost in concealing valuable clues to character, the reticence factor will reduce the consumer surplus generated by biographies if unpublished materials are denied copyright protection.

Productive versus Reproductive Uses

We have thus far been considering only *productive* uses of unpublished materials not intended for publication, uses that improve the published work in

27. See Richard A. Posner, *The Economics of Justice*, ch. 9 (1981).

which the materials are incorporated. We now consider whether copyright law should permit *reproductive* uses, such as publication of letters as a separate volume rather than as constituents of a biography or history. One's instinctive answer is "no" because the publisher is creating a perfect substitute for the author's work and adding no value apart from making that work public. But remember that we are considering works not intended to be published, and so the publisher is not depriving the author of a profit that was his incentive for creating the work in the first place.[28] Nevertheless there are two reasons for giving stronger copyright protection against reproductive than productive uses of unpublished materials. First, a reproductive use will tend to be more detailed and extensive and thereby inflict greater harm. Salinger would doubtless be pained more by publication of his collected letters than by publication of a biography that quoted from them. And if the law makes no distinction between reproductive and productive uses, future Salingers will be more reluctant to write letters.

Second, giving the letter writer control over publication of his letters facilitates a utility-maximizing transaction: the writer will consent to publication if the market value of the letters, commuted into royalties that he receives, exceeds the psychological or reputational harm to him. But isn't this point equally applicable to productive uses of unpublished works? The biographer can buy the right to quote from the letters if he gains more than Salinger is harmed. The difference is that a biographer is likely to want to publish unpublished materials by a number of different people, and if he has to negotiate a license from each the transaction costs will be great. Moreover—and here we are harking back to a point made in the preceding chapter when we were discussing the fair use privilege for book reviews—the credibility of biographies would be impaired if the reader knew that the biographer had been required to obtain the subject's consent in order to be able to publish his letters. For that consent may well have been limited to selected portions of letters that portray the subject in a favorable light, or conditioned on the biographer's deleting the portions of the biography that were critical of the subject. A critical biography would be transformed into an authorized one, which would reduce its value to most readers.

Unpublished Materials Intended for Publication

Obviously the case for broad copyright protection of unpublished works is stronger when the authors intend to publish them, but how much stronger

---

28. We do not consider whether the publication of the materials might reduce their value to collectors as distinct from their publication value. Publication might very well increase their value to collectors by increasing the public's interest in the materials.

depends on the use the copier makes of the as yet unpublished work. Consider a reproductive use of the work, as in the *Nation* case. By substituting for the original work, a reproductive use reduces the market demand for the work it copies and thus the incentive to incur the costs of creating it. It probably lowers social welfare, which we can define for this purpose as $W = N(c + s) - E(N)$, where N is now the number of unpublished works intended for eventual publication but the other terms are as before. These unpublished works enter the social welfare function directly because they will soon be available to consumers. Let $\phi = \phi(z)$ be the probability of a reproductive use by an unauthorized publisher of the unpublished work, the publication being a substitute for later publication authorized by the copyright holder. It is inverse to the degree of copyright protection for unpublished works intended for publication, which we again denote by z. In equilibrium N will increase until the expected producer surplus equals the marginal cost of expression, that is, until $[1 - \phi(z)]s = E_N$.

W is maximized with respect to z when $c + s = E_N$. Substituting $[1 - \phi(z)]s$ for E_N, however, yields $\phi(z) = -c/s$—which is not possible since the probability of a reproductive use obviously is not negative. Given a non-negativity constraint, W will be maximized by making $\phi(z)$ as small as possible, which requires setting $z^* = 1$. If we define copyright protection as the fraction of a work that cannot be copied and assume that works intended for publication will be copied if not prohibited by law (because they yield producer surplus), then $\phi(z) = 1 - z$ and is zero when $z^* = 1$.

The model implies that reproductive uses of unpublished materials intended for publication should be forbidden because they produce no offsetting benefits. But this is overstated. The reproductive use will bring the work to market a little sooner, though the benefit is likely to be less than the sum of the costs of impairing the incentive to create the work in the first place and of the defensive measures that the creator of the original work, like any other trade secret owner, will take to prevent anyone else from publishing it first. A further wrinkle is that a reproductive use may lower the price of copies and hence increase consumer surplus for works that are still created in the face of reproductive uses. This is more likely if the reproductive use involves copying only part of the original work and so does not substitute completely for it. The *Nation* case is an example of such a partial reproductive use; the *Nation* article substituted for the article in *Time* but not for the book itself.

The final category is a productive use of an unpublished work intended for publication. A productive use will have a smaller adverse effect on the expected revenues of the author of the original work than a reproductive one. The effect on expected revenues might even be positive, as in the case of a biography or history that quotes only modest amounts from soon-to-be-published sources. We don't see why the fair use doctrine should be more narrowly construed in such a case than in the ordinary case in which a biographer or historian quotes short passages from published works.

The Cases Revisited

Our analysis has suggested that with regard to unpublished materials not intended for publication, the expected harm from publication of the unpublished materials is normally quite small and is anyway not highly responsive to the scope of copyright protection, so that denying copyright protection is unlikely to dry up to even a slight extent the stream of unpublished materials.[29] The opposite is generally true regarding the publication of unpublished works that their authors intend eventually to publish. These conclusions imply that the fair use doctrine should be applied with particular generosity to unpublished works not intended for eventual publication—thus reversing the presumption in the cases we led off this chapter with, though it is important to bear in mind that the cases were decided before Congress amended the fair use provision of the copyright statute to suggest that publication status per se should not determine the applicability of the fair use privilege.

The *Nation* case, involving the unauthorized publication of unpublished materials intended for eventual publication (and soon, too), was thus correctly decided against fair use. But *Salinger* and *New Era* were not.[30] In both cases the effect of an injunction against publication of the unpublished materials was bound to be to suppress truthful information that was relevant to a matter of public interest, namely the character of a famous writer and of a prominent religious leader, respectively. Just as the tort law of privacy permits publicizing discreditable or embarrassing facts that, whether by virtue of their intrinsic interest or the individual's prominence, are newsworthy—that is, are valuable "goods" in the marketplace of ideas and opinions[31]—so the same dispensation should be granted to publicizing copyrighted though unpublished work not intended for eventual publication.[32] Although copyright

29. Recall, though, our acknowledgment that the quality of the unpublished materials may fall to some extent because of the reticence factor.

30. The injunction sought in *New Era* was denied, but the opinion implies that if it had been sought more promptly it would have been granted, and that is the aspect of the decision that strikes us as wrong.

31. See, for example, Haynes v. Alfred A. Knopf, Inc., 8 F.3d 1222 (7th Cir. 1993); Richard A. Posner, *Overcoming Law*, ch. 25 (1995). Compare the limitations imposed by interpretation of the free-speech clause of the First Amendment on the right of "public figures" to obtain legal remedies against defamation, the theory behind the limitations being that the enhanced public interest in such figures justifies in effect a subsidy for publication about them.

32. And recall our earlier point that the privacy interest is attenuated by the fact that the writer has already compromised his privacy by the disclosure of the embarrassing or discreditable facts to the intended recipient of his letter or to the intended reader of his diary.

does not prevent the publication of the facts and ideas in the unpublished work, the incremental contribution to knowledge made by publication is significant for the reasons stated earlier. That is why Salinger and the Church of Scientology fought tooth and nail to prevent publication. The social benefits of publication are doubtless less than those of disseminating the informational content, but we have seen that the social costs of publication, whether in terms of the impact on the creation of unpublished materials of possible value or on the legitimate interests of the authors of such materials, when properly analyzed, probably are slight. The *Wright* and *Sundeman* cases,[33] in which fair use of unpublished materials not intended for publication was upheld, seem to us closer to the mark.

We end with the curious and difficult case of *Lish v. Harper's Magazine Foundation*.[34] *Harper's* magazine has a section called "Readings" in which it publishes documents that it thinks will interest its readers. The case arose from the inclusion in "Readings" of an unpublished letter, edited down to 52 percent of its original length, by Gordon Lish, a well-known teacher of creative writing. He had sent the letter to forty-nine prospective creative-writing students. The letter is described by the court as "contain[ing] a variety of material ranging from nuts and bolts details about the logistics of the class, instructions as to how students are expected to behave in class, to passages of exuberant rhetoric exhorting students to heroic efforts. The Letter was interesting both for its factual and stylistic content."[35] *Harper's* could have paraphrased the letter without infringement, but that would have missed the way in which, in the words of one of the magazine's witnesses, "the letter swerves from the hifalutin to the ordinary to the slangy. It's a way of demonstrating by these devices the variety of ways in which effects can be produced linguistically."[36] The court rejected the fair use defense. It thought that *Harper's* could have illustrated Lish's style with a few short quotations, and it seemed particularly troubled by the fact that *Harper's* had copied such a large fraction of the letter.

The court rejected the defense even though it also found that the letter had no commercial value to Lish; in other words, it was a case about copying unpublished material not intended ever to be published. Or was it? It seems rather to fall between the two categories of unpublished materials that we have been assuming exhaust the field. For it was really a case of *limited* publication. The letter was sent to forty-nine prospective students. Doubtless Lish sent similar letters to other groups of that kind. The letters are solicitations

33. See notes 11 and 20 above. See also Norse v. Henry Holt & Co., 847 F. Supp. 142 (N.D. Cal. 1994).

34. 807 F. Supp. 1090 (S.D.N.Y. 1993).

35. Id. at 1095.

36. Id. at 1099.

and undoubtedly are drafted and timed with that in mind. Publication of these letters without Lish's authorization threatened to interfere with his preferred mode of publication. The letters might not themselves be salable, as the court found, yet they generated income for Lish indirectly by stimulating demand for his creative-writing course, which is a private venture of his rather than part of a college program. The case is perhaps not so remote from the *Nation* case as it might at first seem. The analysis we have suggested does not appear in the court's opinion, but some intuition of it may have influenced the outcome.

6

Fair Use, Parody, and Burlesque

Parody and burlesque are ancient literary genres—*The Battle of Frogs and Mice* is an ancient Greek parody of the *Iliad*—that depend for their effect on the copying of distinctive features of the original, features without which the meaning of the parody or burlesque would be lost. Here is the beginning of the anonymous "Dental Soliloquy":

> To have it out or not? That is the question;
> Whether 'tis better for the jaws to suffer
> The pangs and torments of an aching tooth,
> Or to take steel against a host of troubles;
> And, by extracting, end them? To pull—to tug!
> No more; and by a tug to say we end
> The tooth-ache, and a thousand natural ills
> The jaw is heir to; 'tis a consummation
> Devoutly to be wished?[1]

And here from Part II of "The Sweeniad" by the pseudonymous "Myra Buttle" is a parody of the opening stanza of *The Waste Land* (footnote omitted):

> Sunday is the dullest day, treating
> Laughter as profane sound, mixing
> Worship and despair, killing
> New thought with dead forms.
> Weekdays give us hope, tempering
> Work with reviving play, promising
> A future life within this one.
> Thirst overtook us, conjured up by Budweisserbrau
> On a neon sign: we counted our dollar bills.
> Then out into the night air, into Maloney's Bar,

1. Quoted in Beate Müller, "Hamlet at the Dentist's: Parodies of Shakespeare," in *Parody: Dimensions and Perspectives* 127, 141 (Beate Müller ed. 1997).

And drank whiskey, and yarned by the hour.
Das Herz ist gestorben, swell dame, echt Bronx.
And when we were out on bail, staying with the Dalai Lama,
My uncle, he gave me a ride on a yak,
And I was speechless. He said, Mamie,
Mamie, grasp his ears. And off we went
Beyond Yonkers, then I felt safe.
I drink most of the year and then I have a Vichy.

This is almost as close a copy as Shakespeare's description of Cleopatra is a copy of North's translation of Plutarch (see Chapter 2), though more words have been changed. And since Eliot's poem remains under copyright, why isn't the parodist an infringer? Because the use a parodist makes of the original may be a fair use. The Supreme Court has confirmed that a parody may be a fair use but has declined to provide further guidance, ruling instead that whether a particular parody is a fair use depends on the circumstances of the individual case.[2] Economic analysis, building on the discussion of the fair use doctrine in Chapter 4, can provide essential guidance but we must first get a clear idea of the nature and purpose of parody, which we can do with the help of literary theorists.[3]

Parody is best understood in terms of one of its synonyms: it is a "take-off"—a takeoff on another work or on a genre of works. It takes characters, incidents, dialogue, or other aspects of the parodied work(s) and moves on from there to create a new work. Generally there is an incongruity between the borrowed and the new elements, as where the parodist sets about to "grasp the essentials of the style of a given [serious] author or a school of authors, and then proceed to concoct an outlandish episode which is expressed in that style."[4] "The highest kind of parody may be defined as a humorous and aesthetically satisfying composition in prose or verse, usually written without malice, in which, by means of a rigidly controlled distortion, the most striking peculiarities of subject matter and style of a literary work, an au-

2. Campbell v. Acuff-Rose Music, Inc., 510 U.S. 569 (1994). The Court reversed the grant of summary judgment in favor of the plaintiff but did not rule definitively that the defendant's parody was a fair use, while hinting broadly that it was. The parody was a rap version of the song "Pretty Woman." It used the tune (though with some changes) and one line of the lyrics. See Anastasia P. Winslow, "Rapping on a Revolving Door: An Economic Analysis of Parody and *Campbell v. Acuff-Rose Music, Inc.,*" 69 *Southern California Law Review* 767 (1996).

3. See, for example, Simon Dentith, *Parody* (2000); Margaret A. Rose, *Parody: Ancient, Modern, and Post-Modern* (1993); Linda Hutcheon, *A Theory of Parody: The Teachings of Twentieth-Century Art Forms* (1985); Seymour Chatman, "Parody and Style," 22 *Poetics Today* 25 (2001); "Symposium on Parody," 13 *Southern Review* 2 (1980); G. D. Kiremidjian, "The Aesthetics of Parody," 28 *Journal of Aesthetics and Art Criticism* 231 (1969); J. G. Riewald, "Parody as Criticism," 50 *Neophilologus* 125 (1966).

4. Kiremidjian, note 3 above, at 235.

thor, or a school or type of writing, are exaggerated in such a way as to lead to an implicit value judgment of the original."[5] Not all parodies are humorous, however, just as not all are free of malice. *The Wind Done Gone* is an unfunny but very pointed parody of *Gone with the Wind* designed to point up what the parodist considered the racism of that famous novel.[6]

The Copyright Issue

So parody involves both a taking from a previous work and an injection of creativity, large or small. Yet often none of the copyrighted elements of the parodied work(s) is taken. This is especially likely if what is being parodied is not a single work, as in the *Hamlet* and *Waste Land* parodies with which we began, but instead a writer's (or painter's or composer's) entire *oeuvre*—in short, his style or outlook. Style is not copyrightable (though it can be trade-marked[7] as a way of preventing plagiarism), nor are ideas or point of view, or an entire genre (for example, the sonnet, the Gothic novel, the musical comedy)—and a distinctive style, point of view, or choice of genre can be conjured up without using a writer's actual words, characters, or story line. Neither is a title copyrightable, or stock characters (for example, the hard-boiled private eye, the miser, the Latin lover), or the standard plots (star-crossed lovers and so forth), so a parodist who took only those features from a copyrighted work would not be an infringer either. Myra Buttle could have done an effective parody of T. S. Eliot, though not of *The Waste Land* per se, without sticking quite so close to the meter and story line of the poem. Max Beerbohm's well-known parodies of Henry James, such as *The Mote in the Middle Distance* and *The Guerdon,* would not be within range of an infringement suit because they are not substantially similar to any specific story or novel of James.

But when the parodist does take copyrighted elements of the parodied work, it is arguable that his taking should be deemed an infringement no matter how great his creative additions. The combination of copyrighted elements with fresh creative input is simply a derivative work, and we know that modern copyright law for good reasons assigns the exclusive right to make and sell derivative works to the owner of the copyright on the original work. The law does not care how much "better," or commercially more valuable, the derivative work is. Transaction costs are minimized when all rights over the original work and its derivative works are concentrated in a single pair of hands.

5. Riewald, note 3 above, at 128–129.

6. See SunTrust Bank v. Houghton Mifflin Co., 268 F.3d 1257 (11th Cir. 2001).

7. See Romm Art Creations, Ltd. v. Simcha International, Inc., 786 F. Supp. 1126 (E.D.N.Y. 1992).

However, a point we made in Chapter 4 in reference to book reviews points to a fair use defense for many parodies. Although reviews sometimes reduce the demand for a book, when this happens the reason is not that the review supplies that demand—rarely is a book review a close substitute for the book itself—but that it points out flaws and so provides valuable information without undermining the rewards for creating *worthwhile* intellectual property. The harm to an author that comes from exposing the weaknesses of his effort—from drawing attention to the *lack* of value of the intellectual property he has created—is not the kind of harm that copyright law should be concerned with preventing. Obviously not all books that contain errors are valueless; indeed, books can have great weaknesses yet still be socially valuable because of offsetting strengths. But such a book will not be devastated by negative book reviews that stress its weaknesses. The marketplace in ideas and opinions will generate a demand for and a supply of other reviews that emphasize the book's strengths. Put differently, critical book reviews are themselves a valuable form of intellectual property but a form that would lose much of its value without a fair use defense.

Parody is often a mode of criticism, criticism by ridicule,[8] whether funny or savage or both, though unlike book reviews parodies are not also a mode of advertising. A review will often serve to introduce a book to the public, but the audience for a parody must already have some and often considerable familiarity with the parodied work in order to get the point—indeed, works are rarely parodied that are not already very well known and thus likely to be recognized by a large number of people, the parodist's potential audience. Hence parodies do not fit into the fair use category of negative harm, implied consent by the author of the original to copying. Unlike reviews, they do not furnish information about experience goods that tends to expand the demand for those goods—the parodied work will already be sufficiently well known that it no longer *is* an experience good. So we would not expect the creators of expressive works, if choosing a copyright regime behind the veil of ignorance, to agree that, like book reviews, parodies should be entitled to a fair use privilege. The basis of the fair use privilege for parodies is their critical function. If a parodist had to get a copyright license to copy from the parodied work, criticism would be impeded. If a license were granted, moreover, this would undermine the credibility of the parody as criticism, just as in the parallel case of the licensed book review. The audience for the parody would wonder whether the parodist had pulled his punches in order to obtain the license at a lower fee.

Parody has been called a limited form of criticism because of its focus on idiosyncrasy:

8. See Kiremidjian, note 3 above, at 234; Dentith, note 3 above, at 32–38.

Parody naturally tends to be the watchdog of established forms, a correction of literary extremes . . . [It thus] tends to confine itself to "writers whose style and habit of thought, being more marked and peculiar, was more capable of exaggeration and distortion." This tendency seriously restricts the scope of critical parody because it seems to ignore the fact that the absence of any "marked and peculiar" style and habit of thought is a symptom of mediocrity rather than of talent.[9]

This is overstated. There are plenty of parodies of mediocrity, as in Joyce's *Dubliners* and the Gerty MacDowell episode in *Ulysses*,[10] among many other examples; mediocrity is often ridiculous. And parodies of the style of great writers, such as Shakespeare's parody in *Hamlet* of Marlowe[11] or Beerbohm's parodies of James and Shakespeare[12] focus on criticizable (whether justly or not) features of the style of the writers parodied—in these examples, Elizabethan bombast and Jamesian convolution. Another example is the parody of the form, conventions—and pretensions—of the epic poem: *Paradise Lost* by Pope's *Rape of the Lock,* for example. And parody can be a method of political criticism, as in *The Wind Done Gone.*

Parodies also differ from book reviews in being more likely to supply a part of the demand for the original work. The movie *Abbott and Costello Meet Frankenstein,* a parody of the earlier movies *Frankenstein, Dracula,* and *The Wolf Man,* reproduces the principal characters and themes of the parodied works in a feature-length format that the viewer might prefer to seeing (or, more likely, seeing for a second or a third time) all three of the original works.[13] *Young Frankenstein* is a similar parody, though just of *Frankenstein,* and *Love at First Bite* is a similar parody of *Dracula.* Most parodies are humorous (as in the examples just given), and many people prefer a humorous to the original serious version, especially when the original was itself intended

9. Riewald, note 3 above, at 132–133 (footnotes omitted).

10. The style of which "owes a considerable debt of parody to the style" of Maria Cummins's novel *The Lamplighter* (1854), whose heroine is named Gerty. Don Gifford, with Robert J. Seidman, *Ulysses Annotated: Notes for James Joyce's Ulysses* 384 n. 1 (2d ed. 1988).

11. In the player's bombastic speech narrating Priam's slaying by Pyrrhus (II.2.450–518), which is a takeoff on Aeneas' narration of the same incident in Christopher Marlowe's play *The Tragedy of Dido, Queen of Carthage* (II.1.518–558).

12. The latter in "'Savonarola' Brown," in Max Beerbohm, *Seven Men and Two Others* 233, 246 (1950).

13. Yet as noted in Don Harries, *Film Parody* 19 (2000), Universal Pictures, which produced *Abbott and Costello Meet Frankenstein,* was the owner of the three earlier horror films that it spoofed. This implies that the parody version was not expected to draw viewers from the parodied films—more precisely, not so many viewers as to make the parody a source of greater loss than gain of revenue. On film parody generally, see, besides Harries's book, Wes D. Gehring, *Parody as Film Genre: "Never Give a Saga an Even Break"* (1999).

purely as entertainment and lacks moral or intellectual pretension. Some parodies are erotic versions of a nonerotic original, and they may supply the demand for the original on the part of the segment of the population that likes its entertainment spiced with sex. We shall call parodies that offer themselves as possible substitutes for the parodied works "burlesques." (Not as perfect substitutes, ordinarily.) Notice, however, that burlesques involve elements of complementarity as well as substitution to the extent that they draw favorable attention to the original and thus provide free advertising for it.

Another distinctive feature of parody that complicates fair use analysis is that it doesn't always ridicule or otherwise criticize the parodied work itself. Instead it may use that work—treating it as the standard of excellence—to disparage something else, as when T. S. Eliot in *The Waste Land* copied passages from St. Augustine, Dante, Shakespeare, Spenser, Marvell, and other classic authors greatly admired by Eliot to show up by way of contrast what Eliot believed to be the sordidness and spiritual emptiness of modern life. In other words, the copied work used in the parody may be the *weapon* rather than the *target*—in which event why should the owner of the original be reluctant to license the parody, especially since it may very well draw favorable attention to the parodied work? The "weapon" form of parody, which the cases tend to call "satire," is illustrated by a case in which the owner of the copyrights on the Dr. Seuss books brought suit against the publisher of a book that—bizarrely—narrated the events of the murder trial of O. J. Simpson in the style of Dr. Seuss. The plaintiff won.[14] Some works are both parody and satire. An example is Jeff Koons's puppy sculpture (see Chapter 9) and probably Manet's *Olympia* (see Chapter 2), in which Titian's *Venus of Urbino* is recycled as a Parisian prostitute. Of course, it is always possible, and often likely, that the copyright owner doesn't want to become associated with satire. But if he denies a license for a burlesque because it would present a misleading picture of his own social views, the denial prevents public confusion and is thus efficient. We shall give an example later.

Like satires, burlesques, illustrated by *Abbott and Costello Meet Frankenstein* (other examples are the movie *Clueless,* a takeoff on Jane Austen's novel *Emma,* and *High Anxiety,* a takeoff on Hitchcock's *Vertigo*), tend not to be critical of the parodied work. A work that criticizes some earlier work is unlikely to be offering itself as a substitute for that work, unless the criticism is of the gentle "making fun of" sort; *Abbott and Costello Meet Frankenstein* makes fun of the originals, but the originals had never been taken seriously by most viewers anyway. To complete the picture, some outright parodies (as distinct from burlesques and from "weapon" parodies), illustrated by Beer-

---

14. See Dr. Seuss Enterprises v. Penguin Books USA, Inc., 109 F.3d 1394 (9th Cir. 1997).

bohm's parodies of James, are only mildly critical or perhaps not critical at all, their main or only object being to amuse, yet without offering themselves as substitutes for the original.

The argument for fair use is stronger if the parody is neither a satire nor a burlesque, stronger still if it is critical and not merely amusing, and stronger too the less of the parodied work the parodist borrows. He should not be allowed to reproduce an entire copyrighted work without the copyright holder's permission simply by giving the original characters funny names or having them speak in comical accents. By doing this he would entice the silly or vulgar members of the audience of the original work—and they may be a substantial fraction of the potential audience. This would be the literary equivalent of multiplying both sides of an equation by -1 or transposing a musical work written in one key into a different key. But this is just another way of saying that the law should distinguish between "real" parody and burlesque and deny the fair use defense to the latter as well as to satire. From here on in we shall generally use "parody" as exclusive of burlesque.

We have said that the amount of material taken from the original work by the parodist is relevant; but its relevance is only evidentiary. The more that is taken, the likelier it is that the so-called parody is actually intended to be and will be received by the public as a substitute for the original. Yet there are cases, just as in the nonparodic Beanie Babies case discussed in Chapter 4, in which the parody will be ineffectual if less than the whole of the original is copied, a controversial example, examined in Chapter 9, being the parodic sculpture of Jeff Koons. In general, the shorter the original the more of it must be copied in order to evoke the original in the minds of the audience. For example, in *Campbell v. Acuff-Rose Music, Inc.*,[15] the defendant could not evoke "Pretty Woman" without "quoting" a substantial part of the tune. A parodist would not have to quote 7 percent of *War in Peace* to evoke it; but if he quoted only 7 percent of a sonnet (that is, a single line), he might lose his intended audience, though this would depend on the sonnet, and on the audience. Bear in mind, too, that even if an alleged parody is actually a satire or burlesque normally not eligible for the fair use privilege, the author will have the usual fair use privilege of *de minimis* quotation from the original, since such limited quotation is more likely to increase than to reduce the demand for the original; it is a teaser, a come-on—a form of free advertising.

We can sharpen our analysis of parody with the aid of the economist's distinction between substitute and complementary goods, introduced in Chapter 2. In general, copying that is complementary to the copyrighted work (in the sense that nails are complements of hammers) is fair use, but copying that

15. See Note 2 above.

is a substitute for the copyrighted work (in the sense that nails are substitutes for pegs or screws) is not.[16] If the price of nails fell, the demand for hammers would rise but the demand for pegs would fall. The hammer manufacturer *wants* there to be an abundant supply of cheap nails, and likewise publishers want their books reviewed—it is free advertising—and wouldn't want reviews inhibited and degraded by a rule requiring the reviewer to obtain a copyright license from the publisher if he wanted to quote from the book. A good and an advertisement for the good are complements,[17] and likewise a book and a book review.

The distinction between complementary and substitutional copying (sometimes—though as it seems to us, confusingly—said to be between "superseding" and "transformative" copies)[18] is also exemplified by the difference between parody and burlesque. A parody is not a substitute for the original work. But it must copy enough of that work to make the parody recognizable, and that amount of copying is deemed fair use.[19] The amount of copying necessary to evoke the original may be very slight, as in several of the examples we have given. The more eccentric the parodied work, the easier it is to evoke without much, perhaps any, actual quotation.

A hostile parody may reduce the demand for the parodied work. But not, as in the usual case of competing goods, because of substitution. One good is a substitute for the other in consumption because it provides the same satisfaction as the first good and at a comparable price. The hostile parody is obviously not a substitute for the original in this sense. In the short run it will have no negative effect on the demand for the original at all, because it is bought mainly by people who have already bought the original work—someone who didn't know the work already would not realize it was being parodied; they wouldn't understand the point of the parody or derive utility from it. In the long run, as word of the parody spreads, it may reduce demand for

---

16. See Davis v. The Gap, Inc., 246 F.3d 152, 175–176 (2d Cir. 2001); SunTrust Bank v. Houghton Mifflin Co., note 6 above, 268 F.3d at 1277 (concurring opinion); Wendy J. Gordon, "Fair Use as Market Failure: A Structural and Economic Analysis of the Betamax Case and Its Predecessors," 82 *Columbia Law Review* 1600, 1643 n. 237 (1982).

17. See Gary S. Becker and Kevin M. Murphy, "A Simple Theory of Advertising as a Good or Bad," 108 *Quarterly Journal of Economics* 941 (1993).

18. See, for example, Campbell v. Acuff-Rose Music, Inc., note 2 above, 510 U.S. at 579. We questioned the utility of this terminology in Chapter 4.

19. See Campbell v. Acuff-Rose Music, Inc., note 2 above, 510 U.S. at 579, 580–581 and n. 14, 588; SunTrust Bank v. Houghton Mifflin Co., note 6 above, 268 F.3d at 1271; Leibovitz v. Paramount Pictures Corp., 137 F.3d 109, 114 (2d Cir. 1998); Dr. Seuss Enterprises, L.P. v. Penguin Books USA, Inc., note 14 above, 109 F.3d at 1400; Melville B. Nimmer and David Nimmer, *Nimmer on Copyright*, vol. 4, § 13.05[C], pp. 13–203 to 13–218 (2002).

the parodied work by making it an object of ridicule and thus inducing consumers to switch to competing works.

A burlesque, in contrast, is usually just a humorous substitute for the original and so cuts into the demand for it by providing a substitute. Burlesques of this character, catering to the humor-loving segment of the original's market, are therefore not fair use.[20] The distinction is implicit in the proposition affirmed in all the parody cases that the parodist must not take more from the original than is necessary to conjure it up and thus make clear to the audience that his work is indeed a parody. This "rule" should not be taken literally; a parodist who copies a great deal of the original yet at every stage ridicules it is not offering the copy as a substitute to readers or viewers who like the original. The point is, rather, an evidentiary one: the more the parodist takes from the original, the likelier he is to be taking audience *away* from the work parodied, not by convincing them that it is no good (for that is not a substitution effect) but by providing a substitute for it.

One test for whether a work is a parody or a burlesque is whether the audience *has* to be aware of the original in order to enjoy the new work. In the case of a burlesque, he does not; probably most people who enjoyed the movie *Clueless* had never read or even heard of Jane Austen's novel *Emma*, of which *Clueless* is a burlesque as we are defining the term. It is only when the original work is criticized[21] that familiarity with the original is required, as one cannot appreciate the force of a criticism without knowing what is being criticized. Concern with substitution is not allayed by this observation, however. If *Emma* were still under copyright, the copyright holder might be unable to interest Hollywood in producing a movie version because it would be "just like" *Clueless*.[22] But this turns out to be a bad example, since in 1996, only one year after *Clueless* was released, a film version of *Emma* starring Gwyneth Paltrow appeared. And we recall that Universal Studios produced a burlesque of its own horror films. Moreover, to sound a frequent note in this book, copyright protection may already be too broad and, if so, then expanding the fair use doctrine to embrace burlesques might, by cutting down the

20. See Benny v. Loew's Inc., 239 F.2d 532, 536–537 (9th Cir. 1956), affirmed by an equally divided Court under the name Columbia Broadcasting System, Inc. v. Loew's, Inc., 356 U.S. 43 (1958) (per curiam); see Nimmer and Nimmer, note 19 above, vol. 4, § 13.05[B][1], pp. 13–194 to 13–195, § 13.05[C]; cf. Campbell v. Acuff-Rose Music, Inc., note 2 above, 510 U.S. at 580–581 and n. 14, 591.

21. The criticism may of course be admiring, may even be better described by another word, such as commentary. Book reviews do not lose their fair use privilege by being favorable! Chatman, note 3 above, argues that Beerbohm's gentle parodies of Henry James can help readers understand the literary function of the convoluted style of James's late novels.

22. This implies, however, that if *Emma* were still under copyright, *Clueless* would infringe the copyright—and that is uncertain.

scope of that protection, improve overall economic welfare. Even so, it would be questionable to cut it down by privileging burlesques over other forms of substitutional copying, thus creating an artificial incentive to make burlesques.

Although burlesque, unlike parody, does not presuppose that the original work is already known to the audience, the only works likely to be burlesqued are well-known, and probably therefore commercially successful, works. It is the proven success of the original work that creates an expectation that a burlesque of it will also be successful. From this it can be argued that the copyright holder will have reaped his just reward and should not be entitled to insist on a share of the profits of the burlesque or parody, viewed as a derivative work. The counterargument focuses on the distinction between the ex ante and the ex post perspective and notes that while viewed ex post a successful work of intellectual property—a Broadway hit, a best-seller, a hit song—may appear to confer a windfall gain on the creator, ex ante the creator faces a distribution of possible outcomes and if the upper tail of the distribution is cut off, the mean of the distribution will be lowered and the incentive to create intellectual property reduced. The counterargument is weak, however, for reasons that we discussed in Chapter 4 in connection with derivative works. We pointed out that control over derivative works provides only *incremental* income to the creator of the original work, and given the uncertainty that *any* copyright protection is necessary in order to create optimal incentives for the creation of expressive works, it is highly speculative to contend that the increment is necessary to optimize these incentives. A burlesque is a derivative work; and what is more, it is, as we have pointed out, usually the derivative of a commercially *successful* original work, which reduces the likelihood that the increment is necessary from an incentive standpoint. However, precisely because a burlesque is a derivative work, the reasons we offered for giving the creator of the original work control over the derivatives as well are equally available in defense of the law's differentiating between parodies and burlesques and withholding the fair use defense from the latter.

One of the authors of this book was as a college student involved in the composition and performance of a college musical entitled *My Ugly Broad*, a burlesque of *My Fair Lady* that though it never became the subject of litigation illustrates the concerns of this chapter in an interesting way. The Lerner and Loewe show (then recent), which was itself a musical version (derivative work) of George Bernard Shaw's play *Pygmalion*, which had in turn been based on Ovid's story "Pygmalion and Galatea" (an example that we gave in Chapter 2 of the derivative nature of much literary creativity), is the story of how a language specialist passes off a Cockney girl as a Hungarian aristocrat. *My Ugly Broad* inverted the story, which became the story of how a fraternity pledge uglifies a beautiful girl so that he can pass her off as a "pig" on the fraternity's "pig night." The burlesque used the tunes from *My Fair Lady* with appropriately revised lyrics. No criticism was intended of Lerner and Loewe's musical or even of the institution of "pig night"; the only objective was to amuse. It was pure burlesque, though it differed in several ways from the burlesques that we discussed earlier, such as *Young Frankenstein* and *Clueless*. If only because of the amateurism of the production, it did not offer itself to any members of the audience as a substitute for the burlesqued original, though its questionable taste would probably have resulted in denial of a copyright license from the owner of the copyright on *My Fair Lady* had a license been sought.

Remember the first factor that section 107 of the Copyright Act directs courts to consider in deciding whether a copying is a fair use—"whether such use is of a commercial nature or is for nonprofit educational purposes"? If weight is placed on the term "commercial nature," factor (1) may help courts to identify situations in which the copy is intended to substitute for rather than to criticize the original work, since the public is relatively uninterested in criticism. Of course there are many exceptions, and in fact most fair use copies are commercial. But we are speaking here just of parodies, and most people either lack sufficient cultural breadth to recognize most original works in parodies, or, not being of a critical disposition, have greatly enjoyed most of the expressive works that they have seen and therefore would not cotton to criticism of them. *My Ugly Broad* was not critical but neither was it a commercial venture, and this was one of the factors behind its not offering itself as a substitute—it wasn't professional enough.

The sort of burlesque typified by *My Ugly Broad* really is *just* a derivative work. There is no reason why, simply because it is humorous, it should be treated any differently from any other derivative work. It is the critical cast of the true parody that argues for a fair use defense. But criticism must be distinguished from offensiveness. A case that did not become a copyright case because the "parodied" material was in the public domain will illustrate this point.[23] The parodied works were pornographic, but artistically distinguished, drawings by the English artist Aubrey Beardsley. An art teacher employed by a community college made copies of the drawings using stained glass and exhibited them in the college lobby. In order to distinguish the figures in the copy he used glass of different colors, and, as it happened, without invidious intent, he used amber glass for women and white for men, which struck the college cleaning staff, who were black, as a racially offensive state-

23. The case is Piarowski v. Illinois Community College District 515, 759 F.2d 625 (7th Cir. 1985).

ment. The college removed the pictures to a somewhat out-of-the-way exhibition room in the college, precipitating a free-speech suit by the teacher, who lost. For our purposes the significance of the case is simply that while the copy may have been offensive, it was not intended as criticism of Beardsley or as satire or other commentary. It was a "pure" derivative work, so if the drawings copied had been under copyright, the copier would not have had a fair use defense.

So burlesques, whether or not they offer themselves as substitutes for the burlesqued originals, do not have a strong claim to the fair use defense. Nor do parodies in which the copied copyrighted work is used as a weapon, whether of social, political, or aesthetic criticism, rather than being the target of the parody's criticism. Granted, freedom of expression will be curtailed if the creation of *any* parody is burdened by the costs of transacting with and paying royalties to copyright holders. But that is true with respect to burlesques as well. And just as writers should not be allowed to steal paper and pencils in order to reduce the cost of satire, there is no compelling reason to subsidize social criticism by allowing writers to use copyrighted materials without compensating the copyright holder. Recall the risk that a burlesque may give a misleading impression of the views of the creator of the original work. Recall also that it is possible to parody an author, a genre, and even, though with greater difficulty, an individual work without copying any copyrighted materials at all, let alone more than is allowed by the fair use privilege to copy brief passages for any purpose.

This is not to suggest that parodies in which the copied work is a weapon rather than a target lack social value, which should in principle be traded off against any diminution in the copyright owner's revenues as a result of the parody's siphoning of the audience for his work. The point is rather that there is no insuperable obstacle to letting the market make the tradeoff, just as in the case of most other derivative works. There may well be an insuperable obstacle to a market solution, however, when the parodied work is a target of the parodist's criticism. For it may be in the private interest of the copyright owner—but it will very rarely be in the social interest—to suppress criticism of the work or to place a tax on criticism, in the form of a license fee demanded by the copyright owner, designed to compensate the person criticized.

The Coase Theorem might be thought to imply that if the social value of a parody exceeds the private harm to the owner of the copyright on the parodied work, the parodist will be able to negotiate a mutually agreeable license fee with the owner. But this is not necessarily so, because the benefits of the criticism will accrue largely to third parties. This is clearest in the case in which the parody will destroy the reputation of the author of the original work and hence the market for his future works; most of the persons who benefit from the disappearance of that market—persons who would have read the author's future works and been disappointed—will not be customers of the parodist. That makes negotiating for a parody license a high-transaction-cost negotiation, which the fair use privilege for parody avoids.

When, however, the parody uses the parodied work as a vehicle for commenting on society at large, a voluntary transaction should be feasible. A particular author may not want to associate himself with social criticism. But there will be plenty of copyrighted works that the parodist can choose from for such a purpose, especially since they need not be recognizable to the audience. So he will probably be able to negotiate a copyright license with someone. In addition, public domain works may be suitable for his purposes, and then no license will be required. But limiting criticism to works in the public domain would be stultifying, since most recent works, as to which criticism would be timely, will still be under copyright.

Trademark Parodies and the Implications for Copyright Law

The parodying of trademarks is common and, as we shall see in the last part of the chapter, more frequently challenged in court than the parodying of copyrighted works. It presents issues similar though not identical to those presented by the latter practice.[24] Three types of trademark parody should be distinguished.

The first consists of comparative advertising that parodies the competitor's trademark, and is illustrated by *Deere & Co. v. MTD Products*.[25] Both parties sold lawn tractors. MTD ran an ad in which Deere's deer symbol runs in fear from MTD's "Yard-Man" tractor and a barking dog. Ordinarily it is not trademark infringement to use a competitor's trademark in comparative advertising because there is no confusion as to source. MTD, however, profited both from comparing its product favorably to Deere's and from impairing consumers' favorable associations with Deere's mark, and the court held that the latter effect infringed Deere's right to prevent the dilution of

24. Parodies have also been challenged as violations of the tort right of publicity. See, for example, White v. Samsung Electronics America, Inc., 971 F.2d 1395 (9th Cir. 1992), where an ad used a robot that resembled Vanna White, the well-known game-show host. The court ruled for White, a result soundly criticized by Judge Alex Kozinski, dissenting from the denial of rehearing en banc. 989 F.2d 1512 (9th Cir. 1993). The defendant was trading on White's celebrity but also making fun of her. On solider grounds was the decision enjoining the use of Johnny Carson's signature phrase "Here's Johnny!" to advertise a portable toilet. Carson v. Here's Johnny Portable Toilets, Inc., 698 F.2d 831 (6th Cir. 1983). There was no criticism of Carson, just an offensive use of his identity to sell a product.

25. 41 F.3d 39 (2d Cir. 1994).

its mark.[26] The court said that although the ad was humorous, it was not a parody because it was being used to sell a product rather than to offer social commentary or entertainment. We are dubious. It *was* a parody, and comparative advertising benefits consumers because it is an efficient way of providing product information.

In the second type of parody, the parodist is again a seller of a competing product but unlike the *Deere* case there is a danger of confusion as to source. For example, if a fast-food chain offers a "McBagel," some customers may think it's doing so under license from McDonald's. If, however, a seller of T-shirts stencils on the shirts "I Like Cocaine" in a style reminiscent of Coca-Cola's advertising slogan,[27] few if any consumers will think that the Coca-Cola Company is the producer or licensor of the shirts, even though the "Coca" in the firm's name comes from the coca leaf, the source of cocaine; until 1903, Coca-Cola actually contained cocaine. That bit of history being unknown to most drinkers of Coca-Cola, "I Like Cocaine" was a trademark parody of a third kind, where, with source confusion not an issue and the parodist not a competitor, the analysis is parallel to that of copyright parodies. The closest fit is probably with satire—the "I Like Cocaine" parody is making fun of "squares," people who love Coke but are shocked by cocaine. The fit is not perfect, however, and a doctrine of trademark law that has no direct counterpart in the copyright field, namely that of tarnishment of a trademark,[28] might give the Coca-Cola Company a remedy.[29]

The idea behind the tarnishment concept is that the company's "goodwill"—roughly, the producer surplus that it obtains because its products have a good reputation for quality and consistency—may be impaired by the association of its trademarks with activities, such as the traffic in illegal drugs, that offend many consumers. If the parodist wants to use the original work in a way potentially offensive to the audience for the original, even if he is not

26. The court invoked the form of dilution called "tarnishment," of which more below and in the next chapter.

27. Cf. Coca-Cola Co. v. Gemini Rising, Inc., 346 F. Supp. 1183, 1189 (E.D.N.Y. 1972).

28. But with moral rights thinking having infiltrated U.S. copyright law (see Chapter 10), there is now a copyright counterpart to trademark tarnishment. More on this shortly.

29. See J. Thomas McCarthy, *McCarthy on Trademarks and Unfair Competition* §§ 24:104, 24:105 (4th ed. 2002). Compare Hormel Foods Corp. v. Jim Henson Productions, Inc., 73 F.3d 497 (2d Cir. 1996). The movie *Muppet Treasure Island* introduced a character in the form of a wild boar named Spa'am. The manufacturer of Spam objected to the Muppet character. Had the character appeared only in the movie, the analysis would have been identical to that of a copyright parody. The producer of the movie, however, also planned to sell merchandise involving the Spa'am character. But not only was the likelihood of confusion between the luncheon meat and the Muppet character nil; there was no tarnishment because Spa'am was a wholesome Muppet, not a junkie, criminal, or other questionable character.

criticizing it, the trademark holder may fear a negative effect on his revenues. This has happened when homosexual groups have tried to use popular trademarks (such as "Pink Panther") to identify themselves.[30] In such cases the invocation of the fair use defense might impair the trademark owner's goodwill, especially if consumers thought the owner had licensed the offensive use. The more interesting case, and the one more difficult to explain on the basis of the usual economic assumption of rational behavior, is why consumers who realized that a homosexual group was using the "Pink Panther" trademark without the authorization of its owner would transfer their negative view of homosexuality to that owner—as some would.

If it is irrational for people to be thus influenced by arbitrary associations, it is an irrationality so deeply rooted in human psychology as to make a claim for recognition by law. It is related to the cognitive quirk that psychologists call the availability heuristic, which refers to the fact that people tend to attach disproportionate weight to salient features of a product, event, or activity.[31] A trademark seeks to economize on information costs by providing a compact, memorable, and unambiguous identifier of a product or service. The economy is less when, because the trademark has other associations,[32] a person seeing it must think for a moment before recognizing it as the mark of the product or service. There is an analogy to the objection that language purists make to using "disinterested" as a synonym for "uninterested": it blurs the original meaning of disinterested (which is "impartial").

Might a similar notion, lacking though it does any name or official standing in copyright law, explain the cases in which erotic or obscene parodies are held to be copyright infringements? The notion would be that the association of, say, Mickey Mouse with sex would blur the image of childish innocence

30. See Rosemary J. Coombe, "Author/izing the Celebrity: Publicity Rights, Postmodern Politics, and Unauthorized Genders," in *The Construction of Authorship: Textual Appropriation in Law and Literature* 101 (Martha Woodmansee and Peter Jaszi eds. 1994).

31. See, for example, Amos Tversky and Daniel Kahneman, "Judgment under Uncertainty: Heuristics and Biases," in *Heuristics and Biases: The Psychology of Intuitive Judgment* 3, 11–13 (Thomas Gilovich et al. eds. 2002); Paul H. Rubin, *Darwinian Politics: The Evolutionary Origin of Freedom* 169–171 (2002). The availability heuristic is not necessarily irrational. "Heuristics" are reasoning shortcuts; they may be quite consistent with rationality, as argued in Gerd Gigerenzer, Peter M. Todd, and ABC (Center for Adaptive Behavior and Cognition) Research Group, *Simple Heuristics That Make Us Smart*, ch. 6 (1999). Specifically, the availability heuristic may be consistent with rationality once one acknowledges that imaginative reconstruction requires more "effort" (that is, cost) than immediate perception; in other words, once thinking is understood to be a costly activity. See Gary S. Becker, "Preferences and Values," in Becker, *Accounting for Tastes* 3, 11 (1996).

32. They need not be offensive, yet, as we'll see in the next chapter, they may still impair the communicative value of the trademark. Such cases fall under the rubric of "blurring" rather than "tarnishment."

that Walt Disney sought to create for his animated cartoon characters. Against this it can be argued that creators of intellectual property should not be allowed to control the public image of their property by forbidding others to suggest variant images of it. The argument becomes decisive when we consider that the application of the concept of dilution to copyrighted works would imply a right of action even if the parodist did not take any of the copyrighted elements of the original work: suppose someone made a movie called *Bambi* but the central character was a prostitute rather than a fawn. This would be an example of a parody that was not a derivative work.

The foregoing discussion points up a difference in the appropriate treatment of copyright and trademark parodies under the doctrine of fair use. A difference not in all cases, because trademarks can be targets of parodic criticism just like copyrighted works,[33] but in cases where, for example, a firm defames or disparages a competitor or its product in the form of a parody, or where a good-natured parody is used to appropriate the goodwill built up by the competitor.[34] However, with the gradual spread of the moral rights doctrine of European law into American law (see Chapter 10), degrading uses of a copyrighted work may become legally problematic, though presumably the critic's privilege, which has First Amendment overtones, will survive.

The Coca-Cola example suggests an argument that would, if accepted, paradoxically recognize a broader defense of fair use for off-color and otherwise disreputable copyright and trademark parodies than for decorous ones. Granted that a shirt stamped "I Like Cocaine" or an obscene version of Walt Disney's cartoons would be a derivative work of the original trademarked or copyrighted work, it is a derivative work that the owner of the original *could not himself* exploit directly or indirectly because of the ill will that would accrue to him from the respectable segment of society. The work can be developed, and its social benefits (for in an economic analysis the preferences of the vulgar count in the calculation of social welfare along with the preferences of the refined) thus realized, only if the trademark or copyright owner is *forbidden* to control disreputable derivative works.

The objections to the proposal include the difficulty of defining "disreputable" for this purpose and the fact that allowing free use of copyrighted works for disreputable parodies would subsidize those parodies at the expense of others. And yet the subsidy might be appropriate to offset the dis-

33. See, for example, Mattel, Inc. v. MCA Records, Inc., 296 F.3d 894, 901, 906–907 (9th Cir. 2002).

34. The latter is a possible interpretation of the defendant's choice of the name "Lardashe" for its line of jeans for large women in Jordache Enterprises, Inc. v. Hogg Wyld, Ltd., 828 F.2d 1482 (10th Cir. 1987).

incentive of the creator of the original work to produce this type of derivative work.

The major objection to allowing the erotic parody to invoke fair use is different. It is, as mentioned earlier, that erotic parodies fill a part of the demand for the parodied work itself and thus reduce the copyright holder's revenues on sales of the original work and not just of derivative works. This is not always the case, however. The article in the pornographic magazine *High Society* entitled "L.L. Beam's Back-To-School-Sex-Catalog" was not a substitute for the L.L. Bean catalog and was therefore correctly held to be within the fair use defense to trademark infringement.[35] Had *Hustler*, say, used the parody to advertise its magazine, the case might have come out differently. For *Hustler* to make fun of the catalog (like the author of the article) was privileged parody. But if *Hustler* were merely using the article to promote sales of its magazine, this would be an infringement, since there would be no obstacle in that case to negotiating a license with the copyright owner.

The Cases

Let us see whether the distinctions suggested by economic analysis are mirrored in the cases. A complete answer would require us to trudge through them one by one, a tedious procedure even though there are remarkably few reported cases involving trademark and copyright parodies—we have found only 77 since 1950 after eliminating duplication (the same case in different procedural stages, or multiple suits to enjoin the same parody).[36] We shall limit ourselves to a few general observations about the cases.

With the exception of the *Koons* litigation, mentioned earlier and discussed at length in Chapter 9, in all the reported cases both the parody and the parodied work belong to popular rather than to high culture even though there is an enormous body of high-brow parody.[37] Such a parody will rarely infringe

35. L.L. Bean, Inc. v. Drake Publishers, Inc., 811 F.2d 26 (1st Cir. 1987).

36. A list of the cases is available from us on request. Twenty-nine of the 77 are appellate decisions (including the one Supreme Court decision, Campbell v. Acuff-Rose Music, Inc., note 2 above), the rest district court decisions. We count as "parody" cases burlesques and satires as well as "pure" parodies. In several cases that we do not include in our count or discuss, either parody though not present is discussed, see, for example, Ty, Inc. v. Publications International Ltd., 292 F.3d 512 (7th Cir. 2002), or the contention that the defendant's work is in any sense a parody (including, to repeat, the broad sense that encompasses satires and burlesques) is correctly rejected. See, for example, Castle Rock Entertainment, Inc. v. Carol Publishing Group, Inc., 150 F.3d 132 (2d Cir. 1998). We also exclude cases in which the parodist is sued for defamation.

37. See, for example, *Parodies: An Anthology from Chaucer to Beerbohm—and After* (Dwight MacDonald ed. 1960); Chatman, note 3 above.

the copyright on the parodied work even prima facie (that is, without regard to the privilege of fair use). The work parodied—whether a work of music, of art, or more commonly of literature—will usually be rich in identifiable stylistic characteristics that can without infringement be copied in order to remind the reader of the original—for remember that style is not copyrightable. Also, high-brow parody is more likely than low-brow to criticize the original work, because high-brow audiences are more interested in issues of tastes and standards, more snobbish, and more critical than popular audiences are.[38] And a high-brow parody rarely replaces the demand for the original. The clearest example is parodies of novels. Few parodies are lengthy because the comic exaggeration that is the essential technique of parody pales rapidly, and so the parody of a novel will usually be too short to replace the original (there is an analogy to the book review). *The Wind Done Gone* is an exception, being of novel length—but then it is not a work of *comic* exaggeration of the parodied original. Finally, when high-brow parody uses an original work as a weapon rather than as a target, often the original is a work in the public domain and the parodist's point is precisely the decline in standards since some Golden Age of refinement. It would not have suited T. S. Eliot's purposes in *The Waste Land* to quote works recent enough for copyright to have subsisted in them.

Trademark cases predominate over copyright cases by a margin of 53 to 33.[39] In both groups the alleged infringer wins in roughly half the cases.[40] Parodies that are erotic or off-color are found in 12 of the 77 cases (7 of the trademark and 6 of the copyright cases)[41]—almost 16 percent. This may seem

38. A low-brow exception is *Mad Comics'* parody of the television series *M.A.S.H.*, discussed in Ziva Ben-Porat, "Method in MADness: Notes on the Structure of Parody, Based on MAD TV Satires," 1 *Poetics Today* 245 (1979). Of a more common type is the parody of the Icelandic sagas in the quondam television series *Monty Python's Flying Circus*. Probably few members of the television audience had heard of the Icelandic sagas, much less read any of them. What the audience saw was not a parody of a literary work but rather a madcap satire of stereotypical Scandinavian ethnic characteristics, such as stolidity and bleakness.

39. The sum exceeds 77 because 9 cases involve charges of both copyright and trademark infringement and so are listed in both groups.

40. The copyright owner won 17 of the 33 copyright cases and the trademark owner won 25 of the 53 trademark cases, so that the overall score was 42 to 44. That in litigation between private parties (as opposed to cases in which the government is a party) the plaintiff will, as in our sample, win about half the cases is predicted on economic grounds in George L. Priest and Benjamin Klein, "The Selection of Disputes for Litigation," 13 *Journal of Legal Studies* 1 (1984). (But we shall discuss a counterexample—patent litigation—in Chapter 12.) By "copyright owner" or "trademark owner" we mean of course the owner of the copyright or trademark on the parodied work. By "won" we mean that the plaintiff obtained either preliminary or final relief, or at least a reversal of a decision for the defendant.

41. Again the sum exceeds the total number of erotic parody cases because of the presence of a dual copyright-trademark case.

a high figure, but is not surprising because such parodies are quite likely to offend the copyright or trademark owner or his audience/customers.

Of particular interest is the breakdown between cases in which the parodied work is a target and cases in which it is a weapon to attack or criticize other things, or perhaps just an effort to create a humorous work. The heavy preponderance of both the copyright and the trademark cases is in the target category: for the copyright cases the figures are 29 target and 5 weapon and for the trademark cases the figures are 51 and 6, so in the sample as a whole target cases predominate by a score of 80 to 11.[42] The explanation may be, as suggested earlier, that a market transaction is feasible in weapon but not in target cases, permitting a sharper definition of property rights and therefore reducing the uncertainty that begets litigation, though a better explanation is probably just the fact that the target form of parody is more harmful to the owner of the parodied work than the weapon form. At all events, the defense of fair use, which qualifies the copyright or trademark owner's property right, has no proper place in a weapon case,[43] and so we are not surprised that the copyright owner won 8 of the 11 weapon cases (73 percent), whereas the parodist won 39 of the 71 target cases (55 percent).[44]

42. Summing to 91 rather than 77 because 9 of the cases involved both trademark and copyright and 5 involved a parodied work that was both a target and a weapon.

43. But prima facie infringement is less likely in a trademark weapon case than in a copyright weapon case, since in a trademark case the issue is not the amount copied as such (unless dilution is charged) but whether consumers are likely to be confused as to the source of the defendant's parody. See Cliff Notes, Inc. v. Bantam Doubleday Dell Publishing Group, Inc., 886 F.2d 490 (2d Cir. 1989). By the same token, however, prima facie infringement is more likely in a trademark parody case than in a copyright parody case if, as in People for the Ethical Treatment of Animals v. Doughney, 263 F.3d 359 (4th Cir. 2001), and Anheuser-Busch, Inc. v. Balducci Publications, 28 F.3d 769 (8th Cir. 1994), the parodist fails to make clear that he is not the author or affiliated with the author of the original work.

44. The weapon and target cases sum to 82 because there are 5 dual cases.

7

The Economics of Trademark Law

Trademarks are a distinct form of intellectual property from patents and copyrights. In some respects trademark law is closer to tort law (indeed, from a technical legal standpoint, trademark law is part of the branch of tort law known as "unfair competition") than to property law, though there is considerable overlap and the basic economics of property continues to be relevant. Not only is trademark law highly amenable to economic analysis, but the legal protection of trademarks has a more secure efficiency rationale than the legal protection of inventive and expressive works.

To oversimplify somewhat, a trademark is a word, symbol, or other signifier used to distinguish a good or service produced by one firm from the goods or services of other firms. Thus "Sanka" designates a decaffeinated coffee made by General Foods, "Windows" a family of computer operating systems manufactured by Microsoft Corporation, and "Xerox" the dry copiers made by Xerox Corporation. "Bib"—the "Michelin Man"—is the symbol of tires made by the Michelin Company. A stylized penguin is the symbol of a line of paperback books published by Penguin Books; a distinctively shaped green bottle is a trademark[1] of the producer of Perrier bottled water; the color pink is a trademark for residential insulation manufactured by Owens-Corning.

The Economic Function of Trademarks

Suppose—admittedly a rather dated example in this era of gourmet coffee—that you happen to prefer decaffeinated coffee made by General Foods. If General Foods' brand had no name, then to order it in a restaurant or grocery store you would have to ask for "the decaffeinated coffee made by General Foods." This takes longer to say, requires you to remember more, and requires the waiter or clerk to read and remember more than if you can just ask for "Sanka." The problem would be even more serious if General Foods

1. In trademark jargon, distinctive packaging and labeling that function as trademarks—in other words, the use of appearance rather than words as the identifier of source—are "trade dress." But to keep our exposition simple we ignore this terminological refinement.

made more than one brand of decaffeinated coffee—as in fact it does. The benefit of the brand name is thus analogous to that of designating individuals by names rather than by descriptions.

To perform its naming function a trademark or brand name (these are rough synonyms) must not be duplicated. To allow another maker of decaffeinated coffee to sell its coffee under the name "Sanka" would destroy the benefit of the name in identifying a brand of decaffeinated coffee made by General Foods. (Whether there might be offsetting benefits we consider later.) But the existence of that benefit presupposes a certain identity or continuity in the brand. Consider the analogy of giving people names in order to make it easier to distinguish among different people. This would be of little value if individuals changed so much from day to day that the person named "John McInerney" was really a different person today from what he had been yesterday. Likewise the benefits of trademarks in reducing the cost to consumers of distinguishing among brands of a product require that the producer of a trademarked good maintain a consistent quality of his output, that is, that he make sure that from the consumer's standpoint it really is the same product from unit to unit and time to time.

Suppose, then, that a consumer has a favorable experience with brand X and wants to buy it again. Or suppose he wants to buy brand X because it has been recommended by a reliable source or because he has had a favorable experience with another brand produced by the same producer. Rather than reading the fine print on the package to determine whether the description matches his understanding of brand X, or investigating the attributes of all the different versions of the product (of which X is one brand) to determine which one is brand X, the consumer will find it much less costly to search by identifying the relevant trademark and purchasing the corresponding brand. For this strategy to work, however, not only must it be cheaper to search for the right trademark than for the desired attributes of the good; past experience also must be a good predictor of the likely outcome of current consumption choices—that is, the brand must exhibit consistent quality. A trademark conveys information that allows the consumer to say to himself, "I need not investigate the attributes of the brand I am about to purchase because the trademark is a shorthand way of telling me that the attributes are the same as that of the brand I enjoyed earlier."[2]

---

2. See John F. Coverdale, "Trademarks and Generic Words: An Effect-on-Competition Test," 51 *University of Chicago Law Review* 868 (1984); and for empirical evidence in support of the consumer-information theory of brand identification that underlies our analysis of trademarks, see I. P. L. Png and David Reitman, "Why Are Some Products Branded and Others Not?" 38 *Journal of Law and Economics* 207 (1995). It should be noted that the benefits of a trademark to the consumer need not depend on whether the trademark identifies a particular brand or the producer of that brand. Consumers benefit even if they are unable to identify the producer of a brand they desire to purchase—even if the good is from a single anonymous source.

The value of a trademark to the firm that uses it to designate its brand is the saving in consumers' search costs made possible by the information that the trademark conveys or embodies about the quality of the firm's brand. The brand's reputation for quality and thus the trademark's value depend on the firm's expenditures on product quality, service, advertising, and so on. Once the reputation is created, the firm will obtain greater profits because repeat purchases and word-of-mouth references will add to sales and because consumers will be willing to pay a higher price in exchange for a savings in search costs and an assurance of consistent quality.

Less obviously, a firm's incentive to invest resources in developing and maintaining (as through advertising) a strong mark depends on its ability to maintain consistent product quality. In other words, trademarks have a self-enforcing feature. They are valuable only insofar as they denote consistent quality, and so only a firm able to maintain consistent quality has an incentive to expend the resources necessary to develop a strong trademark. When a brand's quality is inconsistent, consumers learn that the trademark does not enable them to relate their past to their future consumption experiences; the trademark does not reduce their search costs; they are unwilling to pay more for the branded than for the unbranded good; and so the firm will not earn a sufficient return on its expenditures on promoting the trademark to justify making them. A similar argument shows that a firm with a valuable trademark will be reluctant to lower the quality of its brand because it would suffer a capital loss on its investment in the trademark.[3]

The benefits of trademarks in lowering consumer search costs presuppose legal protection because the cost of duplicating someone else's trademark is small and the incentive to incur this cost in the absence of legal impediments will be greater the stronger the trademark. The free-riding competitor will, at little cost, capture profits associated with a strong trademark because some consumers will assume (at least in the short run) that the free rider's and the original trademark holder's brands are identical. If the law does not prevent it, free riding may destroy the information capital embodied in a trademark, and the prospect of free riding may therefore eliminate the incentive to develop a valuable trademark in the first place.

Some Economics of Language

An entirely different benefit of trademark protection derives from the incentives that such protection creates to invest resources not in maintaining qual-

---

3. See Benjamin Klein and Keith B. Leffler, "The Role of Market Forces in Assuring Contractual Performance," 89 *Journal of Political Economy* 615 (1981).

ity but in inventing new words[4] or symbols or, less clearly, design features used as trademarks, such as the shape and color of the Perrier bottle or the shape of the Ferrari automobile; but for the moment we confine our attention to words. Trademarks improve the language in three ways. They increase the stock of names of things, thus economizing on communication and information costs in the ways just suggested. They create new generic words—words that denote entire products, not just individual brands. "Aspirin," "brassiere," "cellophane," "escalator," "thermos," "yo-yo," "dry ice," and a number of other names of common goods were once trademarks—and, whatever courts may say, "Kleenex," "Xerox," "Velcro," and "Rollerblades" are widely used to denote entire products as well as particular brands.[5] Trademarks further enrich language by creating words or phrases that people value for their intrinsic pleasingness as well as their information value, such as "Pheremon" perfume and "Swan's Down" cake mix. A study in 1985 found that the frequency of brand names in best-selling American novels was increasing rapidly,[6] with generic names achieving an impressive frequency of 160 generic names per 10,000 words (1.6 percent).

The importance of trademarks to language is only modest, however, because the contribution they make to the language is mainly a byproduct of the contribution that the products they designate make to the world of things. "Rolls Royce," though undoubtedly a trademark, has a linguistic value that goes beyond its use as a source identifier, as in such phrases as "the Rolls Royce of baby strollers"—an example, by the way, of how a brand name can add to the language even without becoming generic. But what is important is not the word "Rolls Royce" but the fact that there is a make of automobiles that signifies opulence. It would have to be called *something*, and whatever it was called would occupy the linguistic space actually occupied by "Rolls Royce." This point will help us explain important features of trade-

---

4. A study of 2,000 brand names concludes that they are formed on the same linguistic principles as other words. See Jean Praninskas, *Trade Name Creation: Processes and Patterns* 101 (1968). A fascinating older study that reaches a similar conclusion is Louise Pound, "Word-Coinage and Modern Trade-Names," 4 *Dialect Notes* 29 (1913).

5. See Adrian Akmajian, Richard A. Demers, and Robert M. Harnish, *Linguistics: An Introduction to Language and Communication* 70 (1984), which gives "Kleenex" and "Xerox" as examples of how brand names can become part of ordinary language.

6. See Monroe Friedman, "The Changing Language of a Consumer Society: Brand Name Usage in Popular American Novels in the Postwar Era," 11 *Journal of Consumer Research* 927 (1985). For similar findings relating to plays and popular music, respectively, see Monroe Friedman, "Commercial Influences in Popular Literature: An Empirical Study of Brand Name Usage in American and British Hit Plays in the Postwar Era," 4 *Empirical Studies of the Arts* 63 (1986), and Monroe Friedman, "Commercial Influences in the Lyrics of Popular American Music of the Postwar Era," 20 *Journal of Consumer Affairs* 193 (1986).

mark law—such as the termination of trademark protection if the mark becomes generic—that would be inexplicable if trademarks provided the same sort of intellectual enrichment that patents and copyrights do. But the explanation will require a detour through a neglected area of economics, the economics of language.

The goal of a communication system is to minimize the sum of the costs of avoiding misunderstanding and the costs of communicating. Suppose there is a word for snow and a word for falling, and now the question is, should a word be coined for "falling snow"? In favor of the new word is that unless it is very long, it will take less time to utter, read, and write; against it is that people will have to learn and remember another word. The more common a term is, the likelier that the benefits of having a single word will exceed the costs, not only because the gains from shortening the term will be greater but also because the cost of learning and remembering a word is less if it is in common use. The use of a word rather than a periphrasis to name a brand illustrates the same point.

Both examples are closely related to a statistical observation made many years ago: the length of words is inverse to their frequency.[7] It might seem that rather than frequently used words being shorter than infrequently used ones, all words would be short in order to economize on communication costs. But length is an important dimension along which words vary and so are distinguished one from another, and this dimension would be lost if all words were short. It makes economic sense for frequently used words to be short and infrequently used ones long; then total length is minimized without sacrificing distinctiveness and so increasing the number of errors (misunderstanding). More generally, the drive to make language simple is balanced by the desire to avoid ambiguities and confusions that result from lack of differentiation.[8]

Here are some other examples of efficient language rules.

1. Irregularities of grammar and spelling are more common in frequent than infrequent words.[9] The more frequently used a word is, the easier it is to learn by rote, and hence the less important it is that people be able to

7. See George Kingsley Zipf, *Human Behavior and the Principle of Least Effort: An Introduction to Human Ecology* 24 (1949).

8. See, for example, Jean Aitchison, *Language Change: Progress or Decay?* 201, 226 (1981). Analytically the tradeoff in communication theory between cost (minimized by short words) and accuracy (which requires differentiation, hence long and short words) is similar to the tradeoff in the economics of procedure between error costs (minimized by procedural formality) and administrative costs (minimized by dispensing with formal procedures). See Richard A. Posner, *Economic Analysis of Law*, ch. 21 (6th ed. 2003).

9. See, for example, Theodora Bynon, *Historical Linguistics* 42–43 (1977).

construct the word by the application of a rule. Everyone knows that the past participle of the verb "to be" is "been"; but it is convenient to be able to construct the past participle of "excogitate" by rule rather than have to memorize it.

2. Pronunciation changes faster than spelling because changes in pronunciation do not reduce the intelligibility of existing reading matter, which represents a vast and valuable capital stock of knowledge.

3. Perfect synonyms are rare; they would increase learning costs without adding to the communication resources of the language, except that synonyms make it easier to write poetry that rhymes or has regular meter.

4. Pronouns, which in all languages known to us are short, are an ingenious device for economizing on the length of words, namely the proper nouns that the pronoun substitutes for.

Examples of the efficiency of language rules could be multiplied,[10] but we have said enough to establish the only point that bears importantly on trademarks—that language is created and maintained and creatively altered without a system of property rights in words, grammatical forms, and so on. (Remember that words cannot be copyrighted; neither can grammatical forms.) Of course the costs of enforcing a system of property rights in words—the costs, for example, of a system under which the coiner of a word (such as Jeremy Bentham, who coined "codification," "minimize," and several other words still in common use) obtained a property right in it—would be immense. This may be a sufficient explanation for why there is no such system. But whatever the reason, its absence seems not to be missed. We do not find many people worrying that language may not be an efficient medium of communication after all.

Of particular relevance to the economics of trademarks, the creation of new words for new things seems not to be retarded by the fact that the coiner of a word can obtain no property right. Either the costs of thinking up new words are slight, or the incentives to do so, independent of any direct compensation, are great. The former seems important for proper names (naming a baby, for example) and for terms of art, the latter for trademarks; if a producer wants to market a new brand effectively, he needs a distinctive name—unless he is trying to pass off his brand as someone else's.

It's a good guess, therefore, that we do not need trademark protection just to be sure of having enough words, though we may need patent protection to be sure of having enough inventions or copyright protection to be sure of having enough books, movies, and musical compositions. Computer operating systems, which are a language though one that is "spoken" and "read" by

10. See, for example, Aitchison, note 8 above, at 152–155 and ch. 8.

computer chips and programs rather than by human beings, are copyrightable; maybe any invented language, such as Esperanto, would be. But the investment required to create a whole new language is much greater than that required to create a single new word, so the case for property rights is stronger in the former instance than in the latter.

Our analysis also suggests that the universe from which trademarks are picked is very large. The availability of alternative words, symbols, and so on to those appropriated for use as particular trademarks will play an important role in our formal analysis, where we denote it by W. It turns out that a high W is a precondition to a system of trademarks that is effective in lowering consumer search costs.

The Social Costs of Trademarks

What the law terms a "fanciful" mark, such as "Exxon" and "Kodak," has no information content except to denote a specific producer or brand, and so its appropriation as a designator of the products of particular firms does not deny society access to useful information. Since, as we shall explain, a trademark "goes with" the brand rather than being salable separately, the transfer of the mark is automatically effected by a transfer of the rights to make the branded product, as by a sale or licensing of production rights or assets; there are no additional transaction costs. And unlike the undiscovered continent or hunt for sunken treasure discussed in Chapter 1, rent seeking to stake out a trademark is not a problem, provided that the "banking" of trademarks is not permitted (more on this later). The number of distinctive yet pronounceable combinations of letters to form words that will serve as a suitable trademark is very large,[11] implying a high degree of substitutability and hence only a slight value in exchange. And although the costs of legal enforcement of trademarks are not trivial, they do not include the cost in inefficient resource allocation from driving a wedge between price and marginal cost. A trademark is not a public good; it has social value only when used to designate a single brand. If A develops a strong trademark for his brand that other firms are free to affix to their own brands, which compete with A's, the information capital embodied in A's trademark will soon be destroyed. Unauthorized copies of a copyrighted work (a classic public good), in contrast, will not (unless there are congestion externalities, an issue we take up in the next chapter) destroy

11. Two qualifications, tugging in opposite directions, should be noted. First, not all producers want their trademark to be pronounceable—trademarks that consist of acronyms, such as "MS-DOS," often are not. Second, a producer that wants to market its brand worldwide under the same name will have to avoid letter combinations that are offensive or inappropriate in any of the world's languages; and there are many such combinations. A famous example is Ford's effort to market its "Nova" brand of car in Mexico; in Spanish, "no va" means "doesn't go."

the value of the work, though they may reduce the incentive to create future works.

At least in the case of a fanciful mark, then, the social costs of legal protection of trademarks are modest,[12] both absolutely and in relation to the benefits discussed earlier. Other kinds of mark involve higher but still manageable costs, and marks that involve costs in excess of their benefits are denied legal protection.

But are we ignoring the danger that by fostering product differentiation trademarks create deadweight costs, whether of monopoly or (excessive) competition? We have been assuming that a trademark induces its owner to invest in maintaining uniform product quality; an alternative interpretation is that it induces him to spend money on creating, through advertising and promotion, a spurious image of high quality that enables monopoly rents to be obtained by deflecting consumers from lower-price substitutes of equal or even higher quality. In the case of products manufactured according to a uniform formula, such as aspirin or household liquid bleach, the ability of name-brand goods (Bayer aspirin, Clorox bleach) to command higher prices than generic (nonbranded) goods has seemed to some economists and more lawyers an example of the power of brand advertising to bamboozle the public and thereby promote monopoly.[13] Brand advertising *presupposes* trademarks—they are what enable a producer readily to identify his brand to the consumer.

This concern has gained no foothold in trademark law. The implicit economic model that guides that law is our model, in which trademarks lower consumers' search costs by providing them with valuable information about brands and encourage quality control rather than create social waste and consumer deception. The hostile view of brand advertising anyway is unsound.[14]

---

12. Though this depends on the scope of the protection; but at the moment we are just considering protection against actually or potentially misleading appropriations of a trademark by a competitor.

13. See, for example, Borden, Inc. v. FTC, 674 F.2d 498 (6th Cir. 1982), vacated as moot, 461 U.S. 940 (1983); William S. Comanor and Thomas A. Wilson, *Advertising and Market Power,* ch. 3 (1974); Richard Schmalensee, "On the Use of Economic Models in Antitrust: The *ReaLemon* Case," 127 *University of Pennsylvania Law Review* 994 (1979); Warren G. Lavey, "Patents, Copyrights, and Trademarks as Sources of Market Power in Antitrust Cases," 27 *Antitrust Bulletin* 433, 448–451 (1982). More on this example below and in Chapter 11, where we note the striking example of brand-name drugs that continue to sell at the same high price as when they were under patent after the patent expires and they face competition from chemically identical generics; in such a case the trademark is easily imagined to be the engine of a continued monopoly.

14. See Klein and Leffler, note 3 above, and references cited there; see also Steven N. Wiggins and David G. Raboy, "Price Premia to Name Brands: An Empirical Analysis," 44 *Journal of Industrial Economics* 377 (1996).

The fact that two goods have the same chemical formula does not make them of equal quality to even the most coolly rational consumer. The consumer will not be interested in the formula as such but in the actual manufactured product that he will be consuming, and he may therefore be willing to pay a premium for greater assurance that the product will actually be manufactured to the specifications of the formula.[15] Trademarks enable him to economize on a real cost because he spends less time searching to get the quality he wants. The rejection by trademark law of a monopoly theory of trademarks is thus a mark in favor of the economic rationality of that law.

A Formal Model of the Economics of Trademarks

We define the full price (π) of a good X to the buyer as its money price (P) plus the search costs (H) he incurs in learning about the relevant characteristics of X.[16] That is,

$$\pi = P + H(T, Y, W). \tag{1}$$

H depends in part on information provided by the firm to the buyer by means of its trademark T. The more resources the firm pours into developing and promoting its mark, the stronger the mark will be (that is, the greater T will be) and the smaller H will be.

Two kinds of information are generated by T. The first is information that enables the consumer to identify the source of the good; for example, knowing that Crest toothpaste comes from a single source even if one does not know that Procter and Gamble is that source. Information about source economizes on search costs by lowering the cost of selecting goods on the basis of past experience or the recommendation of other consumers. The second kind of information is information about the product itself. For example, a "descriptive" mark (of which more later) may, in addition to identifying source, describe some properties of the brand; this information also lowers search costs.

15. This is probably a factor in the drug example in note 13 above.

16. Our model is similar to that in Isaac Ehrlich and Lawrence Fisher, "The Derived Demand for Advertising: A Theoretical and Empirical Investigation," 72 *American Economic Review* 366 (1982), which treats advertising as a variable that reduces search costs and thus the full price of the good. Their model builds in turn on the approach to advertising in Gary S. Becker and George J. Stigler, "De Gustibus Non Est Disputandum," 67 *American Economic Review* 76 (1977). More recently, Becker, jointly with Kevin Murphy, has proposed a different theory of advertising, one in which advertisements are complements of the advertised good. See Gary S. Becker and Kevin M. Murphy, "A Simple Theory of Advertising as a Good or Bad," 108 *Quarterly Journal of Economics* 941 (1993). Their article does not discuss trademarks, which we continue to believe are best interpreted by reference to consumer search costs.

H also depends on factors other than *T*, such as the amount of advertising, the technology available to the firm for producing information, the number of competitors (because search costs may be lower the fewer competitors there are, with the result that the benefits of trademarks in providing source information are likely to be lower when there is one or only a few producers), and the cost of the buyer's time. We denote these other factors by *Y*, but because our interest is in trademarks we shall ignore them.

H also, and more importantly, depends on *W*, the earlier-mentioned index of the availability of words and other symbols that the firm can use as its trademark.[17] *W* interacts with the firm's trademark to provide information to consumers on relevant attributes of the firm's product. Most of the time *W* will be too large to affect consumer search costs noticeably. But if a single firm is given the exclusive right to use the word or words that identify an entire product, as distinct from an individual brand of the product, competition with other firms that make the same product will be impaired. Thus, if a particular manufacturer of personal computers could not use the terms "personal computer" or "PC" in its advertising or labeling because another firm had the exclusive right to these terms, it might have to describe its product as "a machine capable of doing word processing and high-speed calculations and other data manipulations, using a central processing unit," etc. An even more elaborate periphrasis would be necessary if "word processing" had also been appropriated. Because it is harder to recall long than short phrases, a lengthy description may well convey less usable information about the firm's product than a single word or a short phrase, so search costs will rise. Thus the greater *W* is (that is, the larger the universe of possible names for *X*) the greater the potential productivity of a trademark in minimizing consumer search costs.

We can write the profit function of the producer of a trademarked good as

$$I = P(T)X - C(X) - RT \tag{2}$$

where *I* is the firm's net income (profit), $P(T)$ is the price the firm charges for its good (X), $C(X)$ is the cost to the firm of producing *X*, and *R* (assumed to be constant) is the cost to the firm of producing a unit of *T*. Because the benefits from a trademark are not exhausted in a single period, a trademark is a form of capital, and so in a more complete model we would have to take account of depreciation, distinguish net from gross investment, and so on. Instead, for the sake of simplicity, we assume a one-period model, but the simplification does not affect our analysis.

We assume a positive and decreasing marginal product for *T* in lowering

17. To simplify notation we write $H = H(T)$ despite the fact that *H* also depends on *Y* and *W*.

search costs (that is, $H_t < 0$ and $H_{tt} > 0$) and an increasing marginal cost for X ($C_x > 0$ and $C_{xx} > 0$). Substituting $\pi - H(T)$ for P yields

$$I = [\pi - H(T)]X - C(X) - RT. \tag{3}$$

Assuming a competitive industry (that is, one in which each firm takes π as given), the firm will maximizes its profits when it picks X and T such that

$$[\pi - H(T)] - C_x = 0 \tag{4}$$

and

$$-H_t X - R = 0. \tag{5}$$

Equation (4) expresses the usual equality between price and marginal cost while equation (5) equates the marginal return from a one-unit increase in T to its cost.[18]

Figures 7.1 and 7.2 help to convey an intuitive understanding of these equilibrium conditions. Figure 7.1 shows that the price of a unit of X is independent of the quantity of X (because the firm is assumed to be operating in a competitive market) but is greater the stronger the firm's trademark ($T^1 > T^* > T^0$), since T in effect substitutes for search costs that would otherwise be borne by the consumer and so makes X more valuable. The firm in Figure 7.1 is operating at the minimum point on its average cost curve (including trademark costs) and is thus earning zero profits. Figure 7.2 shows that the benefits of an additional unit of T depend both on the productivity of T ($=$ the value of $-H_t$) in lowering search costs and on the amount of X sold. An increase in T makes all units of X more valuable to consumers. The profit-maximizing values of X and T in Figures 7.1 and 7.2 are X^* and T^*, and the resulting equilibrium price is P^*.

Although in our model each firm is a price taker with respect to π (the full price of its good), the nominal price of X—the particular firm's brand of the good—will differ among firms. Firms with strong trademarks (lower Hs) will command higher prices for their brands not because of any market power but because the search costs associated with their brand are lower. For example, if

18. In the monopoly case equation (4) becomes

$$P[1 - 1/(e \cdot s)] - C_x = 0,$$

where e denotes the elasticity of demand with respect to π and s denotes P's share of π. Since output (X) is lower under monopoly, so is T (from equation (5)). This is not surprising. The principal benefit of a trademark—source identification—is less if there is only one producer. The monopoly model is less useful in analyzing trademark law than the competitive one because a number of trademark doctrines deal with the effect of granting exclusive rights to one competitor on the ability of others to compete effectively.

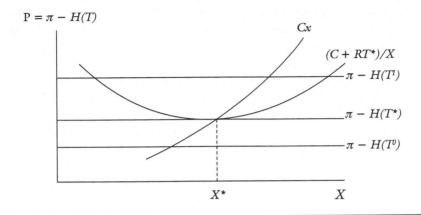

$P = \pi - H(T)$

Cx

$(C + RT^*)/X$

$\pi - H(T^1)$

$\pi - H(T^*)$

$\pi - H(T^0)$

X^* X

Figure 7.1.

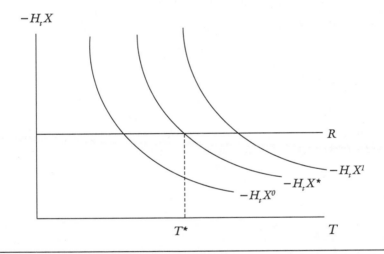

$-H_t X$

R

$-H_t X^1$

$-H_t X^*$

$-H_t X^0$

T^* T

Figure 7.2.

the full price of X is $20, a firm with $H = $10 will sell its brand of X for $10 while a firm with $H = $5 will sell its brand for $15. In general the equilibrium values of X, T, and P will be greater the greater π, the smaller H, the greater the marginal product of T, and the lower the marginal costs of X and T. Also, the greater the availability of words and other identifiers for use as trademarks (the greater W is), the lower will the values of H and H_t tend to be for a given value of T and hence the greater will be the equilibrium values of X, T, and P; and because X is greater, the equilibrium value of π will be lower.

We construct an industry supply curve for X with respect to π in Figure 7.3. For each π we calculate the firm's profit-maximizing values of X and T from equations (4) and (5) and sum the individual firms' outputs at each π to obtain the industry supply curve. It is positively sloped because a higher full price will induce each firm to expand its output of X both through the direct effect of a higher π on P and the indirect effect of the initial increase in X, which leads to a higher T and hence a further increase in P. Figure 7.3 shows the equilibrium full price and output at the intersection of the industry demand and supply curves (D and S).

We can incorporate quality differences among brands into the formal model by redefining the variables π, P, and H on a per unit of quality rather than per unit of output basis. Let Q be an index of quality of good X and $C(Q, X)$ the total cost of the output of the good, which we assume increases at an increasing rate for both Q and X. The firm would then want to maximize

$$I = [\pi - H(T)]QX - C(Q, X) - RT \tag{6}$$

with respect to X, Q, and T. The first-order conditions are

$$PQ - C_X = 0, \tag{7}$$

$$[\pi - H(T)]X - CQ = 0, \tag{8}$$

$$-H_t QX - R = 0. \tag{9}$$

Equation (9) implies that the stronger the firm's trademark, and hence the lower $H(T)$ (search costs as a function of the trademark's strength), the

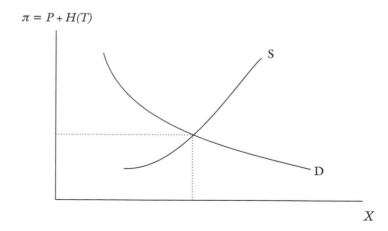

$\pi = P + H(T)$

Figure 7.3.

higher will be the price per unit of quality and hence from equation (8) the higher the quality of the firm's product. Similarly, the higher that quality, the greater the benefits of strengthening one's trademark (equation (9)) and the more therefore will the firm invest in its trademark. Thus a simple extension of our basic model yields the intuitive result that legal protection of trademarks encourages the production of higher-quality products.

Acquisition, Transfer, and Duration of Trademarks

The model will help us analyze specific issues and doctrines in trademark law, beginning with how trademark protection is acquired.

ACQUISITION One of the costs of a property-rights system—the transformation of the rents flowing from possession of a valuable right into costs of acquiring the right in the first place—could be a problem for trademark law as well, depending on how trademark protection is acquired. One way is registration. It resembles the methods for acquiring patents and copyrights and is in use in most of the world outside the United States. A second method, which is the traditional approach of the common law, is a type of "first possession" rule (see Chapter 1). A third is the current American system, a mixture of registration and first possession.

Under the common law approach, ownership of a trademark is obtained by using it in commerce, that is, by selling the trademarked product or service to the public. A first-possession rule, of which this is a variant, has several economic advantages. One, emphasized in Chapter 1, is that it minimizes rent seeking. A firm that by registering could obtain exclusive rights to trademarks without using them might invest substantial resources in thinking up plausible new brand names. Even though the elasticity of supply of such names is very high, the ownership of a vast number of them, and the aggregate licensing revenues that such ownership would command, could be a magnet drawing resources into the activity of creating brand names well beyond the optimal level of such investment. Moreover, letter combinations differ in their value as potential trademarks,[19] and the supply of the most valuable combinations is not perfectly elastic. In addition, firms might register well-known trademarks on products that the original trademark holder was no longer making, in the hope of later licensing the mark back to the original holder— another example of rent-seeking behavior.

---

19. See, for example, Sharon Begley, "New ABCs of Branding," *Wall Street Journal,* Aug. 26, 2002, p. B1.

Apparently the "banking" of trademarks in countries such as Japan that have a pure registration system does occur and has made it more costly to enter consumer markets in those countries.[20] The costs would be particularly great if, like the United States (as we shall see), the countries that permit the banking of trademarks forbade the sale of trademarks apart from the goods they denote. Firms would be forced to adopt less efficient trademarks (those yielding a higher H in our model) because they could not buy trademarks from the bank. The banked trademarks would be available only to the bank's "depositors," when they decided to sell a product for which they needed a trademark, even though some other firm might have an immediate need for one or more of the marks in the bank. It is not surprising that the United States has rejected trademark banking, while the countries that permit it also permit trademarks to be sold apart from the goods they designate.

Additional evidence concerning the effect of permitting the banking of trademarks comes from experience with "cybersquatters." Every Web site or other Internet-accessible computer has a unique Internet address ("domain name"), which includes both the name of the site and a domain designation, which for commercial sites is .com. Addresses with the .com designation are obtainable only from the Internet Corporation for Assigned Names and Numbers (ICANN), which issues them on a first-come, first-served basis for a modest fee. Until the enactment in 1999 of the Anticybersquatting Consumer Protection Act,[21] there was nothing to prevent a person or firm from registering domain names for the sole purpose of selling them to business firms for use in those firms' businesses. The names might be the names of existing firms—one cybersquatter registered more than 200 well-known business names, including "Delta Airlines" and "Neiman-Marcus"—or a term descriptive of a business or activity, such as "stamps.com" or "sex.com." This was classic rent seeking; the costs involved in racing to register well-known trademarks and then selling them back to the original trademark owners or litigating with them had no social product. The Act forbids registering as a domain name another person's distinctive trademark (or a confusingly similar name) with the intention of profiting from the goodwill associated with the mark.

A first-possession rule not only limits rent seeking but also reduces administrative costs compared to a rule that requires determining who invented the

---

20. Japan does provide for cancellation of trademarks that remain unused for three years—and the provision was tightened in 1996 after a survey "showed that 31.8% of all the registered trademarks in Japan (nearly 1.3 million) had never been used and would not be used in the future . . . The large amount of non-used marks have narrowed the choice of marks available for applicants." Masaya Suzuki, "The Trademark Registration System in Japan: A Firsthand Review and Exposition," 5 *Marquette Intellectual Property Law Review* 133, 148–149 (2001).

21. 15 U.S.C. § 1125(d).

trademark. Since trademarks often consist of common words, shapes, and colors, it would often be costly to figure out which party to a trademark dispute had invented the mark first. A cheaper alternative is to determine who *used* it first. Because "use in commerce," for purposes of establishing a right to a trademark, means the sale to the public of the good with the trademark attached, a potential second user will be on notice not to invest resources in an identical or confusingly similar mark. Some risk of duplication remains because there may be an interval between the development and full exploitation of the mark during which another firm (the "junior user") may be developing the same mark unaware of the first ("senior user").[22] But the cost of duplication is lower than in the case of patents because it is cheaper to create a trademark (as distinct from promoting and maintaining it) than to invent a new product or process.[23]

Conditioning trademark rights on use also makes a close fit with the social function of trademarks in identifying and distinguishing goods. If the good is not available for sale, the trademark confers no benefit. It is true that, as with other cases of conditioning ownership on possession, such as the appropriation system of water rights in the western United States, conditioning the legal protection of a trademark on the sale of the trademarked product can lead to the premature introduction of a product. A firm eager to establish its right to a nifty trademark may decide to begin selling the trademarked product earlier than it would otherwise do, merely to stake its claim to the trademark. But few individual trademarks are so valuable apart from the products they name that a firm will make costly marketing decisions just to appropriate a particular name.

The downside to a pure use system of establishing trademark rights is the risk of inadvertent and wasteful duplication in the interval between when a firm begins to develop a trademark and when it satisfies the use requirement; during that interval another firm may begin using the trademark. A trademark registry can enable such mishaps to be avoided, but as we have said a pure registration system or one with a minimal requirement of use has the disadvantage of enabling firms to bank trademarks. Appropriately, therefore, the current American system of establishing trademark rights is a mixture of state common law rights and an optional federal registration system—which is itself a mixture of registration and first-possession principles—created by the Lanham Act.[24] Registration under the Act does not confer a right unless

22. See, for example, Blue Bell, Inc. v. Farah Manufacturing Co., 508 F.2d 1260 (5th Cir. 1975).

23. The function of the patent system in reducing duplication by warning off prospective inventors of the same product or process is emphasized in Edmund W. Kitch, "The Nature and Function of the Patent System," 20 *Journal of Law and Economics* 265 (1977). See Chapter 11.

24. 15 U.S.C. §§ 1051 et seq. The Act also provides remedies for infringement of unregistered (that is, common law) trademarks and for false advertising and labeling.

the trademark is used. Formerly, less use was required than at common law; indeed, a token sale—even if it was just to an employee of the firm—or a single shipment might suffice. But a 1989 amendment restored the common law understanding. Since the trademark registry is public and readily searched, the risk of inadvertent duplication is minimized and widespread use is made a less important method of preventing duplication.

There is still the risk that before use commences, another firm may begin selling its brand under the same trademark. But that risk is minimized by another provision of the Act, authorizing "intent to use" trademark registrations: a firm can register a mark if it has a "bona fide intention" to use it in commerce within the next six months (several extensions are possible). The registration is revoked if sales in commercially significant quantity do not occur within the deadline. The combination of the intent-to-use and registration provisions largely prevents two potentially wasteful outcomes: since registration requires (eventual) use, the social costs associated with banking trademarks are eliminated; and the intent-to-use provision minimizes the risk of inadvertent duplication.

The biggest objection to a pure first-possession rule for intellectual property, and the strongest argument for a system of paper titles (the trademark registry, corresponding to the land or patent registries), is that the thing possessed has no definite physical locus. Suppose that producer A, who makes brand X desk lamps, is at present selling only in New York but has plans to sell eventually throughout the country. May producer B, who operates only in California, continue to sell his desk lamps under the X name even after A enters the California market? The Lanham Act deals with the first problem by making registration presumptive evidence of the registrant's right to use the trademark throughout the United States.[25] So if A registers his desk-lamp trademark, this operates as notice to B that should A expand into B's territory, A will have the superior claim to exclusive use of the trademark there.

In the absence of registration, the court, in deciding whether A may use its mark in B's sales area, will consider the closeness of the relation between A's original and expansion uses, A's unreasonable delay, if any, in enforcing his trademark against B (A's "laches," as it is called), and B's good or bad faith—whether he knew about A's trademark and was copying it or whether it was a coincidence that he began using the same mark.[26] The more alike A's original and expansion uses are, the costlier it will be for A and its customers if A is

25. See 15 U.S.C. § 1057(b); Coach House Restaurant, Inc. v. Coach & Six Restaurants, Inc., 934 F.2d 1551, 1562 (11th Cir. 1991).

26. See, for example, Polaroid Corp. v. Polarad Electronics Corp., 287 F.2d 492 (2d Cir. 1961) (Friendly, J.); Dwinell-Wright Co. v. White House Milk Co., 132 F.2d 822 (2d Cir. 1943) (L. Hand, J.).

forced to use a different mark in the expansion uses. Given the mobility of consumers,[27] many of them may be confused by the fact that the same brand is called one thing in one state and another thing in another. That is why Standard Oil Company of New Jersey came up with a new mark, "Exxon," to replace the Esso, Humble, Standard, and Enco marks that it had used for the identical products sold in different states. Consumers may also be confused if similar goods, such as a hammer and a screwdriver, made by the same producer are sold under different names. So if A in our example is denied the use of his trademark in his expansion markets, geographic or product, he may, like Standard Oil of New Jersey, be forced to adopt a wholly new trademark, thus sacrificing some reputation capital associated with the original mark.

The doctrine of laches (unreasonable delay in suing that is prejudicial to the defendant) forces A to internalize B's cost of duplication when appropriate. If A has reason to know that B is proceeding to develop a similar mark in ignorance of A's prior use, A, unless he has registered his mark, must, on pain of not being able to use it in his expansion markets, warn B off. The cost to A of preventing the collision of the two marks is less than that of B. But if B, rather than proceeding in ignorance of A's prior use (that is, in good faith), has deliberately copied A's mark, the costs of duplication are self-imposed; B is the cheaper cost avoider and the defense of laches to A's suit for infringement is rejected.

The registration system created by the Lanham Act has eased the problem of geographic overlap by in effect extinguishing any good-faith defense to a suit for product infringement if the federal registry indicates that the trademark is already being used to designate a brand of the same product. If the products are different, an inference of good faith is not automatically extinguished by registration because the path of expansion into different, even though related, products is inherently uncertain. B may have no reason to think that A is planning to expand into B's product market. This can be true of geographic expansion as well, but the difference is consumer mobility. Consumers are not chained to one location. In traveling around the country or in moving from one part of the country to another, they may be confused if different brands of the same product are sold under the same name. They are apt to assume that every desk lamp sold under a particular brand name is the same brand, that is, is produced by the same producer.

---

27. Well illustrated by Park 'N Fly, Inc. v. Dollar Park & Fly, Inc., 782 F.2d 1508, 1509 (9th Cir. 1986), where the parties provided services to airline passengers at different airports but the pool of customers was the same. We discuss the determinants of likelihood of confusion in greater detail later.

TRANSFER   U.S. law generally prohibits the sale or licensing of trademarks except as an incident to selling or licensing the right to produce the good that the mark identifies.[28] This rule—that trademarks cannot be transferred "in gross"—may seem puzzling. Why should Coca-Cola not be allowed to sell its trademark while retaining all rights to its secret formula for syrup? The answer relates to the economic function of trademarks in providing information about a good's attributes that would be more costly to obtain elsewhere. If A sells just his trademark (a sale "in gross" or "naked" assignment) to B and consumers know about the sale, B's attaching A's trademark to his own goodwill will not, at least as a first approximation, enable him to obtain a higher price for his good. But consumers may not know about the sale and so may be misled about the quality of B's good. In contrast, if A sells the formula or other assets used to produce the good, this will signify essentially just a change of ownership, so there will be no reason to believe that the quality of the good will be less; thus it makes sense for the trademark to remain attached to the product.

Let ϕ^b denote the probability that consumers correctly believe that A's mark identifies B's inferior good. So $1 - \phi^b$ is the probability that consumers are confused and believe that A's mark, now attached to B's good, designates A's good; that is, they think they are still buying A's good. Provided that $H(T^a)$ is less than $H(T^b)$ (otherwise B will not attach A's mark to his good), B will obtain a higher price for his (pseudo-A) good than he would without confusion. The increase in price will equal $\{[\pi - H(T^a)] - [\pi - H(T^b)]\}(1 - \phi^b)$ and will therefore be greater the greater the likelihood of confusion and the stronger A's trademark is relative to B's.[29]

This analysis is incomplete in three respects, however. First, it ignores the fact that if prevented from selling his mark in gross, A can reduce the quality of his brand and so obtain the same profits from deceiving consumers as he

---

28. See, for example, Pepsico, Inc. v. Grapette Co., 416 F.2d 285 (8th Cir. 1969). A major exception is for "promotional goods," goods that carry the trademark but are not closely related to the goods primarily produced by the trademark owner. An example is a T-shirt with the trademark or emblem of the Chicago Bears football team. The trademark has a value independent of the good it identifies and is thus itself a good. Our analysis of trademarks does not deal with promotional goods. Another exception is the service mark ("Holiday Inn," for example), often used to denote a franchise operation rather than a manufactured good. As there is no manufacturer, the sale of the trademark cannot be tied to the sale of a right to manufacture.

29. The increase in price will be even greater if B's quality is lower than A's (holding constant the probability of consumer confusion). It will equal

$$(1 - \phi^b)\{[\phi - H(T^a)]Q^a - [\phi - H(T^b)]Q^b\},$$

which is greater the greater A's quality is relative to B's (that is, the greater is Q^a relative to Q^b). We assume that consumers are risk-neutral.

could have done if allowed to sell his trademark to *B* for a deceptive purpose, that is, to designate *B*'s inferior good. Trademark law contains a doctrine designed (perhaps not very effectively) to close this loophole. "Since a trademark is not only a symbol of origin, but a symbol of a certain type of goods and services and their level of quality, a substantial change in the nature or quality of the goods sold under a mark may so change the nature of the thing symbolized that the mark becomes fraudulent and/or that the original rights are abandoned."[30]

Second, our analysis ignores the market checks on *A*'s licensing his trademark for a deceptive use by *B*. Once consumers wise up to the fact that *A*'s trademark no longer identifies a good of consistent quality, they will refuse to pay as much for it to either *A* or *B*. In licensing his mark, therefore, *A* will have an incentive to monitor the quality of *B*'s good to make sure *B* does not impair *A*'s reputation by selling an inferior quality of good. Even if there were no prohibition against licensing a trademark in gross, *A* would forfeit his trademark if the licensee attached the mark to a clearly inferior good. For as we just noted, this is the rule when the trademark is licensed lawfully, that is, is licensed along with the right to produce the seller's good. But that rule is costly to administer because it requires the court to assess quality.

We spoke in the preceding paragraph of "licensing" rather than "selling" the trademark because *A*'s incentive to monitor *B* would evaporate if *A* were selling his trademark to *B* and at the same leaving the market in which the trademarked good is sold, as normally he would be if he were selling the trademark together with the assets used to produce the trademarked good. If instead, as would sometimes be true of a transfer of a trademark in gross, the seller were planning to remain in the market, not sharing the trademark with the buyer (the licensing case, already discussed), but selling under a different brand name, he would still have some incentive to monitor quality, because ill will created when consumers discovered that his original trademark was now designating an inferior good might harm his new trademark. It is different if he is either leaving the market in which the trademarked good is sold or going out of business entirely. And either outcome is likelier, in the case of a sale of a trademark in gross, than his remaining in the market, because if, as a purchase in gross implies, the buyer doesn't want the assets that the seller had used to produce the trademarked good, it probably means that those assets are more valuable in some other employment—or perhaps the buyer doesn't want them because he is planning to reduce the quality of the product, enabling him to use cheaper assets to produce it. In either type of last-period

30. J. Thomas McCarthy, *McCarthy on Trademarks and Unfair Competition,* vol. 2, § 17:24 (4th ed. 2002) (footnotes omitted).

sale in gross—the seller is leaving the market or he is going out of business entirely—the seller will not be risking market retaliation for selling a trademark that will be used by another firm to deceive consumers.

This analysis suggests a need for legal control, and it is met by the rule against the transfer of trademarks in gross and by the corollary rule that forbids a creditor to levy on a trademark of the bankrupt company. Unless the buyer of the bankrupt's estate continues the bankrupt's business, the bankrupt's trademarks are deemed abandoned.[31] The rule prevents a creditor from attaching the mark to an inferior good. It is a prophylactic rule because, as we have noted, the mark will be forfeited once it is discovered that it is being attached to an inferior good—but that may take years to discover and consumers will be deceived in the interim.

The third respect in which our formal analysis of transfers is incomplete is that it does not explain B's incentive to try to gull consumers into thinking they are buying a superior brand. If consumers are easily gulled, our earlier rejection of the monopoly theory of product differentiation would be hard to sustain. If they are not easily gulled, B will suffer the same loss of reputation capital as A. In some cases, however, that prospect will not deter B. B may be in its last period; it may have little or no reputation capital to lose; or the cost of producing its inferior product may be so low that its short-run expected gain from deception exceeds its long-run loss of reputation capital.

DURATION One of the striking differences between trademarks on the one hand and copyrights and patents on the other is that trademarks have no fixed term. The difference makes economic sense. If a given name has no scarcity value as a trademark, so that the resources used in promoting and maintaining it yield only a competitive return, perpetual duration cannot create rent-seeking problems even if discount rates are very low (or zero or for that matter negative), or deflect consumers to inferior or more costly alternatives (the traditional deadweight loss from monopoly). Tracing costs, which would plague perpetual patents and to a lesser extent, as we'll see in the next chapter, perpetual copyrights as well, are not a serious problem either. The trademark is tied to physical property—the good that it names—and it usually is easy to discover who the producer of a good, and therefore the trademark owner, is, though we shall consider some exceptions later. Moreover, to make the producer of a good give up the name before he ceased selling the good would impose added search costs on consumers because the information embodied in the trademark would disappear. And when and if he ceases

---

31. See id., vol. 2, § 18:28.

selling the good, the trademark lapses automatically—another illustration of trademark abandonment.

Distinctiveness and Generic Names

Trademark protection is available only for a word or other signifier that identifies the underlying good or service and distinguishes it from that of other producers. Lack of distinctiveness would make the mark incapable of identifying the good and recalling to a consumer the information (generated by previous experience with the good by him or other consumers) that lowers his search costs and enables the producer to charge a higher price. By the same token, no seller would want to free ride on a nondistinctive signifier. The incentive to free ride depends on the difference between the profits generated by the mark—which by assumption are close to zero in the nondistinctive case—and the costs of duplication. But this does not mean that giving legal protection to nondistinctive marks would be harmless. A mark that does not distinguish one brand of a product from another is probably created from words, symbols, shapes, or colors that are used by other producers of the product as well, and so legal protection of the mark would be likely to prevent others from using identifiers that they require in order to be able to compete effectively.

We can explore this point formally by expanding our H function for a particular producer so that

$$H = H(T, Y, W, Z), \tag{10}$$

where Z denotes words used in common with other producers, such as "computer," "electrical," or "heavy," that is, product rather than brand identifiers. In effect, equation (10) redefines W as an index of words for use as trademarks except those (Z) used in common with other producers. Because the Z terms describe features of the product as distinct from features peculiar to each producer's brand, they tend to be limited in number. The variable Z combines with T to produce information that lowers search costs. Allowing a producer to appropriate a nondistinctive mark would enable him to force his competitors to remove Z from their labels, packaging, and product design. The result would be to shift the $-H_r X$ curve in Figure 7.2 downward and to lower T and raise H for those producers no longer permitted to use Z. The amount of X they produced would fall, shifting the supply curve of X to the left. There would be a social loss because consumers would be paying higher prices for a smaller quantity. Our earlier example of a firm allowed to use "personal computer" as its trademark illustrates this point.

The law could try to solve this problem by having the courts inquire in every case into the economic effects of allowing a particular producer to have exclusive rights to a particular mark. But then a trademark case would be like an antitrust case governed by the Rule of Reason. Such cases are very costly to try or even to settle, and the only thing that makes it worthwhile (both privately and socially) to incur these costs is the large private and social costs that some antitrust violations and some mistaken determinations of antitrust violations impose. Since the allocative effects of individual trademark abuses are pretty much limited to raising consumer search costs within narrow product categories, the potential misallocations are smaller than in most antitrust cases and the private stakes usually much smaller as well. So it would not pay to conduct an antitrust-type analysis in most trademark cases, and instead the law has sorted potential marks into a few broad classes according to distinctiveness and has made classification determinative of legality,[32] much as in antitrust cases governed by per se rules. The result is sometimes criticized for its crudeness, but the saving in costs of legal administration probably is offsetting.

The fanciful mark—the made-up name that resembles no other word, such as "Exxon" or "Kodak"—is the most distinctive and therefore the least problematic. Much like a fanciful mark in their economic properties and legal treatment are arbitrary and suggestive marks, the former more clearly so, however. An arbitrary mark is a word in common use that has no meaning descriptive or even suggestive of the product that it is being used to name: "Apple Computer" and "Black & White Scotch" are examples. The elasticity of supply (W in our formal model) of such terms is very high. There are 450,000 words in *Webster's Third New International Dictionary,* and although they are not freely substitutable if one is trying to say something that will be understood, they are freely substitutable if one is uninterested in meaning. Of course many of them are too long to be usable trademarks for most products, but plenty are short and the number of possible word pairs, as in both the examples of arbitrary marks that we have given, is much larger than the number of words. As we noted earlier, some potential identifiers have more consumer appeal than others, but even if the unappealing ones are excluded there are plenty left for sellers to choose among.

Somewhat more problematic are suggestive marks—words that imply characteristics of the goods they are used to name but do not describe them. Examples include "Qualcomm," "Microsoft," and *"Business Week."* The elasticity of supply of suggestive marks is less than that of fanciful and arbitrary marks but not much less than the latter when one considers substitution be-

---

32. Succinctly summarized in Abercrombie & Fitch Co. v. Hunting World, Inc., 537 F.2d 4, 9–11 (2d Cir. 1976).

tween trademark categories. *"Business Week"* competes with *"Forbes"* and *"Barron's"* (arbitrary marks) as well as with the *"Wall Street Journal"*—the last also an example of a suggestive mark.

When we come to the descriptive mark, such as "All Bran," "Holiday Inn," "Beanie Babies," and "American Girl," we find trademark protection allowed only on proof of "secondary meaning"—proof that the consuming public understands the word or phrase as primarily the name of the brand. A given product has only so many attributes that interest buyers. If one producer is allowed to appropriate the word that describes a key attribute, he will obtain rents measured by the higher price he receives for his branded product because he will have made it more costly for his rivals to inform their customers of the attributes of their brands without using the same descriptive word. In time, however, the descriptive meaning of a word may be largely forgotten and the word may come to signify to most people the name of a particular brand. This is a natural progression. A new product may require a descriptive name to introduce the consuming public to it, and if the product turns out to be popular the name may stick to the most popular brand while normal language drift causes substitution of another term to describe the product as a whole. "All Bran" has come to mean not any all-bran cereal but a particular brand of all-bran cereal. Once this happens, allowing the word or expression to be appropriated as a trademark may create net social benefits by reducing search costs more than it raises the costs to competitors, who are no longer permitted to use the same word.

Just as words can be classified into different types of trademark, so can shapes and other signifiers. Similar to fanciful and arbitrary words are unusual symbols and shapes or novel combinations of well-known symbols, shapes, and colors. Similar to descriptive names are common symbols (circles, squares, or hearts) and individual colors (particularly primary colors). To allow a firm to appropriate one of these descriptive signifiers as its trademark would create the parallel danger that after several firms had done this the limited number of attractive symbols and colors would all have been used, making it substantially more costly for other firms to compete. Yet as with descriptive words, there may come a time—especially if the symbol or color in question has been used exclusively over a period of years by the producer of one brand—when the common signifier denotes just that producer's brand to most consumers.[33] It now primarily provides source information; it has acquired secondary meaning.

Consider the trademarking of common shapes and colors of pills sold as

---

33. As confirmed for color in Qualitex Co. v. Jacobson Products Co., 514 U.S. 159 (1995). The Court's opinion in *Qualitex*, written by Justice Breyer, contains a clear statement of the economic rationale for trademark protection and also for the exception for functional (either utilitarian or aesthetic) marks, of which more shortly.

prescription drugs. After a patent on a drug expires, other firms may begin selling the "same" drug under a different brand name or under its generic name while copying the shape and color of the original manufacturer's pill. Despite the lower price charged by the new entrants, many consumers may prefer to stick with the original manufacturer; maybe they had a good experience with the drug and are reluctant to believe claims that the substitute is identical in all material respects. Since a consumer is unlikely to read the fine print on the vial in which a prescription drug is sold at retail that identifies the manufacturer (and it really is fine print), he may rely on the only accessible signifiers—its shape and color—to indicate that it's the pill he wants. So if entrants are allowed to use the same size, shape, and color for their pills, this may lead to deliberate substitution by the druggist, either because the manufacturers of the generic substitute charge the druggist a lower price or because the druggist is temporarily out of the original manufacturer's brand,[34] or to inadvertent substitution because the druggist is careless. In these circumstances, where there are both significant benefits from source identification and high costs of using means other than size, shape, and color to identify the source, we expect, and we find, that courts grant trademark protection to common sizes, shapes, and colors of prescription drugs.[35] They are less likely to do this with other products, including nonprescription drugs, which are sold to the consumer in their original package. The manufacturer can display the brand name prominently on the package; he does not have to use size, shape, and color for source identification.

Generic words cannot be trademarked at all. What is more, if a trademark becomes a generic name, trademark protection immediately ceases. A generic name or term is by definition the name not of a brand but of an entire prod-

34. In some states, druggists are authorized by law to substitute the generic equivalent unless the prescribing physician forbids the substitution, the purpose being to control costs in a market believed deficient in competition because of the prevalence of third-party payment and other circumstances. The prescription drug market may be one in which trademark protection can create significant market power, another reason being the interaction between patent and trademark protection in that industry, which we discuss in Chapter 11.

35. See Ciba-Geigy Corp. v. Bolar Pharmaceutical Co., 747 F.2d 844 (3d Cir. 1984). But the principle, although recognized in subsequent cases, see, for example, SmithKline Beecham Corp. v. Pennex Products Co., 605 F. Supp. 746 (E.D. Pa. 1985), has rarely if ever been successfully invoked since the *Ciba-Geigy* decision. See, for example, Bristol-Myers Squibb Co. v. McNeil-P.P.C., Inc., 973 F.2d 1033 (2d Cir. 1992); American Home Products Corp. v. Barr Laboratories, Inc., 834 F.2d 368 (3d Cir. 1987). Some cases suggest that the risk of confusion is actually less in prescription drug cases than in over-the-counter drug cases because the selection of the prescription drug is made by the consumer's physician, who is more sophisticated than the average consumer. See Pharmacia Corp. v. Alcon Laboratories, Inc., 201 F. Supp. 2d 335, 374 (D.N.J. 2002), and cases cited there.

uct: "airplane" and "computer" are examples. "Personal computer" is an example of a term that began as a brand name but eventually, and indeed rather rapidly, became the name of the product.[36] This is the opposite progression from a descriptive term that eventually acquires secondary meaning. If the producer of one brand could appropriate the name of the product, he would earn rents because of the added cost to his rivals of periphrasis—of describing their products as "heavier-than-air flying machines" or "a programmable electronic device for storing, retrieving, and manipulating data." In other words, he would reduce the amount of Z available to competitors, thus shifting the industry supply curve to the left and creating a deadweight loss equal to the shaded area in Figure 7.4. Since π, the full price of X, increases when the supply curve shifts to the left, the firm appropriating the generic term would earn economic rents equal to the higher price for its brand (recall that $P = \pi - H$) times the number of units of X that it sells.

The monopoly resulting from the appropriation of a generic name would be described as a product monopoly but is more accurately a language monopoly. Unless the owner of the generic name were the lowest-cost producer throughout the entire feasible range of the product's output, he would license the use of the name to competitors and receive rents in the form of license fees. Licensing would limit the deadweight loss to the cross-hatched area in Figure 7.4 by preventing firms from expending resources on developing new ways to denote their products (the license would be cheaper to them). It would thus transform a social cost into a transfer payment to the firm appropriating the generic term. But it would not eliminate all deadweight losses. Besides the cross-hatched area, there would be the costs of negotiating and enforcing the trademark licenses and of obtaining generic trademarks (including costs generated by rent-seeking behavior) in the first place. Even without licensing, although the appropriation of a generic mark would raise the costs of competing firms, it would not necessarily raise them so high that any of those firms left the market. But it might reduce the firms' competitive effectiveness.

The costs of obtaining generic trademarks (if they were allowed) would often merge with the costs of invention, because the firm best situated to appropriate a generic name would be the first producer of the product. The rents from invention would go up because they would include rents from the name of the product. If the current legal protection of inventions is optimal (or is simply assumed to be such by courts unable to investigate the issue),

---

36. Though oddly its meaning remains ambiguous: it can mean either a computer that uses a microprocessor manufactured by Intel or AMD (but not Apple, for example), or any small computer. When called a "PC" it is more likely to be used in the former sense.

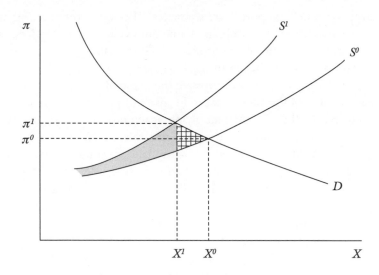

Figure 7.4.

any legal protection for generic names will create socially wasteful opportunities to earn rents.

All this may explain why generic names cannot be trademarked—but why does a trademark that *becomes* a generic name lose trademark protection?[37] Shouldn't a producer clever enough to name his brand with a word that will some day be used as the name of the entire product be rewarded for this valuable addition to the lexicon? Is the language not richer for such words as "thermos," "brassiere," "aspirin," "cellophane," "dry ice"—all well-known examples of trademarks that have become generic names? Our earlier discussion of the economics of language suggests an answer. Property rights are not necessary in order to induce the rapid creation of serviceable new words for new things. Trademarks are a minor though not trivial[38] source of generic names, and we can think of no product whose introduction or diffusion was retarded because the producer couldn't think up a serviceable name. Observe the rapidity with which a large vocabulary of arresting and memorable terms has emerged without significant assistance from trademarks to describe things that are new in the last half-century—medicines, weaponry, political

37. Another example, by the way, of the fact that trademarks are often not perpetual even though they are not subject to fixed expiration dates.

38. See Shawn M. Clankie, "Brand Name Use in Creative Writing: Genericide or Language Right?" in *Perspectives on Plagiarism and Intellectual Property in a Postmodern World* 253 (Lisa Buranen and Alice M. Roy eds. 1999).

and social movements, legal and scientific terms, computers, and so on. The demand for names for new things is very great but the supply cost is trivial, so a large supply is forthcoming without need to offer special monetary inducements to the inventors. Anyway, the mere prospect of a brand name's becoming generic would usually be too slight to give the firm a strong incentive to search for a name that would not have generic potential. What creates such potential is not so much anything about the name itself (and so there should be no scarcity of trademarks with generic potential) but just the success of the branded product and consequent popularity of the trademarked name.

Some marks that have become generic terms began life as fanciful marks (for example, "aspirin," "cellophane," and "frisbee"), others as suggestive or descriptive ones (such as "thermos" and "dry ice"—suggestive—and "all-bran"—descriptive). The latter probably predominate because a fanciful mark is more clearly indicative of a specific producer, whereas a suggestive or descriptive mark is more indicative of a type or class. It might seem that a descriptive mark would never be chosen for a *new* product, since such marks are not appropriable as trademarks until they acquire secondary meaning.[39] But if the product is new in the sense that it has no close substitutes, the firm will not have to worry that a descriptive mark is being used by competing brands—there are none.

Since, however, a suggestive or descriptive mark is more likely than a fanciful or arbitrary one to become a generic name, why would any producer choose such a mark? Because it conveys additional information to the consumer, information about the attributes as well as just the source of the good,[40] and is thus a partial substitute for advertising. The producer will trade off this gain, which may be particularly important precisely in the case of a new product as yet unknown to consumers, against the increased risk of losing the mark because it becomes generic, as well as against its lesser distinctiveness and hence lesser value as source identification than a fanciful or arbitrary mark would have. Our analysis predicts, incidentally, that the shorter the expected life of a brand, the more likely the producer is to use a suggestive mark, while descriptive marks are more likely to be used for brands with a long expected life because it takes time to acquire secondary meaning, a prerequisite to obtaining trademark protection for such a mark.

The negative effect on the supply of trademarks from denying protection to generic terms is slight and almost certainly outweighed by the benefits

39. As a detail, but an important one, we note that color and product design, as distinct from words or symbols, can never be appropriated as trademarks unless secondary meaning is demonstrated. See Wal-Mart Stores, Inc. v. Samara Bros., Inc., 529 U.S. 205 (2000).

40. See John M. Carroll, *What's in a Name? An Essay in the Psychology of Reference* 179 (1985).

from pitching a trademark into the public domain when it becomes generic. For this reduces the costs of communication by making it cheaper for competitors of the (former) trademark owner to inform the consumer that they are selling the same product. And not just competitors. Consider the application of the fair use doctrine of trademark law[41] to the controversy over the use of "Star Wars" to describe President Reagan's "Strategic Defense Initiative." "Star Wars" was the trademarked name of a movie, but the owner of the trademark was refused an injunction against the use of the term to describe the Strategic Defense Initiative.[42] Such a use could not be enjoined in any event under traditional trademark law, which requires proof of at least a likelihood of consumer confusion. But were it not for fair use considerations (specifically in the SDI example the social value of allowing the trademark to be used to describe something completely different from the trademarked product), it might have been enjoinable under antidilution statutes, of which more later.

The trademark owner may, it is true, expend resources on preventing his trademark from becoming generic (another example of an intellectual property counterpart to a fence enclosing a parcel of land). Such an expenditure will not be a pure deadweight loss; it will have the desirable side-effect of reminding consumers of the existence of competing brands. Every time General Foods stresses "Sanka-*brand* decaffeinated coffee," it implies the existence of other brands. This retards the emergence of "Sanka" as a generic name but reinforces "decaffeinated coffee" as a generic name. There is some social cost if "Sanka" would be a cheaper (it certainly is a shorter) generic name, but it is likely to be lower than the social cost of giving legal protection to trademarks that become generic names. General Foods' assiduous effort to prevent "Sanka" from becoming generic worked, and without limiting competition. The generic name has become "decaf," which is as short and snappy as "sanka" would be.

One way of resisting genericness is for the trademark owner himself to sponsor a generic name different from his trademark, in the hope that the generic name will catch on, allowing him to retain his trademark. General Foods actively promoted the term "decaffeinated coffee" and Xerox the terms "photocopy" and "photocopier," both firms hoping to provide attractive alternatives to their trademarks for the generic name of the product.[43] The rule against retaining a trademark once the mark becomes generic actually gives the trademark owner an incentive to enrich the language.

41. 15 U.S.C. § 1115(b)(4).
42. Lucasfilm Ltd. v. High Frontier, 227 U.S.P.Q. 967 (D.D.C. 1985).
43. See Rochelle Cooper Dreyfuss, "Expressive Genericity: Trademarks as Language in the Pepsi Generation," 65 *Notre Dame Law Review* 397, 417 (1990).

There is, however, one significant drawback to terminating trademark protection when a mark becomes generic. A consumer who bought Bayer aspirin at a time when Bayer was the only producer and "aspirin" was its trademark (as it still is in Canada) might have assumed, when other brands came on the market and were allowed to be called "aspirin" too, that they would be identical to Bayer aspirin not only in formula but in every respect, including, for example, quality control. The practical relation between brand and product—how close a substitute the generic is for the brand—is not self-evident and may be difficult to determine in the period of transition from monopoly to competition. Giving generic status to the former brand name may increase the search costs of consumers who believe there are quality differences between the old and the new brands. Overall, however, search costs would be greater if the sellers of the new brands could not use the generic name.

Terminating legal protection when a trademark achieves generic status might be criticized as imposing a dichotomous solution on a continuous problem. Generic status is achieved gradually. There will be an interval during which some consumers will still think of the trademarked name as the name of a particular brand though others are already thinking of it as the name of the product. If the law waits to withdraw legal protection until all consumers think of it as the name of the product, the trademark owner will obtain substantial rents. But if the law withdraws protection as soon as a few consumers understand it as a generic term, this will sow confusion and thus impose substantial consumer search costs. Trademark protection should cease when the costs of continued protection (deadweight losses resulting from higher prices, higher costs to rivals in using alternative words, and the costs of licensing and defending trademarks) exceed the benefits (minimizing consumer confusion and search costs and maximizing the incentive of firms to maintain consistent product quality). The Trademark Clarification Act of 1984 makes "the primary significance of the registered mark to the relevant public" the criterion for whether the mark has become generic.[44] This formulation is vague but does leave room for the kind of cost-benefit approach just sketched, and no better alternative springs to mind; a fixed date of expiration of trademarks would be wholly unsatisfactory for the reasons explained earlier.

Difficult problems of determining whether a trademark has become a generic name are apt to arise in cases in which the trademark owner initially has a product monopoly. Such cases are common, not because monopolies are

---

44. 15 U.S.C. § 1064(g). Thus, "A registered mark shall not be deemed to be the generic name of goods or services *solely* because such mark is also used as a name of or to identify a unique product or service." Id. (emphasis added).

common but because a brand name is most likely to become a generic name when there is only one brand. With one producer, consumers have little incentive to use separate terms to describe the product and the brand or, what is equivalent, to denote product information and source information separately. It is more economical to refer to both an instant camera and its manufacturer as "Polaroid" than to use both terms—until Polaroid ceases to be the only manufacturer. But at that point there is no other generic name. Maybe the presumption in the monopoly case should be in favor of generic status. If the consumer has never had a competitive alternative to A's brand, the brand name is less likely to convey information about the particular attributes of A's good than simply to define the product, because without the comparisons enabled by competition the consumer will not be using A's trademark to lower his costs of searching for the brand he wants. This may be a factor in the limited competition that generics seem to provide to brand-name drugs in the initial period after the latter come off patent even though the generics are much cheaper and, chemically at least, identical to the branded drugs. Another factor, however, is that, as we pointed out earlier, brands that are chemically identical may differ in other respects that are important to consumers. We return to this issue in Chapter 11.

We can make a stab at estimating how good a job the courts are doing of determining when trademarks have become generic, at least if the dictionary can be considered an accurate inventory of words in general use by the relevant publics (perhaps a big if). Of 68 examples in the McCarthy treatise of marks that courts have held to be generic,[45] 29 either do not appear in a current unabridged dictionary[46] or, if they do appear, the meaning held to be generic is not included (for example, "matchbox" is in the dictionary but not as meaning toy cars sold in matchbox-sized boxes). Of 24 examples of trademarks that courts have held not to be generic,[47] 6 nevertheless are listed in the dictionary with the rejected generic meaning. Thus trademarks held to be generic are more likely to show up in the dictionary with their generic definitions than those held not to be generic, but only by a factor of about two—57 percent versus 25 percent.

An interesting variant of the generic-mark issue is the "dual use" issue in *Illinois High School Association v. GTE Vantage Inc.*,[48] from which we quote the court's summary of the facts:

45. See McCarthy, note 30 above, vol. 2, § 12:18. We excluded marks that consist of more than one word.

46. *Merriam-Webster Unabridged,* http://www.m-w.com (visited August 2002).

47. See McCarthy, note 30 above, vol. 2, § 12:19. This is subject to the same qualification as in note 45 above.

48. 99 F.3d 244, 245 (7th Cir. 1996).

Since the early 1940s, the Illinois High School Association, sponsor of the Illinois high school basketball tournament—the premier high school basketball tournament in the United States, we are told—has used the trademark "March Madness" to designate the tournament, held every year in March and sometimes broadcast nationally. IHSA has licensed the use of the trademark on merchandise associated with the tournament. Another basketball tournament—NCAA's "Final Four" championship—is also played in March, spilling over into the early part of April. In 1982, when CBS began televising the "Final Four" championship games, broadcaster Brent Musburger used the term "March Madness" to designate them. The term caught on and is now widely used by the media and the public to denote this basketball tournament as well as IHSA's.

In 1993 or 1994, NCAA began licensing the use of the term "March Madness" to producers of goods and services related to its tournament. [In 1996] one of the licensees, Vantage, began using "March Madness" to promote a CD-ROM game that it calls "NCAA Championship Basketball." The term "March Madness" appears in a circle on the box in which the game is to be sold and in some of the game's computer graphics.

The Illinois High School Association sued Vantage, and lost because the court concluded that IHSA had lost its exclusive right to the trademark when the public, under the influence of the media, adopted "March Madness" as the name of the NCAA's tournament, though some residents of Illinois continue to use the term to designate the IHSA tournament as well. The term had not become generic in the usual sense because it designated not an entire product category or activity (basketball tournaments, for example) but just two, the NCAA's tournament and IHSA's tournament. But because the public for whatever reason called both events by the same name, neither sponsor would be allowed to exclude the other from using it, as the result of such exclusion would be an impoverishment of the language.

Functionality

The concept of functionality, which is mainly important in connection with design features used as trademarks (our Perrier example) or as the basis for design patents (see Chapter 11), is a parallel concept to genericness, as well as to the copyright concept of functional expression discussed in Chapter 4. A functional feature cannot be trademarked, and a trademarked feature loses trademark protection when it becomes functional. The maker of a tire could not trademark its circular shape but could trademark an irregularly shaped hubcap. The maker of a steak knife could not trademark the serrated blade but could trademark an intricate arabesque carved into the handle. A particular shape for a container might initially be subject to being trademarked, but if technological developments made it much cheaper to manufacture than alternative shapes, it would lose its trademark protection.

The concept of functionality can be given a precise economic meaning. A nonfunctional feature, hence one that can be trademarked, is a feature that has perfect (or nearly perfect) substitutes, so that a property right will create no deadweight loss (see Figure 7.4). If it lacks good substitutes, either because the product is worth less without it (the circular tire) or because it makes the product cheaper to produce (the example of container shape), trademark protection will be denied. The feature may of course be a worthwhile addition to the stock of useful knowledge, but, if so, it may be patentable as a utility patent (the normal twenty-year patent, as distinct from the fourteen-year design patent). Trademark protection for a functional feature would circumvent the requirements for, and the durational limit of, utility patents.

The trickiest problem with functionality involves "aesthetic" as distinct from "utilitarian" functionality. The term "utilitarian," as used in this polarity, carries its everyday sense of "practical," "down to earth," "unadorned." The illustrations given in the preceding paragraph were of utilitarian functionality in this sense. Even if a design feature merely makes a product more pleasing, however, it may be deemed functional ("aesthetic functionality") and trademark protection will again be withheld. The concept of aesthetic functionality is premised on the recognition that utility in an economic sense, as distinct from the everyday sense, includes anything that makes a good more valuable to consumers. But because a producer of a consumer product will never deliberately uglify it—and we do not want him to—any design feature that he seeks to trademark will be designed in part to please. The courts thus have the difficult task of disentangling the merely aesthetic ("merely ornamental," as the cases sometimes say)[49] effect of a trademarked design feature from a design feature that is an attribute of the product rather than of just the brand.

We can explore utilitarian functionality by rewriting the profit function of the illustrative firm in our formal model as

$$I = [\pi - H(T)]X - C(X, F) - RT, \tag{11}$$

where C, the cost of production, has been expanded to make it a function not only of the amount of X produced but also of the physical attributes (F) of

49. See McCarthy, note 30 above, vol. 1, § 7:81.

the product that are claimed as trademarks. Assume that if another firm is denied access to F, its marginal cost of producing X will increase; that is, $C_{xf} <$ 0. This will shift the marginal cost of producing X to the left in Figure 7.4, reducing output and producing a deadweight loss. Exclusive rights for functional features of a product and for generic terms have identical effects in our economic model.

A mark is not deemed to be functional just because it makes the product more attractive.[50] A more attractive trademark makes the good to which it is attached of higher quality from the consumer's standpoint. Let $Q(A)$ denote quality and A the attractiveness of the mark ($Q_a > 0$ and $Q_{aa} < 0$), and assume that a more attractive trademark is more costly to produce. Hence the cost of producing a unit of T (R in our notation) is no longer constant but depends on A, as in $R = R(A)$, where $R_a > 0$ and $R_{aa} \geq 0$. While a *strong* trademark increases the price that consumers are willing to pay for the good by lowering search costs ($H_t < 0$), an *attractive* trademark raises price by increasing the utility that consumers get from the good once they have bought it.

Rewriting equation (11) and assuming that the firm can prevent others from copying its attractive trademark yields

$$I = [\pi - H(T)]Q(A)X - C(X, F) - R(A)T. \tag{12}$$

Profit maximization requires

$$[\pi - H(T)]Q(A) - C_x = 0 \tag{13}$$

$$-H_tQ(A)X - R(A) = 0 \tag{14}$$

$$[\pi - H(T)]Q_aX - R_aT = 0 \tag{15}$$

Because a more attractive mark is more expensive to produce, the firm will invest in such a mark only if it is rewarded by obtaining a higher price for each X it sells—the increase in price equaling $[\pi - H(T)]Q_a$ in equation (15). The higher the price, the more units of X the firm will produce (see equation (13)). Other firms are not put at a cost disadvantage, however, as they were by utilitarian functionality, because in the aesthetic case $R(A)$ depends only on the firm's investment in making its mark attractive. In terms of Figure 7.4, allowing a firm to prevent others from duplicating its attractive trademark (so that the level of A increases) increases both output (X) and quality ($Q(A)$) and therefore shifts the supply curve to the right.[51]

A problem arises only if the aesthetic feature becomes an attribute of the product (an F) in the minds of consumers, so that to produce an X equivalent

---

50. See, for example, LeSportsac, Inc. v. K Mart Corp., 754 F.2d 71, 76–78 (2d Cir. 1985).
51. The horizontal axis is QX rather than X.

in the consumer's mind to an X that has this feature a firm would have to incur additional costs, just as in a case of utilitarian functionality. In *Publications International, Ltd. v. Landoll, Inc.*,[52] which involved the alleged infringement of PIL's trademark on a cookbook, the court remarked that

> the color gold on a product or its package is a prime example of aesthetic functionality. This is the case mentioned in *Qualitex Co. v. Jacobson Products Co.*,[53] where "color plays an important role (unrelated to source identification) in making a product more desirable." Gold connotes opulence, and so is a standard element of the décor of food products, such as chocolate, that are valued for their rich taste rather than for their nutritional value. It also has a long history of use in bookbinding; the spine of the book in which this opinion is printed is decorated with gilt. Gold is a natural color to use on a fancy cookbook. A different color on PIL's page ends would have a better claim to be a source signifier; compare a blue container of orange juice with an orange one.[54]

Actually, the consequences of allowing such a feature to be appropriated for a trademark are ambiguous. Appropriability will expand A by giving the firm an incentive to spend the money necessary to produce a more attractive T, but it will reduce the level of F available to competitors and hence raise their costs of producing X. It might seem that the courts in such a case should trade off $Q(A)$, which if trademark protection is denied will fall because of the effect on the incentive of firms to produce more attractive products, against C, the costs of production, which will rise because competing producers will not be able to copy the attractive feature. Rather than attempting this balancing act, the courts deny trademark protection for the attractive feature only if it is indispensable to the marketing of the product, that is, roughly speaking, only if the trademark owner would obtain a product monopoly if he could exclude others from copying the feature. This approach permits legal protection for attractive colors that serve as identifiers, such as the color pink for insulation but not the color yellow for tennis balls or the color brown for peanut butter—or the color yellow for margarine. Consumers considered a nonyellow substitute for butter unattractive, which was why the dairy industry lobbied (at first successfully) for forbidding producers of margarine to color it yellow.

Although appropriability may still be necessary to elicit the expenditures required to create a pleasing product design, just as to create utilitarian functionality, it need not take the form of trademark protection. The grant of de-

52. 164 F.3d 337 (7th Cir. 1998).
53. See Note 33 above, 514 U.S. at 165.
54. 164 F.3d at 342.

sign patents may be preferable to courts' attempting to trade off the design's positive effect on the attractiveness of the seller's brand against the negative effect on the ability of other sellers to compete with him.

Infringement and Confusion

In order to prevent another seller from selling his goods under your trademark, you must (unless you are proceeding under a dilution theory) show that consumers are likely to think either that it is your brand that he is selling or that you have sponsored, approved, or licensed his use of your trademark. This is a lighter burden than having to prove actual confusion. The choice between a "likelihood" and an "actual" standard involves balancing two potential error costs. Under the former standard some similar marks that do not cause confusion will be held infringing.

Requiring proof of confusion, whether likely or actual, makes economic sense. Just as people in different parts of the country or in different occupations can have identical names without causing misunderstanding, so sellers in unrelated product or geographic markets can affix the same names or other marks to their goods without confusing consumers. Suppose A and B produce different brands of product X. A has a strong mark that yields low search costs, denoted by H^a. B adopts a similar mark, which however is weaker, at least at first, because it is new, but there is no likelihood of confusion between the two marks. Both marks then convey accurate information about the reputation of the underlying product (or producer). A's good will command a higher price than B's because $H^a < H^b$ (since $\pi = (P^a + H^a) = (P^b + H^b)$, $P^a > P^b$ if $H^a < H^b$), but this is consistent with competition and with maximizing the sum of consumer and producer surplus in the X market. There is no free riding. B's revenue depends solely on the value of H^b, not H^a, the absence of confusion implying that consumers correctly match the particular H with the firm's product.

Legal intervention to prevent B from using the mark similar to A's could impose heavy costs. A seller might adopt a trademark in all innocence, not knowing that some other seller, selling a different product in a remote area of the country, had adopted the same trademark previously; he might invest substantial resources in advertising his trademarked goods—and he might be forced to write off the entire investment if first use established a nationwide property right covering all products. To avoid such disasters, sellers would have to invest heavily in investigating prior uses of trademarks they were thinking of adopting. These costs are reduced if the original owner must show a likelihood of confusion.

It is consistent with this analysis that, as we noted earlier, the owner of a registered mark bears a lighter burden of proving likelihood of confusion than the owner of an unregistered mark. Registration warns off potential infringers more effectively than mere use, which may not be observed if it occurs in a limited geographical area.

In deciding whether there is a likelihood of confusion, courts look at such things as the similarity in spelling of the original and allegedly infringing trademark (for example, "Exxon" and "Exxene"), the strength of the original mark, the similarity of the products involved, whether the consumers of the products overlap, whether the products are sold through the same retail outlets, and how knowledgeable consumers of these products are. The last point is particularly interesting from an economic standpoint in its implicit acknowledgment that the inputs into the sale of a product include information supplied by buyers as well as by sellers. The cheaper the buyer-produced information is—perhaps because the consumers of a particular product are highly knowledgeable, such as business purchasers of an item essential to their business—the less information the seller must supply, as by making a greater effort to distinguish his trademark from a competitor's.

Formally, a consumer looking at one of two confusingly similar marks will be uncertain whether the search costs associated with it are H^a or H^b (that is, whether he will be receiving A's or B's brand of X).[55] Let the expected value (E) of H^a (that is, $E(H^a)$) equal $\phi^a H^a + (1 - \phi^a)H^b$, where ϕ^a is the probability of correctly relating the trademark to A's good and $1 - \phi^a$ is the probability of mistaking B's for A's good. The corresponding price of A's brand (assuming risk neutrality) will be $P_0{}^a = \pi - E(H^a)$. In the absence of any confusion, A's brand would sell for $P_1{}^a = \pi - H^a$ (where $P_1{}^a > P_0{}^a$, assuming $H^a < E(H^a) < H^b$). The reduction in A's price per unit of X caused by B's adopting a similar mark is

$$P_1{}^a - P_0{}^a = (1 - \phi^a)(H^b - H^a), \tag{16}$$

which will be greater the stronger A's trademark is relative to B's (that is, the higher $H^b - H^a$ is) and the greater the likelihood of confusion $(1 - \phi^a)$.[56]

Consumers will underestimate the search costs associated with B's brand because they will attach a positive probability to its actually being A's brand. This will lead to a higher price for B's product, equal to

$$P_0{}^b - P_1{}^b = (1 - \phi^b)(H^b - H^a), \tag{17}$$

which is larger the greater the likelihood of confusion $(1 - \phi^b)$ and the stronger A's trademark relative to B's.

55. We consider the case of noncompeting goods later.

56. Notice that $1 - \phi^a$ will also tend to be greater the greater the amount of X produced by B relative to A. For example, suppose consumers cannot distinguish between A's and B's mark, and B produces $90X$ and A produces $10X$. Consumers will assume that $\phi^a = .10$ and $1 - \phi^a = .90$.

At first B's adopting a mark confusingly similar to A's may have no effect on consumers as a whole. If the likelihood of incorrectly identifying A's and B's goods is identical $(1 - \phi^a = 1 - \phi^b)$, consumers paying a lower price for A's good will be balanced by consumers paying a higher price for B's good. But confusion between the two marks will soon lower A's profits, and A will respond by reducing both his output of X and his expenditures on T.[57] This will make his brand less valuable. For with lower T, consumers' search costs will be higher because the probability that a consumer assigns to being able to determine that the brand he is purchasing is A's declines as the amount of X produced by A falls relative to the amount produced by B.

The factors that the courts consider in estimating confusion line up well with our analysis. Similarities in the appearance and sound of the two marks, buyers' lack of sophistication, similarity of the underlying product, and overlapping sales territories all raise the probability of confusion $(1 - \phi^a)$, while the stronger A's trademark (the lower H^a) is, the greater will be the drop in the price of A's good if infringement is not prevented.

Thus far we have assumed that firms produce identical physical products (Xs) but different brands and that B's brand has a worse reputation than A's because, for example, of a greater variance in its quality, requiring consumers to search more to be sure of getting the quality they want. Abstracting from physical differences among products simplifies our model but is unrealistic. B, when it adopts a mark similar to A's for the purpose of confusing consumers, is also likely to produce a lower-quality product than A (a lower Q than in the expanded market modeled in equations (6) through (9)). Consumers who confuse B's mark with A's will assume that the quality of the underlying physical good is the same; so if B can cut costs by reducing the quality of his product without consumers noticing, he will have even higher profits than if he maintains the same quality as A. B's incentive to free ride on A's trademark will be greater the higher the quality of the underlying good, adjusted for B's costs of making the physical good appear equivalent to A's. Thus, if stripped

---

57. The reduction in output will lower ϕ^a, further reducing A's output and trademark investment. The firm will cut back on its trademark expenditures (see equation (5) and Figure 7.2) because both the output of X and the marginal product of T will have fallen. (The marginal product of T with confusion is $-\phi^a H_t$, which is less than $-H_t$.) Other responses are also possible; in particular, A may change his trademark to avoid its being confused with B's, but there are costs of doing this, too.

Notice that the harm to A arises because consumer confusion lowers the price A receives for a unit of X. This in turn causes A to reduce X and T. One would also expect confusion to harm A because it would enable B to take sales away from A. This does not occur in our formal model because we assume that each firm (including A) faces a perfectly elastic demand for its output. If we allowed for a negatively sloped firm demand curve, B's infringement would lead A to produce fewer Xs even if the price of X were unchanged.

of trademark protection, *A* would have less incentive either to develop a strong trademark or to produce a high-quality good.

Allowing the quality of the underlying good (that is, of *X*) to differ across firms enables us to explain a case like *Taylor Wine Co. v. Bully Hill Vineyards, Inc.*[58] The defendant added the well-known "Taylor" name to its trademark even though it made higher-quality wines than the plaintiff's Taylor wines. Presumably it thought the gain in consumer recognition would more than offset consumers' expectation of a reduced quality of its product.

Consumers differ in their ability to distinguish among trademarks according to how careful they are in searching for goods and their shopping skills.[59] Suppose a seller adopts a trademark that is similar but not identical to that of a similar product sold by someone else. Careful consumers, defined for our purposes as consumers with low costs of acquiring and processing product information, are not fooled. Careless consumers, equivalent in the economics of tort law to potential accident victims who have above-average costs of taking care, are fooled. Removing all ambiguity from an advertising claim for the sake of the careless may make the advertisement confusing for the careful (or perhaps for some other group of careless consumers who, however, were not deceived by the original claim). That problem is less acute in the trademark context. The second seller should be able to find a trademark that distinguishes his product from the first seller's in the minds of the careless without confusing the careful. We therefore expect courts to be more protective of the careless consumer in trademark cases than in false-advertising cases.

There is a case for protecting even the most careless consumers from being confused by similar trademarks if, as we have been assuming so far, the second seller adopts its similar trademark *intending* to deceive.[60] In that case the cost of preventing confusion is negative—it is the social benefit from the second seller's *not* expending resources on creating a confusing trademark—so that even if the benefits to consumers are small, prevention will be cost-justified unless the costs of using the legal system are very high.[61] If the infringement is unintentional, however—a common situation, especially when the infringed trademark is unregistered—there is no good alternative to some form of cost-benefit analysis. *B*'s trademark provides benefits to consumers who

---

58. 569 F.2d 731, 733–734 (2d Cir. 1978).

59. See Richard Craswell, "Interpreting Deceptive Advertising," 65 *Boston University Law Review* 657, 672–684 (1985).

60. See, for example, American Chicle Co. v. Topps Chewing Gum, Inc., 208 F.2d 560, 563 (2d Cir. 1953) (L. Hand, J.).

61. This is the economic definition of an intentional tort for which no defense of or akin to contributory negligence (that is, no defense of victim fault) should lie. See William M. Landes and Richard A. Posner, *The Economic Structure of Tort Law*, ch. 6 (1987).

are not confused and use his mark to identify his good, thus reducing H^b and raising the amount of X that B produces, but harms consumers who believe they are getting a good produced by A. Only if the additional cost to B of reducing confusion is less than the expected reduction in harm to the confused group from B's abandoning the mark should he be found guilty of infringement.

Consistent with this suggestion, courts in cases of unintentional infringement require the plaintiff to prove that an appreciable (that is, nontrivial, though not necessarily immense) number of ordinarily prudent consumers are likely to be misled by the similarity between the two marks.[62] The more who are misled, the likelier are the costs of confusion to exceed the costs of changing the second mark. The focus on the ordinarily prudent consumer allows for the possibility that the lowest-cost avoider of confusion may be the consuming public itself, in which event the burden of avoiding confusion is placed on consumers by refusing to enjoin the second mark.

Compare the traditional approach taken by the Federal Trade Commission to the parallel problem of false advertising. The Commission's efforts in this area invited a drumbeat of criticism,[63] which the common law of trademark infringement has escaped. In part this was due to the fact that the FTC believed it should protect careless consumers from even innocent misrepresentations,[64] while trademark law, as we have seen, protects the careless consumer only from deliberate misrepresentation. In part it may have been due to the fact that a firm that complains to the FTC bears none of the costs of enforcement (they are borne by the taxpayer if the Commission decides to act on the complaint) and so has less incentive to avoid making frivolous and anticompetitive complaints than it would if it bore part of those costs, as it would in a private lawsuit.[65] Also relevant is the difference between common law and public regulation as methods of promoting the efficient use of resources. Common law—which trademark law mainly is, despite the Lanham Act, which codifies and supplements rather than displaces

---

62. See, for example, McGregor-Doniger, Inc. v. Drizzle, Inc., 599 F.2d 1126 (2d Cir. 1979).

63. See, for example, Richard S. Higgins and Fred S. McChesney, "Truth and Consequences: The Federal Trade Commission's Ad Substantiation Program," 6 *International Review of Law and Economics* 151 (1986).

64. See Craswell, note 59 above, at 697. In 1983 the Commission abandoned its approach, in favor of a "reasonable consumer" standard. See "FTC Policy Statement on Deception" (Oct. 14, 1983), *http://www.ftc.gov/bcp/policystmt/ad-decept.htm*, summarized in Edmund W. Kitch and Harvey S. Perlman, *Intellectual Property and Unfair Competition* 160 (5th ed. 1998).

65. And if the suit is deemed frivolous, the plaintiff will have to pay the defendant's attorney's fees as well as his own. See Blau Plumbing, Inc. v. S.O.S. Fix-It, Inc., 781 F.2d 604, 612 (7th Cir. 1986).

the common law of unfair competition, of which the common law of trade-marks is a part—is for a variety of institutional reasons more likely to be informed by a concern with achieving efficient resource allocation than administrative regulation is.[66]

Dilution, Blurring, and Tarnishment: Trademark Propertized

Suppose a lounge in Boston calls itself "Tiffany" or a peanut vendor in the Bowery calls himself "Rolls Royce Ltd." There is no danger that consumers will think they're dealing with Tiffany or Rolls Royce if they patronize these sellers, so there might seem to be no case for thinking them guilty of trade-mark infringement. Many states, however, would recognize a cause of action for dilution of the Tiffany and Rolls Royce trademarks.[67] There is now an antidilution provision in the Lanham Act, though it is limited to "famous" trademarks.[68] A related problem—where, however, a cause of action is not recognized—is that of cheap copies, as when a perfume manufacturer advertises a very cheap perfume as a copy of Chanel No. 5.[69] A legal doctrinal reason for the difference in outcomes is that the copier is not using the trade-mark to denote his cheap copy, just as we are not using the phrase "Chanel No. 5" to denote any product of ours merely by using the name in this book. In *Smith v. Chanel* the copier was using the phrase to inform consumers about the scent of his perfume. It would have been very costly for consumers to acquire such information before purchasing the copier's perfume because the perfume was sold through the mail.

There are several possible grounds for providing a legal remedy for the use of a trademark without the trademark owner's consent even when the use does not deceive or confuse consumers regarding the source of the product or service that they are buying. Three of these grounds form a cluster: tarnishment, blurring, and pure dilution. When the consumer who has patronized the peanut vendor sees the name "Rolls Royce," he will think both about the auto manufacturer and about the peanut vendor. The Rolls Royce

66. See, for example, Posner, note 8 above, § 12.9 and ch. 19. One of those reasons may be that both sides in a private suit bear litigation expenses, whereas in an administrative proceeding the private complainant is able to shift the cost to the agency.

67. See, for example, Hyatt Corp. v. Hyatt Legal Services, 736 F.2d 1153, 1157–1159 (7th Cir. 1984).

68. See 15 U.S.C. § 1125(c); Ty, Inc. v. Perryman, 306 F.3d 509 (7th Cir. 2002); Nabisco, Inc. v. PF Brands, Inc., 191 F.3d 208 (2d Cir. 1999).

69. See Smith v. Chanel, Inc., 402 F.2d 562 (9th Cir. 1968). On remand, the district court found that the copier had violated section 43(a) of the Lanham Act (false advertising) because its perfume did not in fact have the identical scent as Chanel No. 5, as claimed in its advertising.

image of quality and luxury will thus be overlaid or contaminated by the opposite image that the sight of the peanut vendor creates. Psychologists discuss this phenomenon under the rubric of the "availability heuristic," as we noted in the preceding chapter in discussing trademark parody cases. The converse case, that of favorable associations, is illustrated by the high prices paid for ordinary objects merely because they were once owned by celebrities, such as Jacqueline Kennedy Onassis or the Duke and Duchess of Windsor; a premium is paid for the association. The existence of such premiums makes it plausible to suppose that association with anticelebrities (the peanut vendor, for example) would indeed impose a cost. The clearest cases of tarnishment are those in which the negative premium is particularly high because, as in the parody or travesty cases discussed in the preceding chapter, the association is hateful or offensive, rather than merely ridiculous as in the Rolls Royce example. A similar phenomenon leads some people to change their names if a namesake becomes notorious. Very few people any more are named "Adolf," not because the name would cause confusion but because it has negative associations.

Even if the association is completely neutral, there is a cost to the owner of the trademark. Suppose elite brand names such as "Tiffany" and "Rolls Royce" were appropriated only by producers of equally fine products. Nevertheless the distinctiveness of the marks as identifiers of the products sold by the Tiffany and Rolls Royce companies would be reduced. More mental time and effort—the "imagination cost" to which we referred in Chapter 6—would be required to associate the name with a particular product. The result would be an increase in consumer search costs. This is the "blurring" effect of which the dilution cases speak.

A distinct economic reason for antidilution laws, though not one that has yet gained a foothold in the case law, is based on external benefits. Rolls Royce has made a substantial investment in creating a famous name. This investment has taken the form not only of advertising the name but also and more important of producing a product whose quality has made the name a worldwide symbol of quality. The peanut vendor appropriates some of the benefits of that investment without compensating the investor. There is no confusion; the consumer will not think the vendor's peanuts of higher quality just because he uses the name Rolls Royce for his business. The use of the name is a joke—but it is a joke intended to attract business and it works as a joke only because of the fame of the Rolls Royce name. Suppose there is no blurring or tarnishment either. If the appropriation of the mark without the permission of Rolls Royce were nevertheless forbidden, the benefits of its investment in creating a famous name would be more completely internalized and the amount of investing in creating prestigious names would rise. The common law doctrine of misappropriation, discussed briefly in Chapter 4, might be invoked in support of legal protection in such a case, for it is a pure misappropriation case.[70] Those who believe that "product differentiation" is a bad thing because it creates artificial barriers to entry would not applaud such a result, but as we noted at the beginning of this chapter that belief is mistaken.

There are, however, two good economic objections to legal protection in the pure dilution case, that is, the case in which the goodwill created by a trademark is used by another producer without any element of blurring or tarnishment. ("Dilution" is actually a misnomer in such a case, and even "misappropriation" is misleading, for there is no impairment of the trademark owner's goodwill; it is spread farther without being diminished.) First, the number of prestigious names is so vast that it is unlikely that any of the owners of prestigious trademarks could obtain substantial licensing fees. Competition would drive the fees to zero since, if the name is being used in an unrelated market, virtually every prestigious name will be a substitute for every other in that market. Second, trademark owners already work to prevent their mark from being attached to any brand other than their own. In part this is to preserve the mark by preventing consumer confusion, but in part it is also to prevent the mark from becoming generic. If antidilution law is interpreted as arming trademark owners to enjoin uses of their mark that, while not confusing, threaten to render the mark generic, the social benefits of genericness, in reduced consumer search costs and enhanced competition, are reduced or postponed.

The final economic argument for antidilution laws relates to cheap copies. "Many persons purchase branded goods for the purpose of demonstrating to others that they are consumers of the particular good,"[71] in other words, to impress others. Just as people often conceal their undesirable characteristics in order to create or protect reputation capital,[72] so they flaunt their desirable characteristics. They advertise themselves (much as sellers advertise their goods) by wearing clothes, jewelry, or accessories that tell the world that they are people of refined or flamboyant taste or high income. (The motive is similar to that of many collectors.) If others can buy and wear cheap copies, the signal given out by the purchasers of the originals

70. See Rochelle Cooper Dreyfuss and Roberta Rosenthal Kwall, *Intellectual Property: Cases and Materials on Trademark, Copyright and Patent Law* 137–138 (1996).

71. Richard S. Higgins and Paul H. Rubin, "Counterfeit Goods," 29 *Journal of Law and Economics* 211 (1986).

72. See Richard A. Posner, *The Economics of Justice*, ch. 9 (1981).

is blurred.[73] The perfume you smell may be Chanel No. 5, which tells you something about the wearer, or it may be some cheap copy. It may be difficult or impossible to tell which.

The twist here is that the confusion does not occur in the market for the trademarked good, or in any other product market, but in a "resale" market where consumers of the product compete with other consumers for advantageous personal transactions. Using trademark law to make it harder to market cheap copies (say, by forbidding the maker of the cheap copy of Chanel No. 5 to mention Chanel No. 5 in its advertising) promotes competition in this market while impairing it, perhaps severely, in the product market. The trade-off would be simple only if we were confident that the sole motive for buying the cheap copy was to pass oneself off as having a higher income. Then one could regard the seller of the cheap copy as a kind of contributory infringer who was making it easier for consumers to deceive the people with whom they transact in the market for personal relations and sometimes in the job market as well. But if this is not the sole motive, then the effect of allowing damages for dilution may be to prevent the marketing of imitations, resulting in higher prices because of reduced competition. Suppose someone really could duplicate the scent of Chanel No. 5 (and without violating trade secrecy or infringing a patent); how could he describe his product accurately without mentioning the Chanel brand? Trademark protection would have the same effects as allowing a descriptive mark to be appropriated without proof of secondary meaning.

73. This was the explicit basis for sporadic efforts to regulate luxury in dress in medieval Europe. In the fourteenth century "nothing was more resented by the hereditary nobles than the imitation of their clothes and manners by the upstarts . . . Magnificence in clothes was considered a prerogative of the nobles, who should be identifiable by modes of dress forbidden to others . . . Sumptuary laws were repeatedly announced, attempting to fix what kinds of clothes people might wear." Barbara W. Tuchman, *A Distant Mirror: The Calamitous 14th Century* 19 (1978). See also Gary S. Becker, Edward Glaeser, and Kevin M. Murphy, "Social Markets and the Escalation of Quality: The World of Veblen Revisited," in Gary S. Becker and Kevin M. Murphy, *Social Economics: Market Behavior in a Social Environment* 84 (2000).

8

The Optimal Duration of
Copyrights and Trademarks

In this chapter we undertake a critical examination of the widely accepted proposition that economic efficiency requires that the copyright term be limited[1] and glance at the contrasting case of trademark protection, which as explained in the preceding chapter has no time limit as such although it can be lost by abandonment or laches or by becoming a generic name. The reader may be surprised to find us toying with the idea of "perpetual" copyright, in light of our emphasis on uncertainty that the existing scope of intellectual property rights can be justified economically. But the tradeoff we focus on in this chapter is not life plus seventy years versus forever but life plus seventy years versus short fixed terms renewable as many times as the copyright owner wants if he is willing to pay a renewal fee (which may be substantial) every time. The result might be a larger public domain, and in particular fewer restrictions on copying most works created recently, than under the current system.

We do not consider the possible application of the approach to software copyrights. Indefinite renewal might enable software producers to impede competitors' software development, an unlikely prospect with regard to other types of copyrighted work. In any event, software is excluded from our empirical analysis, which (as will become clear) is necessarily limited to experience under the pre-1976 copyright regime, when there were no software copyrights.

Introduction

The first federal copyright statute, enacted in 1790, specified an initial term of fourteen years plus a renewal term of the same length, provided the author was still living at the end of the initial term. The initial term was lengthened to twenty-eight years in 1831 and the renewal term to twenty-eight years in 1909, forty-seven years in 1962, and sixty-seven years in 1998. The Copyright Act of 1976 switched from a fixed to a variable but still limited term

---

1. See, for example, Brief of George A. Akerlof, et al., as Amici Curiae in Support of Petitioners in Eldred v. Ashcroft, 123 S. Ct. 769 (2003), filed May 20, 2002.

equal to the life of the author plus fifty years, raised to seventy years in 1998 by the Sonny Bono Copyright Term Extension Act. The 1976 Act fixed a term for works of hire[2] of seventy-five years from publication or 100 years from creation, whichever expired first; the Sonny Bono Act extended these terms to ninety-five and 120 years. The 1976 Act also made copyrights on works created after January 1, 1978, nonrenewable, but it allowed assignments and other transfers of copyrights to be terminated by the author or his heirs thirty-five years after the assignment or transfer.

The Constitution authorizes Congress to create copyright and patent protection only "for limited Times."[3] But the legal significance of "limited Times" is unclear, although the motivation—a hostility deeply rooted in Anglo-American law and politics to the conferral of monopolies by the executive branch of government[4]—is clear enough. Any time short of infinity, which is to say any fixed period of years, is "limited" in the literal sense of the word; and even if "limited" means something *far* short of infinity, this limitation might conceivably be got around by allowing repeated extensions of the copyright term. Renewals and extensions of patents and copyrights had been common in England in the eighteenth century, though on an individual rather than a wholesale basis, and it was English practice that provided the model and inspiration for the copyright clause of the Constitution and for the early federal copyright statutes.[5] And since common law copyright is perpetual, states could recognize copyright after the expiration of federal copyright protection if the federal copyright law disclaimed any intention of preempting state law.[6] Moreover, although Congress could not grant perpetual copyright under the authority of the Constitution's copyright clause, maybe it could do so under other grants of power to Congress, such as the power to regulate interstate and foreign commerce. That is unlikely; the framers clearly intended to limit as well as confer congressional authority to grant patents and copyrights. In any event, our concern is with the economics rather than the constitutionality of indefinite renewal.[7]

2. These are works in which the employer, or occasionally other hirers, of the actual author of the work owns the copyright unless the contract with the author provides otherwise. We examine the work for hire doctrine in Chapter 10.

3. On the significance of the term "limited Times," see Edward C. Walterscheid, *The Nature of the Intellectual Property Clause: A Study in Historial Perspective* 271–307 (2002).

4. See, for example, The Case of Monopolies, 11 Co. Rep. 85b, 77 Eng. Rep. 1260 (K.B. 1602).

5. See Walterscheid, note 2 above, at 355–356, 364.

6. See Bonito Boats, Inc. v. Thunder Craft Boats, Inc., 489 U.S. 141, 166–167 (1989).

7. The Supreme Court has recently upheld by a broad margin (7–2) the constitutionality of the Sonny Bono Act, see Eldred v. Ashcroft, 123 S. Ct. 769 (2003), against the claim that it violated the "limited Times" provision. In light of that decision, it is unlikely that a system of indefinite renewals, which has more to commend it than the Sonny Bono Act, would be held unconstitutional.

Although a copyright that could be renewed indefinitely might turn out to be perpetual, this would be unlikely for any but a tiny fraction of all copyrights. We shall see that fewer than 11 percent of the copyrights registered between 1883 and 1964 were renewed at the end of their twenty-eight-year term, even though the cost of renewal was small.[8] And only a tiny fraction of the books ever published are still in print; for example, of 10,027 books published in the United States in 1930, only 174 were still in print in 2001—1.7 percent.[9] These data suggest that most copyrights depreciate rapidly and therefore that few would be renewed if even a slight fee were charged; the sheer bother of applying for renewal appears to be a significant deterrent. Granted, it costs more to keep a book in print than to renew a copyright; and a copyrighted work's derivative works may have commercial value after the original work has lost it. Nevertheless it is apparent that even with an unlimited right of renewal the public domain would remain a vast repository of intellectual "property" (legally, nonproperty) available for use without charge both by consumers and as a source of free inputs into the creation of new intellectual property.

Allowing unlimited renewals might, depending on the length of the initial term and on the fee structure, actually *expand* the number of works in the public domain. The average value of those works would probably fall, since copyright in the most enduringly popular works would be renewed over and over again. But the total value might well rise, and not only because fewer works would remain under copyright for as long a time as under the present system. The public domain is not a fixed supply of works from which any enlargement of copyright protection subtracts. Its size is a positive function of the extent of copyright protection. The more extensive that protection is, the greater the incentive to create intellectual property, some fraction of which will become a part of the public domain when the copyright expires or, under the system we are suggesting, is not renewed. Cutting the other way, though, is the fact that a stiff renewal fee increases the expected cost of copyright and so may deter the creation of some expressive works.

---

8. The renewal fee was $1 from 1909 to 1947, $2 from 1948 to 1965, $4 from 1966 to 1977, $6 from 1978 to 1990, $12 from 1991 to 1992, $20 from 1993 to 1999, and $45 from 2000 to the present. Prior to 1992, a copyright holder who wanted to renew his copyright had to file a renewal application during the last year of the initial copyright term. An amendment that year to the Copyright Act made renewals automatic, although there still are some benefits to filing for renewal registration. See Robert A. Gorman and Jane C. Ginsburg, *Copyright: Cases and Materials* 356–357 (6th ed. 2002).

9. These data were computed from *American Library Annual and Book Trade Almanac for 1872–1957; The Bowker Annual* (same publication, new title) for 1974; and *Books in Print*, at Bowker.com.

The Benefits of Time-Limited Copyrights

Two propositions are widely believed by most economists; it is the tension between them that makes the question of a limited versus indefinite copyright term an interesting and difficult one. The first proposition is that, so far as is feasible, all valuable resources, including copyrightable works, should be owned, in order to create incentives for their efficient exploitation and to avoid overuse. The second proposition is that copyright should be limited in duration. The reasons offered in support of the second proposition should be familiar to the reader from the earlier chapters in this book: (1) tracing costs increase with the length of copyright protection; (2) transaction costs may be prohibitive if creators of new intellectual property must obtain licenses to use all the previous intellectual property they seek to incorporate; (3) because intellectual property is a public good, any positive price for its use will induce both consumers and creators of subsequent intellectual property to substitute inputs that cost society more to produce or are of lower quality, assuming (realistically however) that copyright holders cannot perfectly price discriminate; (4) because of discounting to present value, incentives to create intellectual property are not materially affected by cutting off intellectual property rights after many years, just as those incentives would not be materially affected if, during the limited copyright term, lucrative new markets for the copyrighted work, unforeseen when the work was created, emerged;[10] (5) in any event, retroactive extensions of copyright should not be granted. On the one hand, they can't affect the incentive to create new works, since a retroactive extension affects only the return on works already in existence.[11] On the other hand, the possibility of obtaining retroactive extensions invites rent seeking, as in the Disney Company's lobbying for the Sonny Bono Act, of which more shortly.

Determining the optimal term of copyright protection requires balancing at the margin the incentive effects of a longer term against the administrative and access costs, bearing in mind that the relevant access includes that of future creators of intellectual property as well as that of consumers of the existing property. Since, given discounting and depreciation, the incremental in-

10. One must be cautious, however, in asserting that "unforeseen" opportunities will not affect incentives. A particular new market may be unforeseen or unanticipated yet may be part of a *class* of markets that when the work was created had a foreseen, positive probability of coming into existence and therefore may have influenced the incentive to create the work. See generally Jane C. Ginsburg, "Copyright and Control over New Technologies of Dissemination," 101 *Columbia Law Review* 1613 (2001).

11. This is a slight overstatement. Knowledge of the possibility of a future lengthening of the copyright term might have some, though probably very small, incentive effects.

centive to create new works as a function of a longer term is likely to be very small beyond a term of twenty-five years or so,[12] administrative and access costs will tend to dominate, implying an optimal copyright term considerably shorter than the current term of life plus seventy years.[13] Thus the second proposition denies the first (valuable resources should be owned) and asserts that copyrightable intellectual property should be taken out of private ownership and placed in the public domain after a period of years no longer than required to generate socially efficient incentives to create new works. But is the second proposition always sound? It may be, since from a social standpoint (sometimes from a private one as well) property rights often cost more than they are worth. It has seemed so to most students of copyright law. But we have our doubts.

The argument for limiting copyright duration because of tracing costs is superficial except in explaining why *common law* copyright (largely extinguished, however, by the Copyright Act of 1976) in unpublished works is perpetual: there is usually only one copy of such works, so the cost of determining the copyright holder's identity is trivial unless the copy has passed through many hands.[14] Even in the case of published works, the costs of tracing the ownership of copyrighted works could be reduced to a low level by modest institutional reforms. It is true that enormous tracing costs would be incurred by any would-be publisher of a new translation of the *Iliad* if the heirs of Homer could enforce copyright in the work. But this is only because no one knows who they are. Equally great tracing costs would be required to determine the ownership of a parcel of land if land titles weren't recorded in

---

12. Suppose a copyright on a particular work would yield $1 per year in perpetuity at a discount rate of 10 percent. Under a system of perpetual copyright, the present value of this infinite stream of income would equal $10 $(= 1/r)$. Under a limited copyright term $(= t)$ the present value would be $(1 - e^{-rt})/r$. So if $t = 25$ and $r = .10$, the present value of $1 per year for twenty-five years is $9.18, which is more than 90 percent of the present value of a perpetual copyright. If the value of the copyright depreciates by, say, 5 percent per year, the difference in present value between a perpetual and twenty-five-year copyright is only about 2.5 percent ($6.67 versus $6.51).

13. For empirical evidence that the twenty-year extension of the copyright term by the Sonny Bono Act did not increase the production of copyrightable works, see Kai-Lung Hui and I. P. L. Png, "On the Supply of Creative Work: Evidence from the Movies," 92 *American Economic Review Papers and Proceedings* 217 (May 2002). See also Avishalom Tor and Dotan Oliar, "Incentives to Create under a 'Lifetime-Plus-Years' Copyright Duration: Lessons from a Behavioral Economic Analysis for *Eldred v. Ashcroft*," 36 *Loyola of Los Angeles Law Review* 437 (2002).

14. An example is the discovery of an unpublished manuscript in the library of Harvard University of a novel entitled *Inheritance*, written by Louisa May Alcott in 1849. It had been miscatalogued for many years and no one knew of its existence. Although Alcott was childless, the copyright holders—fourth-generation descendants of Alcott's father—were not difficult to locate. See Lawrence Van Gelder, "Uncovered at Harvard: Alcott's First Novel," *N.Y. Times,* May 1, 1996, p. C15.

public registries. It is not perpetual property rights but absence of registration that creates prohibitive tracing costs.

Were a system of indefinitely renewable copyright to be instituted today, there would be no great difficulty in identifying copyright owners a century or for that matter a millennium hence if, for example, the law required copyright owners to reregister their copyrights every ten or even twenty-five years in some central registry under the name of the copyright holder and to notify the registry in the event the copyright was transferred. (Owners of existing copyrights would be required to register them upon the creation of the new system.) The owner would be required to provide the registry with his address and notify it of any changes of address; a transferee would likewise be required to furnish this information to the registry. Then a search of the registry either under the name of the owner or under the title of the copyrighted work (as the work itself might not reveal the name of the original copyright owner) would reveal the address of the current copyright holder, his agent, etc., from whom a license would have to be sought, just as in the case of the registries in which titles to real estate are recorded and the Uniform Commercial Code registries in which security interests in personal property are recorded. A fee would be charged for renewing a copyright registration to recover the costs imposed on the registry itself and on the searchers by the renewal. The fee could exceed those costs if it were desired to expand the public domain by discouraging renewals of works unlikely to have much commercial value.

Under existing law, when copyright protection begins is relatively unimportant because the duration of protection is determined not by that starting point but instead (except in the case of works for hire) by the death of the author. Under a system of renewals, the starting point becomes critical. So our suggested system would require a return to something like the pre-1976 law, when copyright protection generally began with publication or registration.[15]

There would be no need to require, in addition to registration, that a notice of copyright be placed on copyrighted works indicating the name of the copyright holder and the date of the most recent copyright registration or renewal, as under the 1909 copyright act. The registry should provide adequate notice. And for some works up-to-date notices are either infeasible or simply too costly in relation to the benefits in reducing tracing costs. For example, the seller of a work of art who retains the copyright cannot place an up-to-date copyright notice on the work when it has been out of his possession for many years. There is also a risk of cluttering up a work of art with multiple notices that would detract from the work's artistic merits, unless the

15. This would require the United States to withdraw from the Berne Convention, of which it became a signatory in 1989 and which requires signatories to provide a minimum term of life plus fifty years.

notice had to be placed only on the back of the canvas, or the back of the pedestal on which a sculpture stands.

Joint ownership of copyrights is possible, but we need not worry that the more owners there are, the greater the tracing costs. Since any joint owner of a copyright may license its use subject only to a duty to account for the profits to the other owners, a would-be licensee of a jointly owned copyright need find only one of the joint owners to negotiate with.

The transaction-costs argument against indefinite renewal is stronger than the argument from tracing costs but must not be exaggerated either. Although transaction costs would be incurred each time a copyright was renewed, consisting mainly of the time costs of the copyright holder and the costs of administering the renewal system, they would be slight if most copyrights were not renewed—and the longer the initial term and the higher the renewal fee, the fewer would be renewed. However, the costs incurred in negotiating for the licensing of one or more of that minority of works on which the copyright would be renewed many times would be higher than under the present system, though not when the new work would be copying only one old work—for example, Joyce's *Ulysses* and Homer's *Odyssey*, the movie *Clueless* and the novel *Emma, My Fair Lady* and *Pygmalion, West Side Story* and *Romeo and Juliet, Ragtime* and *Michael Kohlhaas.* But sometimes multiple works are copied, as in Manet's *Déjeuner sur l'herbe* and T. S. Eliot's *The Waste Land,* both celebrated works that would be likely to remain under copyright indefinitely under a system of indefinite renewals. However, a work that borrows from multiple works is unlikely to offer itself as a substitute for any of them, especially when the borrowing from each one is small, and so such a work should probably be shielded from liability in any event by the fair use doctrine, which we argue repeatedly in this book—most pertinently to the present issue in Chapter 9—should be construed generously.[16] Further-

---

16. Consider the following hypothetical example offered in opposition to the Sonny Bono Act: "While interviewing students for a documentary about inner-city schools, a filmmaker accidentally captures a television playing in the background, in which you can just make out three seconds of an episode of 'The Little Rascals.' *He can't include the interview in his film unless he gets permission from the copyright holder to use the three seconds of TV footage.* After dozens of phone calls to The Hal Roach Studios, he is passed along to a company lawyer who tells him that he can include the fleeting glimpse of Alfalfa in his nonprofit film, but only if he's willing to pay $25,000. He can't, and so he cuts the entire scene." Jeffrey Rosen, "Mouse Trap: Disney's Copyright Conquest," *New Republic,* Oct. 28, 2002, p. 12 (emphasis added). We have italicized the sentence that indicates a much too narrow understanding of fair use. The "three seconds" quotation is an example, merely visual rather than verbal, of the kind of brief quotation from copyrighted works that the fair use doctrine, for economic reasons explained in Chapter 4, permits without need for a license from the owner of the copyright. Such misunderstandings are widespread. One of us has encountered an academic publisher who insisted that any quotation of two or more lines of copyrighted poetry requires a license to reprint. That is unsound as a matter of both economics and law.

more, the degree to which even a copy of a single work should be deemed infringing depends on the interpretation given to "substantial similarity," the criterion of infringement as we noted in Chapter 4. Although *Ulysses* is so heavily indebted to the *Odyssey* that it could be regarded as a burlesque of the earlier work, the debts are so well concealed from any but the most learned reader that probably the two works would not be deemed substantially similar. A narrow construal of substantial similarity and a broad construal of fair use would help maintain an ample public domain under a system of indefinite renewals.

Transaction costs under such a system would be greatest for explicitly composite works, such as anthologies of well-known earlier works. Under existing law the publisher of a collection of the world's greatest poems need obtain copyright licenses for only a subset of the poems—none first published before 1923.[17] Under a regime of indefinitely renewable copyright instituted in 1500 A.D., most of the poems in an anthology of popular poetry might still be under copyright and therefore many more licenses would have to be obtained for a new anthology.

The aggregate transaction costs of a system of indefinite copyright renewals would depend on the number and possibly the value of licenses (holding tracing costs constant), the transaction costs per license, and the administrative cost of operating the renewal system. Since the number of licenses would depend in part on the total number of works renewed, aggregate transaction costs could actually fall compared either to a system of automatic renewals or to a single term of life plus seventy years.

Consider now the public-good argument for limiting the duration of a copyright. Copyright law permits a writer or publisher or other producer of an expressive work to charge a price that exceeds marginal cost, which may be very low. To extend the copyright term is to increase the duration of the restriction on output and likewise the producer's revenue. As there is no solid basis for thinking the existing term too short to enable producers of expressive works to cover their full costs, there is no good incentive-based argument for the extension. Even if one thought the current level of copyright protection inadequate, extending the term, as by making copyrights renewable indefinitely, would do little to correct the balance, given discounting to present value. It might seem, therefore, that the only effect of extending the copyright term would be to create access costs by reducing the number of works at any given time that are in the public domain and can therefore be used without need to obtain a license.

17. The copyright on a work first published in 1922 would terminate after seventy-five years (a twenty-eight-year initial term plus a forty-seven-year renewal term), and thus in 1997. The Sonny Bono Act adds an additional twenty years of protection for works that were still under copyright in 1998.

But those costs are unlikely to be great. First, just as future revenues must be discounted to present value to determine their value, so future costs must be discounted similarly to determine their present cost. If the present value of some remote future benefit is trivial, so is the present cost of the equally remote future deadweight loss. It is true that when values cannot be monetized the use of a social discount rate, somehow computed, may be preferable to the use of the private discount rate. But deadweight costs are readily monetizable. Given an estimate of their dollar cost in some future period, government can offset them by investing a sum equal to their present value, computed according to current long-term interest rates, in financial instruments.

The discounting of future deadweight costs ceases to reassure if the question is whether to extend the term of existing rather than future copyrights, at least existing copyrights that, unless extended, will soon expire. Suppose a copyright that was about to expire is extended another twenty years. The deadweight costs will begin to accrue immediately. They still must be discounted, but the present cost will be much greater than if the discounting were of deadweight costs to be incurred in a period first beginning seventy-five years from now.[18] The case for a system of indefinite renewals may thus be stronger if it is limited to copyrights obtained after the system is instituted. However, a potentially offsetting benefit of a system of indefinite renewals not limited to future copyrights—reduced rent seeking—will be noted shortly.

Second, because the scope of copyright protection is narrow, the size of the deadweight loss created by copyright protection will usually be small. The narrow scope of the property right implies the existence of close substitutes, which increase the elasticity of demand for the copyrighted work. In the simple case of a linear demand curve and constant marginal cost, the deadweight loss of monopoly is one-half the amount by which the monopolist's revenue exceeds his cost; the higher the elasticity of demand, the smaller that amount. It has been argued that the optimal duration of a patent would be infinite if the scope of patent protection were narrowed appropriately.[19] Conceivably the scope of copyright protection is already so narrow that an infinite copyright term would not be a source of significant deadweight loss. But this is merely a conjecture (are there good substitutes, for example, for Shakespeare's plays or Mozart's piano concertos?), and one reason the scope is narrow is that the public domain provides a source of free inputs into the

18. This point was emphasized in the economists' amicus curiae brief in the *Eldred* case, note 1 above, at 11.

19. Richard Gilbert and Carl Shapiro, "Optimal Patent Length and Breadth," 21 *RAND Journal of Economics* 106 (1990).

creation of new copyrightable works. If valuable works are withheld from the public domain because the copyright term has been extended, there may be significantly fewer public domain works (weighting number by quality) upon which to draw, which will reduce competition with existing copyrightable works.

Third, indefinite renewal and extending the copyright term are not the same thing. The length of the initial and renewal terms, the fee charged for renewal, and the scope of renewal (would it be limited to a single work, or could it cover a group of works?) are variables that can be adjusted to produce on average whatever de facto copyright term is deemed socially desirable; nor need the length, fee, or scope be the same for all classes of work (books, software, music, etc.). The shorter the initial grant (it could be as short as ten years) and the higher the renewal fee, the shorter would be the de facto copyright term of most works (all, if the renewal fee is high enough—and it could escalate with the number of renewals) and so the fewer the number of works that would be protected by copyright. It is the *composition* of the public domain that would most likely be changed by an indefinite-renewal system because there would be better sorting of works into two categories: (1) valuable works, where the benefits of property rights may well exceed the costs, and (2) works of little value, where the costs of administering copyright protection are very likely to exceed the benefits and a stiff renewal fee would discourage the owner from seeking continuing copyright protection. The public domain would be enlarged, although some valuable works would be excluded that under the present system fall into the public domain eventually.

But the following complication would attend stiff renewal fees. When the fees are very low, the fact that the commercial value of copyrightable works varies enormously is relatively unimportant, except perhaps for photographs, since each photograph is a copyrightable work and serious photographers take many pictures in a single session. But when renewal fees are high, uniform fees can become prohibitive for many copyrighted works—not only photographs. It would be one thing to charge $1,000 to renew the copyright on a movie after ten years, and another to charge $1,000 to renew the copyright on an academic book. But while group renewals of photographs would have to be allowed (as they are under current law), the fact that stiff fees would deter the renewal of copyrights on works having little commercial value is not necessarily a bad thing. By definition these are works unlikely to yield the owners of the copyrights on them a significant return, so it is best that they be placed in the public domain where they can be used as free inputs into the production of new intellectual property, though we shall have to qualify this point later. Still, a single fee for all types of copyrighted work is unlikely to be optimal. An alternative that would minimize legislative and regulatory discretion, and hence rent seeking, would be to make the fee equal to a fixed percentage of the first year's inflation-adjusted revenues from the sale or rental of the copyrighted work.

We have a related response to the argument that under a system of renewals many copyrights would be lost by sheer ignorance or inadvertence on the part of copyright holders. One of the reasons given for the abandonment of the renewal system by the Copyright Act of 1976 was that many copyright holders didn't know they had a renewal right or made fatal errors in filling out the renewal form. (The problem was solved by switching to a system of life plus years, since no one forgets to die.) But ignorance is endogenous; care and information are costly goods, which are not "bought" if the benefits from them are slight. It was because so many copyrights had (and have) so little value that so many copyright holders were not assiduous in protecting their copyrights.[20]

With regard to rent-seeking implications of a switch to a system of indefinite renewals, the first thing to note is that owners of copyrights on old but still commercially valuable works have an incentive to expend resources on lobbying Congress to extend the copyright term on these works. Retroactive extensions do not enhance incentives to create expressive works, so if those incentives are the only benefits from copyright, such extensions will increase transaction and access costs without generating any offsetting value. The costs of Disney's successful efforts to lobby for the Sonny Bono Act that retroactively extended its copyrights by twenty years in order to protect its soon-to-expire copyrights on Mickey Mouse and other cartoon characters,[21] and the costs of the unsuccessful efforts (which seem, however, to have been slight) of competing interests to oppose the extension, were incurred to obtain and limit economic rents, respectively. If there are no offsetting social benefits from retroactive extensions of the copyright term, these costs were wasted from a social standpoint.

20. Granted, the renewal provision of the 1909 Copyright Act was unclear with respect to the prospective assignability of the renewal term and to the respective rights of an assignee and a statutory successor (the provision authorized renewal by the author's heir if the author died before the initial term expired). See Pierre N. Leval and Lewis Liman, "Are Copyrights for Authors or Their Children?" 39 *Journal of the Copyright Society* 1 (1991). These uncertainties, which any law reinstituting renewal could easily dispel, may have been responsible for some failures of renewal.

21. See Janet Wasko, *Understanding Disney: The Manufacture of Fantasy* 85–86 (2001). The Act went into effect on October 27, 1998, four years before the copyright on the original Mickey Mouse would have expired. The Mickey Mouse character has been altered in appearance several times, however, as we'll note in a moment, and the successive versions (which of course are derivative works) copyrighted, so even if the original copyright had been allowed to expire, Disney could have fended off efforts to market an exact duplicate of the current Mickey Mouse.

Rent-seeking activities are a natural consequence of any fixed copyright term, since the Congress that enacts the term cannot prevent future Congresses from increasing it retroactively. There will always be copyright holders whose incomes are diminished when their works fall into the public domain, and they have an incentive to expend resources on seeking retroactive extensions as the end of the copyright term draws near. This rent seeking would be lessened by indefinite renewability, which by eliminating the prospect of losing the income produced by old but still valuable copyrights would largely eliminate the incentive to lobby for copyright extensions. "Largely" rather than "entirely" because some resources might still be expended on lobbying for lower renewal fees and longer renewal terms. But normally it would be cheaper to pay the renewal fee than to try to change the law. And while a system of indefinite renewals limited to future copyrights would not curb the incentive to seek retroactive extensions of existing copyrights, that problem would disappear in time as old copyrights lost their value.

A particularly unfortunate aspect of congressional extensions of the copyright term is that they apply to *all* copyrighted works, not merely those whose owners lobbied for the extensions. Disney might have sought a private bill that would have extended only its copyrights, but a politically more effective strategy was to ally itself with other copyright owners and represent that the legislative relief sought would benefit all creators of intellectual property, not just Disney and a handful of rich heirs. But the result of the blanket extension of the copyright term was that a huge amount of intellectual property having little or no commercial value, yet potential value as a public domain input into future intellectual property, will be kept out of the public domain for another twenty years.

It might be objected that allowing indefinite renewals would eliminate only one form of rent seeking because copyrights have other dimensions of value besides duration, notably scope. But whatever incentive there is for lobbying for enlarged scope exists under the current system; it would not be greater under a system of indefinite renewals. A more serious concern is that copyright holders might renew their copyrights for strategic purposes, hoping one day to "hold up" an author who wanted to copy their work. This practice would resemble strategic patenting, discussed in Chapter 11, and would be a danger posed particularly by software copyrights, which is one reason why we do not discuss the applicability of a system of indefinite renewals to them. With regard to other classes of copyrightable work, a stiff renewal fee, combined with the effect of discounting to present value, should minimize the problem.

If we are correct so far, the *average* copyright duration might be shorter under a system of indefinite renewals than under the current system. Such a system might therefore reduce access costs for most but not all works, compared to the present system. (It probably would not reduce deadweight costs because these presumably are generated mainly by valuable copyrights, which would tend to be renewed.) But whatever the case with regard to costs, it may seem that there could be no social benefits from continuing indefinitely to protect even a small number of valuable works. This assumes, however, that the only justification for copyright protection is the incentives it produces to create new works. This may be wrong, as we consider next.

The Social Benefits of Allowing Some Copyrights to Remain in Effect Indefinitely

We focus here on the relative handful of copyrights that under a system of indefinite renewals could be expected to remain in force for even longer than life plus seventy years. Because of discounting to present value, an increase in the copyright term could not be justified on the ground that it would enhance the incentives to create expressive works. But the economic theory of property rights emphasizes not only their incentive effects, that is, the investment they encourage, but also their effect in optimizing current uses of property. We recall from Chapter 1 that because a natural pasture is not created by human effort, there is no social value in encouraging investments in creating it, but that in the absence of property rights the pasture would be overgrazed; none of the users would take account of the cost that his use imposed on the other users by making their cattle graze more to obtain the same amount of food, and thus gain less weight. Moreover, not all investments in expression are made before copies of a work are sold; some, which we'll call "maintenance" investments, are made afterwards and may be discouraged by durational limits on copyright. So in this part of the chapter we shall be considering congestion externalities and maintenance incentives as arguments for making copyrights indefinitely renewable.

CONGESTION EXTERNALITIES Benefits of property rights analogous to those of property rights in natural pastures have already been recognized in two areas of intellectual property law. One is trademark law, which, as we know, does not impose any fixed limitation on the duration of a trademark, since confusion would result if the same trademark denoted goods of different provenance and quality, and which, through the concept of blurring (a subcategory of dilution), protects trademark owners from the loss of value resulting from nonconfusing duplication of their trademarks, a form of overuse. The other area is the law of publicity rights, which as we noted briefly in Chapter 2 prevents the use of one's name or likeness in advertising or for other commercial purposes without one's permission. The tendency is to make publicity rights inheritable.[22] The motive is not to encourage greater investment in becoming a celebrity (the incremental encouragement would doubtless be minimal),[23] but to prevent the premature exhaustion of the commercial value of the celebrity's name or likeness.[24] The analogy to overgrazing is close. Overgrazing causes crowding in the short run, with a resulting reduction in weight gain, and depletion of the pasture in the long run with similar, though possibly more drastic, results. Similarly, overexposure of a celebrity may turn people off in the short run and truncate the period in which his name or likeness retains commercial value.

Recognition of an "overgrazing" problem in copyrightable works has lagged. Typical is the statement endorsed by many professors of intellectual property law in opposition to the Sonny Bono Act:

> The fundamental difference between tangible and intellectual property is that intellectual property is a nondepletable commons, while tangible property necessarily depletes with use. "The tragedy of the commons" is that failure to recognize perpetual and transferable property rights in tangible property leads inevitably to "overgrazing," as soon as an item of property enters the public domain from which everyone may draw freely. Recognition of perpetual property rights leads to economic efficiency, because a rational owner will optimize the balance between present and future consumption.
>
> There can be no overgrazing of intellectual property, however, because intellectual property is not destroyed or even diminished by consumption. Once a work is created, its intellectual content is infinitely multipliable.[25]

This is overstated, if only because it ignores the trademark and right-of-publicity cases that recognize that intellectual property *can* be diminished by

22. See Huw Beverley-Smith, *The Commercial Appropriation of Personality* 184 (2002); Mark F. Grady, "A Positive Economic Theory of the Right of Publicity," 1 *UCLA Entertainment Law Review* 97, 124–126 (1994). See also Douglas G. Baird, "Does Bogart Get Scale? Rights of Publicity in the Digital Age," 4 *Green Bag* (2d ser.) 357, 363–364 (2001).

23. As argued in Michael Madow, "Private Ownership of Public Image: Popular Culture and Publicity Rights," 81 *California Law Review* 125, 205–215 (1993). For an exception, see Zacchini v. Scripps-Howard Broadcasting Co., 433 U.S. 562 (1977), discussed in Madow, above, at 208 n. 395.

24. See Grady, note 22 above, at 103, 126; Richard A. Posner, *The Economics of Justice* 248 (1981). The English call this "face wearout." Madow, note 23 above, at 222. Madow, however, is skeptical about its empirical significance. See id. at 221–225.

25. Denis S. Karjala, "Statement of Copyright and Intellectual Property Law Professors in Opposition to H.R. 604, H.R. 2589, and S. 505, The Copyright Term Extension Act, Submitted to the Joint Committees of the Judiciary," Jan. 28, 1998, *http://www.public.asu.edu/ ~dkarjala/legmats/1998statement/html.*

consumption. But assessment of the welfare effects of congestion requires distinguishing technological from merely pecuniary externalities (transfer payments). The externality in the pasture case is technological because it imposes a real cost (diminished weight gain) rather than merely altering the distribution of wealth. Refusing to recognize inheritable publicity rights could impose either type of externality or both types. If anyone could use Humphrey Bogart's name or likeness in advertising, the aggregate value of that advertising use might be greater even though Bogart's estate would lose income. Indeed, if the marginal cost of additional copies of his image were zero, the marginal utility would also be zero, even though the total utility could be very great. But the total utility might decline if the lack of excludability and resulting proliferation of the Bogart image led to confusion, the tarnishing of the image, or sheer boredom on the part of the consuming public. Eventually the image might become worthless.

Could this be a problem with regard to copyrightable expression? There is some evidence that it is a concern of the Walt Disney Company with regard to its copyrighted characters, such as Mickey Mouse. "To avoid overkill, Disney manages its character portfolio with care. It has hundreds of characters on its books, many of them just waiting to be called out of retirement . . . Disney practices good husbandry of its characters and extends the life of its brands by not overexposing them . . . They avoid debasing the currency."[26]

Figure 8.1 illustrates the problem. D^0D^0 is the demand schedule in period t for some expressive work. Obviously copyright protection in period t and all future periods would have no effect on whether the work was created in period $t = 0$, but it would create a deadweight cost, illustrated by the triangle $P^0Q^2Q^0$, as a result of the copyright holder's charging P^0 when his marginal cost is zero. Terminating the copyright in t would eliminate the deadweight loss, as the number of uses of the work would increase to Q^2, that is, to the point at which the value of the marginal use equaled zero. But now suppose that contrary to the usual assumption about copyrights, additional uses impose technological externalities. Then terminating the copyright will lead not only to a movement along the demand curve but also to a downward shift (say to D^0D^1) in the overall demand, destroying value equal to the difference between the area under the original demand curve D^0D^0 up to P^0 and the area under D^0D^1 up to a zero price. If the externalities are small, the difference between the two demand curves may be negative, so that terminating the copyright at t would increase value. But if they are large, termination can result in a net loss in value. In the limit, additional uses beyond Q^0 might de-

26. Bill Britt, "International Marketing: Disney's Global Goals," *Marketing*, May 17, 1990, pp. 22, 26.

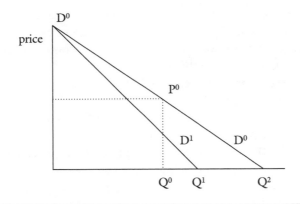

Figure 8.1. Copyright externalities

press the demand curve (as it rotates downward around the point that intersects the vertical axis at D^0) until it coincided with the vertical axis. In that event, terminating the copyright would destroy all its value in period t—the area under $D^0 D^0$ between the point at which it intersects the vertical axis and P^0—and presumably in all future periods as well.

A book or other copyrightable property is conventionally regarded as a public good in the sense that unlike a pasture its use by one consumer does not interfere with its use by any other. This point cannot be decisive, however; a celebrity's name or likeness is a public good in the same sense, yet unlimited reproduction of the name or the likeness could prematurely exhaust the celebrity's commercial value, just as unlimited drilling from a common pool of oil or gas would deplete the pool prematurely. The same could be true of a novel or a movie or a comic-book character or a piece of music or a painting, particularly with regard to copyrights on components of completed works rather than on the completed works themselves. That is why it is better to say that a book or other copyrighted work has public-good characteristics than that it *is* a public good.

If because copyright had expired anyone were free to incorporate the Mickey Mouse character in a book, movie, song, etc., the value of the character might plummet. If this came about only as a result of a movement down the original demand curve, the ordinary consequence of an increase in output, aggregate value would actually increase, by the area under the demand curve between P^0 and a zero price. Alternatively, however, the public might rapidly tire of Mickey Mouse; and his image might also be blurred or even tarnished, as some authors portrayed him as a Casanova, others as catmeat, others as an animal-rights advocate, still others as the henpecked husband of

Minnie. There would thus be both a movement along and a downward shift of the demand curve in Figure 8.1 until Mickey Mouse's commercial value was zero. The same thing would happen in the absence of negative technological externalities, but since the demand curve would be unchanged, total value would increase because there would be no deadweight loss.

To the extent that unauthorized reproductions of Mickey Mouse were classified as parodies, they would be immunized from liability by the fair use doctrine even in a regime of indefinitely renewable copyright. But not all would be parodic. The "Here's Johnny" right-of-publicity case mentioned in Chapter 6 is a good illustration of how an image can be degraded by the context in which it is presented to the public. The "character" in that case was a real human being, not a fiction, but analytically there is no difference between the congestion problem faced by a celebrity and that encountered by a fictitious character. If, as economic analysis of the right of publicity suggests, there is a real congestion problem in the former case, there must be in the latter case as well.

This analysis gains support from the discussion of derivative rights in Chapter 4. One purpose of giving the owner of a copyright a monopoly of derivative works is to facilitate the scope and timing of the exploitation of the copyrighted work—to avoid, as it were, the "congestion" that would result if once the work was published anyone could make and sell translations, abridgments, burlesques, sequels, versions in other media from that of the original (for example, a movie version of a book), or other variants without the copyright owner's authorization. The result could be premature saturation of the market, consumer confusion (for example, as to the source of the derivative works), and impaired demand for the original work because of the poor quality of some of the unauthorized derivative works.

We must not press the congestion argument (or its guilt-by-association cousin, illustrated by the "Here's Johnny" case and by some of the trademark cases discussed in Chapters 6 and 7) too far.[27] While examples can be given of works even of elite culture that may have been damaged by unlimited reproduction (the *Mona Lisa,* the opening of Beethoven's *Fifth Symphony,* and several of Van Gogh's most popular paintings come immediately to mind), there are counterexamples: the works of Shakespeare seem unimpaired by the uncontrolled proliferation of performances and derivative works, some of them kitsch, such as Shakespeare T-shirts and the movie *Shakespeare in Love.* And

27. A technical legal argument for not doing so is that the patent and copyright clause of the Constitution authorizes the grant of patents and copyrights "to promote the Progress of Science and useful Arts," and the elimination of congestion externalities might seem remote from that goal, though we think not, since such externalities impede the efficient functioning of the "Science" and "useful Arts" markets, that is, the markets in intellectual property.

in the field of popular culture, think only of Santa Claus as an example of the power of an iconic character to survive incessant use, apparently undamaged—but with the difference that he is strictly a seasonal character; we have eleven months of respite from him. Much of the Disney Company's own considerable commercial success has been based on its use of fictional characters that are in the public domain, such as Pinocchio, Cinderella, and Quasimodo. Still, the right-of-publicity cases show that there is potentially a legitimate concern here, one that economic analysis should not ignore completely. Think of the role of prominent "literary widows," such as Valerie Eliot and Sonia Orwell, in managing the copyrights of their husbands— would there not have been a danger, had Orwell's copyrights expired on or shortly after his death, of an avalanche of Orwell derivative works that might have made the world tire of him?

In a later chapter we shall express skepticism concerning moral rights doctrine. Among other things, the doctrine confers on creators of intellectual property, mainly artists, the right to prevent their work from being disfigured, even if they have assigned their copyright. We may seem inconsistent in suggesting that copyright owners be entitled to prevent the overuse of their work. There is no inconsistency. Artists can control the use of their work by retaining copyright, since, as we know, the copyright owner has the exclusive right to authorize derivative works: a Mickey Mouse who speaks foul language is a derivative work of the copyrighted Mickey Mouse and so the Disney Company can prevent its creation unless the creator can shelter under the fair use umbrella for parodies. It does not follow that if Disney assigned its copyright, it would still have a right, as under moral rights doctrine (were it available to corporations), to prevent the creation of a degrading version of Mickey Mouse. What is at issue, moreover, in our discussion of congestion externalities is not artistic integrity or reputation, values that may have noncommercial aspects, but a purely economic concern with minimizing economically harmful externalities.

The concern we have expressed regarding congestion externalities may seem to argue for a greatly enlarged concept of trademark dilution, a doctrine that we discussed critically at the end of the preceding chapter. Just as the promiscuous use of Humphrey Bogart's name and likeness in advertising might reduce the aggregate value of that advertising use, so might the promiscuous use of the name Rolls Royce as a trademark reduce the aggregate advertising value of the name even if the consuming public was not confused about the identity of the users. But probably antidilution law is not needed to prevent this problem from arising. The reason is that any widespread use of the mark *would* be confusing. Suppose that a hotel chain adopted the name Rolls Royce. Knowing that modern corporations are often highly diversified and that both automobiles and hotels are part of the travel sector of the economy, many consumers would infer an affiliation between the automobile company and the hotel chain. At the other end of the economic ladder, if, impressed by the success of a Rolls Royce hot-dog vendor, a vendor of roast chestnuts adopted the name Rolls Royce, there would again be a danger of consumer confusion—confusion not with the automobile manufacturer but with the hot-dog vendor; people might think the hot-dog and roast-chestnut vendors affiliates. If, however, somehow without confusion as to source, a prestigious name became so widespread as to threaten supersaturation and resulting loss of value, and thus create a true congestion externality, there would be an argument for invoking the antidilution principle.

MAINTENANCE INCENTIVES   The conventional economic criticism of the length of the copyright term draws too sharp a distinction between creation and copying. Imagine a novel published many years ago in which copyright has expired. The novelist is rediscovered and there is a surge in demand for his novels. Since no publisher could establish a property right in them, the incentives of publishers to publish and promote them might well be inadequate from a social standpoint. Often the demand for particular works of intellectual property is unknown before they actually hit the market.[28] Suppose an enterprising publisher has only a 20 percent chance of success with obscure public domain authors. He publishes the works of five such authors in order to have one success. In the absence of copyright protection, other publishers can wait and see which author sells and then bring out their own versions of his works. Publishers who wait avoid the costs of failure, but their free riding on the market information developed by the first to publish reduces the incentive of any publisher to search for potentially successful public domain works.[29] The tendency would be for only works of already well-known and safe authors whose works were in the public domain to be published.

The gravity of this problem should not be exaggerated. There is plenty of publication of public domain works; we remind the reader of the discussion

28. This has been noted in connection with dolls and other goods portraying dead celebrities. See Ronald Alsop, "Items Portraying Dead Stars Produce Profits Controversy," *Wall Street Journal,* May 10, 1984, p. A37.

29. In other words, "a work's public domain status is far from an unqualified incentive for utilizing it . . . Some of the obvious concerns are whether a copyrighted derivative work will have to compete with other, often low-budget, low quality copies and whether the producer of the copyrighted derivative of a public domain work is likely to have anything unique in the long run." Arthur R. Miller, "Copyright Term Extension: Boon for American Creators and the American Economy," 45 *Journal of the Copyright Law Society* 319, 324 (1998).

in Chapter 2 of the incentives for publication that are independent of intellectual property law. But, grave or trivial, a system of indefinite renewals would ameliorate the problem. It would not solve it, however, since works that were no longer popular would tend not to be renewed many times. Indeed, the problem would exist even if copyright were perpetual. Owners of a perpetual copyright that they considered worthless would not take even modest steps to assure the continued registration (for example, notifying the registry of changes of address) that a system of perpetual, as of indefinitely renewable, copyrights would require be established. A complete solution would require that the saviors of old works on which copyright had expired without renewal, like finders in the law of real property, be allowed to obtain copyright in those works. We consider that possibility later. For now, it is enough to observe that a system of indefinite renewals would, depending on the renewal fee, on whether group renewals were permitted, and on the formalities involved in renewal, somewhat improve the incentives to invest in public domain works.

Under the present regime a publisher has an incentive to make changes in any public domain work that he does revive, since he can copyright the changes. But changes made merely to stake a claim, just like premature introduction of a new product in order to sew up a desired trademark, are inefficient. Extending the copyright term might thus reduce socially excessive product differentiation ("overmaintenance" as it were).

Conversely, if because of its age a newly resuscitated novel were in need of an elaborate scholarly apparatus, re-editing, or other costly additions to make it accessible to a modern readership, publishers might be reluctant to undertake the needed measures, even if they could copyright the scholarly apparatus (which they could not do to the extent it was deemed a matter of ideas rather than expression). They would fear that the cost could not be recouped in the face of competition from cheap, bare-bones editions of the novel. Reviewers might use the scholarly apparatus, of course without paying anything (not even the price of the book, since reviewers generally receive free review copies), to explain the book to the public, who would then buy the bare-bones edition.

Or consider an old movie on which copyright had expired that a studio wanted to issue in a colorized version that would be very expensive to prepare. Promoting the colorized version might increase the demand for the black and white version, a close substitute. Since anyone could copy and sell that version, the studio would have to take into account, in deciding whether to colorize, the increase in demand for the black and white version. As a result the expected revenue from colorization might be less than the private costs and so the studio would decide against it. Indefinite renewal might provide a complete solution, since, given the public's avidity for movies old as well as new, an old movie would be quite likely to have retained enough value to have warranted the expense of renewal.

We conjecture that the reason so few classical composers are recorded and performed is that it is more costly to produce a musical composition than it is, say, to photograph a painting. The recording company that discovered and revived the works of a forgotten or obscure composer would be risking a substantial amount of money in an uncertain venture that could be imitated if successful. Much less expense would be involved in publishing a book or even arranging an exhibition of works of a forgotten or obscure painter. The absence of property rights in the music of well-known classical composers may also explain why many different recording companies record the same public domain works of Beethoven, Mozart, Bach, and other well-known composers.[30] Recording companies differentiate their product by promoting the performer or artist who has signed an exclusive contract with the company. Because a recording company can, for example, copyright the Chicago Symphony Orchestra's recording of Mahler's *First Symphony,* it has an incentive to promote that version; it has little incentive to promote the public domain work of an unknown composer, since it could not appropriate the benefits of its promotional efforts, as distinct from benefits that might accrue from a recorded performance of the unknown composer's work by a popular performer.

Consider also the effect on the recording of a composer's obscure works when his copyrights expire. Our analysis implies that upon the expiration of Puccini's copyrights, the rate at which his obscure works were recorded fell relative to recordings of the best-known works, since an investment in creating a demand for the obscure works would be more difficult to recoup once the works were no longer under copyright.

These examples, unlike those used to illustrate the economic analysis of publicity rights and our extension of that analysis to copyright, show that a case against a definite time limit for copyrights can be grounded in the traditional incentive-based argument for property rights, though with a new twist. The new twist is recognition that the need to invest in intellectual property to maximize its value is not necessarily exhausted in the initial creation of the property. Investment may be necessary to maintain the value of the property and also to resurrect abandoned or otherwise unexploited intellectual prop-

---

30. Eight composers (Mozart, Beethoven, Bach, Brahms, Tchaikovsky, Schubert, Chopin, and Haydn) account for 47 percent of all classical recordings. See F. M. Scherer, "The Innovation Lottery," in *Expanding the Boundaries of Intellectual Property: Innovation Policy for the Knowledge Society* 3, 14 (Rochelle Cooper Dreyfuss, Diane Leenheer Zimmerman, and Harry First eds. 2001).

erty.[31] Magnitudes are critical, however, and in their absence only tentative conclusions are possible.[32] We are told that the Disney Corporation has spent tens of millions of dollars refurbishing the Mickey Mouse character, both by subtle alterations in the character and by situating it in carefully selected entertainment contexts in an effort to increase the appeal of Mickey Mouse to the current generation of young children. The incentive to make such expenditures would be impaired if the copyright expired, allowing anyone to use the character, though the copier could not copy any newly copyrightable features that Disney had added to the original character.[33] This would be an important qualification should it turn out that only the most recent version of the character retains commercial appeal, but that seems unlikely.

If this analysis is correct, the drumbeat of criticisms of the retroactive extension of the Mickey Mouse copyright overlooks valid, although in the present state of knowledge inconclusive, economic arguments for extended copyright protection that are independent of whether the protection is extended

31. "For a work to be commercially successful, it requires effort and investment which, while not 'creative,' is still necessary to generate value. For example, authors employ literary agents, publishers advertise, etc. With musical composition and photographs, the collection, arrangement and indexing of the works adds value. With film, preservation requires constant attention. Even the straightforward act of printing a book entails a risk on investment. Arguably, none of these activities will be pursued as vigorously on behalf of public domain works as they are for works with ownership rights. And, from an economic point of view, these activities 'create' real value." Edward B. Rappaport, "Copyright Term Extension: Estimating the Economic Values" 4 (Congressional Research Service, May 11, 1998).

32. Rappaport states that the effect he describes "may be important in some cases, but, we believe, will more often be marginal." Id. He does not explain the reasoning or evidence that led him to this conclusion.

33. The public legislative history of the Sonny Bono Act contains little discussion of the twenty-year addition to the duration of copyrights on works for hire, such as the Disney copyrights. The main reasons given for the extension for individuals (remember that the Act extended the term for individuals from life plus fifty years to life plus seventy years) were (1) balance of payments and (2) the fact that people are living longer (Irving Berlin being a pertinent example). The second point makes very little sense, since an increase in longevity will automatically increase the length of the copyright term measured from the author's death, unless the concern is with the longevity of his heirs. The first point is mercantilist, reflecting the fact that the United States is a net exporter of intellectual property. One of the committee reports does explain, however, that the extension of the copyright term "will provide the important collateral benefit of creating incentives to preserve existing works [in digital format]." S. Rep. No. 315, 104th Cong., 2d Sess. 13 (1996). This is similar to our colorization example.

The mercantilist argument is not a good one even if a weight of zero is given to foreigners' welfare. Foreign trade is only a small part of the U.S. economy, and most intellectual property produced in the United States is consumed here. Moreover, U.S. producers may be hurt rather than helped by expanded copyright protection because it increases their input costs, as stressed in Chapters 2 and 3.

ex ante or ex post, though, as we have seen, ex post extension involves greater deadweight costs but lower rent-seeking costs. If the method of extension were periodic renewal, then since Congress could cut off the right of renewal at any time, a law authorizing renewals without a number limit would be less vulnerable to a constitutional challenge than a grant of perpetual copyright *ab initio*—the latter being flatly inconsistent with granting a copyright for "limited Times." Periodic renewal would also have the superior economizing properties that we have emphasized.

But it would not address the case in which intellectual property that has fallen into the public domain by abandonment is sought to be revived. Suppose Tobias Smollett had copyrighted his books but after a few renewals his heirs had decided the books had no value and so declined to pay the renewal fee. Our analysis implies that a publisher who wants to publish Smollett's books today should be permitted to take out copyright on them, by analogy to the rule discussed in Chapter 1 that allows finders to obtain title to abandoned (as distinct from merely misplaced) physical property. Unfortunately, the efficient implementation of such a rule would be considerably more complicated in the case of intellectual property. Allowing abandoned physical property to be withdrawn from the public domain unproblematically implements the policy that valuable property should *in general* be owned in order to create the correct incentives for its exploitation. But imagine a "finder" of intellectual property who claimed to have found, and who sought to obtain copyright in and register, all the books in the British Library on which copyright had expired. If the claim were allowed, the situation would resemble the banking of trademarks by listing all possible combinations of the letters of the alphabet, and would thus create the rent-seeking and transaction-cost problems that we discussed in Chapter 7 in relation to such banking.

The problem may not be insoluble. One way to deal with it would be to limit the acquisition of copyright in previously created works to works created after the law authorizing such acquisition was passed. Another would be to require the publication of such a work within a specified period of time after copyright was claimed in it. Another would be to charge a stiff fee for registering such a copyright.

We need to consider one more objection to indefinite renewals and to allowing even limited copyright protection for "found" public domain works. The expenditures that these measures would induce on discovering and disseminating obscure public domain works and on maintaining consumer interest in copyrighted works that were about to fall into the public domain would not be expenditures on creating expressive works; they would be marketing expenditures, which are not within the traditional domain of intellectual property law. Why should a particular subset of such expenditures be singled out for legal protection? Firms that introduce wine and cigar bars, recognize the potential for health clubs that combine workout and social activities, or introduce baggy trousers or pastel colors for clothing cannot prevent other firms from imitating their marketing innovations. Although trademark law may prevent confusingly close imitation and copyright law may protect particular advertising slogans, these laws do not prevent competitors from free riding on the information developed by the market innovators.

But the distinction between expressive works and the marketing of those works is overdrawn. Consider a record company that develops, promotes, and distributes new pop records. Which will be hits and which flops is not knowable in advance. In the absence of copyright protection—and here we are speaking just of protection against the copying of the sound recordings themselves—unauthorized copying could drive the price of the successful recordings down to their cost of manufacture and distribution and leave nothing for covering the costs of developing and promoting recordings of new songs and new performers. Copyright protection enables the record company to earn enough money on the hits to cover both the costs of the hits and the production *and marketing* costs of the many failures. By doing this, copyright indirectly prevents free riding on marketing expenditures similar to those incurred to maintain interest in soon-to-expire copyrighted works.[34] To state this another way, exploring the market for expressive works—the sort of exploration that the measures we are discussing would encourage—is a stage in the creation of intellectual property.

Moreover, marketing expenditures associated with expressive works differ from those associated with the other examples of new products that we gave because it is easier in the case of most expressive works to identify the innovator. Many people might be able to make credible claims of being the first to come up with the idea of baggy pants or pastel shades of clothing or combining exercise and social opportunities under the same roof. Having the legal system try to sort out these competing claims would involve substantial costs that would usually be avoided when someone was seeking to restore a copyright in an obscure public domain work, and the problem would never arise when one was seeking merely to renew an existing copyright.

Finally, many new business ideas may now be legally protectable by business-method patents (see Chapter 10). Such protection is often of marketing

---

34. This concern is explicit in the copyright statute, which discourages free riding on marketing and promotional expenditures of previously unpublished works about to fall into the public domain by conditioning an additional forty-five years of protection on publication. See 17 U.S.C. § 303(a). Thus copyright on works unpublished on January 1, 1978, continues until December 31, 2002, but if they are published by that date protection continues until December 31, 2047.

gimmicks, such as Amazon.com's "one-click shopping," and thus provides incentives for firms to invest in marketing and promotion that would be subject to free riding in the absence of legal protection.

Empirical Analysis

Data on copyright registrations and renewals over the past century are abundant[35] and enable us to add an empirical dimension to our analysis. If it turned out that all or most copyrighted works that antedate the 1976 Copyright Act were renewed, the implication would be that a system of indefinite renewals might approach perpetual copyright, though this would also depend on how steep the renewal fee was. Conversely, if renewals were infrequent even though renewal fees were nominal,[36] probably only a relatively few highly valuable works would remain under copyright beyond the initial term if indefinite renewals were permitted.

The number of registrations is only a proxy for the number of copyrighted works because registration is not a prerequisite for copyright protection. But both the 1909 and 1976 copyright acts created strong incentives to register a copyright and to register it promptly. Not only is registration (or, under the 1976 Act, an application to register) a prerequisite to filing a suit for infringement,[37] but it must be done before the infringement (or within three months of first publication) if the copyright holder wants to recover statutory damages and attorney fees. The 1909 Act fixed the copyright term at twenty-eight years from the date of first publication (or, for works that were copyrighted but not published, from the date of registration), and at the end of the term the copyright could be renewed for an additional twenty-eight years (raised to forty-seven years in 1962 and to sixty-seven years in October 1998) if the copyright holder applied for renewal within the last year of the initial term. Beginning in 1992 renewal became automatic,[38] so renewal registrations were sure to decline after that, but not to zero because there was still an incentive to file: a renewal registration is prima facie evidence of the validity of the copyright during its extended term and of the facts stated in the

35. See *Annual Report of the Register of Copyrights*, various years, published by the U.S. Copyright Office. See also Barbara A. Ringer, "Renewal of Copyright," in *Studies on Copyright: Arthur Fisher Memorial Edition*, vol. 1, p. 503 (1963 [1960]).

36. See note 8 above.

37. Under the Berne Convention Implementation Act of 1988, the registration requirement applies only to a "United States work"—a work first published in the United States or where the author is a U.S. national or lives here. See 17 U.S.C. § 101 for the complete definition.

38. Remember that these are renewals of copyrights that date from before the effective date of the 1976 Act, which gave the copyright owner a nonrenewable term of life plus fifty (later seventy) years.

certificate of renewal. Another statutory change, however, the extension of federal protection by the 1976 Act from published works to all works fixed in a tangible medium, could be expected to increase the number of registrations without any increase in the output of copyrightable works.

Our primary focus is on renewals because they allow us to estimate the expected economic life of a copyright. But we need data on registration as well because the number of initial registrations determines the number of works that are potentially renewable twenty-eight years later. For example, works renewed in 1938 were registered initially in 1910. To obtain the number of 1910 registrations, we have to deduct renewal registrations in 1910 (from works first copyrighted in 1882) because the Copyright Office includes renewal registrations in its tabulation of registration.

Figures 8.2 through 8.4 graph registrations, renewals, and the renewal/registration ratio (which in year t is simply the number of renewals in t divided by the number of initial registrations in $t-28$) over the past century.

Copyright registrations and renewals rose rapidly in the twentieth century, but, as expected, renewals began to decline in 1992 when they became automatic.[39] The rise doubtless reflects an increase in the number of copyrightable works brought about by a growth in the economy's total expressive output, as well as reflecting changes in copyright law. Why then did both registrations and renewals peak in 1991, declining by almost 20 percent by 2000, with the decline concentrated in the last year? The answer may be, in part anyway, that the registration fee doubled in 1991, from $10 to $20, and increased again in 2000, to $30, while the renewal fee doubled to $12 in 1991, rose to $20 in 1993, and more than doubled, to $45, in 2000. Although these fees seem small in relation to the inconvenience of registering and complying with other requirements of registration, such as submission of a copy of the work to the Copyright Office,[40] Figures 8.2 and 8.3 suggest substantial negative responses to higher fees for both original and renewal registrations. The

---

39. Recall that the 1909 Copyright Act (effective July 1, 1909) extended the renewal term from fourteen to twenty-eight years. Works that had been renewed for fourteen years in the period 1895 to 1909 were entitled to a further renewal of fourteen years, for a total renewal period of twenty-eight years. We do not include the fourteen-year extensions in our count of renewals in the 1910 to 1923 period. Our analysis of renewal data begins with the fiscal year ending June 30, 1910, the first fiscal year of the 1909 Act.

40. Another reason for the decline in registrations may be that since 1989 registration has no longer been a condition for bringing an infringement suit for foreign works protected by the Berne Convention and the World Trade Organization, though it remains a prerequisite for seeking statutory damages and attorneys' fees. The fact has little quantitative importance, however, because, as we'll see, foreign works are only a small fraction of copyright registrations. Also, statutory damages and attorneys' fees are significant remedies and so provide significant incentives to continue to register foreign works.

Figure 8.2. Copyright registrations (excluding renewals), 1910–2000

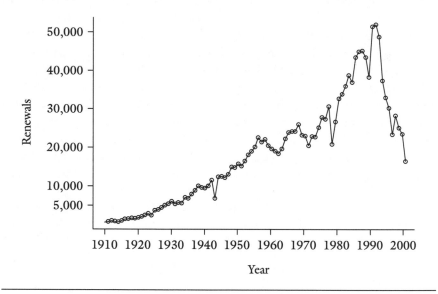

Figure 8.3. Copyright renewals, 1910–2000

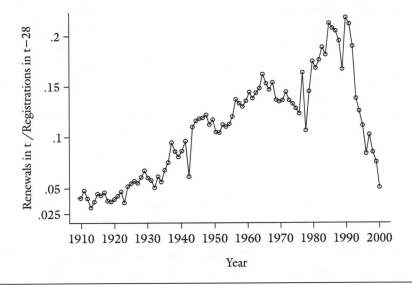

Figure 8.4. Rate of copyright renewal, 1910–2000

effect on renewals is more ambiguous because of the automatic renewal amendment in 1992, although the amendment did not eliminate all incentive to register a renewal; by doing so an author could recapture rights in previously created derivative works.

As Figure 8.4 shows, the fraction of works renewed increased significantly between 1910 and 1991, then plummeted—no doubt mainly because of automatic renewal, though higher fees may also have played a role.[41] Prior to 1992 (the first fiscal year for automatic renewal), renewal rates ranged from a low of .03 in 1914 to a high of .22 in 1991. Although the full cost of renewal includes both a small renewal fee per work (though with some aggregation permitted: a photographer can for a single fee renew his copyrights on a group of fifty photographs whose copyrights all expire on the same date) and

41. We analyze the impact of fee changes in the regression analysis below, but point out here that it would be a mistake to think that the ratio of renewals to registrations should not be expected to change in response to higher fees for *both* renewals and registrations. The ratio of renewals to registrations is calculated from renewals in year t and registrations in year $t-28$, and obviously an increase in fees in 1991 could not affect the number of registrations in 1963, the denominator in the 1991 ratio. The only effect of higher fees on that ratio would come through the effect of a higher renewal fee on the number of renewals that year. Note also that the renewal ratio in Figure 8.4 is biased downward from 1910 to 1937 because data on registrations from 1881 to 1909 include both new registrations and fourteen-year renewal registrations (from works first registered in 1867 to 1895). We account for this bias in our regression analysis.

the monetary equivalent (probably small) of the inconvenience and other costs associated with renewal, the fact that only a small fraction of works are renewed implies that most copyrights have very little economic value after twenty-eight years. A rational decision on whether to renew a copyright depends on a comparison of the discounted value of the expected future revenues from the copyright to the full costs of renewal. So probably the expected economic value of the 80 percent or so of copyrighted works that are not renewed is less than the small cost of renewal. The analysis would not be changed in essentials if, to minimize administrative burden, owners of multiple copyrights make a one-time decision to renew all their copyrights when they expire.

We cannot dismiss the possibility that some fraction of nonrenewals are due to simple oversight or to careless failure to comply with required formalities. Ignorance of renewal formalities is possible even when the work was initially registered; it may have gone out of print (or the equivalent for nonbooks) and the copyright by contract reverted to the author, who may not know about renewal or the renewal date. Still, as we said earlier, ignorance is endogenous; carelessness is evidence that the value of the works in question is less than the full cost of renewal, which includes the cost of informing oneself about the procedures for renewing one's copyright. Nonrenewals by corporations or other owners of works for hire might be a better index of decisions not to renew based on lack of commercial value, but we do not have those data.

Depreciation rates of copyrighted material can be calculated from data on renewals and registrations. Initial registrations constitute one year's stock of copyrighted works; renewal registrations of those works constitute a different, smaller stock of the same works twenty-eight years later (renewals must be registered in the last year of the initial term). The annual rate at which the first stock shrinks to become the second is the depreciation rate of the first stock. That rate is given by the formula $REN_t = (REG_{t-28})e^{-\delta_t 28}$ where REN_t denotes renewals in t of works registered twenty-eight years earlier ($= REG_{t-28}$) and δ_t equals the annual average depreciation rate for copyrights registered in period $t-28$. Figure 8.5 depicts annual depreciation rates, measured in year t, of works registered twenty-eight years earlier; thus the depreciation rate of .054 in 1990 (5.4 percent) is the annual depreciation rate of works registered in 1962. The higher the renewal ratio, the lower the depreciation rate, since we are computing that rate from the fraction of copyrighted works that are renewed.

Notice that the average annual depreciation rate of copyrighted works has ranged from a low of 5.4 percent in 1990 to a high of 12.2 percent in 1914

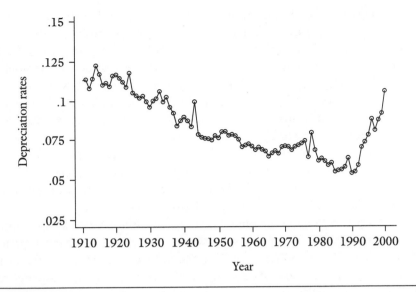

Figure 8.5. Depreciation rates of registered copyrights, 1910–2000

(for works first registered in 1886), the overall average being 8.3 percent.[42] The long-term trend (setting to one side the effect, beginning in 1992, of automatic renewal) is toward lower depreciation, implying that copyrightable works have become more valuable. One reason may be the increase beginning in 1962 in the renewal term from twenty-eight to forty-seven years, which increased the present value of copyrights by extending their potential term. But given discounting, the effect should not have been great, and so it is not surprising that most of the decline in the depreciation rate occurred before 1962.

42. As noted earlier, estimates of depreciation for the years 1910 to 1937 are biased downward because registration data in the period 1881 to 1909 include renewal registrations. Another complication arises from the fact that as a result of the signing of the Berne Convention by the United States, copyright protection was restored for a number of works that were protected in their country of origin but had fallen into the public domain in this country, mainly because of failure to comply with the requirements of notice or renewal. This has two potential effects on the calculation of depreciation. First, if foreign works were less likely to be renewed, or more likely to fall into the public domain because of improper notice, than U.S. works, depreciation of the latter would be lower than shown in Figure 8.5. Second, the size of the public domain would be smaller today. These effects are likely to have only a negligible impact on our empirical analysis because we estimate that foreign works constitute only between 1 and 5 percent of copyright registrations. But we were able to obtain foreign registrations for only some of the years between 1961 and 1977.

Why there was *any* decline in depreciation is unclear. Even if the demand for copyrightable works has been growing, the supply of new works would be expected to grow at about the same rate in order to keep the real value of copyrights approximately constant. One possibility is that new technologies, such as long-playing records, stereo equipment, radio, and television, extended the economic life of copyrights. For example, the growth in demand for prerecorded music made possible by technological advances such as radio and television broadcasting, high-quality home stereo systems, and even the automobile (which increases the number of people listening to radio) should have increased the overall demand for copyrighted music. Some of this demand would be satisfied by older though still copyrighted music, resulting in higher renewal rates and hence a lower depreciation rate.

The reciprocal of depreciation is the average expected life of a copyrighted work. Although the term of a copyright on works first published in the period 1881 through 1972 and renewed for a second term varied from fifty-six to ninety-five years, the commercial life ($= 1/\delta$) of the average copyrighted work was much lower, ranging from 8.2 years to 18.5 years for works first registered in 1886 and 1962, respectively. In the first group, 3.3 percent were renewed (in 1914); in the second, 22 percent were renewed (1990).

It is also possible to estimate the number of works registered in 1934 that retain commercial value today. We chose that year because works first published then could be renewed for forty-seven years in 1962, with another twenty years tacked on in 1998, so that a copyright first registered in 1934 need not enter the public domain until 2029. Yet the estimated depreciation rate of works registered in 1934 is .07, implying that of the works registered that year 50 percent had fully depreciated by 1944, 90 percent by 1977, and 99 percent by 2000; fewer than 1 in 750 works registered in 1934 will have commercial value in 2030. Had renewals been permitted every five or ten years, then after an initial term of twenty or so years about 99 percent of the works registered in 1934 would have fallen into the public domain by the year 2000 because by then their commercial value had fallen below the cost and inconvenience of renewal. Of course, the 1 percent that would still be under copyright would mainly be the more valuable and enduring works.

The Copyright Office publishes separate data on registrations and renewals for books (including, moreover, pamphlets—which account for 80 percent of the category), graphic arts (posters, fine arts, labels, photographs, technical drawings, and maps), and music. As shown in Figure 8.6, the time trend of these three categories closely tracks that of overall registrations (the correlation is .99). This is not surprising, because these categories account for 70 percent of all registrations.

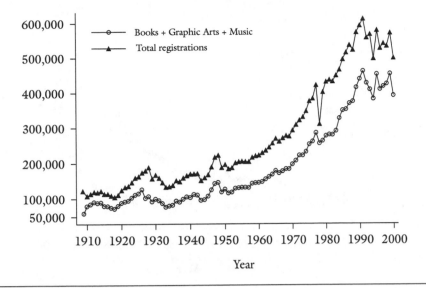

Figure 8.6. Registration of books, graphic arts, and music compared with all copyrights, 1910–2000

Figure 8.7 reveals that the number of musical copyrights has grown the fastest, the number of book copyrights the second fastest, and graphic arts the slowest. We estimated simple regressions of the form $\log y_t = a + rt + u$, where y denotes either book, music, or graphic-art registrations, t time, and u the residual. The coefficient r, which measures the rate of growth per year, equaled .021 (24.5) for books, .025 (41.5) for music, and .014 (7.44) for graphic arts. The t-statistics (in parentheses) indicate that these growth rates are highly significant.[43] The differences in growth rates between any two of the three categories are also statistically significant.

We can also link up renewals with registrations for each of the three categories to estimate category-specific depreciation rates, though since the earliest category-specific registration data we have are for 1909, we can use only renewal data starting in 1937. Figures 8.8 and 8.9 graph the renewal ratio and depreciation rates.

43. However, books include periodicals for the 1909–1926 period, which artificially increases the number of book registrations in that period and so lowers the estimated rate of growth. If we estimate the growth rate from 1927 (rather than 1909) to 2000, the coefficients (and t-statistics) on r are .024 (27.4) for books, .026 (33.3) for music, and .022 (12.8) for graphic arts. Although the growth rates for books and music are much closer, all differences remain statistically significant at the .10 level.

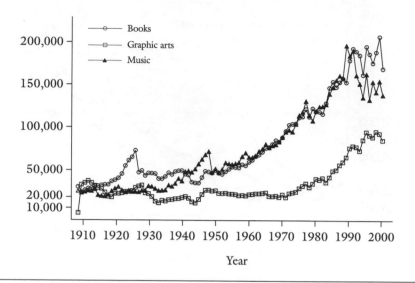

Figure 8.7. Registrations for books, graphic arts, and music

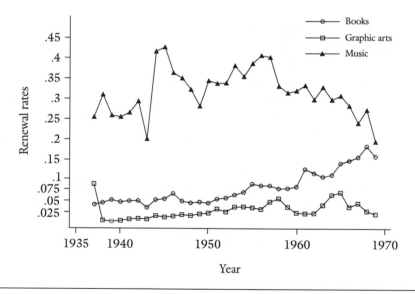

Figure 8.8. Renewal rates of books, graphic arts, and music

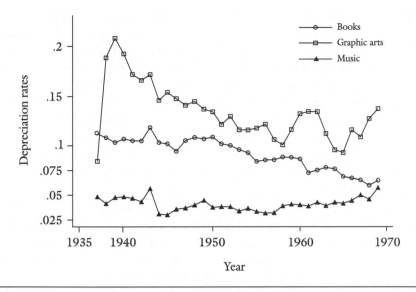

Figure 8.9. Depreciation rates of books, graphic arts, and music

Notice that only about 3 percent of graphic-arts works were renewed after twenty-eight years, compared to 8 percent for books and 32 percent for music (more than 40 percent for works renewed in 1944 and 1956). Music renewal rates have been falling sharply since 1956, while book renewal rates have been rising during this period so that by 1969 renewal rates were greater for books than for music for works first copyrighted in 1942. By the same token, depreciation rates are highest for graphic arts (averaging about 14 percent) and lowest for music (about 4 percent), with books in the middle (above 9 percent).[44] Depreciation rates for both books and graphic arts have declined, while depreciation of music began to increase in the mid-1950s and by 1969 was just slightly below that of books.

What explains these differences? The graphic-arts category is dominated by commercial art, such as advertising layouts and fabric designs for fashion items, the useful life of which tends to be no longer than the advertising cam-

44. We noted earlier that of 10,027 books published in 1930, only 174 were still in print in 2001. An annual depreciation rate of 5.7 percent would produce this more than fifty-fold decline. From our data we estimate a depreciation rate of 8.9 percent for books registered in 1930, but this is the average rate over the period 1930 to 1958 (the date of renewal). Overall, the depreciation rate for books is 9.2 percent for books registered between 1909 and 1941. The probable explanation for the discrepancy between this rate and the 5.7 percent estimate is the fact noted in the text that the book category in our data includes pamphlets and leaflets, which tend to be ephemeral.

paign or latest fashion season. (Mickey Mouse is a dramatic exception.) Photographs are in the graphic-arts category, and this may be part of the explanation for the high depreciation rate. As we noted earlier, although copyright renewal fees are very low for most types of expressive work, they are high for photographs because serious photographers take so many pictures.

At the other extreme in depreciation, music tends to be readily adaptable to changes in taste and context. For example, a song written for a Broadway show may be recorded by many different artists in different styles, tempi, and so on over a long period of time or be used as background music in a movie or a television program.[45] Music is variable in a sense that words are not; a piece of music can be performed in a variety of different ways, but what would it mean to "perform" a novel in a variety of different ways? A related point is that music is less tied to cultural change than purely verbal works, which are often extremely topical and therefore depreciate rapidly. Books are more enduring than most applied art if only because the costs of storing them are relatively low (with digitization, virtually zero) and there is some chance of turning a book into a movie or rekindling interest in the author.

The differences in depreciation rates across categories of expressive work bolster the case for indefinite renewals. Current copyright law does not differentiate among different types of work. All copyrightable works, from computer programs to novels to installation art (which is typically site-specific and lasts only the length of the exhibition), have the identical term despite the large differences in commercial life expectancy. A system of indefinite renewals would automatically distinguish the enduring from the ephemeral. Most works of graphic art probably would not be renewed even if the initial copyright term were only five years. Because books and music are likely to have more lasting value, their renewal rates would be higher.

Multiple regression analysis can be used to estimate the impact on registrations and renewals of changes in fees, statutory changes in copyright law,[46] and changes in the underlying demand for expressive works. The dependent variable in Table 8.1 is the logarithm of the annual number of registrations in the period 1910 to 2000. The independent variables in equations (1.1) and (1.2) are a time trend *(Year)*, the copyright registration or renewal fee *(LogFee)* deflated by the Consumer Price Index (CPI), the expected copyright duration *(LogE(Life))* computed from our estimates of depreciation,

45. Rappaport, note 31 above, at 3 n. 5, remarks that "in the case of music, . . . its 'timeless' quality allows themes to be recycled endlessly." Notice, however, that depreciation rates of music rose in the 1956 to 1969 period, suggesting that more recent popular music is less durable than works created in the 1920s and earlier.

46. We present both OLS (ordinary least squares) and CORC (Cochrane-Orcutt) estimates, the latter to correct for significant autocorrelation.

and annual recreation expenditures *(LogRecExp)*, which include expenditures on expressive (and thus often copyrighted) works of music, movies, books, and periodicals,[47] also deflated by the CPI. The registration, fee, duration, and recreational-expenditure variables are in log form; their regression co-efficients are therefore elasticities. Equations (1.3) and (1.4) add several dummy variables denoting significant changes in the copyright statute that are likely to affect the number of registrations. These include the 1962 amendment extending the renewal term to forty-seven years *(1962RenExt)*, the extension of copyright protection to sound recordings in 1972 *(1972Sound)*, the 1976 Copyright Act, effective in 1978 *(1976Act)*, the 1988 ratification of the Berne Convention effective in 1989 *(1988Berne)*[48] and the 1998 Sonny Bono Act *(1998BonoExt)*, which added twenty years to the copyright term. These variables take a value of 1 for all years in which the given change is in effect and of 0 otherwise.

All four equations reveal a statistically significant growth rate of copyright registrations of about 1 to 2 percent per year. The time trend variable *(Year)* picks up increases in population, income, wealth, and education that are positively correlated with time over the ninety-year period covered by our data and are likely to increase the demand for expressive activities. A positive time trend was visible in Figure 8.2, but regression analysis enables us to conclude that the trend is positively correlated with an increase in the underlying growth in demand for expressive activities rather than with changes in fees, the law, or other policy variables. Although the regression coefficients on rec-reation expenditures are positive in all the equations in Table 8.1, only the OLS (ordinary least squares) estimates (equations (1.1) and (1.3)) are statis-tically significant.

The most interesting result in Table 8.1 is the negative and highly sig-nificant effect of registration fees (t-statistics between 4.6 and 9.1) on regis-trations. The coefficients on fees yield a negative elasticity of around .20, im-plying that a 25 percent increase in fees would reduce copyright registrations by more than 5 percent even though the fees would still be very low. (For ex-ample, the registration fee in 2000 was only $30, and it had averaged only $20.48 in 2000 dollars over the 1910 to 2000 period.) The implication is that most copyrights have negligible expected value, because even very small increases in already very low fees deter many owners of intellectual property

47. We estimate that expenditures on expressive goods account for about 50 percent of the recreation category.

48. The Copyright Act was amended in 1988 (effective in March 1989) to comply with the substantive provisions of the Berne Convention, which sets minimum requirements to which signatory nations are required to conform their copyright laws. The most significant amendment was to make copyright notice optional.

Table 8.1 Regression analysis of registrations (t-statistics in parentheses), 1910–2000

Independent variables	Log registrations			
	OLS (1.1)	CORC (1.2)	OLS (1.3)	CORC (1.4)
Year	.013 (3.71)	.018 (5.44)	.005 (1.88)	.018 (4.78)
LogFee	−.31 (9.06)	−.24 (5.57)	−.19 (5.93)	−.20 (4.67)
LogE(Life)	.07 (.79)	.35 (3.79)	.37 (4.01)	.35 (3.57)
LogRecExp	.20 (2.49)	.03 (.50)	.18 (2.56)	.02 (.26)
1962RenExt	—	—	.08 (2.28)	.02 (.39)
1972Sound	—	—	.16 (3.80)	.03 (.48)
1976Act	—	—	.07 (1.77)	−.14 (2.19)
1988Berne	—	—	.12 (2.86)	.11 (1.86)
1998BonoExt	—	—	.02 (.27)	.06 (1.06)
Constant	−13.8 (2.43)	−24.1 (5.11)	−.92 (.19)	−24.3 (3.47)
Durbin-Watson	.50	2.25	.87	2.11
rho	—	.84	—	.88
R^2	.97	.72	.98	.66
No. observations	90	89	90	89

Note: OLS denotes ordinary least squares and CORC denotes Cochrane = Orcutt corrections for first-order autocorrelation.

from seeking to register it. While registration is now optional rather than a precondition of obtaining a copyright, the remedial advantages that it confers should motivate any copyright holder who thinks his work retains significant commercial value to register his copyright at the earliest opportunity.

The number of registrations is also highly responsive to the expected commercial life *(LogE(Life))* of a work, which for all but a few works is shorter than the statutory copyright term. For example, a 10 percent increase in that expected life leads, other things being equal, to a 3.5 to 3.7 percent increase in registrations in equation (1.4), and this effect is highly significant statistically.[49]

Of the remaining variables, only the 1976 Copyright Act and 1988 Berne Convention dummy variables have statistically significant effects on registrations after we adjust for autocorrelation. Extending the renewal term in 1962 and adding sound recordings to the Copyright Act in 1972 have positive and significant effects on registrations in the OLS but not in the Cochrane-Orcutt estimates. It is not surprising that the term-extension variables (in 1962 and 1998) are insignificant; the expected commercial life of a copyrighted work is so much shorter than the copyright term that it makes a lengthening of the term irrelevant to most potential registrants. Amendments to the Copyright Act that followed U.S. ratification of the Berne Convention are associated with about a 10 percent increase in registrations. These amendments (for example, notice, the need to record some transfers, and licenses all became optional) effectively lowered the full cost (including inconvenience costs) of registration, which in turn should have increased the number of registrations.[50]

One puzzling result is that the 1976 Act seems, after correction for other factors, to have reduced the number of copyright registrations by about 14 percent. Since the Act eliminated common law copyright and brought unpublished works under the federal statute, one would have expected the number of registrations to increase. The negative coefficient on the 1976 Act is the consequence of a sharp drop in registrations in 1978 (the year the Act took effect)—from more than 420,000 in 1977 to 310,742 in 1978, followed, however, by an increase to more than 400,000 the following year. If equation (1.4) is re-estimated treating fiscal year 1979 rather than fiscal year 1978 as the first full year of the 1976 Act, the coefficient on the *1976Act* variable becomes positive and highly significant (.16 with a t-statistic of 3.08), indicating a 16 percent increase in registrations as a result of the Act. There are no changes in the effect of the other variables when we use fiscal year 1979 as the first year of the 1976 Act.

In Table 8.2 the dependent variable is the log of the number of renewals per year. Since renewals depend in part on the number of works registered twenty-eight years earlier, we include two registration variables—one for annual registrations from 1882–1910 and the other for annual registrations from 1911–1972—to account for the fact that data on registrations included both new registrations and renewal registrations through (most of fiscal year)

49. The only exception to the significant effect of *LogE(Life)* is equation (1.1). But that equation is marginal to our analysis because it does not adjust for autocorrelation and excludes five important statutory variables.

50. The offset noted in note 40 above is minor for the reasons explained there.

Table 8.2 Regression analysis of renewals (t-statistics in parentheses), 1910–2000

Independent variables	Log renewals	
	OLS (2.1)	CORC (2.2)
Year	.018 (2.56)	.023 (2.61)
LogFee	−.09 (1.08)	−.22 (2.13)
$LogReg_{t-28}1882–1910$	.95 (10.34)	.86 (5.18)
$LogReg_{t-28}1911–1972$	.99 (10.64)	.89 (5.38)
LogRecExp	−.02 (.14)	−.12 (.67)
1962RenExt	−.07 (.69)	−.06 (.48)
1992AutoRen	−.64 (6.37)	−.47 (3.82)
Constant	−36.4 (3.10)	−44.0 (2.99)
Durbin-Watson	1.08	2.12
rho	—	.55
R^2	.98	−.90
No. observations	90	89

1910. We do not include variables for the 1972, 1976, 1988, and 1998 statutory amendments, as we would not expect them to affect renewals, holding registrations constant. For example, adding twenty years to the renewal term in 1998 increased the expected value (though only slightly) of a renewal but did not affect the incentive to renew because beginning in 1992 renewals had become automatic.

Table 8.2 indicates that renewals are highly responsive to registrations twenty-eight years earlier. Not only are both regression coefficients highly significant, but we cannot reject the hypothesis that the coefficients are both equal to one—that is, that for each 1 percent increase in registrations twenty-eight years earlier, renewals increased by 1 percent. As expected, the automatic renewal amendment in 1992 is statistically significant and indicates that renewals fell by about 50 percent after the amendment. Extending the renewal term from twenty-eight to forty-seven years beginning in 1962 had no significant effect on renewals, but this is not surprising. Consider the copyright holder who has to decide whether to renew his copyright after expiration of the initial term of twenty-eight years. Since the expected additional commercial life of such works is likely to be shorter than twenty-eight years, adding nineteen years to the renewal period should not significantly influence the decision whether to renew.

Turning to the *Year* variable, we find a statistically significant increase in renewals of 2 percent per year (holding registrations eligible for renewal constant). This is consistent with a long-term growth in the demand for and hence in the value of expressive activities, since in response to that growth copyright holders would have a greater incentive to renew their copyrights. After adjusting for this upward trend, we do not find any significant effect of recreation expenditures on renewals.[51]

Like initial registrations, renewals are responsive to changes in fees. Although the coefficient on fees is not statistically significant in equation (2.1), autocorrelation in the OLS estimate produces standard errors that are not unbiased. Equation (2.2) corrects for this bias and reveals a statistically significant effect of fees on renewals: a 10 percent increase in the inflation-adjusted renewal fee results in a 2.2 percent decrease in the number of renewals.[52]

The responsiveness of registrations and renewals to even modest changes in fees implies that (1) the size of the public domain will expand under a system of indefinite renewals compared to the present copyright system; (2) the average value of works in the public domain will decline; (3) the expected economic life of most copyrighted works is short;[53] and (4) a system of indefinite renewals, at least if limited to works copyrighted after the system is created, will separate valuable works in which continued copyright protection may be socially efficient from works in which the cost of continuing that protection exceeds the sum of administrative and access (including transaction) costs.

---

51. This result is expected since there is a .87 correlation between the logarithm of recreation expenditures and *Year.*

52. The reason equations (2.1) and (2.2) do not include an independent variable for the expected life of a copyrighted work is that renewals are used to estimate depreciation and hence expected duration, so that adding the log of expected duration to the right-hand side of the regression equation would place the log of renewals for the same year on both sides of the equation.

53. The actual life of some of these works is longer; an author may err in his estimate of the demand for his work and therefore fail to renew his copyright, though in fact the work has continued value.

Trademark Renewal Rates

We can throw some additional light on the issue of the optimal duration of intellectual property rights by considering renewal rates for trademarks.[54] A trademark has no fixed expiration date. But maintaining a federally registered trademark (which, like copyright registration, is advantageous, as noted in Chapter 6) requires the owner to file an affidavit during the sixth year after registration, and also in every tenth year, stating that the trademark is still in use; he must also file a renewal application every ten years.[55] Prior to the Trademark Law Revision Act of 1988 (effective November 16, 1989), registrations and renewals remained in force for twenty-year periods subject to the owner's having to file an affidavit of continued use every ten years. Thus the Act reduced both the registration and the renewal periods to ten years. Since there is no limit on the number of times a trademark can be renewed, we have in trademark law a model for how a system of indefinite copyright renewals might operate.

Trademark renewals in period t arise from (1) trademarks first registered in $t-20$ and (2) trademarks registered initially in $t-40$, $t-60$, and so on that had been continuously renewed (the last time in $t-20$) and are still in force at time t.[56] Assuming a constant rate of depreciation for trademarks in the interval $t-20$ to t, we have the following identity: $REN_t = (REG_{t-20} + REN_{t-20})e^{-\delta 20}$ where REN and REG denote renewals and registrations respectively, t denotes time, and δ the depreciation rate.

Figures 8.10 and 8.11 plot renewal and depreciation rates for trademarks from 1934 to 1999, the period for which we have data. Trademark renewals averaged 27 percent, annual depreciation was 6.6 percent, and the expected life (equal to the reciprocal of depreciation) was 15.4 years. Trademark renewal rates and the average effective life of a trademark are greater and depreciation lower than the corresponding data for copyrights (Figures 8.4 and 8.5). Between 1934 and 1991[57] trademark renewals averaged 28 percent, depreciation was 6.4 percent, and the expected life was 15.7 years, while the corresponding figures for copyright renewals were 14 percent, 7.3 percent,

54. Though patents are nonrenewable, they have a de facto renewal component. We present patent "renewal" rates in Chapter 11.

55. 15 U.S.C. § 1058.

56. Since our renewal data run through the end of fiscal year 1999 (September 30, 1999), slightly less than a decade after the Trademark Law Revision Act went into effect, all renewals in our sample come from trademarks that had been in force for at least twenty years.

57. We use these dates because 1934 is the earliest year for which we are able to calculate trademark renewal rates (which requires that we have renewals from 1914) and 1991 is the last year for accurately estimating copyright renewals because renewals became automatic starting in 1992.

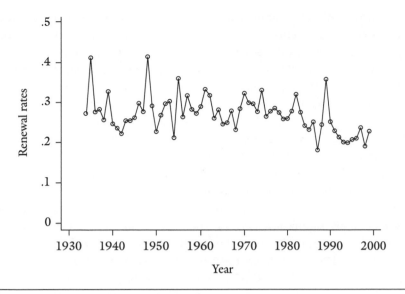

Figure 8.10. Trademark renewal rates, 1934–1999

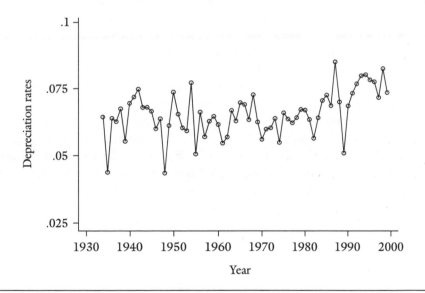

Figure 8.11. Trademark depreciation rates, 1934–1999

and 14 years. Although trademark renewal rates are double copyright renewal rates, the difference in depreciation and in life expectancy is less than 15 percent. In that era (1934–1991), trademarks were renewed after 20 years but copyrights after 28 years, so one would expect higher renewal rates for trademarks than for copyrights even if depreciation were the same.

We also regressed trademark renewals in t (in logs) on registrations and renewals in $t-20$, a time trend *(Year)*, renewal fees adjusted for the CPI, and GNP *(LGNP)* in logs for the period 1935 to 1999. Both registrations and renewals in $t-20$ have positive and highly significant effects on renewals in t; renewal fees have a negative though only marginally significant effect ($t = 1.74$); and neither time nor GNP is significant.[58] It is not surprising that the estimated renewal elasticity with respect to fees is relatively small ($-.06$) and only marginally significant, because there has been very little variation in (nominal) registration fees over the past fifty years. Renewal fees were $15 from 1935 to 1945, $25 from 1946 to 1981, were increased sharply in the next two years (to $150 in 1982 and $300 in 1983), and have remained at $300 since then. There is some evidence that trademark renewal rates declined following the substantial fee increases in 1982 and 1983. Renewal rates averaged .27 in the five-year period 1977–1981 compared to .23 in the five-year period 1984–1988, when the fees were much higher.

The reason depreciation is lower for trademarks than for copyrights is similar to the reason depreciation of copyrighted music is lower than depreciation for books and graphic arts. Like music, a trademark attached to a particular product or service can be extended to new goods and services. A successful trademark signals the reputation of the producer ("goodwill"). Firms have an incentive to capitalize on their goodwill by introducing new and improved products under the same brand name. The Ford Motor Company initially registered the "Ford" trademark in 1909 for automobiles and parts.[59] Since then Ford has introduced hundreds of new automobiles under the Ford name. Similarly, Bayer first registered its trademark in 1908 for use on syn-

---

58. The regression equation is

$$LRen_t = -4.30 + .72 LReg_{t-20} + .14 LRen_{t-20} - .005 \, Year + .06 LFee_t - .40 LGNP + u$$
$$\quad\quad (.66) \quad\quad (11.89) \quad\quad\quad (6.05) \quad\quad\quad (1.02) \quad\quad (1.74) \quad\quad (1.45)$$

$$R^2 = .91 \quad \text{Durbin-Watson Statistic} = 1.80 \quad n = 65$$

The analysis also supports the assumption that the depreciation rates on registrations and renewals in $t-20$ are equal. Since the ratio of renewals to registrations averages about .21 over the 1915–1979 period (the relevant time period for the dependent variable, which runs from 1935 to 1999), equal depreciation rates imply that the renewal elasticity in the above regression should be about 20 percent of the registration elasticity.

59. The Ford trademark was registered fourteen years after its first use in commerce (1895).

thetic coal-tar remedies and later placed the name on numerous pharmaceutical products that hadn't existed in 1908.

This analysis suggests that the depreciation rate of trademarks is likely to be lower than that of books and graphic arts but not necessarily lower than that of musical copyrights, which like trademarks have potential uses, for example in new recordings, beyond their first use. (Of course some books do too—the novel *Gone with the Wind,* for example, later made into a very successful movie.) The data support this conjecture. For the period 1934 to 1991, depreciation rates were 13.4 percent for copyrights on graphic arts, 9.2 percent for copyrights on books, 6.5 percent for trademarks, and 4.1 percent for copyrights on music.[60]

Although trademarks can be renewed indefinitely, their average economic life is only about 15 percent longer than that of the average copyright. The higher renewal fees for trademarks may explain much of this difference. In 2000 it cost $300 to renew a trademark, compared to only $45 to renew a copyright. Another factor, however, is that trademarks lapse unless used, and use is expensive, whereas a copyright can be renewed for a book that is out of print, the hope being that there will be some future interest in it. The indefinite duration of trademarks is less problematic than would be the case for copyrights, because there are no social benefits to public domain trademarks except generic ones—but, as we know, trademarks fall into the public domain when they become generic.

60. These differences are all highly significant statistically.

9

The Legal Protection of Postmodern Art

That a work of art is copyrightable might seem an unarguable proposition of copyright law and economics. But several movements in modern art (actually "postmodern" in the sense of departing radically from classic modernists such as Picasso, Matisse, Mondrian, and Kandinsky in the direction associated with "postmodernist" thought) cast doubt on the proposition. The movement to which we devote our main attention is "Appropriation Art," but in the first part of the chapter we discuss three others, of which one, however, "Pop Art," overlaps Appropriation Art. The analytical focus is also somewhat different in the two parts. In the first, emphasis falls on copyrightability; we ask whether art that is primarily conceptual can be deemed copyrightable without crossing the boundary from expression (copyrightable) to ideas (not). In the second part we assume the copyrightability of Appropriation Art, even though much of it is conceptual, and ask to what extent the appropriation artist should be permitted to copy copyrighted material without having to obtain a license from the owner of the copyright.

But there is a threshold question to be considered, namely how much difference copyright makes in the case of a unique work, such as a painting. The main source of the artist's income and that of intermediaries, such as dealers, typically comes from the sale of the work itself rather than from the sale of copies. The opposite is true of most copyrightable works, such as books, movies, software, musical works, and, in the visual-arts domain, works of graphic art, such as engravings and woodcuts, and certain sculptures—Beanie Babies, for example, which are "soft sculptures" in copyright lingo. Unauthorized copying of unique artworks will, however, reduce the income the artist receives from posters, note cards, puzzles, coffee mugs, mouse pads, T-shirts, and other derivative works that incorporate images from the original work. Although derivative works of this sort are more lucrative when they are derivative from popular rather than elite culture,[1] they have become important sources of income for art museums and galleries as well.[2] Without such income, some of which flows directly to artists and other indirectly by increasing the resources that museums and galleries have for acquiring art, there will be less incentive to create unique works.

How much less? Perhaps not much. Only an artist who is already very successful and therefore well remunerated will find a market for derivative works; that is one reason we didn't emphasize the incentive effects of vesting ownership of derivative works in the holder of the copyright on the original when we discussed that vesting in Chapter 4. There also are substantial benefits both pecuniary and nonpecuniary from recognition as an original artist. Still, the prospect of future ancillary income, however remote, may have a small positive influence on the incentive to create new works.

The point deserving particular emphasis, however, is that copies of works of art often are—or what amounts to the same thing as far as the economic impact of copying is concerned, are perceived to be—greatly inferior in quality to the original. (When copies are good substitutes for an original work, the artist may still be able to charge a higher price for the original to capture some of the benefits from subsequent uses of the work that are not protected by copyright.) When a painting attributed to Vermeer or Van Gogh is discovered to be a forgery, however skillful, its price nosedives. One reason may be that a painting, unlike a piece of music based on a musical score, or a purely verbal work such as a book, cannot be exactly reproduced by copying;[3] and

1. See, for example, Hoepker v. Kruger, 200 F. Supp. 2d 340 (S.D.N.Y. 2002); "The Spider's Bite," *Economist* (U.S. ed.), May 11, 2002, p. 57; Jon Creamer, "Kids TV Tells Toy Story," *Televisual,* May 3, 2002, p. 27; David A. Kaplan, "The Selling of *Star Wars,*" *Newsweek,* May 17, 1999, p. 61.

2. See, for example, Jill I. Prater, "When Museums Act Like Gift Shops: The Discordant Derivative Works Exception to the Termination Clause," 17 *Loyola of Los Angeles Entertainment Law Journal* 97 (1996); Colin Gleadell, "See the Show, Buy the T-Shirt," *Daily Telegraph,* Mar. 2, 2002, p. 7; Laurie J. Flynn, "Licensing Famous Art, Digitally," *New York Times* (late ed.), Aug. 20, 2001, p. C4; Alessandra Stanley, "Modern Marketing Booms at the Vatican Library," *New York Times* (late ed.), Jan. 8, 2001, p. A6; David D'Arcy, "Souvenirs Cashing In on Culture," *Financial Times,* Dec. 30, 1997, arts sec., p. 8; Carol Emert, "SFMOMA Cashes In on Store," *San Francisco Chronicle,* Nov. 22, 1997, p. B1.

3. A book or musical score is an algorithm that generates exact copies; a painting is not. See Nelson Goodman, *Languages of Art: An Approach to a Theory of Symbols* 112–122 (1976). What does correspond to the book or musical score in the visual arts is the mold from which a statue is cast or the engraving from which prints are run off, though the prints will tend to vary in quality, the earlier ones being sharper. For a comprehensive discussion of the mysterious preference for originals over reproductions, see Oswald Hanfling, "The Ontology of Art," in *Philosophical Aesthetics: An Introduction* 76 (Oswald Hanfling ed. 1992).

because there is no "objective" method of determining the quality of works of art, the quality of the nonexact copy is always contestable.[4] This cannot be the entire reason because vintage photographs (prints made at the time the photograph was taken) command a higher price than the identical photograph printed later from the same negative.[5] Another possible reason for the great disparity in price between originals and copies is that the latter, because producible in essentially unlimited quantities, sell at a price equal to their (low) cost of production, whereas the supply of originals is fixed at a low level, so if originals are valued for their scarcity, copies are poor substitutes even at very low prices.[6] But whatever the reasons, the important point for our purposes is simply that copying is a much smaller threat to the ability of artists to recover their fixed costs of expression than it is to the ability of writers and composers to do so.

Even unauthorized reproductions of a painting or sculpture that appear on merchandise will call attention to the original work, and this free publicity may enhance the artist's reputation and increase the value of his works. But the reverse may also happen. Sophisticated collectors may turn away from artists whose images have become too commercial and commonplace. Because the supply of an artist's original works tends to be inelastic (perfectly inelastic when the artist is dead), a reduction in the demand for those works is likely to cause a substantial reduction in their price. This is an example of the problem of congestion externalities that we discussed in the last chapter and provides an argument unrelated to incentives for recognizing copyright in works of art, including the derivative works therefrom. The transaction-cost argument for vesting control over derivative works in the creator of the original is also applicable here. For example, several hundred ancillary products incorporate images from works of art created by Andy Warhol.[7] By concen-

4. See Holger Bonus and Dieter Ronte, "Credibility and Economic Value in the Visual Arts," 76 *Journal of Cultural Economics* 103 (1997).

5. Thus Dorothea Lange's widely reproduced 1930s vintage photograph known as "Migrant Mother" sold at a Sotheby's photography auction on October 7, 1998, for $244,500, Peter Lennon, "Whatever Happened to All These Heroes?" *Guardian,* Dec. 30, 1998, p. 2, although an exhibition-quality print of "Migrant Mother" can be obtained for under $50 from the Library of Congress Photoduplication Service at *http://lcweb.loc.gov/preserve/pds/photo.html.* Edward Weston's vintage 1929 photograph "Pepper" was sold at a Christie's photography auction in 1997 for $74,000, while a print from the same negative, printed by the photographer's son, had been sold at an auction at another gallery eighteen months earlier for only $1,840.

6. See Gary S. Becker, William M. Landes, and Kevin M. Murphy, "The Social Market for the Great Masters and Other Collectibles," in Becker and Murphy, *Social Economics: Market Behavior in a Social Environment* 74, 82–83 (2000).

7. See "The Warhol Store" on the Web site of the Andy Warhol Museum, at *http://www.warholstore.com.*

trating the copyrights in the Warhol Foundation rather than letting each creator of a derivative work own a separate copyright, the law avoids infringement suits involving multiple plaintiffs in which a court might have to decide which of many similar and widely accessible works was the one the defendant had copied. Licensing costs would also rise because a potential licensee would be well advised to seek licenses from all owners of copyrights on derivative works, as well as from the owner of the copyright on the original, in order to avert the risk of being sued by one of them. The copyright on the original Warhol image is sufficient to prevent unauthorized copying of the various derivative works, since copying a derivative work will infringe the copyright on the original work.

But of course one solution would be to deny copyright protection to works of art and their derivative works. The overall case for copyright protection of works of art is weaker than that for copyright protection of most other expressive works. This point should be kept in mind in deciding how the law ought to resolve close questions relating to art copyrights.

Three Schools of Postmodern Art

ABSTRACT EXPRESSIONISM   In Abstract Expressionist paintings of the late 1950s and early 1960s by such artists as Morris Louis, Kenneth Noland, Frank Stella, and Jules Olitski, the notion that a painting is a depiction, even a depiction of abstract shapes, disappears. Painting ceases to be not only representational but also figurative (that is, the distinction between figure and ground is obliterated). Instead it becomes "about" such things as "a conflict between paint and the *support*"[8] or the relation between the painting itself and the framing edge (the borders of the canvas). These paintings are expressive, but arguably what they express is an idea. Suppose, as in a number of Stella's paintings, that what the viewer sees is a series of stripes whose width is identical to the thickness of the support. This is the fundamental design element in the painting. Are other painters free to copy it? If so, they will produce paintings that are virtually indistinguishable from Stella's. Or consider the slightly earlier Abstract Expressionist paintings of Jackson Pollock and Ad Reinhardt. Any painter who adopts Pollock's technique of splashing paint on large canvases spread horizontally on the floor, or who copies Reinhardt's idea of paintings the surface of which is entirely black, will produce paintings that look quite similar to Pollock's and to Reinhardt's, respectively.

8. Michael Fried, "Jules Olitski," in Fried, *Art and Objecthood: Essays and Reviews* 132, 145 (1998) (emphasis in original). The "support" is the rectangular stretched canvas or other object to which the paint is applied.

POP ART The philosopher Arthur Danto has argued that, in Pop Art, art became philosophy.[9] If Andy Warhol has the idea of exhibiting an ordinary box of Brillo in an art museum as if it were a work of art, thus illustrating the philosophical proposition that art has no essence—that anything can be art because the only criterion of art is whether it is accepted as art by the relevant community[10]—then anyone who copies the *idea* of exhibiting a commonplace object in an art museum will produce works of art indistinguishable from Warhol's.[11]

These movements—(late) Abstract Expressionism and (Warholian) Pop Art—are typical of modern art rather than idiosyncratic. A study by the economist David Galenson finds "a generational shift in the prevalent attitude of the leading modern painters toward their enterprise."[12] Formerly, important artists "placed a premium on the development of technique and craftsmanship that would allow them to portray visual sensations, whereas their successors instead emphasized the primary importance of a conceptual approach that would communicate ideas or emotions."[13] Copyright law does not protect ideas.

SUPERREALISM The members of this school strive to produce and sometimes succeed in producing paintings that at first glance are mistaken for photographs. If another artist paints a Superrealist painting of the identical scene, the two paintings may be virtually indistinguishable. Supperrealism differs from the other two movements that we have been discussing because of the emphasis it places on technique, rather to the exclusion of ideas. What unites

9. See Arthur C. Danto, *The Transfiguration of the Commonplace* (1981).

10. "A work such as *Brillo Box* cannot obviously be distinguished, on formalist grounds, from the ordinary object it resembles." Arthur C. Danto, "Introduction," in Danto, *Philosophizing Art: Selected Essays* 1, 8 (1999). See also Morton White, *A Philosophy of Culture: The Scope of Holistic Pragmatism* 120 (2002), similarly distinguishing the functional from the essentialist conception of art. Earlier, Marcel Duchamp had exhibited a standard urinal, which he entitled *Fountain*. Conceptual art is not limited to visual artworks. Consider John Cage's famous piece for "silent piano"—"4'33"—in which the pianist comes on stage, sits down at the piano, and plays nothing for the period indicated by the title of the piece. Cage's New York publisher complained when a British pop music composer and musician named Batt "included a blank, one-minute cut of silence, attributed to Batt-Cage, on the debut record" of a band without intending to pay royalties. "Listen Hard: Silence Is Golden," *Economist*, Aug. 31, 2002, p. 67.

11. We defer consideration of the complications introduced if the design of the Brillo box happens to be copyrighted. Clearly, the brand name and design are trademarked, but Warhol's use is unlikely to create consumer confusion, which is required for establishing a trademark violation other than on a dilution theory.

12. David W. Galenson, *Painting outside the Lines: Patterns of Creativity in Modern Art* 162 (2001).

13. Id.

the three movements is that in all three copyright is problematic, in the first two because the grant of a copyright could be thought to violate the principle that copyright cannot be obtained in ideas and in all three because if a copyright is granted, serious evidentiary problems will confront a court asked to adjudicate a claim of infringement. A "copy," while virtually indistinguishable from the original, will also be virtually indistinguishable, and maybe also derivative, from something else, something that is not copyrightable, whether an idea in the case of Abstract Expressionism or Pop Art or a scene in the case of Superrealism.

The evidentiary objections to copyright are, as we saw in Chapter 4, a muted but significant theme in the doctrines that limit the scope of copyright protection. They argue against recognizing copyright in the brand of minimalist Abstract Expressionism represented by Frank Stella[14] and the brand of Pop Art illustrated by Warhol's *Brillo Box*, though much less strongly against copyright in Superrealism, as it is no more problematic than copyright in photographs.

A shocking suggestion—denying copyright to such famous artists as Frank Stella and Andy Warhol! Yet it is supported by the fact that copyright is not a terribly important factor in artists' incentives. Imagine someone who showed up at an art museum carrying a box of Brillo and offered it as a substitute for *Brillo Box*. The museum would not be interested; nor would any private collector; and so this copying would not reduce the income of Warhol's estate by a penny. The value of *Brillo Box* inheres not in the physical object but in the artist's identity, and so is not impaired by copying. And the identity of the artist is protected by trademark. Given that the market distinguishes sharply between a Stella and a look-alike, or a Warhol and a look-alike, the analysis of trademark law in Chapter 7 implies that confusingly similar copies of original works, unless they carry a clear disclaimer of authenticity, violate the original artist's trademark in his instantly recognizable style.

It is true that increasingly—and dramatically in the case of such celebrity artists as Andy Warhol and Salvador Dali—artists derive substantial income from derivative works (posters, decorative plates, prints, etc.), works that in the absence of copyright could be produced without a license from the artist and therefore without any remuneration to him. But the principal beneficiaries of copyright in these derivative works are artists who already are very successful, and so the incentive effects of the additional income that these works generate for them are likely to be small. However, to the extent that museum shops hold copyright and derive income from it, some less cele-

14. His work of the early 1960s and that of Olitski, Louis, and Noland from approximately the same period are often, indeed, referred to as "Minimalism," although the term is sometimes reserved for a slightly later group of abstract artists, such as Donald Judd.

brated artists may benefit indirectly, because the greater the museum's income the greater its ability to make new acquisitions.

Mention of Warhol and Dali suggests that the strongest argument for copyright in art is the potential for congestion externalities. The uncontrolled proliferation of derivative works of these artists could reduce the aggregate value of the works as the market became saturated and eventually bored to death. The danger is substantial because of the faddish element in the popularity of artists among ordinary people, whose tastes in art are not stabilized by training or experience.

Appropriation Art

A fourth school of postmodern art, "Appropriation Art," unlike the three we have discussed so far, has given rise to significant copyright litigation.[15] Appropriation Art borrows images from popular culture, advertising, the mass media, and other artists and incorporates them into new works of art. Often the artist's technical skills are less important than his conceptual ability to place images in different settings and thereby alter their meaning. Appropriation Art has been described "as getting the hand out of art and putting the brain in." It is legally unproblematic when it copies works that are in the public domain. For example, Marcel Duchamp, an important precursor of Appropriation Art as well as of Pop Art, exhibited ready-made objects such as a urinal, bicycle wheel, and snow shovel as works of art. But when the copied image is copyrighted, the risk of a suit for copyright infringement looms.

Artists and judges tend to have different views about how the law should treat Appropriation Art. The artist perceives legal restraints on borrowing as a threat to artistic freedom:

> Whenever people's response is "how dare you!" I consider that a high compliment. First of all, taking from other artists is not illegal in the art world, as it is in the music industry, and second, it is a direct acknowledgment of how we work in painting. Everything you do is based on what came before and what is happening concurrently. I don't see history as monolithic. I feel very free to take and change whatever I want, and that includes borrowing from my contemporaries. If some people are upset because my work has similarities to what they're doing, that's their problem. And if they take from me, that's great! I don't respect

15. See Niels B. Schaumann, "An Artist's Privilege," 15 *Cardozo Arts and Entertainment Law Journal* 249 (1997); E. Kenly Ames, Note, "Beyond *Rogers v. Koons:* A Fair Use Standard for Appropriation," 93 *Columbia Law Review* 1473 (1993); Lynne A. Greenberg, "The Art of Appropriation: Puppies, Piracy, and Post-Modernism," 11 *Cardozo Arts and Entertainment Law Journal* 1 (1992).

these artificial boundaries that artists and people around artists erect to keep you in a certain category.[16]

Yet from the perspective of copyright law the very term "Appropriation Art" is a provocation; "appropriation" of protected work connotes stealing. And so, rejecting the defense of fair use, *Rogers v. Koons* held that Jeff Koons's well-known sculpture of puppies infringed the plaintiff's copyrighted black and white photograph, which Koons had transformed into a large, colored sculpture that arguably had little new expression since a black and white photograph of the sculpture looked nearly identical to the plaintiff's photograph.[17] The court said that "the essence of Rogers' photograph was copied nearly in toto, much more than would have been necessary even if the sculpture had been a parody of plaintiff's work. In short, it is not really the parody flag that [Koons is] sailing under, but rather the flag of piracy."[18]

We approach the copyright issues presented by Appropriation Art by way of two groups of examples involving disputes over borrowed images. The first involves borrowing by nonartists, the second by artists. The examples in the first group are: (1) *A* copies *B*'s copy of a painting in the public domain; (2) *A* makes and sells a CD-ROM containing copies of *B*'s digital reproductions of old master paintings in the public domain; (3) a museum reproduces its collection of copyrighted and public domain works in digital format and places the reproductions on its Web site, and other individuals download these images and distribute them over the Internet; (4) *A* purchases *B*'s copyrighted note cards, affixes them to tiles, and sells them as decorative objects.[19]

The examples in the second group are: (1) *A* creates a unique collage that

16. Raphael Rubinstein, "Abstraction in a Changing Environment," *Art in America*, Oct. 1994, pp. 102, 103, quoting the artist Richmond Burton.

17. 960 F.2d 301 (2d Cir. 1992).

18. Id. at 310. Koons's sculpture had been prepared for a 1988 exhibition entitled "The Banality Show." Copyright infringement suits were also brought successfully against two other Koons sculptures from the show. See Campbell v. Koons, No. 91CIV.6055, 1993 WL 97381, at *1 (S.D.N.Y. Apr. 1, 1993) (involving a copyrighted photograph of two boys and a pig); United Feature Syndicate v. Koons, 817 F. Supp. 370 (S.D.N.Y. 1993) (involving the character "Odie" from the Garfield comic strip).

19. Example 1 comes from a lawsuit against a firm for making unauthorized copies of an engraver's reproductions of old master paintings. Alfred Bell & Co. v. Catalda Fine Arts, Inc., 191 F.2d 99 (2d Cir. 1951). Example 2 is based on a case rejecting copyright for digital images of works in museum collections. Bridgeman Art Library v. Corel Corp., 25 F. Supp. 2d 421 (1998), amended, 36 F. Supp. 2d 191 (S.D.N.Y. 1999). Example 3 is based on recent proposals for educational fair use of digital images. Conference on Fair Use, *Final Report to the Commissioner on the Conclusion of the Conference of Fair Use* 33–40 (1998). Example 4 is based on copyright suits against a firm for affixing tiles to lawfully acquired copyrighted images and reselling them. Lee v. A.R.T. Co., 125 F.3d 580 (7th Cir. 1997); Mirage Editions, Inc. v. Albuquerque A.R.T. Co., 856 F.2d 1341 (9th Cir. 1988).

includes a copyrighted photograph taken by B; (2) A creates a limited edition series of prints that incorporates B's copyrighted photograph—moreover, reproductions of A's prints appear on posters, calendars, and other mass-produced merchandise; (3) A creates a work that copies the outline of a nude from B's photograph, the distinctive color from C's monochromatic painting, and a miniature yellow square from D's painting; (4) A constructs several identical sculptural works based on B's copyrighted photograph or comic-book character; (5) A creates a work that contains elements substantially similar to one of his earlier works owned by B, who also happens to own the copyright in that work.[20] We begin with the examples in the first group.

1. *Copying a copy of a public domain work.* In *Alfred Bell & Co. v. Catalda Fine Arts*,[21] the defendant reproduced and sold copies of the plaintiff's mezzotint engravings of eighteenth- and nineteenth-century paintings that were in the public domain. The plaintiff's engravings were realistic reproductions that had required great skill and judgment to make. The defendant argued that since they were merely copies of works in the public domain, they failed the originality requirement, so that all he was doing was copying a public domain image, albeit by copying from a copy. The defendant lost the case, as he should have. Originality lay in the art of copying, which required significant expenditures of time, effort, and skill. Free riding by the defendant would undermine the incentive to produce high-quality copies of public domain works. And since copyright law would not have prevented the defendant from hiring engravers to make copies of the same paintings, the decision protected the plaintiff's investment in copying from the public domain without cutting off the defendant's access to the original paintings to make his own copies. Because the plaintiff's copyright prevented free riding but not entry by new firms, it did not enable him to obtain monopoly profits beyond those conferred by any copyright. Entry would occur until the marginal firm just

---

20. The first two examples are based on lawsuits brought by photographers against, among others, Robert Rauschenberg and Andy Warhol for using copyrighted photographs in their works. Both Warhol and Rauschenberg settled out of court. Warhol paid $6,000 in cash and royalties on the print edition of *Flowers* to the photographer Patricia Caulfield, who had threatened to sue Warhol over his flower paintings. Rauschenberg gave the photographer Richard Beebe $3,000 and a copy of the allegedly infringing work worth about $10,000. These cases and others involving the artists Sherri Levine, David Salle, and Susan Pitt are discussed in Ames, note 15 above, at 1484–1485. Example 3 is based on a lawsuit in Germany brought by the well-known photographer Helmut Newton against the artist George Pusenkoff, who claimed that his paintings "quote" rather than borrow from other artists. See Geraldine Norman, "The Power of Borrowed Images," *Art and Antiques,* Mar. 1996, at 123. Example 4 is based on the Koons litigation, notes 17–18 above. Example 5, the case of an artist borrowing from his own works, is based on Franklin Mint Corp. v. National Wildlife Art Exchange, Inc., 575 F.2d 62 (3d Cir. 1978).

21. 191 F.2d 99 (2d Cir. 1951).

covered its full cost of making copies (without free riding) plus a normal return on its investment.

2. *Copying a digital copy of a public domain work.* In *Bridgeman Art Library v. Corel Corp.*,[22] the plaintiff, which produced and marketed color transparencies and digital images of well-known public domain works of art in museum collections, complained that the defendant was selling CD-ROMs that contained images that the defendant had copied from the plaintiff's transparencies. The court likened these transparencies to copies produced by a photocopy machine and held that since photocopying obviously fails the originality requirement of copyright law, modest as it is, so did the transparencies. Left out of account is the fact that, much as in the *Alfred Bell* case, making high-quality transparencies of artworks is a time-consuming process that requires considerable skill on the part of the photographer or copyist.

The court's insistence in *Bridgeman* that a finding of originality requires a "distinguishable variation" between the original and copy that cannot be satisfied by a simple change in medium[23] creates a perverse incentive to produce second-rate or poor-quality copies. Cutting the other way, however, is the consideration that we emphasized in discussing derivative works in Chapter 4—that if the derivative work is indistinguishable from the original work, courts will have a devil of a time determining whether a subsequent work is a copy of the original or of the derivative work, a vital issue if the original work is in the public domain but the derivative work is copyrighted. The incentive to obtain copyright protection by producing a second-rate copy can be curbed by insisting that second-rateness is not a form of originality. (Granted, there is a risk that judges will not be good judges of originality.) So the court's decision may be correct after all.

3. *Copying both public domain and copyrighted works.* Suppose a museum or an educational institution wants to create and distribute digital images of works in its collection. For works created after January 1, 1978, the effective date of the 1976 Copyright Act, the museum will probably have to obtain permission from the copyright holder to reproduce them unless the artist has transferred the copyright to the museum. For works created before 1978, however, there is no easy answer to whether the museum can make copies, for recall that prior to the 1976 Act common law copyright protected unpublished works in perpetuity. Although the Act provides statutory copyright protection from the moment a work is fixed in a tangible form, it further provides that common law copyright in works not yet published when the Act

22. 25 F. Supp. 2d 421 (1998), amended, 36 F. Supp. 2d 191 (S.D.N.Y. 1999).
23. Id. at 196, quoting L. Batlin & Son, Inc. v. Snyder, 536 F.2d 486, 490 (2d Cir. 1976) (en banc).

was passed does not expire until 2002 or, if the work was published after the Act was passed, until 2047.[24] So a nineteenth-century painting could be protected by copyright for a century and a half if it had never been published. But what is "publication" of a work of art? The Act defines "publication" as the distribution of copies (including the first copy that embodies the copyright) to the public and specifies that public display is not a publication.[25] The distribution of reproductions might be treated as either a publication of copies or a derivative work, but publication of a derivative work may not constitute publication of the original work.[26] A further complication is that in some states a museum may own the copyright on a painting or work of art owned by the museum by virtue of the *Pushman* presumption that the transfer of a unique work also transfers the copyright.[27]

In light of these uncertainties and the resulting high costs of determining whether a work is still copyrighted and if so who owns the copyright, there is an argument for expanding the fair use doctrine (a major purpose of which, it will be recalled, is to reduce transaction costs) to embrace museum reproductions of older works. If one is skeptical, as we are inclined to be, that reproduction rights have much impact on the incentive to create works of art, then limiting the ability of educational institutions to make and distribute copies in digital format imposes access costs without offsetting benefits. But a legal response to the problem may be unnecessary because the market has responded in a manner ingeniously designed to minimize transaction costs. There are now organizations—primarily the Visual Artists and Galleries Association and the Artists Rights Society—that help people desirous of reproducing works of art obtain licenses from the copyright holders. Each organization publishes a list of the artists it represents, keeps a slide catalog of works of its members, and acts as the artists' agent in negotiating licenses for reproductions of art in monographs, greeting cards, postcards, merchandise, advertisement, films, and so on.[28]

24. 17 U.S.C. § 303.

25. See 17 U.S.C. § 101.

26. See Academy of Motion Picture Arts and Sciences v. Creative House Promotions, Inc., 944 F.2d 1446 (9th Cir. 1991).

27. See Forward v. Thorogood, 985 F.2d 604 (1st Cir. 1993); Pushman v. New York Graphic Society, 39 N.E.2d 249 (N.Y. 1942). We noted in Chapter 5 that the *Pushman* presumption has been preempted by the Copyright Act of 1976; but copyright in works that had been transferred before that date would have been transferred in accordance with the presumption in those states that accepted it.

28. The Visual Artists and Galleries Association (VAGA) publishes a book entitled *VAGA 2000*, containing an alphabetical listing of the artists represented in the United States by VAGA and the Artists Rights Society. The book is available from VAGA at 350 Fifth Avenue, Suite 6305, New York, New York 10118.

A museum or educational institution also faces the problem of protecting the copies it lawfully makes. This is a variant of the issue in the *Alfred Bell* and *Bridgeman* cases: does the copy satisfy the originality requirement? But here the answer may not matter much. If creating a digital image is not much more expensive than making a copy from a photocopy machine, then copying from a copy will cost about the same as copying from the original. The copier from a copy will have no cost advantage, therefore, and so will not be free riding on the museum's copying. In these circumstances unlimited copying of copies will minimize transaction costs without impairing incentives to create copies in digital format.

4. *Altering and reselling a copyrighted work.* In *Lee v. A.R.T. Co.*,[29] the defendant purchased note cards from the plaintiff, affixed them to tiles, and sold the tiles at retail. Since copying was not involved, the plaintiff claimed that A.R.T. had infringed his right to prepare a derivative work. The statute, we recall from Chapter 4, defines a derivative work broadly to include "any other form in which a work may be recast, transformed or adapted." But the statute also entitles the owner of a lawfully acquired copy to sell or otherwise dispose of the copy without the copyright owner's consent.[30] Applying this "first sale" rule, the court held that A.R.T. had merely placed the equivalent of a mat or frame on a work it had purchased, and had then resold it.[31] The decision makes economic sense. The defendant's activity benefited the plaintiff. The more tiled cards the defendant sold, the more cards he would have to buy from the plaintiff. The plaintiff's position if accepted would give an artist the right to block any minor alteration in a work of his of which he disapproves. This would harm artists in the long run. Costs of contracting over art would rise as galleries, museums, and collectors, in order to avoid copyright liability, sought permission from the copyright owner to mat and frame works of art that they had bought.

So why would a plaintiff sue to stop an activity that benefits him? Maybe it doesn't benefit him; maybe his reputation will be damaged by the alteration in his work. That is the basis of the moral rights doctrine, discussed in the next chapter. But it is unlikely that mounting note cards on tiles would have tarnished Lee's reputation. Nor was it a case of a looming congestion externality. A more plausible explanation is price discrimination. Lee might want to charge higher prices for note cards to firms that affix them to tiles for

---

29. 125 F.3d 580 (7th Cir. 1997).

30. 17 U.S.C. § 109(a). There are exceptions for renting and leasing of sound recordings (CDs, tapes) and computer programs without the copyright owner's authorization. 17 U.S.C. § 109(b)(1)(A).

31. An earlier case involving the same issue and same defendant, Mirage Editions, Inc. v. Albuquerque A.R.T. Co., 856 F.2d 1341 (9th Cir. 1988), had come out the other way.

resale to consumers, because those firms are likely to have a less elastic demand for them than consumers. Arbitrage would make this discrimination infeasible unless the law forbade affixing cards to tiles, or selling the tiles, without the plaintiff's consent. But it is doubtful that enabling artists to engage in this form of price discrimination is needed to give artists adequate incentives. There is no indication that Lee ever contemplated producing tiled note cards or licensing others to do so.

Turning now to our second group of examples, those involving artists' borrowings, we are squarely in the middle of the copyright controversy over Appropriation Art.

1. *Creating a unique work.* Suppose an artist incorporates a copyrighted photograph from a popular magazine into a collage by cutting the photograph out of the magazine, affixing it to a board, and adding other objects, colors, and original images. No copy of the photograph is made, and the photograph itself may constitute only a small part of the collage. This should be an easy case against a finding of copyright infringement. Since the publisher has paid the photographer for his work and charged consumers for copies of its magazine, allowing the photograph to be used in the collage will have no significant impact on incentives to create new commercial photographs or to publish magazines, but it will reduce access and transaction costs.

2. *Creating multiple copies.* Henri Dauman, a French photographer, sued Andy Warhol's estate over Warhol's "Jackie" series of silk-screen prints that incorporated a copyrighted photograph by Dauman of Jacqueline Kennedy that had appeared in *Life* magazine in 1963.[32] Dauman also sued the estate for reproducing the silk-screen images on calendars, posters, and other widely distributed merchandise. We are more sympathetic to the copyright claim here. It might seem arbitrary to draw a bright line between a one-time use of an image lawfully acquired and reproducing that same lawfully acquired image in multiple copies, but the distinction goes to the heart of the economic rationale for copyright. Commercial photographers are in the business of licensing reproduction rights for a variety of unanticipated uses. Without copyright protection the price of copies would be driven down to the cost of copying, leaving nothing to cover the cost of creating the work. Allowing an artist to make multiple copies without authorization poses a more substantial threat to the incentive to create new works than the one-time unauthorized copy, as in our first example.

Warhol had added substantial original expression to the original image, and his silk-screens, one of which sold in 1992 at Sotheby's for more than

32. See Sarah King, "Warhol Estate Sued over Jackie Photo," *Art in America,* Feb. 1997, p. 27. The case was settled.

$400,000, were not likely to cut into the market for the photograph. But remember that he reproduced the silk-screens on posters, calendars, and other merchandise, and these *were* likely to cut into Dauman's market.

3. *Appropriating from multiple sources.* The Russian painter George Pusenkoff included in one of his paintings the outline of a nude from a Helmut Newton photograph, a distinctive bright blue background from an Yves Klein monochromatic painting, and a small yellow square from a painting by the late Russian artist Casimir Malevich.[33] Neither Klein nor Malevich's estate objected to Pusenkoff's borrowing, but Newton did and sought to have the painting destroyed. Pusenkoff's defense was that he had created a unique work rather than made multiple copies, that he had borrowed only the outline of a photograph and not the entire photograph, and that he had transformed the photograph by adding public domain material and altering the medium. Yet he clearly had copied Newton's well-known image without paying for it, and indeed his stated purpose was to copy recognizable elements from other artists—"to make canvases buzz with cultural associations by 'quoting' from other artists—a perfectly respectable postmodernist approach to picture-making."[34]

The German court in which Newton's case was brought held that Pusenkoff's painting was a "free adaptation" rather than a reworking and therefore did not infringe Newton's copyright.[35] Ordinarily an adaptation would be a derivative work and thus infringing if made without the authorization of the owner of the copyright on the original work, and the fact that Pusenkoff's adaptation was a productive or transformative use that did not substitute for the original photograph would be irrelevant. The impact of Pusenkoff's appropriation on Newton's income was surely minute and possibly positive, for Pusenkoff unlike Warhol did not create posters and other merchandise but a unique work; but again that is not the sort of consideration that entitles the making of a derivative work without the authorization of the owner of the copyright on the original. However, by analogy to the "reverse doctrine of equivalents" in patent law (see Chapter 11), it can be argued in defense of the court's decision that creative expression so predominated in Pusenkoff's adaptation that the "derivative" work should be considered an original and the borrowing of Newton's image a fair use.

This suggestion is supported by the fact that Pusenkoff's work borrowed (or "quoted") from more than one previous work. Transaction costs are likely to be high if the law requires artists to obtain permission to appropriate

33. See Norman, note 20 above, at 123.

34. Id.

35. Id. Newton was not happy with the German court's decision, and remarked, "Poor fellow, he hasn't got an idea of his own, so he has to use other people's." Id. at 125. But copyright law does not protect ideas.

from multiple sources, while a work that copies from several sources is less likely to be a substitute for any of them. So the law should be more sympathetic to the artist whose work borrows from multiple copyrighted sources rather than from a single such source. We might even think of Pusenkoff's adaptation as a rough visual-arts counterpart of T. S. Eliot's poem *The Waste Land,* a tissue of quotations from a variety of authors yet regarded by many as the greatest poem of the twentieth century.

4. *Creating sculptures from a single copyrighted source.* This is *Rogers v. Koons.*[36] Koons had bought a note card displaying a photograph of a group of puppies with their owners, had torn off the copyright notice from the card, and had hired an Italian firm to make four large sculptures called *A String of Puppies* based on the photograph. Koons's role was strictly conceptual. He did not make the sculptures himself, although he chose the subject matter, medium, size, materials, and colors. And he did not design the sculptures, at least in the usual sense, for he instructed the studio that they "must be just like photo—features of photo must be captured."[37] Altering the image to avoid a copyright lawsuit would have defeated his purpose of showing that meaning depends on context (this is an example of Arthur Danto's point about art becoming philosophy).

In rejecting the fair use defense, the court emphasized the commercial nature of the copying; the fact (the same point, really) that Koons had earned a substantial sum from the sculptures (three of the four sculptures sold for a total of almost $400,000); that he had faithfully copied the original image; and that the sculptures were likely to impair the market for the copyrighted photograph. Although the copies and the original were sold in different markets, the court believed that Koons's type of appropriation could potentially eliminate an important source of licensing revenues for photographers.

Koons's main argument was that his work should be privileged as a satirical comment or parody. He claimed that by placing the image of the puppies and their owners in a different context from that of the original photograph, he was commenting critically on a political and economic system that in his view (and that of many other social critics and commentators) places excessive value on mass-produced commodities and media images. But we noted in Chapter 6 that a privileged parody requires that the original work be its target. When the parody targets the plaintiff's work, the parties are unlikely to be able to agree on a price that allows the defendant to make fun of, embarrass, or even humiliate the plaintiff. (Of course the photographer might not have realized that Koons's sculptural versions of the photograph *were* parodic.) If the parodist wants to use the parodied work as a weapon to batter

36. See note 17, and accompanying text, above.
37. 960 F.2d at 305, quoting Koons.

society rather than the work, he should have less trouble obtaining a license. But Koons wanted both to comment on the vacuity of modern American culture and—as the court failed to note—to do so by offering the copied work as an *example* of that fatuity. This makes us doubt that the case was correctly decided. There was no chance that Koons's costly sculptures would be substitutes in the market for the plaintiff's note cards. Nor was Koons planning to do Warhol-like reproductions—that would have been inconsistent with the critical message of his parodic copies.

5. *Borrowing from one's own earlier work.* Artists often return to themes that they have used earlier in their careers and even copy from their earlier works. Gilbert Stuart is reported to have painted some seventy-five substantially similar portraits of George Washington.[38] Giorgio de Chirico made numerous copies of many of his best-known early Surrealist works.[39] The examples are not limited to art. Yeats and Auden revised their poems many years after original publication and published the revised versions in collections of their work. A recent review of a variorum edition of poems by Coleridge notes his "revisionary obsession," which resulted for example in there being eighteen different *published* versions of *The Ancient Mariner*.[40] An issue of unlawful appropriation arises only if the artist no longer owns the copyright on the earlier work. This is a reminder of the economic rationale for separating ownership of the copyright on a nonunique work from ownership of the work itself.[41] However, our present subject is unique works, where the artist will often have parted with the copyright. We must consider whether the law should allow him in the name of fair use to produce derivative works.

Such a rule would spare the courts from having to determine whether a new work by the artist was a copy of an earlier work on which he had transferred the copyright or an independently created work substantially similar to his earlier work only because it was by the same person. "If Cézanne painted two pictures of Mont St. Victoire, we should expect them to look more alike than if Matisse had painted the second, even if Cézanne painted the second painting from life rather than from the first painting."[42]

But against this evidentiary point in favor of an expanded fair use privilege is the harm likely to accrue to the artists themselves from retention of a right to make derivative works. The transfer of a copyright is of little value to the transferee if the transferor retains the right to make a derivative work that may destroy the market for the transferred work.

38. See William D. Grampp, *Pricing the Priceless: Art, Artists, and Economics* 6 (1989).
39. See Kim Levin, *Beyond Modernism: Essays on Art from the '70s and '80s* 251–253 (1988).
40. Nigel Leask, "Poems Being Various," *Times Literary Supplement,* July 5, 2002, p. 11.
41. In the case of a unique work, as we saw, there is often a presumption that the copyright is transferred along with the work.
42. Schiller & Schmidt, Inc. v. Nordisco Corp., 969 F.2d 410, 414 (7th Cir. 1992).

10

Moral Rights and the Visual Artists Rights Act

In 1990 Congress enacted the Visual Artists Rights Act (VARA), which amended the Copyright Act to confer attribution and integrity rights, commonly called moral rights, on authors of works of visual art.[1] Attribution rights entitle the artist to claim authorship of a work he created and to disclaim authorship if his work is altered in a manner "prejudicial to his honor or reputation" or incorrectly attributed to him. Integrity rights prohibit the intentional distortion, mutilation, or other alteration of the artist's work that injures his honor or reputation, and make the intentional or grossly negligent destruction of a work of recognized stature actionable.

In contrast to the United States, most countries in Western Europe have a long tradition of recognizing moral rights. France recognized them in the nineteenth century, and since 1928 they have been codified in the Berne Convention, to which the United States became a party in 1989. Before then several states, beginning with California in 1979, had enacted moral rights laws, and the Copyright Act itself had occasionally been interpreted to confer analogous protections.[2]

In this chapter we summarize VARA, explain the economics of moral rights, apply our economic analysis to the cases interpreting the statute, and

1. See 17 U.S.C. § 106A.

2. See Roberta Rosenthal Kwall, "How Fine Art Fares Post VARA," 1 *Marquette Intellectual Property Law Review* 1 (1997). The states are California (1979), Connecticut (1988), Louisiana (1986), Maine (1985), Massachusetts (1984), Pennsylvania (1986), New Jersey (1986), New York (1984), and Rhode Island (1987). All nine states protect both attribution and integrity rights. The major difference among the states is that Louisiana, Maine, New Jersey, New York, and Rhode Island exclude from the integrity right the destruction of a work of art. We omit New Mexico from the group of states that protect moral rights because its statute (enacted in 1995) provides integrity rights only for art incorporated into public buildings. Because of the preemption provision of the Copyright Act, VARA preempts some provisions of state moral-rights statutes, for example a provision forbidding the intentional mutilation of work during the artist's lifetime but not a provision protecting the artist against harm caused him by the display or reproduction of altered works.

finally try to explain why some states passed statutes conferring such rights and with what consequences.

The Statute; Herein of Works Made for Hire

VARA protects works of "visual art" narrowly defined as a unique work or a print, sculpture, or photograph produced in an edition of no more than 200 copies that are signed and consecutively numbered. Unlike the other rights conferred by the Copyright Act (for remember that VARA is an amendment to the Act), the rights conferred by VARA are enforceable only during the artist's lifetime. There are other limitations as well. The artist may not transfer or assign his rights, though he may waive them in a signed document identifying the specific work and uses to which the waiver applies. In the absence of such a waiver, the artist retains his attribution and integrity rights even if he assigns his copyright.

Because the alteration, mutilation, or destruction of a work as a result of negligence, the passage of time, the nature of the materials used in the work, or failed conservation efforts does not violate VARA, an owner of an artwork has no duty to expend resources on preserving a work in good condition. VARA also provides no remedy for injuries to the artist's reputation caused by the presentation, display, or reproduction of his work; he cannot complain that a dimly lit exhibition of his work or a poor-quality reproduction of his work in a pamphlet or Web site violates his integrity or attribution right.[3]

Nor does VARA creates any rights in works made for hire—works prepared by an employee within the scope of his employment.[4] To explain the reason for this exclusion, we shall have to digress to consider the scope and economic purpose of the works for hire provision—a subject of independent interest, however.

The significance of characterizing a work as a work for hire is that unless the parties agree otherwise the employer owns the copyright on the work. A work created pursuant to a formal employment relationship (as when Disney hires an animation artist who is paid a regular wage, receives fringe benefits, and can be assigned to work on different projects) is an unambiguous example of a work for hire. But a commissioned work executed by an independent artist may also be a work for hire if, for example, the commissioning party pays the artist a monthly stipend, pays health and other fringe benefits during the time he works on the project, defrays the cost of materials, and exercises overall though not necessarily daily supervision. The reason that the work for

---

3. See Pavia v. 1120 Avenue of the Americas Associates, 901 F. Supp. 620 (S.D.N.Y. 1995).
4. 17 U.S.C. § 101.

hire concept cannot be limited to formal employment is that an identical relationship can be created by skillful drafting of contracts that purport to treat the (de facto) employee as an independent contractor.

The economic difference between the employment relation and its equivalents, on the one hand, and the relation that exists between a principal and a truly independent contractor, on the other hand, is that in the first case the principal (the employer) directs the worker in the performance of his work rather than merely specifying the output.[5] The direction implies that much of the knowledge and know-how that goes into the worker's creation of a piece of intellectual property comes from the employer, making the employer in effect a co-creator, and often the major co-creator—think of Jeff Koons's role in the creation of the puppy sculptures. Often the employer will be coordinating the expressive production of several or many employees, as in the case of a movie studio (because of the iron hand with which Disney controls its creative product, some of its employees refer to the company as "Mauschwitz") or the atelier of successful artists like Andy Warhol and before him Rembrandt and Rubens. When several artists contribute to creating an integrated expressive work, it is efficient to vest copyright in one person and who better than the initiator and coordinator of the project?[6] Also, the decision to pay a worker a wage rather than contracting for his output is a way of shifting risk from worker to employer, the latter being likely to be less risk-averse. This risk shifting would be highly imperfect if the employer lowered the wage but allowed the employee to retain a financial interest, necessarily highly variable, in the intellectual property that he had a hand in creating. For these reasons one expects that if copyright were vested initially in the employee, the parties would contract to transfer it to the employer. Vesting copyright in the employer in the first instance economizes on transaction costs.

But this is in general and not in every case. It is generally and we think correctly understood that academics, although employees of the university in which they teach and conduct their research, own the copyrights on their academic books and articles.[7] Their decision about what and how to write is their own rather than the university's; they are better informed with regard to

5. See Ronald H. Coase, "The Nature of the Firm," 4 *Economica* (n.s.) 386 (1937); Richard A. Posner, *Economic Analysis of Law* 407–408 (6th ed. 2003).

6. This "better exploiter" rationale of the work for hire doctrine is explored in I. T. Hardy, "An Economic Understanding of Copyright Law's Work-Made-for-Hire Doctrine," 12 *Columbia-VLA Journal of Law and the Arts* 181 (1988).

7. See Hays v. Sony Corp. of America, 847 F.2d 412, 416–417 (7th Cir. 1988); Weinstein v. University of Illinois, 811 F.2d 1091 (7th Cir. 1987); Chanani Sandler, "Copyright Ownership: A Fundamental of 'Academic Freedom,'" 12 *Albany Law Journal of Science and Technology* 231, 240–244 (2001); Robert A. Gorman, "Copyright Conflicts on the University Campus," 47 *Journal of the Copyright Society* 297, 302–305 (2000).

publication outlets; and because academics move around a lot, it would be awkward if each university at which they worked owned the lecture notes, books, and articles, including unpublished manuscripts, that they created when employed by that university. An academic might have to negotiate for licenses from several universities whenever he wanted to teach the same course at a different university, bring out a second edition of a book he had written, or complete and publish a manuscript that he might have been working on for a number of years and in several different university employments.[8]

An intermediate case is the think tank. Most think tanks are more mission-oriented than universities, and the members of their research staff tend to be less peripetetic than professors. So we are not surprised that most though not all think tanks retain copyright in their researchers' work; the Brookings Institution does, for example, though the American Enterprise Institute generally does not.

A rule that may seem in tension with the work for hire provision is that in the case of a collective work, such as a magazine, copyright law vests the copyright on each individual contribution initially in the author of the contribution. However, the owner of the collective work can copyright the work itself (compare the copyrightability of compilations, discussed in Chapter 4) and if he publishes a revised version can include the individual copyrighted contributions without having to obtain new licenses from their authors.[9] The difference between this case and that of a work for hire is that ordinarily the author of the contribution will have been the sole creator of the intellectual property and will know best how to maximize its value through subsequent publication, revision, and so forth, activities unlikely moreover to reduce the demand for the collective work.

The rather unequivocal wording of the collective-works provision of the copyright statute led the Supreme Court in the *Tasini* case[10] to hold that the *New York Times* had infringed the copyrights of freelance contributors of articles to the *Times* when it included the articles in computer databases such as Lexis/Nexis. Those databases, the Court held, were not a "revision" of the original newspaper editions in which the articles had appeared; they were instead a translation from the print medium to an electronic medium. The decision is unfortunate from an economic standpoint. It is bound to result in less complete electronic databases; publishers will have to exclude many older articles that still are or may be under copyright because they will be unable to locate the authors or the authors' heirs. The decision also increases transac-

8. See Rochelle Cooper Dreyfuss, "The Creative Employee and the Copyright Act of 1976," 54 *University of Chicago Law Review* 590 (1987).

9. 17 U.S.C. § 201(c).

10. New York Times Co. v. Tasini, 533 U.S. 483 (2001).

tion costs without significantly enhancing the incentive of writers to produce more or better articles. It conferred a windfall on writers of already published articles, but windfalls do not create incentives.

Future licenses are likely to contain a clause authorizing the *Times* to include the author's article in electronic databases—as its recent licenses already did at the time of the decision—because such a clause minimizes transaction costs; but the Coase Theorem implies that such a clause has no significance for authors' incomes. If the *Times* owns the electronic publication rights to articles not yet created, the authors will receive higher upfront payments for new articles because the articles are worth more to the *Times,* which if the authors own these rights they will sell them back to the publisher by means of the clause. Either way, the author is compensated for the fact that the electronic database is an addition to the market for his article. And either way, the compensation is likely to be negligible. Most newspaper articles have little republication value; they are an ephemeral form of expression. Those that do, usually by virtue of their authors' reputation, are more likely to find a lucrative republication market in printed anthologies by the author or others than in electronic format. Many freelance authors of newspaper articles would if need be pay to have their articles in electronic databases, as it would be a way of advertising their work. There is support for this conjecture in the fact that newspapers with higher circulations generally do not pay their op-ed writers more.

In the Disney example with which we began our examination of the work for hire doctrine, transaction costs would be prohibitive if each artist employed by Disney owned the copyright to his work and so could block or delay publication of a project such as a movie or a comic book that involved the efforts of many creative employees. Aware of the holdout problem, Disney would acquire the separate copyrights before embarking on the project; and so the law's assigning them to Disney at the outset reduces transaction costs. Which brings us back to VARA. For if the individual employee's creative contribution were protected by VARA, then since Disney's use of his contribution might alter, mutilate, or even destroy it, Disney would again insist in advance that the artist waive these rights. Or suppose a developer commissioned a large sculptural work as part of a building project and after the work was completed and installed decorated it with Christmas decorations that the artist regarded as degrading. Anticipating such possibilities, the developer would require a waiver of VARA rights when he commissioned the sculpture. The exemption from VARA for works for hire is thus a way of economizing on transaction costs.

Another important limitation of VARA coverage involves works, installed in buildings, that are likely to be mutilated or destroyed if they are ever removed. VARA provides that there is no integrity right for a work installed after the statute's effective date of July 1, 1991, provided the artist consented in writing to both its installation and the possibility that removal might mutilate or destroy the work, or, in the case of a work installed prior to the effective date, provided the artist consented to its installation. If an installed work can be removed without being mutilated or destroyed, the artist retains his integrity right unless the building owner notifies him that he intends to remove the work and gives the artist a reasonable opportunity to remove it at his own expense.

Consider a building owner who hires an artist to create a site-specific sculptural work for the building's entrance plaza. Their contract is silent on the artist's rights if the sculpture is ever removed, though removal would destroy the sculpture. A new owner acquires the building and wants to tear it down and build a modern office building in its place. Never having consented to the possible destruction of his work, the sculptor would be in a position, given VARA, to extract a substantial payment from the new owner for allowing the project to go forward. The owner might argue that the sculpture was a work for hire, but we have already seen that commissioning a work does not necessarily turn it into such. So building owners would demand written waivers of VARA rights at the time works such as we are discussing were commissioned. If the waiver proved difficult to obtain, building owners might forgo installing artwork in buildings in order to avoid future legal problems.

VARA protects the artist's integrity right only against alterations that injure his "honor or reputation" and against the destruction of his work only if it is of "recognized stature." The terms "honor" and "reputation" were borrowed without attempt at definition from European moral rights laws, but the intended meanings are reasonably clear. Reputation is a matter of what other people think of one, and an artist's reputation is primarily a matter of what art lovers think of the artist's work. An injury to an artist's reputation is likely to affect the prices of his artworks and thus, if he is still active or has retained copyright or ownership of some of his works, his income. Honor is a related concept but includes self-esteem and need have no pecuniary implications. Someone might intentionally mutilate the work of an unknown artist, injuring the artist's self-esteem yet inflicting no financial injury on him because the work had no market value.[11] Finally, the statutory term "work of recognized stature" has been interpreted to require only minimum public acknowledgment of a work's quality or significance.[12]

11. For a bizarre example, see Taliferro v. Augle, 757 F.2d 157 (7th Cir. 1985).

12. See Martin v. City of Indianapolis, 192 F.3d 608 (7th Cir. 1999); Carter v. Hemsley-Spear, Inc., 861 F. Supp. 303 (S.D.N.Y. 1994), reversed on other grounds, 71 F.3d 77 (2d Cir. 1995).

The Economics of Moral Rights

Proponents of moral rights laws argue that these laws create a climate of respect for art and artists that encourages artistic creation. The implication is that such laws increase the quality-adjusted quantity of art. There is no evidence for this conjecture. Artistic innovation in the past half-century has been greater in the United States than in Europe, despite Europe's having moral rights laws during this period and the United States largely not.[13] Economics suggests that integrity rights, though not attribution rights, may do more harm than good and on balance may actually discourage artistic creation.[14]

Attribution rights are closely related to rights against fraud and trademark infringement (and also to the norm against plagiarism), so that much of what they seek to prevent is already forbidden,[15] often by criminal as well as civil law. For example, the laws against fraud would forbid someone who was not Jasper Johns to paint a picture in Johns's style, sign it "Jasper Johns," and attempt to pass it off in the market as Johns's work. And removing Johns's signature from an original Jasper Johns painting and selling it under one's own name would violate trademark and unfair competition law, although such a forgery is unlikely because it would reduce the painting's market value. Not only does VARA add little if anything to the rights that an artist already has in such cases; but those rights, unlike the rights created by VARA, do not expire with the artist's death.

Attribution rights could be used to prevent one type of "fraud" that would escape the reach of conventional fraud law, however. Suppose someone painted a picture in the style of Jasper Johns solely for the purpose of displaying it in his home, and signed it "Jasper Johns." He would be perpetrating a fraud of sorts because he would be trying to gain prestige and status by fooling relatives, friends, and others into believing him wealthier and more cultured than he actually was. His conduct would be similar to that of a poor woman who wears a perfume with the same scent as Chanel No. 5 hoping to be thought wealthy. He might also be infringing copyright, depending on how many features of Johns's art he copied in order to make his forgery dif-

---

13. David W. Galenson and Bruce Weinberg, "Age and the Quality of Work: The Case of Modern American Painters," 108 *Journal of Political Economy* 761 (2000), presents data on the surge in innovative American art that began in the late 1940s.

14. The fullest economic analysis of moral rights is Henry Hansmann and Marina Santilli, "Authors' and Artists' Moral Rights: A Comparative Legal and Economic Analysis," 26 *Journal of Legal Studies* 95 (1997); we discuss their argument for such rights below.

15. See Waldman Publishing Corp. v. Landoll Inc., 43 F.3d 775 (2d Cir. 1994); Robinson v. Random House, Inc., 877 F. Supp. 830 (S.D.N.Y. 1995).

ficult to detect. But neither Johns nor society as a whole has much interest in deterring such activity.

For these reasons we are not surprised to have found no cases in which the plaintiff was seeking to enforce an attribution right. The picture is different when we turn to integrity rights. It is true that, just as with attribution rights, even if there were no moral rights law there would be alternative methods for securing protection of the artist's integrity rights—most obviously contract law (though also copyright law, as we shall note shortly). An artist concerned with the possible future alteration of his work could add a term to the original sales contract giving him the right to approve or veto future modifications of the work. But there would be two drawbacks. Most sales contracts in the art world are oral rather than written.[16] To protect integrity rights the parties would have to incur the added costs of a written contract. And a moral rights provision would not be enforceable against subsequent purchasers of the work unless the original purchaser included it in his contract with the subsequent purchaser and the latter, if he resold it, did likewise.

In any event, there is no indication that contracts for the sale of art commonly contained moral rights clauses prior to VARA or its state law predecessors. Some did; Eero Saarinen, the architect who designed the University of Chicago Law School's building, included in his contract with the University a clause limiting alterations in the appearance of the building without his consent. We would expect such clauses to be more common in contracts for architectural than for other artworks because completed buildings are an essential form of advertising for architects; and while it is true that building owners would be reluctant to agree to such clauses because the benefits of altering a building after it is built will often be considerable, by the same token architects would derive greater benefits from such clauses than other visual artists precisely because the probability that the owner of a painting or sculpture would want to alter it is much lower.[17] It seems odd, therefore, that VARA does not cover architectural works. But probably few architects are artists like Saarinen, and perhaps the real estate industry (developers and building owners are the principal defendants in VARA suits) had enough political clout to block the inclusion of architecture in the new law.

The pre-VARA absence of moral rights clauses from contracts for the sale

16. Sixty-one percent of the respondents to a survey conducted by the Copyright Office stated that oral contracts are more common than written ones in the art world. *Waiver of Moral Rights in Visual Artworks: Final Report of the Register of Copyrights* (U.S. Copyright Office, Mar. 1, 1996) (tab. 3.2).

17. Though not zero. Efforts to restore a painting may involve what the artist or others regard as harmful alterations; and there was a time when paintings and sculptures were frequently altered by their owners by the addition of fig leaves.

of the visual artworks that VARA does cover implies that the expected benefit of such a clause to an artist, which is in any event limited because of the difficulty of binding subsequent purchasers, is less than the sum of the cost of drafting the term, the cost of monitoring compliance with it, and the price reduction that the buyer would demand for giving up the option of modifying or even destroying the work in the future without having to obtain the artist's consent. But because the contractual alternative to VARA is imperfect, the absence of moral rights provisions in contracts for the sale of works of art is not necessarily evidence that these provisions have little value to artists.

Some light is cast on the question by a survey that the Copyright Office conducted in 1994 of the implementation of VARA's waiver provision.[18] If moral rights impose costs that exceed their benefits, we would expect artists to waive these rights following the passage of VARA. The survey showed that 73 percent of the survey respondents were aware of VARA, and this awareness was independent of whether an agent or gallery represented the artist, whether his income from art was more or less than $25,000 a year, whether he had ever been commissioned to create a work of art, and whether he lived in a state that has a moral rights statute.[19] Only 17 percent of the respondents had seen a waiver clause, though 23 percent knew artists who had been asked to waive moral rights.[20] Of those who had seen a waiver clause, 13 percent believed that such clauses are routinely included in artists' contracts—but remember that most such contracts are oral, and to be effective a waiver of moral rights must be written. Only 8 percent of the respondents had actually waived moral rights, though 39 percent believed that such clauses are included in contracts for commissioned work.[21] Thirteen percent said they had turned down a contract because it included such a clause, and only 25 percent of those who previously had waived moral rights said they would do so again.[22]

The very low response rate to the survey[23] makes us hesitate to draw strong inferences from it; but it does provide some evidence that many artists do value their VARA rights. This is puzzling, given the dearth of moral rights clauses before the statute was passed and given also that an artist who retains

18. The Copyright Office mailed some 6,800 surveys nationally to visual artists, art lawyers, agents, and others working in the visual arts; 1,061 individuals responded to the survey, 955 of whom categorized themselves as visual artists within the meaning of the Copyright Act. *Waiver of Moral Rights in Visual Artworks*, note 16 above, at 126, 131. Some of the questions were directed only at the visual artists, and not at the other respondents.

19. Id. at 133 (tab. 2).

20. Id. at 134 (tab. 3.1).

21. Id.

22. Id. at 136 (tab. 4.1).

23. Approximately 16 percent. See note 18 above.

the copyright in his work may be able to preserve most of the same rights conferred by the integrity-rights component of moral rights law simply by enforcing his copyright. Because copyright embraces the exclusive right to make and authorize others to make derivative works, any significant distortion, mutilation, or modification of an expressive work without the artist's consent would infringe his copyright because it would be the unauthorized creation of a derivative work.[24] We explained in Chapter 4 why it makes good economic sense to give the copyright owner control over the making and sale of derivative works from his copyrighted work; and in Chapter 8, in discussing the problem of congestion externalities, we pointed out that such control enables the copyright holder to prevent unauthorized versions of the work that might because of their poor quality reduce the demand for the original— a point that overlaps moral rights concerns. And unlike VARA rights, copyright does not exclude reproductions that expire with the death of the copyright holder; indeed, under current law, the death of the author of the copyrighted work triggers a seventy-year extension of copyright protection.

But VARA retains significance in cases in which the copyright to the artwork is transferred along with the work itself. And the derivative-works provision of the Copyright Act would not prevent the intentional destruction of a work of visual art, as VARA would for works of recognized stature—though it is a little hard to see how this can matter very much. The owner of a work of "recognized stature" would rarely want to destroy it, though this depends on how low the "recognized stature" threshold is set, and we'll see shortly that the tendency of the courts has been to set it very low.

Henry Hansmann and Marina Santilli have offered the following economic argument in favor of moral rights that cannot be subsumed under conventional copyright law.[25] They point out that the value of an artwork depends in part on the artist's reputation, which is embodied in the entire stock of his works, each acting in effect as an advertisement for the others.[26] Mutilating one of them could thus impose a cost on the artist, and it would be a cost ex-

24. See Ty, Inc. v. GMA Accessories, Inc., 132 F.3d 1167, 1173 (7th Cir. 1997); WGN Continental Broadcasting Co. v. United Video, Inc., 693 F.2d 622, 626 (7th Cir. 1982); cf. Gilliam v. American Broadcasting Cos., 538 F.2d 14 (2d Cir. 1976). But see Brian T. McCartney, "'Creepings' and 'Glimmers' of the Moral Rights of Artists in American Copyright Law," 6 *UCLA Law Review* 35, 43–52 (1998), expressing skepticism.

25. See Note 14 above.

26. An analogy in the case of authorship is the typical contract between author and publisher in which the author receives a right to royalties for as long as the publisher continues to sell the book. This form of contract gives the author an additional incentive to do a good job on his subsequent books (and often the publisher will negotiate for a right of first refusal to publish those books) in order to enhance the popularity and hence sales of the previously published book, on which the author is still earning royalties. See Ruth Towse, "Copyright and Economic Incentives: An Application to Performers' Rights in the Music Industry," 52 *Kyklos* 369 (1999).

ternal to the mutilator (assuming he has acquired the work lawfully and so could not be punished for theft or malicious mischief). A moral rights law would cause this cost to be internalized. Yet, cutting the other way, the destruction or mutilation of a single work will reduce the effective supply of the artist's works and by doing so increase rather than reduce the value of the remaining works plus any works that he creates in the future. And as long as it was known that *he* had not committed or condoned the mutilation, all the mutilation would demonstrate was that at least one person disliked the artist's work intensely or wanted to subject it to ridicule—and to prevent such a mutilation would be like forbidding a parody. It is true that the parody does not alter the parodied work and the mutilation does. But why should artists be immunized from this form of criticism, when persons who want to criticize the United States by burning the American flag have a constitutional right to do so?[27] It seems, if anything, particularly fitting that criticism of a visual work should take the form of altering its appearance. A verbal work invites a verbal parody, a visual work a visual one.

A possible reply is that a work of art normally is unique, whereas there are millions of copies of the American flag. Suppose a wealthy collector bought a famous artwork without disclosing his intention to mutilate it. Concealment of his intention might enable him to buy it at a price that fell short of the aggregate willingness to pay of the people who treasure the work in its unmutilated state. The result would be to reduce aggregate welfare. But such cases are too rare to justify the creation and maintenance of a complex body of law (with undesirable side-effects) designed to prevent them from arising. Moreover, there is a mismatch between the problem just identified and VARA, which provides no remedy if the mutilation occurs after the artist's death. There is also the point noted earlier that copyright law itself, even without the VARA amendment, provides some protection for moral rights; it is doubtful that the increment added by VARA can be cost-justified. It is no surprise that in the end Hansmann and Santilli prudently draw back from claiming that moral rights are, on balance, efficient.

The Cases

Our skepticism concerning the social value of moral rights law is reinforced by the case law under VARA. Remarkably, there appear to be only six decisions that turn on whether the defendant violated VARA, though a handful of other cases have been decided without a ruling on the question. The pau-

27. Provided, of course, that a person owns the flag that he burns; the same proviso applies to the destruction or mutilation of a work of art.

city of litigation is evidence that moral rights have little value for most artists. The evidence is not conclusive, if only because most cases are settled. But the settlement rate is unlikely to be very high in a new area of law, where there are no precedents to guide the parties in predicting the outcome of litigation if it is not settled. Nor have we been able to find more than a handful of newsworthy disputes involving moral rights (other than those in the decided cases), and most of these antedate the enactment of moral rights laws in the United States.[28] The infrequency of such disputes is not surprising since self-interest provides a powerful incentive for owners of art not to mutilate or destroy it.

All but one of the decided cases involve disputes between property owners and sculptors. And in only one did the artist prevail, though another has not been finally resolved at this writing. All involve relatively unknown artists who had created (with two exceptions) large-scale sculptural or site-specific works that would have been or were substantially damaged or even destroyed as a result of new construction or renovation. The better known an artist is, the more valuable his work is likely to be and therefore the less likely it is that destroying or mutilating it would be an attractive option for its owner. And paintings and other smaller works are likely to be more valuable than the cost of moving them out of the way of whatever activity endangers them.

Carter v. Helmsley-Spear, Inc.[29] is the best known of the cases. Artists known as the "Three-Js" created a vast lobby sculpture, using more than fifty tons of recycled materials including a school bus, in a commercial building in Queens. The work was never completed, although the artists had worked at it for more than three years. A default by the original owner of the building led

28. The principal disputes are: (1) A massive black and white Calder mobile installed in the rotunda of the Pittsburgh International Airport from 1958 to 1978 was repainted green and gold, the colors of Allegheny County, and motorized to turn at regular intervals. (2) Clement Greenberg, the distinguished art critic and trustee of the David Smith estate, stripped the paint from six of Smith's sculptures after Smith's death because he believed it would improve their aesthetic and market values. (3) A sculpture by Isamo Noguchi that had been displayed in the lobby of the Bank of Tokyo Trust Company in New York was removed, cut into pieces, and destroyed in 1980. (4) Diego Rivera painted a large wall mural in Rockefeller Center in 1933 that included a portrait of Lenin near the center and people marching with red flags past Lenin's tomb—elements that were not part of Rivera's original proposal. Rivera refused a request to replace Lenin's head with Abraham Lincoln's (!). The owners temporarily covered the mural and then destroyed it. (5) Richard Serra's site-specific sculpture "Tilted Arc" was removed from the Federal Plaza in lower Manhattan after complaints that the sculpture was a safety hazard and prevented the public from using the space for recreation. Examples 1 through 3 are taken from *Waiver of Moral Rights in Visual Artworks,* note 16 above, ch. 2. Example 4 comes from Walter Robinson, "Art and the Law: 'Moral Rights' Comes to New York," *Art in America,* Oct. 1983, p. 9, and example 5 from Serra v. U.S. General Services Administration, 847 F.2d 1045 (2d Cir. 1988).

29. 71 F.3d 77 (2d Cir. 1995).

to a change in management, and the new management evicted the artists, who, fearing that the management would destroy the sculpture, sought an injunction under VARA. The district court ruled in their favor but the court of appeals reversed, holding that the sculpture was a work for hire. Although the artists had had full authority in matters of design, color, and style, the building management had retained authority over the location and installation of the work; the artists had received a weekly salary, based on a forty-hour work week, for three years and had received unemployment and health benefits (two of the artists filed for unemployment benefits after the new managers fired them); and payroll and social security taxes had been deducted from their weekly salary checks. Nevertheless the result is questionable. The contract that the Three-Js had signed with the building's original owner stipulated that they retained the copyright to the work, implying that the parties did not consider the sculpture a work for hire.

English v. CFC&R 11th Street LLC[30] involved a group of related artworks, including both sculpture and murals, installed in a community garden on East 11th Street in New York City. A development was planned that would involve moving the sculptures but leaving the murals intact, though it would obstruct the view of the murals. The artists claimed that their work had been conceived as a unity, which the planned development would mutilate. Without deciding whether it was either a single work or one of recognized stature, the court held VARA inapplicable because the artwork had been placed on the property illegally. The previous owner (New York City) had never authorized the artists to put their work on the site, although it had remained there for many years without the city's trying to remove it. The court worried that a ruling for the plaintiffs would entitle artists to freeze real estate development by affixing graffiti[31] to construction sites. The plaintiffs were arguing a variant of adverse possession (see Chapter 1)—that by failing to object to their installation the city had lost its right to remove it. Acceptance of the argument would have forced the city either to incur prohibitive costs of patrolling its many vacant lots continuously or to acknowledge a form of "squatters' rights" that would undermine its property rights. It was more efficient to place the burden on the artists of obtaining the city's explicit consent to their use of the property.

In *Pavia v. 1120 Avenue of the Americas Associates*,[32] the plaintiff's large bronze sculpture, comprising four standing forms, had been on display in the

30. 1997 WL 746444 (S.D.N.Y. 1997), affirmed, 1999 WL 822525 (2d Cir. 1999) (per curiam).

31. At least graffiti that are not purely verbal, in which event, as we shall see shortly, they may not be visual works and therefore may be outside the scope of VARA.

32. 901 F. Supp. 620 (S.D.N.Y. 1995).

lobby of the Hilton Hotel in New York City from 1963 to 1988. The plaintiff had retained the title to and copyright in the work. In 1988 the owner of the hotel removed the sculpture, placing two of the four pieces in storage and displaying the remaining two in a parking garage. Since the artist had retained title to the work, the court held that he had rights under VARA even though the work had been created before the Act's effective date. The court nevertheless rejected the plaintiff's claim because the mutilation had also occurred prior to that date. There was still to be considered the plaintiff's complaint about the display of his mutilated work. VARA does not cover display rights but New York's moral rights law does, and the court held that the plaintiff had a valid claim under that law that was not preempted by the federal statute.

In *Martin v. City of Indianapolis,*[33] the defendant city had destroyed the plaintiff's forty-foot outdoor sculpture as part of an urban renewal project. When installed in 1986 the sculpture had been engineered in such a way that it could be disassembled and removed. Remember that VARA provides that a work created before the Act's effective date may not be destroyed unless the artist is given notice of the impending destruction and an opportunity to remove the work at his own expense. Through a bureaucratic foul-up the artist was notified but not given sufficient time to remove the work. Liability also depended on the work's being of recognized stature, but as to this the court held that the plaintiff had satisfied his burden of proof by submitting local newspaper and magazine articles describing the work. No expert witness testified and there were no critical writings on the work or the sculptor. The dissent argued that more evidence of "recognized stature" should be required since otherwise buyers of works of art would be required in virtually all cases to obtain VARA waivers at the outset or face a risk of violating the statute in the future because the work, obscure when commissioned, later attained the requisite recognition.[34]

In *Flack v. Friends of Queen Catherine Inc.,*[35] still another New York City sculpture case, the sculptor Audrey Flack was commissioned by a group of local boosters, the Friends of Queen Catherine (referred to in the opinion as "FQC"), to design a monumental statue of Catherine of Breganza (a seventeenth-century princess of Portugal and queen of England) for installation in the New York borough of Queens, for which Queen Catherine has some un-

33. 192 F.3d 608 (7th Cir. 1999).

34. Compare *Carter,* note 29 above, where the well-known art critic Hilton Kramer testified for the defense and claimed that the work had no merit and no recognized stature. He based his argument on the fact that there was no literature on either the artists or the sculpture. The judge rejected Kramer's testimony on the ground that Kramer is hostile to all modern art!

35. 139 F. Supp. 2d 526 (S.D.N.Y. 2001).

explained significance. The project was abandoned when it was discovered that Catherine and her family had profited from the slave trade. Flack had created a thirty-five-inch clay model of the statue, and in the commotion attending the abandonment of the project the head of the model had been placed outdoors and suffered damage. FQC, which owned the statue and still wanted it cast in bronze, hired another sculptor to resculpt the face. Flack charged that this sculptor was grossly negligent and had produced "'a distorted, mutilated model' in which . . . the nose, nostrils, eyes and lips are uneven and the wrong size."[36] The court, denying summary judgment for FQC, ruled that if Flack could prove that the substitute sculptor had been grossly negligent she was entitled to prevent FQC from casting the altered head in bronze. As a preliminary to this ruling the court held that the clay model was a work of art in its own right even though it had been intended only to be the mold for casting the bronze statue. Clay models made by recognized sculptors are accepted in the art world as works of art, as the court pointed out. But a more straightforward point is that the bronze casting, though it would not be done by Flack personally, would nevertheless be "her" creation within the most sensible meaning to be assigned to VARA. She would own the copyright in it, and the mutilation would violate her integrity right.

Finally, *Pollara v. Seymour*[37] involved a large "protest" mural (actually a painting—it was not painted on a wall) that in the words of the court "depicted stylized figures of various races and socio-economic situations standing on line outside closed doors to legal offices. The mural also contained the phrases 'Executive Budget Threatens the Right To Counsel' and 'Preserve the Right To Counsel.'"[38] The mural was installed in a state government building in Albany without authorization and the same evening was removed by government employees; in the course of removal, the mural was badly damaged. The court held that because the work "was intended solely as a display piece for a one-time event" and "there was never any intent by the artist to preserve her work for future display," the work lacked the statutorily required "stature."[39] Stated more simply, since the artist herself had not intended the work to endure, the damaging of it inflicted no harm on her. It was not as if the defendant intended to exhibit the mural in its damaged form. It gave it back to the artist after removing it.

One of the cases in which a violation of VARA was alleged but not ruled on makes an interesting bookend with *Pollara*. An artist named Moncada

36. Id. at 530.
37. 206 F. Supp. 2d 333 (N.D.N.Y. 2002).
38. Id. at 335.
39. Id. at 336.

claimed that a gallery owner named Lynn Rubin had assaulted him when he attempted to videotape Rubin's removal of the artist's painted wall mural "I am the best artist, Rene" from a building in Soho located opposite Rubin's gallery.[40] The only question before the court was whether the defendant's liability insurance policy covered an intentional tort, but the facts of the case bring to light interesting questions that may arise in future VARA disputes. First is whether the mural was a work of *visual* art; unlike Pollara's mural it consisted entirely of the plaintiff's signature and a single sentence proclaiming his artistic skill. If this is a work of visual art, how are other writings, such as a student's homework or poem, that obviously are not protected under VARA, to be distinguished from it? This is not to deny that words can be an integral and therefore protected part of a visual work. A famous example is the phrase "Et in Arcadia Ego" in Poussin's painting of that name; the words are painted on a tomb depicted in the painting. In the case of certain non-representational art (and even of some modern representational art, such as Surrealism), even the title, though it is not "in" the painting itself, may be an integral part of it because it establishes the mood in which the painting is to be viewed. Examples are Piet Mondrian's "Broadway Boogie-Woogie" and Frank Stella's "Marrakesh" and "Die Fahne Hoch." It does not follow that *all* graffiti are works of visual art; but harking back to Arthur Danto and our discussion of postmodern art in Chapter 9, we may have to acknowledge that the only test of what is art is what is accepted as art, and maybe Moncada's mural passed that test.

Second, although a tenant may have authorized Moncada to paint the mural, there is no indication that the building owner had authorized it. If a tenant's authorization were sufficient to establish VARA rights (which it surely should not be), VARA might protect an unlimited number of graffiti artists and doodlers who decorate the outside walls of their apartments; so cleaning and repainting walls throughout New York City would risk violating VARA (though if the cleaning or repainting destroyed rather than merely altered the graffito, the "artist" would have a hard time showing that it was a work of recognized stature). This was not an issue in *Pollara* because, as the court noted in an earlier opinion in the case, the complaint was not the removal of the mural from the government building but the damaging of it in the course of removal, and it could have been removed without being damaged, for it was not, despite being called a "mural," built in.[41]

Third, even if the plaintiff could show that the mural was a legally authorized work of visual art, he would have to show that it was of recognized stat-

40. Moncada v. Rubin-Spangle Gallery, Inc., 835 F. Supp. 747 (S.D.N.Y. 1993).
41. Pollara v. Seymour, 150 F. Supp. 2d 393, 396 n. 4 (N.D.N.Y. 2001).

ure, which, given its purely verbal character, might have been difficult—but given our earlier point about the criterion for a work of art, who knows?

Although our sample (more precisely, our universe) is small, we can learn something from it. The cases suggest that VARA disputes are likely to be limited to works of visual art that cannot be moved without damaging or destroying them; that the works are unlikely to be valuable works by well-known artists; and that judges are reluctant to preserve art at the cost of hampering development. Conceivably, too, the cost of obtaining waivers from artists may deter museums and galleries from exhibiting installation art that cannot be removed without destroying it and may deter property owners from commissioning works for installation in open spaces, lobbies, and buildings. The sheer paucity of cases, moreover, suggests that VARA did not fill some yawning gap in liability space. It is not as if the statute were so clear, or the penalties for its violation so draconian, that full compliance could be expected to be achieved immediately, obviating litigation.

The inference from the paucity of VARA cases is reinforced by the extraordinary paucity of cases under state moral rights laws. True, many of their provisions were extinguished by the preemptive force of VARA, but even before then cases were few and far between. We mention two. In *Wojnarowicz v. American Family Association*,[42] the plaintiff had created a series of paintings and other artworks aimed "at bringing attention to the devastation wrought upon the homosexual community by the AIDS epidemic."[43] The defendants, the well-known antihomosexual activist Donald Wildmon and an association affiliated with him, copied the most sexually explicit and otherwise offensive fragments of the plaintiff's work (such as an image of Jesus Christ with a hypodermic needle inserted in his arm) and disseminated them in a pamphlet that denounced federal funding of an exhibition of the plaintiff's works. The court correctly described the pamphlet as a derivative work but held it sheltered by the fair use defense, yet went on to hold that the defendants had violated New York's moral rights law. Such a ruling creates tension with First Amendment values and the principle of the parody cases. Mutilation can be a potent form of criticism, as when Marcel Duchamp painted a mustache on a photograph of the *Mona Lisa*, thus poking fun at the solemnity with which classic works of art are regarded. The other case, *Botello v. Shell Oil Co.*,[44] involved the destruction of the plaintiff's mural when the building to which it was attached was demolished, though there was evidence that it could have

42. 745 F. Supp. 130 (S.D.N.Y. 1990).
43. Id. at 133.
44. 229 Cal. App. 3d 1130 (1991).

been removed without being damaged. The only issue decided by the court was that a mural is indeed an "original painting."

Tension between First Amendment values and laws creating intellectual property rights is not limited to the moral rights domain. The case for a broad fair use defense for parodies, book reviews, and other critical works is reinforced by those values. We do not discuss the First Amendment in this book, although in Chapter 4 we cited an article by Jed Rubenfeld, which argues that the First Amendment invalidates the rule giving a copyright owner control over derivative works. But it should be noted that even if there were no *constitutional* protection of freedom of expression, the social value of speech would continue to influence the shape of intellectual property law, as it did long before anyone thought that the First Amendment placed limits on that law.

An Empirical Analysis of State Moral Rights Laws

If as the preceding discussion suggests, moral rights laws do not benefit the group they are intended to protect, namely artists, why are such laws passed? We shall try to answer that question by means of an empirical analysis of the moral rights laws enacted in nine states prior to the passage of VARA.[45] We use cross-sectional data from 1980 and 1990 to examine the impact of the laws on artists' earnings and on location decisions by artists and appropriations for state art agencies, as well as to explore the factors that may have influenced the passage of these laws. The analysis also provides further insight into the likely effects of VARA and in particular causes us to modify our earlier conclusion that moral rights laws are not in artists' interests.

Table 10.1 defines the variables in our empirical analysis and presents their mean values for both the nine states that passed moral rights laws and the states (plus the District of Columbia) that did not. The category "artists" includes painters, sculptors, craft artists, artist printmakers, and photographers. The data on artists are taken from the U.S. Census, which labels a person an artist only if it is his primary occupation. Excluded are designers (who are three times more numerous than artists but unlikely to produce works covered by moral rights laws) and teachers of art in higher education (including art, drama, and music teachers). Photographers comprise about 40 percent of the "artist" category.

Table 10.1 reveals that the states with moral rights laws have larger populations, a greater percentage of residents living in metropolitan areas, higher per capita incomes, a higher proportion of college graduates, higher per cap-

45. See note 1 above.

Table 10.1 Definition of variables and means for the year 1990

Variable name	Definition of variables	States without laws	States with laws
POP	State population (millions)	3.92	9.24
INCOME	State income ($1,000) per capita	$22.49	$26.90
METRO	Percent state population in metropolitan areas	60.7	83.7
COLLEGE	Percent college graduates in state	12.8	13.9
ARTEXP	Per capita state art agencies appropriation	$1.33	$1.87
GOVEXP	Per capita state and local gov't spending ($1,000s)	$2,816	$2,964
APC_{90}	Artists per 1,000 population in 1990	1.34	1.60
AEARN	Mean annual earnings ($1,000s) of artists (both full- and part-time)	$21.21	$25.77
MR	1 if a state has a moral rights law and 0 otherwise	42 states	9 states
MRDEST	1 if a state has a moral rights law that prohibits the intentional or willful destruction of a work	47 states	4 states

Sources: (The following subscripts refer to the years 1980 and 1990.) $POP_{80\&90}$, $METRO_{80\&90}$, $ARTEXP_{90}$, and $GOVEXP_{90}$ are from tables 27, 33, 402, and 462 of the *Statistical Abstract of the United States* (hereafter "Statistical Abstract") (1992); $ARTEXP_{80}$ and $GOVEXP_{80}$ are from tables 488 and 40 of the Statistical Abstract (1981); $COLLEGE_{80\&90}$ is from table 242 of the Statistical Abstract (1995); $INCOME_{80\&90}$ is from table 706 of the Statistical Abstract (1997); $APC_{80\&90}$ is from Diane C. Ellis and John C. Beresford, *Trends in Artist Occupations: 1970–1990* (1994), tables A-14, 15; and $ARTINC_{90}$ is from *http://govinfo.library.orst.edu/cgi-bin/sstf22-list?rjob=B29&radi=&table=5&rloc=X001*.

Notes: The means are for the year 1990.

Income, appropriations, and expenditures data are in 1999 dollars.

Artists include painters, sculptors, printmakers, and photographers. Teachers of art and designers are separate census classifications and are not included in the artist category.

Income data for artists exclude photographers.

The nine states with moral rights laws are California (1979), Connecticut (1988), Louisiana (1986), Maine (1985), Massachusetts (1984), Pennsylvania (1986), New Jersey (1986), New York (1984), and Rhode Island (1987).

ita state and local government spending, higher per capita appropriations for state art agencies, and relatively more and higher-income artists. A comparison of means thus suggests that larger, richer states with more highly educated populations have relatively more artists and are more likely to enact moral rights laws.

We use multiple regression analysis to test whether these differences are statistically significant and whether one can infer any causal relationships among the variables. In equations (2.1) and (2.2) in Table 10.2 the dependent variable is the average annual earnings of artists (AEARN) in 1990. A dummy variable takes a value of 1 if the state enacted a moral rights law between 1979 and 1987 (MR) and 0 otherwise. We expect that, other things being equal, the passage of a moral rights law reduces the demand for and hence the earnings of artists. Equation (2.2) includes a second moral rights dummy variable (MRDEST), which takes a value of 1 if a state law also prohibits the intentional or willful destruction of works of art and 0 otherwise. MRDEST is expected to have a negative sign too because adding this provision to the law should lead to greater use of waivers and hence higher transaction costs in the art market. Other independent variables are per capita state income (INC), the percentage of the population living in metropolitan areas (METRO), the percentage of college graduates (COLLEGE), population size (POP), and per capita appropriations for state art agencies (ARTEXP). We expect these variables to be positively related to artists' earnings because the demand for art is presumably a positive function of income, education, urbanization (since cities attract more sophisticated people), and public support for the arts.

Equations (2.1) and (2.2) also include the lagged (1980) value of artists' earnings as an independent variable in order to hold constant differences in these earnings (across states) that are independent of the passage of moral rights laws between 1980 and 1990. For if states in which artists had higher earnings were more likely to enact such laws, it would be mistaken to infer from a positive regression coefficient on the MR variable that the laws increased the relative earnings of artists. Causation would more likely run in the opposite direction—from higher earnings to the passage of a moral rights law. By holding constant artists' earnings (as well as appropriations for state art agencies, for which we also include a lagged variable, $ARTEXP_{80}$) prior to the enactment of state moral rights laws, the regressions eliminate this possibility.

None of the coefficients on the moral rights variables is statistically significant in either equation, although the second does provide weak support for the proposition that extending a moral rights law to prohibit the destruction of artworks reduces artists' earnings.[46] Of the remaining variables, INC, METRO, and POP have positive signs but only INC is statistically sig-

---

46. However, MR and MRDEST are jointly insignificant in equation (2.2); an F-test requires us to accept the null hypothesis that a moral rights law that includes a provision banning the destruction of recognized artworks has no significant effect on artists' earnings.

Table 10.2 Regression analysis of state moral rights laws (equation numbers and t-statistics in parentheses)

Independent variables	AEARN$_{90}$ (2.1)	AEARN$_{90}$ (2.2)	APC$_{90}$ (2.3)	ARTEXP$_{90}$ (2.4)	MR (2.5)
INC$_{90}$ ($1,000s)	.601 (2.87)	.679 (3.19)	−.014 (1.48)	.060 (0.67)	−.001 (0.03)
METRO$_{90}$	3.387 (1.17)	3.350 (1.18)	−.122 (0.87)	1.581 (1.20)	.006 (1.55)
COLLEGE$_{90}$	−23.404 (1.05)	−23.508 (1.07)	4.626 (3.76)	−14.02 (1.16)	1.703 (0.27)
POP$_{90}$ (millions)	.139 (1.52)	.165 (1.79)	−.003 (0.59)	−.052 (1.22)	.000 (0.96)
GOVEXP$_{90}$ ($1,000s)	—	—	—	.051 (0.15)	—
ARTEXP$_{90}$	−.078 (0.28)	−.140 (0.51)	.002 (0.11)	—	—
MR	.510 (0.44)	1.458 (1.11)	.118 (1.94)	−.170 (0.32)	—
MRDEST	—	−2.856 (1.47)	—	—	—
APC$_{90}$	—	—	—	1.537 (2.35)	—
APC$_{80}$	—	—	.977 (11.14)	—	−.174 (0.51)
AEARN$_{80}$	.055 (0.47)	.020 (0.17)	—	—	−.0005 (0.05)
ARTEXP$_{80}$	—	—	—	.469 (1.94)	.024 (0.46)
Constant	6.615 (2.24)	5.892 (1.99)	.167 (1.10)	−1.530 (1.15)	—
R^2	.57	.59	.90	.40	.24
n	51	51	51	51	51

Note: Equation (2.5) uses 1980 values for INC, METRO, COLLEGE, and POP although the variable definition column indicates 1990 values.

nificant. Surprisingly, COLLEGE and ARTEXP have negative though statistically insignificant effects on earnings. Also puzzling is the lack of a significant relationship between artists' earnings in 1980 and 1990. But the explanation may lie in the fact that the 1980 artist category is much broader than the 1990 category—it includes entertainers as well as artists

So why do artists support moral rights laws, as undoubtedly they do?[47] Ignorance is not a plausible answer. Artists are relatively well educated and should have no difficulty tumbling to the fact that they will get a lower price for their art if they reserve moral rights, whose value if any will not be realized until some future date. A more plausible explanation is that the rhetoric surrounding these laws and the prestige of the people supporting them signal to the community at large that art is a highly valued social enterprise. This signaling may lead to greater interest in art and a more favorable social environment for artists whether or not their earnings increase; they may not increase, for example, if the more favorable environment attracts additional artists and so increases competition. If the "environmental" benefits of moral rights laws more than offset their direct negative effect on earnings, which equations (2.1) and (2.2) suggest is insignificant, artists will want to work and live in states that have these laws.

We can test this suggestion by assuming that if moral rights laws improve the artist's environment, the relative increases from 1980 to 1990 in the number of artists in a state should be greater in states that passed moral rights laws in the 1980s than in states that did not.[48] Equation (2.3) in Table 10.2 tests this hypothesis. The dependent variable is the per capita number of artists in the state in 1990 (APC_{90}). The lagged independent variables turn out to be both highly significant statistically and not significantly different from 1. The implication is that the number of artists would have remained unchanged in a state in the 1980 to 1990 period had the values of the other (the nonlagged) independent variables remained constant.

Among the other independent variables, the percentage of college graduates (COLLEGE) and whether a state has a moral rights law (MR) have significant coefficients. COLLEGE is positive and highly significant, indicating that the higher the percentage of college graduates in a state, the more artists there are. Since more educated persons have a greater demand for the arts

47. A conclusion reinforced by the Copyright Office's survey that we discussed earlier.

48. All the states except California passed their moral rights laws after 1980. California enacted its law in 1979, and the lagged artist variables are their 1980 values. Conceivably the regression coefficient on the MR variable in equation (2.3) understates the impact of moral rights because the specification implicitly assumes that the 1980 artist values do not reflect the passage of a moral rights law. To test for this we re-estimated the equation with California excluded. The regression coefficients (and t-statistics) were virtually identical to those reported in Table 10.2.

and cultural goods, this finding is not surprising. The coefficient on the moral rights law variable is also positive, though only marginally significant.[49] This is some evidence that artists do prefer working and living in states that have these laws. Quantitatively, the passage of a moral rights law is associated with a 7.3 percent increase in the state's artist population.[50]

Per capita state appropriations for arts agencies (the ARTEXP variable in Table 10.1) average $1.43. The range is great—from $10.07 in Hawaii to only 25 cents in Mississippi. Among states having moral rights laws the range is somewhat narrower—from $4.21 in New York to 27 cents in Louisiana. Appropriations for state art agencies should depend in part on the influence of groups that support the arts, such as the artists themselves (APC_{90}). More educated and sophisticated voters, as proxied by the percentage of college graduates and the percentage of persons living in metropolitan areas, are more likely to be consumers of arts and therefore more likely to support public spending on the arts. In addition, the stronger the preference for state and local government spending in general (GOVEXP), the greater should be the state's appropriations for art agencies. We also include the lagged value for arts agency appropriations ($ARTEXP_{80}$) and a moral rights law variable (MR). Assuming that state appropriations for art agencies respond positively to the relative number of artists in the state, we would expect a positive impact of MR on these appropriations.

Consistent with these predictions, equation (2.4) reveals that the greater the relative number of artists in a state (APC_{90}) and the greater its past spending on art agencies ($ARTEXP_{80}$), the larger the state's appropriations for art agencies in 1990. Of the remaining variables, however, none is significant. We re-estimated equation (2.4) substituting APC_{80} for APC_{90} because the causation may run partly from greater art agency appropriations to an increase in the number of artists rather than the reverse; but the effects of this substitution were negligible. We conclude that passage of a moral rights law has no significant effect on state spending on art agencies.[51]

One might expect states that have more artists, spend more money on the arts, and have a more educated and urbanized population would favor moral

49. We also tested the MRDEST variable in equation (2.3). Its coefficient was .00005 and its t value less than .005. The coefficient on MR was unchanged although its significance was less (the t-statistic fell from 1.94 to 1.66).

50. The percentage increases equal the value of the regression coefficient on MR in equation (2.3) divided by the mean value of the dependent variable in states with laws (that is, .118/1.599).

51. We also re-estimated equation (2.4) using both the MR and MRDEST variables. The coefficients on both moral rights variables were highly insignificant and the results for the other variables were virtually unchanged.

rights legislation, assuming as we have reason to do that these laws promote a favorable environment for artistic activity. Equation (2.5) tests this hypothesis by means of a probit regression, since the dependent variable in equation (2.5) is dichotomous (1 if a state passed a moral rights law and 0 if it did not), which attempts to predict the passage of moral rights laws in states between 1979 and 1987 from 1980 values for the independent variables. None of the variables turns out to be statistically significant. Even the per capita number of artists (APC_{80}) has no significant effect on whether a state passes a moral rights law.[52]

52. We also estimated several variations of equation (2.5), including substituting 1990 for 1980 values of the independent variables and substituting MRDEST for MR. In no case were the variables statistically significant.

11

The Economics of Patent Law

The standard rationale of patent law is that it is an efficient method of enabling the benefits of research and development to be internalized, thus promoting innovation and technological progress. We suggest in this chapter that a more illuminating way of thinking about the patent system is as a response to economic problems inherent in trade secrecy and market structure.

The Economic Logic of Patents and Patent Law

PATENT VERSUS COPYRIGHT   In light of the emphasis in so many of the preceding chapters on copyright law, we begin by noting the similarities between patents and copyrights—but also the important legal and economic differences. The conventional rationale for granting legal protection to inventions as to expressive works is the difficulty that a producer may encounter in trying to recover his fixed costs of research and development when the product or process that embodies a new invention is readily copiable. A new product, for example, may require the developer to incur heavy costs before any commercial application can be implemented, so that a competitor able to copy the product without incurring those costs will have a cost advantage that may lead to a fall in the market price to a point at which the developer cannot recover his fixed costs.

A twist not present in the copyright area (with some exceptions noted later) is that in the absence of legal protection for an invention, the inventor will try to keep the invention secret, thus reducing the stock of knowledge available to society as a whole. Patent law combats this incentive by requiring, as a condition of the grant of a patent, that the patent application (which becomes a public document if and when the patent is issued, and often in any event, as we'll note in Chapter 13, eighteen months after filing) disclose the steps constituting the invention in sufficient detail to enable readers of the application, if knowledgeable about the relevant technology, to manufacture the patented product themselves. Of course they may not use the information to make or sell or use the patented product or process itself without a license from the patentee. But they may use it for any other purpose, including attempting to "invent around" the patented invention—that is, to achieve the technological benefits of the patent without duplicating the particular steps constituting it and thus without infringement. Inventing around facilitated by the required disclosure of the patented invention is a limitation on the monopoly power that the patent right confers. Patent law often yields broader protection than trade secrecy in respects that will become clearer in Chapter 13 and saves the inventor the cost of keeping his invention secret. But in return it exacts disclosures that facilitate inventing around. The swap is not advantageous for all inventors, which is one reason why trade secrecy abounds even in domains of inventive activity in which patent protection is obtainable. Another reason is that by teaching how to make the invention, the required disclosure teaches would-be infringers how to infringe, creating a risk that the patentee will have to defend the validity of the patent in expensive litigation.

A patent is more difficult to obtain than a copyright because a lengthy (though, as we'll point out in the next chapter, not very demanding) examination of the patent application by the Patent and Trademark Office is required, and because the drafting of patent claims that will at once withstand a court challenge to their validity yet not be so narrowly drawn as to offer little protection against competitors requires considerable legal skill. But at the same time a patent can confer greater value on its owner than a copyright does, even though the term of a patent is much shorter (its greater breadth is a reason *why* the term is shorter) and even though patent protection does not extend to the patent counterpart of the derivative work, which is the improvement patent. One reason patent protection can be more valuable than copyright protection is that a patent protects against any duplication of the patented invention rather than merely forbidding the copying of it. As we noted in Chapter 4, it usually is feasible to search the patent register for previous inventions, but it is not feasible to search the Library of Congress for previously copyrighted works that a new work might duplicate, especially now that a copyrighted work need be deposited in the Library of Congress only if the owner wants to register his copyright. But there is another important difference. Simultaneous or nearly simultaneous discovery or invention is much more common in the case of ideas, which are (more precisely, a subset of which are) what patents protect from duplication, than in the case of expression, the domain of copyright law. That is why there are patent races but not copyright races. If patents did not protect against independent duplication, an inventor who had spent enormous sums to be the first to discover some useful new idea might find himself unable to recoup his costs because someone else, working independently toward the same goal, had duplicated his discovery within weeks or months after he made it. Patent law prevents such disappointments but at the same time, of course, fosters patent races and the rent-seeking costs that such races can impose.

Another reason patent protection tends to confer greater value on the patentee than copyright protection confers on the copyright holder is that, as just mentioned, patents protect ideas, which have potentially vast commercial application, rather than protecting merely a particular verbal or aural or visual configuration of ideas that are in the public domain—for remember that copyright law does not forbid copying the ideas in a copyrighted work.

With greater legal protection for patentees than for copyright holders comes a greater danger that the inventor will be enabled to charge a higher price than he needs to recover the fixed costs of his invention, thereby restricting access to the invention more than is necessary. This fear may explain why the term of a patent has always been shorter—it is now much shorter—than the term of a copyright, although proper comparison requires discounting to present value. At a discount rate of 10 percent, the present value of a constant stream of income to be received for twenty years[1] is 85 percent of the same stream received in perpetuity, so that in effect the patent statute allows the patentee to realize a maximum of 85 percent of the market value of his invention. At the same discount rate the present value of a constant stream of income to be received for 110 years (the copyright term if the author was forty years old when he created the copyrighted work and died at eighty) is 99.997 percent of what it would be if the term were unlimited.

These calculations are sensitive to the choice of discount rate[2] and to the assumption that the stream is constant forever. But if, as would be more realistic, we assumed that the stream of income would decline after a time—in

---

1. Since 1995 the patent term has been twenty years from the date of the patent application. Before then, and going right back to the first federal patent statute, enacted in 1790, the term had been seventeen years from the date the patent was granted. Since patent applications pend in the Patent and Trademark Office for anywhere from one to five years (sometimes, though rarely, longer), it is not certain that the change in the length of the term actually enlarged patentees' rights. However, a study of patents issued under the old law concludes that the patentees would have received on average a net increase of 253 days of patent protection had the new law been in effect instead. See Mark A. Lemley, "An Empirical Study of the Twenty-Year Patent Term," 22 *American Intellectual Property Law Association Quarterly Journal* 369, 385 (1994). See also id. at 392.

2. At a discount rate of 5 percent, the percentage figures in the text fall to 62.3 and 99.5. But the higher discount rate seems more appropriate in light of the uncertainty associated with income from intellectual property.

other words, assumed that the patent or copyright would depreciate, as we assumed for copyrights and trademarks in Chapter 8—the percentages just calculated would be even higher. Later in this chapter we estimate the depreciation rate of the average patent to be 6 percent. If this figure were plugged into the present-value formula, the twenty-year patent term would yield almost 95 percent of the value of the patent in perpetuity at a 10 percent discount rate. Granted, the 95 percent estimate is too high because the twenty years run from the date of application, not the date of issuance, of the patent. Some patents will get about nineteen years of protection, but others only about fifteen; the average is likely to be eighteen (see note 1). If we substitute eighteen for twenty years, the 95 percent estimate falls—but only to 93 percent.

A FORMAL ECONOMIC MODEL   How far the law should go in protecting an inventor from competition and the related question of how patents affect the incentives to invent can be illuminated with the aid of a simple model. We illustrate with a process patent that reduces the cost of making an existing product (X) rather than with a patent on a new product. The model could easily be extended to a patent on a new product, however, since the new product can be analyzed as the special case of an invention that brings the cost of a new product down from a prohibitive level (that is, at which the supply curve lies everywhere above the demand curve) to a level at which the product can be profitably produced.

In Figure 11.1, DD is the demand curve for X, MR the marginal revenue curve, MC_1 the industry marginal cost or supply curve before the cost-reducing innovation, and MC_0 the marginal cost curve of the firm (assumed to be constant throughout the range of feasible outputs) that develops the cost-reducing invention. The difference between the two marginal cost curves is the cost savings at each unit of output brought about by using the new technology. To simplify, we assume that many firms can produce X at MC_1 (implying a perfectly elastic industry supply curve equal to MC_1), yielding the pre-invention equilibrium outcome of price P_1 and output X_0. The conventional analysis of patents implies (with a limited exception noted below) no significant change in industry output or price as a result of the process patent. (In contrast, a product innovation will always lead to a greater output, since the pre-innovation output is zero.) Instead the patent holder maximizes his profits per period[3] (the cross-hatched area in the diagram) either by produc-

---

3. The diagram depicts only one period. The full profit from (also social gain from, as noted below in the text) the invention is the present value of the cost savings in the current and future periods minus the cost of the invention.

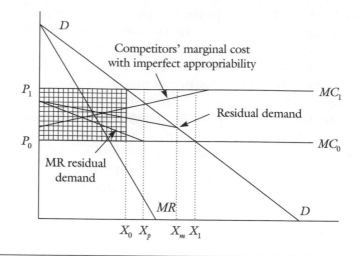

Figure 11.1. Effect of patent protection on copying

ing the entire industry output X_0 at a price slightly below P_1 or by licensing the patent to existing firms at a royalty rate just below $P_1 - P_0$.[4] Although output and price are essentially unchanged, the invention still yields a net social gain equal to the cost saving (the cross-hatched area) minus the cost of developing the invention. If, however, the demand elasticity at the competitive output is sufficiently large, marginal revenue will be above P_0 at X_0, which will lead the patent holder to cut price below P_1 and expand output beyond X_0. In general, the more elastic demand is at X_0 and the bigger the cost reduction resulting from the invention, the more likely price is to be below P_1 and output above X_0.

The conventional analysis that we have just sketched overlooks a key feature of patent law, however, by assuming that the patented innovation has no impact on the cost structure of other firms in the industry. As we noted earlier, the law requires that the patent application disclose the innovation in sufficient detail to enable persons of ordinary skill in the relevant technology to practice the invention. (Not that they are allowed to, of course, while the patent is in force, without the patentee's permission.) Once the patent is issued, and often earlier, the application is publicly available, and the information contained in it will help competing firms to invent around the patent and thus lower their costs of production without infringing the patent. (Presum-

4. The patent holder equates marginal cost to marginal revenue, which coincides with P_1 up to X_0 and with MR at outputs greater than X_0. At X_0 marginal revenue is discontinuous, because it equals P_0 just before X_0 and MR just after X_0.

ably, the more information a firm uses from the patent application, the lower its costs but the greater the risk of being sued for infringement.) In addition to facilitating inventing around, the information in the patent application will help the competitor to determine the feasibility of a process improvement without having to incur the cost of experimenting to obtain this information. It may even enable him to get away with a certain amount of infringement. The patent holder may be reluctant to sue for infringement because of the risk that the court will hold that the patent is invalid. He may therefore tolerate modest levels of infringement.

The requirement of public disclosure creates a situation of *incomplete appropriability* by the patent holder, which in Figure 11.1 will cause the marginal cost curve of the patentee's competitors to fall below MC_1. Of course it is unlikely to fall all the way to MC_0, the patentee's marginal cost. In addition, it will probably become upward sloping rather than perfectly elastic as it falls because firms will differ among themselves in the costs of inventing around the patent, infringing the patent without being sued, and so on (recall the parallel example of copiers' upward-sloping supply curve in Chapter 3). If the competitors are price takers and the patentee acts as a dominant firm, the patentee will face a downward-sloping residual demand curve equal to the difference between *DD*—the overall demand for *X*—and the quantity that would be supplied by competitors at every different price of *X*. The patentee maximizes profits by equating MC_0 to the marginal revenue derived from his residual demand curve, yielding in equilibrium a total output of X_m consisting of the patentee's output of X_p and the competitors' output of $X_m - X_p$. The market price will lie between P_1 (the pre-invention price) and P_0 (the patentee's marginal cost). In short, output will be greater than the pre-patent output of X_0 and price will be lower than P_1. This contrasts with the conventional analysis, in which output and price before and after the innovation are (with the qualifications noted) unchanged.

The greater patent protection is, the smaller the benefit to competitors from the information contained in the patent grant because the less they can do with it. They will face greater difficulty and higher costs in inventing around the patent, a higher probability of losing a patent infringement suit, and greater sanctions if they lose. Their marginal cost curve will be steeper or, equivalently, the elasticity of supply lower, making the residual demand curve less elastic and thus enabling the patentee to charge a higher price and capture a greater share of the post-invention market.[5]

---

5. The elasticity of the residual demand curve can be written as $\varepsilon_r = \varepsilon_d/s + \varepsilon_s(1 - s)/s$, where ε_d is the elasticity of the demand curve, ε_s the elasticity of the competitors' supply curve, and s and $1 - s$ the patentee's and the competitors' output shares, respectively. The greater are ε_d and ε_s and the smaller is s, the greater ε_p will be. The patentee's profit-maximizing ratio of P/MC_0 is $[\varepsilon_d/s + \varepsilon_s(1 - s)/s]/[\varepsilon_d/s + \varepsilon_s(1 - s)/s - s]$ and thus is greater the lower ε_s and ε_d are.

Whether a given degree of patent protection is socially desirable depends on the patentee's fixed costs, the inherent difficulty of inventing around the patent (that is, holding constant the degree of patent protection), and the extra profits that the patentee can expect to receive from greater protection. The greater the fixed costs of research and development and the easier it is to invent around the patent, the greater will be the degree of patent protection required to create adequate incentives to invest in developing the invention in the first place. The patent system makes no effort, however, to match the degree of patent protection to those variables. A patentee's monopoly markup, which of course is influenced by the degree of patent protection, bears no direct relation to the fixed costs that he actually incurred in creating the patented invention. If the elasticity of demand is low because competitors find it very difficult to invent around or, in the case of a new product, because the product provides benefits to consumers not available from other products, the patentee will be able to charge a high price relative to marginal cost and thus obtain revenues that may greatly exceed what may be modest total costs. Not only will access to the patented invention be restricted to a greater degree than would be necessary to create incentives for optimal invention, but the prospect of such windfalls will induce rent-seeking behavior, with a resulting waste of resources illustrated by patent races, which are discussed below. Copyright has no direct analog to a patent race, but there is an indirect one: the "dry hole" phenomenon, discussed in Chapter 2, that may lead to the overproduction of books and other expressive works.

The length of a patent illustrates the potential disjunction between actual and optimal patent protection. If as we suggested earlier a patent enables the patentee to retain 85 percent of the profit generated by it even if there is no depreciation, the twenty-year patent term is excessive if a perpetual patent would be expected to overcompensate the patentee by more than 17.6 percent (.15 ÷ .85).[6] If we factor in depreciation at 6 percent, the twenty-year term is excessive if a perpetual patent would overcompensate the patentee by more than 5.3 percent (.05 ÷ .95). There is no theoretical or empirical basis for supposing that any of these figures approximates the level at which the average patentee would recover the cost of invention but no more.

PATENT RACES A patent race is a race among competing firms to be the first to discover and patent some new idea having commercial potential. Such

---

6. See George J. Stigler, "A Note on Patents," in Stigler, *The Organization of Industry* 123 (1968). (For example, if the market value of the patent if perpetual is $1 million and the patentee should have received only $850,000, $150,000 represents excess compensation and it is 17.6 percent of the $850,000 that he should have received.) The percentage in the text rises to 25 percent under the seventeen-year term in force before 1995 if the difference between the date of patent application and the date of grant is disregarded.

a race can generate costs of invention that exceed the social benefits,[7] because the first competitor to reach the finish line will obtain the patent and thus the full value of the invention (minus the part that is externalized by the limitation on the length of the patent term, but we have seen that under plausible assumptions that part is small) even if he beat his competitors by only a day. Suppose the present discounted value of the patent is $10 million, three firms are in the race, and if each spends $2 million each will have a 33 percent chance of being the first to invent. Assume further that the social surplus is maximized if each firm spends just $2 million on trying to come up with the invention. From a private standpoint, any of the competitors that thinks that by spending another $5 million on research and development he can be the first to come up with the invention by even just one day may have an incentive to make that expenditure. We say "may" rather than "will" because the decision will depend on the competitor's expectations concerning the likely reaction of the other firms. He may fear that they will counter his expenditure of $5 million with expenditures of their own that will cause his expenditure to be a poor investment. On the other hand, he may think he can conceal the expenditure from his rivals. Among still other possibilities, each of the competitors may invest a smaller amount in the race or one may drop out of the race and each of the others spend $5 million. In any event, it is quite possible that more than the optimum total of $6 million (3 × $2 million) will be spent on R&D. This assumes that the additional costs, unless trivial, incurred in trying to beat rivals by one day to the patent finish line will exceed the social benefits of having come up with the invention one day earlier, but this is a plausible assumption—especially since the earliest inventor is not necessarily the one who can produce the product or process embodying the invention the fastest. He may be better at inventing than at producing. If so, after winning the race he may decide to license the fastest or most efficient producer, in which event the transaction cost incurred in the licensing process will be still another cost of the race.

Two qualifications to the economic criticism of patent races should be noted. First, the research expenditures by the losers of the race may not be wasted even if the race does not accelerate the inventive process by a day, for the expenditures will generate information that the losers may be able to use in other projects. Second, patent races need not produce any social waste at all in cases, which are particularly common in the pharmaceutical drug industry, in which there are as it were multiple prizes and hence more than one winner. For example, SSRIs (selective serotonin reuptake inhibitors), such as

---

7. See, for example, Dennis W. Carlton and Jeffrey M. Perloff, *Modern Industrial Organization* 522–526, 536–540 (3d ed. 2000), summarizing an extensive literature illustrated by Partha Dasgupta and Joseph Stiglitz, "Uncertainty, Industrial Structure, and the Speed of R&D," 11 *Bell Journal of Economics* 1 (1980).

Prozac, Zoloft, and Paxil, are competing antidepressant drugs, but they are based on different chemicals and so are separately patentable.

RULES THAT REDUCE THE SOCIAL COSTS OF PATENT PROTEC-TION Patent law employs a number of devices to minimize social costs, besides the previously discussed requirement of public disclosure. The patent's limited term is, of course, one of the devices. This limitation may, as we have pointed out, be largely illusory because of discounting to present value and its interaction with depreciation. But not completely. A byproduct of patent racing is that patents frequently are obtained well before commercial development is complete (famous examples are the jet engine, radio and television, and fluorescent lighting), which reduces the economically significant length of the patent term below twenty years. Unlike a copyright or a trademark, a patent can be obtained before there is a working model of the patented product or process—it's as if one could obtain a copyright on a book on the basis of an outline, or a trademark without having a product to sell. The early grant of a patent not only shortens the time in which the inventor can charge a monopoly price because the patent term runs from the application for or (before 1995) from the grant of a patent rather than from the commencement of production and sale; it may also minimize wasteful duplication of effort by competing inventors.[8] The early grant serves the same purpose as privatizing a common pasture or as the committed-searcher doctrine, which allows the first searcher who commits himself to search for an abandoned piece of property to prevent others from obtaining title to it for as long as his search is being conscientiously pursued (see Chapter 1). But the doubt expressed when we said "*may* also minimize wasteful duplication" bears emphasizing; like so many other propositions about patent law, this one can be questioned—and will be shortly.

Inventions are not patentable unless they are useful, novel, and non-obvious. Let us try to give economic meanings to these terms. The requirement of utility can be understood to have three economic purposes. One is to rule out patents on basic research, and another is to delay the point in the development of a new product or process at which a patent may be obtained; we'll return to both these points. The third is to reduce the cost of patent searches by screening out useless inventions by cranks or amateurs, or by inventors hoping to blanket an area of research with patents in the hope of forcing researchers who come up with useful inventions within the area to seek licenses from them. In other words, the requirement of utility serves to

8. This is the "prospect theory" of patent law, proposed in Edmund W. Kitch, "The Nature and Function of the Patent System," 20 *Journal of Law and Economics* 265 (1977).

limit strategic patenting—a serious problem of the patent system, as we shall note. An alternative to requiring proof of utility, however, would be to increase the patent fee.

The requirement of novelty prevents getting a patent on something known to have been invented already. Unlike many foreign patent systems, the U.S. system gives the right to patent to the first inventor (with a qualification noted later) rather than to the first filer of a patent application. The effect is to economize on search costs, broadly defined. There are two ways of searching for an idea that one might patent. One is to search the prior art, including unpatented as well as patented inventions, to see whether the invention has already been made. That requires a search of technical articles as well as of the patent registry. The other method is to search just the patent registry and if one doesn't find a patent on the invention, to conduct the necessary R&D. The second method is more costly in those cases in which an invention is part of the prior art but not already patented; for there is wasteful duplication in that case. The U.S. rule encourages the first method of search, since if the invention is in the prior art even though it is not patented, an application for a patent will fail for want of novelty.[9]

There is an ambiguity in the concept of novelty that is related to the discussion in Chapter 1 of abandonment. We are not interested in the metaphysical question whether ideas, lacking as they do spatial or temporal bounds, can be said to have existed before they were discovered and therefore to lack novelty: it has always been the case that a certain sequence of steps would enable a heavier-than-air structure to fly. Our concern is with the practical question whether property rights should be recognized in otherwise patentable inventions that have been abandoned. The patent statute is not much help here. The requirement of novelty bars the grant of a patent if before the date of the invention sought to be patented the invention was "known or used by others."[10] Read literally this would bar the grant of a patent on an abandoned invention. But the Supreme Court long ago held that if knowledge of an invention has been completely lost, the re-inventor can patent it.[11] In addition,

9. See Robert Patrick Merges and John Fitzgerald Duffy, *Patent Law and Policy: Cases and Materials* 419–422 (3d ed. 2002).

10. 35 U.S.C. § 102(a). We examine in Chapter 13 the significance of this requirement for the patentability of an invention that someone else made and used earlier but kept as a trade secret. Use is vital. Under the U.S. first-to-invent rule an inventor does not forfeit his right to patent his invention by virtue of not having filed a patent application promptly after having made the invention, though if he publishes the invention he must then apply for a patent on it within one year.

11. Gayler v. Wilder, 51 U.S. (10 How.) 477 (1850). See also Corona Cord Tire Co. v. Dovan Chemical Corp., 276 U.S. 358 (1928); Allen v. W. H. Brady Co., 508 F.2d 64 (7th Cir. 1974).

abandonment can be evidence that the first inventor was unable to reduce his idea to practice and so was not really the first inventor in the sense relevant to patent law; he failed the test of utility.

Were "nonobviousness" interpreted literally, it would add little to the requirements of utility and novelty, since if an invention is both useful and obvious, why hasn't it been discovered already? Maybe because an unexpected shift in demand and supply has suddenly made it useful and *someone* has to be the first to grasp the fact; but that is a special case. A more illuminating approach ties nonobviousness to uncertainty and cost.[12] Invention is a matter of adding to the stock of useful knowledge and so of reducing uncertainty. What is already known is not something waiting to be invented. But sometimes an idea is unknown not because it would be costly to discover but because it has no value. If some exogenous shock gives it value, it will be discovered more or less simultaneously by a number of those who can exploit it; there is no need to give exclusive rights to the first discoverer. But if it is costly to dispel uncertainty, then since the cost is incurred before a product embodying the invention can be brought to market, competitors will be tempted unless blocked by patents to sit back and wait until the invention is made and then sell copies, thus free riding on the inventor's cost of invention. Uncertainty and cost interact, in other words, as we also noted in regard to expressive works in Chapter 2. Uncertainty implies the likelihood of failures en route to success. Those failures are costly, and since the costs are incurred before the successful invention can be patented and marketed, they are additional fixed costs that the inventor must recover in the revenues generated by his patent.

Uncertainty has a further significance. In his classic article on the economics of invention, Kenneth Arrow pointed out that risk aversion would result in underinvestment, from a social standpoint, in risky undertakings, such as invention.[13] This point balances Arnold Plant's argument that patentability draws resources from what might be socially more valuable productive activities that do not offer monopoly returns. Unfortunately, the weights of these two offsetting factors are unknown.

To the extent that the requirement of nonobviousness succeeds in prevent-

---

12. On the cost element, see Edmund W. Kitch, "*Graham v. John Deere Co.*: New Standards for Patents," 1966 *Supreme Court Review* 293; Roberts v. Sears, Roebuck & Co., 723 F.2d 1324, 1344 (7th Cir. 1983) (en banc) (separate opinion). On the uncertainty element, see Robert P. Merges, "Uncertainty and the Standard of Patentability," 7 *High Technology Law Journal* 1 (1992).

13. See Kenneth J. Arrow, "Economic Welfare and the Allocation of Resources for Invention," in *The Rate and Direction of Inventive Activity: Economic and Social Factors* 609, 610–614 (1962).

ing the patenting of inventions that would not cost a lot to discover and perfect, it limits patent races, which are more costly the greater the net expected gain from winning. There is also an evidentiary argument for the requirement of nonobviousness. Inventions that are obvious are likely to mark only small advances over the prior art. This will make it difficult, when a patent expires, to determine whether someone who appears to be using the invention covered by the expired patent may actually be infringing a later patent, not yet expired, that made a tiny improvement over the invention covered by the expired patent. Here the requirement of establishing that one's invention is not obvious serves the same evidentiary function that we identified in Chapter 4 for the requirement that a derivative work of a copyrighted work, to be copyrightable itself, have significant originality.

There is a growing tendency, fostered by the Federal Circuit (the court with exclusive jurisdiction over patent appeals—see Chapter 12), to use commercial success as a proxy for nonobviousness. The theory is that if an invention is both obvious *and* lucrative, why wasn't it thought of earlier? The tendency has been criticized for failing to distinguish between invention itself and marketing, the latter involving inputs other than the invention that are not protected by intellectual property law.[14] Courts cannot readily disentangle the contribution of the invention to the commercial success that attends its marketing. It is odd, though, that use of commercial success as a proxy for nonobviousness should be encouraged by the Federal Circuit, since evidence of commercial success is the sort of evidence that courts with no technical knowledge feel comfortable with, and the Federal Circuit has that knowledge, or at least to a greater extent than other U.S. courts do. It is a further indication that, as we shall see in the next chapter, the Federal Circuit has a bias in favor of patentability.

An important limitation of patent law is that fundamental ideas, such as physical laws, cannot be patented. The domain of this rule is different from that of the parallel limitation in copyright law. The "ideas" found in an expressive work that are ineligible for copyright protection are standard plots, stock characters, verse forms, literary and musical genres, schools of painting, dramatic conventions, iconography, and the like. The ideas that patent law excludes are fundamental scientific (including mathematical) and technological principles. The two classes of idea (call them "expressive" and "inventive") are related, however, both in the enormous potential for rent seeking that would be created if property rights could be obtained in them and in the enormous transaction costs that would be imposed on would-be

14. See Robert P. Merges, "Commercial Success and Patent Standards: Economic Perspectives on Innovation," 76 *California Law Review* 805 (1988).

users.[15] The transaction costs would be enormous because the scope of either kind of idea, the expressive or the inventive, often is extremely difficult to pin down, and this would make it difficult for newcomers to know when they needed to get a license. Apart from uncertainty, the more elements out of which a new expressive work or new invention could be made that were owned by someone (in other words, the more the public domain shrank) and therefore had to be licensed by the newcomer, the greater would be the transaction costs that he would incur.

The shorter the patent term, the lower the social costs of allowing fundamental principles to be patented. Basic research is distinguished from applied research mainly by lacking *immediate* commercial applications. Hence if the patent term were very short, the social costs of allowing the patenting of basic research findings would be minimal—though so would be the incentive for such research that patentability would impart. The patent term is not short, and the interval between basic research and commercial applications is shrinking;[16] so making basic research findings patentable could impose heavy social costs. The shorter the interval, however, the harder it is to deny patents on basic research. If commercial applications of some piece of basic research are immediately foreseeable, a patent on the research will pass the test of utility.

The distinction between fundamental idea and patentable invention is being further eroded by the rise of the business-method patent, for which such fundamental-seeming algorithms as the Black-Scholes options-pricing model would have been a plausible candidate had it been invented after the new type of patent was recognized.

An enormous amount of basic research is produced every year in the United States and other advanced countries without benefit of patentability. This is not in itself a compelling reason against extending patent protection to basic research, because it overlooks the role of government in funding such research. In 1999 half of all basic research in the United States was funded by the federal government, and of the balance 29 percent was financed by universities and other nonprofit research establishments out of their own funds.[17] In effect, basic research is incentivized by a reward system

15. There is also a considerable area of overlap between copyright-related ideas and patent-related ideas that is due to the many important technological innovations in the expressive media, including new methods of painting, color photography, and special effects in movies.

16. See Robert P. Merges, "Property Rights Theory and the Commons: The Case of Scientific Research," *Social Philosophy and Policy,* Summer 1996, p. 145 (1996).

17. Computed from NSF/SRS, *National Patterns of R&D Resources: 2000 Data Update,* tab. 2: National Expenditures for Basic Research from Funding Sectors to Performing Sectors— 1993–2000, *http://www.nsf.gov/sbe/srs/nsf01309/start.htm.*

that involves prestigious academic appointments, lecture fees, grants that reduce teaching loads, and the prospect of Nobel and other prizes, while applied research (including, however, instruments and other tools used to conduct basic research) is incentivized by intellectual property rights. If patent protection extended to basic research, government would reduce its funding, taxes would be lower, and the allocative distortions caused by taxes would be smaller. However, a great deal of this research has no near-term commercial application and so could not be financed by patenting. In addition—and in tension with the point made above that patents on basic research would generate disproportionate rewards—because basic research has commercial value only as an input into further (applied) research activity, it would be very difficult to calculate license fees for patents on basic research, in which event patents might not be an effective method of eliciting such research.

Moreover, universities have strong incentives to support basic research—the leading universities are called "research universities" and regard the conduct of basic research as their main mission—while a system of government grants for basic research that supplement university resources operates better than it would in the commercial arena because politicization of basic research is less likely. Money for strictly scientific research conducted in universities is more likely to be allocated in accordance with objective scientific criteria. A scheme of financial support for commercial innovations would undoubtedly attract strong pressure from interest groups eager to persuade the government to give this or that industry a leg up by financing its R&D. Basic research by definition does not have immediate commercial applications, so it is less attractive to business groups and therefore they can be expected to exert less pressure on the government agencies that fund such research. Less is not zero; and universities themselves engage in lobbying, a form of rent seeking, for government grants.

Reference to basic research brings out a contrast between the role of nonpecuniary incentives in the creation of expressive works and in the creation of inventions. The principal rewards of aesthetic achievement flow to the authors (composers, painters, etc.) of the expressive works themselves rather than to the creators of the "ideas" reflected in them. Odd as it may seem, not much celebrity attaches to being the inventor or discoverer of perspective, the fugue, the sonnet, the obtuse narrator, the rhymed couplet, the opera, and so forth, as opposed to the perfecters of the form. How many people know that Monteverdi invented the opera? Even among those who do know this, he is far less celebrated than such operatic composers as Mozart, Wagner, and Verdi. The situation is the opposite in scientific and technological fields. There fame, a potent motivator with often a cash value to boot, goes to the discoverer of basic ideas rather than to the individuals who perfect their application.[18] This is an argument for providing greater legal protection and therefore economic rewards to applicators than to discoverers in the scientific and technological as opposed to the cultural domain, and that is approximately the line drawn by the patent law. However, the line is eroding. As we mentioned, the shortening of the time between scientific discovery and technological application is, among other factors, enabling more and more fruits of basic research to be patented.

The nonpatentability of basic ideas is related to the distinction that patent law draws between discovery of that which has always existed and invention, denying patent protection to the former.[19] Superficially the relation is that basic ideas fit the concept of discovery better than that of invention; one supposes that $E = mc^2$ is a discovery about the structure of matter rather than an invention of Einstein's, although some philosophers of science would disagree. But the real point, which takes us back to the continental-discovery example of Chapter 1, is that when something is known to exist and is just waiting to be found, the danger of a wasteful race to find it is increased because the probability of success, and hence the expected gain, is greater.

The limitations that patent law imposes on the obtaining of a patent are procedural as well as substantive. In particular, one can't just assert a patent, as one can a copyright or trademark. One must submit a patent application to the Patent and Trademark Office (PTO) for determination whether the invention satisfies all the preconditions for patentability. The alternative would be to allow an inventor to assert a patent and let the courts decide whether the patent was valid. In fact the courts *do* decide, since the grant of a patent by the PTO creates only a rebuttable presumption of the patent's validity. So the difference between the patent and copyright regimes is that the former has two tiers of review and the latter just one. Even if the patent statute were amended to eliminate the preliminary review function of the PTO, there would doubtless still be a patent registry and patent searches so that inventors wouldn't waste their time on inventions that would not stand up in court if challenged. That is why the PTO also maintains a registry of trademarks, even though applications for trademark registration do not receive in-depth review.

The argument for administrative scrutiny of patent applications is that without it the patent registry would be clogged by patents of very dubious

18. On the motivations of scientists, see Paula E. Stephan, "The Economics of Science," 34 *Journal of Economic Literature* 1199, 1201–1203 (1996).

19. See Robert P. Merges et al., *Intellectual Property in the New Technological Age* 146–149 (2d ed. 2000).

validity asserted often for anticompetitive purposes. It *was* clogged between 1793 and 1836 when there was no patent examination—an experiment that failed in part because of patent registrations seemingly designed to extract rents from serious inventors.[20] This is not a *general* problem with copyright, though the qualification is important. The narrow scope of a copyright makes it infeasible for a publisher, say, to throw a monkey wrench into the business of a competitor by registering copyright on a host of books that have no commercial value but might occupy a competitor's entire field of prospective operation so that the competitor's efforts to exploit the field would be blocked by copyright; it also frustrates collusion between competitors to cross-license copyrights. There are exceptions: only a limited number of pleasing tunes can be constructed from a short series of notes,[21] and only a limited number of short sequences of computer code is possible. In both these cases it might be feasible to obtain, and at rather little cost, an immense number of copyrights that would tend to block subsequent composers and software writers. The law has been alert to the problem in the computer software context.[22] Recall from Chapter 4 the holding of the *Sega* case that the fair use privilege allows software to be copied without the copyright holder's permission when the copying is necessary for reverse engineering the software to generate the same functionality (unprotected by copyright law) by means of a different sequence of code. In the case of musical copyrights, the plaintiff must show that the defendant had access to the plaintiff's work and that the two works are substantially similar. And even if that is the case, the defendant can rebut the inference of copying by showing that he independently created the work. That showing is easier to make the more limited the alternatives open to composers, so that, unless a musical work that the com-

20. The Senate report accompanying the bill to reinstate patent examinations contains a vivid account of the country being "flooded with patent monopolies, embarrassing to bona fide patentees, whose rights are thus invaded on all sides . . . Out of this interference and collision of patents and privileges, a great number of lawsuits arise . . . It is not uncommon for persons to copy patented machines in the model-room; and, having made some slight immaterial alterations, they apply in the next room for patents." S. Rep. No. 338, 24th Cong., 1st Sess. 3 (1836).

21. In a sequence limited to four notes in a major scale that are then repeated four times, the total number of combinations is more than 4,000, but not all of these combinations will yield tunes sufficiently pleasing to have commercial value.

22. The "cover" and "jukebox" rules for musical copyrights, see 17 U.S.C. §§ 115–116, are addressed to a different problem. The cover rule allows performers to record copyrighted works without the copyright owner's permission, once he has authorized a distribution of his work in recorded form. The jukebox rule allows jukebox owners to place whatever recordings they want in their jukeboxes without permission of the copyright owners. These are examples of compulsory licensing, and in both cases the copyright owner is entitled to a fee.

poser is alleged to have infringed is widely performed, he is likely to have a strong defense of independent creation.

The administrative review process in the Patent and Trademark Office is lax (see Chapter 12). The consequence may be the creation of "patent thickets" that retard innovation, as we shall point out shortly.

Is Patent Law Socially Cost-Justified?

The most important economic question about the patent system is whether on balance, with the various twists and turns that we have mentioned, it increases or reduces economic welfare. Although there are powerful economic reasons in favor of creating property rights in inventions, there are also considerable social costs and whether the benefits exceed the costs is impossible to answer with confidence on the basis of present knowledge. The *relative* quality of patents can be estimated because patent applications are required to cite prior patents of which the applicants are aware on which the current application is based, and so the number and character of the citations to a given patent, much like the number and character of citations to a judicial opinion or a scholarly article, can be used as a proxy of quality.[23] Citation data can also be used to evaluate some policy issues relating to the inventive process. For example, the federal government has for a number of years now been encouraging its research laboratories to focus more on research having commercial applications.[24] One would like to know whether the new policy has been effective—and a study has found that government research is indeed

23. See Bronwyn H. Hall, Adam B. Jaffe, and Manuel Trajtenberg, "The NBER Patent Citation Data File: Lessons, Insights and Methodological Tools" (National Bureau of Economic Research Working Paper No. 8498, Oct. 2001).

24. This is part of a broader program of encouraging the commercial exploitation of government-conducted or -supported research. Another part of the program, the Bayh-Dole Act of 1980, authorizes universities and other research entities to patent the fruits of research supported by federal funds. See Rebecca S. Eisenberg, "Public Research and Private Development: Patents and Technology Transfer in Government-Sponsored Research," 82 *Virginia Law Review* 1663 (1996). Previously such fruits were in the public domain. A foreseeable and, it appears, an actual effect of the change in policy has been to provide windfalls to universities in the form of royalties for inventions financed in large part by the federal taxpayer and to encourage universities to shift their research emphasis from basic to applied research. See id. at 1708–1714; Peter S. Arno and Michael H. Davis, "Why Don't We Enforce Existing Drug Price Controls? The Unrecognized and Unenforced Reasonable Pricing Requirements Imposed upon Patents Deriving in Whole or in Part from Federally Funded Research," 75 *Tulane Law Review* 631, 668 (2001), and references cited there. That shift in emphasis shows, however, that patentability does affect research incentives. The effect is complex. By increasing the university's revenues, the patenting of the fruits of applied research generates funds that can be used to support basic research, and by providing additional income to university researchers may avoid losing them to industry.

being cited more frequently in private patents, which suggests that the answer is yes.[25]

But citations to patents do not reveal whether an invention would have been made without the prospect of its being patented. Even assessments of the relative value of patents on the basis of citations are of limited reliability, especially if social rather than private value is the concern. The usual method of assessment is to deem a patent more valuable the more various the areas of technology it is cited in. But the broader a patent's reach, the more likely it is both to impede inventive activity by increasing the likelihood that a new invention will infringe an existing patent (the same concern we expressed in Chapter 2 with regard to broad copyright protection) and to cover basic research.

Patent "renewal" rates are another potentially illuminating but ultimately inconclusive body of data.[26] We use scare quotes because a U.S. patent cannot be renewed after the expiration of its twenty-year statutory term. To keep it in force for the full twenty years, however, the patentee must pay maintenance fees of $880 at 3.5 years, $2,020 at 7.5 years, and $3,100 at 11.5 years after the patent has been issued. In effect, a patent holder gets to enjoy the full twenty-year term only if he "renews" his patent three times. One study finds that 82.6 percent of patents were still in force (that is, had been "renewed") after four years, 57.4 percent after eight years, but only 37 percent after twelve years.[27] Using the same methodology as in Chapter 8, we have estimated depreciation rates from these data of 4.8 percent over the first four years after issue, 6.9 percent from five to eight years, and 8.3 percent thereafter. Over the entire twenty-year period the depreciation rate is about 6 percent. Put differently, we estimate an average economic life for a patent (given maintenance fees) of about 16.6 years, including a full twenty-year term for about 30 percent of issued patents.

25. See Adam B. Jaffe, Michael S. Fogarty, and Bruce A. Banks, "Evidence from Patents and Patent Citations on the Impact of NASA and Other Federal Labs on Commercial Innovation," 46 *Journal of Industrial Economics* 183 (1998). The authors cite several previous studies of patent citations. Id. at 185. The authors tried to verify the accuracy of the citations, and found that 75 percent were meaningful, the rest essentially noise. Id. at 202. Laura M. Baird and Charles Oppenheim, "Do Citations Matter?" 20 *Journal of Information Science* 2, 7 (1994), estimates that at least 20 percent of patent citations are erroneous.

26. Many foreign countries grant renewable patents. For a summary of studies of such renewals, see Jean O. Lanjouw, Ariel Pakes, and Jonathan Putnam, "How to Count Patents and Value Intellectual Property: The Uses of Patent Renewal and Application Data," 46 *Journal of Industrial Economics* 405 (1998); for an illustrative study, see Mark Schankerman and Ariel Pakes, "Estimates of the Value of Patent Rights in European Countries during the Post-1950 Period," 96 *Economic Journal* 1052 (1986).

27. Mark A. Lemley, "Rational Ignorance at the Patent Office," 95 *Northwestern University Law Review* 1495, 1503–1504 (2001) (1998 data).

Since the "renewal" fees are pretty stiff (certainly compared to comparable fees respecting copyrights and trademarks), our estimates of patent depreciation, combined with data on depreciation of copyrights, provide some basis for thinking that patents create substantial private values—but by the same token that they may confer greater monopoly power than copyrights do, as indeed we would expect given the nature of the two types of right. In Chapter 8 we estimated for the period 1934 to 1991 depreciation rates of 13.4 percent for graphic-arts copyrights, 9.2 percent for copyrights on books, 6.5 percent for trademarks, and 4.1 percent for copyrights on music, compared to our 6 percent estimate in this chapter for patents. The interesting comparison is between patents, trademarks, and music copyrights, on the one hand, and book and graphic-arts copyrights on the other. The depreciation rates are much lower in the first triad even though patent and trademark renewal fees are much higher than copyright renewal fees. We speculated that trademark depreciation rates were lower than those of most classes of copyright because a trademark can readily be transferred to another product or service; the trademark right thus has "breadth." The depreciation rate of music copyrights is low, we suggested, because music, often lacking words (and even when there are words, they are often an unimportant element of the piece) and susceptible of an indefinite number of different arrangements, is more adaptable to different tastes and times than books are, while graphic-arts works, with the occasional exception (such as Mickey Mouse), tend to be highly ephemeral because they usually are tied to particular advertising campaigns or product cycles. The low depreciation rate of patents is particularly striking because of the stiff fees; the combination of low fees and the high elasticity of renewals to fees persuaded us in Chapter 8 that most copyrights have little commercial value. Evidently patents are on average much more valuable than copyrights, and comparison with trademarks and music copyrights suggests that part of the reason is that they indeed cover more ground than copyrights do, other than music copyrights.

Do they cover more ground because otherwise the inventor could not recover his fixed costs? The question is empirical and the evidence inconclusive. Many highly progressive, research-intensive industries, notably including the computer software industry, do not rely heavily on patents as a method of preventing free riding on inventive activity.[28] For there are alterna-

---

28. See, for example, Richard C. Levin et al., "Appropriating the Returns from Industrial Research and Development," *Brookings Papers on Economic Activity* 783 (1987); Mark Schankerman, "How Valuable Is Patent Protection? Estimates by Technology Field," 29 *RAND Journal of Economics* 77 (1998); Robert Mazzoleni and Richard R. Nelson, "The Benefits and Costs of Strong Patent Protection: A Contribution to the Current Debate," 27 *Research Policy* 273, 275–276 (1998); Wesley M. Cohen, Richard R. Nelson, and John P. Walsh, "Protecting Their Intellectual Assets: Appropriability Conditions and Why U.S. Manufacturing Firms Patent (or Not)" (National Bureau of Economic Research Working Paper No. 7552, 2000).

tive ways of preventing free riding on valuable inventions. Recall from our initial discussion of copyright, in Chapter 2, that the likelihood that copying will actually prevent the creator of intellectual property from recovering his fixed costs depends on the cost of copying. That cost is often high in the case of industrial innovations because of the learning curve. If the cost of using some process or making some product decreases (up to a point) with time as the user becomes more skilled and experienced in the use of the process or the manufacture of the product, the imitator will find himself at a cost disadvantage in competing at the manufacturing stage. This disadvantage may offset the imitator's advantage in not having borne any of the costs of the innovation itself.

May, but also may not. In the case of new drugs, whose manufacturers are avid in seeking patent protection,[29] the fixed costs of research and development are very high, in part because of stringent regulatory requirements, but marginal costs are very low, including the marginal costs of imitators. (The same thing is true of computer software, but trade secrecy and copyright law give software manufacturers alternative intellectual property protection to patents.) On a present-value after-tax basis, R&D is 30 percent of the total cost of a new drug,[30] although questions have been raised about the social productivity of much of this R&D.[31] It is also the case that some drug patents are unusually difficult to invent around,[32] which may make them too lucrative. Recall that, as illustrated by Figure 11.1, the more difficult it is for competitors to invent around a patent, the less elastic will be the patentee's residual demand curve and hence the higher will be the markup of price over marginal cost and so the greater the gross profits generated by the patent.

The difficulty of inventing around drug patents is not solely technological. There is evidence that when branded drugs, the patents on them having expired, must compete with much cheaper generic drugs (cheaper because they are free riders on the R&D of their brand-name predecessors), their prices

29. "In only one industry, drugs, were product patents regarded by a majority of respondents as strictly more effective than other means of appropriation." Levin et al., note 28 above, at 796.

30. Patricia M. Danzon, *Pharmaceutical Price Regulation: National Policies versus Global Interests* 5 (1997).

31. About two-thirds of drug R&D is academic and federal rather than industry, Darren E. Zinner, "Medical R&D at the Turn of the Millennium," *Health Affairs,* Sept./Oct. 2001, pp. 202, 205 (exh. 4), and it has been argued that most drug breakthroughs are due to academic and federal rather than industry research. See, for example, Public Citizen Congress Watch, "Rx R&D Myths: The Case against the Drug Industry's R&D 'Scare Card'" 8–10 (Washington, D.C., July 2001).

32. See Eric von Hippel, *The Sources of Innovation* 53 (1988); Levin et al., note 28 above, at 798.

tend not to fall.[33] As we noted in Chapter 7, the patent monopoly accustoms doctors and patients to the name-brand product (trademark reinforcing patent), and when the patent expires and a generic substitute becomes available at much lower cost, they remain reluctant to substitute for the familiar brand an unknown (un)brand, which though certified as chemically identical may differ in some subtle way, perhaps involving quality control. The sales of the branded drug will fall, as the manufacturer in effect cedes the low-price segment of the market to the generics, but profit per unit will remain high, and aggregate profits, though smaller than before, will remain healthy. One study found only a gradual decline in market share upon patent expiration,[34] though analysis of the welfare effects is complicated by the possibility that a patentee, in order to perpetuate its monopoly, will invest in brand loyalty by reducing the price of the patented product in the pre-expiration period.[35]

Much of the evidence relating to drug patents predates, however, the passage of the Hatch-Waxman Act in 1984. The Act allows generic-drug manufacturers to begin the required FDA testing of their drug before the patent on the brand-name equivalent expires, without being guilty of patent infringement. Apparently the Act, along with other initiatives private as well as public to control spiraling costs of health care, has produced a large increase in generics' market share.[36] However, the Act also extended the patent term for pharmaceutical drugs by the amount of time (up to a maximum of five

33. See, for example, Roger D. Blair and Thomas F. Cotter, "Are Settlements of Patent Disputes Illegal Per Se?" 47 *Antitrust Bulletin* 491, 496–501 (2002); Dong-Churl Suh et al., "Effect of Multiple-Source Entry on Price Competition after Patent Expiration in the Pharmaceutical Industry," 35 *Health Services Research* 529 (2000); F. M. Scherer, "Pricing, Profits and Technological Progress in the Pharmaceutical Industry," *Journal of Economic Perspectives,* Summer 1993, pp. 97, 101–102. Furthermore, if the patentee obtains a follow-on patent during the patent term and claims that the generic will infringe it, the FDA will automatically grant repeated thirty-month stays of approval of the generic until the patent dispute is resolved. See, for example, Robert Langreth and Victoria Murphy, "Perennial Patents," *Forbes,* Apr. 2, 2001, p. 52. This practice is under attack and may soon be changed by regulation or legislation.

34. See Meir Statman, "The Effect of Patent Expiration on the Market Position of Drugs," 2 *Managerial and Decision Economics* 61 (1981). There is even evidence that branded-drug prices rise when patent protection ceases because the manufacturers, writing off the high-elasticity segment of the market, increase their marketing efforts in the low-elasticity segment. See Ernst R. Berndt, "Pharmaceuticals in U.S. Health Care: Determinants of Quantity and Price," *Journal of Economic Perspectives,* Fall 2002, pp. 45, 63; Steven J. Davis, Kevin M. Murphy, and Robert H. Topel, "Entry, Pricing and Product Design in an Initially Monopolized Market" (National Bureau of Economic Research Working Paper No. 8547, Oct. 2001).

35. See Gideon Parchomovsky and Peter Siegelman, "Towards an Integrated Theory of Intellectual Property," 88 *Virginia Law Review* 1455 (2002).

36. See Berndt, note 34 above, at 62–63; Henry Grabowski, "Patents and New Product Development in the Pharmaceutical and Biotechnology Industries" 6–8 (Duke University Department of Economics, July 2002). See also Jay P. Bae, "Drug Patent Expirations and the Speed of Generic Entry," 32 *Health Services Research* 87 (1997).

years) that it takes for the drug to be approved by the Food and Drug Administration for sale to the consuming public.

In creating a testing exception to infringement, the Hatch-Waxman Act expanded, though only in the pharmaceutical domain, the long-standing but narrowly interpreted "experimental use" doctrine of patent law, the counterpart to the fair use doctrine of copyright law. It has been urged that the experimental use doctrine be expanded to allow scientists to use patented research tools (such as gene fragments, and the tumor-prone oncomouse used, as its name implies, in cancer research) without license. The main argument is that the number of patented research tools required to conduct experiments is often so great that the transaction costs of obtaining licenses for all of them are prohibitive.[37] The doubts that we have expressed concerning the social benefits of the existing level of patent protection argue for generous construal of fair use principles in patent law as in copyright law.

That the patent term for new drugs may be too long is not refuted by evidence that, contrary to widespread belief, the profits of the U.S. pharmaceutical industry do not significantly exceed the industry's cost of capital.[38] The evidence is consistent with government regulation that limits the ability of drug manufacturers to charge monopoly prices to certain segments of the population. It also suggests that the manufacturers of differentiated drugs are competing with each other—an example of monopolistic competition, the situation in which each seller (which might be as humble as a barber shop enjoying a slight locational monopoly) in a market faces a downward-sloping demand curve but because entry is unimpeded, the firms in the market have zero monopoly profits, price being equal to average cost.[39] Competition for monopoly rents will, as we know, tend to transform them into costs without necessarily producing commensurate social benefits. In the example in Chapter 1 of a race to be the first to discover and appropriate a new continent, the ten competitors as a group had zero profits, but because they were competing for rents their costs were higher than otherwise and exceeded the benefit, generated by the higher costs, of discovering the continent a year earlier. For the same reason, the fact that much drug research fails to generate products that recoup the cost of the research is consistent with rent seeking. The prospect of large profits enabled by patent protection provides a lure for investment in research, yet the resources devoted to that research conceivably

---

37. See Janice M. Mueller, "No 'Dilletante Affair': Rethinking the Experimental Use Exception to Patent Infringement for Biomedical Research Tools," 76 *Washington Law Review* 1 (2001).

38. See Henry G. Grabowski and John M. Vernon, "Returns to R & D on New Drug Introductions in the 1980s," 13 *Journal of Health Economics* 383 (1994). See also Scherer, note 33 above, at 103–106.

39. See Carlton and Perloff, note 7 above, at 454–457.

might be socially more productive in an industry in which innovation is not rewarded with a monopoly.

Nevertheless the strongest case for patents in something like their present form is said to be found in a subset of the drug industry: "The collection of small and medium sized firms in the American biotechnology industry is, of course, a striking example of enterprises that would not have come into existence without the prospect of a patent, and which depend on patent protection to make their profits, and to attract capital."[40] Yet there is concern that the extent of patent protection of biological research tools may be such as to impede biotechnological progress. For example, the existence of separate patents on complementary gene fragments may make the transaction costs of assembling genetic material needed for research very high. More generally, the licensing of research tools is complicated and therefore costly for reasons similar to why patent licensing of basic research would be complicated and therefore costly.[41] At the same time, the industry has a valid concern that a "fair use" (or broadened experimental use) exception for research tools developed and patented by industry would enable academic researchers to use the tools—and thus free ride on the industry R&D—to create and obtain their own patents on new drugs.

A natural experiment on the effects of patents is the federal government's encouragement of applied research by universities, which has resulted in a great increase in university patenting. But the implications for industry are unclear. Universities are unusual in being engaged in research but not production. It was natural that they would focus on basic research, and it would have been difficult for them to profit from conducting applied research if the fruits could not be patented, since they could not profit by embodying the research in products or processes that they could insulate from competition by trade secrecy or first-mover advantages, but only by licensing their inventions. Being able to earn substantial income from patent licensing has, it appears, induced universities to substitute away from basic research,[42] and the result may have been a net social loss.

The difficulty of evaluating the social benefits of the patent system can be

40. Mazzoleni and Nelson, note 28 above, at 276. Nelson is a leading economist-skeptic about patents, so the quoted statement carries particular weight.

41. See *Report of the National Institutes of Health (NIH) Working Group on Research Tools*, June 4, 1998, *www.nih.gov/news/researchtools/index.htm*; Michael A. Heller and Rebecca S. Eisenberg, "Can Patents Deter Innovation? The Anticommons in Biomedical Research," 280 *Science* 698 (1998). But see the contrary arguments, reflecting the industry view, in Richard A. Epstein, "Steady the Course: Property Rights in Genetic Material" (University of Chicago Law School, John M. Olin Law and Economics Working Paper No. 152 [2d ser.], June 2002).

42. See note 24 above.

illustrated by reference to another legal limitation on patents as compared to copyrights. An inventor can obtain a patent on an improvement that he makes to someone else's patent—provided the improvement satisfies the normal requirements for patentability, including utility, novelty, and nonobviousness—without obtaining a license from the original patentee. It's as if the owner of a derivative work could copyright it without a license from the owner of the copyright on the original. The patentee of the improvement probably won't be able to use his patent without infringing the original patent, but by the same token the original patentee cannot make the improvement without infringing the improver's patent. This is the situation of blocking patents; it forces a negotiation between the patentees if the most efficient technology is to be employed.[43] Whether the extra negotiation costs offset the potential incentive benefits from encouraging independent firms to develop improvement patents is unclear. A full analysis would also require consideration of the possible diminished incentives of the original patentee to develop an improvement patent, and the saving in licensing and search costs if the patentee had these rights to begin with and sought out other firms to improve his patent.

Awareness of the problem of bilateral monopoly, and more broadly of transaction costs, in the patent setting explains the "reverse doctrine of equivalents."[44] Under that doctrine, if the contribution made by the improvement *greatly* exceeds the contribution made by the original patented invention, the improver is allowed to practice his invention without being deemed an infringer, even though he is making use of the prior invention without a license from the patentee. Under the "doctrine of equivalents," discussed below—a secure part of patent law—small differences between a patented invention and an alleged infringing invention are not a defense to infringement. The rationale of the reverse doctrine is that requiring the improver to negotiate a license from the original inventor would impede a potentially valuable improvement; this is a transaction-costs rationale. It reflects fair use thinking transposed from copyright to patent law: when the improver makes only a trivial use of the patented invention, transaction costs swamp the social benefit of allowing the patentee to exact a licensing fee.

This raises the question whether copyright law should emulate patent law's

43. See Westinghouse v. Boyden Power Brake Co., 170 U.S. 537 (1898); Robert P. Merges and Richard R. Nelson, "On the Complex Economics of Patent Scope," 90 *Columbia Law Review* 839 (1990); Howard F. Chang, "Patent Scope, Antitrust Policy, and Cumulative Innovation," 26 *RAND Journal of Economics* 34 (1995).

44. See, for example, Merges and Nelson, note 43 above. The doctrine has received a frosty reception from the Federal Circuit, but this may be changing. See Amgen Inc. v. Hoechst Marion Roussel, Inc., 314 F.3d 1313, 1351 (Fed. Cir. 2003).

treatment of improvements. There is a clue to the answer in the rules on co-ownership. Patent law allows any co-owner of a patent to use it without the permission of the other co-owners. This is similar to the rule of copyright law that any of the coauthors of a joint work may exercise the full rights of a copyright holder (to use the work, license its use to others, etc.), subject to having to share the profits from the license or other use with his coauthors (share equally, in the absence of an agreement specifying the parties' respective shares). Both are rules designed to minimize bilateral monopoly. The patent rule differs from the copyright rule, however, in not requiring an accounting for profits to the co-owners (unless they agree to share the profits). The reason may be that technological advance is a continuous process of improvement, and transaction costs are minimized if a patentee can work on the patented invention or license others to do so without sharing the profits with his co-owners. Continuous improvement is less common in expressive works, though of course not unknown—musical arrangements, cartoon characters, and of course computer software are examples of copyrightable works that often undergo a process of continuous development.

Even though transaction costs would be minimized in one sense if patent improvements were treated like derivative works in copyright law, they would be increased in another sense if one assumes that the original patentee and his licensees (if any) cannot always be depended on to recognize opportunities for improvements to his invention. Many students of innovation believe that it is best understood as a quasi-Darwinian process—a process almost of trial and error in which the market selects from among diverse approaches whose relative promise cannot be assessed in advance.[45] This approach implies that a multiplicity of independent sources of inventive activity is superior to a centralized process directed by the patentee. Although the patentee has an incentive to license inventors of improvements in its patents, its ability to act on that incentive may be impeded by firm culture, management style, the hierarchic, bureaucratic structure of a large firm, the quirks of particular employees, and other factors that may be difficult to control and that vary from firm to firm.[46] There is only so much diversity that an organization can tolerate, as we learn from the frequent failure of mergers because the merging firms turn out to be unable to meld their distinct cultures. Intrafirm diversity in invent-

45. See, for example, Richard R. Nelson and Sidney G. Winter, *An Evolutionary Theory of Economic Change* (1982); Nelson and Winter, "Evolutionary Theorizing in Economics," *Journal of Economic Perspectives,* Spring 2002, pp. 23, 33–39; Merges and Nelson, note 43 above, at 873–879.

46. "Firms facing the same market signals respond differently, and more so if the signals are relatively novel." Nelson and Winter, *An Evolutionary Theory of Economic Change,* note 45 above, at 276.

ing or in licensing inventors is thus an imperfect substitute for interfirm diversity. The Darwinian theories of invention provide economic support for the improvement patent,[47] which encourages firms to do R&D on technologies dominated by patents held by other firms.

The same approach could be taken to copyrights, and derivative works thus made copyrightable without license from the owner of the copyright on the original work.[48] We have acknowledged in this chapter that some copyrighted works undergo continuous improvement, and we acknowledged in Chapter 4 that allowing unauthorized derivative works to be copyrighted might lead to increased creativity. But there is considerable potential for confusion in such an approach because of the low cost of making many types of derivative work and the fact that they are not screened in advance for originality, or held to a high standard of originality if challenged in court, as patents are, and copyrighting costs literally nothing because copyright attaches automatically to a copyrightable work. The mischief potential of "blocking" copyrights would therefore be high. In contrast, it is costly to obtain a patent (apart from the major cost, that of R&D, it costs about $10,000 to $30,000 in filing fees, attorneys' fees, and other expenses to prepare a patent application and get it approved by the Patent and Trademark Office),[49] including a patent on an improvement. Money costs to one side, because trivial improvements will flunk the criteria for patentability, the danger that optimal development of a patented technology will be blocked (in the blocking-patents sense) by trivial improvements, resulting in high transaction costs without offsetting benefits in enhanced innovation, is minimized.

The Darwinian theories of innovation have a further significance for analysis of the patent system. They cast doubt on Edmund Kitch's prospect theory,[50] which commends the patent system for centralizing the inventive process in the original "prospector." The original prospector may have a flawed conception of the optimal path of development. If as Kitch believes it is the *reduction* in the amount of duplication of inventive activities that is the prime merit of the patent system, the system may, while effecting some economies, actually be retarding technological progress. Another objection to Kitch's theory is that while its objective is to reduce rent seeking, specifically patent races, by increasing the benefits to being the original prospector, the theory if

47. See Merges and Nelson, note 43 above, at 873–879; Mark A. Lemley, "The Economics of Improvement in Intellectual Property Law," 75 *Texas Law Review* 989 (1997).

48. As argued by Professor Lemley in the article cited in the preceding note.

49. See Lemley, note 27 above, at 1498. And the cost in attorneys' fees is likely to be higher if it is a valuable patent and the owner therefore wants to maximize the likelihood that it will withstand a court challenge.

50. See Merges and Nelson, note 43 above, at 872–875.

implemented might engender wasteful races to be that prospector. The earlier the patent is granted, the broader its protection is likely to extend (because there will be less prior art to be skirted by narrowing the claims in the patent application)—making it more valuable and inciting a greater expenditure on trying to be first to obtain the patent.

Furthermore, patents often are sought not because the applicant considers patenting a more effective method of recapturing his fixed costs of innovation than trade secrecy or lead time (his head start over competitors and the resulting learning-curve advantage that will persist after his competitors imitate him), but because he wants to prevent others from obtaining a patent that might be used to prevent him from using his innovation without paying someone else a licensing fee.[51] The more readily patents are granted and are upheld in court and the broader the legal protection they confer, the greater the incentive for defensive patenting of the kind just described, patenting not motivated by inability to recover the fixed costs of invention by other means.

Defensive patenting must be distinguished from patent suppression.[52] The

51. See Adam B. Jaffe, "The U.S. Patent System in Transition: Policy Innovation and the Innovation Process," 29 *Research Policy* 531, 539–540 (2000); John R. Allison and Mark A. Lemley, "Who's Patenting What? An Empirical Exploration of Patent Prosecution," 53 *Vanderbilt Law Review* 2099, 2104 n. 17 (2000); Nancy T. Gallini, "The Economics of Patents: Lessons from Recent U.S. Patent Reform," *Journal of Economic Perspectives,* Spring 2002, pp. 131, 140, 149; Levin et al., note 28 above, at 798 n. 29. An alternative is simply to publish one's invention in the hope that this will convince the PTO to turn down any application to patent it on the ground that it lacks novelty. See Douglas Lichtman, Scott Baker, and Kate Kraus, "Strategic Disclosure in the Patent System," 53 *Vanderbilt Law Review* 2175 (2000).

52. A recent statement by a patent attorney for Hewlett Packard, though it uses language of suppression, appears to be referring, rather, to defensive patenting: "'We get patents not to protect our own products, but because it gives us power to exclude in areas where others might want to participate,' he recently told about a dozen H-P researchers and scientists gathered near the company's headquarters here. 'We assume our competitors are filing for patents in all different areas. We don't want to be the last ones on the block.'" Pui-Wing Tam, "More Patents, Please! Tech Companies Urge Staffers to Submit Innovative Ideas; Cash Awards, Plaques at H-P," *Wall Street Journal,* Oct. 3, 2002, p. B1. For a more explicit description of the defensive strategy, see Russell L. Parr, "IP Leverage: Facilitating Corporate Value Creation," in *From Ideas to Assets: Investing Wisely in Intellectual Property* 271, 282 (Bruce Berman ed. 2002): "A defensive strategy is simple. Patent everything in sight and threaten competitors with infringement litigation when they come too close to making products or doing business in a similar fashion. Licensing income is not a goal that is part of this strategy." The importance of defensive patenting is suggested (no stronger word is possible) by the estimate that "at any given time, over about 95 percent of patents are unlicensed and over about 97 percent are generating no royalties." Samson Vermont, "The Economics of Patent Litigation," in id. at 327, 332. Cf. Bronwyn H. Hall and Rosemarie Ham Ziedonis, "The Patent Paradox Revisited: An Empirical Study of Patenting in the U.S. Semiconductor Industry, 1979–1995," 32 *RAND Journal of Economics* 101, 125 (2001). The role of patents in facilitating cartelization is an old story, but a true one; we discuss it in Chapter 14.

defensive patentee is not trying to prevent the emergence of a new technology. But there are a number of well-documented cases of firms' acquiring or developing a new technology, patenting it, and then deciding not to make or license the patented product even though it is commercially promising.[53] Such patent suppression can be economically rational behavior.[54] Suppose A and B are competitors, and A believes that there is a new technology that would be compatible with B's production methods but not with his own and that if adopted by B would give B a decisive competitive advantage. A might in these circumstances have a rational incentive to expend some resources on preventing B from adopting the new technology, by patenting it first. An alternative would be to license the use of the patent to B at a royalty rate high enough to extract most of the benefit of the technology to B. But A might be reluctant to do that because of fear that in working with the new technology B would develop still better technology and so steal a march on A. It might be costly to calculate a license fee that would protect A from being harmed by such an eventuality—or to negotiate the fee without revealing A's concern to B.

Probably the most common reason for patent suppression, however, is innocent: after obtaining the patent the patentee gets cold feet, doubting that the expense of actually producing the new product or adopting the new process is commensurate with the expected return. Licensing remains an option but involves, as just suggested, significant transaction costs.

We need not delve any deeper into the issue of patent suppression.[55] Our point is only that patents are sometimes suppressed, and this is an example of how they can actually impede technological progress.

Defensive and suppressive patenting may be grouped together as prime examples of "strategic" patenting, the subject of a substantial business literature that casts additional doubt on the efficiency of the patent system as a means of optimizing the rate and direction of inventive activity. In that literature we come across frequent remarks of the sort that "invention is not the point of most valuable patents. Instead, most patents are obtained for the proper business purpose of keeping competitors away from the market for a new product

53. See the exhaustive treatment in Kurt M. Saunders, "Patent Nonuse and the Role of Public Interest as a Deterrent to Technology Suppression," 15 *Harvard Journal of Law and Technology* 389 (2002).

54. See Carlton and Perloff, note 7 above, at 538; Paul Stoneman, *The Economic Analysis of Technology Policy* 113–114 (1987).

55. Thus we need not consider the interesting suggestion in Julie S. Turner, Comment, "The Nonmanufacturing Patent Owner: Toward a Theory of Efficient Infringement," 86 *California Law Review* 179 (1998), that a patent owner who does not intend to use his patent should not be entitled to enjoin infringers, but instead should be remitted to his remedy in damages—which would be slight in most cases, at least if monopoly profits generated by patent suppression were not thought to be the kind of loss for which patent law should authorize damages.

or service."[56] "The opposite of building a patent wall around your product—or clustering, as it is sometimes called—is bracketing the patents of your competitors."[57] "Companies have been said to use a technique of patent 'flooding' or 'blanketing' a technology area . . . The typical scenario is that a new technology is patented by a first company, and a second company . . . if the stakes are high enough, can assign enough resources literally to blanket all of the potential improvements to the invention by filing patents on these improvements. The first company is then essentially forced into some type of cross-licensing agreement if they want a business to grow."[58] There may well be exaggeration here; aggressive rhetoric comes easily to business executives and consultants and often has no economic significance. And the improvements patented by these "bracketers" or "blanketers" are not worthless—if they were not real improvements the original inventor would have no incentive to seek to license them. Yet it might be more efficient to leave the improvements to be made, at a slower pace but at a lower cost, by the original inventor.

Mention of improvement patents brings into view the question of what shall count as an infringement, a question that further and deeply complicates the assessment of the patent system's overall economic effects. We pointed out in Chapter 4 that from an economic standpoint whether a new expressive work infringes a copyrighted work should depend on whether the extent of the copying of the old work by the new is sufficient to make the new a close substitute for the old in the marketplace. The same is true regarding patents. But substitution is a matter of degree, and it is unclear whether patent grants should be interpreted broadly, by an expansive construal of the "doctrine of [patent] equivalents,"[59] or narrowly. The doctrine of equivalents corresponds to the concept of substantial similarity used to determine whether a copy of an expressive work is close enough to infringe the copyright on that work. It is nicely illustrated by *International Nickel Co. v. Ford Motor Co.*[60] International Nickel had a patent on "modular iron," which involved a .04 percent addition of magnesium to molten iron. Ford began making its own version of modular iron, which solely differed from International Nickel's in containing only .02 percent magnesium. The court held that Ford had infringed International Nickel's patent; Ford's variant was "equivalent" to the patented product. Had Ford made a substantial improvement and otherwise satisfied

56. Stephen C. Glazier, *Patent Strategies for Business* 11 (3d ed. 2000).

57. Kevin J. Rivette and David Kline, *Rembrandts in the Attic: Unlocking the Hidden Value of Patents* 110 (2000).

58. H. Jackson Knight, *Patent Strategy for Researchers and Research Managers* 42–43 (1996).

59. Reaffirmed recently in Festo Corp. v. Shoketsu Kinzoku Kogyo Kabushiki Co., 535 U.S. 722 (2002).

60. 166 F. Supp. 551 (S.D.N.Y. 1958), discussed in Merges and Nelson, note 43 above, at 853–854.

the requirements of patentability, it could have obtained an improvement patent.

The practical test for equivalence requires supposing that the patentee's patent application had contained a claim for the very invention that he now claims is equivalent to the patent that he did obtain, and then asking whether such a claim would have been barred by a previous patent or other prior art.[61] This is similar to asking in a copyright case whether the copyright holder is seeking protection for expression or for an idea. If the latter—if for example he is seeking to prevent someone else from using some standard plot on the ground that (in patent jargon) the defendant's use of that plot makes the defendant's work "equivalent" to his own though not identical to it—the judicial response would be that he could not have copyrighted the element that he claims makes the defendant's work equivalent to his.

The doctrine of equivalents enables patent applicants to economize on description. It thus invites comparison to doctrines of contract law that by supplying standard terms economize on the costs of drafting contracts. Without a doctrine of equivalents, patent applicants would have to include much greater detail concerning the extent of the patent protection sought. The doctrine is susceptible, however, to the following abuse: apply for as broad a patent as possible, that is, be as abstract as possible. (Recall, again from Chapter 4, the correlation between breadth and abstractness.) If the broad patent is granted, you may have gotten yourself a very substantial monopoly. Samuel Morse, the inventor of the telegraph, applied for a patent on "the use of the motive power of . . . electro-magnetism, however developed[,] for making or printing intelligible characters at any distance." A patent so broad might have returned Morse profits vastly in excess of his fixed costs of invention, especially if he could in effect have extended his seventeen-year patent term by patenting improvements made during the term.[62] If the PTO balks at the breadth of the patent protection sought, the applicant can amend the application to narrow the scope—and then after the application is granted reassert the abandoned claims under the doctrine of equivalents (that is, argue that any patent containing any of those claims is equivalent to his own patent). This maneuver is blocked by the doctrine of "prosecution history estoppel," which as recently interpreted by the Supreme Court presumptively forbids the patentee to invoke the doctrine of equivalents with respect to any claim that the PTO, in the course of insisting on a narrower application, rejected as failing to satisfy one or more of the requirements for patentability.[63] Another check

61. See Wilson Sporting Goods Co. v. David Geoffrey & Associates, 904 F.2d 677 (Fed. Cir. 1990).

62. See O'Reilly v. Morse, 56 U.S. (15 How.) 62 (1853), discussed in Merges and Nelson, note 43 above, at 850–851.

63. In the *Festo* case, note 59 above.

on overclaiming in a patent is the statutory rule that a patent claim is invalid if it is indefinite; an indefinite claim would tend to enlarge the practical scope of the patent beyond its lawful bounds by imposing legal risks on competitors, who would be buying an infringement suit if they mistook those bounds because the patent claim was unclear. The requirement would be less important if there were a defense of independent creation, as in copyright law; since there is not, the potential infringer is entitled to a clear warning of the scope of the patentee's rights, so that he does not infringe inadvertently.

Broad interpretation of a patent's scope increases the patentee's power to exclude competition. But at the same it "forces other firms, if they want to compete in the broad product field, to work on alternatives that may be very different from what is already patented."[64] It may also (shades of Kitch) reduce patent racing,[65] though, alternatively, it may just shift the patent race to an earlier period (the race for the broad patent). Narrow interpretation can increase transaction costs: subsequent inventors may have to get licenses from more patentees[66]—though the other side of the coin is that the narrower the existing patents are, the less likely a new invention is to infringe any of them. It has been argued that narrow interpretation may, in addition, actually increase the deadweight loss from the patentee's monopoly pricing by making it easier to create close substitutes that cost considerably more to make than the patentee's product.[67] Suppose the marginal cost of that product is $1 and the price $3, but if the patent grant is construed narrowly a competitor can make a close substitute at a cost of $2. Consumers will be deflected to the competitor. The patentee may respond by reducing his price in an effort to win them back. Whether this process enhances social welfare is uncertain. On the one hand, deadweight losses from output restrictions are reduced; on the other hand, production costs are higher when both the original patentee and a competitor or competitors produce two products than when a product is produced by the patent holder alone. Another consideration is that to the extent the competitor is successful, the patent reward is reduced and the patentee may be unable to recoup his fixed costs of invention. If instead, as a consequence of a broad interpretation of the patent, the substitute

---

64. Mazzoleni and Nelson, note 28 above, at 275.

65. See, illustrative of a large literature, Vincenzo Denicolò, "Patent Races and Optimal Patent Breadth and Length," 44 *Journal of Industrial Economics* 249 (1996). We do not discuss the tradeoff between breadth and duration of patents; in effect, we treat the existing duration (generally twenty years) as exogenous to our analysis.

66. See Robert P. Merges, "Institutions for Intellectual Property Transactions: The Case of Patent Pools," in *Expanding the Boundaries of Intellectual Property: Innovation Policy for the Knowledge Society* 123 (Rochelle Cooper Dreyfuss, Diane Leenheer Zimmerman, and Harry First eds. 2001).

67. See Paul Klemperer, "How Broad Should the Scope of Patent Protection Be?" 21 *RAND Journal of Economics* 113 (1990).

is deemed infringing, fewer consumers will substitute away from the patented product because they will be denied access to the closest substitute.[68]

But the analysis is incomplete. A broad patent, by greatly limiting substitution, will enable the patentee to charge a higher price than if the patent were narrow.[69] Because a profit-maximizing monopolist will always raise his price to a point within the elastic range of his demand curve, the higher price will deflect some consumers to substitutes, albeit poor ones, offsetting (to what extent cannot be determined a priori) the effect of a broad patent in compressing the range of available substitutes.

Here is another equivocal benefit of broad interpretation: in increasing the frequency of defensive patenting, it increases the number of patents, and the more patents that are issued, the more disclosure of technological ideas is made that other inventors may be able to use.[70] But if defensive patenting is a major factor in the increase in the number of patents in the last two decades (see the statistics in Chapter 12), and thus an indirect result of the strengthening of patent protection over this period that may underlie the increase, further doubt is cast on whether more patents mean more and better innovation.

Broad patent protection has still another, and fundamental, double-edged effect: it increases the return to the first inventor, which encourages invention, but increases the cost of invention to his successors, which discourages invention. The analogy to our discussion of copyright in Chapters 2 and 3, where we pointed out that the broader copyright protection is, the costlier the subsequent creation of expressive works becomes because earlier works are inputs into later ones, should be apparent. A related point is that the more exacting the requirement of novelty and so the harder it is to get a patent, the easier it is for subsequent inventors to obtain patents (although they will be narrow too) but the less information useful to them will be disclosed in patent applications because there will be fewer of them.[71]

The analogy of patent to copyright invites an adaptation of the formal model in Chapter 3 to patents, going beyond Figure 11.1 and the accompanying discussion. Indeed, at the formal level, the parallelism is so close that we could use the identical model, deriving the identical results, with just a

68. A similar argument was made with respect to copyright in Ian E. Novos and Michael Waldman, "The Effects of Increased Copyright Protection: An Analytic Approach," 92 *Journal of Political Economy* 236, 244–245 (1984). Recall that our own doubts about broad copyright protection are not based on underutilization (that is, reduced access by consumers), but on transaction costs and input costs, which the Novos and Waldman article does not discuss.

69. We ignore the complications introduced by price discrimination; they would not alter the analysis fundamentally.

70. See Gallini, note 51 above, at 140.

71. See Suzanne Scotchmer and Jerry Green, "Novelty and Disclosure in Patent Law," 21 *RAND Journal of Economics* 131 (1990). A further argument for narrow interpretation of patents is presented in the next chapter.

relabeling of the variables: p would be the price of a unit of output of the patented product, $q(p)$ the market demand for that output, x and $y(p, z)$ the number of units produced by the patentee and the duplicators (where y depends on both p and z, the amount of protection against duplication conferred by patent law), c the patentee's marginal cost, e the cost of creating the patented invention in the first place, and so forth. The implications for patent law and inventions would with minor adjustments be similar to those listed at the end of Chapter 3 for copyright law and expressive works.

But wouldn't there have to be a major adjustment to reflect the boon that patents confer on subsequent patentees by forcing disclosure of the steps constituting the invention? This might seem to alleviate the tension between earlier and later innovators that we emphasized in the copyright setting. But the appearance is misleading. For if we set unpublished materials and some computer software[72] to one side for the moment, copyright law evokes disclosure just as patent law does. With the exceptions just mentioned, copyrighted works are fully public and subsequent authors can use any of the information (that is, ideas) contained in them to help them in making their own such works. There is even a term for this use—"managed copying." The differences between patent and copyright law, and between expression and invention, are great, but not at the level of abstraction at which our formal model was pitched.

Patent Law as a Response to Trade Secret Law and Monopoly

The foregoing analysis suggests grounds for skepticism that the existing level of patent protection is essential to enabling inventors to recover their fixed costs. These grounds are reinforced by a growing body of empirical studies illustrated by a study of Japanese patent law that, using patent citations and other proxies for evaluating the relative contribution of different patents to technological progress, found that Japan's expansion of patent rights in 1988 had no effect on innovation or R&D.[73] There is also evidence that the patenting of computer software actually retards innovation because most software

72. Object code (machine code), as distinct from source code, is not readable by a human being or otherwise usable by him unless he has access to the source code. If, therefore, a software manufacturer copyrights only the object code, retaining the source code as a trade secret, public access to the copyrighted code will not generate information that other software writers can use.

73. See Mariko Sakakibara and Lee Branstetter, "Do Stronger Patents Induce More Innovation? Evidence from the 1988 Japanese Patent Law Reforms," 32 *RAND Journal of Economics* 77 (2001). Other studies are cited and summarized in id. at 98–99. Mazzoleni and Nelson, note 28 above, summarize the arguments for doubting that the expansion of patent protection in recent decades has promoted a net increase in economic welfare. And Jaffe, note 51 above, at 555, after a careful survey of the economic literature concerning the expansion, concludes: "There is widespread unease that the costs of stronger patent protection may exceed the benefits. Both theoretical and, to a lesser extent, empirical research suggest this possibility."

innovation both builds on and complements existing software. Without the retardation introduced by patenting and the resulting need to negotiate licenses, software manufacturers would innovate more rapidly and each would benefit from the others' innovations, which, because of the sequential and complementary nature of the innovations in this industry, would enhance the value of the existing products.[74]

We do not question the importance of technological progress to economic welfare, the relation of R&D expenditures to such progress, or that because of positive externalities the social return to R&D exceeds the private return.[75] The issue is the effect of the actual patent system that we have, and of feasible variants that can be imagined, on R&D, weighting quantity of R&D by quality. The positive correlation between the strength of a nation's intellectual property laws and the nation's economic growth, capital-labor ratio, per capita income, and government funding of R&D[76] similarly does not establish causal relations.

One study found that "while the aggregate value of patent rights appears to be quite high, it is estimated to be only on the order of 10 to 15 percent of total national expenditures on R&D. Hence it is unlikely to be the major factor in determining the overall level of expenditures."[77] If this is right, then incremental increases in patent protection are unlikely to influence inventive activity significantly and incremental reductions might actually enhance economic welfare. Notice in this regard that any increase in patent protection, to the extent it succeeds in its objective of inducing additional inventive activity, creates additional competition, since patented products are often substitutes for other patented products. The additional competition will reduce the profitability of inventive activity, and hence the resources devoted to it, blunting the effect of the enhanced patent protection in preventing the manufacture of close substitutes for patented products and thus the incentive effect of the enhanced protection.[78] There is support for this proposition in the

74. See James Bessen and Eric Maskin, "Sequential Innovation, Patents, and Imitation" (MIT Sloan School of Management and Princeton University, July 2002).

75. See Charles I. Jones and John C. Williams, "Measuring the Social Return to R&D," 113 *Quarterly Journal of Economics* 1119 (1998).

76. See Dennis W. Carlton, "A Critical Assessment of the Role of Imperfect Competition in Macroeconomics," in *Market Behaviour and Macroeconomic Modelling* 73, 84–86 (Steven Brakman, Hans von Ees, and Simon K. Kuipers eds. 1998).

77. Zvi Griliches, Ariel Pakes, and Bronwyn H. Hall, "The Value of Patents as Indicators of Inventive Activity," in *Economic Policy and Technical Performance* 97, 120 (Partha Dasgupta and Paul Stoneman eds. 1987).

78. See Tomas Philipson and Frank R. Lichtenberg, "The Dual Effects of Intellectual Property Regulations: Within- and Between-Patent Competition in the US Pharmaceuticals Industry" (University of Chicago, George J. Stigler Center for the Study of the Economy and the State, Working Paper No. 178, Oct. 12, 2002). This is a point that we made in Chapter 4 with reference to increased copyright protection.

next chapter, where we find that the pro-patent policies of the Federal Circuit seem to have had at best only a small, though positive, impact on research and development expenditures.

The strongest economic arguments for the patent system (or at least *a* patent system, not necessarily the one we have and possibly one that would grant less protection to inventors) are four—and none is directly related to the traditional cost-internalization arguments for property rights in inventions. Three of the four are related to economic problems created by trade secrecy, and the fourth to the problem of monopoly (economic, not patent).[79]

1. In the absence of a patent option, inventors would invest many more resources in maintaining trade secrecy (and competitors in unmasking them) and inventive activity would be inefficiently biased toward inventions that can be kept secret.[80] This is one point rather than two because the bias in inventive activity would be the result of inventors' trying to minimize their costs of maintaining secrecy.

Concern about biasing the direction of inventive activity is also, we digress briefly to note, the economic argument for business-method patents,[81] such as Amazon.com's "one-click" method of ordering books and other products. Allowing such innovations to be patented goes some way toward correcting the potential distortion in the allocation of resources to inventive activity that arises from limiting patent protection to products of scientific and technological rather than marketing ingenuity. Against the validity of business-method patents (which has yet to be determined by the Supreme Court), however, it

79. Patents may have an additional value, again unrelated (or only obliquely related) to internalizing the costs of invention, in signaling the quality of a firm's technical knowledge. See Clarisa Long, "Patent Signals," 69 *University of Chicago Law Review* 625 (2002). The distinction noted in the text between an "economic monopoly" and a "patent monopoly" is pursued in Chapter 14, where we discuss antitrust issues presented by intellectual property.

80. See Steven N. S. Cheung, "Property Rights in Trade Secrets," 20 *Economic Inquiry* 40 (1982).

81. See, for example, Robert P. Merges, "As Many as Six Impossible Patents before Breakfast: Property Rights for Business Concepts and Patent System Reform," 14 *Berkeley Technology Law Journal* 577, 579–588 (1999). The validity of business-method patents was affirmed by the Federal Circuit in State Street Bank & Trust Co. v. Signature Financial Group, Inc., 149 F.3d 1368 (Fed. Cir. 1998). The method in question, in the court's words, consisted of "a data processing system (the system) for implementing an investment structure which was developed for use in Signature's business as an administrator and accounting agent for mutual funds. In essence, the system, identified by the proprietary name Hub and Spoke (R), facilitates a structure whereby mutual funds (Spokes) pool their assets in an investment portfolio (Hub) organized as a partnership. This investment configuration provides the administrator of a mutual fund with the advantageous combination of economies of scale in administering investments coupled with the tax advantages of a partnership." Id. at 1370. In other words, it was an algorithm, like the Black-Scholes option-pricing formula, though longer.

can be argued that the research and development of new methods of marketing are not such costly activities as to require legal protection. Despite the unavailability of business-method patents until quite recently, there has been no shortage of marketing innovations. Think back to the analysis of obviousness earlier in this chapter, and apply it to the "one-click" patent. All that is involved is that when a purchaser types in his order, an Amazon.com computer combines the order information with stored purchaser information (address, credit card number, and so forth), so that with one click the purchaser signals the computer to ship and bill accordingly.[82]

2. A patent option facilitates efficiency in manufacturing. The possessor of a secret process for manufacturing a product may not be the most efficient manufacturer of it. In principle, he can license the trade secret to a more efficient manufacturer. But licenses of trade secrets are even more costly than patent licenses because the risk of inadvertent disclosure or unprovable theft of the secret is greater if the trade secret is licensed than if it is kept within a single organization. So absence of patent protection would cause inefficiencies in manufacture.[83]

3. Suppose a firm invents a process that has value in the manufacture not only of its own products but also of products in other industries. If the process is kept secret from the world, the firm may never even learn of the other potential applications. And if it does learn of them, what is it to do?[84] One possibility is to enter the other industries in which the process could be employed profitably and begin manufacturing their products. But apart from the delay involved in such a course of action, the firm may lack the requisite skills, knowledge, or other resources for operating effectively in those industries, even if it is a highly efficient manufacturer in its own industry, and so it either will not enter at all or, if it does, will incur needlessly high manufacturing costs. The alternative is to license the process to the firms already in those industries, but licensing of trade secrets is, as we just noted, costly because the secret is more likely to leak out the more people who are in on it. This is also a reason to doubt that merger with a firm already in the target industry is a feasible alternative to unilateral entry into the industry.

82. See Walter G. Hanchuk, "How to 'Read' a Patent: Understanding the Language of Proprietary Rights," in *From Ideas to Assets,* note 52 above, at 27, which contains the text of Amazon.com's patent application.

83. See Gallini, note 51 above, at 141–144, and studies cited there. The broader point is that patent law may overcome the high transaction costs associated with trade secrets. See F. Scott Kieff, "Property Rights and Property Rules for Commercializing Inventions," 85 *Minnesota Law Review* 697 (2001); Paul J. Heald, "A Non-Incentive Theory of Patent Law" (University of Georgia Law School, 2002).

84. Cf. Dennis W. Carlton, "The Law and Economics of Rights in Valuable Information: A Comment," 9 *Journal of Legal Studies* 725 (1980).

This discussion suggests that patent law may benefit small firms. They are least likely to have the resources to be able to manufacture products based on their inventions.

The arguments for patent law that are based on the limitations of trade secrets might be thought to imply that trade secrecy law, as an alternative to patent law, should be abolished.[85] But without either trade secrecy or patents, concerns about the adequacy of incentives for invention would be magnified. And as we shall see in Chapter 13, while trade secrecy law perhaps could be trimmed a bit, a core of trade secrecy certainly should remain legally protected, namely the protection of trade secrets against appropriation by means of force or fraud (burglary, trespass, assault, threats, false pretenses, wiretapping, bribery, and so forth), because of the rent seeking that the abolition of such protection would incite. Anyway, even if trade secrecy *should* be abolished, it is not about to be, and so patent law can be defended as a second-best solution to the problems that trade secrecy law creates.

4. Without patents a boost might be given to the organization of markets along monopolistic rather than competitive lines. Suppose that because of superior efficiency or economies of scale, a firm is the sole producer of some product. If in a world without patents the firm invents a process that reduces its costs of production, or an improved version of its product that creates additional surplus, it will be able in the first case to increase its profits by reducing its price and in the second case to increase its profits by increasing its price. In neither case will the effect be to make entry into its market more attractive. (In the second case, although price is higher, the higher price reflects the superior quality of the product; the quality-adjusted price may be no higher.) A process can often be concealed, and an invention embodied in a new product may not be easily discoverable by reverse engineering. Moreover, as we have emphasized, an inventor has lead-time and learning-by-doing advantages (the first reinforced by trademark, in the case of consumer products) that do not depend on legal protection. In all these respects, a monopolistic innovator may not need patent protection in order to internalize the benefits of his innovation. Competitive firms, however, lack these advantages and so are more dependent on patents than monopolists are to take advantage of technological opportunities for cost reduction or product improvement.

Unfortunately, the arguments for patent law that we have just presented, although they strike us as compelling in the aggregate, do not enable us to determine whether patent protection should be broader or narrower than it

85. This might seem impossible to do without unreasonable invasions of business privacy; but long steps toward abolition could be taken by such measures as overruling *E. I. du Pont de Nemours & Co. v. Christopher*, repealing the semiconductor law, refusing to enforce employee covenants not to compete, and forbidding encryption—all matters discussed in Chapter 13.

is, or along what dimension. There are different ways in which the scope of a patent right can vary. Although breadth and duration are often contrasted, they are substitutes; the longer the patent term, the greater the amount of inventive activity by others that will be excluded save by leave of the patentee. Breadth or scope can be contracted or expanded by tinkering with the doctrine of equivalents and its obverse, the doctrine of reverse equivalents (obverse because in effect it denies enforceability to the original patent if it is just a trivial variation of the improvement patent); by requiring more or less detail in the patent application; by raising or lowering the threshold of obviousness; and by being more or less permissive with regard to the inclusion of "functional" language in the claims made in the patent application. A claim is functional when it defines an invention by what it does rather than by what it is (its structure or material). A functional claim is apt to be broader because if allowed it will cover all the different ways of performing the function, even though they may involve structures or materials completely different from those of the applicant's own invention. The choice among methods of broadening or narrowing patent protection is not determined by the observation that we need patent law in order to place limits on trade secrecy.

We consider finally whether a parallel argument to the argument for patent law that is based on the desire to trim the sails of trade secrecy is available for copyright law. Common law copyright corresponds to trade secrecy, as do the contractual restrictions that software producers can impose on direct-buying customers to prevent further disclosure of their software. Novelists commonly keep elaborate journals in which they jot down ideas, character sketches, snatches of conversation, descriptions, and other expressive materials that they later work into novels. They invariably want to conceal the journal from the world. One reason is that if it were published it might, even though an inferior substitute for the eventual novel, undermine demand for the novel; the reader might think he'd gotten the gist of the novel or, more likely, would doubt that the novel would be a big improvement over the inferior mock-up of it. So the parallel to trade secrecy is close, though there are two important differences. The novelist cannot profit from the secret contents of his journal without eventual disclosure in the form of the completed, published novel. And the journal may contain material that if made public would embarrass him and even subject him to lawsuits for publishing libelous material. Knowing this, the author may decide against keeping a journal in the first place.

Although it is not obvious how copyright law can induce disclosures that would otherwise be indefinitely concealed the way industrial trade secrets may remain indefinitely concealed, we gave some examples in Chapter 2. Three possibilities are potentially important. One involves dramatic works. In the absence of copyright, a playwright would, at least in the era before the pocket tape recorder, be reluctant to publish his play, since it would be difficult for someone who merely attended a performance to reconstruct the text sufficiently to be able to put on his own performance of the play. This may have been a factor in Shakespeare's not publishing any of his plays. A related example is building plans, given the difficulty of reconstructing a building on the basis of its appearance (see Chapter 4). The third case is that of the software producer who can use contract to limit the disclosure of his software—but he is likely to do so copyright or not, because much software is easy to invent around. In summary, the existence of a form of trade secrecy in the domain of expressive works does not provide as strong an argument for statutory copyright as the parallel argument for some kind of patent law.

A Note on Design Patents

Our discussion to this point has been confined to "utility" patents, that is, patents on useful inventions. They are by far the most common type of patent, but not the only type. About 10 percent of the patents issued each year by the Patent and Trademark Office are "design" patents, which confer a fourteen-year nonrenewable term on novel, nonobvious, nonfunctional, or ornamental features of manufactured products.[86] Examples would be an ornamental hub cap, a lighting fixture's distinctive shape, and a telephone in the form of a tiger. The overlap of design patents with both copyrights and trademarks is great, because the distinctive design of a branded product is an expressive work and because it is also a common way in which the producer identifies his brand to consumers; such an identifying feature is called "trade dress" and, as noted in Chapter 7, is protected by trademark law. As we also noted there, a design feature can have value in itself as well as value as a source identifier, and it is the former, intrinsic value that design patents protect. The best economic argument for design patents resembles the best economic argument for utility patents: avoidance of distortions created by another body of intellectual property law.

Were there no design patents, manufacturers could still prevent copying of design features by using them as trade dress[87] or, to a lesser extent, by copy-

---

86. See 17 U.S.C. § 171; Steven A. Church, "The Weakening of the Presumption of Validity for Design Patents: Continued Confusion under the Functionality and Matter of Concern Doctrines," 30 *Indiana Law Review* 499 (1997). The remaining category of patents, which we do not discuss, consists of patents on plants.

87. Even conspicuous disclaimers by competitors, designed to prevent confusion by consumers over source, would not defeat the originator's trademark claim, given the dilution ground of trademark protection.

righting them. Yet these may not be the most efficient means of protecting a design. Consider first the trade-dress route. The Rolls-Royce automobile has a distinctive hood ornament—a statue of the "Spirit of Ecstasy." Rolls-Royce might not want to use that ornament in its advertising to identify the automobile, but at the same time it would not want the ornament copied even by a manufacturer of an automobile that no one would suppose a Rolls-Royce.

Design patents are also a way around the doctrine of aesthetic functionality discussed in the trademark chapter. The competitive advantage conferred by a design feature is just what design patents protect. The requirements of demonstrating novelty and nonobviousness serve to confine such patents to designs likely to have been so costly to create that they justify the conferral of a temporary monopoly that will enable the creator to recover that cost. The shorter term (fourteen versus twenty years) reflects the lower cost of designing ornamental versus functional components of commercial products and hence the more limited monopoly required to recover them.

The copyrighting of a design is a cheaper method of obtaining legal protection than patenting it, and the term is much longer. The problem is that a design is copyrightable "only if, and only to the extent that, such design incorporates pictorial, graphic, or sculptural features that can be identified separately from, and are capable of existing independently of, the utilitarian aspects of the article."[88] The "Spirit of Ecstasy" would probably be copyrightable under this standard because it is easily imagined as a free-standing sculpture detached from the hood; the distinctive shape of a container or a lamp housing would not be, however, because it could not readily be imagined as a free-standing sculpture.

88. 17 U.S.C. § 101.

12

The Patent Court:
A Statistical Evaluation

On October 1, 1982, the U.S. Court of Appeals for the Federal Circuit was created by the merger of the appellate section of the U.S. Court of Claims (a court whose jurisdiction was limited to cases in which the federal government is the defendant) with the Court of Customs and Patent Appeals. It has been said that "whether intentional or not, the creation of the [new court] will surely be seen as a watershed event by future historians of the patent system."[1]

The new court inherited the appellate jurisdiction of the CCPA, which was limited however, so far as patents were concerned, to appeals from decisions by the Patent and Trademark Office. But in addition it was given exclusive jurisdiction over appeals from federal district courts in patent infringement cases. Before then such appeals had gone to the regional court of appeals in which the district court whose decision was being appealed was located. This system was criticized because of the inconsistent results to which it gave rise. The regional courts of appeals differed widely in their attitude toward patent validity, the difference reflecting the tug of war (to be discussed in Chapter 14) between those who thought patents essential to technological progress and those who thought them mainly a tool for stifling competition. The preponderant attitude seems to have been negative, as only about 35 percent of patents whose validity was challenged in court survived the challenge.[2] The intercircuit differences fomented forum shopping, which was possible because there would often be multiple alleged infringers. There was even a risk of inconsistent rulings concerning the same patent, since a judgment upholding the validity of a patent would not bind an alleged infringer who had not been a party to the suit in which the judgment was rendered.

Writing shortly after the creation of the new court, one of us expressed

1. Robert P. Merges, Peter S. Menell, and Mark A. Lemley, *Intellectual Property in the New Technological Age* 130 (2d ed. 2000).
2. See Gloria K. Koenig, *Patent Invalidity: A Statistical and Substantive Analysis* 4-18 to 4-19, 4-22 to 4-23 (rev. ed. 1980); P. J. Federico, "Adjudicated Patents: 1948–54," 38 *Journal of the Patent Office Society* 233, 236 (1956).

concern about specialized federal courts in general[3] and a patent court in particular (though, since the Federal Circuit's jurisdiction is not limited to patent cases, it is only semispecialized and indeed is less specialized than the two courts from which it was created).[4] Patent law was "riven by a deep cleavage, paralleling the cleavages in antitrust law, between those who believe that patent protection should be construed generously to create additional incentives to technological progress and those who believe that patent protection should be narrowly construed to accommodate the procompetitive policies of the antitrust laws."[5] Because of the limitations of knowledge concerning the economic effects of patents that we emphasized in the preceding chapter, the division of opinion between the pro- and anti-patent camps could be explained only as reflecting different answers to "questions of value, which cannot be answered by consulting an expert observer, neutrally deploying his value-free knowledge."[6]

A specialized or even semispecialized court would be more inclined than a court of generalists to take sides on the fundamental question whether to favor or disfavor patents, especially since interest groups would be bound to play a larger role in the appointment of the judges of such a court than they would in the case of the generalist federal courts. It would be difficult to get the patent bar excited about the appointment of an appellate judge who might hear only two or three patent appeals a year, but if the judge was going to be a member of the court that heard *all* patent appeals, the patent bar and its clients would exert themselves to influence the selection. The side of the fundamental controversy that a patent court would be likelier to take would be the pro-patent side, simply because a court that is focused, like an administrative agency (invariably specialized), on a particular government program is more likely than a generalist court to identify with the statutory scheme that it is charged with administering. This, by the way, has been the bent of the Patent and Trademark Office (PTO) itself, as we shall note later in this chapter.

The Federal Circuit has indeed turned out to be a pro-patent court in comparison to the average of the regional courts that it displaced in the patent domain. In a careful review of the first six years of the new court's patent jurisprudence, Rochelle Dreyfuss concluded that the court "has taken on a

---

3. See Richard A. Posner, *The Federal Courts: Crisis and Reform* 147–160 (1985).

4. Only about 30 percent of the judges of the court in recent years have had a patent background, see John R. Allison and Mark A. Lemley, "How Federal Circuit Judges Vote in Patent Validity Cases," 27 *Florida State University Law Review* 745, 751 (2000), but they have written 63 percent of the patent opinions, see id. at 752–753, suggesting that their influence on the court's patent jurisprudence has been preponderant.

5. Posner, note 3 above, at 152–153.

6. Id.

decidedly pro-patent bias."[7] She did not consider the court to be as biased as its critics claimed, and she rightly noted that its bias might be less reflective of its specialized character than of changes in the economic *Zeitgeist* that occurred in the 1980s. Those changes included a sharp retrenchment in antitrust law by the Justice Department and the courts and an intensified concern with the international competitiveness of U.S. industry. (We return to these ideological and political developments in Chapter 15.) The unification of patent appeals had had the desired effect of reducing inconsistency and forum shopping; and on the whole, she concluded, the court had been a good idea and was doing a good job.

Since the publication of Dreyfuss's article in 1989, the Federal Circuit has continued to lean in favor of patent rights, most notably in its recognition of business-method patents, although the major changes engineered by the court took place in the 1980s. The court has managed to avoid substantial public controversy over its patent jurisprudence,[8] in part perhaps because of the general drift toward expanded protection of intellectual property. Indeed, given the political pressure for such expansion, the fact that the court has avoided substantial controversy is another bit of evidence that it is indeed leaning in favor of patent validity. Academic criticism of the court's patent decisions continues, however, and the empirical study that constitutes the balance of this chapter supports some of that criticism.

Patent Applications and Patent Grants

Our empirical study estimates, to begin with, the impact of the Federal Circuit on the number of patent applications, the number of patents issued, and the probability that an application will be granted. We also examine, by estimating the court's impact on research and development (R&D) expenditures, whether the Federal Circuit has stimulated technological progress. This is a better test of technological progress than whether the number of patents has increased, because the latter increase might reflect a substitution away from trade secret protection without a net increase in technological progress, or an increase in the amount of defensive and other strategic patenting, with again no net beneficial effect on progress. Just the fact that there

7. Rochelle Cooper Dreyfuss, "The Federal Circuit: A Case Study in Specialized Courts," 64 *New York University Law Review* 1, 26 (1989). An example from the period covered by Dreyfuss's study was the court's decision in Roche Products, Inc. v. Bolar Pharmaceutical Co., 733 F.2d 858 (Fed. Cir. 1984), which defined the experimental use exception to patent infringement in the narrowest possible terms, precipitating the enactment of the Hatch-Waxman Act, discussed in Chapter 11. For analysis and conclusions similar to Dreyfuss's, see Gerald Sobel, "The Court of Appeals for the Federal Circuit: A Fifth Anniversary Look at Its Impact on Patent Law and Litigation," 37 *American University Law Review* 1087 (1988).

8. See Richard A. Posner, *The Federal Courts: Challenge and Reform* 253 (1996).

are so many patents "out there" increases the cost of invention. As F. M. Scherer points out, the Federal Circuit has "rendered decisions greatly strengthening the presumption of patent validity and broad scope in contested cases and [has] increased to occasional billion-dollar thresholds the amount of damages awarded when infringement is proved. These changes bolster incentives for innovators in one respect. But they also make innovation more dangerous—indeed, much like walking through a mine field—in technologies with complex and overlapping patents of uncertain scope. The net effect on incentives is neither obvious nor known."[9]

The Federal Circuit would influence the number of patent applications and the number of applications granted by means of the precedents that it issued. Many cases and of course even more patents and patent applications were in the pipeline when the court was created, and the behavior of parties to those matters with regard to patenting, to infringing, and to bringing and defending a lawsuit would not have been significantly influenced by any change in the direction of patent law brought about by the new court. Hence if the percentage of patents held valid shot up, this would presumably be due to the fact that the court had different policies from the regional courts that it had supplanted. Eventually, however, those policies, reflected in the court's decisions, would influence patent applications, patent grants, and patent suits, and direct comparisons with the pre–Federal Circuit era would no longer be meaningful. For example, if the court took a hard line against patent validity, fewer weak patents would be sought or granted, so the percentage of patents held valid by the court might be no lower than in the old days. But if we confine our attention to the first five years or so after the creation of the Federal Circuit, we will be on pretty safe ground in attributing any change in outcomes to the policies of the new court rather than to adaptations by inventors and the PTO to those policies.

From a comprehensive study of both published and unpublished decisions of the Federal Circuit[10] we cull the following statistics regarding the court's

9. F. M. Scherer, *New Perspectives on Economic Growth and Technological Innovation* 87 (1999).

10. See Donald R. Dunner, J. Michael Jakes, and Jeffrey D. Jarceski, "A Statistical Look at the Federal Circuit's Patent Decisions: 1982–1994," 5 *Federal Circuit Bar Journal* 151 (1995). Our statistics are computed from charts 1D–3D, id. at 162, 167, 172, which deal with validity decisions based on 35 U.S.C. §§ 102 (novelty), 103 (nonobviousness), and 112 (enablement—that is, the requirement that the description in the patent application be sufficient to enable someone who is skilled in the relevant technology to actually make the invention). We exclude cases remanded for further proceedings and appeals from the Patent and Trademark Office, which would not have gone to the regional courts of appeals before the creation of the Federal Circuit. The number of cases in Table 12.1 does not correspond to the actual number of cases because the authors report their data on a per-patent basis. For a further description of their methodology, see Dunner, Jakes, and Jarceski, above, at 153–154.

Table 12.1 Percentage of cases in which Federal Circuit upheld validity of patent, 1982–1992

Year	Cases	Percentage of patents held valid
1982–83	22	45
1983–84	99	67
1984–85	62	58
1985–86	122	76
1986–87	70	70
1987–88	79	70
1988–89	73	63
1989–90	100	69
1990–91	40	65
1991–92	17	67

decisions on validity. We report these statistics in Table 12.1 for the first ten rather than five years of the court's existence to test for evidence of adaptive behavior.

Notice that in the first five years of the new court the percentage of cases in which the validity of a challenged patent was upheld increased enormously over the pre–Federal Circuit era, in which, as we noted earlier, only 35 percent of patents had been held valid compared to a weighted average of 67 percent for the first ten years of the Federal Circuit.[11] These statistics provide dramatic confirmation of the court's pro-patent leanings but not conclusive evidence. It is widely believed that while the court is indeed prone to uphold the validity of patents, it is loath to find infringement.[12] There is support for this belief in the court's narrow interpretation of the doctrine of equivalents[13] and in its broad interpretation of prosecution-history estoppel, which the Supreme Court modified in the *Festo* decision discussed in the preceding chapter. We know from that chapter that the effects of narrow construal of patents

11. Another study, using a different methodology and not limited to the early period of the Federal Circuit, found that the court was holding patents valid only 54 percent of the time. See John R. Allison and Mark A. Lemley, "Empirical Evidence on the Validity of Litigated Patents," 26 *American Intellectual Property Law Association Quarterly Journal* 185, 205–206 (1998). These authors' data, which are probably more comparable to those in the studies of the pre–Federal Circuit era than the data in Table 12.1, nevertheless reveal a sizable increase in the percentage of patents held valid following the creation of the Federal Circuit. From another study with a similar database, we calculate that the court has been holding patents valid in 53 percent of the cases. See Robert L. Harmon, *Patents and the Federal Circuit* 160 (5th ed., 2002 supp.).

12. See Dunner, Jakes, and Jarceski, note 10 above, at 152.

13. See, for example, Johnson & Johnson Associates, Inc. v. R.E. Service Co., 285 F.3d 1046 (Fed. Cir. 2002) (en banc) (per curiam).

are very complex. But it is possible that the net protection of inventors by the court is not much, perhaps not any, greater than that of the regional courts of appeals when they had jurisdiction over patent appeals, though this seems unlikely,[14] in part because of the Federal Circuit's receptivity to novel theories of patentees' damages.[15]

But quite apart from the Federal Circuit's net effect on the protection of inventors, there is much to be said for combining a greater willingness to uphold the validity of patents with a reluctance to find them infringed. It is a curiosity of patent law that the sanction for an improper patent grant lacks gradations: it is invalidity or nothing. One might think that if a patent's claims were overbroad and thus duplicated prior art, the claims would be narrowed; but instead they are invalidated; and likewise if the claim is not adequately described. Because invalidity is such a severe sanction, there is a reluctance to impose it, and an attractive alternative is to construe patents narrowly, so that they survive but do not impede the legitimate competition of other inventors.

The data in Table 12.1 provide no evidence of adaptive behavior. Comparing 1982–1987 (in which we are on pretty safe ground in assuming that any change in outcomes was due to the policies of the new court rather than to adaptations by inventors and the PTO to those policies) to 1987–1992, we find that the percentage of patents held valid in the two periods was almost identical—68 percent in the first versus 67 percent in the second.

Figure 12.1 graphs the number of patent applications filed and patents issued since 1960.[16] If the Federal Circuit's pro-patent orientation had an effect on patent activity, we would expect it to show up first in patent applications, and later, because of the time that it takes for the Patent and Trademark Office to act on an application, in the number of patents issued. We might expect patent applications to be affected within two or three years of the creation of the new court and patents issued to be affected within four or five years.[17]

Figure 12.1 reveals little growth in patent applications until the creation of

14. See Merges, Menell, and Lemley, note 1 above, at 130.

15. See id. at 330–333. For other evidence of the Federal Circuit's pro-patent leanings, see Allison and Lemley, note 11 above, at 252; Robert P. Merges, "Commercial Success and Patent Standards: Economic Perspectives on Innovation," 76 *California Law Review* 805 (1988).

16. The source of the data in Figure 11.1 is U.S. Patent and Trademark Office, "U.S. Patent Activity 1790–Present," *http://www.uspto.gov/web/offices/ac/ido/oeip/taf/reports.htm*. See also 1979, 1992, 2000, and 2001 annual reports of the Commissioner of Patents and Trademarks (workload table).

17. The average interval between the filing of the patent application and the issuance of the patent is 864 days. See Mark A. Lemley, "An Empirical Study of the Twenty-Year Patent Term," 22 *American Intellectual Property Law Association Quarterly Journal* 369, 385 (1994) (tab. 1).

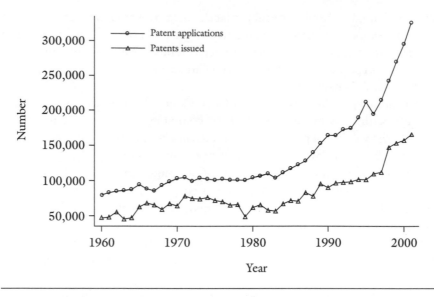

Figure 12.1. Patent applications and patents issued, 1960–2001

the Federal Circuit but rapid growth thereafter. Patent applications grew by an annual rate of only 1.5 percent from 1960 to 1982 but at an annual rate of 5.7 percent from 1982 to 2001. If we assume that the Federal Circuit did not begin to have an effect on the number of patent applications until two years after the court was created, the 5.7 percent annual growth rate for 1982 to 2001 becomes a 6.3 percent annual growth rate for 1984 to 2001. The pattern is similar for the number of patents granted. Allowing for a four-year lag in the effect of the Federal Circuit on this number (because of the average interval of two years between the filing and grant of a patent application), we have annual growth rates of 1.6 percent from 1960 to 1986 and 5.7 percent from 1986 to 2001. These statistics suggest that the Federal Circuit has had a significant positive effect on both the number of patent applications and the number of patent grants.

Contrary to what one might have supposed, these increases are not the result of the advent of the business-method patent. Despite the notoriety of this class of patents and the fact that they would not have flourished without the Federal Circuit's blessing, the number applied for and issued were, until 2000, extremely modest and could not begin to explain the overall increase in patent applications and grants that began in the early and mid-1980s.[18] As

---

18. See U.S. Patent and Trademark Office, "Class 705 Application Filing and Patents Issued Data for FY 95–01," *http://www.uspto.gov/web/menu/pbmethod/applicationfiling.htm*.

late as 1995 only 330 business-method patent applications were filed and only 126 were granted. The reason doubtless is that *State Street,* the decision by the Federal Circuit that approved the business-method patent (see Chapter 11), was not issued until 1998. By 1999 the figures for applications and grants had jumped to 2,821 and 585, respectively, and the following year they reached 7,800 and 899.

We can use regression analysis to get a better fix on the impact that the Federal Circuit has had on the number of patent applications and patents issued. Table 12.2 tests the hypothesis that the rate of patent applications and grants increased after the establishment of the Federal Circuit. We estimated spline regressions of the following form:

$$LApp_t = b_0 + b_1 Y_1 + b_2 Y_2 + b_3 LGDP_{t-1} + b_4 LRD_{t-1} + u_t.$$

$$LGrant_t = b_0 + b_1 Y_1 + b_2 Y_2 + b_3 LApp_{t-2} + b_4 LRD_{t-3} + w_t.$$

$LApp_t$ and $LGrant_t$ denote the logarithm of patent applications filed and patents granted in year t. Y_1 denotes years prior to the date on which the Federal Circuit could first have influenced the number of patent applications or patents issued (we'll call this the "effective date"), and takes a constant value thereafter. Y_2 denotes years after that date, so that if 1984 is assumed to be the earliest year in which the Federal Circuit could first have influenced the number of patent applications filed, then $Y_2 = 1$ in 1984, 2 in 1985, and so on. $LGDP$ is the logarithm of real gross domestic product adjusted by the GDP deflator. LRD denotes the logarithm of real R&D expenditures in 2000 dollars one year earlier in equation (1) in Table 12.2, and three years earlier in equation (3), to reflect the time lags between research expenditures, patent applications, and patent grants; u_t is the residual term.[19] The regression coefficients b_1 and b_2 denote the rate of growth of patent applications and patents issued in Y before and after the effective date of the Federal Circuit, and b_3 and b_4 denote the elasticity of Y with respect to GDP and to R&D expenditures, respectively. If the Federal Circuit has had a positive impact on the number of patent applications and grants, we would expect $b_2 > b_1$.

In equation (1) in Table 12.2 we expect both b_3 and b_4 to be positive, since patenting activity should be positively related both to GDP and to R&D expenditures lagged one period to reflect the passage of time before GDP and R&D expenditures would influence patent applications. Equation (2) includes patent applications lagged two periods as an independent variable, but deletes GDP, which should have no independent effect on patent grants once

19. For R&D expenditures, see U.S. Census Bureau, *Statistical Abstract of the United States* 603 (2000) (tab. 978). For conversion to year 2000 dollars, see U.S. Department of Labor, *CPI Inflation Calculator, http://data.bls.gov/cgi-bin/cpicalc.pl.*

Table 12.2 Spline regression analysis of patent applications and patents issued, 1960–2001 (t-statistics in parentheses)

Independent variables	Patent applications		Patent grants	
	OLS (1)	OLS (2)	OLS (3)	OLS (4)
$Year_1$	−.01 (1.17)	−.01 (1.04)	−.02 (2.96)	−.02 (3.63)
$Year_2$	.04 (6.62)	.04 (5.59)	−.004 (0.20)	−.04 (1.56)
$Year_3$	—	.04 (5.34)	—	.02 (0.77)
$LGDP_{t-1}$	.53 (2.42)	.51 (2.15)	—	—
LRD_{t-1}	.04 (0.38)	.05 (0.50)	.80 (3.55)	1.15 (4.69)
$LApp_{t-2}$	—	—	.64 (1.59)	.48 (1.29)
Constant	22.9 (1.88)	21.7 (1.69)	33.4 (3.49)	36.8 (4.13)
Durbin-Watson	1.31	1.31	1.47	1.72
R^2	.99	.99	.89	.91
No. observations	40	40	39	39

Notes: OLS denotes ordinary least squares. Equations (1) and (2) assume that the effective starting date of the Federal Circuit (the $Year_2$ variable) is the end of 1984 or the beginning of 1985 and equations (3) and (4) assume that the starting date is the end of 1985 or the beginning of 1986. Equations (2) and (4) divide the period following the effective date of the Federal Circuit into two subperiods: $Year_2$ runs from the beginning of 1985 to 1991 in equation (2) and from the beginning of 1986 to 1991 in equation (4), and $Year_3$ from the beginning of 1992 to 2001 in both equation (2) and equation (4). R&D is lagged three periods in equations (3) and (4).

we control for the number of patent applications. Equation (2) also lags R&D two additional periods to account for the average time it takes to get a patent application approved.[20]

The regressions reveal no significant growth in patent applications from 1960 to 1984 but a positive and highly statistically significant growth of 4 percent per year starting in 1985. The difference between the no-growth and

20. We experimented with lags of different periods as well, without significantly affecting our results. Although the Federal Circuit was established in 1982, we experimented with several different effective dates (as defined above), ranging from 1983 to 1986 for applications and 1984 to 1987 for patents issued; our results are not sensitive to the different dates.

4 percent rate is also highly significant. When we divide the post-Federal Circuit period into two periods, 1985–1991 and 1992–2001 (*Year₂* and *Year₃* respectively in equation (2)), we find that applications grew by about 4 percent per year in both subperiods; there has been no observable decline in growth since 1992. The advent of business-method patents contributed, though modestly, to continued growth in the later period, but probably a more important factor has been an accumulation of pro-patent precedents that convinced inventors and their lawyers that patent applications would indeed receive a warmer welcome than in the pre–Federal Circuit era. Of the two other variables in regressions (1) and (2), only GDP (lagged one period) has a positive and statistically significant impact on patent applications. The R&D expenditures variable (lagged one period), though positive, is not statistically significant.

At first glance the patent-issued regressions yield dramatically different results from the applications regressions. Four of the five coefficients of the year variables in equations (3) and (4) are negative, although only the coefficients for the period prior to the creation of the Federal Circuit are statistically significant. This translates into a roughly 2 percent statistically significant annual decline in patents issued in the 1962 to 1985 period compared to a statistically insignificant decline in the subsequent period. This in turn suggests that the Federal Circuit arrested a decline in the annual number of patents issued during the twenty or so years before the effective date of the new court. It is true that the raw number of patents issued increased slightly during the pre–Federal Circuit period, as shown in Figure 12.2, but our regressions suggest that this was due to increases in patent applications and R&D expenditures, which more than offset a negative impact possibly due to the hostility of some appellate courts to patents before the loss of their patent jurisdiction to the Federal Circuit. Put differently, the patent-issued regressions imply that had those courts been as favorably disposed to patentees as the Federal Circuit has proved to be, there would have been a 2 percent higher rate of growth in the number of patents issued annually between 1960 and the end of 1985.

The coefficients of the R&D variables are highly significant, suggesting that increases in R&D expenditures improve the average quality of patent applications, which in turn leads to a higher success rate. The elasticity of patents issued to R&D is not significantly different from 1, implying that a 10 percent increase in R&D increases the number of patents issued by 10 percent, holding constant the number of patent applications.

The annual patent success rate (the ratio of patents issued in year t to applications in year $t-2$) has averaged .65 (ranging between .48 and .79) over the period from 1962 to 2001. Figure 12.2 graphs the success rate, which appears to have trended slightly downward.

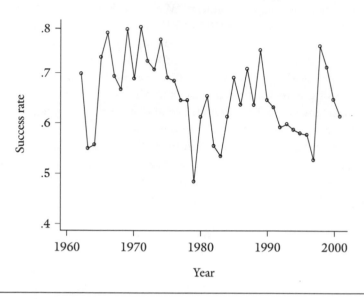

Figure 12.2. Patent success rate, 1962–2001

In Table 12.3 we regress patent success on R&D (lagged three years), patent applications (lagged two years), and $Year_1$ and $Year_2$ to separate the pre– and post–Federal Circuit periods. As expected, we find a significant positive effect of R&D expenditures on patent success. We also find a significant decline in the patent success rate of about 2 percent per year in the period prior to the establishment of the Federal Circuit, and, consistent with the patent-issued regressions in Table 12.2, we find that the Federal Circuit arrested this decline. We find no evidence that an increase in the number of patent applications, which might suggest a decline in the average quality of the applications, is negatively related to the patent success rate.[21]

21. We re-estimated the success-rate regression in Table 12.3 by adding $LGDP_{t-3}$ as an independent variable; it had a positive and highly significant impact on the success rate and increased the adjusted R^2 from .26 to .39. *LRD* continued to be highly significant and of the same magnitude, although both $Year_1$ and $Year_2$ took on greater negative values: $-.07$ (3.82) for $Year_1$ and $-.05$ (1.99) for $Year_2$ (t-statistics in parentheses). We still find a roughly 2 percent greater decline in patents granted before the creation of the Federal Circuit. Two previous studies reached conflicting conclusions on whether the advent of the Federal Circuit had increased the rate of patenting. Compare Bronwyn H. Hall and Rosemarie Ham Ziedonis, "The Patent Paradox Revisited: An Empirical Study of Patenting in the U.S. Semiconductor Industry, 1979–1995," 32 *RAND Journal of Economics* 101, 125 (2001), finding that it did, with Samuel Kortum and Josh Lerner, "Stronger Protection or Technological Revolution: What Is Behind the Recent Surge in Patenting?" 48 *Carnegie-Rochester Conference Series on Public Policy* 247 (1998), finding that it did not.

Table 12.3 Spline regression analysis of logarithm of patent success rate, 1962–2001 (t-statistics in parentheses)

LRD_{t-3}	$LApp_{t-2}$	$Year_1$	$Year_2$	Constant	R^2
.80	−.36	−.02	−.004	33.4	.26
(3.55)	(0.89)	(2.96)	(0.20)	(3.49)	

Notes: The Durbin-Watson statistic of 1.91 indicates the absence of first-order autocorrelation. *Year₁* runs from 1962 to the end of 1985 and *Year₂* from the end of 1985 through 2001. There are 39 observations.

Research and Development Expenditures

A pro-patent Federal Circuit might initially stimulate R&D expenditures by strengthening property rights in inventions, yet the effect might well dissipate in the long run. Stronger patent protection will increase the cost of R&D by curtailing the amount of borrowing from patented work, though at the same time it may lead firms to prefer patenting an invention to keeping it a trade secret and this will increase the availability of scientific knowledge, increase the returns from research, and so ultimately lead to increased expenditures on R&D.

Figure 12.3 reveals an upward trend in real (that is, inflation-adjusted) R&D expenditures over the past forty years. A simple regression of the log of

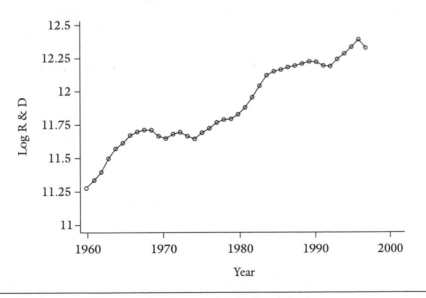

Figure 12.3. Logarithm of R&D expenditures, 1960–2000 (in 2000 dollars)

R&D expenditures on time yields a highly significant growth rate of 2.5 percent per year. Could this be a result of the Federal Circuit's favorable attitude toward patents? That issue is explored in the regressions in Table 12.4, but the results are inconclusive and depend on the particular specification of the regression model. We estimate spline regressions in equations (1) and (2) that include as independent variables $Year_1$ and $Year_2$, where $Year_1$ runs from 1960 through the end of 1982 and $Year_2$ runs from the beginning of 1983 through 1999 (the last year for which we have R&D data), and the log of real GDP (LGDP). In equation (2) we add the lagged value of R&D as a separate independent variable, and in equations (3) and (4) we substitute for the two year variables a time trend variable *(Year)* and a Federal Circuit dummy variable (which takes the value 1 starting in 1983 and 0 for the earlier years). Equations (1) and (2) ask whether R&D expenditures grow more rapidly after than before the creation of the Federal Circuit, while equations (3) and (4) estimate a single time trend for the entire time period and ask whether R&D expenditures increase after the creation of the Federal Circuit.[22]

No significant difference in the trend of R&D expenditures before and after the creation of the Federal Circuit is revealed in regressions (1) and (2). There is no time trend at all in R&D when GDP and R&D are held constant (equation (2)). R&D is positively related to GDP, although the coefficient is only marginally significant in equation (2).[23] There is no time trend in R&D in equations (3) and (4) either, but in these regressions the creation of the Federal Circuit is associated with a positive and significant (equation (4)) or marginally significant (equation (3)) increase in R&D expenditures of 6 to 9 percent. In other words, while the creation of the Federal Circuit does not appear to have increased the rate of growth of R&D, it may have increased the overall level of these expenditures.[24]

22. All regressions were corrected for significant first-order autocorrelation in the residuals, though the correction was only partially successful in equations (1) and (2). All the equations assume that the Federal Circuit's impact, if any, on R&D begins the year after the court's creation. This might appear too soon to expect decisions of the Federal Circuit to influence firms' behavior. But given the lags between R&D expenditures and patent applications and grants, firms would have an incentive to adjust their R&D if they anticipated the court's pro-patent decisions. As it turns out, however, our results are not sensitive to substituting alternative starting dates for the Federal Circuit of 1984 or 1985 for 1983.

23. The regression coefficient on lagged R&D is positive—a 10 percent increase in last period's R&D leads to a 5 to 6 percent increase in the current period—and highly significant. This finding is not surprising because research programs often extend beyond a single period, so that a decision to undertake a research project today is likely to involve expenditures over several time periods.

24. The regression equations in Table 12.4 specify 1983 as the effective date of the Federal Circuit. We experimented with other effective dates (for example, 1984 and 1985), but without altering the results in the table.

Table 12.4 Regression analysis of logarithm of R&D expenditures, 1960–1999 (t-statistics in parentheses)

Independent variables	R&D expenditures			
	CORC (1)	CORC (2)	CORC (3)	CORC (4)
Year$_1$	−.01 (0.78)	−.003 (0.41)	—	—
Year$_2$	.003 (0.38)	−.004 (0.40)	—	—
Year$_3$	—	—	−.001 (0.14)	.001 (0.14)
Fed. Circuit	—	—	.06 (1.71)	.09 (2.95)
LGDP	.64 (2.31)	.43 (1.59)	.66 (2.49)	.12 (0.51)
LRD$_{t-1}$	—	.55 (3.38)	—	.64 (5.59)
Constant	24.8 (1.10)	8.65 (15.2)	.67 (0.59)	1.32 (0.11)
Durbin-Watson	.92	1.31	1.13	1.61
rho	.89	.82	.87	.45
R^2	.38	.73	.54	.97
No. observations	39	38	39	38

Note: CORC denotes Cochrane-Orcutt corrections for first-order autocorrelation.

Amount of Patent Litigation

Other things being equal, the more certain law is, the less likely is litigation. The effect of the Federal Circuit on the certainty of patent law is likely to have been complex. Uncertainty might increase initially because there would be fewer precedents to base predictions on, since the Federal Circuit had not yet ruled on many issues. This effect, however, would tend to diminish over time as the new court decided more cases and issues, and eventually to be overcome by the reduction in variance when one court, instead of twelve, is deciding patent disputes at the appellate level.

Figure 12.4 presents data on the annual number of patent cases filed in the district courts and the annual number of attorneys and agents registered to practice before the Patent and Trademark Office in the period from 1960 to

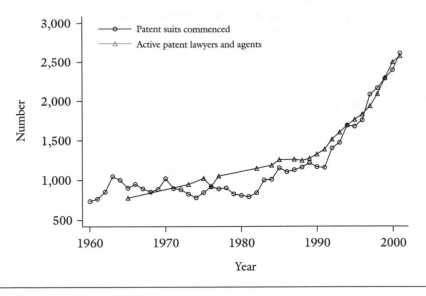

Figure 12.4. Patent cases filed in federal district courts/patent attorneys and agents registered, 1960–2001

2001.[25] The correlation between the two variables (in logarithms) is .97, and a regression of the number of attorneys and agents on patent suits filed, for the twenty-three periods in which we have data on the number of attorneys and agents, yields a coefficient of .86 and a t-ratio of 17.6, indicating a very high level of statistical significance. In other words, the ratio of patent lawyers to patent cases seems not to have increased as a result of the advent of the Federal Circuit. Had the court succeeded in simplifying the law, one might have expected the ratio to fall; but any such effect might easily be swamped by increases in the average stakes and complexity of a patent case. Perhaps both effects have been at work and have offset each other, but this is conjecture.

Figure 12.5 contains data on the annual number of civil cases filed in federal district courts between 1960 and 2001.[26] A comparison of the two

25. We have data only on attorneys and agents for selected months and years over the 1965 to 2001 period. We have taken the last month in a year as the value for that year—for example, if August 1985 is the last month for which we have data in 1985, we used that number as the 1985 figure. To facilitate comparison with the number of cases filed, we have divided the number of attorneys and agents by 10. The data consist of published and unpublished statistics of the PTO; we thank Samson Vermont for his invaluable assistance in obtaining these data for us. A caveat: the number of attorneys and agents registered with the PTO is only an approximation of the number of lawyers involved in patent litigation in the courts, but we cannot find data on the latter number.

26. The source for these data is the 1982 and 2000 annual reports of the Administrative Office of the U.S. Courts (app. tab. C-2), Washington, D.C.

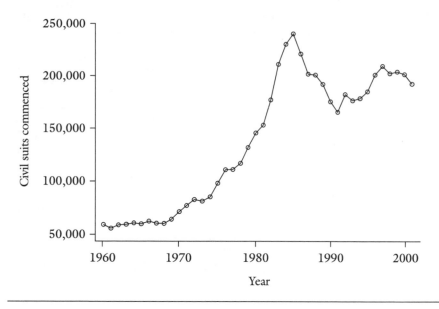

Figure 12.5. Civil cases filed in federal district courts, 1960–2001

graphs reveals that the growth in patent litigation is not simply a result of an overall increase in civil litigation. Patent litigation remained roughly flat until the early 1980s and then increased by nearly 300 percent over the next twenty years, while civil litigation increased steadily from 1960 to 1985 and then fell by about 20 percent over the next fifteen years.

In Table 12.5 we test the hypothesis that the Federal Circuit has been responsible for the increase (or part of it) in patent litigation. We again use a spline regression in which $Year_1$ and $Year_2$ denote the years before and starting in 1983 (the first full year of the Federal Circuit), and divide $Year_2$ into two subperiods, 1983 to 1991 and 1992 to 2001, to allow us to test the hypothesis that after ten years the Federal Circuit would have developed a large enough body of precedents to eliminate the uncertainty associated with the creation of a new court. The other independent variables in the regression analysis include the number of civil suits commenced in the federal district courts (to control for overall trends in civil litigation), real GDP (to test whether litigation tends to increase with income), and the total number of patents issued over the previous three years, this last variable being a rough proxy for the stock of potential patent disputes that may ultimately lead one party to file a suit; the greater the stock, the greater the number of suits filed, other things being equal.

We also present results based on a different specification for the Federal Circuit variables. Here we include an overall time trend variable *(Year)* and

Table 12.5 Regression analysis of logarithm of patent suits commenced in federal district courts, 1962–2001 (t-statistics in parentheses)

Independent variables	R&D expenditures			
	OLS (1)	OLS (2)	OLS (3)	CORC (4)
LPatents	.37 (2.94)	.20 (1.64)	.24 (0.83)	.26 (1.07)
LCivil suits	.64 (5.62)	.53 (4.89)	−.24 (1.14)	.44 (2.09)
LGDP	−.07 (0.21)	−.15 (0.46)	−.32 (0.37)	.15 (0.29)
Year$_1$	−.05 (3.55)	−.04 (2.81)	—	—
Year$_2$	.04 (3.69)	.04 (4.05)	—	—
Year$_3$	—	.06 (5.14)	—	.001 (0.14)
Year	—	—	.02 (0.59)	.05 (2.14)
FC$_1$	—	—	.29 (3.53)	.07 (0.93)
FC$_2$	—	—	.34 (3.26)	.11 (1.53)
Constant	96.1 (3.88)	74.5 (3.21)	−26.7 (0.50)	−103.5 (2.43)
Durbin-Watson	1.31	1.64	.54	2.21
rho	—	—	—	.94
R^2	.98	.98	.88	.47
No. observations	39	39	39	38

Definition of variables: LPatents = the logarithm of the sum of the number of patents issued in year $t-1$, $t-2$, and $t-3$; *LCivil suits* = the logarithm of the number of civil suits commenced in all federal district courts in year t; *LGDP* = the logarithm of real GDP in year t; *Year$_1$* takes the year value up to 1982 and 1982 thereafter; *Year$_2$* takes the value 0 through 1982, 1 to 19 beginning in 1983 and ending in 2001 in equation (1) and 1 to 9 ending in 1991 in equation (2) and 9 thereafter; *Year$_3$* takes the value 0 through 1991 and 1 to 10 beginning in 1992 and ending in 2001; *Year* takes the value of the year; *FC$_1$* is a dummy variable that equals 1 from 1983 to 1991 and 0 otherwise; and *FC$_2$* equals 1 from 1992 to 2001 and 0 otherwise.

two dummy variables to denote the Federal Circuit: FC_1 takes the value 1 in the period 1983–1991 and 0 otherwise, and FC_2 takes the value 1 in the period 1992–2001 and 0 otherwise. The purpose of the latter variable is to test whether litigation begins to taper off once the Federal Circuit creates a stock of precedents; if so, we should observe a negative coefficient on FC_2.

In equations (1) and (2), there is a highly statistically significant increase in the rate of growth of patent litigation of about 4 percent per year starting in 1983, as expected. But, surprisingly, equation (2) indicates that the rate of increase is significantly greater *after* 1992 (6 percent compared to 4 percent),[27] despite the accumulation of Federal Circuit precedents by this period. Could the problem be an omitted variable? But we have controlled for several variables that are likely to be important determinants of patent litigation. Both *LPatents* and *LCivil suits* are positively and significantly (or marginally significantly) correlated in regressions (1) and (2) with the number of patent suits. The coefficients of the civil litigation variable indicate that a 10 percent increase in civil suits is associated with a 5 to 6 percent increase in patent litigation. We have also controlled for the overall level of economic activity (the GDP variable), but its effect on patent litigation is insignificant.[28]

In regressions (3) and (4) (which are identical except that (4) corrects for significant first-order autocorrelation), we substitute a single time trend variable for the 1962 to 2001 period (the *Year* variable) and estimate the Federal Circuit's impact by including two dummy variables—FC_1 for the 1983–1991 period and FC_2 for the 1992–2001 period. The dummy variable approach hypothesizes a constant percentage change in patent litigation each year. This hypothesis, however, is rejected in both regressions, which reveal a significant positive growth rate of patent litigation. Although the coefficients of the two dummy variables are positive, they are statistically significant only in the OLS regression. Because the coefficients on the two dummy variables are roughly the same in regression (3), we cannot reject the hypothesis that the Federal Circuit's impact on patent litigation was the same in both periods. Once we correct for autocorrelation, the coefficients on both dummy variables are insignificant. The coefficients on the remaining variables are generally posi-

27. An F test rejects the null hypothesis at the .01 level that the regression coefficients of *Year₂* and *Year₃* are equal in equation (2).

28. This is not surprising; *LGDP* is highly correlated with both the patent stock and civil litigation variables (.86 with *LPatents* and .89 with *LCivil suits*). In comparison, the correlation between *LPatents* and *LCivil suits* is .56. GDP could have a significant impact on overall civil litigation even if it has an insignificant effect on patent litigation. We tested this hypothesis by regressing *LCivil suits* on *Year* and *LGDP*. The regression coefficient on *LGDP* was negative and statistically insignificant (a t-statistic of only .39).

tive but only the civil litigation and time trend variables are statistically significant.

In short, the regression analysis provides some though not strong support for the hypothesis that the creation of the Federal Circuit increased the rate of growth of patent litigation.[29]

To summarize our empirical study, the creation of the Federal Circuit appears to have had a positive and significant impact on the number of patent applications, the number of patents issued, the success rate of patent applications, the amount of patent litigation, and possibly the level of R&D expenditures—though remember that such an increase cannot be equated with an increase in the rate of technological advance. Even more clearly, for reasons explained in Chapter 11, an increase in patents applied for and granted cannot be taken as a reliable proxy for technological advance.

An aggravating factor is the institutional bias of the Patent and Trademark Office in favor of granting patent applications. Apart from the obvious fact that patent application proceedings are usually ex parte, which creates a bias in favor of granting the application because there is no opponent, patent examiners "are compensated in part based on the number of final dispositions of patents that they accumulate. Because it is easier and faster to secure a final disposition by allowing a patent application than by denying it, there is an incentive to allow applications."[30] What is more, the examiner must write up his reasons for denying a patent application but not for granting one; and in addition the PTO is entirely supported by patent applicants' fees rather than by congressional appropriations, a fact that naturally predisposes the office in favor of the applicants.[31] These built-in tendencies to bias are exacerbated by the Federal Circuit's own bias in favor of upholding the validity of patents. However, it should be noted that a frequent result of the PTO review process is that the patent granted is narrower than the application sought. This narrowing reduces the likelihood of patent infringement litigation.

One might at least have thought that the centralization of patent appeals would, after an initial transition period, reduce the rate of growth in the number of patent lawsuits by making case outcomes more predictable. However, the opposite appears to be true.

---

29. An earlier study of patent litigation between 1971 and 1991 found no net effect of the creation of the new court on the amount of patent litigation. See Jon F. Merz and Nicholas M. Pace, "Trends in Patent Litigation: The Apparent Influence of Strengthened Patents Attributable to the Court of Appeals for the Federal Circuit," 76 *Journal of the Patent and Trademark Office Society* 579 (1994)

30. Arti K. Rai, "Facts, Law, and Policy: An Allocation-of-Powers Approach to Patent System Reform" 21 (University of Pennsylvania Law School, 2002).

31. Id.

We do not wish to end on a critical note. The study reported in this chapter is preliminary because we have not attempted to disaggregate our patent data by industry, and so we cannot exclude the possibility that the results of our analysis may have been influenced by exogenous changes in the relative size of industries that differ in their dependence on patent protection. However, in subsequent research[32] we correct for several additional factors that may have influenced the results of our study, such as changes in patent filing fees; the Hatch-Waxman Act (see Chapter 11), which affected patent practices in the pharmaceutical industry and went into effect at the same time as our assumed date for when the Federal Circuit court would first have influenced patent applications; and a recent tendency for software manufacturers to substitute patent for copyright protection. In addition, we decompose U.S. patent applications between U.S. and foreign (particularly Japanese) residents, and also trace patent applications in foreign nations (Canada and Japan), all with a view toward determining whether our patent court variable may actually be picking up effects due to a surge of innovation by U.S. companies occurring at the same time as the patent court came on line. The result of these various adjustments is that our basic conclusions are unchanged.

We have not attempted to assess the accuracy of the Federal Circuit's patent decisions in relation to that of the patent decisions of the regional courts of appeals in the pre–Federal Circuit era, or to consider whether the Federal Circuit should have done more to individuate patent doctrine to differing conditions in different industries. These are challenging issues for future research.

32. See William M. Landes and Richard A. Posner, "An Empirical Analysis of the Patent Court" (forthcoming in *University of Chicago Law Review*).

13

The Economics of Trade Secrecy Law

Despite the importance of trade secrets to the business community, trade secrecy law has attracted relatively little attention from economists or economically minded lawyers.[1] In this chapter[2] we sketch an approach to the economics of trade secrecy law that connects it both to other areas of intellectual property and to broader issues in the positive economic theory of the common law.[3] Our analysis sheds additional light on the argument of Chapter 11 that the best economic justification for patent law is that it solves certain problems of trade secret law; put differently, that it curbs certain inefficiencies unavoidably created by trade secret law.

A trade secret is an item of information—commonly a customer list, business plan, recipe, or manufacturing process—that has commercial value and that the firm possessing the information wants to conceal from its competitors in order to prevent their duplicating it. It is questionably described as "property" in a Supreme Court decision that upheld a conviction for fraud under a statute (the federal mail-fraud statute) that at the time required that

1. Exceptions are Edmund W. Kitch, "The Law and Economics of Rights in Valuable Information," 9 *Journal of Legal Studies* 683 (1980), and Steven N. S. Cheung, "Property Rights in Trade Secrets," 20 *Economic Inquiry* 40 (1982). See also the following note.

2. The chapter is based on an article that we coauthored with David D. Friedman (see Introduction). Professor Friedman of course is not to be charged with responsibility for our revisions. For significant contributions since our article was published in 1991, see Robert G. Bone, "A New Look at Trade Secret Law: Doctrine in Search of Justification," 86 *California Law Review* 241, 260–283 (1998); Pamela Samuelson and Suzanne Scotchmer, "The Law and Economics of Reverse Engineering," 111 *Yale Law Journal* 1575 (2002). Bone marshals the arguments and evidence against trade secrecy law, criticizing our original analysis for underestimating the social costs of trade secrecy. His criticism has influenced our further thought on the subject. Samuelson and Scotchmer's contribution is discussed later.

3. By "common law" we mean, as explained in the Introduction, law made primarily by judges. Although there is federal as well as state common law, trade secret law is a part of the latter rather than the former. It is no longer a pure common law area, because a number of states have adopted the Uniform Trade Secret Act. But like many other uniform laws, the Act is for the most part codification rather than repudiation of the common law.

the fraud deprive the victim of something tangible—something like property but unlike the right to honest service.[4] A trade secret is not property in the same sense that real and personal property and even copyrights and patents are because it is not something the possessor has the (more or less) exclusive right to use or enjoy.[5] If through accident the secret leaks out, or if a competitor unmasks it by reverse engineering, the law gives no remedy. The law does give a remedy if the secret is lost through a breach of contract—say, by a former employee who had promised not to disclose what he learned on the job—or through a tort, such as trespass. But the violation is not of a property right to the secret but of a common law right defined without regard to trade secrets or to information in general.

Hence in a sense there is no law of trade secrets, though we can see one trying to emerge in the well-known though strangely isolated case of *E. I. du Pont de Nemours & Co. v. Christopher*.[6] A competitor of DuPont hired a pilot to photograph a plant that DuPont was building. The goal was to uncover secrets of DuPont's manufacturing process. Although the court found no trespass by the overflying aircraft, it held that the competitor had violated DuPont's common law rights. Since there was no trespass, the "rights" invaded could only have been rights to the trade secrets themselves rather than a right to prevent trespass, conversion, breach of contract, or other conventional common law wrongs. An alternative interpretation, however, is that the opinion in effect enlarged the concept of a trespass, much as do Fourth Amendment (search and seizure) cases that classify wiretapping as a form of search even though there is technically no trespass because the wiretap is placed on the telephone line outside the suspect's premises.

4. Carpenter v. United States, 484 U.S. 19 (1987). The statute has since been amended to eliminate the requirement.

5. The qualification is in recognition of the manifest limitations that the law imposes on the untrammeled enjoyment of property. Recall, for example, that a copyright does not protect against duplication as such, even though duplication may completely destroy the value of the original, but only against copying.

6. 431 F.2d 1012 (5th Cir. 1970). The decision was cited by the Supreme Court in Kewanee Oil Co. v. Bicron Corp., 416 U.S. 470, 476 n. 5 (1974), for the proposition (not pertinent to *Kewanee* itself, however, where the trade secret was obtained through a breach of contract) that the improper means of obtaining a trade secret that are actionable under trade secret law include "aerial reconnaissance." It has also been cited approvingly in subsequent Fifth Circuit cases, notably Phillips v. Frey, 20 F.3d 623, 630 (5th Cir. 1994), and Alcatel USA, Inc. v. DGI Technologies, Inc., 166 F.3d 772, 784–785 (5th Cir. 1999), but both were cases in which the trade secret was obtained by a misrepresentation. Another Fifth Circuit decision, Hurst v. Hughes Tool Co., 634 F.2d 895 (5th Cir. 1981), contains a ringing endorsement of *Christopher*, but the court found that the defendant had used no improper methods to obtain the plaintiff's trade secret. We have not discovered any cases that are like *Christopher* in the sense of finding misappropriation despite the absence of either a breach of contract or a violation of a common law tort.

There are two other respects in which our statement that there is no law of trade secrets was too bold. The first, which however is not very interesting, is that even though in general an appropriation of a trade secret is unlawful only if it was effectuated through the commission of an independent common law wrong, when it comes time to assess damages or award some other remedy the court will take account of the trade secret's commercial value. But this is no different in principle from valuing personal property in a suit for conversion. Second, it has been argued—and there is nothing to prevent courts from accepting the argument, since common law principles are created by courts and can be revised by them in light of changed circumstances or new understandings—that reverse engineering should be a forbidden method of unmasking a trade secret when it is very cheap to do.[7] When it is costly, the possessor of the trade secret enjoys a measure of de facto protection from the appropriation of his investment in creating the secret; when it is cheap, secrecy fails as protection. We shall see, however, that there are objections to taking this path.

We organize our analysis of trade secrecy law around three questions. The first is why anyone would choose not to patent his trade secret. The second, which is closely related, is why the law permits the possessor of the secret to elect between patent and trade secrecy protection when the secret is of a sort that would be patentable. The third, which turns out to be not merely related but inseparable from the second, is why the law has been reluctant to protect trade secrets as such, or, what is nearly the same question, why it does not provide a remedy against the loss of trade secrets by accident or by reverse engineering.

Incentives for Trade Secrecy

Judges and lawyers have sometimes reasoned that because trade secret law provides less protection to the inventor than patent law does, no rational person who makes a patentable invention would fail to seek a patent; and therefore trade secret law *must* protect a class of lesser inventions, as well as things like customer lists that are not inventions at all. That reasoning is unsound, as we can see by considering three types of case. In the first, the disclosure required by patent law would render the invention worthless; a customer list (an "invention" in the sense of the creation of valuable new information, though not in the ordinary sense of the word) is an example. In the second type of case, the inventor has a patentable invention that he believes no one else would come up with within twenty years (the term of a patent). In the

---

7. See Samuelson and Scotchmer, note 2 above.

third case he has a nonpatentable invention but believes that competitors will require so much time to invent it on their own that he can obtain a substantial return by keeping the invention secret.

The inventor's choice between patent and trade secrecy may seem obvious not only in the first and third cases, where the choice of trade secrecy is foreordained, but also in the second; for does not a patent confer greater protection than secrecy? Not necessarily. The disclosure required by patent law may enable a competitor to invent around the patent in less time than it would take him to discover the inventor's secret. In addition, the required disclosure instructs competitors on how to infringe. Not only is patent litigation very costly,[8] but by suing an infringer a patentee puts his patent at risk of being held invalid, and we know from the last chapter that even under the hospitable regime of the Federal Circuit a high percentage of all challenged patents are held invalid. The net expected benefits of patent infringement must sometimes be positive, or there would be little or no patent infringement litigation. One way to avoid infringement is not to patent.

An invention, moreover, may have only modest value, and obtaining patent protection involves nontrivial fixed costs of preparing the patent application as well as the substantial maintenance fees that we discussed in Chapter 11. Protecting a trade secret avoids these costs. And while it requires expenditures on preventing disclosure of the secret, these should be roughly proportional to the value of the secret to prospective appropriators (only roughly because other factors affect the cost of keeping an invention secret, such as how many people within the company must be privy to it in order for it to be exploited effectively). More resources will be devoted to trying to discover a trade secret the more valuable the secret is believed to be. Since the cost of defense is therefore likely to be low when the secret is of modest value, trade secret protection will often be cheaper than patent protection and the difference may exceed the difference in benefits arising from the fact that patent protection is broader and, in the posited case, lasts longer. In addition, the cost of obtaining a patent must be incurred in every case in which a patent is obtained, regardless of the patent's commercial value, whereas the cost of establishing trade secret protection is incurred only if the secret turns out to be sufficiently valuable to incite someone to try to steal it. Then too, "lasting longer" is not always a source of significant additional value because of discounting to present value, technological change, or shifting consumer prefer-

8. Only about 2 percent of patents are challenged in litigation, but when there is a patent suit and it is not quickly settled, the cost is considerable. The average cost to each party has been estimated at $799,000 through the end of discovery and $1.5 million through trial and appeal. See Mark A. Lemley, "Rational Ignorance at the Patent Office," 95 *Northwestern University Law Review* 1495, 1502 and n. 28 (2001).

ences, and because head-start, learning-curve, and trademark effects may give a first inventor a durable competitive advantage even if he lacks legal protection against duplication.

If we set to one side any difference in cost between obtaining a patent and preserving trade secrecy, the inventor's choice is between patenting the invention for stronger protection and keeping it a trade secret for what he hopes will be a longer time. The existence of the invention will usually lower the expected cost to others of reinventing it, because they will know that reinvention is feasible and so they will not have to budget as much for likely failure. So failure to reinvent will be some evidence that others would not have come up with the invention independently and hence that it is nonobvious and deserving of some legal protection. The law of trade secrets enables this demonstration by increasing the likelihood that anyone who does duplicate the invention will do so by reinventing rather than by stealing it.

Tugging the other way, however, is the possibility that the existence of the invention will reduce the return to reinvention—on the theory that any duplicator would face competition from the original inventor—and hence the incentive to try to reinvent it. But this is unlikely because we are speaking of patentable inventions and the duplicator would be able to get a patent and so (as we'll point out) force the original inventor to abandon his use of the invention. The duplicator's application would not flunk the test of novelty because, as noted in Chapter 11, an invention is not considered one "known or used by others" if the prior knowledge and use were not public. What will tend to delay duplication is that competitors will be denied the benefit of disclosure of the steps composing it, a disclosure that might enable them to invent around it, a form of duplication.

The case of the nonpatentable invention expected by its inventor to yield a substantial return only if it can be kept secret is similar. The fact that the invention is unpatentable probably means that patent law deems it or the class of inventions to which it belongs lacking in utility or novelty, or obvious. By keeping his unpatentable invention secret, the inventor offers to demonstrate that the patent law is wrong. If instead *he* is wrong and the invention turns out to have no commercial applications or someone else invents the same thing the next year (either because his invention is obvious or because it is not novel—it was part of the prior art all along), this proves the government right; so it's as if the inventor had been denied a patent and the patent law preempted trade secret law. But if the inventor is right and there is no duplication, then he gets the approximate reward he would have gotten if the invention were patentable—as he should, at least given the premises of patent law (an important qualification), for he has shown that the government was mistaken in thinking the invention unworthy of patent protection.[9]

This case need not reflect a disagreement between the inventor and the patent authorities, though we have posed it that way. It may simply reflect the fact that patent law cannot be tailored finely enough to cover every case. Everyone may agree that some invention will be made by someone else within six years but since patent law contains no provision for patents that expire in six years, awarding the inventor a patent would substantially overreward him. The Patent and Trademark Office correctly refuses the patent—and the inventor correctly uses trade secret protection instead.

Welfare Effects of Allowing an Inventor to Opt for Trade Secrecy over Patent Protection

To summarize the preceding discussion, rational inventors choose trade secret protection when they think that patent protection is too costly in relation to the value of their invention or will yield them a profit substantially less than that value (as reflected, in part, by the length of time it takes before anyone else duplicates the invention), either because it is not patentable or because the length or breadth of patent protection is insufficient. By preserving the trade secret the inventor demonstrates that his belief was correct. In effect, then, the common law has plugged several economic holes in the patent statute. The holes are big ones, judging from survey results that suggest that on the whole secrecy is preferred to patenting as a method of protecting an invention against being duplicated.[10]

But we have been discussing just the private incentives for trade secrecy and must consider now the social benefits and costs. The longer it takes to duplicate an invention the greater its social value is likely to be; the lag implies that the inventor really made a difference to technological progress, rather than just having discovered something a day before someone else would have discovered it. It does not follow, however, that he should receive a longer period of legal protection. Even though it is desirable that inventive efforts be channeled toward inventions that really matter to society, the extension of protection beyond the twenty-year patent term is un-

9. This was one of the reasons the Supreme Court gave in *Kewanee*, note 6 above, for rejecting the argument that the patent statute preempts the states' common law of trade secrets. See 416 U.S. at 487, 491.

10. See Wesley M. Cohen, Richard R. Nelson, and John P. Walsh, "Protecting Their Intellectual Assets: Appropriability Conditions and Why U.S. Manufacturing Firms Patent (or Not)" (National Bureau of Economic Research Working Paper No. 7552, 2000).

likely to have significant incentive effects, because of discounting to present value.

But it would be a mistake to place too much weight on the effect of trade secret law in sometimes giving an inventor a longer period of legal protection than he would have had he gone the patent route. A more important consideration is that the patent route, because of its cost and required disclosures, often just is not attractive to an inventor of a patentable invention, so that to abolish or curtail trade secrecy would undermine incentives to innovate.

It might seem that the clearest case for trade secrecy would be the invention that is not patentable yet cannot be duplicated quickly without access to its secret. The effect of trade secrecy in encouraging invention in this case must be balanced, however, against the cost that it imposes. That cost is the loss of the information elicited by the disclosure requirement of patent law or revealed by other means—or that would be revealed by other means if there were neither patent law nor trade secrecy law and if the costs of maintaining secrecy, for example by hiring security guards and enforcing employees' covenants not to compete, were prohibitive. Such covenants, by the way, are a common device for protecting trade secrets because it is easier to determine whether a former employee is competing with his former employer than whether he is competing with him with the aid of his former employer's trade secrets. We discuss these covenants further later in this chapter.

Edmund Kitch's prospect theory (see Chapter 11) conceives of a patent as a device for establishing property rights over regions of partially unexplored inventions. From this standpoint the public disclosure that is a condition for obtaining a patent is essentially a boundary marker, serving to head off wasteful duplication of inventive efforts by alerting the competition to the existence of a privileged developer. There is, of course, no public disclosure of a trade secret; so if the goal of patent law is to bring about early and full disclosure while preserving incentives to invent, it may seem that the possessor of a trade secret should be forced to choose between patenting the invention and losing all legal protection. This could be done by a rule making federal patent law preempt state trade secret law, or more precisely bar the use of state common law remedies by possessors of trade secrets. That approach was rejected in the *Kewanee* case.[11] Is its rejection consistent with the prospect theory?

Because an inventor is not ineligible to obtain a patent merely because someone else has made, but has secreted, the invention, the endeavors of the second inventor do not have the futility of endeavors in which an inventor will not be allowed to use his invention because a competitor patented it a day earlier. Indeed, the first inventor, the one who is keeping his invention a

11. See note 6.

secret, cannot patent it once the one-year grace period in which an inventor may use his invention without applying for a patent has expired.[12] Thus trade secret law does not let an inventor play dog in the manger. If he takes the trade secret path and thus (after a year) forfeits his right to seek a patent, he cannot prevent a subsequent inventor from patenting the invention and knocking him out of the market.[13]

Still, and in tension with the prospect theory, if the first inventor were forced to disclose the invention the second inventor would save resources. To that extent trade secret law encourages a duplication of effort that patent law discourages. A further round of analysis, however, suggests that trade secret law may not encourage as much duplication of inventive effort as patent law does. A prime cause of excessive investment by those seeking patent protection is, as we know, that the first to invent will receive the entire profit of the invention (except insofar as that profit is truncated by the limited term of the patent). He will receive it even if he beat the second inventor by only a day, in which event his incremental contribution to social welfare will be much smaller than the value of the invention. The excessive investment resulting from this divergence between private and social benefits is most wasteful when the cost of making the invention is falling rapidly over time; for then, from a social though not a private standpoint, the making of the invention probably should be deferred, though this depends on how great the benefits of the invention are and on the discount rate. Trade secret protection, unlike patent protection, pushes toward the correct social outcome in such a case because the faster the cost of making an invention is falling, the less valuable the invention will be as a trade secret, as the falling cost will increase the likelihood that it will soon be reinvented.

We should consider more carefully the rule mentioned earlier that enables an inventor who manages to duplicate an invention protected only by trade secrecy to patent the duplicate and by doing so prevent the original inventor from continuing to use his invention.[14] This rule, announced by the Federal Circuit in the *Gore* case[15] (and another example of the Federal Circuit's bias in favor of patents), diverges from the rule prevailing in most other countries,

12. See 35 U.S.C. § 102(b); Metallizing Engineering Co. v. Kenyon Bearing & Auto Parts Co., 153 F.2d 516 (2d Cir. 1946) (L. Hand, J.).

13. See W. L. Gore & Associates v. Garlock, Inc., 721 F.2d 1540, 1550 (Fed. Cir. 1983).

14. For an interesting discussion and references, see Vincenzo Denicolò and Luigi Alberto Franzoni, "Patents, Secrets, and the First Inventor Defense" (University of Bologna, Department of Economics, Sept. 2002).

15. See note 13 above. In the First Inventor Defense Act, 35 U.S.C. § 273, a part of the American Inventors Protection Act (1999), Congress adopted what we are calling the foreign rule, but just for business-method patents.

which allows the second inventor to get a patent but the first inventor to continue using the invention without having to obtain a license from the patentee. The effect of the foreign rule is to create a duopoly.

The foreign rule seems preferable on economic grounds to the "American" rule announced in *Gore*. On the one hand, the American rule discourages inventors from going the trade secret route by reducing the expected return from the trade secret, even though that route has private and social advantages over patents for many types of invention. On the other hand, it overrewards the second inventor, who after all has not added to the stock of knowledge but merely duplicated an existing invention—one would have to set an awfully high value on the disclosures required by patent law to think that they make it worthwhile to give a mere reinventor a monopoly. Moreover, the American rule produces the anomaly that the period of monopoly is lengthened while the incentive to innovate is actually diminished. Suppose the first inventor manages to keep his invention secret for ten years, at the end of which time the second inventor obtains a patent. Then the monopoly period will have been extended from twenty years (the term of a patent) to thirty years, yet the original inventor's incentive to invent is reduced by the American rule, as we have seen, while the second inventor is a Johnny-come-lately rather than a real innovator. The American rule does, however, reduce subsequent inventors' incentive to reverse engineer the first invention; and reverse engineering can be costly. The foreign rule reduces the return to the second inventor and (conditional on the second inventor's receiving a patent) enhances competition in the market in which the trade secret and the patent are utilized. This, in turn, lowers prices and increases consumer surplus and thereby increases social welfare.

Another new rule that affects the choice between patent and trade secrecy involves publication of the patent application. Many foreign countries, but not the United States, have long required that the patent application be made public eighteen months after it is filed, whether or not the patent is granted. This creates a strong incentive to go the trade secrecy route, since if the holder of a trade secret is denied a patent he will not be able to fall back on secrecy to protect his invention. In 1999 Congress took a step toward adoption of the foreign rule by providing for making U.S. patent applications public after eighteen months unless the applicant certifies that he is not seeking patent protection in a country that has the eighteen-month rule.[16] It is a small step because an inventor who has applied for a foreign patent has by do-

---

16. See 35 U.S.C. § 122(b); Robert Patrick Merges and John Fitzgerald Duffy, *Patent Law and Policy: Cases and Materials* 62–63 (3d ed. 2002).

ing so assumed the risk that if the patent is denied he will lose his trade secret; and it is a step taken by Congress, not by the pro-patent Federal Circuit.

The Economic Rationale of the Limitations of Trade Secrecy Law

Before we can attempt an overall assessment of trade secret law, we must consider why it is for the most part confined to protecting innovators against conduct that is independently wrongful—that is, that violates some legal principle unrelated to inventive activity. As we know from Chapter 1, the owner of physical property does not lose his property right if he loses the property; there is no legal principle of "finders keepers," although finders may have some rights and property can be lost by abandonment. The owner of a patent does not lose his property right merely because someone else is clever enough to duplicate his invention either by completely independent discovery or by reverse engineering his product without consulting the files of the Patent and Trademark Office, where the invention will be described for all who wish to read. Why does the law deny these rights to the lawful possessor of a trade secret? And should it?

There are two possible answers, or classes of answer. The first focuses on the economic character of a trade secret as information and the second on the economic effects of the different methods of appropriating someone's trade secret.

THE ECONOMIC CHARACTER OF A TRADE SECRET Consider by way of analogy the distinction in international law between lawful and unlawful espionage, a distinction founded in turn on the cooperative nature of the production of information. To ferret out another nation's secrets by patient collation of its published statistics and its newspaper articles or by photography from a spy satellite or by the diligence of one's military attachés stationed in the nation's capital illustrates lawful espionage. The unlawful kind is illustrated by bribery of government employees, by extortion, by kidnapping, and by burglary—in other words, by common law offenses. In part the legal difference is due to the greater cost of preventing espionage of the first kind, and there is a nearly exact parallel in the choice made in trade secret "law" of what tactics of espial to forbid. But that will not explain the tolerance of international law for the military attaché's nosing about. The explanation must be reciprocity. We allow other nations to station military attachés in our country as a condition of their allowing us to station our military attachés in their countries. This reciprocity yields net gains because a nation that wants to deter its adversaries must be able to communicate a credible, if inexact, notion of its strength. It does this by opening itself part way to the first-hand scrutiny of its adversaries' trained professionals. This is a more credible mode of demonstrating strength than bragging about it. A nation that refused to allow foreign military attachés would be communicating either weakness or that it was planning a surprise attack and so wanted at once to look weak and to conceal its preparatory measures.

The qualification in "part way" should be stressed. No nation wants to reveal all its secrets, lest this invite countermeasures by potential enemies. Revealing all might signal strength yet would beget weakness. The military-attaché system allows some secrets to be kept.

Corresponding to considerations of reciprocity that lead nations to agree to provide some but not all information to their competitors are considerations of reciprocity in the inventive process that arise from the fact that every producer of information is also a consumer of information. As we have emphasized throughout this book, a basic input into the production of information is other information. Ex ante, every producer of information wants access to his competitors' information as well as protection of his own.[17] The law strikes a balance between these inconsistent desires in the domain of trade secrets by prohibiting only the most costly means of unmasking such secrets. They are costly in major part because of the defensive maneuvers they incite.[18] For example, if the law refused to enforce contracts in which employees promise not to spill their employer's' trade secrets (or not to compete with their employer), employers might be led to reorganize their businesses in a manner that might be grossly inefficient were it not for the imperative of secrecy. They might move their operations to jurisdictions that protect trade secrecy, pay much higher wages so that employees would be reluctant to quit (taking the employer's trade secrets with them), split up tasks among more employees so that each knows less, or employ family members even though they may be less competent, counting on them to be loyal out of altruism or because the family setting often enables effective, informal retaliation against the disloyal, members of a family being in an ongoing relationship, unlike the employer and an unrelated former employee. With the possessor of a trade secret unable to protect it even imperfectly by licensing, there would be

17. The point is made with reference to patents in Suzanne Scotchmer, "Standing on the Shoulders of Giants: Cumulative Research and the Patent Law," *Journal of Economic Perspectives,* Winter 1991, p. 29.

18. See Kewanee Oil Co. v. Bicron Corp., note 6 above, 416 U.S. at 485–487. *Kewanee,* and an earlier opinion of the Second Circuit, written by Judge Henry Friendly, Painton & Co. v. Bourns, Inc., 442 F.2d 216 (2d Cir. 1971), are good treatments of the economics of trade secret law. For a list of defensive measures, see Randy Kay, "A Distance Runner's Guide to Trade Secret Protection—Maintaining Secrecy," *San Diego Business Journal,* June 5, 2000, p. 31.

no way in which his invention could be used in other industries—or indeed by anyone except himself,[19] even, as we noted in Chapter 11, if he were an inefficient producer; so there would be underspecialization. Legal protections of trade secrets are an attractive substitute for such costly defensive maneuvers.

But not all the possible legal protections. Suppose the law forbade reverse engineering, a common method of unlocking trade secrets. Such a prohibition would eliminate the social benefits arising from the fact that when manufacturers are permitted to reverse engineer each other's products they learn things that they can put to use in their own design of new products. To forbid reverse engineering would inhibit the development of products that do not even compete with the one that has been reverse engineered. This cannot be the last word, however, since the cheaper reverse engineering is, the more limited the protection that trade secrecy law gives new inventions. To the extent that trade secrecy allows socially valuable but nonpatentable inventions to be protected from immediate duplication, reverse engineering is a mixed blessing from a social as well as a private standpoint. We shall have to come back to this issue.

Employees' covenants not to compete with their former employer for a period of years are an important method of protecting trade secrets, because it is easier to detect and prove a violation of such a covenant than it is to discover and prove that a competitor's discovery of one's trade secret is the result of unlawful appropriation rather than of independent research. A well-known study compares high-tech firms located along Route 128 outside of Boston with similar firms in Silicon Valley.[20] Massachusetts enforces employee covenants not to compete; California does not. The study finds as one would expect that in Silicon Valley employees move around more among firms, no doubt often taking some of their previous employers' trade secrets with them. The resulting pooling of knowledge may, however, contribute more to technological progress than the greater internalization of new technological ideas that a more effective scheme for the protection of trade secrets would contribute, provided that employers in Silicon Valley do not substitute for the unenforceable covenants not to compete even more costly methods of protecting trade secrets; but we have not heard this suggested. In principle, competitors possessing "blocking" trade secrets can share them through cross-licensing, but negotiation and enforcement of licenses for the use of valuable confidential information are quite costly; as we noted earlier,

---

19. He could sell the secret, but how do you do that when there is no legal protection of trade secrets, without revealing it to the prospective purchaser?

20. AnnaLee Saxenian, *Regional Advantage: Culture and Competition in Silicon Valley and Route 128* (1994).

it is a very delicate art to negotiate for the revelation of a secret without the negotiation itself unmasking it.[21] The informal pooling that comes from the unenforceability of employee covenants not to compete may be on balance more efficient. The point is closely related to the suggestion in Chapter 11 that patents may be counterproductive in an industry in which innovation is sequential and complementary—and in fact the study we cited there was of the software industry, the major high-tech industry in Silicon Valley.

THE ECONOMIC CHARACTERISTICS OF THE METHODS OF AP-PROPRIATING TRADE SECRETS AND OF PREVENTING THEIR AP-PROPRIATION   We have already begun considering these, but a formal model will be helpful in moving the analysis toward a conclusion. Assume that a firm can lose its trade secret either through theft or other common law wrong on the one hand or through accidental disclosure or reverse engineering on the other. We denote the loss in either case by L and the probability that the loss will occur through a common law wrong by p, which is lower the greater the scope of legal protection and the greater the firm's own expenditures (x) on preventing the loss. The probability of loss through accidental disclosure or reverse engineering we denote by q and the firm's expenditures on preventing this type of loss by y.

The firm wants to minimize the sum of its expected loss from losing the trade secret and its costs of preventing that loss, a sum we denote by L^*. Assuming for simplicity that the firm sells a single unit of output having a cost that is independent of the costs of protecting the firm's trade secrets, and at a given price, we can rewrite L^* as

$$L^* = [p(x)(1 - q(y)) + q(y)(1 - p(x)) + q(y)p(x)]L + x + y. \quad (1)$$

To minimize L^* (assuming diminishing marginal effects of x and y), the firm will choose an x and a y such that

$$p_x(1 - q)L + 1 = 0 \text{ and } q_y(1 - p)L + 1 = 0. \quad (2)$$

Thus the greater the value of the trade secret (that is, the greater L is), and so the more productive the expenditures on preventing its being lost whether through theft or other common law wrong on the one hand or through accident or reverse engineering on the other hand, the more resources the firm will invest in protecting the trade secret.

Consider the effect of a law that prohibits theft or other common law wrong (theft for short) but not loss through accident or through reverse en-

---

21. Such licenses appear to be rare. See Cheung, note 1 above, at 45; also Bone, note 2 above, at 280.

gineering. Such indeed is American trade secret law, and if enforced should reduce x compared to a world without any legal protection of trade secrets. Since the threat of legal sanctions will deter at least some potential thieves, the probability of losing the secret through a common law wrong will be lower with that law in effect. The assumption of diminishing marginal effect suggests in turn that the lower p is, the less productive will units of x be. In theory, public and private expenditures on preventing theft could be complements rather than substitutes. But this is unlikely. Even without a law against the outright theft of trade secrets (for example, by burglary), a firm could do a lot to reduce the probability of such thefts, for example by screening employees more carefully and by installing more effective security systems. It will do less if the threat of legal sanctions deters the theft of its trade secrets.

A more interesting point is that x will probably be lower if trade secret law does not provide a remedy against loss through accident or reverse engineering than if it does. If it does not, the probability of the trade secret's being lost in that way may be high, and since the trade secret is therefore likely to be lost regardless of expenditures on preventing theft, the productivity of those expenditures is reduced. As for y (expenditures on reducing the probability of the loss of a trade secret through accident or reverse engineering), it will be higher than if the law protected against accidental loss and reverse engineering as well as against theft. With theft unlawful and therefore less frequent, the gains from preventing loss by accident or reverse engineering are greater because the trade secret is not likely to be lost anyway—that is, by theft—which would reduce the productivity of expenditures on preventing its loss by other means.

The welfare effects of trade secret law in the model are complicated, but they do not imply that protection of trade secrets should be greater than under existing law. One component of L^*, namely L, the lost profit of the holder of the trade secret if the secret is revealed, is a private but not necessarily a social cost. Competitors could make productive use of the information embodied in the trade secret; society would benefit from this use; and the benefit would offset part of the loss to the inventor and maybe all of it. Thus the theft of a trade secret does not have the identical economic significance as an ordinary theft. Apart from the greater difficulty of determining by the methods of litigation whether the seeming appropriation of information is actually a theft rather than independent rediscovery, which is hardly a problem in the case of theft of physical property, there is the fact that the trade secret "thief" brings about a social gain not present in thefts of physical property (with trivial exceptions). The social gain is approximated by the reduction in cost or the improvement in quality brought about by the greater competition that comes from eliminating the information monopoly of the possessor of the trade secret. But this gain is likely to be offset by the sum of the social cost (similar in the two types of case) imposed by the theft, measured by the resources expended on attempting and opposing an involuntary transfer of wealth, and of the reduction in the incentive to invent.

The other component of L^* is the cost of preserving secrecy $(x + y)$, and we have seen that if trade secrets are protected only against theft, the first component is likely to be smaller than if the legal protection is broader, although the second component is likely to be larger.

In sum, there is no compelling reason for enlarging trade secret protection; and a reason for not doing so is that in a regime in which trade secrets were protected against appropriation by such means, the costs that competitors would have to incur in order to avoid infringing would be likely to exceed y, the cost to the possessor of the secret of preventing its disclosure. This is clearer in the case of accidental loss than of reverse engineering, so let us begin there.

Firms would find it very costly to sift through all the information they received in order to determine whether some of it might be information that the possessor of a trade secret had accidentally "mislaid." This is a case in which, unlike the finder cases discussed in Chapter 1, the cost of care is so much lower to the potential victim (the owner of the trade secret) than to the potential injurer (the competitor) that a rule of no liability is more efficient than a liability rule. Recognition of this point is implicit in the rule that the possessor of a trade secret cannot complain even about its deliberate theft unless he has taken meaningful measures to preserve its secrecy.[22] This is an exception to the principle that there is no defense of contributory negligence to an intentional tort. If A steals B's wallet, he has committed the tort of conversion, and it is no defense that B was careless to leave his wallet in a place where it could easily be stolen. The exception recognizes that a trade secret is not visible physical property (like the wallet, or like a fenced piece of land or for that matter a piece of land whose boundaries are specified in a deed in a land registry), but merely information that the possessor wants to keep secret. Most information that people and firms possess they do not care about keeping secret and the use of that information by others without the possessor's consent is therefore not wrongful. But these others cannot know what information the possessor considers a trade secret unless he makes it clear by taking measures to prevent unauthorized persons from learning it. That is why the accidental appropriation of a trade secret is a real possibility

22. See, for example, Pioneer Hi-Bred International v. Holden Foundation Seeds, Inc., 35 F.3d 1226, 1235–1236 (8th Cir. 1994); Rockwell Graphic Systems, Inc. v. DEV Industries, Inc., 925 F.2d 174 (7th Cir. 1991).

and the burden of avoiding it placed on the possessor of the secret rather than on potential appropriators.

In the case of the appropriation of a trade secret by theft, in contrast, not only would self-protection by potential victims involve heavy expenditures, but the cost to the potential injurer of committing an intentional tort, that is, the cost of *not* investing resources designed to effect a transfer of wealth, is actually negative, since real resources are consumed in the measures taken to accomplish the theft.[23] This point has to be balanced, however, against the point in the preceding paragraph about requiring the possessor of a trade secret to take some precautions against its unmasking because otherwise no one will know it is secret rather than public information. We want him to take *some* precautions, but not too many. The *Christopher* case struck the right balance. The fact that DuPont did not roof its construction site could not reasonably be interpreted as a signal that everything going on at the site was public information. A decision in favor of Christopher would have induced firms in DuPont's position to invest heavily in roofing their construction sites. In addition, Christopher expended resources on hiring an airplane and pilot in order to appropriate DuPont's trade secret. Liability would deter him in the future from incurring such costs and would eliminate DuPont's incentive to expend resources on building a roof for the sole purpose of discouraging rent-seeking activities of competitors.

We cannot be as confident about the economically correct legal treatment of reverse engineering as we are about that of accidental loss. A competitor will usually know when he is engaged in reverse engineering and he should therefore be able to comply readily enough with a prohibition against the practice, as would not be true of liability for accidental appropriation of a trade secret. If reverse engineering is allowed, the possessor of a trade secret may incur costs in design or production intended to make his product more difficult to reverse engineer. And there is the argument by Pamela Samuelson and Suzanne Scotchmer that when reverse engineering is very cheap, trade secrecy ceases to be a viable means of enabling inventors to recover the fixed costs of inventing.[24]

There are, however, two arguments against imposing legal liability for reverse engineering. First, if a competitor duplicates someone's trade secret, it will often be difficult to prove or disprove that he did it by reverse engineering rather than by independent research; and the error costs of the litigation process are an important constraint on the optimal scope of legal liability.

23. See William M. Landes and Richard A. Posner, *The Economic Structure of Tort Law*, ch. 6 (1987).

24. See note 2.

Second, as we noted earlier, reverse engineering will often generate knowledge about the product being reverse engineered that will make it possible to improve it or develop or improve other products. Here the analogy to our espionage case, to the case of incremental creativity in copyright, and to the patentability of improvements is close. Ex ante, the members of an industry might agree to allow reverse engineering of each other's products, knowing that all would have a net expected gain since reverse engineering frequently results in product improvements. Recognition of this point in the semiconductor industry has given rise to a distinction, codified in the Semiconductor Chip Protection Act of 1984,[25] between piracy and acceptable reverse engineering—the latter involving substantial investment and innovation.[26]

The fact that reverse engineering usually is quite costly, moreover, automatically cuts down on the amount of free riding on the first inventor. But of course this is the basis for the argument that reverse engineering when cheap should be prohibited in order to enhance incentives for inventive activity. Indeed, from an economic standpoint there is little distinction between *really* cheap reverse engineering on the one hand and piracy on the other. And it could be that the only reason *observed* reverse engineering is usually costly is that when it is cheap the inventions that can be reverse engineered are not developed in the first place or are patented.

A law that forbade deliberately appropriating trade secrets by either theft or reverse engineering would be closely analogous to copyright law, which penalizes copying. It would provide less protection of intellectual property than patent law does because it would still allow independent invention, as patent law does not; but it would go further than copyright law, which allows the copying of ideas and forbids only the copying of expression. A law that forbade without limitation of term the copying of productive ideas would thus impose greater access costs than copyright law does; whether there would be commensurate benefits is unknown. Such a law might even be more protective of inventors than patent law, since it would confer rights of unlimited duration and not require public disclosure, although it would not bar independent discovery. Use of trade secret law, a body of state law, to create such superpatents would pose serious problems of conflict with patent law and so present an issue of preemption of state by federal law.

Notice that in both the copyright and trade secret cases an alternative to allowing extensive copying is to rely on voluntary transactions. An author who

25. 17 U.S.C. §§ 901 et seq. See also id., § 906.
26. See Leo J. Raskind, "Reverse Engineering, Unfair Competition, and Fair Use," 70 *Minnesota Law Review* 385 (1985). Compare the Digital Millennium Copyright Act, which as we noted in Chapter 2 forbids reverse engineering of encryption devices to facilitate unauthorized electronic copying of copyrighted recordings.

wanted to use a plotline in another author's novel could negotiate a license from him, and firms that wanted to reverse engineer each other's products could enter into cross-licensing agreements permitting this; these would be like R&D joint ventures. Transaction costs might well be high, however, and those costs would make theft of trade secrets a more attractive substitute for contract than it is under current law.

One possible solution to these uncertainties would be to forbid reverse engineering but have a broad fair use defense for cases in which the reverse engineering involved a significant investment and produced significant new information; but such an approach would involve a high degree of uncertainty in application and so give rise to substantial costs of judicial administration. So about all that is clear concerning the appropriate scope of trade secrecy law is that obtaining a trade secret by force or fraud (what together we are describing as "theft") should be punishable because of the heavy costs that would be incurred in self-help remedies against such incursions if they were lawful and the damage to the incentive to invent that would be produced. It is not clear that reverse engineering should be forbidden or even limited. It is not even clear that enforcing employee covenants not to compete generates social benefits in excess of its social costs. We do support, however, the slight extension of trade secrecy law represented by the *Christopher* case, though it could be regarded as really just a slight extension of the law of trespass to take account of the fact that in the age of flight the concept of trespass may require redefinition. One can imagine similar extensions, for example to limit the use of nontrespassory means of electronic surveillance of a competitor's secret processes.

Once it is conceded that there should be legal remedies against the appropriation of trade secrets at least by force or fraud, the argument for having some kind of patent law is greatly strengthened even if the social benefits of patents in internalizing innovation externalities are sharply discounted for the reasons discussed in Chapter 11. For as we noted at the end of that chapter, if trade secrecy were the only way of preventing the appropriation of significant classes of commercially valuable information—if obtaining a patent were never an alternative—heavy costs arising from measures to maintain and uncover trade secrets would be incurred, inventive activity would be excessively biased in favor of projects that could be concealed, and transfers of technology across industries would be inhibited. The point emphasized in this chapter is that the complementarity of patent and trade secret law runs in both directions. Not only does patent law solve problems of trade secret law, but trade secret law plugs gaps and softens rigidities in patent law.

14

Antitrust and Intellectual Property

Many important antitrust cases have involved intellectual property; and the rights of owners of intellectual property have been shaped (mostly limited) to a great degree by antitrust law. Then, too, it is widely believed that intellectual property law and antitrust law are enemies—that intellectual property authorizes patent and copyright (and perhaps also trademark and trade secret) monopolies that offend antitrust principles. A consideration of the economics of intellectual property would be seriously incomplete without some discussion of the intersection between intellectual property law and antitrust law.[1]

Patent Tie-Ins and Other Forbidden Attempts to "Extend" the Patent Monopoly

In general, though with numerous exceptions, the older cases that apply antitrust principles to intellectual property involve patents and the newer ones copyrights. The oldest cases were technically not antitrust cases at all but patent misuse cases. Patent misuse is a judge-made doctrine that forfeits patent protection (or provides other relief, if forfeiture is infeasible, as in the *Brulotte* case that we'll be discussing shortly) if the patent owner uses the patent in an improper way. The principal patent misuse cases that presented issues of antitrust policy were cases in which the patent owner conditioned the use of his patented process or product on the licensee's buying another, unpatented product from him, as when the patentee of a mimeograph machine required his licensees to agree to buy the ink they used in the machine from him.[2] After the enactment of section 3 of the Clayton Act in 1914,[3]

1. We can only scratch the surface of what has become an enormous field in its own right. See Herbert Hovenkamp, Mark D. Janis, and Mark A. Lemley, *IP and Antitrust: An Analysis of Antitrust Principles Applied to Intellectual Property Law* (2002) (two volumes).
2. Henry v. A. B. Dick Co., 224 U.S. 1 (1912).
3. 15 U.S.C. § 14.

cases challenging the tying of unpatented to patented products were generally brought as federal antitrust suits rather than litigated under the patent misuse doctrine.[4] The theory of these cases was that by denying the buyer the use of the tying product (the patented product or process) unless he agreed to buy a separate product from the seller as well, the seller was trying to "leverage" or "extend" his monopoly to the market for that separate product—only extending it in product space rather than in time. This reasoning does not make good economic sense. If the seller tries to charge a monopoly price for the separate product, the buyer will not be willing to pay as much for the tying product as he would if the separate product, which he has to buy also, were priced lower. The two products are complements; raising the price of one reduces the demand for the other. Acquiring monopoly power in the tied-product market thus comes at the expense of losing profits in the tying-product market.

Tie-ins are a fact, but they are adopted (when allowed by the law) not to enable a seller to use his existing monopoly to acquire a second monopoly but for other reasons, such as to facilitate price discrimination. In the *Dick* (mimeograph) case,[5] the price that licensees of the mimeograph machine were willing to pay for its use was probably more or less proportional to the amount of use they envisaged and so to the amount of ink they used. Requiring them to buy the ink from Dick enabled Dick to vary the effective price they paid for the machine according to their elasticity of demand, as proxied by the amount of ink they consumed; the more they used the machine the more value they were getting from it, and so the more they were willing to pay for it in the absence of a competitively priced close substitute. Since the law permits price discrimination (with immaterial exceptions), there is no reason why it should forbid tie-ins and thus force sellers to resort to less efficient means of discrimination—if they were more efficient, a prohibition would be unnecessary[6]—unless the tie-in has a sinister purpose; we shall see that sometimes it may.

Tie-ins can be adopted for other reasons that, like price discrimination, should not raise antitrust hackles. These reasons are easiest to grasp when the

4. See, for example, International Business Machines Corp. v. United States, 298 U.S. 131 (1936); Morton Salt Co. v. G. S. Suppiger Co., 314 U.S. 488 (1942); International Salt Co. v. United States, 332 U.S. 392 (1947).

5. See note 2.

6. Benjamin Klein and John Shepard Wiley, Jr., "Competitive Price Discrimination as an Antitrust Justification for Refusals to Deal" (UCLA Department of Economics and School of Law, 2002), explains the ways in which price discrimination by means of tie-ins or other oblique-seeming means can be more efficient than merely charging different prices to different groups of buyers.

tying product is not a patent or copyright but either a trademark or a product embodying a trade secret. The owner of a trademark, as we know from Chapter 7, cannot preserve his right to use the trademark unless he maintains consistent quality. This may be easier to do by supplying complementary products himself than by licensing their manufacture. The owner of a trade secret may be reluctant to license the manufacture of complementary products lest in specifying his requirements he give away his secret or at least make reverse engineering easier.[7] Moreover, the tied product may itself embody trade secrets (suppose the effectiveness of Dick's mimeograph machine depended on Dick's secret process for manufacturing ink that would work best in the machine), and as noted in earlier chapters it is costly to license a trade secret.

Most copyrights, trademarks, and trade secrets confer little in the way of monopoly power. The situation is less clear regarding patents (though we noted in Chapter 11 estimates that fewer than 3 percent of all patents generate any royalties and fewer than 5 percent are licensed), and so it is not surprising that courts in the early patent tie-in cases tended to confuse patent "monopolies" with monopolies that have economic consequences grave enough to warrant the invocation of antitrust prohibitions. This confusion led judges to suppose that there is an inherent tension between intellectual property law, because it confers "monopolies," and antitrust law, which is dedicated to overthrowing monopolies. That was a mistake. At one level it is a confusion of a property right with a monopoly. One does not say that the owner of a parcel of land has a monopoly because he has the right to exclude others from using the land. But a patent or a copyright is a monopoly in the same sense. It excludes other people from using some piece of intellectual property without consent. That in itself has no antitrust significance. Arnold Plant was mistaken to think that rights in physical property alleviate scarcity and rights in intellectual property create it (see Introduction). Information is a scarce good, just like land. Both are commodified—that is, made excludable property—in order to create incentives to alleviate their scarcity. Talk of patent and copyright "monopolies" is conventional; we have used this terminology ourselves in this book. The usage is harmless as long as it is understood to be different from how the same word is used in antitrust analysis.

What is true, as correctly observed by Plant, is that the grant of an exclusive right to intellectual property may restrict access to the property more than is necessary to secure the social advantages of property rights. When it does so, the exclusive right is monopolistic in an invidious sense. The *average* patent, however, confers too little monopoly power on the patentee in a

---

7. See Philip E. Areeda, *Antitrust Law: An Analysis of Antitrust Principles and Their Application*, vol. 9, ¶ 1716f, pp. 207–211 (1991).

meaningful economic sense to interest a rational antitrust enforcer, and sometimes it confers no monopoly power at all—think of defensive patents, and of the many patents that are never licensed or if licensed never produce royalties for the licensor. Of course a patentee could not discriminate, and therefore would not adopt a tie-in, if he faced a perfectly elastic demand curve. But as long as it is not perfectly elastic, price discrimination will, depending on its cost (including the cost of preventing arbitrage), be feasible, because for a demand curve not to be perfectly elastic *means* that different customers are willing to pay different prices, or the same customers different prices for different quantities, or both. Price discrimination is common in industries that though competitive do not sell a totally uniform, fungible product—and is pervasive in markets for intellectual property, even though those markets usually are competitive—yet has no known adverse effects on efficiency sufficient to warrant the expense and uncertainty of antitrust liability. Think of so paltry an example of an intellectual property "monopoly" as a book published by an academic press dealing with the Black Sea grain trade during the first decade of the Roman Empire. The press might have a choice between charging $30 per copy with an expected sale of 600 copies and $50 with an expected sale of 300 copies; this would show that it faced a downward-sloping demand curve.

Edmund Kitch rejects this way of analyzing the issue of intellectual property "monopolies." Quoting a statement in an article by us that "the demand curve for copies of a given book is . . . negatively sloped because there are good but not perfect substitutes for a given book," he argues that while "it is obviously true that one book is not an exact copy of another . . . that does not mean that two or more books are not economic substitutes for each other"; and he accuses us of contradicting ourselves in maintaining both that the demand for a given copyrighted book is not perfectly elastic and that copyrights rarely confer monopolies.[8] He denies that tie-ins are a form of price discrimination, arguing that the belief that they are is an artifact of how the product is described; if it is described not as the number of machines sold but as "number of hours of use, amount of throughput, or machine cycles," the price is uniform.[9]

Kitch makes the mistake of treating monopoly and competition as dichotomous. He thinks (or at least by his choice of words implies) that if a product has "economic substitutes," it is a perfectly competitive product like wheat and so the producer cannot price discriminate. But monopoly and perfect

8. Edmund W. Kitch, "Elementary and Persistent Errors in the Economic Analysis of Intellectual Property," 53 *Vanderbilt Law Review* 1727, 1734–1735 (2000).
9. Id. at 1738.

competition do not exhaust the economic universe. This becomes clear as soon as the focus is switched from the question of monopoly versus competition to the question how elastic is the demand for a given good.[10] If demand is highly elastic, this implies the existence of very close substitutes and as a result too little monopoly power to worry about, with perfect competition (infinite elasticity) being the limiting case. The less elastic the demand, the poorer the substitutes and the greater the concern with monopoly power, that is, with a divergence between price and marginal cost brought about by the seller's reducing his output in order to create an artificial scarcity that will increase the market price of his good.

The possible price range is broad. The formula for the profit-maximizing monopolist's markup over the competitive price (assuming that marginal cost is constant over the full output range between the monopoly and competitive outputs) is

$$\frac{P_m}{P_c} = \frac{\varepsilon}{\varepsilon - 1} \tag{1}$$

Thus if the elasticity of demand (ε) for the firm's product is 100 (technically, -100, since price and demand are inverse), the monopoly price will exceed the competitive price by roughly 1 percent, while if the elasticity of demand is 2 the monopoly price will be twice the competitive price.

If demand elasticities for intellectual property were very high, particularly in the short run, no such property would be created in a free-market system. A producer of intellectual property cannot recover his fixed costs by selling his product at a price equal to marginal cost, and intellectual property cannot be created without incurring fixed costs, namely the costs of creating it before sales commence.[11] We emphasize short-run elasticity because if the elasticity is low in the short run though high in the long run, the producer may

10. We are speaking of course of elasticity of demand with respect to price.

11. A qualification should be noted: it is the ratio of fixed to variable (and hence marginal) costs that makes pricing equal to marginal cost unremunerative, not the existence of fixed costs itself. A firm in a perfectly competitive market may have substantial fixed costs. A wheat farmer, for example, is likely to have substantial fixed costs in the form of land and buildings, but as long as he faces rising marginal costs he need have no difficulty covering his fixed costs even though competition constrains him to set a price equal to his marginal cost. Suppose the cost of producing his first unit of output is $1, his second $2, his third $3, and so forth; his fixed costs are $10; and the market price is $5. Then he will produce five units, incurring total variable costs of $15 ($1 + $2 + $3 + $4 + $5), but obtaining a revenue of $25 ($5 x 5), enough to cover his fixed costs of $10. If, however, the variable cost of each of the first four units were $4, so that his total variable costs were $21 (4 x $4 + $5), he could recover only $4 of his fixed costs ($25 − $21). That is the typical situation faced by producers of intellectual property, with the limiting case being the one in which marginal cost is zero at all levels of output.

be able to recover his fixed costs during the brief period in which he has a "monopoly" or to use that period to obtain a learning-curve advantage that will enable him to outcompete his competitors when they begin to imitate him. Possibilities such as this make it difficult to be confident that either copyright or patent law is actually necessary to create incentives for the production of an optimal quantity of intellectual property. But our only point is that since the demand for a given piece of intellectual property will invariably be downward sloping, and since price discrimination will usually be profit maximizing if arbitrage can be limited at reasonable cost, intellectual property will often be priced discriminatorily even though most of it has "economic substitutes."

Kitch's redescription of tying as the charging of a uniform price for an appropriately recharacterized product is also mistaken. It confuses price with utility. The fact that some people get more use from their mimeograph machine and as a result get greater value from it does not mean, in any sense relevant to economic analysis, that they are buying a different product from the low-volume users. It is because different users get different utility from the *same* product that the producer, if he can at reasonable cost prevent arbitrage or other substitution, can increase his profits by charging different prices to different users even though his cost of serving the different users is identical, as implied by its being the same product. Of course there are cases in which because of location, creditworthiness, volume, or other factors the cost of selling the same product varies across customers; but a cost-based price difference, unlike one based on a difference in the elasticity of demand of different customers, is not price discrimination, at least in an economic sense. But it makes no economic sense to say that if A drives his car 100,000 miles a year and B drives an identical car 10,000 miles per year, then if the manufacturer charges A \$50,000 and B \$5,000 there is no price discrimination because each buyer pays the same price per mile driven.

A related but more sophisticated criticism of our position is made by Benjamin Klein and John Wiley.[12] They recognize that tying is a method of price discrimination and that the ability to discriminate presupposes that the firm doing the discriminating faces a downward-sloping demand curve. But they urge a distinction between a firm's power over its own price and a firm's power to affect the market price, and they would reserve the term "market power" (or monopoly power) for the latter situation. The firm is part of the market, however, and so its price and therefore output decisions will affect the market price and output. Suppose that by discriminating the firm reduces its output (a possible though not inevitable outcome of discrimination, as we noted in Chapter 2, where we pointed out that the effect of discrimination on output is indeterminate, unless the discrimination is perfect, which is impossible). If the other firms in the market face upward-sloping marginal cost curves, so that expanding output would require them to raise their price, the output of the entire market will be reduced and average price will rise. This is obvious if the elasticity of supply is zero, but the point holds so long as that elasticity is not infinite.

We are not suggesting that price discrimination be forbidden. In a competitive market it may well expand output by enabling a seller to pick up some buyers who were unwilling to pay his initial, uniform price but are willing to pay a lower price that is, however, above his marginal cost; and competition may prevent him from raising his price significantly to less elastic demanders. That would illustrate Klein and Wiley's thesis. The larger the market share of the discriminating firm, however, the greater the likelihood that price discrimination will enable it to charge higher as well as lower prices by segmenting its market, with indeterminate impact on its overall output. Klein and Wiley point out that, precisely because that impact is indeterminate, price discrimination of intellectual property increases the incentive effects of intellectual property protection without reducing (on average) access. But that is not a compelling argument for price discrimination, since, as we have emphasized throughout this book, no one knows whether the present level of intellectual property protection is optimal. Remember that increasing the incentive to create intellectual property beyond the level necessary to induce the socially optimal production of such property will result in socially costly rent-seeking activities. In general, it seems better to consider price discrimination a neutral phenomenon from a normative economic standpoint rather than something to be discouraged or encouraged.

In any event, market power is pervasive. Recall the discussion of monopolistic competition in Chapter 11. A barber shop has a locational monopoly, so each shop is able to charge a price above marginal cost and can therefore discriminate, for example by charging the same price for cutting the hair of a balding man as of a bushy-haired one.[13] If transportation improvements eliminated these locational monopolies, barber shop prices would be lower and more uniform; discrimination would cease. Obviously, in the absence of such improvements, no one is going to worry about the pricing of barbers' services, but still it is higher than it would be were it not for the presence of market power. The "no worry" point is fundamental, however, to analyzing the antitrust implications of intellectual property, because the vast majority of

---

13. Charging the same price for two goods that have different marginal costs is the same phenomenon from an economic standpoint as charging different prices for two goods that have the same marginal cost.

copyrights, patents, and other intellectual property rights confer no more monopoly power on the owner of the right than owning the only barber shop within a five-block radius does. We therefore welcome a recent decision by the Federal Circuit that has been criticized as declaring open season on copyright tying.[14]

A different objection to casual talk about patent and copyright "monopolies" is that it implicitly views competition as the state in which there are many firms competing to sell the same product rather than as the state in which society's scarce resources are being exploited as efficiently as possible. From the latter standpoint, which is more directly related to economic welfare, excluding others from the use of property either physical or intellectual may be procompetitive even if the result is a reduction in the number of competitors or a divergence from perfect competition (that is, pricing at marginal cost). If making intellectual property excludable creates value, the efficient allocation of resources may be improved even if an economic and not merely a nominal legal monopoly is created. This is the insight that underlies Joseph Schumpeter's influential theory of innovation.[15] Suppose a market has ten competitors each selling their output at a price equal to their marginal cost (which also equals each firm's minimum average cost) of $5, and along comes an innovator who discovers how to produce the product for only $2. He charges a price just below $5 and as a result takes over the entire market because he is charging a price below the existing firms' cost, and he is prevented from raising his price above $5 by the threat of inducing re-entry by the former competitors or new entry by another innovator. Although monopoly has replaced competition and price has soared above marginal cost, resources have been freed up for use in other economic production even though price may have fallen only slightly or not at all. In short, economic welfare—the goal of a competitive economy—has risen compared to the pre-innovation state. The concern about monopoly pricing is misplaced in such a case. To argue that economic welfare would be even higher if all firms had access to the innovation at zero cost ignores the fact that the innovation

---

14. See In re Independent Service Organizations Antitrust Litigation, 203 F.3d 1322 (Fed. Cir. 2000). Actually the case did not involve tying as such, but instead a refusal by Xerox to supply patented replacement parts and diagnostic software to firms that would use them to impede Xerox's efforts to prevent arbitrage, and would thus undermine Xerox's discriminating in price. But analytically such a refusal to deal is the same thing as tying, as will become clearer as the discussion in this chapter proceeds.

15. Schumpeter's theory is updated, refined, and extended in Richard R. Nelson and Sidney G. Winter, *An Evolutionary Theory of Economic Change,* pt. 5 (1982). See also Albert N. Link, "Firm Size and Efficient Entrepreneurial Activity: A Reformulation of the Schumpeter Hypothesis," 88 *Journal of Political Economy* 771 (1980).

might not be developed if the innovator did not receive a property right in the innovation.

The same thing is true if the innovation is not cost reducing but rather demand increasing. Suppose that by dint of investing in product improvements, an innovator succeeds in differentiating his product from the products of his competitors. The result will be to increase the demand for his product and as a result increase his price. Both consumer and producer surplus will increase, provided the increase in demand is less than the cost increase of the innovation. An act that simultaneously increases a firm's market power and creates new consumer and producer surplus is not a strong candidate for condemnation under antitrust law.

The most dubious application of the thinking that informed the early patent tie-in cases came in the Supreme Court's much later decision in *Brulotte v. Thys Co.*,[16] which held that a patent owner may not enforce a contract for the payment of patent royalties beyond the patent's expiration date.[17] The Court reasoned that by extracting a promise to continue paying royalties after expiration of the patent, the patentee had extended the patent beyond the statutory term and therefore in violation of the law. That is wrong. After the patent expires, anyone can make the patented process or product without being guilty of patent infringement. As the patent can no longer be used to exclude anybody from such production, expiration has accomplished what it was supposed to accomplish. If the licensee agrees to continue paying royalties after the patent expires, the royalty rate will be lower during the period before expiration. The duration of the patent fixes the limit of the patentee's power to extract royalties; it is a detail whether he extracts them at a higher rate over a shorter period of time or at a lower rate over a longer period of time. Charging royalties beyond the term of the patent merely alters the timing of royalty payments, as would be obvious if a patent-licensing agreement obligating the licensee to pay royalties for the next 100 years went into effect a day before the patent expired. The royalty *rate* would be minuscule because of the imminence of the patent's expiration. And, to repeat, as soon as it expired, regardless of the payment terms, competitors would be free to use the patented process or product.

The rule of *Brulotte* has become particularly anomalous since a 1988

16. 379 U.S. 29 (1964).

17. The decision has attracted a drumbeat of criticism, beginning with Justice Harlan's dissent. Id. at 34. See also USM Corp. v. SPS Technologies, Inc., 694 F.2d 505, 510–511 (7th Cir. 1982); Scheiber v. Dolby Laboratories, Inc., 293 F.3d 1014 (7th Cir. 2002); Phillip E. Areeda et al., *Antitrust Law*, vol. 10, §§ 1782c2–1782c3, pp. 506–511 (1996); Harold See and Frank M. Caprio, "The Trouble with *Brulotte:* The Patent Royalty Term and Patent Monopoly Extension," 1990 *Utah Law Review* 813, 814, 851; Rochelle Cooper Dreyfuss, "Dethroning *Lear:* Licensee Estoppel and the Incentive to Innovate," 72 *Virginia Law Review* 677, 709–712 (1986).

amendment to the patent statute that provides that "no patent owner other-wise entitled to relief for infringement . . . shall be . . . deemed guilty of mis-use or illegal extension of the patent right by reason of his having . . . condi-tioned the license of any rights to the patent or the sale of the patented product on the acquisition of a license to rights in another patent or purchase of a separate product" unless the patentee has market power in the market for the conditioning product.[18] The effect is to confine the doctrine of the patent tie-in cases to ones in which the patentee has real market power, not merely the technical monopoly (right to exclude) that every patent confers. This is a welcome curtailment of the doctrine but unfortunately falls short of overrul-ing the *Brulotte* decision. It places a limit merely on defenses to patent in-fringement suits, and a patentee seeking to enforce an agreement to pay post-expiration royalties can't be suing for patent infringement; his patent has expired. And although the rationale of *Brulotte* is the same as that of the dis-credited tying cases—the Court even said in *Brulotte* that to "use that lever-age [the power conferred by the monopoly] to project those royalty pay-ments beyond the life of the patent is analogous to an effort to enlarge the monopoly of the patent"[19]—and not a whit stronger (probably even weaker, since there is only one product), the new statutory defense is limited to tying, as its language makes clear.

The kind of thinking reflected in the early tie-in cases and *Brulotte* also un-derlies the "repair versus reconstruction" doctrine of patent misuse law. Of-ten a patent consists of a combination of elements some of which (sometimes all of which) are not separately patented. An early example was a patented combination of a patented fixture for holding a roll of toilet paper with the roll itself, which was not patented.[20] The Court held that it was not an in-fringement for the purchaser of the product to replace the roll when it was used up. The purchaser had the right to maintain the product in use (the right of "repair," in an extended sense of the word). It would be different if, after the fixture had worn out at the end of its normal useful life, the pur-chaser had reassembled it from unpatented components; that would be "re-construction" and would constitute an infringement.

As the Federal Circuit has recognized in holding that a patentee can pro-vide in the patent license that the licensee can use the product only once (or a limited number of times),[21] the repair-reconstruction distinction has nothing

18. 35 U.S.C. § 271(d)(5).
19. Brulotte v. Thys Co., note 16 above, 379 U.S. at 33.
20. See Morgan Envelope Co. v. Albany Perforated Wrapping Paper Co., 152 U.S. 425 (1894).
21. Mallinckrodt, Inc. v. Medipart, Inc., 976 F.2d 700 (Fed. Cir. 1992). Actually, the court was merely returning to the original understanding of the repair doctrine, see Wilson v. Simpson, 50 U.S. (9 How.) 109 (1850), which had become submerged by the growth of hostility to pat-ents as sources of monopoly power.

to do with patent policy. It is solely a matter of interpreting the license. If the patentee forbids the licensee to repair the patented product, he will not be able to charge as high a license fee because the product will have a shorter useful life; so there is no economically meaningful sense in which the prohibition "extends" the patent. Cases that regarded patentees' efforts to prevent the licensee from replacing components of the patented article as a form of tying (of the components to the patent)[22] presumably have gone down the same drain as the tying cases themselves.

Other Patent Cases

All this said, patents and other intellectual property rights can be sources of genuine antitrust problems, a possibility obscured by the fact that patent monopolies in an economically meaningful sense can coexist with competition in its sense of rivalry, as the Supreme Court failed to understand in the gasoline-cracking case.[23] The defendants were accused of restricting competition in the gasoline industry by pooling the patents that they held on the "cracking" method of manufacturing gasoline. Since only about a quarter of all gasoline was produced by this method, the Court concluded that the pooling could not have had anticompetitive consequences. If as is likely there were diseconomies of scale in producing gasoline by the cracking method, the defendants could not have supplied the entire market at a lower cost than their competitors. But had they competed with each other rather than eliminating competition among themselves by the pooling and cross-licensing of their patents, they would have supplied a larger fraction of the market at a lower cost, producing a social cost savings without any reduction in the price of gasoline.[24]

This is not to suggest that patent pooling and cross-licensing are always, or characteristically, or even often anticompetitive, at least in the sense of the term that implies a reduction in economic welfare. They are methods of reducing transaction costs, and the reduction may well dominate any anticompetitive effect. A patent pool in which, typically, owners of related patents transfer them to a central organization and are then free to use any of the patents in the pool, with or without having to pay a royalty (assessed by the pool), is the counterpart to the blanket copyright licenses of the performing-rights organizations in the music industry. And recall the equivocal welfare

22. Such as Aro Manufacturing Co. v. Convertible Top Replacement Co., 365 U.S. 336 (1961), discussed in "The Supreme Court, 1962 Term," 75 *Harvard Law Review* 40, 242 (1961).

23. Standard Oil Co. (Indiana) v. United States, 283 U.S. 163 (1931).

24. See Richard A. Posner and Frank H. Easterbrook, *Antitrust: Cases, Economic Notes, and Other Materials* 274–276 (2d ed. 1981).

effects of patent races: if the racers merge, or pool their R&D, the effect may be to eliminate wasteful rent seeking—or it may be to eliminate a healthy diversity of inventive approaches. The former effect is likely to dominate if there are economies of scale in R&D, the latter if there are diseconomies of scale.

In principle, arrangements whereby competing firms pool, license, or cross-license their patents should receive careful antitrust scrutiny. This may be rather empty advice, however, if the consequences of these transactions cannot be determined with reasonable accuracy and expedition, and at reasonable cost, by the methods of litigation. Still, there are easy as well as difficult cases. Suppose a market contains four firms each of which has a patented process for making the market's product. If each licenses its patent to the others in exchange for a royalty payment, the effect will be similar to that of a cartel that decided to raise the market price by the same amount. A more difficult case is where the patents are blocking patents: each covers a part of the manufacturing process and only a manufacturer with rights to all of them can produce the market's product efficiently. If they are truly blocking, forbidding their joint use would be inefficient. That joint use could be brought about either by the sale of all the patents to a single firm (whether one of the patentees or a different firm altogether) or by a cross-licensing agreement that would permit each of the firms to use all the patents. The former may be the more efficient solution to the problem of blockage because it enables further research and development of the manufacturing process to be centralized; if so, cross-licensing agreements would be suspect as cartelizing devices—the patents may not in fact be blocking.[25] That is an example of economies of scale in R&D. But the Darwinian theories of innovation, as we know from Chapter 11, imply that cross-licensing of blocking patents may be more efficient than pooling because it creates multiple centers of competing research. That is an example of diseconomies of scale. A merger among patent racers provides, as we have already seen, a similarly indeterminate evaluative issue.

The most troubling aspect of patent pooling and cross-licensing from an antitrust standpoint is that it discourages challenges to the validity of particular patents. Remember that the issuance of a patent is merely prima facie evidence of the patent's validity. If competitors are in the best position to determine whether a patent is valid but are bought off by licensing agreements having generous terms, the result may be to disguise a cartel as a lawful patent monopoly. The General Electric lightbulb case illustrates the problem.[26] General Electric licensed its principal competitor, Westinghouse, to manufac-

25. See id. at 288.
26. United States v. General Electric Co., 272 U.S. 476 (1926).

ture lightbulbs using the GE patent. GE had 69 percent of the market, Westinghouse 16 percent, and other licensees of GE 8 percent, for a total of 93 percent, so the effect of the licensing agreement was to solidify the monopoly conferred by GE's patent. The license fixed a minimum price at which Westinghouse could sell the lightbulbs. The royalty rate was only 2 percent but was to rise to 15 percent if Westinghouse's share of the lightbulb market reached 15 percent, which, as the figures above reveal, had happened by the time the case was tried. The very low starting royalty rate suggests that the right to use the patent was not worth a lot to Westinghouse, and the rate escalation keyed to Westinghouse's market share suggests that the parties were trying to minimize competition.

Nor is it immediately apparent how fixing a minimum price for sales by a licensee of products embodying the patented invention is an effective method of exploiting a valid patent, though it is an effective method of preventing price competition. If the licensee is a less efficient producer than the patentee, the patentee will produce the product embodying the invention himself rather than license the production to others. If the licensee is the more efficient producer, the patentee will be able to charge him a royalty that will exceed the profit the patentee would obtain if he manufactured the product himself. This is the obverse of the tie-in case. Because the product and the patent are complements, a reduction in the price of the product, made possible by the producer's efficiency, will increase the demand for the patent and thus increase the patentee's income—dramatically so since the only cost incurred by the patentee in licensing his patent is the cost of negotiating the licensing agreement.

As in the cracking case, the patentee might be the more efficient manufacturer but only up to a point. Even so, the effect of putting a floor under its licensees' price would be, as in the cracking case itself (or at least our interpretation of it), to increase the total costs of manufacture, to the detriment of the patentee qua patentee. This is another reason for thinking that the Westinghouse license was a device by which the parties raised the price of lightbulbs, dividing the market between them; for remember that the more Westinghouse sold, the higher the royalty, which would limit its ability to outcompete GE along some dimension other than price (fixed in the license agreement).

But there is a consideration tugging the other way and thus undermining the foregoing analysis. When both the patentee and a licensee (or licensees) are selling the patented product, it will be difficult to specify in the license agreement terms that protect the patentee against future uncertainties. The licensee might turn out to be more efficient than expected and be able to undersell the patentee despite a stiff royalty. The patentee would obtain greater royalties as a result of the licensee's greater output, but might lose more if, for example, it were unable to sell any of its own output at a price that covered its costs. This is one reason why, as we noted in Chapter 11, patent licenses are costly to negotiate.

This point may hold the key to explaining why even though the firms in the *General Electric* case were competitors and price-fixing agreements between competitors are standardly treated as illegal per se, the Supreme Court upheld GE's right to fix Westinghouse's price. The Court reasoned that the efficient exploitation of patents might be thwarted if licensees had a legal right to undersell the patentee and by doing so perhaps drive the patentee out of business. Although the rational patentee wants the patented product manufactured by the most efficient producer, there is a danger that during the period in which the licensing agreement, providing for a specified royalty, is in effect the licensee's cost will fall unexpectedly, giving the licensee a price advantage in the sale of the patented product that will prevent the patentee from recouping his fixed costs of manufacturing. The patentee could achieve the same protection by charging a royalty that varied with the licensees' sales (not market share), so that any loss of anticipated sales would be offset by higher royalties. But this would make for a more complicated and so an even more costly licensing agreement.

Merger policy under modern antitrust law focuses on the effect of a challenged merger on the level of concentration in the market of the merged firms. If the merger increases that level appreciably, it is likely to be condemned, on the theory that a reduction in the number of significant firms in a market facilitates collusion, whether tacit or express, and collusion creates deadweight and rent-seeking losses by enabling the colluding firms to raise price and reduce output. Should the antitrust authorities and the courts also consider the possible effect of such a merger on innovation? If, for example, innovation were positively correlated with concentration, perhaps on the theory that restrictions on price competition deflect competition into other channels, one of which is product or process innovation, the social benefits from a merger that increased concentration might exceed the conventional social costs associated with collusion-facilitating concentration. However, after many years of study, it remains completely uncertain in both theoretical and empirical analysis whether concentration promotes, reduces, or does not affect innovation.[27] So effect on innovation is probably something that should be ignored in the administration of merger law.

---

27. See, for example, Dennis W. Carlton and Robert H. Gertner, "Intellectual Property, Antitrust and Strategic Behavior" 14 (National Bureau of Economic Research Working Paper No. W8976, June 2002).

Copyright Cases and End-Product Royalty Arrangements

One of the most interesting of the older copyright antitrust cases is *Broadcast Music, Inc. v. Columbia Broadcasting System, Inc.*[28] The Supreme Court in that case upheld the blanket licenses issued by the music performing-rights organizations against the charge that such licenses are a per se violation of antitrust law because they eliminate price competition. The blanket license entitles the licensee, for a flat fee, to play any song in the organization's inventory as many times as he likes during the term of the license. The organization allocates the receipts among its member composers roughly in proportion to the relative frequency with which their songs are played. In effect, the organization is an exclusive sales agency for a group of competitors, and by setting the price for the performing rights of its stable of composers it eliminates price competition among them. But by eliminating the heavy transaction costs that the direct licensing of music from the copyright holders would involve, the blanket license offers users a more attractive product at a lower price than competitive licensing would offer. It is another example of how restricting competition can actually enhance economic welfare. This conclusion is reinforced by the fact that the blanket license is nonexclusive; the composer is free to negotiate an individual license with a prospective user of his music.

Suppose that before the performing-rights organization was formed, competition among copyright holders drove the price of individual licenses down to $1,000 but there were in addition licensing transaction costs borne by the licensee of $500. Suppose further that licensees would have been willing to pay up to $2,000 for a license. Hence they received $500 of consumer surplus ($2,000 − $1,000 − $500). A performing-rights organization that acquired exclusive licensing rights from its members might be able to charge users the full $2,000 for the blanket license because it would have a monopoly (assuming no other performing-rights organization provides effective competition). If, however, the organization acquires only nonexclusive rights, the most it can charge is $1,500, the $1,000 competitive price plus the $500 saving in transaction costs, since users have the option of going around the blanket license and acquiring licenses directly from the copyright holders. Thus users are no worse off, and the composers are better off, so there is a welfare gain that could not be achieved if the blanket license were prohibited as a form of price fixing (which it is). It is no surprise that the blanket license has escaped the usual per se condemnation of price fixing.

The *BMI* case has implications for the patent-antitrust interface as well, specifically for the question whether a patentee should be permitted to base

28. 441 U.S. 1 (1979).

royalties on the licensees' revenues from the end product that incorporates the patented input.[29] To explain, an additional economic virtue of the blanket licenses besides economizing on transaction costs is that they avoid the misallocation of resources that would occur if some musical compositions, being unique and protected from competition by copyright, were priced far above marginal cost; for this method of pricing would create an incentive for potential customers to substitute compositions that might cost society more per unit of quality to produce or disseminate. An end-product royalty has the same virtue; the licensee's decision on how much of the patented unit to use relative to other inputs is not distorted by the unit's being priced above its marginal cost, because the amount of the royalty is invariant to the quantity of the input used. The legal objection, which we shall take up shortly when we discuss bundling, is that end-product royalties are the carrot to tying's stick. Because it costs the licensee nothing to substitute the patented input against the other inputs that he might use to produce the final product, he is irresistibly induced, once he decides to buy some of the patented input (the "tying quantity," call it), to buy the rest of those inputs from the patentee as well (the "tied quantity"). Tie-ins are normally harmless, however, and the same is probably true of end-product royalties.

Consider Microsoft's former practice of basing the fee that it charged manufacturers of PCs for the right to install its operating system on their computers on the manufacturers' total computer sales. This meant that if a manufacturer wanted to install Microsoft's system on at least some of its computers, the marginal cost of installing them on the rest was zero. The effect was almost the same as if Microsoft had required the manufacturers to install its operating system in all the computers they sold, which could be analyzed as a tying arrangement in which the tying product consists of the number of copies of the Microsoft operating system that the manufacturers want to install and the tied product (the product they must take to get the tying product) consists of the number of copies they would prefer not to install. The antitrust objection to Microsoft's practice (which the company under pressure from the Justice Department agreed in a consent decree to abandon) is bound up with the special issue of network externalities, on which more shortly.

Another very interesting older copyright antitrust case, and one that turns out to be related both to blanket licenses and to tie-ins, is *United States v. Loew's, Inc.*,[30] where the Supreme Court invalidated "block booking" in the movie industry as a form of illegal tying. Block booking refers to the movie

---

29. See Louis Kaplow, "The Patent-Antitrust Intersection: A Reappraisal," 97 *Harvard Law Review* 1813, 1881–1885 (1984).

30. 371 U.S. 38 (1962).

studios' practice of charging distributors a price for a bundle of movies rather than pricing them separately. In other words, the purchase of any movie in the bundle is conditioned on the purchase of the others; so there is a close analogy to a tie-in. And the motives are similar, as an example will show. Suppose a movie studio sells two films, X and Y, that are worth different amounts to different moviegoers and hence to distributors. Assume the studio has two distributors, A and B, that are interested in the films. A is willing to pay $8,000 for X and $2,500 for Y, while B is willing to pay $7,000 for X and $3,000 for Y. If the studio were to price X and Y separately, its best price for X would be $7,000 and for Y $2,500, and so its total revenue would be $19,000. If it sells X and Y as a package, however, it can charge $10,000 for the package and thus obtain a total revenue of $20,000.[31] When the products are priced separately, the price is depressed by the buyer who values each one less than the other buyer does; the bundling eliminates this effect. The profitability of bundling is greater the more products that can be bundled.[32] For this makes it more likely that the package will contain products that consumers place opposite valuations on, as in our numerical example, where A values X more than B does while B values Y more than A does.

As in this example, bundling, like tying, is often, perhaps characteristically, a method of price discrimination, unless the bundle could not be unbundled without a substantial cost penalty—imagine selling each component of an automobile, the carburetor, brakes, radiator, axles, etc., separately to the consumer. But like the blanket licenses in the music industry, it reduces transaction costs and, like both those licenses and end-product-royalty patent-licensing agreements, it eliminates monopoly as a factor distorting the choice of goods within the bundle. Bundling, like tying, end-product royalty agreements, and related contractual methods, including exclusive dealing and full-requirements contracts, may, as we'll point out shortly, have anticompetitive effects in particular settings. But not in general; and so the main effect of the tying and bundling rules is merely to increase the cost of price discrimination. For remember that price discrimination is not in general unlawful, which means that firms engage in tying or bundling when that is the cheapest or most effective method of discrimination. To the extent that prohibiting these practices leads not to a reduction in discrimination but merely to an increase in the cost of discrimination, the prohibition imposes a net social cost.

31. See George J. Stigler, "A Note on Block Booking," in Stigler, *The Organization of Industry* 165 (1968). An alternative explanation of block booking is presented in Roy W. Kenney and Benjamin Klein, "The Economics of Block Booking," 26 *Journal of Law and Economics* 497 (1983). Their explanation is unrelated to monopoly or discrimination, but instead emphasizes transaction-cost savings and optimization of marginal incentives, much as in the *BMI* case.

32. See Yannis Bakos and Eric Brynjolfsson, "Bundling and Competition on the Internet," 19 *Marketing Science* 63 (2000).

In some cases, it is true, most clearly when there are no feasible alternative methods of discrimination to tying or bundling, the prohibition of these practices may, by reducing or eliminating discrimination, reduce the rent seeking and other costs that discrimination imposes. This may be a good thing. Discrimination produces on average, so far as anyone knows, no net social benefits. The motive and consequence are to increase profits, and the costs incurred in discriminating, which include not only those mentioned already but also distortions in competition between favored and disfavored purchasers from the discriminating seller, are, on average, a net social cost, since, on average, discrimination does not improve resource allocation (it does when it increases output over the single-price monopoly output). However, as we are about to see, these reservations about the efficiency of discrimination have little force in a situation in which a seller's average total cost of some product is higher than his marginal cost, a common—indeed the typical—situation in the intellectual property field.

Because a patent or copyright presupposes both the existence of a differentiated product (and thus a downward-sloping demand curve) and a high ratio of fixed to variable costs, pricing equal to marginal cost is quite likely not to cover the seller's full costs, and one alternative is discrimination. Like any other form of monopoly pricing, price discrimination, except when it increases output over the single-price monopoly output, reduces allocative efficiency by driving a wedge between price and marginal cost, compared to the charging of a single price equal to marginal cost; there are also the administrative costs and secondary distortions that we just mentioned. But the "first best" option of pricing equal to marginal cost is not open to a seller who by virtue of having declining average total costs cannot recover his total costs by setting a price equal to marginal cost. If he sets a (single) price equal to his average total cost, he will be deflecting customers who would have paid a lower price, but still one equal to or greater than marginal cost, to inferior or more costly substitutes. He may be able to retain these customers if he discriminates.

Or may not; the point is not that discriminatory pricing is more efficient than average-cost pricing in the case of a firm with declining average total costs. It may or may not be, depending on the particular schedule of prices chosen by the seller to maximize his profits. When the seller substitutes a range of prices for a single price, the part of the range below the former price attracts some new customers and elicits more purchases by old customers, but the part above repels some old ones and causes others to buy less, and it is impossible to say a priori which effect will dominate. Discrimination is sometimes defended on the ground that, under certain configurations of cost and demand, there may be no single price that enables the firm to recover its total costs. But in such a case, the firm's output probably generates little in the way of consumer surplus, and in that event the resources used in producing that output might have a higher social product in another use.

The point is simply that when a firm is operating under conditions of declining average costs, there is no reason in general to suppose discriminatory pricing *less* efficient than pricing equal to average total cost, which—not marginal-cost pricing—is the only feasible alternative. And so there is no good reason for antitrust intervention aimed at preventing discrimination, and this is regardless of the precise form of discrimination—whether explicit, or implicit as in tying and bundling—unless the implicit has an additional effect that is exclusionary. We turn next to that possibility.

Antitrust and Intellectual Property in the New Economy

In recent years the focus of antitrust in regard to intellectual property has been on firms in the "new economy," mainly manufacturers of computer chips, such as Intel, and of software, such as Microsoft, and Internet-based businesses (Internet access providers, Internet service providers, and Internet content providers), such as AOL and Amazon.com. They differ markedly from the type of enterprise whose practices traditionally provided the grist for the antitrust mill, but they differ in ways that should by now be thoroughly familiar to the reader. The traditional industries were characterized by multiplant and multifirm production (indicating that economies of scale are limited at both the plant level and the firm level, or in other words that average total costs are, beyond relatively modest output levels, rising), stable markets, heavy capital investment, modest rates of innovation, and slow and infrequent entry and exit. The new-economy industries tend to be characterized instead by falling average costs (on a product, not firm, basis) over a broad range of output, modest capital requirements relative to what at least until recently was available for new enterprises in the global capital market, very high rates of innovation, quick and frequent entry and exit, "instant scalability" (the ability of a firm to multiply the output of a product very rapidly with no increase in marginal cost), and economies of scale in consumption ("network externalities," as they are more commonly called), the realization of which may require either monopoly or interfirm cooperation in standards setting.

The key to understanding these industries is that their principal output is indeed intellectual property, namely computer code, rather than physical goods, although the intellectual property may be shipped on a disk or other physical product (not necessarily: software is increasingly shipped to the purchaser over the Internet). This is obviously the case for computer software but is also true to a large extent of computer chips, which are technologically highly advanced and also come with their own software to interface with operating-system software, and Web-based services. The ability of any business offering such services to take and fill orders and carry out the other operations (such as marketing, billing, handling returns, tracing missing shipments, responding to customer questions and complaints, and allaying the customer's privacy and security concerns) that are required to furnish its customers with whatever goods or services the business provides is a function to a large extent both of the sophistication of the business's computer software and of its trademarks and copyrights. Recall our discussion in Chapter 11 of Amazon.com's patented "one-click shopping"; it is a computer application.

Trade secrecy is important in some branches of the software industry, notably the manufacture of computer operating systems. Even though an operating system can be patented or copyrighted, provided it satisfies the requirements imposed by the patent and copyright statutes (such as utility, novelty, and nonobviousness in the case of patents, and minimal creativity and independent creation in the case of copyrights), a computer scientist who studies the system with the aid of its source code can pick up clues on how to write a program that will have the same functionality as the copyrighted system but not infringe because it will use a different arrangement of code. Microsoft's Windows 98 operating system and its Windows 2000 Professional operating system have almost indistinguishable functionality but the code that generates this functionality is radically different in the two systems. Hence Microsoft until its recent antitrust troubles was assiduous in its efforts to maintain the source code for its operating systems (the human-readable code that constitutes the instructions for creating the machine-readable operating-system code) as a trade secret rather than relying on patent or copyright protection alone.

Yet software manufacturers do seek copyright protection as well, and the extension of copyright protection to software is controversial (and likewise patent protection, but we shall not discuss that separately). Controversial not because software is "read" by a computer rather than by a human being, for a program has the generic characteristics of an expressive work, being a unique combination of symbols generating functionality that is not itself copyrightable, just as the author of a conventional expressive work cannot copyright the ideas that the work communicates. The antitrust concern, rather, is that copyright may create excessive protection for software, resulting in monopoly prices far higher than necessary to recover the costs of writing the software, as a consequence of difficulties of inventing around code that has become an industry standard. We had a glimpse of this concern (which incidentally exists in some tension with the argument that it is the very ease of such inventing around that causes software manufacturers often to rely on trade secrecy, instead of copyright or patent protection, to ward off competitors) in Chapter 4, in discussing user interfaces. The characteristic desktop display of the modern computer, with its icons, trash bin, drop-down menus, and so on, has much the appearance of a picture, the sort of thing that would normally be copyrightable. But this "picture" is also the method by which the user of the computer interfaces with its programs, and once he has become thoroughly accustomed to this method it will be costly for him to switch to another method, just as it would be a huge bother to switch from driving a car on the right to driving it on the left, even though there is no inherent superiority to driving on the right.

The user-interface copyright issue could well be thought a case in which the superiority of one method of expressing an idea (the "idea" being the various functions that the computer performs) is so great—not necessarily intrinsically superior; it might be superior just because of high switching costs—that control over it confers control over the idea and therefore copyright protection should be denied on the authority of the doctrine of functional expression, discussed in Chapter 4. But as we know from that chapter, this is a monopoly problem that can be and is handled by copyright law, without need to invoke antitrust law; remember *Sega Enterprises Ltd. v. Accolade, Inc.* A similar case is *Lotus Development Corp. v. Borland International, Inc.*, where Judge Boudin's concurring opinion helpfully points out the anticompetitive implications of allowing the owner of a copyright on code that has become a standard to block competitors from using that code.[33]

The same thing is true with regard to interfaces between application programs (such as word processing) and a computer's operating system, or between servers and PCs (these interfaces are called "protocols") linked by telecommunications lines in a network. Provided that a new computer application program satisfies the other requirements of copyrightability, the programmer is allowed to copy the interface or protocol without which the program, however creative, is likely to be unmarketable because it cannot be conveniently accessed by computer operators. Again this result is reached under copyright law,[34] but antitrust considerations are salient;[35] in the presence of network externalities, a supplier that is denied access to the network is at a profound competitive disadvantage.

The main issues in the government antitrust suit against Microsoft arose from the claim that Microsoft had sought to prevent Netscape's Web browser

33. 49 F.3d 807, 820 (1st Cir. 1995), affirmed by an equally divided Court, 516 U.S. 233 (1996).

34. See, for example, Computer Associates International v. Altai, Inc., 982 F.2d 693 (2d Cir. 1992).

35. See Peter S. Menell, "An Epitaph for Traditional Copyright Protection of Network Features of Computer Software," 43 *Antitrust Bulletin* 651 (1998).

from becoming installed in PCs running Microsoft's Windows operating system. Microsoft's concern was that the browser might, in conjunction with the application-programming computer language known as Java, become a platform for applications programs that would otherwise run directly on Windows—a platform, moreover, compatible with any operating system. Then Windows might lose its principal competitive advantage over other operating systems, which is that most application programs are written first (and sometimes only) for Windows because of its dominant share of the operating-system market. And with the browser supplying much of the functionality of the operating system, operating systems might become commodities— cheap, simple, and easily manufactured—and as a result Windows would cease to be a source of monopoly profits. Applications writers would not write programs for Java-Netscape, however, until it was installed on most PCs, and that, it is charged, is what Microsoft tried to prevent.[36] We shall see that this kind of exclusionary conduct can be in the rational self-interest of a monopolist.

Network externalities cast a sidelight on the issue of software piracy, which we discussed briefly in Chapter 2. Suppose a potential pirate has a choice between stealing software that is en route to becoming a standard and buying the software of a competing producer. If he decides to pirate, he will be at once reducing the competitor's income and increasing the network externalities of the dominant producer. In this case the pirated producer not only is not hurt by piracy (as we suggested in Chapter 2 would often be the case); he is helped by it.[37]

A further antitrust concern regarding intellectual property rights in software is that the methods of distributing software often enable the creator to obtain by contract even more protection than copyright law gives him. Copyright gives the copyright owner a property right in his intellectual property even when it is in the hands of a person with whom he has no contract, such as the purchaser of a copyrighted book from a bookseller. To the extent that the software manufacturer contracts directly with the ultimate purchaser, for example by selling over the Web, he can impose by means of contract tighter restrictions than the copyright law would allow him to do in the absence of contract;[38] for example, he can forbid the purchaser to make an extra copy for

36. See United States v. Microsoft Corp., 253 F.3d 34, 66–67 (D.C. Cir. 2001) (en banc) (per curiam).

37. See Lisa N. Takeyama, "The Welfare Implications of Unauthorized Reproduction of Intellectual Property in the Presence of Demand Network Externalities," 42 *Journal of Industrial Economics* 155 (1994).

38. See Mark A. Lemley, "Beyond Preemption: The Law and Policy of Intellectual Property Licensing," 87 *California Law Review* 111, 124–134 (1999).

his own use, as copyright law permits, or (the point we emphasized in Chapter 2) forbid fair use copying. It is true that a contract is unlikely to have the same duration as copyright protection. But length of protection is academic in the case of software, which becomes obsolete long before the copyright on it expires. It is also true, however, that the manufacturer will have to compensate the purchaser for consenting to restrictions on the purchaser's use of the software.

The possibility that the combination of copyright and contract gives software manufacturers too much market power in the economic sense, that is, causes a lessening rather than an increase in the quality-adjusted output of software, creates a natural concern with any further practice that might increase a manufacturer's power over price. It is at this point that another feature of the new economy, namely economies of scale in consumption, becomes troublesome from an antitrust standpoint, as we have already glimpsed in discussing the Microsoft case. Economies of scale in manufacture are familiar; up to a point, the longer the production run, the lower the average total cost as fixed costs get spread over a larger and larger output. Economies of scale in consumption describe the situation in which the larger the firm's output is, up to some point, the more valuable that output is to the firm's customers. Telephony is the most easily understood example. Telephone service is worthless if there is only one subscriber; he would have no one to talk to. The more subscribers there are, the more valuable the service is to each one, or at least to many of them. Interactive services, such as e-mail and online auctions, are similar. Likewise the sharing of computer programs, as where two or more academics collaborate on writing a scholarly article by means of word-processing and spreadsheet programs. Literal networking or sharing to one side, computer programs tend to be more valuable the more people use them because training, support by information-technology personnel, and standardization of equipment and procedures are facilitated. It is the same reason that the typewriter keyboard is standardized.

Economies of scale in consumption presuppose uniformity rather than a common source. The international telephone system is a single network, but its components are owned by a vast number of separate firms and individuals. The components have been standardized to assure interoperability, in much the same way that the gauge of the railroad track has been standardized. A firm that manufactures one of the essential components of a network would prefer to be the exclusive source of that component rather than be required to disclose the information that would enable competitors to duplicate it. If the component is protected by patent, copyright, contract, or trade secrecy law from being appropriated by a competitor, the requisite uniformity is more likely to be achieved by monopoly provision than by standardization.

The features of the new economy that we have been describing tug it toward monopoly yet, oddly, also toward competition. The more protection from competition a firm that succeeds in obtaining a monopoly will enjoy, the more competition there will be to become that monopolist; and provided that the only feasible or permitted means of obtaining the monopoly are socially productive, this competition may be wholly desirable rather than a form of wasteful rent seeking. A firm that will have the protection both of intellectual property law and of economies of scale in consumption if it is the first to come up with an essential component of a new-economy product or service will have a lucrative monopoly, and this prospect should accelerate the rate of innovation, just as, other things being equal, the more valuable a hoard of buried treasure is, the more rapidly it will be recovered.

What is more, the successful monopolist is likely to be a firm that initially charges a very low price for the new product that it has created. Think back to the telephone. Since every new subscriber increases the value of the service to the existing subscribers, a telephone company has an incentive to provide price inducements to new subscribers, as the money it will lose on them may be more than made up by the higher price that existing subscribers will pay for access to a larger network. This is especially likely if the network will be a natural monopoly, in the sense that no competitor would find it feasible to duplicate it—then the faster the network reaches maturity, the longer the monopolist will be protected from challenges to its monopoly. The prospect of obtaining a network monopoly should thus induce not only a high rate of innovation but also a low-price strategy that induces early joining and compensates the early joiners for the fact that eventually the network entrepreneur may be able to charge a monopoly price.

Traditional networks such as the telephone system and the railroads required enormous capital investments and were therefore difficult to duplicate. The owner of such a network, or of an important part of it, had a pretty secure monopoly. The less capital investment the creation of a substitute network involves, the less secure the network monopolist's monopoly is. Because of the extraordinary rate of innovation in the new economy and the rapidity with which new networks that are primarily electronic can be put into service, new-economy networks may not be secure against competition, as a series of new-economy monopolists, such as Wang and IBM, learned to their sorrow. And in that event the gale of creative destruction that Schumpeter described, in which a sequence of temporary monopolies operates to maximize innovation, conferring social benefits far in excess of the social costs resulting from the short-lived monopoly prices that the process entails, may be a reality. This is especially likely because quality competition tends to dominate price competition in the software industry. The quality-adjusted price of software has fallen steadily simply because quality improvements have vastly outrun price increases. And it is kept low by the desire to increase the value of a network by maximizing the number of users.

We must be careful not to paint too bright a picture, forgetting that there is such a thing as too rapid a rate of innovation, resulting from too great an investment of resources in innovation. Innovation is sometimes a form of socially wasteful rent seeking; that is the criticism of patent races. R&D resources that would be socially more productive elsewhere in the economy might be sucked into the new economy only because higher economic rents were available there.

The feasibility of challenging an existing network monopolist emerges as a critical issue in the rosy Schumpeterian picture. The threat and occasional reality of entry will limit expected monopoly profits and thereby curb rent seeking. We remarked that network monopolies in the new economy may be insecure. But they may also be too secure despite the high rate of innovation and the modesty of the capital investments required to create a purely electronic monopoly. Even if the only way to become a network monopolist in the new economy is to be the first to come up with a new technology that benefits consumers, the existence of the monopoly may discourage subsequent technological innovation by other firms. If network externalities are large, they may give the monopolist a natural-monopoly cost advantage that exceeds the benefit of a superior new technology. This is the issue of "path dependence": an industry may be stuck with an inferior technology because of the cost advantage of the existing network.[39]

The gravity of the problem should not be exaggerated. There appear to be few well-documented cases.[40] But the antitrust concern with network externalities is not centrally about technological inferiority but about barriers to entry. Suppose that a network monopolist and a potential entrant into the

39. See, for example, Stanley M. Besen and Joseph Farrell, "Choosing How to Compete: Strategies and Tactics in Standardization," *Journal of Economic Perspectives,* Spring 1994, p. 117; Joseph Farrell and Garth Saloner, "Installed Base and Compatibility: Innovation, Product Preannouncements, and Predation," 76 *American Economic Review* 940 (1986); Michael L. Katz and Carl Shapiro, "Technology Adoption in the Presence of Network Externalities," 94 *Journal of Political Economy* 822 (1986). A closely related source of path dependence is "switching costs": having learned how to use one computer, a consumer may be reluctant to switch to a different type of computer even if it is superior, because of the cost of learning how to operate a different type. See Paul Klemperer, "Competition When Consumers Have Switching Costs: An Overview with Applications to Industrial Organization, Macroeconomics, and International Trade," 62 *Review of Economic Studies* 515, 517–523 (1990). See generally Jean Tirole, *The Theory of Industrial Organization* 404–409 (1994).

40. See the discussion of the debate over the typewriter keyboard in Richard A. Posner, *Public Intellectuals: A Study of Decline* 96–97 (2001).

monopolist's market have identical costs but that because of the benefit of the network to consumers they are willing to pay $X more for the monopolist's service than they would pay for the new entrant's network-less service. Then the monopolist can charge a price equal to his cost plus $X without inducing entry; the $X is a monopoly-price increment.

The difficulty of entry into network industries creates a legitimate antitrust concern with methods by which a firm that has a monopoly share of some market in an industry characterized by network externalities might attempt to mobilize, as it were, those externalities against new entrants. This concern arose long before the term "new economy" entered the lexicon, in the *Standard Fashion* case[41] decided by the Supreme Court in the 1920s. The case is a surprisingly apt model for antitrust policy toward the new economy.

The defendant manufactured a very popular line of women's dress patterns, which retailers thought it essential to be able to carry. The defendant required retailers to agree not to carry competing lines. Competing manufacturers could in principle create their own retail outlets, but who would shop there if the most popular brand could not be found? They would have to create a line as long and as popular as Standard Fashion's line and that would be a risky and costly undertaking.

What distinguished *Standard Fashion* from a garden-variety exclusive-dealing case was the existence of economies of scale at the distribution level. Consumers didn't want to traipse from store to store. They wanted a full line in each store, so anyone entering the dress-patterns business had to provide the full line if it was excluded from stores that carried the dominant firm's line. Restricting its retailers no doubt cost Standard Fashion something; they would demand compensation in the form of a lower wholesale price in exchange for agreeing to curtail their purchasing options. But the added cost to Standard Fashion might be less than the increase in its expected monopoly profits from forestalling new entry by compelling prospective entrants to enter on a full-line basis. The point is not that the new entrant would have to invest more capital, since capital is not in short supply, but that it would have to embark on a riskier undertaking, that of creating not a single successful or niche product but a whole line of such products. It's as if one couldn't make commercial aircraft without making military aircraft as well.

The analogy to a new-economy network externality should be plain. The network corresponds to the full-line retail store in *Standard Fashion*. A firm may wish to enter the market by producing one component of the network or one value-added service, but if a competitor by virtue of owning or having an exclusive-dealing contract with the network refuses to cooperate with the

---

41. Standard Fashion Co. v. Magrane-Houston Co., 258 U.S. 346 (1922).

firm, it will have to duplicate the entire network in order to get distribution of its product.

Piecemeal entry is the norm in most industries. A department store carries the products of many producers, most of whom do not offer a full line of products. One can imagine a number of designers of women's dress patterns, each specializing in one pattern, and the department store assembling the different patterns into a full line to compete with Standard Fashion's full line. The riskiness of entry to each designer would be minimized. The *Standard Fashion* case was decided in 1922, however, and many towns may not have had department stores. We may be in a similar stage in the development of the new economy: distribution facilities may be sufficiently limited to create bottlenecks that monopolists can exploit to perpetuate monopoly. However, the Internet is eliminating many distribution bottlenecks by expanding the geographical scope of distribution markets; one can now enter such a market without having a physical outlet proximate to the customers.

It is important to note that a monopolist would have no incentive to engage in exclusionary conduct, since it is costly, unless his monopoly were fragile, that is, vulnerable to new entry. This point is missed in Robert Bork's criticism of the *Standard Fashion* decision.[42] He argues that Standard Fashion couldn't extract a monopoly price from its dealers twice, first by charging them what the market would bear and then by forcing them to enter into exclusive-dealing contracts. That's true, but what Standard Fashion may have been able to do was to extend the duration of its monopoly, which might have collapsed sooner otherwise.[43] Such extensions can be enormously profitable, as we shall note shortly.

Assuming that Standard Fashion's exclusive dealing would have delayed entry at least somewhat, though it would not have prevented it, we have the exquisitely difficult case of a practice that is at once exclusionary and efficient. For it is easy to find efficiency justifications for exclusive dealing.[44] Apart from the benefits in encouraging the dealer to commit himself to the manufacturer's brand, exclusive dealing limits style piracy. These turn out to be closely related benefits. Unless constrained by an exclusive-dealing contract,

---

42. Robert H. Bork, *The Antitrust Paradox: A Policy at War with Itself* 305–307 (2d ed. 1993).

43. Bork's more cogent criticism of the decision is that Standard Fashion didn't have a monopoly; its share of the patterns market was only 40 percent. True, that was its nationwide share, and the Supreme Court pointed out that in many small towns it was the only supplier of patterns. Still, 60 percent of the nation was open to a piecemeal competitor to obtain distribution.

44. See Benjamin Klein and Kevin M. Murphy, "Vertical Restraints as Contract Enforcement Mechanisms," 31 *Journal of Law and Economics* 265, 287–288 (1988); Howard P. Marvel, "Exclusive Dealing," 25 *Journal of Law and Economics* 1, 11–18 (1982).

a dealer might use Standard Fashion patterns to attract customers to his store, then switch them to cheaper brands that resembled the patterns (perhaps being copies of them), the dealer's incentive to do this being a very low wholesale price for those brands. The price would be low because the manufacturer of a cheap brand, by taking a free ride on Standard Fashion's investment in creating popular dress patterns that he could copy, would have lower costs than Standard Fashion.

Balancing the costs and benefits of an exclusionary practice that also has efficiency characteristics may well be beyond the capacity of the courts. But here is a possible approach. If the practice is one employed widely in industries that resemble the monopolist's but are competitive, there should be a presumption that the monopolist is entitled to use it as well. For the widespread adoption of the practice implies that it has significant economizing properties, which implies in turn that to forbid the monopolist to use it will drive up his costs and so (if they are marginal costs) his profit-maximizing monopoly price. The burden should shift to the plaintiff to show that, nevertheless, forbidding the use of the practice will offset the effect of the prohibition on the monopolist's costs by increasing the rate or speed of new entry. Or, if this is deemed too difficult an issue for a court to resolve, proof that the challenged practice is widespread in competitive industries should be a complete defense.

The likelihood that the monopoly profits obtained during the extension period (as we may call the length of time for which a monopoly is extended by means of exclusionary practices) will exceed the costs of the exclusionary practice to the monopolist is enhanced when, as in both *Standard Fashion* and parallel new-economy cases, the monopoly is of intellectual property. (Remember that Standard Fashion was selling dress patterns, not the dresses themselves; that was why it faced a danger of piracy, which is just a pejorative term for unauthorized copying.) It is this that makes efforts at delaying the entry of competitors into a monopolized new-economy market properly suspect from an antitrust standpoint. The marginal cost of intellectual property is often much lower than the market price. In the extreme case, which is approximated in some software markets, marginal cost is close to zero, meaning that almost all the revenues earned by a firm that monopolizes the market (and they may be great since, as we know, the monopolist's price is determined by the elasticity of demand as well as by marginal cost) go directly to the bottom line. This makes it quite plausible that the profit from extending the monopoly another year or two will exceed the cost of the exclusionary practices required to obtain the extension.

Suppose the development of a new software product costs $10 million, incurred entirely in year t. Marginal cost is $1, the profit-maximizing price is

$15, and at that price output is 1 million units per year. The monopoly is expected to last one year if entry is not forestalled, two years if it is. If the monopoly lasts one year, the monopolist's profit will be $4 million ($15 million − $10 million − [1 million units × $1]). If it lasts two years, his profit will soar to $18 million ($30 million − $10 million − [2 million units x $1]). The second-year profit is thus $14 million (actually a little less because of the need to discount future profits to present value), and the monopolist will be willing to spend up to that amount to delay entry by one year.[45] The figures are arbitrary, but high ratios of price to marginal cost are common in intellectual property markets, such as computer software, and so there can be no basis for confidence that the cost of an exclusionary practice in such markets will always exceed the additional monopoly profits that the practice makes possible.

Exclusive dealing, the specific practice in *Standard Fashion,* is analytically similar to tying, so that much of what we have said about the case applies to tying as well. Exclusive dealing ties distribution to manufacture; equivalently, tying is exclusive dealing in the tied product. So all we need is sensible law on exclusive dealing in order to be able to deal sensibly with tying cases. Suppose there are economies of scale in the manufacture or sale of the tied product, corresponding to the economies of scale in distribution that is the key to understanding *Standard Fashion* as a case that may have involved a genuinely exclusionary practice. Then a firm that wants to enter the market for the tying product but because of the tying arrangement is denied access to existing producers of the tied product (they are owned, or contractually controlled, by the monopoly producer of the tying product), and so has to produce the tied product as well, will have higher costs than the monopolist. This will reduce his expected gain from entering the market for the tying product. If, moreover, as is normally the case, the tying and the tied products are complements, the cost of the arrangement to the seller may not be great, and this opens up the possibility of asymmetric costs to monopolist and entrant, a situation in which an exclusionary practice is more likely to be a rational tactic for a monopolist to employ than if the firms operated under the same cost conditions.

The reason for the possible asymmetry is that reducing the price of a product because its cost has fallen increases the demand for its complements—that is the definition of complementary. This is best seen in the bundling variant of tying, discussed earlier in this chapter in connection with block booking, where instead of requiring purchasers to buy a complementary product the

---

45. How much he will actually spend will depend on the slope of the marginal-cost curve for blocking entry. If it is very steep, he may spend much less than $14 million.

monopolist gives it away. A monopolist of hammers, desiring to prevent entry into the hammer market, might decide to offer purchasers of its hammers all the nails they want, for free. This reduction in the price of nails would increase the demand for hammers, so the monopolist would make up some of his losses on nails in greater sales of hammers. Modern computer operating systems are sold as bundles of separate programs that could be (in fact that used to be) priced and sold separately. This makes it difficult for the manufacturer of one of these programs to interest consumers in it. For example, Microsoft bundles its browser into its operating system; this made it difficult for Netscape to charge consumers for its browser, and it had to look for other sources of revenue, such as using the browser to direct consumers to the Netscape home page and selling advertising on that page. The effect of bundling is similar to that of refusing to sell each program in the operating system separately to the consumer (tying). Microsoft did not recover the costs of developing the browser directly by raising the price of the operating system, but because the browser made the operating system more valuable there was doubtless some indirect cost recovery. In raising these points we of course do not deny that there are many practical objections to subjecting design decisions, such as whether to sell a product as a unit or as separately priced components, to antitrust review.

The plaintiff won in *Standard Fashion,* and the decision remains good law. Its principle (whether or not it was soundly applied to its facts) is not limited to exclusive dealing but extends to any business method calculated to exclude an equally or more efficient competitor. The illegality of predatory pricing is likewise settled antitrust doctrine, which is fortunate, since there is a greater danger of predatory pricing in new-economy than in old-economy industries.[46] The reasons are that high-volume manufacture is so cheap and that predatory pricing is so difficult to distinguish by the methods of litigation from network-building pricing, in which the early customers might actually be charged a negative price to reflect the value that they confer on the network. Sales to them at such a price would only appear to be below cost in an invidious sense; they would no more be predatory than run of the mill loss-leader selling. Regarding the first of these points, a firm whose output consists of computer code does not have to worry that supplying the entire market will require a large capital investment in manufacturing capacity; and so the possibility of using predatory pricing not merely to defend but to obtain a monopoly is enhanced.

---

46. Granted that verified instances of predatory pricing are few and far between, there is no solid theoretical basis for denying that it is sometimes a rational business strategy—or at least would be if it were lawful. See Richard A. Posner, *Antitrust Law* 207–223 (2001).

We conclude that antitrust doctrine is sufficiently supple, and sufficiently informed by economic theory, to cope effectively with the distinctive-seeming antitrust problems presented by the new economy—the most striking example of the rise of intellectual property to the pinnacle of the American economic system. What is troublesome, but would take us beyond the scope of the book to discuss adequately, is the institutional structure of antitrust enforcement. It is not well adapted to deal swiftly and surely with technically complex activities. The practices of a rapidly changing, highly technical industry such as computer software place enormous strains on the antitrust system.

15

The Political Economy of
Intellectual Property Law

It should be apparent by now that intellectual property rights have undergone a significant expansion that began, roughly speaking, with the Copyright Act of 1976.[1] How is that expansion to be explained? Under the rubric of "public choice," economists try to explain legislation, and the political and governmental process more generally, by modeling government action as the result of the workings of demand and supply.[2] In Chapter 10 we tried, though without conspicuous success, to explain state moral rights statutes in these terms. Particular emphasis is placed in the public-choice literature on the role of interest groups in overcoming the free-rider problem inherent in the fact that legislation and policy are for the most part nonexcludable public goods. A person can enjoy the full benefit of the statute, regulation, or other policy in question without having contributed a dime to the collective effort that was necessary to get it promulgated.[3] This free-rider problem, like the parallel problem that besets cartelists (a seller that remains outside the cartel, undercutting the cartel price slightly, can increase his net profits, provided free riding does not destroy the cartel), can be overcome if the benefits of the collective effort required to get the legislation enacted are great and the costs small or, if large, either widely diffused or imposed on politically impotent groups. These conditions are most likely to be satisfied if the legislation is backed by

---

1. This is only approximate, as there were significant expansions before then, such as the extension of the copyright renewal term to forty-seven years beginning in 1962 and the extension of copyright protection to sound recordings in 1972.

2. For useful summaries of public-choice theory, see Robert D. Cooter, *The Strategic Constitution* (2000); Daniel A. Farber and Philip P. Frickey, *Law and Public Choice: A Critical Introduction* (1991); Jonathan R. Macey, "Public Choice and the Law," in *The New Palgrave Dictionary of Economics and the Law*, vol. 3, p. 171 (Peter Newman ed. 1998).

3. In contrast, intellectual property is an excludable public good.

(but not opposed by) a compact interest group that has a lot to gain from the legislation.[4]

Public-choice theory has had only limited success in explaining political behavior and government action. Limited is not zero; the theory has made significant contributions to the understanding of public utility and common carrier regulation, certain other forms of regulation including occupational licensure and other labor-market (including safety and health) regulation, and tariffs. But it has not, for example, succeeded in explaining the forces that brought into being the system of property rights that is fundamental to a capitalist economy. Can it say anything about the extension of that system to encompass intellectual property, and the spurt in intellectual property protection that we have dated to the 1976 copyright statute?[5] We find it helpful to approach the question by first considering another trend that began at roughly the same time: the deregulation movement.

Beginning in the late 1970s and continuing almost to the present day, a number of important industries in the transportation, communications (including broadcasting), energy, and financial-services (including banking) sectors—industries that until then had long been subject to comprehensive public regulation mainly of the public utility or common carrier variety—were wholly or entirely deregulated. Significant partial deregulation has occurred in other industries, including legal services. Probably the greatest success of public-choice theory had been in explaining the pattern of regulation that existed *before* deregulation took hold. Public-choice theory showed that the principal effect of such regulation was to enable or shore up producers' cartels, and it identified the demand and supply factors that explained the success of some producers and the failure of others in obtaining such regulation. Those factors turned out to be much the same, as we have suggested, as the factors that facilitate purely private cartels. The more concentrated the cartelists' market and the more diffuse the buyer side of the market, the easier it is for the cartelists to overcome the free-rider problems that bedevil cartels—

---

4. On the role of interest groups in public policy, see, for example, George J. Stigler, *The Citizen and the State: Essays on Regulation* (1975); Stephen P. Magee, William A. Brock, and Leslie Young, *Black Hole Tariffs and Endogenous Policy Theory: Political Economy in General Equilibrium* (1989); Richard A. Posner, "Theories of Economic Regulation," 5 *Bell Journal of Economics and Management Science* 335 (1974).

5. These are not the only questions about intellectual property law that public-choice theory might be able to shed light on. Josh Lerner, "150 Years of Patent Protection," 92 *American Economic Review Papers and Proceedings* 221 (May 2002), finds that patent protection is greater in wealthier and in more democratic countries than in poorer and less democratic ones. Wealthy countries are more likely to be producers as well as consumers of intellectual property, creating a demand for intellectual property protection; and democratic countries are more hospitable to innovative thinking than less democratic ones.

and if they can overcome those problems in the private marketplace, they may be able to overcome parallel problems in the political marketplace, where legislation is "bought." The difference between the private and the regulatory cartel is that firms able to collude effectively without interference from the antitrust authorities (as will usually be the case if their collusion is tacit) have less demand for regulatory backing than firms facing greater obstacles to private cartelization. That is why, for example, farmers are more likely to seek legislation limiting agricultural competition than producers of cement are likely to seek regulation of the cement industry.

Public-choice theory has proved better at explaining regulation than at explaining deregulation.[6] But it can help us identify the factors that, taken together, may explain the latter phenomenon, though it cannot provide all the help we need.[7] One factor is the economic malaise of the seventies—a period of slow economic growth combined with a high rate of inflation—which created a demand for economic reform. That malaise, moreover, produced the election of Ronald Reagan, an economic liberal in the nineteenth-century sense, that is, a believer in free markets, and a magnet for other such believers, a number of whom received executive or judicial appointments. Even before that, with the election of Richard Nixon in 1968, free-market thinking had begun to take hold in the government. Though Nixon himself was not an economic liberal, some of his appointees were, to a degree anyway, including three of his four Supreme Court appointees (Burger, Rehnquist, and Powell). Another factor, and again one related to the economic distress (the "stagflation") of the seventies, was the rise of the Chicago School of economic analysis. The most influential figure of the Chicago School was Milton Friedman, and his prestige and influence rose with the apparent failure of Keynesian economics, of which he was the leading critic.

These political and intellectual currents, though almost certainly a factor in deregulation,[8] might not have sufficed by themselves to bring about widespread deregulation. But in addition many of the regulated firms were becoming restive under regulation. One reason was the high rate of inflation in the 1970s, which interacted with regulatory control over rates, and particularly regulatory lag in granting rate increases, to impede needed pricing flexibility. A more important reason, this one solidly rooted in public-choice and cartel theory, is the tendency of cartelization, including cartelization by regulation, to transform cartel profits into costs. A cartelized market is not

6. As argued in Steven K. Vogel, *Freer Markets, More Rules: Regulatory Reform in Advanced Industrial Countries,* ch. 1 (1996).

7. For an excellent discussion, see Organisation for Economic Co-Operation and Development (OECD), *Regulatory Reform in the United States* 18–20 (1999).

8. See Martha Derthick and Paul J. Quirk, *The Politics of Deregulation* 238–245 (1985).

in equilibrium. Because price exceeds marginal cost, there are unexploited profit opportunities. If price competition is prevented by agreement or regulation, the members of the cartel will vie for additional sales by increasing the quality of their product until at the margin the cost of the product equals the price. At this point regulation becomes all costs and no benefits, at least to the most efficient firms, whose expansion is inhibited by the protectionist philosophy of the regulators.[9]

Against this background, let us now consider the simultaneous trend toward ever-greater legal protection of intellectual property. Should intellectual property law be thought a form of regulation? In that case, the trend toward deregulation in other sectors of the economy was being bucked, as it were, by an equal and opposite regulation trend. That would not be a unique phenomenon, for the regulation of health and safety, and of employment, has increased during the era of deregulation; but those forms of regulation had begun well before the deregulation movement. It is only the movement for greater protection of intellectual property that has actually coincided with the deregulation movement. We must try to explain this coincidence.

That there has been a trend toward greater protection of intellectual property cannot be doubted. It began, we said, with the Copyright Act of 1976, which significantly lengthened the copyright term. It continued with the creation of the U.S. Court of Appeals for the Federal Circuit in 1982 to be the exclusive patent appellate court, in the expectation (which has been fulfilled, as we saw in Chapter 12) that it would interpret and apply the patent statute in a way that would strengthen inventors' rights. The trend accelerated in the 1990s, with the Visual Artists Rights Act, the Architectural Works Protection Act, the Sonny Bono Act, the Digital Millennium Copyright Act, and other statutes, some not even mentioned in this book. Further complicating analysis, however, is the fact that the expansion of intellectual property has not been linear. Remember the 1992 amendment to the fair use provision of the Copyright Act, which provided that the same general standard should govern the application of the fair use defense to unpublished as to published materials; the 1989 restoration to the Lanham Act of the common law requirement of commercially meaningful rather than merely token sales to establish trademark protection;[10] the Trademark Clarification Act of 1984 that established

---

9. See id. at 19–20; Joseph D. Kearney and Thomas W. Merrill, "The Great Transformation of Regulated Industries Law," 98 *Columbia Law Review* 1323, 1394–1397 (1998). "All costs and no benefits" is something of an exaggeration, however, since if the marginal-cost curve of nonprice competition is steeply upward sloping, the total costs expended on that competition may not be great. See George J. Stigler, "Price and Nonprice Competition," in Stigler, *The Organization of Industry* 23 (1968).

10. At the same time, however, the 1989 amendments authorized "intent to use" trademark registration. See Chapter 7.

an implicit cost-benefit analysis for determining when a trademark has become a generic name; the anticybersquatting statute that prevents an especially inefficient form of banking of trademarks; the statute creating a limited antitrust immunity for patent tie-ins; and the Hatch-Waxman Act that expanded the experimental use defense to patent infringement? These all seem to have been economically efficient legislative interventions into the existing body of intellectual property law.

Setting aside those interventions for the moment, let us consider whether there might be a public-choice explanation for the expansion of intellectual property rights. One possibility is that there is an inherent asymmetry between the value that creators of intellectual property place on having property rights and the value that would-be copiers place on freedom to copy without having to obtain a license from the author or publisher of the original work or (in the case of patents) the inventor. The enforcement of an exclusive right to intellectual property can shower economic rents on the holder of that right, but copiers can hope only to obtain a competitive return. This would make it easier to organize a collective effort of copyright and patent owners to expand intellectual property rights than to organize a copiers' interest group to oppose such an expansion. The music performing-rights organizations, mentioned several times in this book, illustrate the ability of owners of intellectual property to organize coalitions to protect their ownership rights. It is noteworthy that "most of the statutory language" of the Copyright Act of 1976 "was not drafted by members of Congress or their staffs at all. Instead, the language evolved through a process of negotiation among authors, publishers, and other parties with economic interests in the property rights the statute defines."[11]

The asymmetry of stakes between originators and copiers of intellectual property becomes especially pronounced when, as has been true of every copyright law, an extension of the copyright term is made applicable to existing works as well as to those created after the extension. Since the costs of creating the existing works have already been borne, the additional revenue generated by the extension of their copyrights is almost entirely profit, that is, economic rent. In contrast, those opposing the extension do so on behalf of intellectual property that they have yet to create and that can be expected to yield them only a normal, competitive return. So they have less to gain from a successful outcome to the struggle than the supporters of the extension.

On this theory one might expect continuous, inexorable pressure from such owners to strengthen such rights. Tugging the other way, however, is the fact that most creators of intellectual property use intellectual property

11. Jessica D. Litman, "Copyright, Compromise, and Legislative History," 72 *Cornell Law Review* 857, 860–861 (1987).

created by others as inputs into the creation of their own intellectual property—a point that we have emphasized throughout this book. Any law that strengthens rights to such property beyond the level necessary to assure an adequate supply is likely to increase those input costs. This prospect may retard efforts by producers of intellectual property to press for expanding legal protection of such property; conceivably, it might even align their interest with that of society as a whole.

Consider the question whether businesses that value patent protection would prefer the Patent and Trademark Office to be lax or strict in its review of patent applications. The obvious answer is lax, but it may be incorrect. If the PTO is known to be lax, courts will give less weight to the presumption of validity of patents; moreover, the makers of valuable inventions may find themselves impeded in obtaining patents by the existence of a large number of patents already issued in their area of research. So again the public and private interest in effective regulation of the patent process may coincide.

But this is unlikely to be a *general* feature of intellectual property law because there is a persisting asymmetry with regard to the private benefits from recognizing versus denying intellectual property rights. We have clues to the existence of this asymmetry in the absence of serious opposition to the bill that became the Sonny Bono Copyright Term Extension Act; in the difficulty that Lawrence Lessig encountered in finding a plaintiff to challenge the constitutionality of the Act;[12] and in the fact that the Disney Company was the Act's strongest supporter even though many of its most successful characters and movies have been based on public domain works, such as *Cinderella* and *The Hunchback of Notre Dame*. One possible explanation is that despite Disney's experience, the public domain really isn't worth much—that we have been exaggerating the dependence of authors and inventors (especially the former) on previously created works. But this suggestion confuses private with social value. Public domain works have less private value than copyrightable works because they cannot be appropriated. Some of them have great social value. It is true that most creators of expressive work do not want to appropriate any part of the public domain; they just want to incorporate some of it into their work without having to negotiate for a license. But the immediate effect of the Sonny Bono Act was not to remove anything from the public domain. It was merely to postpone the addition to the public domain of works on which the copyright would expire earlier were it not for the Act. In effect, all the Act did, so far as increasing the costs of future creators of intellectual property is concerned, was to reduce the rate at which the public domain would be expanding. The expected private benefits of such expan-

---

12. See Steven Levy, "The Great Liberator," *Wired*, Oct. 2002, pp. 140, 155. Lawrence Lessig was the lead counsel for the plaintiff in Eldred v. Ashcroft. See Chapter 8.

sion were likely to be smaller than the expected private benefits of retaining copyright on certain highly valuable properties, such as the Mickey Mouse character;[13] this may explain Disney's seeming, by its support of the Sonny Bono Act, to be turning its back on the public domain, from which it has derived such profit.

There is a sense in which the Sonny Bono Act is *too* good an example of the asymmetry between the private value of intellectual property rights and the private value of the intellectual public domain. If the Act had been limited to expressive works created after its date of passage, producers of intellectual property such as Disney would have balanced the higher input costs resulting from the prospective shrinkage of the public domain against the increased revenue stream from a longer period of copyright protection, and given discounting to present value the tradeoff would probably not have favored the extension. But because the Act applied to all existing intellectual property as well, it conferred a windfall on owners of existing intellectual property that distorted the balance. Compare bankruptcy reform. Ex ante, debtors and creditors have a shared interest in optimal bankruptcy law. If creditors have suboptimal remedies against defaulting debtors, interest rates will be very high and debtors as a whole will suffer. If creditors have excessively severe remedies against defaulting debtors, people will be afraid to borrow and both the volume of and interest rates on loans will fall, to the detriment of creditors. But ex post, debtors may benefit from a law expanding bankruptcy exemptions or otherwise tilting the balance in favor of debtors, and creditors may benefit from the opposite tilt, because, in either case, the interest rate is fixed so far as currently outstanding credit is concerned. The possibility of retroactive legislation is a candle to rent-seeking moths. This is a strong argument in favor of making legal reform prospective only, and it is as applicable to intellectual property law as it is to bankruptcy law.

Sony's Betamax system (see Chapter 4) was a relatively rare example of a product that had great commercial value but only if intellectual property protection was relaxed, as otherwise Sony would have owed enormous amounts of money in damages for contributory infringement. Having won its case, however, Sony, and other producers of products bought to a considerable extent by infringers of intellectual property rights, no longer had a strong incentive to seek legislative protection. In those situations in which concentrated economic interests would be adversely affected by expansion of intellectual property rights, such expansion is likely to be resisted effectively.[14] An important example is the "passive carrier" exemption in the Copyright Act,

---

13. See Robert P. Merges, "One Hundred Years of Solicitude: Intellectual Property Law, 1900–2000," 88 *California Law Review* 2187, 2236–2237 (2000).

14. See id. at 2237–2238.

which protects telecommunications companies from being sued for contributory infringement when they carry infringing materials, such as copyrighted music transmitted by infringers across the Internet.[15] The rampant piracy of copyrighted music and other copyrighted materials by users of the Internet has spurred a movement to limit the exemption, and this is a dispute that ranges interest groups on both sides of a controversy over the scope of intellectual property rights. The conflict between trademark owners and cybersquatters, resolved in favor of the former, is a similar example; another is the conflict between copyright owners and Internet service providers over "caching," resolved in the Digital Millennium Copyright Act in favor of the latter.[16]

An even better example, because it relates directly to the Sonny Bono Act, concerns the fees that ASCAP and BMI charge restaurants and other retail establishments for a blanket license to play the copyrighted music controlled by these organizations. Passage of the Act was stymied until a provision was added excusing restaurants, bars, and other retailers of limited square footage from having to pay the license fee for recorded music broadcast on their premises.

A further consideration of a public-choice character, this one also emphasized in the legislative history of the Sonny Bono Act (see Chapter 8), is mercantilist. As noted in the Introduction, the United States has a very large positive balance of trade in intellectual property. This means that the access costs imposed whenever intellectual property rights are enforced are shifted in part to foreigners, who neither vote in nor are permitted to make campaign contributions in U.S. elections. Export industries have often obtained special protection or assistance from government. Mercantilism to one side, a nation that has a comparative advantage in producing intellectual property is more likely to favor intellectual property rights than one that does not, and we noted in Chapter 11 evidence that patent rights are correlated with measures of economic development in general and R&D expenditures in particular.[17]

We might try to get an angle on the role of interest groups in the formula-

15. See 17 U.S.C. § 111(a)(3).

16. "Caching" refers to the temporary copy that an Internet service provider makes of transmitted material on a local server so that the subscriber can, after looking at the material, look at it again by clicking "Back" on his browser rather than by having to get it transmitted to him long distance from the original sender.

17. See Juan C. Ginarte and Walter G. Park, "Determinants of Patent Rights: A Cross-National Study," 26 *Research Policy* 283 (1997). The article rejects the alternative hypothesis that patent protection is responsible for the higher level of economic development and higher R&D expenditures in the countries that enforce expansive patent rights. That rejection is consistent with our argument in Chapter 11 concerning the indeterminacy of the economic effects of expanding patent rights.

tion of intellectual property law by examining amicus curiae briefs in the Supreme Court in intellectual property cases. Although an amicus curiae brief can be filed by an individual, most are filed by organizations, and most individual filers are in fact representatives of organizations. Hence amicus curiae briefs provide a rough clue to interest-group activity. Since 1980 the Supreme Court has decided 32 intellectual property cases that presented substantive issues of intellectual property law and in which amicus curiae briefs were filed; another case is, at this writing, awaiting decision. In these 32 cases, a total of 287 amicus curiae briefs supporting or opposing intellectual property protection were filed[18]—and, as we would expect, a majority, 162, support intellectual property rights. However, this majority is due mainly to the 11 patent cases in the sample, in which 82 briefs were filed in support of patent protection and only 48 against. In the other 21 cases, the score is 80 in support of the intellectual property right and 77 against. Patent law is the area in which we suggested that the pressure against expansive intellectual property protection should be as great as the pressure for, given the ways documented in Chapter 11 in which patents can harm corporate interests as well as helping them. Our data do not support this hypothesis. The ratio of amicus curiae briefs favoring and opposing intellectual property rights is 1.71:1 in the patent cases and only 1.03:1 in the copyright cases, while the average number of amicus curiae briefs per patent case is 11.8 and the corresponding number for copyright cases only 7.5.

By way of comparison, in the 34 cases decided by the Supreme Court since 1980 in which substantive issues of antitrust law were presented and amicus curiae briefs were filed, 89 of the amicus briefs supported a finding that the antitrust laws had been violated and 96 opposed the finding. Comparison with the statistics on amicus briefs in the intellectual property cases indicates less support among filers of amicus briefs for antitrust "rights" than for intellectual property "rights." This is as expected, since the period since 1980 has been one during which the scope of antitrust liability has contracted rather than, as in the case of intellectual property, expanded.

We must not ignore the possibility that there is a significant public-interest component in intellectual property law in general and perhaps even in the expansion of that law in recent decades. Not even the most dyed-in-the-wool public-choice theorist would be likely to deny that many laws serve the public interest or, more precisely, serve a *conception* (quite possibly erroneous) of the public interest, rather than the interest of some narrow interest group. Many of these theorists would further concede that interest-group pressures are not always necessary to procure the passage of efficient legislation or the

---

18. A list of the cases is available from the authors.

formulation by judges of efficient common law rules. It is hard to believe, for example, that interest groups are necessary for the enactment of laws protecting property rights or punishing criminal behavior. If the benefit-cost ratio is high enough, collective action becomes feasible even in the absence of interest groups.

Think back to the discussion of property rights in Chapter 1. Harold Demsetz, an economist distinctly unsympathetic to public-interest explanations of legislation, nevertheless argued that the rise of property rights was due not to the machinations of interest groups but to rising scarcity that had increased the value of property rights relative to the costs. He did not propose a causal mechanism connecting a perceived increase in the social benefits of a property-rights system with its adoption via the political process, but such theories exist. In Joseph Schumpeter's theory of democracy,[19] for example, politicians vie for office by offering voters attractive policies in much the same way that sellers of ordinary goods vie for sales by offering consumers attractive terms. If they fail to deliver, they may be voted out of office, as happened to Jimmy Carter in 1980 and to George Bush in 1992. The perceived ineffectuality of Democratic Party politicians to repress crime was a factor in the defeat of Democratic presidential candidates in 1968 and in the 1980s. If property rights and crime suppression are important to enough voters, successful politicians will supply these goods without the promptings or pressures of interest groups. Mention of Carter is particularly apropros because his failure to win reelection in 1980 was due in significant part to the "stagflation" of the 1970s. Advocates of expanding intellectual property rights argued that by increasing the pace of innovation, such an expansion would help to bring the nation out of the economic doldrums.

If we think about the history of intellectual property law since the Middle Ages, we can, just as with Demsetz's theory of the emergence of property rights in physical property, easily tell a "Whiggish" (history as progressive) story in which the growth of intellectual property rights is explained by reference to material and social changes that increased the social value of such rights. As we noted in Chapter 2, when copying is expensive relative to the cost of expression—and here we add, bringing inventions into the picture, when duplicating an invention is expensive relative to the cost of developing the invention—the value of intellectual property rights will be limited; authors and inventors will not need them in order to be protected from copying that is so fast and cheap that it prevents them from recovering their fixed costs of expression or invention. The expansion of trademark rights over the

19. See Joseph A. Schumpeter, *Capitalism, Socialism, and Democracy*, chs. 22–23 (1942). For a summary of his theory, see John Medearis, *Joseph Schumpeter's Two Theories of Democracy* (2001); for elaboration of it, see Richard A. Posner, *Law, Pragmatism, and Democracy*, chs. 4–6 (2003).

past century can also be explained as a response to market forces. With the reduction in transportation costs and the growth of specialization in markets, buyers have less and less contact with sellers or information about them. In such markets, trademarks provide consumers with an economical means of acquiring information on the reputation of sellers and the quality of goods sold. A reinforcing factor in the overall expansion of intellectual property is that, as we have stressed throughout the book, intellectual property rights tend to be costly to define and enforce. These costs are likely to be particularly high in an unsophisticated legal system.

As the system becomes more sophisticated in the sense of better able to resolve disputes that involve difficult issues (such as whether two expressive works are substantially similar or whether a new invention duplicates an old one), as the cost of copying falls and its speed increases as a consequence of technological developments, as moreover technological progress becomes more highly valued and originality in general more highly prized, the costs of intellectual property rights fall and the benefits rise, leading us to expect intellectual property rights to expand even in a political regime oriented toward promoting the public interest. By the time the U.S. Constitution was drafted in 1787, twelve of the thirteen states had already adopted copyright laws, and common law patents were widely recognized. The Constitution's grant of power to Congress to enact national patent and copyright laws was uncontroversial, and patent and copyright statutes were passed by the first Congress.[20] The parallel to the rise of rights over physical property and the concomitant decline of common property, a decline dramatically symbolized by the enclosure movement discussed in Chapter 1, is apparent. It is interesting to note in this connection that developing countries gave their (grudging) assent to the World Trade Organization Agreement on Trade-Related Aspects of Intellectual Property Rights (the TRIPs Agreement, as it is known), which greatly strengthened the international enforcement of intellectual property rights, in part because they anticipated such benefits as a greater willingness by the developed countries to transfer technology to them and a greater spur to production of intellectual property by their own enterprises.[21]

But the history that we have been recounting, while it might explain not

20. See Bruce W. Bugbee, *Genesis of American Patent and Copyright Law* (1967); Frank D. Prager, "Historic Background and Foundation of American Patent Law," 5 *American Journal of Legal History* 309 (1961); Irah Donner, "The Copyright Clause of the U.S. Constitution: Why Did the Framers Include It with Unanimous Approval?" 36 *American Journal of Legal History* 361 (1992).

21. See Duncan Matthews, *Globalising Intellectual Property Rights: The TRIPs Agreement*, ch. 5 (2002). Evidence concerning these and other benefits of intellectual property rights protection to developing countries is summarized in Keith E. Maskus, "Intellectual Property Rights and Economic Development," 32 *Case Western Reserve Journal of International Law* 447, 478–488 (2000).

only TRIPs but also the enactment of the Digital Millennium Copyright Act in response to technological advances that have made exact copying of digital files virtually costless and virtually instantaneous as well, does not explain why 1976 should be an inflection point, marking the beginning of a sudden and unprecedented growth in the legal protection of intellectual property in general.[22] If, however, we consider carefully the political and ideological forces that were about to precipitate the deregulation movement, we shall discover some clues to a possible answer. Free-market ideology is friendly to property rights. In extreme versions of that ideology, the goal of economic liberalism is total commodification—everything of economic value owned by someone. Even short of this, an important and worthwhile goal of the deregulation movement was to substitute, so far as possible, market-based solutions for economic problems for solutions based on direct regulation. "Free market environmentalism," for example, proposed that conservation of scarce natural resources, whether ocean fisheries or the electromagnetic spectrum, could be achieved most efficiently by broader recognition of property rights, while pollution could be best controlled by such market-oriented, rights-based measures as tradeable permits for emission of pollutants such as sulphur dioxide.[23] Markets and property rights go hand in hand. Property rights provide the basic incentives for private economic activity and also the starting point for transactions whereby resources are shifted to their most valuable use.

Given the historically and functionally close relation between markets and property rights, it was natural for free-market ideologists to favor an expansion of intellectual property rights. Natural—and it would have been clearly right either if intellectual property rights had identical economic properties to physical property rights, which we have seen throughout this book that they do not, or if a system of direct regulation of expressive and inventive activity had been in place and the proposal had been to substitute a system based on property rights. If in 1976 there had been no patent system but instead a system of direct government awards to successful inventors or direct government financing of R&D by private companies; if royalties in licenses of intellectual property had been fixed by government rather than by contract; if

22. The point is not so much that the 1976 Act itself brought about a fundamental change in copyright law, though it substantially extended the copyright term for individuals as well as in essence federalizing what had been state common law copyright, but that in the years since there has been an unprecedented number of new intellectual property statutes and judicial doctrines.

23. See, for example, Terry L. Anderson and Donald R. Leal, *Free Market Environmentalism* (1991); Symposium, "The Law and Economics of Property Rights to Radio Spectrum," 41 *Journal of Law and Economics* 521 (1998); Elisabeth Krecké, "Environmental Policies and Competitiveness," 16 *Homo Oeconomicus* 177 (1999). For other references, see Elinor Ostrom, *Governing the Commons: The Evolution of Institutions for Collective Action* 12–13 (1990).

the publication of books had been a government monopoly; if the prices of books, drugs, and other goods that embody intellectual property were fixed by a regulatory agency; if to minimize access costs intellectual property was given away for free and its costs subsidized by the government—if any of these things had been true, substitution of patent and copyright and trade secret and trademark law, in short of intellectual property rights, would have been a giant step in the right direction from the standpoint of economic efficiency and a major plank in the platform of the deregulation movement. But none of these things *was* true. Intellectual property was already "deregulated" in favor of a property-rights system, and the danger that the system would be extended beyond the optimal point was as great as the danger that it would be undone by a continuing decline in the cost (especially the quality-adjusted cost) of copying.

A point that we made at the end of Chapter 1 is relevant here: equating intellectual property rights to physical property rights overlooks the much greater governmental involvement in the former domain than in the latter, at least in a mature society in which almost all physical property is privately owned, so that almost all transactions involving such property are private. Government is continuously involved in the creation of intellectual property rights through the issuance of patents, copyrights, and trademarks. Skeptics of government should hesitate to extend a presumption of efficiency to a process by which government grants rights to exclude competition with the holders of the rights. Did not Friedrich Hayek, than whom no stronger defender of property rights can easily be imagined, warn that "a slavish application [to intellectual property] of the concept of property as it has been developed for material things has done a great deal to foster the growth of monopoly and . . . here drastic reforms may be required if competition is to be made to work. In the field of industrial patents in particular we shall have seriously to examine whether the award of a monopoly privilege is really the most appropriate and effective form of reward for the kind of risk-bearing which investment in scientific research involves."[24]

Another political or ideological factor in the sharp increase in the scope of intellectual property protection that we are dating from 1976 was the belief that one of either the causes or consequences of the economic malaise of the 1970s was a decline in the competitiveness of U.S. industry attributable to a loss of technological momentum to competing nations, notably Japan. This became a rationale for increasing patent protection through creation of a court that would have exclusive jurisdiction over patent appeals, although of course Japanese and other inventors would be free to seek U.S. patents. We

24. Friedrich A. Hayek, *Individualism and Economic Order* 114 (1948).

saw in Chapter 12 that the patent appellate system that preceded the creation of the Federal Circuit apparently did cause a decline in the number of patents issued, after correction for other factors; some inkling of this may have played a role in the creation of the court, given concern about the rate of technological progress. The expansion of intellectual property rights was also doubtless propelled by a desire to alleviate our chronic trade deficits by increasing the income of owners of copyrights and other intellectual property, most of those owners being American.

Earlier we mentioned Nixon's Supreme Court appointments. These appointees found the economic critique of traditional antitrust policy persuasive. And so during the 1970s and 1980s, the Supreme Court, joined in the Reagan years by the Department of Justice and the Federal Trade Commission, backtracked from the antitrust hawkishness of previous decades. Recall that one component of that hawkishness had been hostility to intellectual property rights, which were viewed as sources of monopoly power (which they are, but rarely to a degree having any antitrust significance). So the shift in antitrust policy, as well as increased favor for property rights, created an increasingly hospitable climate for intellectual property rights.

Whether the increases in the legal protection of intellectual property since 1976 have conferred net benefits on the U.S. economy is uncertain. But the political forces and ideological currents that we have described, abetted by interest-group pressures that favor originators of intellectual property over copiers, may explain the increases. An additional factor is the growth in the size of the market for intellectual property, indicated by the statistics in the Introduction. That growth cannot be dated to 1976; but there is no doubt that recent decades have seen a marked growth in that market, as the economies of the advanced nations shifted from being "industrial" economies to "information" economies. This growth increased the potential economic rents from intellectual property rights, and so may have increased the asymmetry of incentives that we have been stressing between supporters and opponents of expanded intellectual property rights.

The analysis is further complicated, however, by the fact that legal policy toward intellectual property rights is shaped by judicial as well as legislative action. Public-choice analysis has focused on legislation because the play of interest groups in the legislative process is widely acknowledged and it thus becomes plausible to view legislation as a product demanded by and supplied to influential interest groups in exchange for political support, including campaign contributions. The judicial process, in contrast, is structured to minimize the role of interest groups; interest groups can file amicus curiae briefs, but judges have little incentive to give much weight to such briefs. For these and other reasons economic analysis of legal institutions has tended to distinguish between common law and legislative policymaking and to argue that the former is, for a variety of reasons including judicial incentives and constraints, more likely than the latter to be economically efficient.[25] We find this pattern in intellectual property law as well, to a considerable extent though not completely. The most efficient areas of intellectual property law appear to be the largely common law fields of trademark, trade secrecy, and publicity rights law,[26] plus common law copyright and the very important doctrine of fair use in copyright law—still largely common law though codified in the Copyright Act of 1976. Similarly, though the vitally important nonobviousness requirement of patent law was not codified until the Patent Act of 1952, judges had long been invalidating patents for obviousness. On the whole, then, the judge-made parts of intellectual property law seem pretty efficient; it is not the judges who are to be blamed for setting the copyright and patent terms, abolishing copyright renewals in favor of a single very long term, importing moral rights doctrine into the copyright statute, or making buildings as well as building plans copyrightable. As in previous economic analyses of judge-made law, we have noted numerous instances of economic ingenuity displayed in judge-made rules and judicial decisions.

Yet the 1992 amendment to the fair use provision of the copyright statute was aimed at cases that we have criticized (*Salinger* and *New Era*), and in previous chapters we have taken potshots at other cases as well, such as *Rogers v. Koons* (though the fault may have lain in the failure by Koons's lawyer to characterize the puppies sculpture as a "target" parody and not just a "weapon" parody); *Tasini* (the *New York Times* electronic database case—but there the fault may have been the too-exact language of the collective-works provision of the copyright statute); the business-methods patent jurisprudence of the Federal Circuit; and *Brulotte v. Thys* (the case that forbade licens-

---

25. This was a principal theme of our book *The Economic Structure of Tort Law* (1987). See also Richard A. Posner, *Economic Analysis of Law* (6th ed. 2003), esp. pt. 2. The term "common law" requires definition, however. In its narrowest sense, it refers to the bodies of law administered by the common law courts of England in the eighteenth century and thus excludes admiralty law, domestic relations law, and equity jurisprudence. In a broader sense it refers to any body of law that is judge-created. In its broadest sense, and the one in which we use it in this book, it refers not only to judge-created bodies of law but also to judge-created doctrines that fill gaps or resolve ambiguities in statutes or constitutions. In this sense much of antitrust law, much of constitutional law, and much of patent and copyright law are common law. As mentioned in the text, several areas of intellectual property law are common law in the second sense as well, statutes being absent or merely being codifications of common law principles.

26. The main trademark statute, the federal Lanham Act, is quite detailed, but many of its most significant provisions merely codify judge-created doctrines, such as functionality, 15 U.S.C. § 1053(e)(5), or the nontransferability of a trademark "in gross," that is, without the assets for making the trademarked product. Id., § 1060.

ing a patent on condition that the licensee pay royalties beyond the expiration date of the patent), one of the all-time economically dumb Supreme Court decisions and yet merely the culmination of decades of foolish patent and copyright tie-in and bundling decisions.

Because of the role that the Federal Circuit has played in expanding patent protection, a satisfactory explanation for why the legal protection of intellectual property has been expanding in recent decades would require consideration of the distinctive political economy of specialized as distinct from generalist judges. Not that the Federal Circuit is completely specialized; its jurisdiction ranges well beyond patent cases. Nevertheless patent cases are the most important part of its jurisdiction, and, as we explained in Chapter 12, a specialized court is more likely to have a "mission" orientation than a generalist court. That has been the experience with the Federal Circuit; it has defined its mission as promoting technological progress by enlarging patent rights.

A difficult question is why there has been more legislative activity in the field of copyrights than in that of patents, given that, as we pointed out in Chapter 11, patents offer the potential of greater economic rents than copyrights. The proximate answer is that copyright and patent law have a different structure. Copyright law tends to specify the nature of the protected work (for example, books), whereas patent law protects inventions more broadly. So when new types of expressive works arise (such as sound recordings) or old types are thought in need of copyright protection (such as buildings, as distinct merely from architectural plans), new legislation may be necessary to bring them under the copyright umbrella. How then to explain the difference in structure? One possibility is that patent law is drawn more broadly because a patent is applied for rather than asserted; there is a filtering machinery, the proceeding before the Patent and Trademark Office, to prevent the most questionable patent applications from being granted. Copyright is asserted. So if copyright law defined copyrightable materials simply as "expressive works," yet without requiring (because of the difficulty discussed in Chapter 4 of conducting a search of previously copyrighted matter) the Copyright Office to review a copyright application for novelty, nonobviousness, and so on, there would be a great deal of litigation-fomenting confusion about what was validly covered by copyright and what was in the public domain.

An alternative explanation for why there is less legislative activity in the patent area, which is, however, related, is that the structure of the patent law leaves more discretion to the courts, meaning today primarily the Federal Circuit, which we know is hospitable to patent rights, so patentees have less demand for legislative largesse. This would also tend to explain our amicus curiae statistics, which showed greater effort to obtain patent than copyright protection through the judicial process. Still another possible explanation, though a weaker one and one in tension with our amicus curiae statistics, is that while *in principle* patents provide more legal protection and greater rent opportunities than copyright, the balance may have shifted because of the steps the law has taken to curb that potential, as by making the patent term short (by copyright standards), imposing the requirement that the steps necessary to enable duplication of the invention be disclosed in the patent application, charging high maintenance fees, and making the patent applicant run the gauntlet of a PTO proceeding; in addition there is the alternative of trade secrecy, which diminishes the demand for patent protection. As a result of all this, it is possible that today, given the very long copyright term and the very low costs of duplication of many types of copyrighted work, there are *greater* potential rents from copyright in many areas than from greater patent protection. However, this is not a compelling explanation, as it leaves unexplained why patent holders have not obtained modifications of the patent statute that would give them rights more nearly equivalent to those that copyright holders now enjoy.

In sum, the body of intellectual property law and its expansion in recent decades seem explicable only by a combination of public-interest and public-choice theories of the political process. What is more, it seems necessary to add political and ideological factors to the combination, and to blur the sharp distinction in some of the previous literature between the efficiency orientations of legislatures and of courts.

Conclusion

We shall not attempt to summarize the book, but shall instead by way of conclusion emphasize eight points that emerge from our analysis.

1. Economics is a great simplifier of law. Intellectual property law consists of numerous separate fields—copyright law, patent law, trademark law, trade secrecy law, the tort right of publicity, and the common law of misappropriation—that involve different statutes, different accretions of judge-made rules and doctrines, and different legal vocabularies. Moreover, the subject matter of intellectual property law covers an enormous range of different industries and activities. Nevertheless, economic analysis reveals a great deal of common ground beneath the legal and empirical variety. There are more distinctions in law than there are meaningful differences. Economic analysis enables intellectual property law to be grasped as a whole and the many commonalities among the different fields and cases to be seen clearly, along with the significant differences.

Economics has enabled us, for example, to explain the reciprocal relation of patent and trade secret law, each solving serious problems of the other, neither remotely satisfactory without the other. It has enabled us to discern the importance of congestion externalities, heretofore explicitly recognized only with regard to the right of publicity, in justifying some degree of copyright protection (though perhaps less than under present law), and to relate those externalities to the copyright owner's monopoly of derivative works, to the concept of moral rights, to the copyrighting of unique works of art even though copies of such works are not good substitutes, and to the copyrightability of conceptual art despite the principle that copyright law does not protect ideas. Economic analysis has also enabled us to identify a relation between musical copyrights on the one hand and trademarks and patents on the other; to trace the permeation of the fair use principle throughout intellectual property law; to relate copyright renewals to strategic patenting; to explain the difference between the rights of co-owners of patents and of copyrights and the different treatment of improvement patents by patent law and of derivative works by copyright law; and to propose a new system for determining the duration of copyrights.

2. The economic analysis that unifies the different fields of intellectual property law also unites intellectual property law with ordinary property law. In Chapter 1 we discussed the economics of property law and intellectual property law interchangeably, and throughout the book we have referred frequently to parallel legal treatments of the two types of property. More is involved than analogy. The basic economics of property applies equally to intellectual property and to physical property. The many differences between the two bodies of law can to a great extent be explained simply by the different values of the relevant variables in a unified economic model. For example, transaction costs are generally much greater with respect to intellectual property than physical property. This difference has significance for particular legal solutions, but does not affect the analytic model. For a basic hypothesis of that model is that the higher transaction costs are, the less likely the law is to seek to regulate transactions by means of broadly defined property rights, since a property right, being a right against the world—that is, a right to insist that anyone wanting it negotiate with the owner for it—can be reallocated from lower- to higher-valued users only through voluntary transactions. If such transactions are infeasible because of high transaction costs, the law will narrow the property right.

That is why we expect (and find) a much broader fair use doctrine (which in effect permits an uncompensated taking of property) in intellectual property law than in the law of physical property.[1] It is why we expect finders' rights to be broader too, and the extinction of a property right by the passage of time to be more common. It is why possessors of trade secrets are required to build higher "fences" than possessors of land. These examples could be multiplied at will. We look forward to a time when professors of property law will consider intellectual property a natural extension of their interest and when intellectual property professors will take a turn at teaching the basic property law course. To our knowledge, such crossover ventures are at present rare.[2]

1. Although the term is not used in the ordinary law of property, the concept exists and is illustrated by the doctrine of "trespass of necessity." If you swerve onto a person's vacant lot in order to avoid hitting a child, you are not guilty of a trespass even though you lacked the property owner's permission. In the jargon of intellectual property, we would term your use of his property fair use and therefore privileged. Although we have emphasized fair use in copyright law, there is also a fair use doctrine in trademark law, and patent law contains fair use elements too, as in the treatment of improvement patents.

2. For an interesting example of one, see Richard A. Epstein, "*International News Service v. Associated Press:* Custom and Law as Sources of Property Rights in News," 78 *Virginia Law Review* 85 (1992).

3. Economic analysis has come up short of providing either theoretical or empirical grounds for assessing the overall effect of intellectual property law on economic welfare. There is least doubt about the value of trademark law, which we explained in Chapter 7 as a rationally designed system for minimizing consumer search costs,[3] and about the core of trade secrecy law (see Chapter 13). It is a reasonable surmise as well that some core patent and copyright protection is welfare-improving. But there is no basis for confidence that the existing scope and duration of either patent or copyright protection are optimal. The doubt is not whether the protection is too meager but whether it is too great, imposing access and transaction costs disproportionate to the likely benefits from enhancing the incentives to produce socially valuable intellectual property. Doubt is deepened by a point we've harped on continually—that expanding intellectual property rights can actually reduce the amount of new intellectual property that is created by raising the creators' input costs, since a major input into new intellectual property is existing such property.[4] This is true in both the patent and copyright areas and makes us skeptical about proposals to enlarge intellectual property rights in those areas. Any further enlargement would increase access and transaction costs and could at the same time weaken rather than strengthen the incentives to create new intellectual property.

4. It might be thought that if economics cannot answer the fundamental question how extensive the legal protection of intellectual property should be, the efficiency of particular rules, doctrines, statutory provisions, or cases cannot be determined either. But that is not correct. Some economic points are clear however the fundamental question is answered; and it is possible also to be "realistic" and, taking the approximate present level of intellectual property protection as a given (approximate because there is surely some play in the joints), ask what rules, doctrines, and so forth are correct on that assumption. For example, it seems clear that whether or not copyright law goes too far in protecting authors, the doctrine of fair use ought to be given a generous construal with regard to unpublished materials not intended by their authors to be published; as we explained in Chapter 5, denying the use of such works by subsequent authors is unlikely to deter the creation of such materials significantly. Similarly, even if we do not know whether the current

---

3. Though we did express doubt about the social benefits of "pure" antidilution law.

4. This was a novel point with regard to copyright when we first made it in our article "An Economic Analysis of Copyright Law," 18 *Journal of Legal Studies* 325 (1989). It had long been familiar to students of patents, since it was obvious that technological advance is a cumulative process. Literature and the arts are less frequently understood in those terms, the tendency being to think (mistakenly) of the creators of works of the imagination as solitary geniuses rather than as improvers of previous work.

copyright term is too long (though we suspect it is), we showed in Chapter 8 that a system of renewable copyright terms would probably be superior on efficiency grounds to the single very long term established by the Copyright Act of 1976 and further lengthened by the Sonny Bono Copyright Term Extension Act. And whether or not works of visual art should be copyrightable at all—given that the main effect is probably just to give the most successful artists some additional income from derivative works—the moral rights doctrine embodied in the Visual Artists Rights Act seems plainly inefficient.

We argued for trade secret and patent law on grounds unrelated to the question whether the patent term is too long or patent protection too broad. And our analysis of the benefits of trademarks in reducing consumer search costs (without, as our detour into the economics of language showed, impoverishing the language) is untouched by uncertainty over whether intellectual property is being overprotected; for the access and transaction costs imposed by patent and copyright law are not a significant factor in trademark law even where that law has been "propertized" by antidilution statutes. As these points illustrate, and indeed as we have emphasized throughout the book, there is much more to economic analysis of intellectual property law than a concern with providing incentives to create such property.

5. Another element of our analysis that is worth stressing is what might be called the "interlock" thesis. Given that some degree of legal protection of intellectual property is necessitated by the static and dynamic benefits that property rights confer, the specific doctrines of that law that have emerged often reflect the need to check the distortions that efforts to create, define, and enforce intellectual property rights inevitably give rise to. The durational limitations of patent and copyright law are obvious examples; another is the ubiquitous doctrine of fair use. We mentioned the reciprocal relation of patent and trade secrecy law, and we also pointed out that design patents can be understood as responding to problems created by the protection of trade dress by trademark law.

6. Intellectual property is notably diverse. There are four major fields of intellectual property law (patents, copyrights, trademarks, and trade secrets), but far more than four economically distinct forms of intellectual property. It is far from obvious that the same basic set of legal rules is apt for popular songs and computer software, customer lists and industrial processes, electronic databases and Beanie Babies, new drugs and ornamental hood ornaments, the oncomouse and one-click ordering over the Web. In particular, scientific and technological advances have placed what is essentially an eighteenth-century system of property rights and regulations under increasing strain. A more radical restructuring of intellectual property law than considered in this book, better informed by scientific and technological under-

standing and more heavily focused on current and likely scientific and technological advances (particularly in computerization, telecommunications, and biotechnology), may be overdue.

7. As we have noted throughout this book, but particularly in the last chapter, the last quarter-century has witnessed a considerable though not uniform expansion in the extent of intellectual property rights. We explored the possible causes of this trend with rather inconclusive results. Although we identified some economically efficient interventions, both legislative and judicial, into the existing body of intellectual property law, no public-interest explanation for the evolution of intellectual property law over this period seems plausible. Public-choice theory, which emphasizes the role of interest groups in determining public policy, has not as yet come up with a convincing explanation for this evolution either. The importance of such an explanation is practical as well as theoretical, for without it the path of feasible reform cannot be discerned nor steps taken down it. Along with answering the fundamental question of how extensive a system of intellectual property rights is required in order to generate adequate incentives for the creation of expressive and inventive activity, explaining the evolution of intellectual property law is the most important unfinished business of economic analysis of intellectual property.

8. Another unresolved issue is that of the relative efficiency of judge-made and statutory law. While on the whole the judge-made parts of intellectual property law seem pretty efficient, and we noted numerous instances of economic ingenuity displayed in judge-made rules and judicial decisions, a number of legislative interventions have been efforts to rectify economically unsound decisions, such as the patent and copyright tie-in and bundling decisions. The solution to the puzzle of why intellectual property protection has been expanding in recent decades will require consideration of, among other difficult issues, the difference in perspectives, constraints, and incentives between judges and legislators and how these two bodies of decision-makers have interacted to produce the fascinating, colorful, problematic, complex, immensely important, and quintessentially economic body of law that has been the subject of this book.

Acknowledgments

The book draws on our previous writings, both joint and separate, on intellectual property, but with extensive revisions, including updating, rearrangement, amplification, and rethinking. The discussion of patent law in Chapters 11 and 12 is completely new, as are the Introduction, the Conclusion, and Chapter 15. Chapters 1 and 14 are largely new, and all the other chapters are revised, expanded, and updated versions of our previous work; in particular, Chapters 2, 4, and 9 contain a great deal of new material. The previous writings on which we draw that are jointly authored by us are "Trademark Law: An Economic Perspective," 30 *Journal of Law and Economics* 265 (1987); "The Economics of Trademark Law," 78 *Trademark Reporter* 267 (1988); "An Economic Analysis of Copyright Law," 18 *Journal of Legal Studies* 325 (1989); "Some Economics of Trade Secret Law," *Journal of Economic Perspectives*, Winter 1991, p. 61 (coauthored with David D. Friedman); and "Indefinitely Renewable Copyright," 70 *University of Chicago Law Review* 471 (2003). Authored by Landes alone are "Copyright Protection of Letters, Diaries, and Other Unpublished Works: An Economic Approach," 21 *Journal of Legal Studies* 79 (1992); "Copyright, Borrowed Images, and Appropriation Art: An Economic Approach," 9 *George Mason University Law Review* 1 (2000); and "What Has the Visual Rights Act of 1990 Accomplished?" 25 *Journal of Cultural Economics* 283 (2001). Authored by Posner alone are "When Is Parody Fair Use?" 21 *Journal of Legal Studies* 67 (1992); *Law and Literature*, ch. 11 (revised and enlarged ed. 1998); *Frontiers of Legal Theory*, chs. 1, 6 (2001); and *Antitrust Law*, ch. 9 (2d ed. 2001).

We thank William Baude, Peter Broadbent, Carolyn Chong, Bryan Dayton, Brian Grill, David Kitchen, and Carl LeSueur for very helpful research assistance, and Michael Aronson, Erica Benton, Dennis Carlton, Edward Cramer, Christopher DeMuth, Rochelle Dreyfuss, Michael Green, Scott Hemphill, Scott Kieff, Benjamin Klein, Elisabeth Landes, Mark Lemley, Lawrence Lessig, Pierre Leval, Douglas Lichtman, Robert Merges, William Patry, Steven Shavell, John Thorne, Samson Vermont, Timothy Wu, and Tzachi Zamir for very helpful comments on an earlier draft. We also thank, for their many helpful comments, the audience at the Thirty-Second Annual Donald C. Brace Memorial Lecture, sponsored by the Copyright Society of the USA, where Posner presented a version of Chapter 8 on November 18, 2002; the audience at the 2002 AEI-Brookings Joint Center Distinguished Lecture on November 19, 2002, where he presented a version of Chapter 15; and participants in the law and economics workshop at Harvard Law School, and the intellectual property workshop at Boston University Law School, where he presented versions of Chapters 11 and 12, and a version of Chapter 8, respectively, on March 4 and 6, 2003. And finally we thank the participants in workshops and conferences at which versions of the articles that formed the basis for some chapters were presented for their helpful comments.

Case Index

A&M Records, Inc. v. Napster, Inc., 120–121

Abercrombie & Fitch Co. v. Hunting World, Inc., 188n

ABKO Music Inc. v. Harrisongs Music, Ltd., 88n

Academy of Motion Picture Arts and Sciences v. Creative House Promotions, Inc., 264n

Alcatel USA., Inc. v. DGI Technologies, Inc., 355n

Alfred Bell & Co. v. Catalda Fine Arts, 261n, 262, 263, 265

Allen v. W. H. Brady Co., 303n

American Chicle Co. v. Topps Chewing Gum, Inc., 204n

American Geophysical Union v. Texaco, 48n

American Home Products Corp. v. Barr Laboratories, Inc., 190n

Amgen Inc. v. Hoechst Marion Roussel, Inc., 317n

Anderson v. Stallone, 109n

Anheuser-Busch, Inc. v. Balducci Publications, 165n

Aro Manufacturing Co. v. Convertible Top Replacement Co., 382n

Baker v. Selden, 97–104

Benny v. Loew's, Inc., 155n

Blau Plumbing, Inc. v. S.O.S. Fix-It, Inc., 205n

Blue Bell, Inc. v. Farah Manufacturing Co., 181n

Board of Trade v. Dow Jones and Co., 105–106

Bonito Boats, Inc. v. Thunder Craft Boats, Inc., 211n

Borden, Inc. v. FTC, 173n

Botello v. Shell Oil Co., 286–287

Bridgeman Art Library v. Corel Corp., 261n, 263, 265

Bristol-Myers Squibb Co. v. McNeil-P.P.C., Inc., 190n

Broadcast Music Inc. v. Columbia Broadcasting System, Inc., 386–387, 388n

Brulotte v. Thys Co., 372, 380–381, 417

Campbell v. Acuff–Rose Music, Inc., 148n, 153, 154n, 155n, 163n

Campbell v. Koons, 261n

Carpenter v. United States, 355n

Carson v. Here's Johnny Portable Toilets, Inc., 159n, 226

Carter v. Helmsley-Spear, Inc., 275n, 281–282, 283n

Castle Rock Entertainment, Inc. v. Carol Publishing Group, Inc., 163n

Ciba-Geigy Corp. v. Bolar Pharmaceutical Co., 190n

Cliff Notes, Inc. v. Bantam Doubleday Dell Publishing Group, Inc., 165n

Coach House Restaurant, Inc. v. Coach & Six Restaurants, Inc., 182n

Coca-Cola Co. v. Gemini Rising, Inc., 160n, 162

Columbia Broadcasting System, Inc. v. Lowe's, Inc., 155n

Computer Associates International v. Altai, Inc., 392n

Corona Cord Tire Co. v. Dovan Chemical Corp., 303n

Davis v. The Gap, Inc., 154n

Deere & Co. v. MTD Products, 159–160

Demetriades v. Kaufmann, 100n, 101n

Dr. Seuss Enterprises, L.P. v. Penguin Books USA, Inc., 152, 154n

Durham Industries, Inc. v. Tomy Corp., 113n

427

Dwinell–Wright Co. v. White House Milk Co., 182n

E. I. du Pont deNemours & Co. v. Christopher, 330n, 355, 355n, 369, 371
Eldred v. Ashcroft, 210n, 211n, 218n, 231, 408n
English v. CFC&R 11th Street LLC, 282
Estate of Martin Luther King, Jr., Inc. v. CBS, Inc., 124n

Feist Publications, Inc. v. Rural Telephone Service Co., 103–104
Festo Corporation v. Shoketsu Kinzoku Kogyo Kabushiki Co., 322n, 323n, 338
Flack v. Friends of Queen Catherine Inc., 283–284
Forward v. Thorogood, 264n
Franklin Mint Corp. v. National Wildlife Art Exchange, Inc., 262n

Gaylor v. Wilder, 303n
Gilliam v. American Broadcasting Cos., 279n
Gracen v. Bradford Exchange, 113n

Harper & Row Publishers, Inc. v. Nation Enterprises, 125, 126, 130, 143–144, 146
Haslem v. Lockwood, 17n, 35
Haynes v. Alfred Knopf, Inc., 144n
Hays v. Sony Corp. of America, 272n
Henry v. A. B. Dick Co., 372n, 373–374
Hoepker v. Kruger, 255n
Hormel Food Corp. v. Jim Henson Productions, Inc., 160n
Hurst v. Hughes Tools Co., 355n
Hyatt Corp. v. Hyatt Legal Services, 206n

Illinois High School Assocation v. GTE Vantage, Inc., 33, 196–197
Imperial Homes Corp. v. Lamont, 100n
In re Independent Service Organizations Antitrust Litigation, 379n
International Business Machine Corp. v. United States, 373n
International News Service v. Associated Press, 4, 105, 107, 421n
International Nickel Co. v. Ford Motor Co., 322–323
International Salt Co. v. United States, 373n

Johnson & Johnson Associates, Inc. v. R. E. Service Co., 338
Jordache Enterprises, Inc. v. Hogg Wyld, Ltd., 162n

Kewanee Oil Co. v. Bicron Corp., 355n, 359n, 360, 364n

L. Baitlin & Son, Inc. v. Snyder, 113n, 263n
Lee v. A.R.T. Co., 108n, 261n, 265
Leibovitz v. Paramount Pictures Corp., 154n
L. L. Bean, Inc. v. Drake Publishers, Inc., 163n
LeSportsac, Inc. v. K Mart Corp., 199n
Lish v. Harper's Magazine Foundation, 145–146
Lotus Development Corp. v. Borland International, Inc., 392
Lucasfilm Ltd. v. High Frontier, 194n

Mallinckrodt, Inc. v. Medipart, Inc., 381n
Martin v. City of Indianapolis, 275n, 283
Mattel, Inc. v. MCA Records, Inc., 162n
McGregor-Doniger, Inc. v. Drizzle, Inc., 205n
Metallizing Engineering Co. v. Kenyon Bearing & Auto Parts Co., 361n
Minnear v. Tors, 91n
Mirage Editions, Inc. v. Albuquerque A.R.T. Co., 261n, 265n
Moncada v. Rubin-Spangle Gallery, Inc., 284–285
Morgan Envelope Co. v. Albany Perforated Wrapping Paper Co., 381n
Morrisey v. Proctor and Gamble Co., 97n
Morton Salt Co. v. G. S. Suppiger Co., 373n
Mucha v. King, 27n

Nabisco, Inc. v. PF Brands, Inc., 206n
Nadalin v. Automobile Recovery Bureau, Inc., 28n
National Basketball Association v. Motorola, Inc., 106–108
New Era Publications v. Henry Holt & Co., 125–126, 126n, 130, 135n, 144, 417
New York Times v. Tasini, 273, 417

O'Reilly v. Morse, 323n

Painton & Co. v. Bourns, Inc., 364n
Park 'n Fly, Inc. v. Dollar Park & Fly, Inc., 183n
Pavia v. 1120 Avenue of the Americas Associates, 271n, 282–283
People for the Ethical Treatment of Animals v. Doughney, 165n
Pepsico, Inc. v. Grapette Co., 184n
Pharmacia Corp. v. Alcon Laboratories, Inc., 190n

Phillips v. Frey, 355n
Piarowski v. Illinois Community College District 515, 157n
Pickett v. Prince, 109n, 113n
Pioneer Hi-Bred International v. Holden Foundation Seeds, Inc., 368n
Polaroid Corp. v. Polarad Electronics Corp., 182n
Pollara v. Seymour, 284–285
Publications International, Ltd. v. Landoll, Inc., 200
Pushman v. New York Graphic Society, 127, 264

Qualitex Co. v. Jacobson Products Co., 189n, 200

Richmond Homes, Inc. v. Raintree, Inc., 101n
Roberts v. Sears, Roebuck, & Co., 304n
Robinson v. Random House, Inc., 276n
Roche Products, Inc. v. Bolar Pharmaceutical Co., 336n
Rockwell Graphic Systems, Inc. v. DEV Industries, Inc., 368n
Rogers v. Koons, 163, 261, 268–269, 272, 417
Romm Art Creations, Ltd. v. Simcha International, Inc., 149n

Salinger v. Random House, Inc., 125, 126, 129, 130, 135n, 144, 417
Scheiber v. Dolby Laboratories, Inc., 380n
Schiller and Schmidt, Inc. v. Nordisco Corp., 269n
Sega Enterprises Ltd. v. Accolade Inc., 100, 102, 121n, 309, 392
Serra v. U.S. General Services Administration, 281n
Sheldon v. Metro-Goldwyn Pictures, 88n
Smith v. Chanel, 206, 206n
SmithKline Beecham Corp. v. Pennex Products Co., 190n
Sony Corporation of America v. Universal Studios, Inc., 118–119, 123, 409
Standard Fashion Co. v. Magrane-Houston Co., 397–401
Standard Oil Co. (Indiana) v. United States, 382
State Street Bank & Trust Co. v. Signature Financial Group, Inc., 328n, 341

Sunderman v. Seajay Society, Inc., 135n, 145
SunTrust Bank v. Houghton Mifflin Co., 149, 154n

Taliferro v. Augle, 275n
Taylor Wine Co. v. Bully Hill Vineyards, Inc., 204
Treasure Salvors, Inc. v. Unidentified Wrecked & Abandoned Sailing Vessel, 17
Ty, Inc. v. GMA Accessories, Inc., 279n
Ty, Inc. v. Perryman, 206n
Ty, Inc. v. Publications International Ltd., 121–122, 163n

UMG Recordings, Inc. v. MP3.com, Inc., 121n
United Feature Syndicate v. Koons, 261n
United States v. General Electric Co., 383–385
United States v. Loew's, 387–388
United States v. Microsoft Corp., 393–394
Universal Studios, Inc. v. Corley, 43n
U.S. Golf Association v. St. Andrews System, Data–Max, Inc., 106n
USM Corp. v. SPS Technologies, Inc., 380n

Waldman Publishing Corp. v. Landoll, Inc., 276n
Wal-Mart Stores, Inc. v. Samara Bros., Inc., 193n
Weinstein v. University of Illinois, 272n
Westinghouse v. Boyden Power Brake Co., 317n
WGN Continental Broadcasting Co. v. United Video, Inc., 279n
White v. Samsung Electronics America, Inc., 159n
White-Smith Music Publishing Co. v. Apollo Co., 19n
Williams v. Broadus, 109n
Wilson v. Simpson, 381n
Wilson Sporting Goods Co. v. David Geoffrey & Associates, 323n
W. L. Gore & Associates v. Garlock, Inc., 361–362
Wojnarowicz v. American Family Association, 286
Wright v. Warner Books, Inc., 129n, 145

Zacchini v. Scripps-Howard Broadcasting Co., 223n

Author Index

Aitchison, Jean, 170n, 171n
Akerlof, George A., 210n
Akmajian, Adrian, 169n
Alchian, Armen A., 42n
Alford, William P., 52n
Allison, John R., 320n, 335n, 338n, 339n
Alsop, Ronald, 228n
Ames, E. Kenly, 260n
Anderson, Bentley J., 7n
Anderson, Terry L., 11n, 414n
Areeda, Philip E., 374n, 380n
Arno, Peter S., 310n
Arrow, Kenneth J., 304

Bae, Jay P., 314n
Baird, Douglas G., 105n, 223n
Baird, Laura M., 311n
Baker, Scott, 320n
Bakos, Yannis, 388n
Banks, Bruce A., 311n
Becker, Gary S., 154n, 161n, 174n, 209n, 256n
Begley, Sharon, 179n
Ben-Porat, Ziva, 164n
Berman, Bruce, 320n
Berndt, Ernst, 314n
Besen, Stanley M., 46n, 126n, 396n
Bessen, James, 327n
Beverley-Smith, Huw, 64n, 105n, 223n
Bevington, David, 59n
Bhagwati, Jagdish, 47n
Blair, Roger D., 7n, 314n
Bloom, Harold, 59n
Bone, Robert G., 354n, 366n
Bonus, Holger, 256n
Bork, Robert H., 398n
Bouckart, Boudewijn, 2n
Boudin, Michael, 392
Boyle, James, 13n

Brakman, Steven, 327n
Branstetter, Lee, 326n
Breit, William, 42n
Breyer, Stephen G., 9n, 21n, 189n
Britt, Bill, 224n
Brock, William A., 404n
Brown, Cynthia J., 51n
Brynjolfsson, Eric, 388n
Bugbee, Bruce W., 51n, 413n
Bullough, Geoffrey, 58n
Buranen, Lise, 61n, 192n
Bynon, Theodora, 170n

Caprio, Frank M., 380n
Carlton, Dennis W., 40n, 117n, 301n, 315n, 321n, 327n, 329n, 385n
Carroll, John M., 193n
Caves, Richard E., 38n
Chang, Howard F., 317n
Chatman, Seymour, 148n, 155n, 163n
Cheung, Steven N. S., 328n, 354n, 366n
Church, Steven A., 332n
Clankie, Shawn M., 192n
Clark, T. J., 68n
Coase, Ronald H., 14n, 23n, 91, 92, 95–97, 102, 272n
Cohen, Wesley M., 312n, 359n
Comanor, William S., 173n
Coombe, Rosemary J., 161n
Cooter, Robert D., 403n
Cotter, Thomas F., 7n, 314n
Coverdale, John F., 167n
Craswell, Richard, 204n, 205n
Creamer, Jon, 255n
Cross, Eric, 67n

Dahlman, Carl J., 12n
Dale, S. S., 67n
Danto, Arthur C., 258n

Danzon, Patricia M., 313n
D'Arcy, David, 255n
Dasgupta, Partha, 301n, 327n
Davis, Michael H., 310n
Davis, Steven J., 314n
De Geest, Gerrit, 2n
Demers, Richard A., 169n
Demsetz, Harold, 14n, 412
Denicolò, Vincenzo, 10n, 324n, 361n
Dentith, Simon, 148n, 150n
Derthick, Martha, 405n
Donner, Irah, 413n
Dreyfuss, Rochelle Cooper, 194n, 208n, 230n, 273n, 324n, 335–336, 380n
Duffy, John Fitzgerald, 7n, 303n, 362n
Dunner, Donald R., 337n, 338n

Easterbrook, Frank H., 382n, 383n
Ehrlich, Isaac, 174n
Eisenberg, Rebecca S., 310n, 316n
Ellickson, Robert C., 17n
Emert, Carol, 255n
Epstein, Richard A., 15n, 105n, 316n, 421n

Farber, Daniel A., 403n
Farrell, Joseph, 396n
Feather, John, 51n
Federico, P. J., 334n
First, Harry, 230n, 324n
Fisher, Lawrence, 174n
Flynn, Laurie J., 255
Fogarty, Michael S., 311n
Frank, Björn, 56n
Franzoni, Luigi Alberto, 361n
Frickey, Philip P., 403n
Fried, Michael, 68n, 257n
Friedman, David D., 354n
Friedman, Monroe, 169n
Friendly, Henry, 364n
Fruman, Norman, 59n
Frye, Northrop, 60

Galenson, David W., 258, 276n
Gallini, Nancy T., 5n, 9n, 320n, 325n, 329n
Gehring, Wes D., 151n
Gertner, Robert H., 385n
Gifford, Don, 151n
Gigerenzer, Gerd, 161n
Gilbert, Richard, 218n
Gilovich, Thomas, 161n
Ginarte, Juan C., 410n
Ginsburg, Jane C., 212n, 213n
Ginsburgh, Victor A., 27n

Glaeser, Edward, 209n
Glazier, Stephen C., 322n
Gleadell, Colin, 255n
Goldreyer, Elizabeth, 48n
Goldstein, Paul, 109n, 113n
Goodman, Nelson, 255n
Gordon, Wendy J., 4n, 118n, 154n
Gorman, Robert A., 212n, 272n
Grabowski, Henry G., 314n, 315n
Grady, Mark F., 223n
Grampp, William D., 269n
Green, Jerry, 325n
Green, Michael Steven, 93n, 97n, 104n
Greenberg, Abraham S., 1n
Greenberg, Lynne A., 260n
Griliches, Zvi, 327n
Gurnsey, John, 57n
Gutterman, Alan S., 7n

Hadfield, Gillian K., 2n
Hall, Bronwyn H., 310n, 320n, 327n, 344n
Hamermesh, Daniel, 48n
Hanchuk, Walter G., 329n
Hand, Learned, 88n
Hanfling, Oswald, 16n, 255n
Hansmann, Henry, 276n, 279–280
Hardy, I. T., 272n
Harlan, John Marshall, 380n
Harmon, Robert L., 338n
Harnish, Robert M., 169n
Harries, Don, 68n, 151n
Hausman, Jerry A., 40n
Hayek, Friedrich 415
Heald, Paul J., 329n
Heller, Michael A., 316n
Higgins, Richard S., 205n, 208n
Hochman, Harold M., 42n
Holloway, Lynette, 54n
Holmes, Oliver Wendell, 19n, 27n, 28n
Holzhauer, Rudi, 4n
Horton, Andrew, 68n
Hotelling, Harold, 19
Hovencamp, Herbert, 372n
Hui, Kai-Lung, 214n
Hurt, Robert M., 9n
Hutcheon, Linda, 148n

Jaffe, Adam B., 9n, 21n, 310n, 311n, 320n, 326n
Jakes, J. Michael, 337n, 338n
Janis, Mark D., 372n
Jarceski, Jeffrey D., 337n, 338n
Jaszi, Peter, 51n, 161n

Johnson, George, 48n
Jones, Charles I., 327n
Jones, Eric L., 12n

Kahneman, Daniel, 161n
Kaplan, Benjamin, 52n
Kaplan, David A., 125n, 255n
Kaplow, Louis, 387n
Karjala, Denis S., 223n
Katz, Michael L., 396n
Kay, Randy, 364n
Kearney, Joseph D., 406n
Kenney, Roy W., 388n
Kieff, F. Scott, 329n
King, Sarah, 266n
Kirby, Sheila Nataraj, 46n, 126n
Kiremidjian, G. D., 148n, 150n
Kitch, Edmund W., 10n, 116n, 181n, 205n, 302n, 304n, 319, 324, 354n, 360, 375
Klein, Benjamin, 46n, 164n, 168n, 173n, 373n, 377–378, 388n, 398n
Klemperer, Paul, 324n, 396n
Klenz, William, 67n
Kline, David, 322n
Knight, Frank, 12n
Knight, H. Jackson, 322n
Koenig, Gloria K., 334n
Kortum, Samuel, 344n
Kraus, Kate, 320n
Krecké, Elisabeth, 414n
Kuipers, Simon K., 327n
Kwall, Roberta Rosenthal, 208n, 270n

Langreth, Robert, 314n
Lanjouw, Jean O., 311n
Lavey, Warren G., 173n
Leahey, Jack, 48n
Leal, Donald R., 414n
Leask, Nigel, 269n
Leffler, Keith B., 168n, 173n
Lemley, Mark A., 4n, 109n, 296n, 311n, 319n, 320n, 334n, 335n, 338n, 339n, 357n, 372n, 393n
Lennon, Peter, 256n
Lerner, Andres V., 46n
Lerner, Josh, 344n, 404n
Lessig, Lawrence, 9n, 45n, 120n, 408
Leval, Pierre N., 135n, 220n
Levin, Kim, 269n
Levin, Richard C., 312n, 313n, 320n
Levmore, Saul, 28n
Levy, Steven, 408n

Lichtenberg, Frank R., 91n, 327n
Lichtman, Douglas G., 89n, 105n, 114n, 119n, 320n
Liebowitz, S. J., 46n
Liman, Lewis, 220n
Lindenbaum, Peter, 52n
Link, Albert N., 379n
Litman, Jessica D., 407n
Locke, John, 4
Loewenstein, Joseph, 51n
Long, Clarisa, 328n
Lueck, Dean, 26n

MacDonald, Dwight, 163n
Macey, Jonathan R., 403n
Machlup, Fritz, 9n
MacKie-Mason, Jeffrey K., 40n
Madow, Michael, 223n
Magee, Stephen P., 404n
Mallon, Thomas, 59n
Martin, Henri-Jean, 51n
Marvel, Howard P., 398n
Maskin, Eric, 327n
Maskus, Keith E., 413n
Masterson, Salathiel C., 51n
Matthews, Brander, 51n
Matthews, Duncan, 413n
Maurer, Stephen M., 104n
Mazzoleni, Robert, 312n, 316n, 324n, 326n
McCarthy, J. Thomas, 160n, 185n, 196n, 198n
McCartney, Brian T., 279n
McChesney, Fred S., 11n, 205n
McCloskey, Donald (Deirdre) N., 12n, 96n
McDougal, Stuart Y., 68n
McKenzie, Matt, 120n
Medearis, John, 412n
Medema, Steven G., 96n
Mehra, Salil Kumar, 112
Meltzer, Françoise, 59n
Menell, Peter S., 2n, 4n, 99n, 334n, 339n, 392n
Menger, Pierre-Michel, 27n
Merges, Robert Patrick, 4n, 9n, 303n, 304n, 305n, 306n, 308n, 317n, 318n, 319n, 322n, 324n, 328n, 334n, 339n, 362n, 409n
Merrill, Thomas W., 33n, 406n
Merz, Jon F., 352n
Miller, Arthur R., 228n
Mueller, Janice M., 315n
Müller, Beate, 147n

Murphy, Kevin M., 46n, 154n, 174n, 209n, 256n, 314n, 398n
Murphy, Victoria, 314n

Nelson, Richard R., 216n, 312n, 317n, 318n, 319n, 322n, 324n, 326n, 359n, 379n
Newman, Peter, 26n, 38n, 403n
Nimmer, David, 67n, 109n, 154n, 155n
Nimmer, Melville B., 67n, 109n, 154n, 155n
Norman, Geraldine, 262n, 267n
Novos, Ian E., 325n

Oliar, Dotan, 214n
Oppenheim, Charles, 311n
Ostrom, Elinor, 414n

Pace, Nicholas M., 352n
Pakes, Ariel, 311n, 327n
Parchomovsky, Gideon, 314n
Park, Walter G., 410n
Parker, William N., 12n
Parr, Russell L., 320n
Patterson, Lyman Ray, 1n, 51n, 52n
Penrose, Edith, 9n
Perlman, Harvey S., 205n
Perloff, Jeffrey M., 38n, 40n, 117n, 301n, 315n, 321n
Philipson, Tomas, 91n, 327n
Picker, Randal C., 118n, 119n
Plant, Arnold, 1n, 2, 2n, 8, 20, 21n, 22–23, 51n, 304, 374
Png, I. P. L., 167n, 214n
Pound, Louise, 169n
Prager, Frank D., 413n
Praninskas, Jean, 169n
Prater, Jill I., 255n
Priest, George L., 164n
Putnam, Jonathan, 311n

Quirk, Paul J., 405n

Raboy, David G., 173n
Rai, Arti K., 352n
Rappaport, Edward, 231n, 244n
Raskind, Leo J., 370n
Reichman, J. H., 104n
Reitman, David, 167n
Richtler, Mordechai, 134n
Ricks, Christopher, 59n, 61n
Riewald, J. G., 148n, 149n, 151n
Ringer, Barbara A., 234n

Rivette, Kevin J., 322n
Robinson, Joan, 39n, 40n
Robinson, Walter, 281n
Romer, Paul, 66n
Ronte, Dieter, 256n
Rose, Carol M., 13n, 34n
Rose, Margaret A., 148n
Rose, Mark, 51n
Rosen, Jeffrey, 216n
Rosen, Sherwin, 49n
Ross, David, 39n, 40n
Roy, Alice M., 61n, 192n
Rubenfeld, Jed, 112n, 287n
Rubin, Paul H., 161n, 208n
Rubinstein, Raphael, 261n

Sakakibara, Mariko, 326n
Saloner, Garth, 396n
Salop, Steven C., 73n
Samuelson, Pamela, 104n, 354n, 356n, 369
Samuelson, Paul A., 39n
Sandler, Chanani, 272n
Santilli, Marina, 276n, 279–280
Saunders, David, 51n
Saunders, Kurt M., 321n
Saxenian, AnnaLee, 365n
Schankerman, Mark, 311n, 312n
Schaumann, Niels B., 260n
Scheffman, David T., 73n
Scherer, F. M., 39n, 40n, 230n, 314n, 315n, 337
Schjeldahl, Peter, 68n
Schmalensee, Richard, 40n, 173n
Schuchman, Robert M., 9n
Schumpeter, Joseph, 379, 379n, 412
Scotchmer, Suzanne, 5n, 9n, 104n, 325n, 354n, 356n, 364n, 369
See, Harold, 380n
Seidman, Robert J., 151n
Seifert, Fedor, 51n
Shapiro, Carl, 218n, 396n
Shavell, Stephen, 9n
Siegelman, Peter, 314n
Siwek, Stephen E., 3n
Sobel, Gerald, 336n
Stanley, Alessandra, 255n
Statman, Meir, 314n
Steiner, Peter O., 40n
Stephan, Paula E., 308n
Stigler, George J., 18n, 174n, 300n, 388n, 404n, 406n
Stiglitz, Joseph, 301n

Stoneman, Paul, 321n, 327n
Suh, Dong-Churl, 314n
Suzuki, Masaya, 180n
Swidler, Steve, 48n

Takeyama, Lisa N., 393n
Tam, Pui-Wing, 320n
Thurow, Lester, 2n
Tirole, Jean, 40n, 396n
Todd, Peter M., 161n
Topel, Robert H., 314n
Tor, Avishalom, 214n
Towse, Ruth, 4n, 279n
Trajtenberg, Manuel, 310n
Tuchman, Barbara W., 209n
Tuckman, Howard P., 48n
Turner, Julie S., 321n
Tversky, Amos, 161n

Van Gelder, Lawrence, 214n
van Ypersele, Tanguy, 9n
Varian, Hal R., 40n
Vermont, Samson, 320n
Vernon, John M., 315n
Vogel, Steven K., 405n
von Ees, Hans, 327n
von Hippel, Eric, 313n

Waldman, Michael, 325n
Walsh, John P., 312n, 359n
Walterscheid, Edward C., 211n
Wasko, Janet, 220n
Weinberg, Bruce, 276n
Weisbrod, Burton, 48n
White, Morton, 258n
Wiggins, Steven N., 173n
Wiley, John Shepard Jr., 373n, 377–378
Williams, John C., 327n
Willig, Robert D., 40n
Wilson, Thomas A., 173n
Winslow, Anastasia P., 148n
Winter, Sidney G., 318n, 379n
Wittenberg, Philip, 52n
Woodmansee, Martha, 51n, 161n
Wordie, J. R., 12n

Yen, Alfred C., 4n
Young, Leslie, 404n

Ziedonis, Rosemarie Ham, 320n, 344n
Zimmerman, Diane Lennheer, 230n, 324n
Zinner, Darren E., 313n
Zipf, George Kingsley, 170n

Subject Index

Abandonment of property, 17–18, 28–29, 31–35; intellectual versus physical property, 32, 232, 303–304

Academic research. *See* Basic research; Universities

Advertising, 117–118, 154; as complement of advertised good, 174n; comparative, 159–160; false, 204–206. *See also* Brand names; Marketing; Product differentiation; Trademarks

American Investors Protection Act, 361n

Anthologies, 217. *See also* Copyrights, compilations

Anticybersquatting Consumer Protection Act, 180, 410

Antitrust and intellectual property: blanket licenses, 386–387; block booking, 387–388; bundling, 388, 400–401; end-product royalties, 386–388; exclusive dealing, 397–400; felt tension between the two fields of law, 335, 372, 416; merger law, 385; Microsoft litigation, 387–393, 400–401; minimum-price patent licenses, 384–385; patent pooling, 382–383; patents as cartelization devices, 383–385; predatory pricing, 401; software markets, 390–402; tying arrangements, 372–390 passim, 400

Architectural Works Protection Act of 1990, 101–102, 406

Architecture, 100–102, 277. *See also* Architectural Works Protection Act; Copyrights, architects' plans; Copyrights, buildings

Art (visual), 16, 24, 99, 114–115, 254–293; Abstract Expressionism, 257–259; Appropriation Art, 254, 260–262, 266–269; artists' incomes from derivative works, 254–255, 259–260; artists' support for moral rights laws, 278–279, 291; conceptual, 6, 254; congestion externalities, 256, 260; derivative works from, 254–257; graffiti, 285; museum shops, 24, 41, 46, 255; Pop Art, 254, 258–259; postmodern, 254–269, 285; price of originals versus price of copies, 41, 255–256; publication of, 264; re-creation as copying, 85n; sale contracts, 277–279; sculptors' clay models, 284; stolen, 35–36, 124; Superrealism, 258–259; vintage photographs, 256. *See also* Manet; Moral rights; Warhol

Artists Rights Society, 264

ASCAP. *See* Performing-rights organizations

Authorship, 64; academic, 48, 53, 65, 97, 272–273; authors' incentives, 48, 53, 65; royalties as method of compensating, 38–39, 48, 279n. *See also* Plagiarism

Availability heuristic, 161, 207

Basic research, 97, 305–308, 310n

Bayh-Dole Act of 1980, 310n

Berne Convention, 234n, 235n, 239n, 245–247, 270

Biography, 131–144

Biotechnology. *See* Pharmaceutical drugs

Blurring. *See under* Dilution

Book reviews, as advertising, 117–118, 154. *See also under* Fair use

Brand loyalty. *See* Brand names; Trademarks

Brand names, 64–65, 166–167, 169n, 195–196; pharmaceutical, 54, 173, 196, 313–314. *See also* Product differentiation; Trademarks

Broadcasting, 106–108. *See also* Television

Burlesques, 152–158, 163, 217

Celebrities, 207, 223; dead, 223–224, 228n; incomes of, 54–55. *See also* Publicity rights; Superstars

Censorship, 52

Circumvention. *See* Encryption

Clayton Act, section 3, 372–373

Coase Theorem, 52, 92, 96, 158–159, 274

Common law: defined, 417n; economic analysis of, 10, 87, 417; tendency of, toward efficiency, 205–206, 417; trademark law as, 179, 205–206; trade-secrets law as, 355–356. *See also* Copyrights, common law

Commons. *See* Public domain

Communication theory, 170–172

Competition, 23; for monopoly, 22–23, 315–316; monopolistic, 315, 378–379; perfect, 375–376. *See also* Antitrust and intellectual property; Monopoly

Compulsory licensing, 7, 9n

Computers, 42, 387; computer chips, 370, 390–391; electronic databases, 104–105, 273–274, 417; Semiconductor Chip Protection Act, 370; switching costs, 396n. *See also* Digitization; File sharing; Internet; Software

Congestion externalities, 13–14, 20, 70, 222–228; in art, 256, 260, 279

Constitution. *See* U.S. Constitution

Consumer search costs, 168, 173–174, 202–203, 422–423; careful versus careless consumers, 204–205. *See also* Trademarks

Contracts, 43–44, 52, 91n, 118–119, 393–394; breach of contract as theft of trade secret, 355; for sale of art, 277–279; complementary versus substitutional, 153–154

Copying: economics of, 41–51; intermediate, 100; managed, 326; modern technology of, 42, 49, 140. *See also* Copyrights

Copyright Act of 1909, 129, 215, 234, 235n

Copyright Act of 1976, 129, 214, 220, 234–235, 245–247, 263–264, 403, 406–407, 414n, 417; section 101, 103n, 108n, 234n, 271n, 333n; section 102(a)(8), 101n; section 102(b), 91n, 100n; section 103, 103n; section 106A, 270n; section 106(2), 108; section 107, 115, 126n, 129, 157; sections 109(a) and (b)(1)(A), 265n; section 111(a)(3), 410; sections 115 and 116, 309n; sections 117(a)(1) and (b), 109n; section 201(c), 273n; section

303(a), 233n; sections 408, 411–412, and 504–505, 86n

Copyright Clearance Center, 116n

Copyrights, 5; adverse-possession analogy, 33–34; and antitrust, 379, 387–388, 392; architects' plans, 100, 332; artworks, 127, 254–293; block booking of, 387–388; books, 240–244, 253; breadth, 324n; buildings, 100–102; collective works, 273–274; common law, 124, 127, 129, 211, 214, 247, 263, 331; compilations, 103–104; contract substitutes for, 43–44, 52, 393–394; contributory infringement, 43, 118–121; copyright infringement versus plagiarism, 60–61; cover rule, 309n; databases, 273–274; deposit of copy in Library of Congress, 295; depreciation of, 212, 238–244, 312; dilution, 161–162; dramatic works, 42–43, 57, 331–332; duration, 33–34, 69–70, 210–249, 394, 419; economic model of, 55–56; effect on, of encryption, 44; effects of, on cost of expression, 66–70; English practice, 1, 51–52, 211; evidentiary considerations, 88–90, 113–114, 155, 257, 259, 263; facts versus expression, 102–104, 107; fees, 219–220, 235–237, 245–246, 249; first-sale rule, 265; foreign copyright law, 270; foreign residents, 239n; formal model, 71–84, 90–91, 131–141; and free speech, 158, 162, 287; government documents, 15–16, 24; graphic arts, 240–244, 253, 312; history of, 1, 51–52, 84; ideas versus expression, 83, 91–103, 107, 132n, 257–259, 305–307, 322, 392; indefinite renewals of, 210–249; independent creation versus copying, 85–91, 102–103, 355n; of industry standards, 100, 392; infringement of music copyrights, 88; invented languages, 172; joint ownership, 30, 216, 318; jukebox rule, 309n; maintenance-incentives argument for, 228–230; marketing expenditures, 232–233; merger doctrine, 97–101, 104; music, 54n, 66, 88, 240–247, 252–253, 309–310, 312; notice, 34, 215; originality requirement, 89–90, 262–263, 265, 319; ownership of copyright versus ownership of copy of copyrighted work, 126–128; passive-carrier defense, 409–410; patronage as alternative, 53, 65; photographs, 112–113, 237, 262–263, 266–269; preemption, 107, 129, 211,

270n; preservation-incentives argument, 230–231; and privacy, 141; publication requirement, 129, 264; reclaiming from assignee, 38; registration, 86, 129, 215, 234–249, 295; remedies for infringement, 86n, 119; renewals, 212, 219–220, 234–249, 252–253; retroactive extension, 220–221, 409; right to make copy for own use, 394; and Romantic theories of creativity, 63–64; short phrases, 89, 99; software, 96–97, 99–101, 109, 265, 309, 326, 332, 391–392, 394; sound recordings, 245–247, 265n, 403n; sporting events, 107; statutory history, 210–211; structural difference between copyright and patent law, 418–419; substantial-similarity test of infringement, 67, 89–91, 217, 322; think tanks, 273; tracing costs, 213–216; trade-secret analogies, 331–332; transaction costs, 216–217; transfers of, 127, 264; tying arrangements by owners of, 379; unique works of art, 127, 254–257; unpublished works, 87, 124–146, 247, 263–264, 273, 326, 331, 422; user interfaces, 100, 392; versus design patents, 332–333; versus patents, 294–297; welfare effects of, 80–84; works fixed in tangible form, 129; works made for hire, 211, 271–275, 282. *See also* Antitrust and intellectual property; Art (visual); Derivative works; Fair use; Intellectual property; Patents, compared with copyrights; Performing-rights organizations; U.S. Constitution, patent and copyright clause

Copyright Term Extension Act, 211, 213, 214n, 217n, 220, 223, 245–247, 406, 408–410; legislative history, 231n, 410; mercantilist argument for, 231n, 410

Credence goods, 65

Derivative works, 24, 41, 68, 90, 108–115, 121, 212, 226–227; adaptations as, 267; in art, 254–269 passim; burlesques as, 155, 157–158; copyright versus patent, 317–319; copyrightability of, 110–114; disreputable, 162–163, 279; economic rationale for author's monopoly of, 109–114; exceptions to author's monopoly, 109n, 267–268; and moral rights law, 279–280; parodies as, 149–150; publication of, 264; from public-domain works, 113, 263; scope of concept, 109, 114–115; software,

109; versus improvement patents, 111–112, 319

Diaries. *See* Copyrights, unpublished works

Digital Millennium Copyright Act, 43–44, 370n, 406, 410, 414

Digitization, 43–45, 49, 62n, 87, 263–265, 414

Dilution, 160n, 206–209; blurring, 161n, 207, 221; cheap copies, 208–209; famous marks, 206; pure, 207–208, 227–228; tarnishment, 160–161, 206–207

Disney corporation, 220–221, 272, 274, 408–409. *See also* Mickey Mouse

Droit de suite, 4, 38

Drugs. *See* Patents, pharmaceutical

Economic analysis of law, 3–4, 10, 87

Eliot, T. S., copying by, 59, 60n, 61, 152, 164, 216, 268

E-mail, 128

Enclosure movement, 12–13, 413

Encryption, 43–45

English Copyright Act of 1710, 1, 52

Externalities, technological versus pecuniary, 20, 224–226. *See also* Congestion externalities; Network externalities; Public goods

Facts, intellectual property in, 102–108

Fair use, 44–46, 59, 61, 115–123, 216n, 306, 417; and First Amendment, 287; book reviews, 117–118, 150, 155n; by biographers, 131–144; borrowing from one's own earlier work, 269; copying of industry standards as, 100, 392; copyright parodies versus trademark parodies, 162, 165; Jeff Koons's puppy sculpture, 260–261, 268–269, 417; museum reproductions, 264; unpublished works, 125–126, 128–146; productive or transformative versus reproductive or superseding use, 123, 130–131, 141–142, 154; trademarks, 194. *See also* Parodies

Federal Circuit, 2, 7, 305, 328, 334–353, 357, 406, 415–416; approval of business-method patents, 341, 417; damages determinations, 339; impact of, on R&D expenditures, 345–347; impact on amount of patent litigation, 347–352; impact on number of patent applications, 340–345; impact on number of patents granted, 340–345; infringement determinations,

Federal Circuit (continued)
338; origin, 334; pro-patent orientation, 335–353, 361, 418; specialization, 334–335, 418; validity determinations, 337–339

Federal Trade Commission, regulation of false advertising, 205–206

File sharing, 46–47, 120–121

Film. See Movies

First Inventor Defense Act, 361n

Food and Drug Administration, 314–315

Generic names. See under Trademarks

Hatch-Waxman Act, 314–315, 335n, 353, 407

Imagination costs, 161n, 207

Information costs, 65; experience versus search goods, 117n. See also Trademarks, economic function of

Innovation: bearing of risk aversion, 304; causes of, 327; Darwinian theory of, 318–320, 383; effect of market structure on, 385; effect of patents on, 326–328, 345–347, 383; inventors' incentives, 307–308; pharmaceuticals, 313–316; Schumpeterian theory of, 379–380, 395–396. See also Basic research; Patents; Universities

Intellectual property: access-incentive tradeoff, 11, 20–22, 213–214; China, 52; commonalities across different fields of, 420–421; common law versus legislative, 417, 424; developing countries, 413; economic analysis of, 1–4, 8–10; elasticity of demand facing producers, 376–377; foreign laws, 7, 270, 303, 311n, 326–327, 353, 361–362; foreign trade in, 3, 231n, 410; growth as law field, 2–3; growth in legal protection of, 412–413; growth in market for, 2–3, 249, 416; income generated by, 54–55; noneconomic perspectives, 4–5; remedies for infringement, 7–8; rewards systems for, 9, 24; role in economic growth, 2; social value of intellectual-property rights, 21–24, 422; trend toward greater protection of, 406–407. See also Antitrust and intellectual property; Property; specific fields of intellectual property law

Interest groups. See Public-choice theory

Internet, 7, 410; antitrust concerns regarding Internet-related markets, 390–402;

cybersquatting, 180, 410. See also File sharing

Inventions. See Innovation; Patents

Joint ownership, 29–30. See also under Copyrights; Patents

Koons, Jeff, 152–153, 261, 268–269

Language: economics of, 168–172, 192–193; generic words, 169, 192

Lanham Act, 181–183, 205–206, 406, 417n; antidilution provision of, 206; section 43(a), 206n. See also Trademarks

Letters. See Copyrights, unpublished works

Literature: character of ideas in, 94; concepts of literary creativity, 58–61, 63–64, 422n; contribution of trademarks to, 169, 192; extensive quotation in literary analysis, 135n; modernist, 59. See also Eliot; Milton; Shakespeare

Manet, Edouard, 67–68, 152, 216

Marketing, copyright protection of, 232–233

Mickey Mouse, 220, 224–227, 231, 244, 312. See also Disney corporation

Milton, John, copying by, 61, 63, 67

Misappropriation, doctrine of, 5, 62–63, 104–108, 207

Monopoly, 15n, 22–23; different concepts of, 374–379; and generic names, 195–196; industry standards issue, 99–100, 392, 394; monopolistic competition, 315, 378–379; of complementary good, 122; patent monopoly versus economic monopoly, 328n, 374–375; and product differentiation, 173–174; versus property right, 374. See also Antitrust and intellectual property; Competition

Moral rights, 4, 63, 160n, 162, 227, 270–293, 423; attribution rights, 270, 276–277; foreign law, 270; integrity rights, 270, 276–287; noteworthy disputes over, 281n; overlap with derivative-works doctrine, 279–280; public-choice analysis of, 287–293; state law, 270, 286–293; and trademark tarnishment, 160n; waivers of, 278–279, 286; works of recognized stature, 275, 279, 282–283

Movies: block booking, 387–388; colorization, 229–230; copying in, 68. See also Disney corporation

Music, conceptual, 258n; copying ("quotation") in classical music, 67–68; cover and jukebox copyright rules, 309n; marketing expenditures, 233; parody, 148n, 153; popular, 169n; recording of classical music, 230. *See also* Copyrights, music; Copyrights, sound recordings; Recording industry

Napster, 47, 120, 121n
Network externalities, 46, 394. *See also under* Software

Parodies, 61, 147–165, 226, 261, 280, 287; erotic, 161–165; parody defined, 148–149; as political criticism, 151; and publicity rights, 159; target versus weapon, 152, 165, 268–269; trademark parodies, 159–165
Patent Act: section 102, 337n; section 102(a), 303n; section 102(b), 361n; section 103, 337n; section 112, 337n; section 122(b), 362n; section 171, 332n; section 271(d)(5), 381n; section 273, 361n
Patents, 27, 91n; on abandoned inventions, 303–304; adverse-possession analogy, 33–34; as alternatives to trade secrets, 328–331, 336, 345, 356–363; American rule on rights of second inventor if first invention is trade secret, 361–362; applications for, 308–309, 337–345, 357, 362–363; basic versus applied research, 96–97, 302; blanketing and bracketing, 322; blocking, 317; broad versus narrow, 323–325, 331, 338–339; business-method, 23n, 95n, 98, 233–234, 306, 328–329, 336, 340–341, 343, 361n; as cartelization tools, 383–385; citations as measure of quality, 310–311; clustering, 322; commercial success as evidence of nonobviousness, 305; compared with copyrights, 96–98, 294–297, 325–326; competitive effects of, 327–328, 330; cross-licensing, 383; defensive patenting, 320–322, 325, 336, 375; depreciation, 297, 302, 311–312; design, 100n, 200–201, 332–333; doctrine of equivalents, 114, 317, 322–323, 331, 338; duration, 21, 33–34, 296–297, 300, 302, 306, 314–315, 331, 333, 362, 380–381; economic effects, 10n, 326–328, 331–332, 410; economic rationale for granting, 294–300; enablement (disclosure) requirement,

294, 298–299, 326, 337n, 356–357, 360–361; end-product royalties, 386–388; evidentiary considerations, 305; examination, 86, 308–309, 319, 320n, 323–324, 352, 357, 418; expense, 303, 311–312, 316, 357, 360; experimental use, 315–316, 335n, 407; fair-use analogy, 315–316; fees, 303, 311–312, 319; first-to-file rule, 303; first-to-invent rule, 303; foreign patent laws, 303, 311n, 326–327, 361–362; foreign patenting, 353; foreign-resident U.S. patenting, 353; formal model of, 297–299; functional versus structure or material claims, 331; ideological controversy over, 335–336; improvement, 112, 295, 317–319, 322; incomplete appropriability, 299; indefinite, 324; independent discovery, 86, 90, 295–296, 324; industry demand for, 312–316; inventing around, 295, 298–299, 313, 357; joint ownership, 30, 318; licensing of, 307, 316, 320–321, 374, 381–385; litigation cost, 357n; litigation over, 334–353, 357n; minimum-price licenses, 384; novelty, 89–90, 303–304, 320n, 358; number granted, 339–345; number granted as function of R&D expenditures, 344–345; number of patent lawyers, 347–348; obviousness, 21, 304–305, 417; one-year grace period, 360–361; patent-misuse doctrine, 372–373, 380–382; patent monopolies versus economic monopolies, 328n, 374–375; patent races, 18, 93, 296, 300–302, 324, 382–383; pharmaceutical, 54, 173n, 300–301, 313–316; plant, 332n; pooling, 382–383; preemption by federal of state law, 359n, 360, 370; prior invention, 87, 360–361; product versus process, 297; prosecution history estoppel, 323–324, 338; prospect theory, 181n, 302, 319–320, 324, 360–361; publication of application, 362; publication of prior art, 320; recent increase in number of, 325; remedies, 321n; renewals, 311–312; repair versus reconstruction, 381–382; requirement of proving utility, 302–303; research tools, 315–316; reverse doctrine of equivalents, 267, 317, 331; royalties, 320n, 374; royalties after patent expires, 380–381, 417–418; searching prior art, 303; as signals of quality of firm's technical knowledge, 328n; software, 86, 96–97, 327–328; strategic patenting,

Patents *(continued)*
302–303, 320–322, 336; structural difference between patent and copyright law, 418–419; suppression of, 320–321; types of, 332; validity determinations, 337–339, 383. *See also* Federal Circuit; Innovation; Intellectual property; U.S. Patent and Trademark Office
Performing-rights organizations, 9n, 29–30, 116–117, 120, 382, 386–387, 407, 410
Pharmaceutical drugs, competition between, 313–316; R&D, 313. *See also under* Patents
Photography. *See* Art, vintage photographs; Copyrights, photographs
Piracy, 46–47, 410; style, 399. *See also under* Software
Plagiarism, 52, 59–66; and moral rights law, 276
Price discrimination, 39, 46n, 122, 265–266, 373, 377–378, 388–390; in declining average-cost industries, 389–390; output effects, 40, 389–390; perfect, 40; prerequisite of, 375; versus Ramsey pricing, 40n
Privacy, 22; business, 330n; private versus social benefits of, 141; right of, in tort law, 64, 130, 134, 141, 144. *See also* Copyrights, unpublished works; Publicity rights
Product differentiation, 173–174, 207. *See also* Brand names; Trademarks
Property: adverse possession, 21, 31–34; committed-searcher doctrine, 17–18, 26, 27n, 302; economics of, 8, 11–36; finders' rights, 27–29, 229, 232, 368, 421; first-possession rules, 179–182; how acquired, 25–36; ideology of property rights, 414–415; nature of property right, 355, 363, 367, 374, 421; physical versus intellectual, 8, 11–20, 25–36, 44, 414–415, 421; relation of, to trade secrets, 355, 363, 367; rise of property rights, 412; static versus dynamic benefits of, 11–14, 222–224; trespass, 355. *See also* Abandonment of property
PTO. *See* U.S. Patent and Trademark Office
Public-choice theory, 403–419, 424; application to copyright statutes, 220–221; application to moral rights laws, 287–293; asymmetric stakes of contending interests, 407–411; deregulation movement, 404–406; versus ideological theory of expansion of intellectual property protection, 414–415; versus "malaise" theory of expansion of intellectual property protection, 415–416; versus public-interest theory of expansion of intellectual property protection, 412–413
Public domain: appropriation of public-domain works, 229, 232; how composition would be affected by system of indefinite renewals, 219, 249; how nourished by copyright, 69–70, 212; intellectual versus physical, 13, 31–32; private versus social value of, 408–409; protection of, by copyright statute's preemption provision, 107; publication of public-domain works, 53–54; social value of, 14–15
Public goods, 14, 19–20, 23–24, 217, 225; excludable versus nonexcludable, 14, 24, 403
Publicity rights, 54n, 64, 105n, 159n, 222–227; heritability of, 223–224
Publishing, academic, 53, 56, 375; e-books, 120n; economics of, 23, 38–57, 228–230, 273–274; newspapers, 105, 273–274. *See also* Authorship
Pushman presumption, 127, 264

Recording industry. *See* Copyrights, music; Encryption; File sharing; Performing-rights organizations
Rent seeking, 17–18, 220–221; by banking trademarks, 180. *See also* Patents, patent races; Public-choice theory
Research and development (R&D), 345–347; economies and diseconomies of scale in, 383. *See also* Basic research; Innovation; Patents, economic effects
Reverse engineering, 44, 100, 309, 330, 362–363. *See also under* Trade secrets

Salvage, maritime, 17, 26
Satire, 152–153, 160, 163
Semiconductor Chip Protection Act of 1984, 370
Shakespeare, William, copying by, 52, 58–61, 64, 66–67
Software, 41, 43, 57, 99–101, 171–172, 210, 221, 312, 318, 366; antitrust concerns related to, 390–402; browsers, 393, 401; computer operating systems, 391, 393, 401; interfaces and protocols, 100, 392; network externalities, 392–402; overlapping copyright and patent

protection of, 96–97, 353; piracy of, 46–47, 98, 393. *See also under* Patents
Sonny Bono Copyright Term Extension Act. *See* Copyright Term Extension Act
Stationers' Company, 1, 51–52
Statute of Anne. *See* English Copyright Act of 1710
Superstars, economics of, 49–50, 55

Tarnishment. *See under* Dilution
Television: video recorders, 118–119. *See also* Broadcasting
Tie-ins. *See* Antitrust and intellectual property, tying arrangements
Time shifting (Betamax case), 118–119, 123
Trade dress, 166n, 332–333. *See also* Patents, design
Trademark Clarification Act of 1984, 195, 406
Trademark Law Revision Act of 1988, 250
Trademarks, 6, 9, 25, 31, 64, 413, 422, 423; acquisition of, 179–183; adverse-possession analogy, 33; aesthetic functionality, 97, 199–201, 332; arbitrary, 188, 193; artists', 258n, 259, 276; banking of, 180–182; banking of, in Japan, 180; cancellation of, in Japan, 180n; colors as, 189–190, 193n, 200; common law of, 205–206; competitive effects of, 330; contribution of, to language, 168–172, 193–194; depreciation, 250–253, 312; descriptive, 189, 193, 209; doctrine of laches, 182–183; dual use, 196–197; duration, 186–187, 222; economic function of, 161, 166–168, 173–174; fair use, 194; fanciful, 172–173, 188, 193; fees, 253; forfeiture by reason of quality degradation, 185; formal model of, 174–179; functionality doctrine, 197–201; generic names, 190–197, 208; geographic scope, 182–183, 201; inadvertent infringement, 86; intentional versus unintentional infringement, 204–205; intent-to-use registrations, 182, 406n; licensing versus sale of, 185–186; and monopoly, 173–174; parodies of, 159–165; pharmaceutical, 54, 173n, 190, 196, 314; plagiarism as trademark infringement, 63; and product quality, 168, 185, 203–204; promotional goods, 184n; proof of likelihood of confusion, 201–206; registration of, 27, 86, 179–183, 201–202, 204, 250, 308; renewals, 250–253;

secondary meaning, 193; service marks, 184n; shapes as, 189–190, 197–201; social costs of, 172–174; status of, in bankruptcy, 186; suggestive, 188–189, 193; as source of product differentiation, 173–174; transfer of, 184–186; transfers in gross, 184–186; as trying product, 374; use-in-commerce requirement (token versus commercially significant), 86, 179–182, 406; utilitarian functionality, 198–200; versus design patents, 332–333. *See also* Brand names; Dilution; Intellectual property; Internet, cybersquatting; Lanham Act; Trade dress
Trade secrets, 22, 30, 36, 124, 354–371; adverse-possession analogy, 33; aerial reconnaisance as theft of, 355, 369, 371; analogized to military secrets, 363–365; blocking, 365–366; breach of contract as theft of, 355; common law of, 355–356; complementarity of patent and trade secret law, 328–331, 356–363, 423; contractual protection of, 360, 364–365; copyright analogies, 331–332, 370–371; defined, 354; duration, 356–360; effect on market structure, 330; employee covenants not to compete as method of protecting, 360, 364–366, 371; fair use, 371; formal model of, 366–368; inventor's choice between patents and trade secrets, 356–363; licensing of, 329, 365–366, 371; loss of, by accident, 33, 366–369; relation of, to concept of property, 355, 363, 421; relation of, to copyright and patent law, 370–371; reverse engineering of, 355–356, 365–371; in software, 391; theft of contrasted with theft of physical property, 367; transaction costs of, 329n; trespass as theft of, 355; and tying arrangements, 374
Transaction costs, 8, 12, 16–17, 21, 31–33, 216–217, 305–306, 421; Coase's analysis of, 14; derivative works, 110–111; of trade secrecy, 329. *See also* Coase Theorem; Fair use
TRIPs Agreement (World Trade Organization Agreement on Trade-Related Aspects of Intellectual Property Rights), 413–414
Tying arrangements. *See under* Antitrust and intellectual property

Uniform Trade Secret Act, 354n
Universities: applied research by, 310–311,

316; patent policies of, 310n; role of, in pharmaceutical research, 313n; support of basic research by, 306–307, 316. *See also* Authorship, academic

Unpublished works. *See* Copyrights, unpublished works; Fair use, unpublished works

U.S. Constitution, patent and copyright clause, 1, 211, 226n, 232, 413

U.S. Court of Appeals for the Federal Circuit. *See* Federal Circuit

U.S. Court of Claims, 334

U.S. Court of Customs and Patent Appeals, 334

U.S. Patent and Trademark Office (PTO), 86, 295, 296n, 308–310, 319, 320n, 323–324, 334–335, 337n, 358, 408, 418; procedures and incentives, 352; trademark registry, 308

Visual Artists and Galleries Association, 264

Visual Artists Rights Act, 270–271, 274–287, 406, 423

Warhol, Andy, 256–260, 262n, 266–267, 269, 272